UNITED STATES GOVERNMENT

Policy and Supporting Positions

Committee on Homeland Security
and Governmental Affairs

United States Senate

118th Congress, 2d Session

NOVEMBER 12, 2024

Available via http://www.govinfo.gov

Printed for the use of the
Committee on Homeland Security and Governmental Affairs

U.S. GOVERNMENT PUBLISHING OFFICE

WASHINGTON, D.C. : 2024

COMMITTEE ON HOMELAND SECURITY
AND GOVERNMENTAL AFFAIRS

GARY C. PETERS, Michigan, *Chairman*

THOMAS R. CARPER, Delaware
MAGGIE HASSAN, New Hampshire
KYRSTEN SINEMA, Arizona
JACKY ROSEN, Nevada
JON OSSOFF, Georgia
RICHARD BLUMENTHAL, Connecticut
LAPHONZA BUTLER, California

RAND PAUL, Kentucky
RON JOHNSON, Wisconsin
JAMES LANKFORD, Oklahoma
MITT ROMNEY, Utah
RICK SCOTT, Florida
JOSH HAWLEY, Missouri
ROGER MARSHALL, Kansas

DAVID M. WEINBERG, *Staff Director*
ALAN S. KAHN, *Chief Counsel*
WILLIAM E. HENDERSON III, *Minority Staff Director*
CHRISTINA N. SALAZAR, *Minority Chief Counsel*
LAURA W. KILBRIDE, *Chief Clerk*

FOREWORD

Every four years, just after the Presidential election, the "United States Government Policy and Supporting Positions," commonly known as the *Plum Book*, is published, alternately, by the Senate Committee on Governmental Affairs and the House Committee on Government Reform.

This publication contains data (as of July 16, 2024) on over 7,000 Federal civil service leadership and support positions in the legislative and executive branches of the Federal Government that may be subject to noncompetitive appointment (e.g., positions such as agency heads and their immediate subordinates, policy executives and advisors, and aides who report to these officials). The duties of many such positions may involve advocacy of Administration policies and programs and the incumbents usually have a close and confidential working relationship with the agency head or other key officials.

Following are the major categories of positions listed:

- Executive Schedule and salary-equivalent positions paid at the rates established for levels I through V of the Executive Schedule;

- Senior Executive Service (SES) "General" positions;

- Senior Foreign Service positions;

- Schedule C positions excepted from the competitive service by the President, or by the Director, Office of Personnel Management, because of the confidential or policy-determining nature of the position duties; and

- Other positions at the GS–14 and above level excepted from the competitive civil service by law because of the confidential or policy-determining nature of the position duties.

See Appendix 2 for more details on SES appointments and Appendix 3 for more details on Schedule C appointments. Additional information on the positions listed and the Federal salary schedules under which they are paid is provided in the appendices. The Legend on the following page shows the codes and acronyms used in this publication.

DISCLAIMER

The information for this committee print was provided by the U.S. Office of Personnel Management [OPM].

LEGEND

_____

Position Location (Column 1)

Listed are the cities, States/Provinces and foreign countries in which the positions are located. Countries and cities (or other subdivisions) are shown for overseas posts. Note that "Washington, DC" includes positions in the entire metropolitan area and therefore may include certain cities and counties in the States of Maryland and Virginia.

Position Title (Column 2)

Listed are the position titles and the names of the organizations in which they are located.

Name of Incumbent (Column 3)

Listed are the names of individuals serving under other than career appointments. The phrase "Career Incumbent" is shown for positions incumbered by career appointees. The term "Vacant" is shown for positions that were not occupied on July 16, 2024, the "as of" date of this publication.

Note the law requires "member" positions in certain agencies (e.g., boards, committees, and commissions) be filled on a bipartisan basis. For such positions, the following letter codes are shown in parentheses following the name of the incumbent:

(D) = Democrat   (I) = Independent   (R) = Republican

Type of Appointment (Column 4)

Listed are letter codes that denote the type of appointment under which the position incumbent is serving. Note that several categories of positions can be filled by more than one type of appointment, e.g., SES positions listed in this publication may be filled by using career, noncareer, limited emergency, or limited term appointment authorities. Therefore, no "Type of Appointment" is shown for such positions when they are vacant.

PAS	=	Presidential Appointment with Senate Confirmation
PA	=	Presidential Appointment (without Senate Confirmation)
CA	=	Career Appointment
NA	=	Noncareer Appointment
EA	=	Limited Emergency Appointment
TA	=	Limited Term Appointment
SC	=	Schedule C Excepted Appointment
XS	=	Appointment Excepted by Statute

Pay Plan (Column 5)

Listed are letter codes that denote the Federal salary schedule or pay system under which the position incumbents are going to be paid. Tables showing the salary range for major pay systems are contained in Appendix 4.

AD	=	Administratively Determined Rates
ES	=	Senior Executive Service
EX	=	Executive Schedule
FA	=	Foreign Service Chiefs of Mission
FE	=	Senior Foreign Service
FP	=	Foreign Service Specialist
GS	=	General Schedule
PD	=	Daily Pay Rate* (per diem)
SL	=	Senior Level
TM	=	Federal Housing Finance Board Merit Pay
VH	=	Farm Credit Administration Pay Plan
WC	=	Without Compensation*
OT	=	Other Pay Plan* (all those not listed separately)

* Although not pay plans, these codes are shown for information purposes.

Level, Grade, or Pay (Column 6)

Listed are numerical and letter codes that denote the level, grade or salary of the position incumbered:

Levels I through V of the Executive Schedule

Grades 1 through 15 of the General Schedule

Annual Salary in Dollars

Daily Pay Rate in Dollars

If there is no entry in this column, the position does not have an established level, grade, or pay rate. For example, the pay rate for Senior Executive Service and Senior Level positions is "personal," i.e., attached to the incumbent, not the position. The pay rate for each new appointee is set by the appointing authority (usually the agency head) on a case-by-case basis. Annual salary schedules and pay ranges for such positions are shown in Appendix 4.

Tenure (Column 7)

Listed are the terms or durations of the appointment in years. If there is no entry in this column, the appointment has no fixed term.

Expires (Column 8)

Listed are the expiration dates for time-limited appointments. If there is no entry in this column, the incumbent is not serving under a time-limited appointment. However, many member positions on agency advisory boards, councils, and commissions are filled initially for a fixed term, but the incumbents may (and often do) serve beyond the expiration date until they are replaced. In such cases, no expiration date is shown.

CONTENTS

APPENDICES

LEGISLATIVE BRANCH

ARCHITECT OF THE CAPITOL

Location	Position Title	Name of Incumbent	Type of Appt.	Pay Plan	Level, Grade, or Pay	Tenure	Expires
Washington, DC	Architect of the Capitol..	Thomas E. Austin.................	PAS	OT	....	....	....

GOVERNMENT ACCOUNTABILITY OFFICE

Location	Position Title	Name of Incumbent	Type of Appt.	Pay Plan	Level, Grade, or Pay	Tenure	Expires
	OFFICE OF THE COMPTROLLER GENERAL						
Washington, DC	Comptroller General...	Gene L Dodaro	PAS	EX	II	15	12/29/25
Washington, DC	Deputy Comptroller General	Vacant	....	EX	....	....	....

GOVERNMENT PUBLISHING OFFICE

Location	Position Title	Name of Incumbent	Type of Appt.	Pay Plan	Level, Grade, or Pay	Tenure	Expires
	Office of the Director						
Washington, DC	Director..	Hugh Nathaniel Halpern.....	PAS	EX	II	10	12/05/29
Washington, DC	Deputy Director	Brian Pearl	XS	EX	III	....	....
	Superintendent of Documents						
Washington, DC	Superintendent of Documents	Scott A Matheson	XS	OT	....	....	....
	Office of the Inspector General						
Washington, DC	Inspector General	Nathan Deahl......................	XS	OT	....	....	....

LIBRARY OF CONGRESS

Location	Position Title	Name of Incumbent	Type of Appt.	Pay Plan	Level, Grade, or Pay	Tenure	Expires
	OFFICE OF THE LIBRARIAN						
Washington, DC	Librarian of Congress..	Carla Hayden	PAS	EX	II	10	09/14/26
	AMERICAN FOLKLIFE CENTER BOARD OF TRUSTEES						
Washington, DC	Ex Officio Member, Secretary of the Smithsonian Institution.	Lonnie Bunch	XS	WC	....	....	....
Washington, DC	Ex Officio Member, Secretary of Veterans Affairs.	Denis G McDonough	XS	WC	....	....	....
Washington, DC	Ex Officio Member, Chairperson, National Endowment for the Humanities.	Shelly Lowe	XS	WC	....	....	....
Washington, DC	Ex Officio Member, Chairperson, National Endowment for the Arts.	Maria Rosario Jackson	XS	WC	....	....	....
Washington, DC	Ex Officio Member, President of the American Folklore Society.	Amy Skillman......................	XS	WC	....	....	....
Washington, DC	Ex Officio Member, President Of The Society For Ethnomusicology.	Melvin Butler	....	....	....	....	....
Washington, DC	Ex Officio Member, Director, Institute Of Museum And Library Services.	Vacant	....	WC	....	....	....
Washington, DC	Board Member	Sara C Bronin	PA	WC	....	6	06/01/28
Washington, DC	Board Member	Jessica Looman	PA	WC	....	6	06/01/30
Washington, DC	Board Member	Rachel Leland Levine	PA	WC	....	6	06/01/28
Washington, DC	Board Member	Charles F Sams...................	PA	WC	....	6	06/01/28
	LIBRARY OF CONGRESS TRUST FUND BOARD						
Washington, DC	Ex Officio Member, Secretary of the Treasury ..	Janet Yellen	XS	WC	....	....	....
Washington, DC	Member...	Eric Mindich........................	PA	OT	....	5	03/08/28
Washington, DC	Member...	Virginia L Thomas	PA	WC	....	5	03/08/25

LIBRARY OF CONGRESS—Continued

Location	Position Title	Name of Incumbent	Type of Appt.	Pay Plan	Level, Grade, or Pay	Tenure	Expires
	PERMANENT COMMITTEE FOR THE OLIVER WENDELL HOLMES DEVISE						
Washington, DC	Committee Member	Risa Goluboff	PA	WC	....	8	03/08/31
Washington, DC	Committee Member	Martha S Jones	PA	WC	....	8	03/08/31
Washington, DC	Committee Member	Trevor Morrison	PA	WC	....	8	03/08/31
Washington, DC	Committee Member	Kenneth Mack	PA	WC	....	8	10/10/24

EXECUTIVE BRANCH

EXECUTIVE OFFICE OF THE PRESIDENT

Location	Position Title	Name of Incumbent	Type of Appt.	Pay Plan	Level, Grade, or Pay	Tenure	Expires
	EXECUTIVE OFFICE OF THE PRESIDENT						
	WHITE HOUSE OFFICE						
Washington, DC	Assistant to the President and Chief of Staff ...	Jeffrey Zients......................	PA	AD	....	....	....
Washington, DC	Assistant to the President and Homeland Security Advisor and Deputy National Security Advisor.	Elizabeth Sherwood-Randall.	PA	AD	....	....	....
Washington, DC	Assistant to the President and Senior Advisor to the President and Director of the Office of Public Engagement.	Stephen Benjamin...............	PA	AD	....	....	....
Washington, DC	Assistant to the President and Senior Advisor to the First Lady.	Anthony Bernal...................	PA	AD	....	....	....
Washington, DC	Assistant to the President and Director of the National Economic Council.	Lael Brainard	PA	AD	....	....	....
Washington, DC	Assistant to the President and Senior Advisor to the President.	Anita Dunn..........................	PA	AD	....	....	....
Washington, DC	Assistant to the President and Staff Secretary and Director of the Office of Gun Violence Prevention.	Stefanie Feldman	PA	AD	....	....	....
Washington, DC	Assistant to the President and Principal Deputy National Security Advisor.	Jonathan Finer....................	PA	AD	....	....	....
Washington, DC	Assistant to the President and Director of the Office of Legislative Affairs.	Shuwanza Goff	PA	AD	....	....	....
Washington, DC	Assistant to the President and Press Secretary.	Karine Jean-Pierre...............	PA	AD	....	....	....
Washington, DC	Assistant to the President and Co-Chair and Executive Director of the White House Gender Policy Council.	Jennifer Klein......................	PA	AD	....	....	....
Washington, DC	Assistant to the President and Director of Communications.	Benjamin Labolt..................	PA	AD	....	....	....
Washington, DC	Assistant to the President and Director of Scheduling and Advance.	Ryan Montoya	PA	AD	....	....	....
Washington, DC	Assistant to the President and Director of Management and Administration and Director of the Office of Administration.	David Noble	PA	AD	....	....	....
Washington, DC	Assistant to the President and Senior Advisor to the President and Director of the Office of the Intergovernmental Affairs.	Thomas Perez	PA	AD	....	....	....
Washington, DC	Senior Advisor to the President for International Climate Policy.	John Podesta........................	PA	AD	....	....	....
Washington, DC	Assistant to the President and Deputy Chief of Staff.	Natalie Quillian...................	PA	AD	....	....	....
Washington, DC	Assistant to the President and Director of the Office of Presidential Personnel.	Gautam Raghavan	PA	AD	....	....	....
Washington, DC	Assistant to the President and Director of Speechwriting.	Vinay Reddy	PA	AD	....	....	....
Washington, DC	Assistant to the President and Deputy Chief of Staff.	Bruce Reed..........................	PA	AD	....	....	....
Washington, DC	Assistant to the President and Counselor to the President.	Steven Ricchetti	PA	AD	....	....	....
Washington, DC	Assistant to the President and Director of Oval Office Operations.	Richard Ruffner...................	PA	AD	....	....	....
Washington, DC	Assistant to the President and Director of Political Strategy and Outreach.	Emmy Ruiz...........................	PA	AD	....	....	....
Washington, DC	Assistant to the President and Cabinet Secretary.	Evan Ryan	PA	AD	....	....	....
Washington, DC	Assistant to the President and White House Counsel.	Edward Siskel	PA	AD	....	....	....
Washington, DC	Assistant to the President for National Security Affairs.	Jacob Sullivan	PA	AD	....	....	....
Washington, DC	Assistant to the President and Domestic Policy Advisor.	Neera Tanden	PA	AD	....	....	....
Washington, DC	Assistant to the President and Director of Digital Strategy.	Christian Tom......................	PA	AD	....	....	....
Washington, DC	Assistant to the President and Deputy Chief of Staff.	Annmarie Tomasini..............	PA	AD	....	....	....

EXECUTIVE OFFICE OF THE PRESIDENT—Continued

Location	Position Title	Name of Incumbent	Type of Appt.	Pay Plan	Level, Grade, or Pay	Tenure	Expires
Washington, DC	Assistant to the President and National Climate Advisor.	Ali Zaidi	PA	AD	....	....	....
Washington, DC	Deputy Assistant to the President and Director of Policy and Projects for the First Lady.	Mala Adiga............................	PA	AD	....	....	....
Washington, DC	Deputy Assistant to the President and Communications Director for the First Lady.	Elizabeth Alexander.............	PA	AD	....	....	....
Washington, DC	Deputy Counsel to the President	Russell Anello.......................	PA	AD	....	....	....
Washington, DC	Deputy Assistant to the President and Senior Deputy Press Secretary.	Andrew Bates	PA	AD	....	....	....
Washington, DC	Deputy Assistant to the President and Deputy Director of Political Strategy and Outreach.	Dennis Cheng	PA	AD	....	....	....
Washington, DC	Deputy Assistant to the President and Principal Deputy Director of the Office of Public Engagement.	Jamison Citron	PA	AD	....	....	....
Washington, DC	Deputy Assistant to the President and Deputy for Clean Energy Innovation and Implementation.	Kristina Costa	PA	AD	....	....	....
Washington, DC	Deputy Counsel to the President	Rachel Cotton	PA	AD	....	....	....
Washington, DC	Deputy Assistant to the President and Deputy Director of the National Economic Council.	Brendan Danaher.................	PA	AD	....	....	....
Washington, DC	Deputy Assistant to the President and Deputy Director of the National Economic Council.	Navtej Dhillon	PA	AD	....	....	....
Washington, DC	Deputy Counsel to the President	Tyeesha Dixon	PA	AD	....	....	....
Washington, DC	Deputy Assistant to the President and Deputy Director of the National Economic Council and Director for Competition Council Policy.	Jonathan Donenberg............	PA	AD	....	....	....
Washington, DC	Deputy Assistant to the President and Deputy Director of the Office of Presidential Personnel.	Stacy Eichner	PA	AD	....	....	....
Washington, DC	Deputy Assistant to the President and Social Secretary.	Carlos Elizondo	PA	AD	....	....	....
Washington, DC	Deputy Counsel to the President and Legal Advisor to the National Security Council.	Joshua Geltzer......................	PA	AD	....	....	....
Washington, DC	Deputy Assistant to the President for Economic Mobility.	Robert Gordon	PA	AD	....	....	....
Washington, DC	Deputy Assistant to the President and Deputy Director of the National Economic Council.	Daniel Hornung...................	PA	AD	....	....	....
Washington, DC	Deputy Assistant to the President and Deputy Director of Legislative Affairs and House Liaison.	Meredith Jones.....................	PA	AD	....	....	....
Washington, DC	Deputy Assistant to the President and Senior Advisor to the Director of the Office of Public Engagement.	Jennifer Kaplan...................	PA	AD	....	....	....
Washington, DC	Deputy Assistant to the President and Deputy Director of the Gender Policy Council.	Katherine Keith	PA	AD	....	....	....
Washington, DC	Deputy Assistant to the President and Deputy Director of the Office of Intergovernmental Affairs.	Daniel Koh...........................	PA	AD	....	....	....
Washington, DC	Deputy Assistant to the President and Deputy Director of Digital Strategy.	Tericka Lambert..................	PA	AD	....	....	....
Washington, DC	Deputy Assistant to the President for Immigration.	Elisabeth Lawrence..............	PA	AD	....	....	....
Washington, DC	Deputy Assistant to the President and Senior Advisor for Political Engagement.	John McCarthy......................	PA	AD	....	....	....
Washington, DC	Deputy Assistant to the President and Asian American and Native Hawaiian/Pacific Islander Senior Liaison.	Erika Moritsugu...................	PA	AD	....	....	....
Washington, DC	Deputy Assistant to the President and Principal Deputy Communications Director.	Kristen Orthman.................	PA	AD	....	....	....
Washington, DC	Deputy Assistant to the President for Racial Justice and Equity.	Kylie Patterson.....................	PA	AD	....	....	....
Washington, DC	Deputy Assistant to the President and Senior Advisor to the Chief of Staff.	Rosa Po.................................	PA	AD	....	....	....
Washington, DC	Deputy Assistant to the President and Deputy National Climate Advisor.	Mary Repko	PA	AD	....	....	....
Washington, DC	Deputy Assistant to the President and Senior Advisor to the White House Counsel.	Ian Sams..............................	PA	AD	....	....	....
Washington, DC	Deputy Assistant to the President for Infrastructure Implementation.	Samantha Silverberg	PA	AD	....	....	....
Washington, DC	Deputy Assistant to the President and Senior Deputy Press Secretary.	Emilie Simons	PA	AD	....	....	....

EXECUTIVE OFFICE OF THE PRESIDENT—Continued

Location	Position Title	Name of Incumbent	Type of Appt.	Pay Plan	Level, Grade, or Pay	Tenure	Expires
Washington, DC	Deputy Assistant to the President and Deputy Director of the Office of Legislative Affairs.	Lee Slater	PA	AD	....	....	....
Washington, DC	Deputy Assistant to the President and Senior Advisor for Digital Strategy.	Patrick Stevenson.................	PA	AD	....	....	....
Washington, DC	Deputy Counsel to the President	Karl Thompson.....................	PA	AD	....	....	....
Washington, DC	Deputy Assistant to the President and Director of Strategic Outreach and Senior Advisor.	Ashley Williams...................	PA	AD	....	....	....
Washington, DC	Deputy Assistant to the President for Health and Veterans Affairs.	Christen Young....................	PA	AD	....	....	....
Washington, DC	Special Assistant to the President and Associate Counsel.	Magdey Abdallah................	PA	AD	....	....	....
Washington, DC	Special Assistant to the President and House Legislative Affairs Liaison.	Alma Acosta Garcia	PA	AD	....	....	....
Washington, DC	Special Assistant to the President for Candidate Recruitment and Congressional Outreach.	Mariana Adame...................	PA	AD	....	....	....
Washington, DC	Special Assistant to the President for Climate Policy, Finance and Innovation.	Nana Ayensu	PA	AD	....	....	....
Washington, DC	Special Assistant to the President and Director of Partnerships and Private Sector.	Kathryn Balcerzak..............	PA	AD	....	....	....
Washington, DC	Special Assistant to the President and Senior Counsel.	Kevin Barstow......................	PA	AD	....	....	....
Washington, DC	Special Assistant to the President for Climate Policy, Industrial Sector, and Community Investment.	Benjamin Beachy	PA	AD	....	....	....
Washington, DC	Special Assistant to the President for Agriculture and Rural Policy.	Kelliann Blazek...................	PA	AD	....	....	....
Washington, DC	Special Assistant to the President and Senior Counsel.	Phillip Brest	PA	AD	....	....	....
Washington, DC	Special Assistant to the President and Associate Counsel.	Sophia Brill........................	PA	AD	....	....	....
Washington, DC	Special Assistant to the President for Economic Policy.	Rachel Brown	PA	AD	....	....	....
Washington, DC	Special Assistant to the President and Director of White House Personnel.	Dalmyra Caesar	PA	AD	....	....	....
Washington, DC	Special Assistant to the President for Education.	Jessica Cardichon...............	PA	AD	....	....	....
Washington, DC	Special Assistant to the President and House Legislative Affairs Liaison.	Colleen Carlos	PA	AD	....	....	....
Washington, DC	Special Assistant to the President and Senior Counsel.	Megan Ceronsky..................	PA	AD	....	....	....
Washington, DC	Special Assistant to the President and Director of Broadcast Media.	Muriel Chase	PA	AD	....	....	....
Washington, DC	Special Assistant to the President and House Legislative Affairs Liaison.	Jim Cho...............................	PA	AD	....	....	....
Washington, DC	Special Assistant to the President and Senior Counsel.	Sean Crotty.........................	PA	AD	....	....	....
Washington, DC	Special Assistant to the President and Senate Legislative Affairs Liaison.	Elizabeth Darnall................	PA	AD	....	....	....
Washington, DC	Special Assistant to the President for Infrastructure Implementation.	Minelly De Coo....................	PA	AD	....	....	....
Washington, DC	Special Assistant to the President and Director of Presidential Correspondence.	Geraldine De Puy................	PA	AD	....	....	....
Washington, DC	Special Assistant to the President for Tax Policy.	William Debot......................	PA	AD	....	....	....
Washington, DC	Special Assistant to the President and Senior Labor Advisor.	Erika Dinkel-Smith..............	PA	AD	....	....	....
Washington, DC	Special Assistant to the President and Senior Associate Counsel.	Osasumwen Dorsey..............	PA	AD	....	....	....
Washington, DC	Special Assistant to the President and Deputy Staff Secretary.	Adele El-Khouri...................	PA	AD	....	....	....
Washington, DC	Special Assistant to the President for Domestic Agency Personnel.	Analysse Escobar	PA	AD	....	....	....
Washington, DC	Special Assistant to the President for Gender Policy.	Rhea Fernandes...................	PA	AD	....	....	....
Washington, DC	Special Assistant to the President and Senior Presidential Speechwriter.	Aviva Feuerstein	PA	AD	....	....	....
Washington, DC	Special Assistant to the President and Chief of Staff to the Senior Advisor to the President.	Jordan Finkelstein	PA	AD	....	....	....
Washington, DC	Special Assistant to the President and Chief of Staff of the National Economic Council and Senior Advisor for Communications.	Robert Friedlander..............	PA	AD	....	....	....

EXECUTIVE OFFICE OF THE PRESIDENT—Continued

Location	Position Title	Name of Incumbent	Type of Appt.	Pay Plan	Level, Grade, or Pay	Tenure	Expires
Washington, DC	Special Assistant to the President and Senior Communications Advisor for Economic Messaging.	Robert Friedlander................	PA	AD	....	....	....
Washington, DC	Special Assistant to the President for Manufacturing and Industrial Policy.	Monica Gorman....................	PA	AD	....	....	....
Washington, DC	Special Assistant to the President and Chief of Staff and Senior Advisor to the Deputy Chief of Staff.	Sheila Grant........................	PA	AD	....	....	....
Washington, DC	Special Assistant to the President for Strategy and Operations.	Alexandra Greenstein..........	PA	AD	....	....	....
Washington, DC	Special Assistant to the President and Director of Presidential Scheduling.	Camilo Haller.....................	PA	AD	....	....	....
Washington, DC	Special Assistant to the President and Senior Advisor for Domestic Preparedness and Response (Detailee to the Office of Pandemic Preparedness and Response Policy).	Chandresh Harjivan	PA	AD	....	....	....
Washington, DC	Special Assistant to the President and White House Coordinator for CHIPS Implementation and Investment.	Ryan Harper.........................	PA	AD	....	....	....
Washington, DC	Special Assistant to the President and Deputy Director of the Office of Public Engagement.	Michael Hayes......................	PA	AD	....	....	....
Washington, DC	Special Assistant to the President for Economic Agency Personnel.	Ryan Hubbard	PA	AD	....	....	....
Washington, DC	Special Assistant to the President for Presidential Boards and Commissions.	Meredith Jachowicz..............	PA	AD	....	....	....
Washington, DC	Special Assistant to the President and Deputy Director of the Office of Gun Violence Prevention.	Gregory Jackson	PA	AD	....	....	....
Washington, DC	Special Assistant to the President and House Legislative Affairs Liaison.	Audra Jackson......................	PA	AD	....	....	....
Washington, DC	Special Assistant to the President for Economic Development and Industrial Strategy.	Alejandro Jacquez	PA	AD	....	....	....
Washington, DC	Special Assistant to the President and House Legislative Affairs Liaison.	Diala Jadallah-Redding	PA	AD	....	....	....
Washington, DC	Special Assistant to the President for Climate and Science Agency Personnel.	Sara Jordan	PA	AD	....	....	....
Washington, DC	Special Assistant to the President and Legislative Affairs Liaison.	Peter Kenny.........................	PA	AD	....	....	....
Washington, DC	Special Assistant to the President and Senior Communications Advisor for Economic Messaging.	Michael Kikukawa	PA	AD	....	....	....
Washington, DC	Special Assistant to the President and Director of Political Engagement.	Phillip Kim	PA	AD	....	....	....
Washington, DC	Special Assistant to the President for Economic Policy.	Michael Konczal	PA	AD	....	....	....
Washington, DC	Special Assistant to the President and Senior Associate Counsel.	Jeremy Kreisberg	PA	AD	....	....	....
Washington, DC	Special Assistant to the President and Senior Communications Advisor.	Elena Kuhn..........................	PA	AD	....	....	....
Washington, DC	Special Assistant to the President and Chief of Staff for the Office of Legislative Affairs.	Garrett Lamm	PA	AD	....	....	....
Washington, DC	Special Assistant to the President and Director of Technology.	Austin Lin...........................	PA	AD	....	....	....
Washington, DC	Special Assistant to the President and Chief of Staff for the Office of Public Engagement.	Erica Loewe	PA	AD	....	....	....
Washington, DC	Special Assistant to the President and Director of Political Engagement.	Colleen Loper.......................	PA	AD	....	....	....
Washington, DC	Special Assistant to the President for Housing and Urban Policy.	Chad Maisel.........................	PA	AD	....	....	....
Washington, DC	Special Assistant to the President for National Security Agency Personnel.	Salem Mariam.....................	PA	AD	....	....	....
Washington, DC	Special Assistant to the President and Chief of Staff for the Office of Presidential Personnel.	Brooks Mears.......................	PA	AD	....	....	....
Washington, DC	Special Assistant to the President and Senior Associate Counsel.	Jonathan Meltzer	PA	AD	....	....	....
Washington, DC	Special Assistant to the President and Senate Legislative Affairs Liaison.	Benjamin Merkel..................	PA	AD	....	....	....
Washington, DC	Special Assistant to the President for Leadership Development and Appointee Engagement.	Vanessa Millones..................	PA	AD	....	....	....

EXECUTIVE OFFICE OF THE PRESIDENT—Continued

Location	Position Title	Name of Incumbent	Type of Appt.	Pay Plan	Level, Grade, or Pay	Tenure	Expires
Washington, DC	Special Assistant to the President and Deputy Director of Communications.	Jennifer Molina	PA	AD	....	....	....
Washington, DC	Special Assistant to the President and Director of Research.	Terrance Moynihan	PA	AD	....	....	....
Washington, DC	Special Assistant to the President and Associate Counsel.	Elizabeth Mueller.................	PA	AD	....	....	....
Washington, DC	Special Assistant to the President and Director of Regional Media.	Dhara Nayyar.....................	PA	AD	....	....	....
Washington, DC	Special Assistant to the President for Economic Policy.	Michael Negron	PA	AD	....	....	....
Washington, DC	Special Assistant to the President for Community Public Health and Disparities.	Catherine Oakar	PA	AD	....	....	....
Washington, DC	Special Assistant to the President for Racial and Economic Justice.	Andrea O'Neal......................	PA	AD	....	....	....
Washington, DC	Special Assistant to the President and Deputy Director of Management and Administration.	Elizabeth Pan	PA	AD	....	....	....
Washington, DC	Special Assistant to the President and Director of Coalitions Media.	Luisana Perez Fernandez	PA	AD	....	....	....
Washington, DC	Special Assistant to the President and Chief of Staff to the Office of White House Counsel and Senior Counsel.	Michael Posada....................	PA	AD	....	....	....
Washington, DC	Special Assistant to the President and Director of Political Operations.	Ryan Quinn	PA	AD	....	....	....
Washington, DC	Special Assistant to the President and Chief of Staff for Cabinet Affairs.	Sanam Rastegar	PA	AD	....	....	....
Washington, DC	Special Assistant to the President and Deputy Director of Oval Office Operations.	Julia Reed	PA	AD	....	....	....
Washington, DC	Special Assistant to the President and Director of Employee Engagement and Leadership Development.	Lauren Reyes......................	PA	AD	....	....	....
Washington, DC	Special Assistant to the President and Senior Associate Counsel.	Ricardo Rios.......................	PA	AD	....	....	....
Washington, DC	Special Assistant to the President and Senior Advisor to the Deputy Chief of Staff.	Molly Ritner........................	PA	AD	....	....	....
Washington, DC	Special Assistant to the President and Chief of Staff for the Office of Scheduling and Advance.	Paawee Rivera	PA	AD	....	....	....
Washington, DC	Special Assistant to the President and Director of Finance.	Courtney Rizzo	PA	AD	....	....	....
Washington, DC	Special Assistant to the President and Senior Presidential Speechwriter for the First Lady.	Mary Robbins	PA	AD	....	....	....
Washington, DC	Special Assistant to the President for Labor Policy.	Cassandra Robertson	PA	AD	....	....	....
Washington, DC	Special Assistant to the President and Director of the White House Office of Faith-Based and Neighborhood Partnerships.	Melissa Rogers	PA	AD	....	....	....
Washington, DC	Special Assistant to the President and Director of Confirmations.	Heather Samuelson..............	PA	AD	....	....	....
Washington, DC	Special Assistant to the President and Director of Strategic Planning and Senior Policy Advisor for the Office of the First Lady.	John Scanlon	PA	AD	....	....	....
Washington, DC	Special Assistant to the President for Health Care.	Jessica Schubel.....................	PA	AD	....	....	....
Washington, DC	Special Assistant to the President and Senior Advisor for Communications to the Chief of Staff.	Saloni Sharma	PA	AD	....	....	....
Washington, DC	Special Assistant to the President and Senate Legislative Affairs Liaison.	Dana Shubat........................	PA	AD	....	....	....
Washington, DC	Special Assistant to the President and Chief of Staff for the Office of Management and Administration.	Jennifer Sjogren	PA	AD	....	....	....
Washington, DC	Special Assistant to the President and Personal Aide to the President.	Jacob Spreyer	PA	AD	....	....	....
Washington, DC	Special Assistant to the President for Intergovernmental Affairs.	Stephanie Sykes..................	PA	AD	....	....	....
Washington, DC	Special Assistant to the President for Veterans Affairs.	Terri Tanielian.....................	PA	AD	....	....	....
Washington, DC	Special Assistant to the President and Director of Political Outreach.	Victoria Taylor	PA	AD	....	....	....

EXECUTIVE OFFICE OF THE PRESIDENT—Continued

Location	Position Title	Name of Incumbent	Type of Appt.	Pay Plan	Level, Grade, or Pay	Tenure	Expires
Washington, DC	Special Assistant to the President for Climate and Senior Advisor for Strategic Planning.	Frances Thomas	PA	AD	....	....	....
Washington, DC	Special Assistant to the President and Associate Counsel.	Raymond Tolentino	PA	AD	....	....	....
Washington, DC	Special Assistant to the President for Democracy and Civic Participation.	Justin Vail.............................	PA	AD	....	....	....
Washington, DC	Special Assistant to the President and Press Secretary for the First Lady.	Vanessa Valdivia	PA	AD	....	....	....
Washington, DC	Special Assistant to the President and Chief of Staff for the Office of Management and Administration.	Andrea Valverde...................	PA	AD	....	....	....
Washington, DC	Special Assistant to the President and Senior Advisor to the Deputy Chief of Staff.	Vivek Viswanathan	PA	AD	....	....	....
Washington, DC	Special Assistant to the President and Deputy Director for Global Gender Policy.	Rachel Vogelstein	PA	AD	....	....	....
Washington, DC	Special Assistant to the President and Senate Legislative Affairs Liaison.	Andrew Wallace...................	PA	AD	....	....	....
Washington, DC	Special Assistant to the President for Labor and Workers.	Rachel West	PA	AD	....	....	....
Washington, DC	Special Assistant to the President and Deputy Director of Management and Administration.	Jeffrey Wexler......................	PA	AD	....	....	....
Washington, DC	Special Assistant to the President and Senior Advisor for States and Implementation.	Ryan Whalen	PA	AD	....	....	....
Washington, DC	Special Assistant to the President and Deputy Director of the Office of Gun Violence Prevention.	Robert Wilcox.......................	PA	AD	....	....	....
Washington, DC	Special Assistant to the President and Chief of Staff for the Domestic Policy Council.	Brent Woolfork	PA	AD	....	....	....
Washington, DC	Special Assistant to the President and Director of the White House Visitors Office.	Ethan Yake	PA	AD	....	....	....
Washington, DC	Special Assistant to the President for Clean Energy Implementation.	Avi Zevin..............................	PA	AD	....	....	....
Washington, DC	Special Assistant to the President and Deputy Director of Communications.	Herbert Ziskend	PA	AD	....	....	....
Washington, DC	Special Assistant to the President for Economic Policy.	Joshua Zoffer	PA	AD	....	....	....
	OFFICE OF THE VICE PRESIDENT						
Washington, DC	Assistant to the President and Chief of Staff to the Vice President.	Lorraine A Voles...................	PA	AD	....	3	....
Washington, DC	Assistant to the President and National Security Advisor to the Vice President.	Philip H Gordon	PA	AD	....	3	....
Washington, DC	Deputy Assistant to the President and Communications Director to the Vice President.	Kirsten N Allen	PA	AD	....	3	....
Washington, DC	Deputy Assistant to the President and Chief of Staff to the Second Gentleman.	Jessica W Killin....................	PA	AD	....	3	....
Washington, DC	Deputy Assistant to the President and Principal Deputy National Security Advisor to the Vice President.	Rebecca R Lissner...............	PA	AD	....	3	....
Washington, DC	Deputy Assistant to the President and Domestic Policy Advisor to the Vice President.	Kristine J Lucius..................	PA	AD	....	3	....
Washington, DC	Deputy Assistant to the President and Counsel to the Vice President.	Erica K Songer	PA	AD	....	3	....
Washington, DC	Deputy Assistant to the President and Deputy Chief of Staff to the Vice President.	Erin S Wilson	PA	AD	....	3	....
Washington, DC	Special Assistant to the President and Press Secretary to the Vice President.	Ernesto Apreza	PA	AD	....	3	....
Washington, DC	Special Assistant to the President and Director of Management and Administration for the Office of the Vice President.	Cynthia R Bernstein............	PA	AD	....	3	....
Washington, DC	Special Assistant to the President and Deputy Director of the Office of Public Engagement and Intergovernmental Affairs.	Gabriela C Cristobal............	PA	AD	....	3	....
Washington, DC	Special Assistant to the President and Deputy Chief of Staff to the Second Gentleman.	Joshua J Dickson	PA	AD	....	3	....
Washington, DC	Special Assistant to the President and Deputy Domestic Policy Advisor to the Vice President.	Christopher Fisk	PA	AD	....	3	....
Washington, DC	Special Assistant to the President and Senior Advisor for Congressional Affairs and Strategic Outreach.	Andrew J Flick	PA	AD	....	3	....

EXECUTIVE OFFICE OF THE PRESIDENT—Continued

Location	Position Title	Name of Incumbent	Type of Appt.	Pay Plan	Level, Grade, or Pay	Tenure	Expires
Washington, DC	Special Assistant to the President and Director of Speechwriting for the Vice President.	Steven P Kelly......................	PA	AD	....	3	....
Washington, DC	Special Assistant to the President and Deputy National Security Advisor to the Vice President for Strategic Communications and Speechwriting.	Dean K Lieberman...............	PA	AD	....	3	....
Washington, DC	Special Assistant to the President and Director of Scheduling and Advance for the Vice President.	Kelsey L Smith....................	PA	AD	....	3	....
Washington, DC	Special Assistant to the President and Personal Aide to the Vice President.	Opal A Vadhan	PA	AD	....	3	....
	OFFICIAL RESIDENCE OF THE VICE PRESIDENT						
Washington, DC	Associate Director for Events	Felicity G Hector-Bruder	SC	GS	11	....	....
	COUNCIL OF ECONOMIC ADVISERS						
Washington, DC	Chairman, Council of Economic Advisers..........	Jared Bernstein....................	PAS	EX	II	....	....
Washington, DC	Member, Council of Economic Advisers	Heather Marie Boushey.......	PA	EX	IV	....	....
Washington, DC	Member, Council of Economic Advisers	Clement Jackson	PA	EX	IV	....	....
Washington, DC	Chief of Staff, Council of Economic Advisers.....	Amy Ganz	XS	AD	....	....	....
Washington, DC	Director of Macroeconomic Forecasting	Career Incumbent	CA	ES	....	....	....
	COUNCIL ON ENVIRONMENTAL QUALITY						
Washington, DC	Chair, Council on Environmental Quality	Brenda Mallory	PAS	EX	II	....	....
Washington, DC	Chief of Staff and Director of Policy and Programs.	Matthew Lee-Ashley	XS	AD	....	....	....
Washington, DC	General Counsel	Emma Cheuse	XS	AD	....	....	....
Washington, DC	Deputy Chief of Staff and Senior Advisor to the Chair.	Alyssa Roberts.....................	XS	AD	....	....	....
Washington, DC	Deputy General Counsel....................................	Vacant	....	AD	....	....	....
Washington, DC	Senior Advisor to the Chair	Corey Solow	XS	AD	....	....	....
Washington, DC	Senior Director for Water....................................	Sara Gonzalez-Rothi	XS	AD	....	....	....
Washington, DC	Senior Director for Lands	Stephenne Harding.............	SC	GS	15	....	....
Washington, DC	Senior Director for Chemical Safety and Plastic Pollution Prevention.	Jonathan Black....................	XS	AD	....	....	....
Washington, DC	Senior Director for Resilience............................	Crystal Bergemann.............	XS	AD	....	....	....
Washington, DC	Director for Public Engagement	Elise Gout	XS	AD	....	....	....
Washington, DC	Director of Communications	Justin Weiss........................	XS	AD	....	....	....
Washington, DC	Director of Congressional and Intergovernmental Affairs.	Kaitlyn Montan	SC	GS	13	....	....
Washington, DC	Senior Advisor for Engagement and Operations.	Emily McAuliffe	SC	GS	13	....	....
Washington, DC	Communications Advisor and Speechwriter.....	Mai McNicholas...................	SC	GS	12	....	....
Washington, DC	Policy Advisor for Clean Energy and Infrastructure.	Bianca Majumder................	SC	GS	11	....	....
Washington, DC	Special Assistant to the Chair...........................	Chetan Hebbale..................	SC	GS	9	....	....
Washington, DC	Staff Assistant for Environmental Justice	Abedlkareem Ihmeidan	SC	GS	7	....	....
Washington, DC	Member (Council on Environmental Quality)...	Vacant	....	EX	....	....	....
Washington, DC	Member (Council on Environmental Quality)...	Vacant	....	EX	....	....	....
Washington, DC	Deputy Director	Vacant	....	EX	....	....	....
	INTELLECTUAL PROPERTY ENFORCEMENT COORDINATOR						
Washington, DC	Intellectual Property Enforcement Coordinator.	Vacant	....	SL	....	....	....
Washington, DC	Legal Advisor	Career Incumbent	CA	ES	....	....	....
	NATIONAL SECURITY COUNCIL						
Washington, DC	Special Assistant to the President and Executive Secretary and Deputy Chief of Staff.	Dilpreet Sidhu	PA	EX	IV	....	....
	NATIONAL SPACE COUNCIL						
Washington, DC	Deputy Assistant to the President and Executive Secretary of the National Space Council.	Chirag R Parikh	PA	AD	....	....	....
	OFFICE OF ADMINISTRATION						
Washington, DC	Assistant to the President and Director, Office of Administration, and Director, Office of Management and Administration.	David Noble	PA	AD	....	....	....
Washington, DC	Deputy Assistant to the President and Deputy Director.	Sarah Feldmann...................	PA	AD	....	....	....
Washington, DC	Special Assistant to the President and Chief of Enterprise Applications.	Bindu Gakhar.......................	PA	AD	....	....	....

EXECUTIVE OFFICE OF THE PRESIDENT—Continued

Location	Position Title	Name of Incumbent	Type of Appt.	Pay Plan	Level, Grade, or Pay	Tenure	Expires
Washington, DC	Special Assistant to the President and Chief Financial Officer.	Viquar Ahmad	PA	AD	....	....	....
Washington, DC	Special Assistant to the President and Chief People Officer.	Danielle Melfi	PA	AD	....	....	....
Washington, DC	Special Assistant to the President and Chief Operations Officer.	Deborah Aguilar	PA	AD	....	....	....
Washington, DC	Special Assistant to the President and Director of White House Information Technology.	Austin Lin..............................	PA	AD	....	....	....
Washington, DC	Special Assistant to the President and General Counsel.	Raheemah Abdulaleem	PA	AD	....	....	....
Washington, DC	Chief of Staff...	Priyal Amin	PA	AD	....	....	....
Washington, DC	Deputy Chief Operations Officer......................	Allison Panther McIntee......	PA	AD	....	....	....
Washington, DC	Senior Advisor and Leadership Coach	Daniel Mulhern	PA	AD	....	....	....
	OFFICE OF MANAGEMENT AND BUDGET						
	Office of the Director						
Washington, DC	Director Office of Management and Budget......	Shalanda Delores Young......	PAS	EX	I	....	....
Washington, DC	Chief of Staff...	Karen De Los Santos	NA	ES	....	....	....
Washington, DC	Tribal Advisor	Elizabeth Edna Molle-Carr...	SC	GS	15	....	....
Washington, DC	Deputy Chief of Staff.....................................	Joshua David May................	SC	GS	13	....	....
Washington, DC	Special Assistant...	Zoriana Moulton...................	SC	GS	9	....	....
Washington, DC	Deputy Director Office of Management and Budget.	Nani Ann Coloretti..............	PAS	EX	II	....	....
Washington, DC	Executive Associate Director	Jacob David Leibenluft........	NA	ES	....	....	....
Washington, DC	Special Assistant...	Allison Toledo	SC	GS	9	....	....
Washington, DC	Deputy Director for Management	Jason S Miller......................	PAS	EX	II	....	....
Washington, DC	Senior Coordinator for Management.................	Julia Brinn Siegel	NA	ES	....	....	....
Washington, DC	Advisor to the Deputy Director for Management.	Sophie Maher	SC	GS	12	....	....
Washington, DC	Made in America Director...............................	Livia Shmavonian	NA	ES	....	....	....
Washington, DC	Senior Advisor, Office of Federal Procurement Policy (OFPP).	Christine Harada	NA	ES	....	....	....
Washington, DC	Associate Director for Performance Management.	Loren Schulman	NA	ES	....	....	....
Washington, DC	Confidential Assistant....................................	Makaila Ranges...................	SC	GS	9	....	....
	Legislative Affairs						
Washington, DC	Associate Director for Legislative Affairs	Wintta Woldemariam...........	NA	ES	....	....	....
Washington, DC	Deputy Associate Director for Legislative Affairs.	Janice Marong Nsor............	SC	GS	14	....	....
Washington, DC	Deputy to the Associate Director for Legislative Affairs and Senior Advisor for Public Engagement.	Benjamin Adam Ward..........	SC	GS	14	....	....
Washington, DC	Deputy to the Associate Director for Legislative Affairs.	Matthew Pastore	SC	GS	12	....	....
Washington, DC	Confidential Assistant....................................	Shelby Talton......................	SC	GS	9	....	....
	General Counsel						
Washington, DC	General Counsel...	Daniel Jacobson...................	NA	ES	....	....	....
Washington, DC	Deputy General Counsel	Adam Grogg........................	NA	ES	....	....	....
Washington, DC	Senior Counsel for Oversight............................	Tara Pugera Ganapathy	SC	GS	15	....	....
Washington, DC	Senior Counsel..	Samuel Callahan.................	SC	GS	15	....	....
Washington, DC	Confidential Assistant....................................	Abegael Admete...................	SC	GS	9	....	....
	Communications						
Washington, DC	Associate Director for Communications and Strategy.	Shelby Wagenseller	NA	ES	....	....	....
Washington, DC	Senior Advisor for Communications..................	Vacant	....	ES	....	....	....
Washington, DC	Deputy Associate Director for Communications.	Alexandra Bell......................	SC	GS	14	....	....
Washington, DC	Deputy Associate Director for Communications.	Christina Wilkes..................	SC	GS	14	....	....
Washington, DC	Advisor..	Nicholas Batman.................	SC	GS	11	....	....
	Office of Management and Budget						
Washington, DC	Associate Director for Economic Policy..............	Wesley Eu-Kwang Yin	NA	ES	....	....	....
	Climate, Energy, Environment and Science Programs, Not "Staff Offices"						
Washington, DC	Associate Director, Climate, Energy, Environment, and Science Programs (CEESP).	Laura Gillam	NA	ES	....	....	....
Washington, DC	Confidential Assistant....................................	Megan Kosai........................	SC	GS	7	....	....

EXECUTIVE OFFICE OF THE PRESIDENT—Continued

Location	Position Title	Name of Incumbent	Type of Appt.	Pay Plan	Level, Grade, or Pay	Tenure	Expires
	General Government Programs						
Washington, DC	Associate Director for General Government Programs.	Joseph Carlile......................	NA	ES	....	....	....
Washington, DC	Confidential Assistant...	Samuel Apostolopoulos	SC	GS	7	....	....
	Education, Income Maintenance and Labor Programs						
Washington, DC	Program Associate Director, Education, Income, Maintenance and Labor (EIML).	Amanda Perez	NA	ES	....	....	....
Washington, DC	Confidential Assistant...	Christopher Clayton.............	SC	GS	9	....	....
	Health Division						
Washington, DC	Program Associate Director for Health Programs.	Rose Melody Sullivan	NA	ES	....	....	....
Washington, DC	Confidential Assistant...	Nancy Khasungu Makale	SC	GS	9	....	....
	National Security Programs						
Washington, DC	Associate Director for National Security Programs.	Edward F Meier	NA	ES	....	....	....
Washington, DC	Advisor to the Associate Director for National Security Programs.	Patrick K Sullivan...............	SC	GS	12	....	....
	Office of Federal Financial Management						
Washington, DC	Controller, Office of Federal Financial Management.	Vacant	....	EX	....	....	....
	Office of Federal Procurement Policy						
Washington, DC	Confidential Assistant...	Benjamin Schwartz..............	SC	GS	7	....	....
Washington, DC	Administrator Office of Federal Procurement Policy.	Vacant	....	EX	....	....	....
	Office of Information and Regulatory Affairs						
Washington, DC	Administrator, Office of Information and Regulatory Affairs.	Richard Revesz	PAS	EX	III	....	....
Washington, DC	Associate Administrator, Office of Information and Regulatory Affairs.	Samuel Kryzan Berger	NA	ES	....	....	....
Washington, DC	Counselor to the OIRA Administrator	Varun Mohan Jain	SC	GS	15	....	....
Washington, DC	Senior Counselor to the OIRA Administrator ...	Martha G Roberts	NA	ES	....	....	....
Washington, DC	Confidential Assistant...	Dianelda Pulido...................	SC	GS	9	....	....
	Office of E-government and Information Technology						
Washington, DC	Administrator E-Government and Information Technology.	Clare Martorana...................	PA	EX	III	....	....
Washington, DC	Federal Chief Information Security Officer.......	Vacant	....	ES	....	....	....
Washington, DC	Confidential Assistant...	Leah Milhander...................	SC	GS	11	....	....
Washington, DC	Confidential Assistant...	Kevin O'Connor...................	SC	GS	7	....	....
Washington, DC	Administrator, United States Digital Service (USDS).	Mina K Hsiang.....................	SC	SL	....	....	....
Washington, DC	Senior Advisor for Delivery (USDS)..................	Andrew Michael Nacin	SC	GS	15	....	....
	OFFICE OF THE NATIONAL CYBER DIRECTOR						
Washington, DC	National Cyber Director....................................	Harry Coker........................	PAS	AD	....	....	....
Washington, DC	Deputy National Cyber Director	Vacant	....	AD	....	....	....
Washington, DC	Chief of Staff..	Michael Hochman	XS	AD	....	....	....
Washington, DC	Assistant National Cyber Director for Strategy and Research.	James Krejsa	XS	AD	....	....	....
Washington, DC	Assist National Cyber Director for Legislative Affairs.	Elliott Phaup	XS	AD	....	....	....
Washington, DC	Assistant National Cyber Director for Public Affairs.	Victoria Dillon	XS	AD	....	....	....
Washington, DC	Assistant National Cyber Director for Cyber Policy and Programs.	Nicholas Leiserson	XS	AD	....	....	....
Washington, DC	Assistant National Cyber Director for Supply Chain and Tech Security.	Anjana Rajan.......................	XS	AD	....	....	....
Washington, DC	Assistant National Cyber Director for Stakeholder Engagement.	Jennifer Sara Berlin	XS	AD	....	....	....
Washington, DC	Assistant National Cyber Director for Workforce, Training, and Education.	Seeyew Mo	XS	AD	....	....	....
Washington, DC	Assistant National Cyber Director for Federal Cyber.	Philip Stupak.......................	XS	AD	....	....	....
Washington, DC	Attorney-Advisor...	Vacant	....	AD	....	....	....
Washington, DC	Chief Counsel for Regulatory Harmonization and Senior Advisor to the National Cyber Director.	Jonathan Feigelson	XS	AD	....	....	....
Washington, DC	Dep Assist National Cyber Director for Legislative Affairs.	Elliott Phaup	XS	AD	....	....	....

EXECUTIVE OFFICE OF THE PRESIDENT—Continued

Location	Position Title	Name of Incumbent	Type of Appt.	Pay Plan	Level, Grade, or Pay	Tenure	Expires
Washington, DC	Deputy Assistant National Cyber Director for Stakeholder Engagement.	Caroline Chang	XS	AD	....	....	....
Washington, DC	Deputy Assistant National Cyber Director for Stakeholder Engagement.	Faith Lowe	XS	AD	....	....	....
Washington, DC	Deputy Assistant National Cyber Director for Public Affairs and Press Secretary.	Vacant	....	AD	....	....	....
Washington, DC	Deputy Chief of Staff...	William Xavier Doerrer	XS	AD	....	....	....
Washington, DC	Deputy Executive Secretary	Chloe Sztabnik	XS	AD	....	....	....
Washington, DC	Deputy Assistant National Cyber Director for Technology and Ecosystem Security.	Vacant	....	AD	....	....	....
Washington, DC	Deputy Assistant National Cyber Director for Strategy and Budget.	Drenan Dudley	XS	AD	....	....	....
Washington, DC	Director for Strategy and Budget......................	Nikolis Robert Smith	XS	AD	....	....	....
Washington, DC	Director for Strategy	Lauryn Williams...................	XS	AD	....	....	....
Washington, DC	Director of Special Projects...............................	Michaela Lee	XS	AD	....	....	....
Washington, DC	Deputy Executive Secretary	Christina Coleburn	XS	AD	....	....	....
Washington, DC	Executive Secretary and Senior Advisor...........	Vacant	....	AD	....	....	....
Washington, DC	General Counsel	James Halpert	XS	AD	....	....	....
Washington, DC	Policy Advisor..	Jackson Reid......................	XS	AD	....	....	....
Washington, DC	Policy Advisor..	Xavier Ortega	XS	AD	....	....	....
Washington, DC	Press Assistant..	Vacant	....	AD	....	....	....
Washington, DC	Principal Senior Advisor	Julie Klein	XS	AD	....	....	....
Washington, DC	Senior Advisor (National Cybersecurity)..........	Caitlin Clarke......................	XS	AD	....	....	....
Washington, DC	Senior Advisor (National Cybersecurity)..........	Vacant	....	AD	....	....	....
Washington, DC	Senior Advisor (National Cybersecurity)..........	Stephen Vina	XS	AD	....	....	....
Washington, DC	Senior Advisor (Technology and Ecosystem Security).	Oumou Ly	XS	AD	....	....	....
Washington, DC	Senior Advisor, Legislative Affairs	Nury Rodriguez	XS	AD	....	....	....
Washington, DC	Senior Strategy and Research Advisor	Vacant	....	AD	....	....	....
Washington, DC	Special Advisor...	Haley Ring	XS	AD	....	....	....
Washington, DC	Special Advisor...	Vacant	....	AD	....	....	....
Washington, DC	Special Advisor...	Vacant	....	AD	....	....	....
Washington, DC	Special Advisor...	Eitan Geller-Montague	XS	AD	....	....	....
Washington, DC	Special Advisor...	Jennifer Hughes	XS	AD	....	....	....
Washington, DC	Special Assistant..	Charlotte Bradsher	XS	AD	....	....	....
Washington, DC	Special Assistant..	Vacant	....	AD	....	....	....
Washington, DC	Special Assistant..	Adrianna Perez....................	XS	AD	....	....	....
Washington, DC	Special Assistant..	Adriana Lobo	XS	AD	....	....	....
Washington, DC	Special Assistant (National Cybersecurity).......	Sterlin Waters.....................	XS	AD	....	....	....
Washington, DC	Special Assistant (Stakeholder Engagement)....	Vacant	....	AD	....	....	....
Washington, DC	Special Assistant (Stakeholder Engagement)....	Vacant	....	....	....	....	....
Washington, DC	Special Assistant to the Deputy National Cyber Director for Technology and Ecosystem Security.	Vacant	....	AD	....	....	....
	OFFICE OF THE NATIONAL DRUG CONTROL POLICY						
	Office of the Director						
Washington, DC	Director...	Rahul Gupta	PAS	EX	I	....	....
Washington, DC	Deputy Director, Office of National Drug Control Policy.	Adam W Cohen....................	PA	EX	II	....	....
Washington, DC	Chief of Staff..	Ali Haider Bokhari...............	NA	ES	....	....	....
Washington, DC	Attorney-Advisor (General)...............................	Brian Skinner......................	NA	ES	....	....	....
Washington, DC	Senior Advisor (International Relations and Supply Reduction).	Career Incumbent	CA	ES	....	....	....
Washington, DC	Confidential Assistant	Ruhan Syed	SC	GS	9	....	....
	Office of External and Legislative Affairs						
Washington, DC	Assistant Director, Office of External and Legislative Affairs.	Jude McCartin.....................	NA	ES	....	....	....
Washington, DC	Communications Director, Public Affairs...........	Elizabeth Marie Smalley	SC	GS	14	....	....
Washington, DC	Public Affairs Specialist (Press Secretary)........	Samar Ahmad......................	SC	GS	11	....	....
Washington, DC	Legislative Analyst	Amanda Guiliano	SC	GS	13	....	....
Washington, DC	Legislative Analyst	Elisabeth Eyre.....................	SC	GS	13	....	....
Washington, DC	Engagement Specialist.....................................	Erin Sezgin	SC	GS	7	....	....
	Office of Performance and Budget						
Washington, DC	Deputy Assistant Director for Performance and Budget.	Career Incumbent	CA	ES	....	....	....
	Office of Operations						
Washington, DC	Assistant Director, Office of Operations	Career Incumbent	CA	ES	....	....	....

EXECUTIVE OFFICE OF THE PRESIDENT—Continued

Location	Position Title	Name of Incumbent	Type of Appt.	Pay Plan	Level, Grade, or Pay	Tenure	Expires
	Office of Homeland Interdiction and Supply Disruption						
Washington, DC	Assistant Director, Office of Homeland Interdiction and Supply Disruption.	Career Incumbent	CA	ES	....	....	....
	Office of Public Health						
Washington, DC	Assistant Director, Office of Public Health........	Vacant	....	ES	....	....	....
Washington, DC	Senior Advisor (Public Health)	Vacant	....	ES	....	....	....
	Office of Translational Research						
Washington, DC	Assistant Director, Translational Research	Vacant	....	ES	....	....	....
	Office of Commercial Disruption and International Relations						
Washington, DC	Assistant Director, Office of Commercial Disruption and International Relations.	Career Incumbent	CA	ES	....	....	....
	OFFICE OF PANDEMIC PREPAREDNESS AND RESPONSE POLICY						
Washington, DC	Deputy Assistant to the President and Director of the Office of Pandemic Preparedness and Response Policy.	Paul Friedrichs	PA	EX	II	....	....
	OFFICE OF SCIENCE AND TECHNOLOGY POLICY						
Washington, DC	Assistant to the President for Science and Technology, and Director of the Office of Science and Technology Policy.	Arati Prabhakar	PAS	EX	....	....	....
Washington, DC	United States Chief Technology Officer, and Associate Director of Office of Science and Technology Policy.	Vacant	....	EX	....	....	....
Washington, DC	Associate Director, National Security and International Affairs.	Vacant	....	EX	....	....	....
Washington, DC	Associate Director, Science....................	Vacant	....	EX	....	....	....
Washington, DC	Associate Director, Technology........................	Vacant	....	EX	....	....	....
Washington, DC	Special Assistant to the President and Chief of Staff and Deputy Director for Strategy.	Asad Ramzanali	NA	ES	....	....	....
Washington, DC	Special Assistant to the President and Principal Deputy Director for Science, Society, and Policy.	Kei Koizumi..........................	NA	ES	....	....	....
Washington, DC	General Counsel	Vacant	....	ES	....	....	....
Washington, DC	Deputy Chief Technology Officer......................	Vacant	....	ES	....	....	....
Washington, DC	Deputy Director for Industrial Innovation	Justina R Gallegos	SC	GS	15	....	....
Washington, DC	Director of Communication................................	Jacqueline McGuinness	SC	GS	15	....	....
Washington, DC	Director for Legislative Affairs........................	Alexandrine De Bianchi.......	SC	GS	15	....	....
Washington, DC	Deputy Chief of Staff....................................	John Cumming-Meininger...	SC	GS	14	....	....
Washington, DC	Confidential Assistant....................................	Gabriela Giro......................	SC	GS	9	....	....
Washington, DC	Chief of Staff	Vacant	....	ES	....	....	....
Washington, DC	Principal Deputy Director for Policy....................	Vacant	....	ES	....	....	....
Washington, DC	Special Assistant to the President and Principal Deputy U.S. Chief Technology Officer and Deputy Director of Office of Science and Technology Policy.	Vacant	....	ES	....	....	....
	OFFICE OF THE UNITED STATES TRADE REPRESENTATIVE						
	Office of the Ambassador						
Washington, DC	United States Trade Representative....................	Katherine Chi Tai	PAS	EX	I	....	....
Washington, DC	Senior Advisor to the United States Trade Representative.	Elizabeth Baltzan.................	NA	ES	....	....	....
Washington, DC	Senior Advisor to the United States Trade Representative.	Cara Morrow	NA	ES	....	....	....
Washington, DC	Senior Advisor to the United States Trade Representative.	Jamila Thompson	NA	ES	....	....	....
Washington, DC	Chief of Staff....................................	Vacant	....	ES	....	....	....
Washington, DC	Deputy Chief of Staff....................................	Vacant	....	....	....	....	....
Washington, DC	Deputy Chief of Staff....................................	Vacant	....	AD	....	....	....
Washington, DC	Director of Scheduling and Advance Coordinator.	Angelica Zen Annino............	SC	GS	13	....	....
Washington, DC	Deputy Executive Secretary	William Shih........................	XS	AD	....	....	....
Washington, DC	Special Assistant to the United States Trade Representative.	Vacant	....	AD	....	....	....
Washington, DC	Special Advisor for Strategic Planning.............	Keziah Clarke......................	XS	AD	....	....	....
Washington, DC	Special Assistant to the United States Trade Representative.	Lauren Brown	XS	AD	....	....	....
Washington, DC	Special Advisor for Strategic Planning.............	Devontae Freeland	XS	AD	....	....	....

EXECUTIVE OFFICE OF THE PRESIDENT—Continued

Location	Position Title	Name of Incumbent	Type of Appt.	Pay Plan	Level, Grade, or Pay	Tenure	Expires
	Deputy United States Trade Representative (1)						
Washington, DC	Deputy United States Trade Representative (Rank of Ambassador).	Vacant	....	EX	....	....	....
Washington, DC	Special Assistant to the Deputy	Vacant	....	AD	....	....	....
Washington, DC	Special Assistant to the Deputy	Claire Blanton	XS	AD	....	....	....
	Deputy United States Trade Representative (2)						
Washington, DC	Deputy United States Trade Representative (Rank of Ambassador).	Vacant	....	EX	....	....	....
Washington, DC	Special Assistant to the Deputy	Vacant	....	AD	....	....	....
	Chief Agricultural Negotiator						
Washington, DC	Chief Agricultural Negotiator (Rank of Ambassador).	Douglas McKalip	PAS	EX	III	....	....
Washington, DC	Special Assistant to the Chief Agricultural Negotiator.	Jonathan Hurst	XS	AD	....	....	....
	Geneva						
Geneva, Swit	Deputy United States Trade Representative (Rank of Ambassador).	Maria L Pagan.....................	PAS	EX	III	....	....
	Public and Media Affairs						
Washington, DC	Assistant United States Trade Representative for Public Affairs.	Samuel Michel.....................	XS	AD	....	....	....
Washington, DC	Deputy Assistant United States Trade Representative for Public Affairs.	Dylan Hewitt	SC	GS	13	....	....
Washington, DC	Deputy Assistant United States Trade Representative for Public Affairs.	Khalid Sarsour	XS	AD	....	....	....
Washington, DC	Writer-Editor (Speech)	Sung Chang	SC	GS	15	....	....
Washington, DC	Press Secretary	Angela Perez........................	XS	AD	....	....	....
Washington, DC	Digital Coordinator (Press Assistant)	Catherine White	XS	AD	....	....	....
	General Counsel						
Washington, DC	Attorney-Advisor (General Counsel)	Vacant	....	ES	....	....	....
Washington, DC	Deputy General Counsel	Vacant	....	ES	....	....	....
Polk, FL	Special Assistant to the General Counsel..........	Diamonde Cruz.....................	XS	AD	....	....	....
	Congressional Affairs						
Washington, DC	Assistant United States Trade Representative for Congressional Affairs.	Daniel McCarthy	SC	GS	15	....	....
Washington, DC	Deputy Assistant United States Trade Representative for Congressional Affairs.	Samuel Tedla Negatu...........	XS	AD	....	....	....
Washington, DC	Congressional Affairs Specialist.........................	Jillian McGrath	XS	AD	....	....	....
Washington, DC	Congressional Affairs Specialist.........................	Matthew Hoeck	XS	AD	....	....	....
	Intergovernmental Affairs and Public Engagement						
Washington, DC	Assistant United States Trade Representative for Intergovernmental Affairs and Public Engagement.	Roberto Carlos Soberanis	SC	GS	15	....	....
Washington, DC	Deputy Assistant United States Trade Representative for Intergovernmental Affairs and Public Engagement.	Vacant	....	AD	....	....	....
Washington, DC	Director of Intergovernmental Affairs and Public Engagement.	Christopher Gundermann ...	XS	AD	....	....	....
Washington, DC	Director for Intergovernmental Affairs and Public Engagement.	Anthony Reyes......................	XS	AD	....	....	....
	Textiles and Apparel						
Washington, DC	Chief Textiles and Apparel Negotiator...............	Katherine White...................	SC	GS	15	....	....

DEPARTMENTS

DEPARTMENT OF AGRICULTURE

Location	Position Title	Name of Incumbent	Type of Appt.	Pay Plan	Level, Grade, or Pay	Tenure	Expires
	OFFICE OF THE SECRETARY						
Washington, DC	Secretary	Thomas James Vilsack	PAS	EX	I		
Washington, DC	Chief of Staff	Katharine Ferguson	NA	ES			
Washington, DC	Deputy Chief of Staff for Policy	Sean Babington	NA	ES			
Washington, DC	Deputy Chief of Staff	Justo Robles	NA	ES			
Washington, DC	Senior Advisor	Linda A Delgado	NA	ES			
Washington, DC	Senior Advisor	Vacant		ES			
Washington, DC	Senior Advisor	Sivakumar Chandran	NA	ES			
Washington, DC	Director, Office of Tribal Relations	Vacant		ES			
Washington, DC	Senior Advisor for Racial Equity	Dewayne Goldmon	NA	ES			
Washington, DC	Senior Advisor for Climate	Vacant		ES			
Washington, DC	Chief Diversity and Inclusion Officer	Career Incumbent	CA	ES			
Washington, DC	Principal Senior Advisor	Career Incumbent	CA	ES			
Washington, DC	Trade Counsel	Career Incumbent	CA	ES			
Washington, DC	Director of Scheduling	Lauren Atzenbeck	SC	GS	15		
Washington, DC	Director of Advance	Juan Dominguez	SC	GS	15		
Washington, DC	Senior Advisor	Gregory Jaffe	SC	GS	15		
Washington, DC	Senior Advisor	Regina Marie Black	SC	GS	15		
Washington, DC	Senior Advisor	Silvia Fabela-Leyva	SC	GS	15		
Washington, DC	Senior Advisor	Tien Nguyen	SC	GS	15		
Washington, DC	Deputy White House Liaison	Hunter Henderson	SC	GS	13		
Washington, DC	Scheduler	Erin Sandlin	SC	GS	13		
Washington, DC	Special Advisor	Caitlin Balagula	SC	GS	13		
Washington, DC	Advance Lead	Emily Campbell	SC	GS	12		
Washington, DC	Special Assistant	Claudia Meng	SC	GS	12		
Washington, DC	Special Assistant	Fabiola Torres-Lara	SC	GS	11		
	Office of the Deputy Secretary						
Washington, DC	Deputy Secretary of Agriculture	Xochitl Torres Small	PAS	EX	II		
Washington, DC	Chief of Staff to the Deputy Secretary	Russellie Bongolan	NA	ES			
Washington, DC	Senior Advisor	Steffanie Bezruki	NA	ES			
Washington, DC	Special Advisor	Tharun Vemulapalli	SC	GS	13		
Washington, DC	Special Advisor	Diamond Rodriguez	SC	GS	12		
	Office of the Assistant Secretary for Congressional Relations						
Washington, DC	Assistant Secretary for Congressional Relations.	Adrienne Wojie Wojciechowski.	PAS	EX	IV		
Washington, DC	Deputy Assistant Secretary for Congressional Relations.	Vacant		ES			
Washington, DC	Deputy Assistant Secretary for Congressional Relations.	Rodolfo Soto	NA	ES			
Washington, DC	Director of Oversight	Ramon Correa-Colon	SC	GS	15		
Washington, DC	Director, Faith Based and Neighborhood Outreach.	Samantha Joseph	SC	GS	15		
Washington, DC	Director of External Affairs	Brian Sowyrda	SC	GS	15		
Washington, DC	Chief of Staff	Valerie McMakin	SC	GS	15		
Washington, DC	Senior Legislative Advisor	Tracy Fox	SC	GS	15		
Washington, DC	Legislative Advisor	Kiara Tringali	SC	GS	14		
Washington, DC	Legislative Advisor	Gabriela Foster	SC	GS	13		
Washington, DC	Special Advisor	Fernando Brigidi De Mello..	SC	GS	13		
Washington, DC	Legislative Advisor	Varun Butaney	SC	GS	12		
Washington, DC	Legislative Analyst	Cody Baynori	SC	GS	11		
Washington, DC	Special Assistant	Maria Espinoza	SC	GS	11		
Washington, DC	Special Assistant	John Dunn	SC	GS	11		
Washington, DC	Special Assistant	Bryan Bravo	SC	GS	11		
	Office of the Assistant Secretary for Civil Rights						
Washington, DC	Assistant Secretary for Civil Rights	Vacant		EX			
Washington, DC	Deputy Assistant Secretary for Civil Rights	Penny Brown Reynolds	NA	ES			
Washington, DC	Deputy Assistant Secretary for Civil Rights	Vacant		ES			
Washington, DC	Associate Assistant Secretary for Civil Rights..	Career Incumbent	CA	ES			
Washington, DC	Chief of Staff	Conisha Hackett	SC	GS	15		
Washington, DC	Special Assistant	Xochilt Andrade	SC	GS	11		
	Office of Civil Rights						
Washington, DC	Director, Office of Civil Rights	Career Incumbent	CA	ES			
Washington, DC	Deputy Executive Director for Civil Rights	Vacant		ES			

DEPARTMENT OF AGRICULTURE—Continued

Location	Position Title	Name of Incumbent	Type of Appt.	Pay Plan	Level, Grade, or Pay	Tenure	Expires
	Office of the Assistant Secretary for Administration						
Washington, DC	Assistant Secretary for Administration	Malcom Allen Shorter	PA	EX	IV	....	....
Washington, DC	Deputy Assistant Secretary for Administration.	Vacant	....	ES	....	....	....
Washington, DC	Deputy Assistant Secretary for Administration.	Yeshimebet Abebe	NA	ES	....	....	....
	Departmental Administration						
Washington, DC	Director, Office of Property and Fleet Management.	Career Incumbent	CA	ES	....	....	....
Washington, DC	Chief Learning Officer	Career Incumbent	CA	ES	....	....	....
Washington, DC	Director Customer Experience	Career Incumbent	CA	ES	....	....	....
Washington, DC	Executive Director	Career Incumbent	CA	ES	....	....	....
	Office of Human Resources Management						
Washington, DC	Chief Human Capital Officer.............................	Career Incumbent	CA	ES	....	....	....
	Office of Small and Disadvantaged Business Utilization						
Washington, DC	Director, Office of Small and Disadvantaged Business Utilization.	Career Incumbent	CA	ES	....	....	....
	Office of the General Counsel						
Washington, DC	General Counsel	Vacant	....	EX	....	....	....
Washington, DC	Deputy General Counsel (Principal)	Mary Beth Schultz	NA	ES	....	....	....
Washington, DC	Deputy General Counsel	Eric Womack........................	NA	ES	....	....	....
Washington, DC	Deputy General Counsel	Prescott Martin	NA	ES	....	....	....
Washington, DC	Assistant General Counsel, International Affairs, Food Assistance, and Farm and Rural Programs Division.	Vacant	....	ES	....	....	....
Washington, DC	Assistant General Counsel, Civil Rights, Labor and Employment Law Division.	Vacant	....	ES	....	....	....
Washington, DC	Assistant General Counsel, Marketing, Regulatory and Food Safety Programs Division.	Career Incumbent	CA	ES	....	....	....
Washington, DC	Assistant General Counsel, International Affairs, Food Assistance and Farm and Rural Programs Division.	Career Incumbent	CA	ES	....	....	....
Washington, DC	Assistant General Counsel, Marketing, Regulatory and Food Safety Division.	Career Incumbent	CA	ES	....	....	....
Washington, DC	Assistant General Counsel, General Law and Research Division.	Career Incumbent	CA	ES	....	....	....
Washington, DC	Associate General Counsel, Natural Resources and Environment Division.	Career Incumbent	CA	ES	....	....	....
Washington, DC	Associate General Counsel, Regulatory and Marketing.	Vacant	....	ES	....	....	....
Washington, DC	Associate General Counsel, Civil Rights Litigation.	Career Incumbent	CA	ES	....	....	....
Washington, DC	Associate General Counsel, International Affairs and Commodity Programs and Food Assistance.	Vacant	....	ES	....	....	....
Washington, DC	Associate General Counsel, International Affairs, Food Assistance, and Farm and Rural Programs Division.	Career Incumbent	CA	ES	....	....	....
Washington, DC	Director, Office of Ethics	Career Incumbent	CA	ES	....	....	....
San Francisco, CA...	Regional Attorney	Career Incumbent	CA	ES	....	....	....
Albuquerque, NM....	Regional Attorney	Career Incumbent	CA	ES	....	....	....
Kansas City, MO	Regional Attorney	Career Incumbent	CA	ES	....	....	....
Atlanta, GA	Regional Attorney	Vacant	....	ES	....	....	....
Denver, CO	Regional Attorney	Vacant	....	ES	....	....	....
Washington, DC	Senior Oversight Counselor	Nathaniel West....................	SC	GS	15	....	....
Washington, DC	Senior Counselor..	Jeremiah Chapin..................	SC	GS	15	....	....
Washington, DC	Confidential Assistant	Clarissa Marconi Alvarez	SC	GS	9	....	....
	Office of Communications						
Washington, DC	Director of Communications	Catherine E Cochran	NA	ES	....	....	....
Washington, DC	Deputy Director of Communications.................	Marissa Perry	SC	GS	15	....	....
Washington, DC	Speech Writer..	Nina Anand	SC	GS	15	....	....
Washington, DC	Senior Advisor for Strategic Communications ..	William Clement	SC	GS	14	....	....
Washington, DC	Press Secretary	Allan Rodriguez..................	SC	GS	14	....	....
Washington, DC	Special Advisor...	Paige Blanchard	SC	GS	12	....	....
Washington, DC	Press Assistant	Geoffrey Preudhomme	SC	GS	9	....	....
Washington, DC	Press Assistant	Matthew Spata	SC	GS	9	....	....
Washington, DC	Press Assistant	Alexis Posel..........................	SC	GS	9	....	....

DEPARTMENT OF AGRICULTURE—Continued

Location	Position Title	Name of Incumbent	Type of Appt.	Pay Plan	Level, Grade, or Pay	Tenure	Expires
	Office of the Chief Information Officer						
Washington, DC	Chief Information Officer...................................	Career Incumbent	CA	ES	....	....	....
Washington, DC	Chief Data Officer..	Career Incumbent	CA	ES	....	....	....
Washington, DC	Associate Chief Information Officer..................	Career Incumbent	CA	ES	....	....	....
Washington, DC	Associate Chief Information Officer for Policy, E-Government and Fair Information Practices.	Career Incumbent	CA	ES	....	....	....
Washington, DC	Associate Chief Information Officer, Client Technology Services.	Career Incumbent	CA	ES	....	....	....
Washington, DC	Associate Chief Information Officer, International Security Operations Center, Cyber.	Career Incumbent	CA	ES	....	....	....
	OFFICE OF THE CHIEF FINANCIAL OFFICER						
Washington, DC	Chief Financial Officer....................................	Vacant	....	EX	....	....	....
Washington, DC	Associate Chief Financial Officer, Financial Operations/Comptroller.	Career Incumbent	CA	ES	....	....	....
Washington, DC	Chief of Staff..	Wesley Swanzy	SC	GS	15	....	....
	National Finance Center						
New Orleans, LA....	Director, National Finance Center	Career Incumbent	CA	ES	....	....	....
New Orleans, LA....	Director, Government Employee Services Division.	Career Incumbent	CA	ES	....	....	....
	Office of Budget and Program Analysis						
Washington, DC	Associate Director...	Career Incumbent	CA	ES	....	....	....
Washington, DC	Deputy Director for Program Analysis	Career Incumbent	CA	ES	....	....	....
Washington, DC	Director, Budget Control and Analysis Division.	Vacant	....	ES	....	....	....
	Office of Partnerships and Public Engagement						
Washington, DC	Director Office of Partnerships and Public Engagement.	Career Incumbent	CA	ES	....	....	....
	Office of the Chief Economist						
Washington, DC	Chief Economist...	Career Incumbent	CA	ES	....	....	....
	OFFICE OF THE UNDER SECRETARY FOR RURAL DEVELOPMENT						
Washington, DC	Under Secretary for Rural Development...........	Basil I Gooden	PAS	EX	III	....	....
Washington, DC	Deputy Under Secretary for Rural Development.	Farah Ahmad......................	NA	ES	....	....	....
Washington, DC	Chief of Staff..	Sarah M Dietch	NA	ES	....	....	....
Washington, DC	Chief Risk Officer...	Vacant	....	ES	....	....	....
Washington, DC	Senior Advisor for Rural Engagement Delivery and Prosperity.	Cynthia Axne......................	SC	GS	15	....	....
Washington, DC	Senior Counselor for Rural Energy	Clare Sierawski...................	SC	GS	15	....	....
Washington, DC	Special Advisor...	Liliiana Valdes Gamboa.......	SC	GS	12	....	....
	Rural Development						
Washington, DC	Chief Operating Officer...................................	Career Incumbent	CA	ES	....	....	....
Washington, DC	Chief Risk Officer...	Career Incumbent	CA	ES	....	....	....
Washington, DC	Chief Innovation Officer..................................	Career Incumbent	CA	ES	....	....	....
Washington, DC	Director of State Operations............................	Deidre Robert	NA	ES	....	....	....
St Louis, MO	Director, National Financial and Accounting Operations Center.	Career Incumbent	CA	ES	....	....	....
Washington, DC	Deputy Chief Operating Officer	Vacant	....	ES	....	....	....
St Louis, MO	Associate Director, Asset and Business Operations.	Career Incumbent	CA	ES	....	....	....
St Louis, MO	Associate Director..	Vacant	....	ES	....	....	....
Washington, DC	Senior Advisor..	James Dahman....................	SC	GS	14	....	....
Washington, DC	Special Assistant..	Aidan Miller	SC	GS	11	....	....
Montgomery, AL	State Director - Alabama	Nivory Gordon	SC	GS	15	....	....
Palmer, AK..............	State Director - Alaska....................................	Julie Hnilicka	SC	GS	15	....	....
Little Rock, AR	State Director - Arkansas	Jill Floyd...........................	SC	GS	15	....	....
Lakewood, CO	State Director - Colorado	Crestina Martinez...............	SC	GS	15	....	....
Gainesville, FL	State Director - Florida	Lakeisha Hood....................	SC	GS	15	....	....
Honolulu, HI...........	State Director - Hawaii	Chris Jun Kanazawa...........	SC	GS	15	....	....
Indianapolis, IN	State Director - Indiana	Terry Goodin......................	SC	GS	15	....	....
Champagne, IL........	State Director - Illinois	Pamela Monetti	SC	GS	15	....	....
Des Moines, IA	State Director - Iowa	Theresa Greenfield..............	SC	GS	15	....	....
Morehead, KY.........	State Director - Kentucky	Thomas Carew....................	SC	GS	15	....	....
Dover, DE................	State Director - Maryland/Delaware.................	Andrew Dinsmore	SC	GS	15	....	....
Bangor, ME.............	State Director - Maine	Rhiannon Hampson	SC	GS	15	....	....
Amherst, MA...........	State Director - Massachusetts	Scott J Soares....................	SC	GS	15	....	....
St Paul, MN............	State Director - Minnesota	Mary Colleen Landkamer....	SC	GS	15	....	....

DEPARTMENT OF AGRICULTURE—Continued

Location	Position Title	Name of Incumbent	Type of Appt.	Pay Plan	Level, Grade, or Pay	Tenure	Expires
Jackson, MS.............	State Director - Mississippi	Trina N George	SC	GS	15	....	....
Columbia, MO	State Director - Missouri	Kyle Wilkens.......................	SC	GS	15	....	....
Raleigh, NC	State Director - North Carolina	Reginald Speight.................	SC	GS	15	....	....
Cheyenne, WY	State Director - Wyoming...................................	Glenn Pauley	SC	GS	15	....	....
Morgantown, WV	State Director - West Virginia	Ryan Thorn.........................	SC	GS	15	....	....
Richmond, VA	State Director - Virginia	Perry Hickman	SC	GS	15	....	....
Salt Lake City, UT ..	State Director - Utah	Michele Weaver	SC	GS	15	....	....
Bismarck, ND..........	State Director - North Dakota...........................	Erin Hill Oban....................	SC	GS	15	....	....
Columbus, OH	State Director - Ohio	Jonathan McCracken	SC	GS	15	....	....
Stillwater, OK.........	State Director - Oklahoma................................	Kenneth Corn	SC	GS	15	....	....
Portland, OR...........	State Director - Oregon.....................................	Margaret Hoffmann	SC	GS	15	....	....
Huron, SD................	State Director - South Dakota...........................	Nicole Gronli.......................	SC	GS	15	....	....
Nashville, TN	State Director - Tennessee	Arlisa Armstrong.................	SC	GS	15	....	....
Temple, TX..............	State Director - Texas.......................................	Lillian Elizabeth Salerno.....	SC	GS	15	....	....
Athens, GA	State Director - Georgia	Reggie Taylor	SC	GS	15	....	....
Bozeman, MT	State Director - Montana	Kathleen Williams...............	SC	GS	15	....	....
Montpelier, VT........	State Director - Vermont/New Hampshire	Sarah Waring.......................	SC	GS	15	....	....
Syracuse, NY	State Director - New York..................................	Brian Murray	SC	GS	15	....	....
Topeka, KS	State Director - Kansas	Christy Davis.......................	SC	GS	15	....	....
Albuquerque, NM....	State Director - New Mexico..............................	Patricia Dominguez..............	SC	GS	15	....	....
Harrisburg, PA.......	State Director - Pennsylvania...........................	Robert H Morgan	SC	GS	15	....	....
Olympia, WA	State Director - Washington	Helen Price Johnson	SC	GS	15	....	....
Carson City, NV	State Director - Nevada	Lucas Ingvoldstad	SC	GS	15	....	....
Stevens Point, WI....	State Director - Wisconsin	Julie Lassa...........................	SC	GS	15	....	....
Mt Laurel, NJ	State Director - New Jersey	Jane Asselta.........................	SC	GS	15	....	....
Davis, CA................	State Director - California	Maria Gallegos Herrera......	SC	GS	15	....	....
Phoenix, AZ	State Director - Arizona	Charlene Fernandez.............	SC	GS	15	....	....
Boise, ID	State Director - Idaho	Richard Rush.......................	SC	GS	15	....	....
East Lansing, MI	State Director - Michigan	Brandon Fewins	SC	GS	15	....	....
Hato Rey, Puer	State Director - Puerto Rico	Maximiliano Trujillo	SC	GS	15	....	....
	Rural Housing Service						
Washington, DC	Administrator, Rural Housing Service..............	Joaquin Altoro	NA	ES	....	....	....
Washington, DC	Deputy Administrator, Community Programs...	Career Incumbent	CA	ES	....	....	....
Washington, DC	Assistant Chief Information Officer..................	Career Incumbent	CA	ES	....	....	....
Washington, DC	Deputy Chief Financial Officer.........................	Vacant	....	ES	....	....	....
Washington, DC	Executive Director	Career Incumbent	CA	ES	....	....	....
Washington, DC	Director, Budget	Vacant	....	ES	....	....	....
Washington, DC	Senior Advisor..	Olugbenga Ajilore.................	SC	GS	15	....	....
Washington, DC	Chief of Staff..	Yvonne F Hsu	SC	GS	15	....	....
Washington, DC	Deputy Chief of Staff..	Samuel Marquez	SC	GS	13	....	....
Washington, DC	Special Assistant..	Maria Salmeron Melendez ..	SC	GS	11	....	....
	Rural Business Service						
Washington, DC	Administrator, Rural Business-Cooperative Service.	Kathryn Dirksen Londrigan.	NA	ES	....	....	....
Washington, DC	Chief Enterprise Officer.....................................	Vacant	....	ES	....	....	....
Washington, DC	Chief of Staff..	Leroy Garcia........................	SC	GS	15	....	....
Washington, DC	Policy Advisor...	John McAuliff......................	SC	GS	13	....	....
Washington, DC	Special Advisor...	Robert Lyons.......................	SC	GS	12	....	....
Washington, DC	Special Assistant..	Jobeth Delawder..................	SC	GS	11	....	....
	Rural Utilities Service						
Washington, DC	Administrator, Rural Utilities Service..............	Andrew Berke......................	PA	EX	IV	....	....
Washington, DC	Assistant Administrator - Electric Program......	Career Incumbent	CA	ES	....	....	....
Washington, DC	Assistant Administrator, Water and Environmental Programs.	Career Incumbent	CA	ES	....	....	....
Washington, DC	Assistant Director, Telecom Programs	Career Incumbent	CA	ES	....	....	....
Washington, DC	Chief of Staff..	Jason Lumia	SC	GS	15	....	....
Washington, DC	Senior Advisor..	Jaime Jackson	SC	GS	15	....	....
Washington, DC	Senior Advisor..	Alysia Peters.......................	SC	GS	15	....	....
Washington, DC	Senior Advisor for Energy..................................	Aliza Drewes.......................	SC	GS	15	....	....
Washington, DC	Special Advisor...	Asna Ashfaq........................	SC	GS	12	....	....
	OFFICE OF THE UNDER SECRETARY FOR MARKETING AND REGULATORY PROGRAMS						
Washington, DC	Under Secretary for Marketing and Regulatory Programs.	Jennifer Moffitt	PAS	EX	III	....	....
Washington, DC	Deputy Under Secretary for Marketing and Regulatory Programs.	Eric Deeble	NA	ES	....	....	....
Washington, DC	Deputy Under Secretary for Marketing and Regulatory Programs.	Katherine Zenk	NA	ES	....	....	....
Washington, DC	Senior Advisor for Fair and Competitive Markets.	Andrew Green	NA	ES	....	....	....

DEPARTMENT OF AGRICULTURE—Continued

Location	Position Title	Name of Incumbent	Type of Appt.	Pay Plan	Level, Grade, or Pay	Tenure	Expires
Washington, DC	Chief of Staff.................................	Victoria Maloch	SC	GS	14	....	....
Washington, DC	Special Assistant............................	Jewelene Meneses	SC	GS	11	....	....
	Animal and Plant Health Inspection Service						
Washington, DC	Administrator, Animal and Plant Health Inspection Service.	Career Incumbent	CA	ES	....	....	....
Washington, DC	Associate Administrator................	Career Incumbent	CA	ES	....	....	....
Washington, DC	Associate Administrator (Economics)................	Vacant	....	ES	....	....	....
Washington, DC	Deputy Administrator, Policy and Program Development.	Vacant	....	ES	....	....	....
Washington, DC	Associate Deputy Administrator for International Services.	Career Incumbent	CA	ES	....	....	....
Washington, DC	Associate Deputy Administrator, International Services.	Vacant	....	ES	....	....	....
Washington, DC	Associate Deputy Administrator, Wildlife Services.	Vacant	....	ES	....	....	....
Washington, DC	Executive Director, Strategy and Policy.............	Career Incumbent	CA	ES	....	....	....
Washington, DC	Senior Policy Advisor..........................	Ethan Holmes.....................	SC	GS	15	....	....
	Plant Protection and Quarantine Service						
Washington, DC	Deputy Administrator, Plant Protection and Quarantine.	Career Incumbent	CA	ES	....	....	....
Raleigh, NC	Associate Deputy Administrator, Field Operations.	Career Incumbent	CA	ES	....	....	....
	Veterinary Services						
Fort Collins, CO	Associate Deputy Administrator (Strategy and Policy).	Career Incumbent	CA	ES	....	....	....
	Agricultural Marketing Service						
Washington, DC	Administrator, Agricultural Marketing Service.	Career Incumbent	CA	ES	....	....	....
Washington, DC	Chief of Staff.................................	Georgette Furukawa	SC	GS	15	....	....
	OFFICE OF THE UNDER SECRETARY FOR FOOD SAFETY						
Washington, DC	Under Secretary for Food Safety........................	Jose E Esteban	PAS	EX	III	....	....
Washington, DC	Deputy Under Secretary for Food Safety...........	Sandra Eskin.....................	NA	ES	....	....	....
	Food Safety and Inspection Service						
Washington, DC	Administrator..................................	Career Incumbent	CA	ES	....	....	....
Washington, DC	Assistant Administrator, Office of Planning, Analysis and Risk Management.	Career Incumbent	CA	ES	....	....	....
Washington, DC	Deputy Assistant Administrator, Office of Planning, Analysis and Risk Management.	Vacant	....	ES	....	....	....
	OFFICE OF THE UNDER SECRETARY FOR FOOD, NUTRITION AND CONSUMER SERVICES						
Washington, DC	Deputy Under Secretary, Food, Nutrition and Consumer Services.	Vacant	....	ES	....	....	....
Washington, DC	Director of Regulatory and Policy Coordination.	Anne Decesaro.....................	TA	ES	....	....	....
Alexandria, VA	Administrator..................................	Cynthia A Long	NA	ES	....	....	....
Washington, DC	Chief of Staff-Director of Policy........................	Vacant	....	ES	....	....	....
Washington, DC	Chief of Staff.................................	Deborah Swerdlow	SC	GS	15	....	....
Washington, DC	Special Assistant............................	Walter E Hill	SC	GS	12	....	....
	Food and Nutrition Service						
Alexandria, VA	Deputy Administrator for Supplemental Nutrition and Safety Programs.	Career Incumbent	CA	ES	....	....	....
Washington, DC	Deputy Administrator, Policy Support	Career Incumbent	CA	ES	....	....	....
Washington, DC	Deputy Administrator, Center Nutrition and Programs.	Vacant	....	ES	....	....	....
Alexandria, VA	Deputy Administrator, Center for Nutrition Policy and Programs.	Vacant	....	ES	....	....	....
Alexandria, VA	Deputy Administrator, Child Nutrition Programs.	Career Incumbent	CA	ES	....	....	....
Alexandria, VA	Associate Administrator for Supplemental Nutrition Assistance Program.	Career Incumbent	CA	ES	....	....	....
Chicago, IL	Associate Administrator................	Career Incumbent	CA	ES	....	....	....
Washington, DC	Associate Administrator................	Vacant	....	ES	....	....	....
San Francisco, CA...	Regional Administrator, San Francisco, California.	Career Incumbent	CA	ES	....	....	....
Dallas, TX	Regional Administrator, Dallas, Texas	Career Incumbent	CA	ES	....	....	....
Robbinsville, NJ	Regional Administrator - Robbinsville, New Jersey.	Career Incumbent	CA	ES	....	....	....
Atlanta, GA	Regional Administrator, Atlanta, Georgia..........	Career Incumbent	CA	ES	....	....	....

DEPARTMENT OF AGRICULTURE—Continued

Location	Position Title	Name of Incumbent	Type of Appt.	Pay Plan	Level, Grade, or Pay	Tenure	Expires
Chicago, IL	Regional Administrator (Chicago), Food and Nutrition Service.	Career Incumbent	CA	ES	....	....	....
Denver, CO	Regional Administrator (Denver), Food and Nutrition Service.	Vacant	....	ES	....	....	....
Boston, MA	Regional Administrator - Northeast Region	Career Incumbent	CA	ES	....	....	....
Washington, DC	Chief Information Officer....................................	Vacant	....	ES	....	....	....
Alexandria, VA	Assistant Chief Information Officer..................	Career Incumbent	CA	ES	....	....	....
Alexandria, VA	Program Manager...	Timothy Stock	NA	ES	....	....	....
Washington, DC	Senior Advisor for Tech and Delivery	Rebecca Piazza	SC	GS	15	....	....
Alexandria, VA	Senior Policy Advisor......................................	Alberto Gonzalez	SC	GS	15	....	....
Alexandria, VA	Senior Advisor...	Shavana Howard....................	SC	GS	15	....	....
Alexandria, VA	Senior Advisor...	Jayme Holliday......................	SC	GS	15	....	....
Alexandria, VA	Senior Policy Advisor......................................	Sakeenah Shabazz	SC	GS	14	....	....
Washington, DC	Confidential Assistant...	Natalia Guzman	SC	GS	11	....	....
	OFFICE OF THE UNDER SECRETARY FOR TRADE AND FOREIGN AGRICULTURAL AFFAIRS						
Washington, DC	Under Secretary for Trade and Foreign Agricultural Affairs.	Alexis Taylor.........................	PAS	EX	III	....	....
Washington, DC	Chief of Staff..	Jamal Michael Habibi..........	SC	GS	15	....	....
	Foreign Agricultural Service						
Washington, DC	Administrator, Foreign Agricultural Service	Career Incumbent	CA	ES	....	....	....
Washington, DC	Associate Administrator..	Elaine Trevino	NA	ES	....	....	....
Washington, DC	Associate Administrator..	Brooke Jamison	NA	ES	....	....	....
Washington, DC	Deputy Administrator, Trade Programs.............	Career Incumbent	CA	ES	....	....	....
Rome, Italy	Minister Counselor of Agriculture......................	Ellen Luger............................	SC	GS	15	....	....
Washington, DC	Senior Policy Advisor......................................	Malikha Daniels	SC	GS	15	....	....
Washington, DC	Senior Advisor...	Kathleen Waters..................	SC	GS	14	....	....
Washington, DC	Confidential Assistant..	Rakan Alzarqa	SC	GS	9	....	....
	OFFICE OF THE UNDER SECRETARY FOR RESEARCH, EDUCATION, AND ECONOMICS						
Washington, DC	Under Secretary for Research, Education and Economics.	Chavonda J Jacobs Young ...	PAS	EX	III	....	....
Washington, DC	Deputy Under Secretary for Research, Education and Economics.	Sanah Pervaiz Baig..............	NA	ES	....	....	....
Washington, DC	Chief of Staff..	Jeremy Adamson	NA	ES	....	....	....
Washington, DC	Senior Advisor...	Billy Bridgeforth	SC	GS	15	....	....
Washington, DC	Special Advisor..	Tyler Tucker	SC	GS	12	....	....
	Agricultural Research Service						
Washington, DC	Administrator...	Career Incumbent	CA	ES	....	....	....
Beltsville, MD..........	Director, National Agricultural Library.............	Vacant	....	ES	....	....	....
	National Institute of Food and Agriculture						
Washington, DC	Director..	Manjit Misra.........................	PA	EX	II	....	....
Washington, DC	Associate Director for Operations	Career Incumbent	CA	ES	....	....	....
Washington, DC	Associate Director for Programs.......................	Career Incumbent	CA	ES	....	....	....
Kansas City, MO	Deputy Director, Institute of Youth, Family and Community.	Vacant	....	ES	....	....	....
Kansas City, MO	Deputy Director, Institute of Food Production and Sustainability.	Career Incumbent	CA	ES	....	....	....
Washington, DC	Senior Advisor...	Colin Finan...........................	SC	GS	15	....	....
	OFFICE OF UNDER SECRETARY FOR NATURAL RESOURCES AND ENVIRONMENT						
Washington, DC	Under Secretary for Natural Resources and Environment.	Homer L Wilkes	PAS	EX	III	....	....
Washington, DC	Deputy Under Secretary for Natural Resources and Environment.	Meryl Liebowitz Harrell	NA	ES	....	....	....
Washington, DC	Chief of Staff..	Andrea Delgado Fink...........	SC	GS	15	....	....
Washington, DC	Special Advisor..	Cori Lopez.............................	SC	GS	13	....	....
	Forest Service						
Washington, DC	Chief Forester..	Career Incumbent	CA	ES	....	....	....
Washington, DC	Deputy Chief for State and Private Forestry	Career Incumbent	CA	ES	....	....	....
Washington, DC	Associate Deputy Chief, Business Operations...	Career Incumbent	CA	ES	....	....	....
Washington, DC	Associate Deputy Chief, Research and Development.	Career Incumbent	CA	ES	....	....	....
Washington, DC	Director, Strategic Planning and Budget Accountability.	Career Incumbent	CA	ES	....	....	....
Albuquerque, NM....	Director, Albuquerque Service Center-Budget and Finance.	Career Incumbent	CA	ES	....	....	....

DEPARTMENT OF AGRICULTURE—Continued

Location	Position Title	Name of Incumbent	Type of Appt.	Pay Plan	Level, Grade, or Pay	Tenure	Expires
Washington, DC	Director, Civil Rights Staff..................................	Vacant	....	ES	....	....	....
Lakewood, CO	Director, National Job Corps.............................	Career Incumbent	CA	ES	....	....	....
Washington, DC	Director Work Environment and Performance..	Career Incumbent	CA	ES	....	....	....
Washington, DC	Director, Sustainability and Climate Change....	Vacant	....	ES	....	....	....
Washington, DC	Chief Information Officer..................................	Career Incumbent	CA	ES	....	....	....
Washington, DC	Associate Chief Financial Officer.....................	Career Incumbent	CA	ES	....	....	....
Washington, DC	Chief of Staff..	Career Incumbent	CA	ES	....	....	....
Lakewood, CO	Senior Advisor..	Career Incumbent	CA	ES	....	....	....
	National Forest System						
Washington, DC	Deputy Chief, National Forest System	Career Incumbent	CA	ES	....	....	....
Washington, DC	Associate Deputy Chief, National Forest System.	Career Incumbent	CA	ES	....	....	....
Washington, DC	Director, Recreation and Heritage Resources....	Career Incumbent	CA	ES	....	....	....
Washington, DC	Associate Deputy Chief, National Forest System.	Career Incumbent	CA	ES	....	....	....
Washington, DC	Associate Deputy Chief, National Forest System.	Career Incumbent	CA	ES	....	....	....
	State and Private Forestry						
Washington, DC	Associate Deputy Chief, State and Private Forestry.	Career Incumbent	CA	ES	....	....	....
Washington, DC	Associate Deputy Chief, State and Private Forestry.	Career Incumbent	CA	ES	....	....	....
	Field Units						
Washington, DC	Associate Deputy Administrator	Career Incumbent	CA	ES	....	....	....
Missoula, MT...........	Regional Forester, Region 1, Northern Region, Missoula.	Career Incumbent	CA	ES	....	....	....
Lakewood, CO	Regional Forester, Rocky Mountain Region.......	Career Incumbent	CA	ES	....	....	....
Albuquerque, NM....	Regional Forester, Region 3, Southwest Region, Albuquerque.	Career Incumbent	CA	ES	....	....	....
Ogden, UT	Regional Forester, Region 4, Intermountain Region, Ogden.	Career Incumbent	CA	ES	....	....	....
San Francisco, CA...	Regional Forester, Region 5, Pacific Southwest Region, Vallejo.	Career Incumbent	CA	ES	....	....	....
Portland, OR...........	Regional Forester, Region 6, Pacific Northwest Region, (Portland).	Career Incumbent	CA	ES	....	....	....
Atlanta, GA	Regional Forester, Region 8,Southern Region, Atlanta.	Career Incumbent	CA	ES	....	....	....
Milwaukee, WI	Regional Forester, Region 9, Eastern Region	Career Incumbent	CA	ES	....	....	....
Juneau, AK..............	Regional Forester, Region 10, (Juneau).............	Career Incumbent	CA	ES	....	....	....
	International Forest System						
Washington, DC	Director of International Programs...................	Career Incumbent	CA	ES	....	....	....
	Research						
Washington, DC	Deputy Chief, Research and Development	Career Incumbent	CA	ES	....	....	....
	OFFICE OF THE UNDER SECRETARY FOR FARM PRODUCTION AND CONSERVATION						
Washington, DC	Under Secretary for Farm Production and Conservation.	Robert Bonnie......................	PAS	EX	III	....	....
Washington, DC	Deputy Under Secretary for Farm Production and Conservation.	Gloria Montano-Greene	NA	ES	....	....	....
Washington, DC	Chief of Staff..	Timothy John Gannon	NA	ES	....	....	....
Washington, DC	Senior Advisor for Climate and Conservation...	Bidisha Bhattacharyya	SC	GS	15	....	....
Washington, DC	Senior Advisor..	Alyssa Charney	SC	GS	15	....	....
Washington, DC	Special Assistant..	Daelon Harkins	SC	GS	11	....	....
	Farm Production and Conservation - Business Center						
Washington, DC	Director of Organizational Management and Cultural Transformation.	Vacant	....	ES	....	....	....
Washington, DC	Chief, Policy Accounting and Reporting............	Vacant	....	ES	....	....	....
Washington, DC	Senior Advisor..	Monica Rainge.....................	NA	ES	....	....	....
Washington, DC	Chief Operating Officer....................................	Career Incumbent	CA	ES	....	....	....
Washington, DC	Chief Financial Officer.....................................	Career Incumbent	CA	ES	....	....	....
Washington, DC	Chief Economist...	Career Incumbent	CA	ES	....	....	....
Washington, DC	Chief Human Capital Officer............................	Career Incumbent	CA	ES	....	....	....
Washington, DC	Chief Information Solutions Services Del Ops..	Career Incumbent	CA	ES	....	....	....
Washington, DC	Deputy Chief Operations Officer......................	Vacant	....	ES	....	....	....
Washington, DC	Deputy, Chief Operating Officer (Enterprise Services).	Vacant	....	ES	....	....	....
Washington, DC	Director Management Services..........................	Career Incumbent	CA	ES	....	....	....

DEPARTMENT OF AGRICULTURE—Continued

Location	Position Title	Name of Incumbent	Type of Appt.	Pay Plan	Level, Grade, or Pay	Tenure	Expires
Washington, DC	Director, Performance, Accountability and Risk.	Vacant	....	ES	....	....	....
Washington, DC	Director, Office of Acquisition	Career Incumbent	CA	ES	....	....	....
Washington, DC	Director, Environmental Activities....................	Career Incumbent	CA	ES	....	....	....
Washington, DC	Assistant Chief Information Officer..................	Vacant	....	ES	....	....	....
Washington, DC	Assistant Director, Homeland Security and Emergency Management.	Career Incumbent	CA	ES	....	....	....
Washington, DC	Deputy Director for Communications	Career Incumbent	CA	ES	....	....	....
Washington, DC	Deputy Director, Legislative Liaison..................	Career Incumbent	CA	ES	....	....	....
	Farm Service Agency						
Washington, DC	Administrator..	Zachary Ducheneaux	NA	ES	....	....	....
Washington, DC	Associate Administrator...........................	Career Incumbent	CA	ES	....	....	....
Washington, DC	Deputy Administrator for Field Operations	Marcus Graham	NA	ES	....	....	....
Washington, DC	Deputy Administrator for Farm Programs	William Marlow....................	NA	ES	....	....	....
Washington, DC	Senior Advisor..	John Schmidt........................	NA	ES	....	....	....
Washington, DC	Senior Advisor..	Mike Schmidt	NA	ES	....	....	....
Washington, DC	Director, Information Technology Services Division.	Vacant	....	ES	....	....	....
Albuquerque, NM....	State Executive Director - New Mexico.............	Jonas Moya..........................	SC	GS	15	....	....
Bozeman, MT	State Executive Director - Montana	Maureen Wicks.....................	SC	GS	15	....	....
Annapolis, MD........	State Executive Director - Maryland	Clarence Sullivan	SC	GS	15	....	....
Columbia, MO	State Executive Director - Missouri	Joseph Aull	SC	GS	15	....	....
Amherst, MA	State Executive Director - Massachusetts.........	Daniel Smiarowski...............	SC	GS	15	....	....
Tolland, CT..............	State Executive Director - Connecticut.............	Emily Cole	SC	GS	15	....	....
St Paul, MN.............	State Executive Director - Minnesota...............	Whitney Place......................	SC	GS	15	....	....
Lakewood, CO	State Executive Director - Colorado.................	Kent Peppler.......................	SC	GS	15	....	....
College Station, TX .	State Executive Director - Texas......................	Kelly Adkins	SC	GS	15	....	....
Columbia, SC...........	State Executive Director - South Carolina........	Laurie Funderburk	SC	GS	15	....	....
Palmer, AK..............	State Executive Director - Alaska	Amy Pettit............................	SC	GS	15	....	....
Phoenix, AZ	State Executive Director - Arizona....................	Ginger Torres.......................	SC	GS	15	....	....
Little Rock, AR........	State Executive Director - Arkansas.................	Doris Washington	SC	GS	15	....	....
Davis, CA................	State Executive Director - California................	Blong Xiong	SC	GS	15	....	....
Dover, DE................	State Executive Director - Delaware.................	Robin Talley........................	SC	GS	15	....	....
Honolulu, HI...........	State Executive Director - Hawaii	Joy Kono	SC	GS	15	....	....
Springfield, IL	State Executive Director - Illinois....................	Scott Halpin........................	SC	GS	15	....	....
Indianapolis, IN	State Executive Director - Indiana	Julia Ann Wickard	SC	GS	15	....	....
Des Moines, IA	State Executive Director - Iowa	Matthew Russell	SC	GS	15	....	....
Manhattan, KS........	State Executive Director - Kansas	Dennis McKinney................	SC	GS	15	....	....
Lexington, KY	State Executive Director - Kentucky	Dean Schamore	SC	GS	15	....	....
Jackson, MS............	State Executive Director - Mississippi..............	Thaddeus Fairley.................	SC	GS	15	....	....
Lincoln, NE..............	State Executive Director - Nebraska	John J Berge........................	SC	GS	15	....	....
Reno, NV.................	State Executive Director - Nevada	Janice Kolvet	SC	GS	15	....	....
Concord, NH............	State Executive Director - New Hampshire......	Jeffrey Holmes.....................	SC	GS	15	....	....
Warwick, RI.............	State Executive Director - Rhode Island	Jon Scherer..........................	SC	GS	15	....	....
Huron, SD................	State Executive Director - South Dakota	Steven Dick.........................	SC	GS	15	....	....
Syracuse, NY...........	State Executive Director - New York	James R Barber...................	SC	GS	15	....	....
Madison, WI	State Executive Director - Wisconsin................	Eugene Shriefer...................	SC	GS	15	....	....
Richmond, VA.........	State Executive Director - Virginia...................	Ronald Howell	SC	GS	15	....	....
Spokane, WA	State Executive Director - Washington.............	Jon Wyss	SC	GS	15	....	....
Morgantown, WV	State Executive Director - West Virginia..........	Johnny Perdue.....................	SC	GS	15	....	....
Casper, WY	State Executive Director - Wyoming	William Bunce	SC	GS	15	....	....
Fargo, ND	State Executive Director - North Dakota	Marcy Svenningsen.............	SC	GS	15	....	....
Stillwater, OK.........	State Executive Director - Oklahoma	George Kouplen	SC	GS	15	....	....
Harrisburg, PA........	State Executive Director - Pennsylvania...........	Heidi Secord	SC	GS	15	....	....
Salt Lake City, UT ..	State Executive Director - Utah........................	Mark A Gibbons	SC	GS	15	....	....
Nashville, TN	State Executive Director - Tennessee	John Litz.............................	SC	GS	15	....	....
Burlington, VT	State Executive Director - Vermont	John Roberts.......................	SC	GS	15	....	....
Bangor, ME.............	State Executive Director - Maine	Sherry Hamel	SC	GS	15	....	....
Montgomery, AL	State Executive Director - Alabama	Clifton Warren	SC	GS	15	....	....
Columbus, OH	State Executive Director - Ohio	John Patterson	SC	GS	15	....	....
Alexandria, LA	State Executive Director - Louisiana.................	Ronald Guidry	SC	GS	15	....	....
Raleigh, NC	State Executive Director - North Carolina........	Bobby Ray Etheridge	SC	GS	15	....	....
Gainesville, FL	State Executive Director - Florida	Deborah Tannenbaum..........	SC	GS	15	....	....
Athens, GA	State Executive Director - Georgia	Arthur Tripp........................	SC	GS	15	....	....
Boise, ID	State Executive Director - Idaho......................	Arnold Hernandez...............	SC	GS	15	....	....
Hamilton Square, NJ.	State Executive Director - New Jersey	Robert Andrzejczak	SC	GS	15	....	....
Tualatin, OR............	State Executive Director - Oregon	Gail McSpadden Greenman.	SC	GS	15	....	....
Washington, DC	Senior Policy Advisor..................................	Kelcy Schaunaman...............	SC	GS	13	....	....
Washington, DC	Special Assistant..	Victoria Molina....................	SC	GS	12	....	....
Washington, DC	Policy Advisor..	Shawn Campbell	SC	GS	12	....	....

DEPARTMENT OF AGRICULTURE—Continued

Location	Position Title	Name of Incumbent	Type of Appt.	Pay Plan	Level, Grade, or Pay	Tenure	Expires
Washington, DC	Special Advisor..........................	Ethan Tsui...........................	SC	GS	11	....	....
	Natural Resources Conservation Service						
Washington, DC	Chief, Natural Resources Conservation Service.	Terry Cosby........................	NA	ES		....	....
Beltsville, MD..........	Deputy Chief Soil Survey and Resource Assessment.	Vacant	....	ES		....	....
Washington, DC	Deputy Chief, Management and Strategy	Career Incumbent	CA	ES		....	....
Washington, DC	Deputy Chief for Science and Technology.........	Career Incumbent	CA	ES		....	....
Washington, DC	Associate Chief for Conservation....................	Career Incumbent	CA	ES		....	....
Madison, MS............	Director, Gulf of Mexico Ecosystem Restoration Team.	Vacant	....	ES		....	....
Washington, DC	Director Resource Inventory and Assessment Division.	Career Incumbent	CA	ES		....	....
Davis, CA................	State Conservationist, (California)....................	Career Incumbent	CA	ES		....	....
Temple, TX..............	State Conservationist, Temple, Texas	Career Incumbent	CA	ES		....	....
Washington, DC	Regional Conservationist (Central)..................	Vacant	....	ES		....	....
Washington, DC	Regional Conservationist (West)......................	Career Incumbent	CA	ES		....	....
Washington, DC	Regional Conservationist -South East	Career Incumbent	CA	ES		....	....
Washington, DC	Assistant Chief....................................	Kenneth Walker	SC	GS	15	....	....
Washington, DC	Chief of Staff......................................	Alexandra Lawrence	SC	GS	15	....	....
Washington, DC	Senior Advisor External Communications........	Michele Jan Altemus	SC	GS	15	....	....
Washington, DC	Senior Advisor.....................................	Thomas O Halleran.............	SC	GS	15	....	....
Washington, DC	Senior Policy Advisor............................	George Ellis Collier.............	SC	GS	14	....	....
Washington, DC	Policy Advisor.....................................	Maya Cohn.........................	SC	GS	13	....	....
Washington, DC	Policy Advisor.....................................	Maya Johnson.....................	SC	GS	13	....	....
Washington, DC	Special Advisor....................................	Hannah Peyton....................	SC	GS	12	....	....
	Risk Management Agency						
Washington, DC	Administrator, Risk Management Agency	Marcia Bunger.....................	NA	ES		....	....
Washington, DC	Associate Administrator............................	Vacant	....	ES		....	....
Washington, DC	Associate Administrator............................	Career Incumbent	CA	ES		....	....
Washington, DC	Chief of Staff......................................	Toby Cain...........................	SC	GS	14	....	....
	Commodity Credit Corporation						
Washington, DC	Member..	Xochitl Torres Small	PAS	OT		....	....
Washington, DC	Member..	Robert Bonnie.....................	PAS	OT		....	....
Washington, DC	Member..	Alexis Taylor......................	PA	OT		....	....
Washington, DC	Member..	John Rapp..........................	PA	OT		....	....
Washington, DC	Member..	Jennifer Moffitt...................	PA	OT		....	....
Washington, DC	Member..	Gary Washington.................	PA	OT		....	....
Washington, DC	Member..	Tom Vilsack	PA	OT		....	....

DEPARTMENT OF COMMERCE

Location	Position Title	Name of Incumbent	Type of Appt.	Pay Plan	Level, Grade, or Pay	Tenure	Expires
	IMMEDIATE OFFICE						
Washington, DC	Secretary	Gina Raimondo....................	PAS	EX	I	....	....
Washington, DC	Chief of Staff......................................	Christopher Slevin	NA	ES	....	....	....
Washington, DC	Executive Assistant to the Secretary and Associate Director of Operations.	Ana Martinez Campos	SC	GS	13	....	....
Washington, DC	Senior Advisor for Strategic Initiatives	Virginia McQuade	SC	GS	14	....	....
	OFFICE OF THE DEPUTY SECRETARY						
Washington, DC	Deputy Secretary	Don Graves	PAS	EX	II	....	....
Washington, DC	Special Advisor....................................	Eliana Loya	SC	GS	12	....	....
Washington, DC	Chief of Staff to the Deputy Secretary	Tonya Williams....................	NA	ES		....	....
Washington, DC	Senior Advisor for Policy and Program Integration.	Career Incumbent	CA	ES		....	....
Washington, DC	Senior Advisor.....................................	Jeremiah Boyle....................	SC	GS	15	....	....
Washington, DC	Senior Advisor.....................................	Miguel Estien	NA	ES	....	....	....
Washington, DC	Special Assistant..................................	Julia Murphy.......................	SC	GS	11	....	....
Washington, DC	Strategic Advisor to Enterprise Services...........	Career Incumbent	CA	ES		....	....
	Office of the Chief of Staff						
Washington, DC	Deputy Chief of Staff (External)	Brittany Anne Caplin	NA	ES		....	....
Washington, DC	Deputy Chief of Staff (Internal)	James V Secreto	NA	ES		....	....
Washington, DC	Counselor to the Secretary	Samuel Marullo...................	NA	ES		....	....
Washington, DC	Senior Advisor to the Chief of Staff..................	John David Grom	NA	ES		....	....
Washington, DC	Senior Advisor for Strategy, Operations and Engagement.	Rory Michael Slatko.............	SC	GS	15	....	....

DEPARTMENT OF COMMERCE—Continued

Location	Position Title	Name of Incumbent	Type of Appt.	Pay Plan	Level, Grade, or Pay	Tenure	Expires
Washington, DC	Special Advisor................................	Emma Turner......................	SC	GS	12	....	....
Washington, DC	Protocol and Advance Specialist........................	Danielle John......................	SC	GS	11	....	....
Washington, DC	Senior Advisor for Women in Construction	Latifa Lyles...........................	NA	ES	....	....	....
Washington, DC	Director of Native American Business Development.	Shaun Deschene..................	SC	GS	14	....	....
Washington, DC	Senior Counselor to the Secretary	Luis Antonio Jimenez..........	NA	ES	....	....	....
Washington, DC	Senior Advisor................................	James Wise	SC	GS	15	....	....
Washington, DC	Deputy Director of Advance and Protocol.........	James Cody........................	SC	GS	14	....	....
Washington, DC	Associate Director of Protocol and Advance	Miriam Young	SC	GS	13	....	....
Washington, DC	Associate Director of Scheduling.......................	Sydney Vermilyea..................	SC	GS	13	....	....
Washington, DC	Special Advisor................................	David Baler........................	SC	GS	12	....	....
Washington, DC	Special Advisor................................	Kobe Dumas	SC	GS	12	....	....
	Office of Advance, Scheduling and Protocol						
Washington, DC	Associate Director of Scheduling.......................	Karina Rigel	SC	GS	13	....	....
	Office of the White House Liaison						
Washington, DC	White House Liaison..........................	Miguel Juanito L'Heureux...	NA	ES	....	....	....
Washington, DC	Deputy White House Liaison............................	Michael Woicekowski	SC	GS	14	....	....
Washington, DC	Special Assistant...............................	McKenzie Estep..................	SC	GS	11	....	....
	Office of Policy and Strategic Planning						
Washington, DC	Special Assistant...............................	Nahyun Lee	SC	GS	11	....	....
Washington, DC	Director................................	Nell Abernathy	SC	GS	15	....	....
Washington, DC	Counselor to the Secretary	Edward McMichael Dean	SC	GS	15	....	....
Washington, DC	Counselor for Equity	Ines Hernandez-Siqueira......	SC	GS	15	....	....
Washington, DC	Senior Policy Advisor........................	Daniel Clark	SC	GS	15	....	....
Washington, DC	Policy Advisor................................	Nathanael Jo	SC	GS	12	....	....
Washington, DC	Policy Advisor for Equity in Economic Development.	Meron Yohannes..................	SC	GS	13	....	....
Washington, DC	Policy Advisor for Chips Implementation..........	Diana Cricien	SC	GS	13	....	....
Washington, DC	Special Assistant...............................	Bailey Patterson	SC	GS	11	....	....
Washington, DC	Special Advisor................................	Henry Schulz	SC	GS	12	....	....
Washington, DC	Policy Advisor................................	Monica Palid	SC	GS	12	....	....
	Office of the Executive Secretariat						
Washington, DC	Director, Executive Secretariat........................	Alia S Awadallah..................	NA	ES	....	....	....
Washington, DC	Deputy Director	Serame Castillo	SC	GS	14	....	....
Washington, DC	Special Assistant...............................	Maria Leon	SC	GS	11	....	....
Washington, DC	Special Assistant...............................	Carlee Goldberg..................	SC	GS	11	....	....
Washington, DC	Special Assistant...............................	Gabriella Lieberman............	SC	GS	11	....	....
	Office of Business Liaison						
Washington, DC	Director of External Programming	Patrick Hobart......................	SC	GS	14	....	....
Washington, DC	Director, of Faith Based and Neighborhood Partnerships and Advisor for Inclusive Partnerships.	Andres Chong-Qui Torres....	SC	GS	15	....	....
Washington, DC	Director, Public Engagement	Laura O'Neill......................	NA	ES	....	....	....
Washington, DC	Special Assistant...............................	Sarah Yoon...........................	SC	GS	11	....	....
	Office of Public Affairs						
Washington, DC	Director of the Office of Public Affairs..............	Sarah Weinstein	SC	GS	15	....	....
Washington, DC	Director of Digital Strategy and Deputy Director of Public Affairs.	Brendan Cohen....................	SC	GS	14	....	....
Washington, DC	Deputy Press Secretary.......................	Valerie Keys........................	SC	GS	12	....	....
Washington, DC	Deputy Speechwriter...........................	Christopher Groneng	SC	GS	12	....	....
Washington, DC	Speechwriter	Andrew Odgren	SC	GS	13	....	....
Washington, DC	Press Secretary and Deputy Director of Public Affairs.	Charles Andrews II..............	SC	GS	14	....	....
Washington, DC	Press Assistant	Rodrigo Santos Legaspi	SC	GS	11	....	....
	Office of the Chief Information Officer						
Washington, DC	Chief Information Officer..............................	Vacant	....	ES	....	....	....
Alexandria, VA	Office Director- Application Engineering and Development.	Vacant	....	ES	....	....	....
	Office of Legislative and Intergovernmental Affairs						
Washington, DC	Assistant Secretary for Legislative and Intergovernmental Affairs.	Susie Feliz...........................	PAS	EX	IV	....	....
Washington, DC	Director of Legislative Affairs	Thomas Lowdermilk	SC	GS	15	....	....
Washington, DC	Director of Legislative Affairs for Intelligence and National Security.	Feras Sleiman......................	SC	GS	15	....	....
Washington, DC	Director of Oversight........................	Rachit Choksi	NA	ES	....	....	....
Washington, DC	Legislative Advisor	Brendon Maloney	SC	GS	12	....	....
Washington, DC	Special Assistant...............................	Jose Leoncio........................	SC	GS	11	....	....

DEPARTMENT OF COMMERCE—Continued

Location	Position Title	Name of Incumbent	Type of Appt.	Pay Plan	Level, Grade, or Pay	Tenure	Expires
	Office of Deputy Assistant Secretary for Legislative and Intergovernmental Affairs						
Washington, DC	Deputy Assistant Secretary for Legislative and Intergovernmental Affairs.	Rosemarie Laughlin	NA	ES			
	Office of the Chief Financial Officer and Assistant Secretary for Administration						
Washington, DC	Chief Financial Officer and Assistant Secretary for Administration.	Vacant		EX			
Washington, DC	Deputy Assistant Secretary for Intelligence and Security.	Vacant		ES			
Washington, DC	Senior Advisor for Administration and Management.	Vacant		ES			
Washington, DC	Chief of Staff	Calynn Jenkins	SC	GS	15		
Washington, DC	Special Assistant	Jaqucline Revivo	SC	GS	11		
Washington, DC	Special Assistant	Chloe Liu	SC	GS	11		
	Office of the Chief Financial Officer for Financial Management						
Washington, DC	Director, Financial Management Systems	Career Incumbent	CA	ES			
	Office of the Deputy Assistant Secretary for Administration						
Washington, DC	Director, Office of Performance Excellence	Career Incumbent	CA	ES			
Washington, DC	Deputy Assistant Secretary for Administration.	Career Incumbent	CA	ES			
	Office of Privacy and Open Government						
Washington, DC	Director, Office of Privacy and Open Government.	Career Incumbent	CA	ES			
	Office of Civil Rights						
Washington, DC	Director, Office of Civil Rights	Career Incumbent	CA	ES			
Washington, DC	Senior Advisor to the Director of Ocr	Career Incumbent	CA	ES			
	Office of the General Counsel						
Washington, DC	General Counsel	Leslie Kiernan	PAS	EX	IV		
Washington, DC	Deputy General Counsel	Blake Roberts	NA	ES			
Washington, DC	Assistant General Counsel for Legislation and Regulation.	Career Incumbent	CA	ES			
Washington, DC	Assistant General Counsel for Litigation, Employment, and Oversight.	Career Incumbent	CA	ES			
Washington, DC	Chief Counsel for Trade Enforcement and Compliance.	Career Incumbent	CA	ES			
Washington, DC	Chief Counsel for International Commerce	Career Incumbent	CA	ES			
Washington, DC	Chief, Employment and Labor Law Division	Career Incumbent	CA	ES			
Washington, DC	Chief Counsel for Economic Affairs	Career Incumbent	CA	ES			
Washington, DC	Chief, General Law Division	Career Incumbent	CA	ES			
Washington, DC	Chief Counsel for Commercial Law Development Program.	Career Incumbent	CA	ES			
Washington, DC	Chief Counsel for Economic Development Administration.	Career Incumbent	CA	ES			
Washington, DC	Chief Counsel for Minority Business Development Agency.	Career Incumbent	CA	ES			
Washington, DC	Senior Counsel	Ravi Doshi	SC	GS	15		
Washington, DC	Counsel	Elias Kim	SC	GS	15		
Washington, DC	Counsel	Matthew Ryan	SC	GS	15		
Washington, DC	Counsel	Jessica Fuhrman	SC	GS	15		
Washington, DC	Assistant General Counsel for Transactions and Technology.	Career Incumbent	CA	ES			
Washington, DC	Deputy General Counsel for Strategic Initiatives.	Reema Shah	NA	ES			
Washington, DC	Deputy General Counsel for Technology and Economic Growth.	Paige Herwig	NA	ES			
Washington, DC	Counsel	Liani Balasuriya	SC	GS	15		
Washington, DC	Chief Counsel	Career Incumbent	CA	ES			
BUREAU OF INDUSTRY AND SECURITY							
Washington, DC	Under Secretary of Commerce for Industry and Security.	Alan Estevez	PAS	EX	III		
Washington, DC	Deputy Under Secretary for Industry and Security.	Eric Beane	NA	ES			
Washington, DC	Counselor to the Under Secretary	Steven Craig Emme	NA	ES			
Washington, DC	Director, Office of Nonproliferation and Treaty Compliance.	Vacant		ES			
Washington, DC	Senior Advisor	Aiysha Hussain	SC	GS	15		
Washington, DC	Senior Advisor	Lorand Laskai	SC	GS	15		

DEPARTMENT OF COMMERCE—Continued

Location	Position Title	Name of Incumbent	Type of Appt.	Pay Plan	Level, Grade, or Pay	Tenure	Expires
Washington, DC	Chief of Staff	Benjamin Haas-Hawkings	SC	GS	15		
Washington, DC	Deputy Chief of Staff and Advisor	Abigale Belcrest	SC	GS	13		
Washington, DC	Special Advisor	Jackson Hettler	SC	GS	12		
Washington, DC	Deputy Chief of Staff	Saraswati P Shah	SC	GS	14		
Washington, DC	Deputy Director of Public Affairs	Katherine Schneider	SC	GS	14		
Washington, DC	Deputy Director of Congressional Affairs	Qais Roshan	SC	GS	15		
Washington, DC	Congressional and Public Affairs Advisor	Christ-Shamma Matalbert	SC	GS	12		
Washington, DC	Special Advisor	Sara McNaughton	SC	GS	12		
Washington, DC	Director of Public Affairs	Jessica Stallone	SC	GS	15		
	OFFICE OF THE ASSISTANT SECRETARY FOR EXPORT ENFORCEMENT						
Washington, DC	Assistant Secretary for Export Enforcement	Matthew Axelrod	PAS	EX	IV		
	OFFICE OF THE ASSISTANT SECRETARY FOR EXPORT ADMINISTRATION						
Washington, DC	Assistant Secretary for Export Administration	Thea D Kendler	PAS	EX	IV		
Washington, DC	Deputy Assistant Secretary for Export Administration.	Vacant		ES			
Washington, DC	Director, Office of National Strategic and Technology Transfer Controls.	Career Incumbent	CA	ES			
Washington, DC	Director Office of Exporter Services	Career Incumbent	CA	ES			
	DEPUTY ASSISTANT SECRETARY FOR AD/CVD OPERATIONS						
Washington, DC	Deputy Assistant Secretary for Antidumping and Countervailing Duty Operations.	Vacant		ES			
	ECONOMIC DEVELOPMENT ADMINISTRATION						
Washington, DC	Assistant Secretary of Commerce for Economic Development.	Alejandra Ybelisse Castillo	PAS	EX	IV		
Washington, DC	Senior Advisor	William A Ramos	SC	GS	15		
Washington, DC	Senior Advisor	Vacant		ES			
Washington, DC	Chief of Staff	Maryam Janani-Flores	SC	GS	15		
Washington, DC	Director of Public Affairs	Jonathan Lovitz	SC	GS	15		
Washington, DC	Special Assistant	Sarah Rolling	SC	GS	11		
	Office of the Deputy Assistant Secretary						
Washington, DC	Deputy Assistant Secretary for Economic Development and Chief Operating Officer.	Vacant		ES			
	Office of the Assistant Secretary for Economic Development						
Washington, DC	Deputy Assistant Secretary for Policy and External Affairs.	Cristina Killingsworth	NA	ES			
Washington, DC	Chief of Staff	Meghan Maury	SC	GS	15		
Washington, DC	Director of External Affairs	Christopher J Epps	SC	GS	15		
Washington, DC	Special Assistant	Sarah Laga	SC	GS	11		
	Regional Offices						
Seattle, WA	Regional Administrator, West Coast Region	Career Incumbent	CA	ES			
Gloucester, MA	Regional Administrator, Greater Atlantic Region.	Career Incumbent	CA	ES			
St Petersburg, FL	Regional Administrator Southeast Region	Career Incumbent	CA	ES			
Juneau, AK	Regional Administrator, Alaska Region	Career Incumbent	CA	ES			
	Bureau of Economic Analysis						
Washington, DC	Chief Economist	Vacant		ES			
Suitland, MD	Chief of Communications	Career Incumbent	CA	ES			
Suitland, MD	Chief Data Officer	Career Incumbent	CA	ES			
	BUREAU OF THE CENSUS						
Suitland, MD	Chief of Congressional Affairs	Rodrick T Owens	NA	ES			
Suitland, MD	Chief Administrative and Customer Services Division.	Career Incumbent	CA	ES			
Suitland, MD	Senior Advisor for 2030 Census	Vacant		ES			
	Office of the Director						
Suitland, MD	Director of the Census	Robert Santos	PAS	EX	IV		
Suitland, MD	Deputy Director	Career Incumbent	CA	ES			
Suitland, MD	Chief of Staff	Career Incumbent	CA	ES			
Suitland, MD	Senior Advisor to the Deputy Director	Career Incumbent	CA	ES			
Suitland, MD	Assistant Director for Communications	Career Incumbent	CA	ES			
Suitland, MD	Associate Director for Communications	Ditas Katague	NA	ES			

DEPARTMENT OF COMMERCE—Continued

Location	Position Title	Name of Incumbent	Type of Appt.	Pay Plan	Level, Grade, or Pay	Tenure	Expires
	OFFICE OF THE UNDER SECRETARY FOR ECONOMIC AFFAIRS						
Washington, DC	Under Secretary for Economic Affairs	Vacant	....	EX	....	....	....
	OFFICE OF THE CHIEF ECONOMIST						
Washington, DC	Deputy Chief Economist	Vacant	....	ES	....	....	....
	OFFICE OF REGIONAL AFFAIRS						
Washington, DC	Deputy Assistant Secretary for Regional Affairs.	Career Incumbent	CA	ES	....	....	....
	INTERNATIONAL TRADE ADMINISTRATION						
Washington, DC	Director of the Supply Chain Center	Marti Flacks	NA	ES	....	....	....
Washington, DC	Counselor and Chief Negotiator	Sharon Yuan	NA	ES	....	....	....
Washington, DC	Counselor to the Under Secretary....................	Keigan Mull......................	NA	ES	....	....	....
Washington, DC	Counselor to the Under Secretary....................	Margaret Jackson...............	NA	ES	....	....	....
Washington, DC	Deputy Assistant Secretary for Travel and Tourism.	Alexander Lasry...................	NA	ES	....	....	....
Washington, DC	Executive Director for Europe	Vacant	....	ES	....	....	....
Washington, DC	Chief of Staff and Senior Advisor....................	Zachary Learner...................	NA	ES	....	....	....
Alexandria, VA	Chief of Staff and Advisor................................	Vacant	....	ES	....	....	....
Washington, DC	Senior Advisor...	Jonathan J Prutow..............	SC	GS	15	....	....
Washington, DC	Senior Advisor...	Sahar Hafeez	SC	GS	15	....	....
Washington, DC	Senior Advisor...	Jonathan Hillman	SC	GS	15	....	....
Washington, DC	Senior Advisor...	Georgette N Brammer	SC	GS	15	....	....
Washington, DC	Senior Advisor...	Julian Beach......................	SC	GS	15	....	....
Washington, DC	Director of Legislative Affairs	Caitlin Kovalkoski...............	SC	GS	15	....	....
Washington, DC	Director of Public Affairs	Tyrik B McKeiver..............	SC	GS	15	....	....
Washington, DC	Deputy Chief of Staff.......................................	Susannah Marshall.............	SC	GS	13	....	....
Washington, DC	Deputy Chief of Staff (Internal)	Katherine Canavan.............	SC	GS	13	....	....
Washington, DC	Speechwriter and Policy Advisor.....................	Ryan Lee............................	SC	GS	14	....	....
Washington, DC	Policy Advisor...	Lelia Jo Dusthimer	SC	GS	12	....	....
Washington, DC	Communications Specialist.............................	Ethan Wolf.........................	SC	GS	12	....	....
Washington, DC	Legislative Specialist......................................	Naomi Zeigler......................	SC	GS	13	....	....
Washington, DC	Special Advisor and Director of Strategy and Operations.	Camilo Manjarres	SC	GS	13	....	....
Washington, DC	Special Advisor...	Marco Sanchez......................	SC	GS	12	....	....
Washington, DC	Special Assistant..	Ardeshir Pirzadeh	SC	GS	11	....	....
	OFFICE OF THE UNDER SECRETARY						
Washington, DC	Under Secretary for International Trade	Marisa Lago.........................	PAS	EX	III	....	....
Washington, DC	Deputy Assistant Secretary for Ad/Cvd Policy and Negotiations.	Ryan Michael Majerus.........	NA	ES	....	....	....
	Assistant Secretary for Enforcement and Compliance						
Washington, DC	Assistant Secretary for Enforcement and Compliance.	Vacant	....	EX	....	....	....
Washington, DC	Deputy Assistant Secretary for Enforcement and Compliance.	Career Incumbent	CA	ES	....	....	....
	Assistant Secretary for Industry and Analysis						
Washington, DC	Assistant Secretary for Industry and Analysis .	Grant Harris......................	PAS	EX	IV	....	....
Washington, DC	Deputy Assistant Secretary for Services	Neema S Guliani..................	NA	ES	....	....	....
Washington, DC	Deputy Assistant Secretary for Europe	Career Incumbent	CA	ES	....	....	....
Washington, DC	Deputy Assistant Secretary for Manufacturing.	Heather Evans	NA	ES	....	....	....
Washington, DC	Deputy Assistant Secretary for Industry and Analysis.	Career Incumbent	CA	ES	....	....	....
Washington, DC	Executive Director for Manufacturing..............	Career Incumbent	CA	ES	....	....	....
Washington, DC	Executive Director for Services	Career Incumbent	CA	ES	....	....	....
Washington, DC	Senior Advisor...	Andrew Spinelli...................	SC	GS	15	....	....
	DIRECTOR GENERAL OF THE U.S AND FOREIGN COMERCIAL SERVICE AND ASSISTANT SECRETARY FOR GLOBAL MARKETS						
Washington, DC	Director General of the United States and Foreign Commercial Service and Assistant Secretary for Global Markets.	Arun Venkataraman	PAS	EX	IV	....	....
Washington, DC	Deputy Assistant Secretary for Global Markets.	Career Incumbent	CA	ES	....	....	....
Washington, DC	Executive Director of Select USA.....................	Jasjit Singh Kalra	NA	ES	....	....	....
Washington, DC	Deputy Assistant Secretary for China...............	Career Incumbent	CA	ES	....	....	....
Washington, DC	Director of Communications and Outreach.......	Alexandra Bucaciuc	SC	GS	14	....	....
Washington, DC	Senior Advisor...	Ike Umunnah	SC	GS	15	....	....

DEPARTMENT OF COMMERCE—Continued

Location	Position Title	Name of Incumbent	Type of Appt.	Pay Plan	Level, Grade, or Pay	Tenure	Expires
	Deputy Assistant Secretary for Africa, the Middle East and South Asia						
Washington, DC	Executive Director for Middle East and Africa .	Career Incumbent	CA	ES	....	....	....
	Deputy Assistant Secretary for U.S. Field						
Washington, DC	Deputy Assistant Secretary for U.S. Field.........	Kendee Yamaguchi...............	NA	ES	....	....	....
Washington, DC	National Field Director	Career Incumbent	CA	ES	....	....	....
	Deputy Assistant Secretary for Textiles and Apparel						
Washington, DC	Deputy Assistant Secretary for Textiles, Consumer Goods, and Materials.	Vacant	....	ES	....	....	....
	Deputy Assistant Secretary for Western Hemisphere						
Washington, DC	Deputy Assistant Secretary for Western Hemisphere.	Vacant	....	ES	....	....	....
	Deputy Assistant Secretary for Trade, Policy and Analysis						
Washington, DC	Deputy Assistant Secretary for Trade Policy and Analysis.	Vacant	....	ES	....	....	....
Washington, DC	Director, Office of Trade and Economic Analysis.	Career Incumbent	CA	ES	....	....	....
	Deputy Assistant Secretary for Policy and Negotiations						
Washington, DC	Executive Director for Anti-Dumping and Subsidies, Policy and Negotiation.	Career Incumbent	CA	ES	....	....	....
Washington, DC	Executive Director for Trade Agreements Policy and Negotiations.	Career Incumbent	CA	ES	....	....	....
	Advocacy Center						
Washington, DC	Director, Advocacy Center	Vacant	....	ES	....	....	....
	Office of Policy Analysis and Development						
Washington, DC	Associate Administrator for Policy Analysis and Development.	Vacant	....	ES	....	....	....
Washington, DC	Deputy Associate Administrator for Policy Analysis and Development.	Vacant	....	ES	....	....	....
	MINORITY BUSINESS DEVELOPMENT AGENCY						
Washington, DC	Deputy Under Secretary	Eric Morrissette	NA	ES	....	....	....
Washington, DC	Under Secretary of Commerce for Minority Business Development.	Vacant	....	EX	....	....	....
Washington, DC	Counselor to the Under Secretary......................	Leopoldo Martinez Nucete...	SC	GS	15	....	....
Washington, DC	Senior Advisor to the Under Secretary Minority Business Development Agency.	Career Incumbent	CA	ES	....	....	....
Washington, DC	Chief of Staff...	Vacant	....	ES	....	....	....
Washington, DC	Deputy Chief of Staff...	Roosevelt Holmes	SC	GS	15	....	....
Washington, DC	Director of Legislative Affairs	Curtis Doster, Jr.	SC	GS	15	....	....
Washington, DC	Communications Director	Sheyla Asencios	SC	GS	15	....	....
Washington, DC	Director for the Office of Customer Experience.	Career Incumbent	CA	ES	....	....	....
Washington, DC	Special Advisor..	Hyerim Song........................	SC	GS	12	....	....
	NATIONAL OCEANIC AND ATMOSPHERIC ADMINISTRATION						
Washington, DC	Chief of Staff...	Karen Hyun	NA	ES	....	....	....
Washington, DC	Deputy Assistant Secretary for International Affairs.	Susan Ruffo	NA	ES	....	....	....
Washington, DC	Director, Platform and Infrastructure Acquisition Division.	Vacant	....	ES	....	....	....
Silver Spring, MD ...	Senior Advisor for Human Resources	Vacant	....	ES	....	....	....
Silver Spring, MD ...	Big Data Project Director..................................	Vacant	....	ES	....	....	....
Washington, DC	Senior Advisor...	Zachary Penney....................	SC	GS	15	....	....
Washington, DC	Senior Advisor...	Renee Stone	NA	ES	....	....	....
Washington, DC	Senior Advisor...	Jessica Grannis	SC	GS	15	....	....
Washington, DC	Director of Legislative Affairs	Makeda Okolo.......................	NA	ES	....	....	....
Washington, DC	Senior Advisor...	Shalini Mohleji	SC	GS	15	....	....
Washington, DC	Policy Advisor..	Christine Joseph....................	SC	GS	13	....	....
Washington, DC	Speechwriter and Advisor.................................	Marisa Giselle Aleguas........	SC	GS	14	....	....
Washington, DC	Legislative Advisor...	Andrea Daly.........................	SC	GS	13	....	....
Washington, DC	Legislative Specialist...	Liam Burke..........................	SC	GS	12	....	....
Washington, DC	Senior Advisor to the Assistant Administrator of NMFS.	Katie Westfall......................	SC	GS	15	....	....
Washington, DC	Senior Advisor...	Adena Leibman	SC	GS	15	....	....

DEPARTMENT OF COMMERCE—Continued

Location	Position Title	Name of Incumbent	Type of Appt.	Pay Plan	Level, Grade, or Pay	Tenure	Expires
Washington, DC	Policy Advisor..	Lauren Gibson....................	SC	GS	13	....	....
	Office of General Counsel						
Washington, DC	General Counsel	Walker B Smith..................	NA	ES			
Washington, DC	Assistant General Counsel for Fisheries	Career Incumbent	CA	ES			
Washington, DC	Chief Counsel for Industry and Security..........	Vacant	....	ES			
Silver Spring, MD ...	Deputy General Counsel	Career Incumbent	CA	ES			
Washington, DC	Associate Deputy General Counsel	Vacant	....	ES			
	OFFICE OF UNDER SECRETARY						
Washington, DC	Under Secretary Oceans and Atmosphere (Administrator National Oceanic and Atmospheric Administration).	Richard W Spinrad..............	PAS	EX	III	....	
Washington, DC	Assistant Secretary of Commerce for Oceans and Atmosphere.	Jainey K Bavishi..................	PAS	EX	IV	....	
Washington, DC	Assistant Secretary of Commerce for Environmental Observation and Prediction.	Michael Morgan..................	PAS	EX	IV	....	
Washington, DC	Deputy Assistant Secretary for International Fisheries.	Kelly Anne Kryc	NA	ES		....	
Washington, DC	Chief Scientist..	Sarah Kapnick....................	PA	EX	V	....	
Washington, DC	Senior Advisor	Perry Brody	SC	GS	15	....	
Washington, DC	Director of Communications	Lori Arguelles	NA	ES		....	
Washington, DC	Deputy Director, Office of Communications	Career Incumbent	CA	ES		....	
	OFFICE OF DEPUTY UNDER SECRETARY						
Washington, DC	Deputy Under Secretary for Operations...........	Career Incumbent	CA	ES			
	DEPUTY ASSISTANT SECRETARY FOR ASIA						
Washington, DC	Deputy Assistant Secretary for Asia	Career Incumbent	CA	ES		....	
	DEPUTY GENERAL COUNSEL FOR ATMOSPHERIC AND OCEAN RESEARCH AND SERVICES						
Washington, DC	Deputy General Counsel for Atmospheric and Ocean Research and Services.	Career Incumbent	CA	ES		....	
	NATIONAL WEATHER SERVICE						
Silver Spring, MD ...	Director, Surface and Upper Air Division.........	Career Incumbent	CA	ES		....	
	OFFICE OF THE ASSISTANT ADMINISTRATOR FOR WEATHER SERVICES						
Silver Spring, MD ...	Assistant Administrator for Weather Services..	Career Incumbent	CA	ES		....	
Washington, DC	Deputy Assistant Administrator for Weather Services.	Career Incumbent	CA	ES		....	
Silver Spring, MD ...	Senior Advisor for Advanced Modeling Systems.	Career Incumbent	CA	SL		....	....
	OFFICE OF ASSISTANT ADMINISTRATOR SATELLITE, DATA INFORMATION SERVICE						
Washington, DC	Assistant Administrator for National Environmental Satellite Data and Information Services.	Career Incumbent	CA	ES		....	
Silver Spring, MD ...	Deputy Assistant Administrator, Nesdis...........	Career Incumbent	CA	ES		....	
	OFFICE OF SATELLITE AND PRODUCT OPERATIONS						
Suitland, MD...........	Director, Office of Satellite and Product Operations.	Career Incumbent	CA	ES		....	
	OFFICE OF ASSISTANT ADMINISTRATOR, OCEAN AND ATMOSPHERIC RESEARCH						
Washington, DC	Assistant Administrator for Oceanic and Atmospheric Research.	Career Incumbent	CA	ES		....	
Silver Spring, MD ...	Deputy Assistant Administrator for Programs and Administration.	Vacant	....	ES		....	
	NATIONAL MARINE FISHERIES SERVICE						
Silver Spring, MD ...	Assistant Administrator for Marine Fisheries ..	Janet Coit	NA	ES		....	
Silver Spring, MD ...	Deputy Assistant Administrator for Regulatory Programs.	Career Incumbent	CA	ES		....	
Silver Spring, MD ...	Director, International Affairs and Seafood Inspection.	Career Incumbent	CA	ES		....	....

DEPARTMENT OF COMMERCE—Continued

Location	Position Title	Name of Incumbent	Type of Appt.	Pay Plan	Level, Grade, or Pay	Tenure	Expires
Washington, DC	**OFFICE OF INTERNATIONAL AFFAIRS** Associate Administrator, Office of International Affairs.	Career Incumbent	CA	ES	....	....	....
Washington, DC	**NATIONAL OCEAN SERVICE** Assistant Administrator for Ocean Services and Coastal Zone Management.	Career Incumbent	CA	ES	....	....	....
Silver Spring, MD ...	**OFFICE OF NATIONAL MARINE SANCTUARIES** Director, Office of National Marine Sanctuaries.	Career Incumbent	CA	ES	....	....	....
Washington, DC	**OFFICE OF AIR AND SPACE COMMERCIALIZATION** Director, Office of Space Commerce	Richard Dalbello..................	NA	ES	....	....	....
Washington, DC	Deputy Director, Office Space Commerce	Career Incumbent	CA	ES	....	....	....
Washington, DC	**NATIONAL TELECOMMUNICATIONS AND INFORMATION ADMINISTRATION** Spectrum National Security Systems Program Manager.	Career Incumbent	CA	ES	....	....	....
Washington, DC	Deputy Associate Administrator for Broadband Equity, Access, and Deployment.	Evan Feinman	TA	ES	....	....	03/13/25
Washington, DC	Senior Advisor	Philip Murphy	NA	ES	....	....	....
Washington, DC	Senior Advisor............................	Vacant	....	ES	....	....	....
Washington, DC	Senior Advisor (Special Representative for Broadband).	Vacant	....	ES	....	....	....
Washington, DC	Office Director- Application Engineering and Development.	Grace Abuhamad..................	SC	GS	15	....	....
Washington, DC	Director of Congressional Affairs	Parul Desai	SC	GS	15	....	....
Washington, DC	Director of Public Engagement...........................	Francella Ochillo	SC	GS	15	....	....
Washington, DC	Director of Public Affairs	Charles Meisch, Jr	SC	GS	15	....	....
Washington, DC	Director of Intergovernmental Affairs	Herbert Tyson......................	SC	GS	15	....	....
Washington, DC	Deputy Director of Congressional Affairs	Bennett Butler.....................	SC	GS	14	....	....
Washington, DC	Deputy Director of Public Engagement	Mara Reardon......................	SC	GS	14	....	....
Washington, DC	Deputy Director for External Affairs	Rachel Niemerski.................	SC	GS	14	....	....
Washington, DC	Senior Advisor	Lucy Moore	SC	GS	14	....	....
Washington, DC	Senior Advisor for Public Affairs......................	Margaret Harding McGill....	SC	GS	14	....	....
Washington, DC	Special Advisor for Public Engagement............	Viola Niyizigama	SC	GS	12	....	....
Washington, DC	Special Advisor...................................	Cindy Lin	SC	GS	12	....	....
Washington, DC	Special Advisor...................................	Michelle Flores	SC	GS	12	....	....
Washington, DC	Special Assistant for Public Engagement..........	Daniel James Ii	SC	GS	11	....	....
Washington, DC	Press Assistant	Lucas Wood-Gluck	SC	GS	11	....	....
Washington, DC	*Office of the Assistant Secretary for Communications and Information* Assistant Secretary for Communications and Information.	Alan Davidson	PAS	EX	IV	....	....
Washington, DC	Deputy Assistant Secretary for Communications and Information.	Vacant	....	ES	....	....	....
Washington, DC	Deputy Associate Administrator for Planning and Program Development.	Susannah Spellman	TA	ES	....	....	04/19/25
Washington, DC	Associate Administrator for Telecommunications and Information Applications.	Career Incumbent	CA	ES	....	....	....
Washington, DC	*Office of Spectrum Management* Associate Administrator Spectrum Management.	Career Incumbent	CA	ES	....	....	....
Washington, DC	Deputy Associate Administrator for Spectrum Management.	Vacant	....	ES	....	....	....
Washington, DC	Deputy Associate Administrator for Spectrum Planning and Policy.	Career Incumbent	CA	ES	....	....	....
Reston, VA	*First Responder Network Authority* Executive Director, First Responder Network Authority.	Career Incumbent	CA	ES	....	....	....
Reston, VA	Deputy Executive Director, First Responder Network Authority.	Career Incumbent	CA	ES	....	....	....
Reston, VA	Chief Customer Officer	Career Incumbent	CA	ES	....	....	....
Washington, DC	**NATIONAL INSTITUTE OF STANDARDS AND TECHNOLOGY** Under Secretary of Commerce for Standards and Technology.	Laurie E Locascio..................	PAS	EX	III	....	....
Gaithersburg, MD ...	Director, Chips R and D Metrology Program	Career Incumbent	CA	ES	....	....	....
Washington, DC	Director of Public Engagement........................	Jessica Stoneman	SC	GS	15	....	....

DEPARTMENT OF COMMERCE—Continued

Location	Position Title	Name of Incumbent	Type of Appt.	Pay Plan	Level, Grade, or Pay	Tenure	Expires
Washington, DC	Director of Legislative Affairs	Rebecca Callahan	SC	GS	15	....	....
Washington, DC	Director of Intergovernmental Affairs	Cynthia Aragon	SC	GS	15	....	....
Washington, DC	Director of External and Government Affairs...	Atissa Ladjevardian	NA	ES	....	....	....
Washington, DC	Deputy Communications Director.....................	Madeline Broas	SC	GS	14	....	....
Washington, DC	Communications Director	Geoffrey Burgan	SC	GS	15	....	....
Washington, DC	Public Engagement Advisor..............................	Matthew McPartlin	SC	GS	13	....	....
Washington, DC	Legislative Advisor	Denise Pizano-Reyes	SC	GS	13	....	....
Washington, DC	Public Engagement Specialist	Sophia Rubio	SC	GS	13	....	....
Washington, DC	Senior Advisor for External Affairs...................	Michael Patrick Dillon	NA	ES	....	....	....
	OFFICE OF THE DEPUTY UNDER SECRETARY						
Washington, DC	Deputy Under Secretary for International Trade.	Career Incumbent	CA	ES	....	....	....
Washington, DC	Chief Information Officer....................................	Vacant	....	ES	....	....	....
	NATIONAL TECHNICAL INFORMATION SERVICE						
Bethesda, MD..........	Director, National Technical Information Service.	Career Incumbent	CA	ES	....	....	....
	OFFICE OF PROTECTED RESOURCES						
Washington, DC	Director Office of Protected Resources..............	Career Incumbent	CA	ES	....	....	....
	OFFICE OF TRADEMARK TRIAL AND APPEAL BOARD						
Alexandria, VA	Attorney-Examiner (Trademark)........................	Vacant	....	OT	....	....	....
Alexandria, VA	Attorney-Examiner (Trademark)........................	George C Pologeorgis	XS	OT	....	....	....

DEPARTMENT OF COMMERCE OFFICE OF THE INSPECTOR GENERAL

Location	Position Title	Name of Incumbent	Type of Appt.	Pay Plan	Level, Grade, or Pay	Tenure	Expires
	DEPARTMENT OF COMMERCE OFFICE OF THE INSPECTOR GENERAL						
Washington, DC	Office of Inspector General	Vacant	....	EX	....	....	....

DEPARTMENT OF DEFENSE

OFFICE OF THE SECRETARY OF DEFENSE

Location	Position Title	Name of Incumbent	Type of Appt.	Pay Plan	Level, Grade, or Pay	Tenure	Expires
	OFFICE OF THE SECRETARY OF DEFENSE						
Arlington, VA	Secretary of Defense	Lloyd James Austin	PAS	EX	I		
Arlington, VA	Deputy Secretary of Defense	Kathleen A Hicks	PAS	EX	II		
Arlington, VA	Deputy Chief of Staff to the Secretary of Defense.	Caroline Zier	NA	ES			
Arlington, VA	Special Assistant to the Secretary of Defense, Director of Protocol.	Sarah S Farnsworth	NA	ES			
Arlington, VA	Chief of Staff to the Secretary of Defense	Derek Chollet	NA	ES			
Arlington, VA	Chief of Staff to the Deputy Secretary of Defense.	Heather King	NA	ES			
Arlington, VA	Deputy Chief of Staff to the Deputy Secretary of Defense.	Erol Yayboke	NA	ES			
Arlington, VA	Special Assistant to the Secretary of Defense for White House Liaison.	Veronica M Valdez	NA	ES			
Arlington, VA	Director of Speechwriting and Senior Advisor	Warren Bass	NA	ES			
Arlington, VA	Deputy Director of Protocol	Kathy Chung	SC	GS	15		
Arlington, VA	Confidential Assistant to the Secretary of Defense.	Ramona D Campbell	SC	GS	15		
Arlington, VA	Special Assistant to the Secretary of Defense	Carrie A Kagawa	SC	GS	15		
Arlington, VA	Special Assistant to the Deputy Secretary of Defense.	Laura J Kupe	SC	GS	15		
Arlington, VA	Director, Travel Operations	Valentine Sanders	SC	GS	15		
Arlington, VA	Special Assistant (Policy) to the Deputy Secretary of Defense.	David L Vorland	SC	GS	15		
Arlington, VA	Senior Advisor	John Francis Kirby	NA	ES			
Arlington, VA	Special Assistant	Adham Sahloul	SC	GS	13		
Arlington, VA	Special Assistant to the Secretary of Defense (Strategy).	Thomas Barron	SC	GS	15		
Arlington, VA	Senior Advisor	Nicolas Mitchell	NA	ES			
Arlington, VA	Advance Officer	Matthew Michael Harney	SC	GS	15		
Arlington, VA	Senior Advisor to the Deputy Secretary of Defense for Strategic Engagements.	Margaret Mullins	SC	GS	15		
Arlington, VA	Advance Officer	Claire-Ellen Marie Vidinghoff.	SC	GS	13		
Arlington, VA	Protocol Officer	Jill Bartscht Kent	SC	GS	15		
Arlington, VA	Advance Officer	Keenen Geter	SC	GS	14		
Arlington, VA	Special Assistant to the Secretary of Defense	Kim Quarantello	SC	GS	15		
Arlington, VA	Protocol Officer	Andrew Carpenter	SC	GS	12		
Arlington, VA	Deputy White House Liaison	Stephanie Cherkezian	SC	GS	15		
Arlington, VA	Staff Assistant to the Deputy Secretary of Defense.	Habiba Ahmed	SC	GS	12		
Arlington, VA	Special Assistant to the Deputy Secretary of Defense.	Sara Plana	SC	GS	15		
	NATIONAL SECURITY AGENCY						
Fort Meade, MD	Inspector General of the National Security Agency.	Vacant		EX			
	OFFICE OF THE UNDER SECRETARY OF DEFENSE (RESEARCH AND ENGINEERING)						
Arlington, VA	Under Secretary of Defense (Research and Engineering).	Heidi Shyu	PAS	EX	III		
Arlington, VA	Deputy Under Secretary of Defense (Research and Engineering).	David A Honey	PAS	EX	IV		
Arlington, VA	Director, Strategic Capabilities Office	Career Incumbent	CA	ES			
Alexandria, VA	Director, Test Resource Management Center	Career Incumbent	CA	ES			
Arlington, VA	Deputy Director Engineering	Krishnan Aiyer	NA	ES			
Arlington, VA	Executive Director, Business Operations	Career Incumbent	CA	ES			
Arlington, VA	Senior Advisor to the Under Secretary of Defense (Research and Engineering).	Bess Dopkeen	NA	ES			
Arlington, VA	Principal Deputy Executive Director, Systems Engineering and Architecture.	Career Incumbent	CA	ES			
Arlington, VA	Deputy Director, People, Finance, and Management Operations.	Career Incumbent	CA	ES			
Arlington, VA	Deputy Director, Policy and Government Partnerships.	Aditi Kumar	NA	ES			
Arlington, VA	Director, Developmental Test and Evaluation	Career Incumbent	CA	ES			
Arlington, VA	Special Assistant to the Under Secretary of Defense for Research and Engineering.	Riya Patel	SC	GS	15		
Arlington, VA	Special Assistant	Daniel Lapadula	SC	GS	13		

DEPARTMENT OF DEFENSE—Continued

OFFICE OF THE SECRETARY OF DEFENSE—Continued

Location	Position Title	Name of Incumbent	Type of Appt.	Pay Plan	Level, Grade, or Pay	Tenure	Expires
Arlington, VA..........	Senior Advisor to the Under Secretary of Defense (Research and Engineering).	Jongsun Alice Kim	NA	ES	....	....	....
Arlington, VA..........	Special Assistant..	Matthew Padilla..................	SC	GS	15	....	....
Arlington, VA..........	Special Assistant..	Griffin Cannon	SC	GS	11	....	....
Arlington, VA..........	Chief of Staff of the Office of Strategic Capital.	Corey Jacobson	SC	GS	15	....	....
	Office of the Assistant Secretary of Defense (Critical Technologies)						
Arlington, VA..........	Deputy Chief Technology Officer (Critical Technologies).	Maynard A Holliday............	NA	ES	....	....	....
Arlington, VA..........	Principal Deputy Assistant Secretary of Defense (Critical Technologies).	Career Incumbent	CA	ES	....	....	....
Arlington, VA..........	Deputy Assistant Secretary of Defense (Enabling Technology).	Career Incumbent	CA	ES	....	....	....
Arlington, VA..........	Special Assistant..	Alexander Sarti	SC	GS	12	....	....
	Office of the Assistant Secretary of Defense (Mission Capabilities)						
Arlington, VA..........	Deputy Chief Technology Officer (Mission Capabilities).	Thomas Browning	NA	ES	....	....	....
Arlington, VA..........	Principal Deputy Assistant Secretary of Defense (Mission Capabilities).	Career Incumbent	CA	ES	....	....	....
Arlington, VA..........	Deputy Assistant Secretary of Defense (Mission Integration).	Career Incumbent	CA	ES	....	....	....
Arlington, VA..........	Deputy Assistant Secretary of Defense (Multi-Domain Joint Operations).	Career Incumbent	CA	ES	....	....	....
Arlington, VA..........	Deputy Assistant Secretary of Defense (Prototypes and Experiments).	Career Incumbent	CA	ES	....	....	....
	Office of the Assistant Secretary of Defense (Science and Technology)						
Arlington, VA..........	Assistant Secretary of Defense (Science and Technology).	Aprille Ericsson	PAS	EX	IV	....	....
Arlington, VA..........	Deputy Chief Technology Officer (Science and Technology).	Barbara McQuiston.............	NA	ES	....	....	....
Arlington, VA..........	Principal Deputy Assistant Secretary of Defense (Science and Technology).	Career Incumbent	CA	ES	....	....	....
Alexandria, VA	Administrator, Defense Technical Information Center.	Career Incumbent	CA	ES	....	....	....
Alexandria, VA	Deputy Assistant Secretary of Defense (Science and Technology Foundations).	Career Incumbent	CA	ES	....	....	....
Arlington, VA..........	Deputy Assistant Secretary of Defense (Science and Technology Futures).	Vacant	....	ES	....	....	....
Arlington, VA..........	Deputy Assistant Secretary of Defense (Science and Technology Program Protection).	Career Incumbent	CA	ES	....	....	....
Arlington, VA..........	Director, Basic Research.........................	Career Incumbent	CA	ES	....	....	....
Arlington, VA..........	Director, Maintaining Technology Advantage....	Career Incumbent	CA	ES	....	....	....
Arlington, VA..........	Director, Technology Industrial Innovation Base.	Career Incumbent	CA	ES	....	....	....
	OFFICE OF THE ASSISTANT SECRETARY OF DEFENSE (ACQUISITION AND SUSTAINMENT)						
Arlington, VA..........	Under Secretary of Defense (Acquisition and Sustainment).	William A Laplante.............	PAS	EX	III	....	....
Arlington, VA..........	Deputy Under Secretary of Defense (Acquisition and Sustainment).	Vacant	....	EX	....	....	....
Alexandria, VA	President, Defense Acquisition University	Career Incumbent	CA	ES	....	....	....
Arlington, VA..........	Executive Director, Business Operations..........	Career Incumbent	CA	ES	....	....	....
Arlington, VA..........	Special Assistant to the Under Secretary of Defense (Acquisition and Sustainment).	Esther Sperling	SC	GS	13	....	....
Arlington, VA..........	Special Advisor for Climate	Michael McGhee...............	TA	ES	....	....	....
Arlington, VA..........	Special Assistant..	James Santos......................	SC	GS	13	....	....
Arlington, VA..........	Special Assistant..	Simone Williams..................	SC	GS	14	....	....
	Office of the Assistant Secretary of Defense (Acquisition)						
Arlington, VA..........	Assistant Secretary of Defense (Acquisition)	Cara L Abercrombie............	PAS	EX	IV	....	....
Arlington, VA..........	Principal Deputy Assistant Secretary of Defense (Acquisition).	Career Incumbent	CA	ES	....	....	....
Arlington, VA..........	Deputy Assistant Secretary of Defense (Strategic, Space, and Intelligence Portfolio Mgmt).	Career Incumbent	CA	ES	....	....	....

DEPARTMENT OF DEFENSE—Continued

OFFICE OF THE SECRETARY OF DEFENSE—Continued

Location	Position Title	Name of Incumbent	Type of Appt.	Pay Plan	Level, Grade, or Pay	Tenure	Expires
Arlington, VA............	Director, Office of Economic Adjustment	Career Incumbent	CA	ES	....	....	....
Arlington, VA............	Executive Director, Joint Rapid Acquisition Cell.	Career Incumbent	CA	ES	....	....	....
Arlington, VA............	Prin Dep Dir, Performance Assessment and Root Cause Analyses/Dep Dir, Root Cause Analyses.	Career Incumbent	CA	ES	....	....	....
Arlington, VA............	Director, Cyber Warfare..	Career Incumbent	CA	ES	....	....	....
Arlington, VA............	Director, Electronic Warfare...............................	Career Incumbent	CA	ES	....	....	....
Arlington, VA............	Director, Surface Warfare....................................	Career Incumbent	CA	ES	....	....	....
	Office of the Assistant Secretary of Defense (Energy, Installations and Environment)						
Arlington, VA............	Assistant Secretary of Defense (Energy, Installations and Environment).	Brendan Owens	PAS	EX	IV	....	....
Arlington, VA............	Principal Deputy Assistant Secretary of Defense (Energy, Installations, and Environment).	Career Incumbent	CA	ES	....	....	....
Arlington, VA............	Deputy Assistant Secretary of Defense (Energy Resilience and Optimization).	Career Incumbent	CA	ES	....	....	....
Arlington, VA............	Deputy Assistant Secretary of Defense (Environmental Mgmt and Resilience).	Career Incumbent	CA	ES	....	....	....
Arlington, VA............	Deputy Assistant Secretary of Defense (Housing).	Mark Colon	NA	ES	....	....	....
Arlington, VA............	Deputy Assistant Secretary of Defense (Infrastructure Modernization and Resilience).	Career Incumbent	CA	ES	....	....	....
Arlington, VA............	Special Assistant..	Katie Carol Greenberg.........	SC	GS	13	....	....
	Office of the Assistant Secretary of Defense (Industrial Base Policy)						
Arlington, VA............	Assistant Secretary of Defense (Industrial Base Policy).	Laura Taylor-Kale	PAS	EX	IV	....	....
Arlington, VA............	Principal Deputy Assistant Secretary of Defense (Industrial Base Policy).	Career Incumbent	CA	ES	....	....	....
Arlington, VA............	Deputy Assistant Secretary of Defense (Industrial Base Resilience).	Carla Zeppieri......................	NA	ES	....	....	....
Arlington, VA............	Deputy Assistant Secretary of Defense (International and Industry Engagement).	Travis Langster	NA	ES	....	....	....
Alexandria, VA	Director, Small Business Programs....................	Farooq A Mitha.....................	NA	ES	....	....	....
Arlington, VA............	Principal Director, Global Investments and Economic Security.	Career Incumbent	CA	ES	....	....	....
Arlington, VA............	Deputy Director, Planning, Programs and Analysis.	Career Incumbent	CA	ES	....	....	....
Arlington, VA............	Director, Manufacturing Capability Expansion and Investment Prioritization.	Career Incumbent	CA	ES	....	....	....
	Office of the Assistant Secretary of Defense (Nuclear, Chemical and Biological Defense Programs)						
Arlington, VA............	Assistant Secretary of Defense (Nuclear, Chemical and Biological Defense).	Deborah G Rosenblum.........	PAS	EX	IV	....	....
Arlington, VA............	Principal Deputy Assistant Secretary of Defense (Nuclear Chemical and Biological Defense Programs).	Career Incumbent	CA	ES	....	....	....
Arlington, VA............	Deputy Assistant Secretary of Defense (Chemical and Biological Defense).	Career Incumbent	CA	ES	....	....	....
Arlington, VA............	Deputy Assistant Secretary of Defense (Threat Reduction and Arms Control).	Kingston Reif........................	NA	ES	....	....	....
	Office of the Assistant Secretary of Defense (Sustainment)						
Arlington, VA............	Assistant Secretary of Defense (Sustainment)..	Christopher J Lowman	PAS	EX	IV	....	....
Arlington, VA............	Deputy Chief Sustainability Officer..................	Rachel Ross..........................	NA	ES	....	....	....
Arlington, VA............	Chief of Staff to the Chief Sustainability Officer.	Daniel Parnes	SC	GS	15	....	....
Arlington, VA............	Principal Deputy Assistant Secretary of Defense for Sustainment (Logistics).	Career Incumbent	CA	ES	....	....	....
Arlington, VA............	Deputy Assistant Secretary of Defense (Logistics).	Career Incumbent	CA	ES	....	....	....
Arlington, VA............	Deputy Assistant Secretary of Defense (Materiel Readiness).	Vacant		ES	....	....	....
Arlington, VA............	Deputy Assistant Secretary of Defense (Product Support).	Career Incumbent	CA	ES	....	....	....

DEPARTMENT OF DEFENSE—Continued

OFFICE OF THE SECRETARY OF DEFENSE—Continued

Location	Position Title	Name of Incumbent	Type of Appt.	Pay Plan	Level, Grade, or Pay	Tenure	Expires
	OFFICE OF THE UNDER SECRETARY OF DEFENSE (POLICY)						
Arlington, VA..........	Under Secretary of Defense (Policy)..................	Vacant	....	EX	....	....	....
Arlington, VA..........	Deputy Under Secretary of Defense (Policy).....	Vacant	....	EX	....	....	....
Arlington, VA..........	Special Assistant..	Kevin Fashola....................	SC	GS	13	....	....
Arlington, VA..........	Foreign Relations and Defense Policy Manager.	Vacant	....	ES	....	....	....
Arlington, VA..........	Chief Operating Officer....................	Career Incumbent	CA	ES	....	....	....
Arlington, VA..........	Senior Advisor (Career Broadening)	Career Incumbent	CA	ES	....	....	....
Arlington, VA..........	Senior Advisor to the Deputy Assistant Secretary of Defense (South and Southeast Asia).	Jamie Morgan......................	SC	GS	15	....	....
Arlington, VA..........	Special Assistant..	Joseph Federici....................	SC	GS	13	....	....
Arlington, VA..........	Foreign Relations and Defense Policy Manager.	Career Incumbent	CA	ES	....	....	....
Arlington, VA..........	Senior Advisor (Career Broadening)	Daniel Porter Erikson..........	NA	ES	....	....	....
Arlington, VA..........	Senior Coordinator for Afghanistan	Vacant	....	ES	....	....	....
Arlington, VA..........	Senior Advisor (Career Broadening)	Nathaniel Adler....................	NA	ES	....	....	....
Arlington, VA..........	Foreign Relations and Defense Policy Manager.	Career Incumbent	CA	ES	....	....	....
Arlington, VA..........	Special Assistant..	Elizabeth Stockton	SC	GS	15	....	....
	Office of the Assistant Secretary of Defense (Cyber Policy)						
Arlington, VA..........	Principal Deputy Assistant Secretary of Defense (Cyber Policy).	Career Incumbent	CA	ES	....	....	....
Arlington, VA..........	Deputy Assistant Secretary of Defense (Cyber Policy).	Mieke Eoyang......................	NA	ES	....	....	....
Arlington, VA..........	Senior Advisor, Cyber Policy	Leah Dreyfuss	SC	GS	15	....	....
	Office of the Assistant Secretary of Defense (Homeland Defense and Hemispheric Affairs)						
Arlington, VA..........	Assistant Secretary of Defense (Homeland Defense and Hemispheric Affairs).	Vacant	....	EX			
Arlington, VA..........	Principal Deputy Assistant Secretary of Defense (Homeland Defense and Hemispheric Affairs).	Sarah Zimmerman	NA	ES	....	....	....
Arlington, VA..........	Deputy Assistant Secretary of Defense (Arctic and Global Resiliency).	Iris Anneva Ferguson...........	NA	ES	....	....	....
Arlington, VA..........	Deputy Assistant Secretary of Defense (Defense Continuity and Mission Assurance).	Career Incumbent	CA	ES	....	....	....
Arlington, VA..........	Deputy Assistant Secretary of Defense (Homeland Defense Integration and Defense Support of Civil Authorities).	Career Incumbent	CA	ES	....	....	....
Arlington, VA..........	Deputy Assistant Secretary of Defense (Western Hemisphere Affairs).	Ana-Janaina Nelson............	NA	ES	....	....	....
Arlington, VA..........	Senior Advisor to the Assistant Secretary of Defense (Homeland and Hemispheric Affairs) (Climate).	Emily Burlinghaus...............	SC	GS	14	....	....
Arlington, VA..........	Senior Advisor to the Deputy Assistant Secretary of Defense (Homeland Defense Integration and Defense Support of Civil Authorities).	Career Incumbent	CA	ES	....	....	....
Arlington, VA..........	Special Assistant..	Victor Esteves Garcia	SC	GS	14	....	....
	Office of the Assistant Secretary of Defense (Indo-Pacific Security Affairs)						
Arlington, VA..........	Assistant Secretary of Defense (Indo-Pacific Security Affairs).	Ely Ratner	PAS	EX	IV	....	....
Arlington, VA..........	Principal Deputy Assistant Secretary of Defense (Indo-Pacific Security Affairs).	Career Incumbent	CA	ES	....	....	....
Arlington, VA..........	Deputy Assistant Secretary of Defense (China).	Michael Chase	NA	ES	....	....	....
Arlington, VA..........	Deputy Assistant Secretary of Defense (East Asia).	Anka Lee..............................	NA	ES	....	....	....
Arlington, VA..........	Deputy Assistant Secretary of Defense (South and Southeast Asia).	Vacant	....	ES	....	....	....
Arlington, VA..........	Principal Director, East Asia	Career Incumbent	CA	ES	....	....	....
Arlington, VA..........	Special Assistant..	Christopher Estep................	SC	GS	14	....	....

DEPARTMENT OF DEFENSE—Continued

OFFICE OF THE SECRETARY OF DEFENSE—Continued

Location	Position Title	Name of Incumbent	Type of Appt.	Pay Plan	Level, Grade, or Pay	Tenure	Expires
	Office of the Assistant Secretary of Defense (International Security Affairs)						
Arlington, VA..........	Assistant Secretary of Defense (International Security Affairs).	Celeste A Wallander.............	PAS	EX	IV	....	....
Arlington, VA..........	Principal Deputy Assistant Secretary of Defense (International Security Affairs).	Tressa S Guenov	NA	ES	....	....	....
Brussels, Belg..........	Defense Advisor to the U.S. Ambassador to NATO.	Rachel Ellehuus	NA	ES	....	....	....
Arlington, VA..........	Deputy Assistant Secretary of Defense (African Affairs).	Maureen Farrell	NA	ES	....	....	....
Arlington, VA..........	Deputy Assistant Secretary of Defense (Middle East).	Daniel Shapiro.....................	NA	ES	....	....	....
Arlington, VA..........	Deputy Assistant Secretary of Defense (Europe and North Atlantic Treaty Organization Policy).	Lisa Sawyer	NA	ES	....	....	....
Arlington, VA..........	Deputy Assistant Secretary of Defense (Russia, Ukraine and Eurasia Policy).	Career Incumbent	CA	ES	....	....	....
Arlington, VA..........	Principal Director, African Affairs......................	Career Incumbent	CA	ES	....	....	....
Arlington, VA..........	Principal Director for Russia, Ukraine and Eurasia.	Emma Borden......................	SC	GS	15	....	....
Arlington, VA..........	Senior Advisor to the Assistant Secretary of Defense (International Security Affairs).	Career Incumbent	CA	ES	....	....	....
	Office of the Assistant Secretary of Defense (Space Policy)						
Arlington, VA..........	Assistant Secretary of Defense (Space Policy) ..	Vacant	....	EX	....	....	....
Arlington, VA..........	Principal Deputy Assistant Secretary of Defense (Space Policy).	Vipin Narang......................	NA	ES	....	....	....
Arlington, VA..........	Deputy Assistant Secretary of Defense (Nuclear and Countering Weapons of Mass Destruction Policy).	Richard C Johnson...............	NA	ES	....	....	....
Arlington, VA..........	Deputy Assistant Secretary of Defense (Space Policy).	Career Incumbent	CA	ES	....	....	....
Arlington, VA..........	Principal Director, Space Policy and Missile Defense.	Vacant		ES	....	....	....
	Office of the Assistant Secretary of Defense (Strategy, Plans, and Capabilities)						
Arlington, VA..........	Assistant Secretary of Defense (Strategy, Plans, and Capabilities).	Vacant	....	EX	....	....	....
Arlington, VA..........	Principal Deputy Assistant Secretary of Defense (Strategy, Plans, and Capabilities).	Career Incumbent	CA	ES	....	....	....
Arlington, VA..........	Deputy Assistant Secretary of Defense (Global Partnerships).	Christopher Mewett.............	NA	ES	....	....	....
Arlington, VA..........	Deputy Assistant Secretary of Defense (Force Development and Emerging Capabilities).	Michael Horowitz	NA	ES	....	....	....
Arlington, VA..........	Deputy Assistant Secretary of Defense (Plans and Posture).	Vacant	....	ES	....	....	....
Arlington, VA..........	Deputy Assistant Secretary of Defense (Strategy and Force Development).	Eric A Ridge........................	NA	ES	....	....	....
Arlington, VA..........	Special Assistant..	Leon Ratz.............................	SC	GS	15	....	....
Arlington, VA..........	Special Assistant..	Lauren Speranza.................	SC	GS	15	....	....
	OFFICE OF THE UNDER SECRETARY OF DEFENSE (COMPTROLLER)						
Arlington, VA..........	Under Secretary of Defense (Comptroller)	Michael J McCord	PAS	EX	III	....	....
Arlington, VA..........	Deputy Under Secretary of Defense (Comptroller).	Kathleen S Miller.................	PAS	EX	IV	....	....
Arlington, VA..........	Deputy Comptroller (Program/Budget)..............	Career Incumbent	CA	ES	....	....	....
Arlington, VA..........	Deputy Comptroller for Budget and Appropriations Affairs.	Mitchell Souter....................	NA	ES	....	....	....
Arlington, VA..........	Assistant Deputy Comptroller (Program/Budget).	Career Incumbent	CA	ES	....	....	....
Arlington, VA..........	Assistant Deputy Chief Financial Officer..........	Career Incumbent	CA	ES	....	....	....
Arlington, VA..........	Director for Financial Management Policy and Reporting.	Career Incumbent	CA	ES	....	....	....
Arlington, VA..........	Director for Human Capital and Resource Management.	Career Incumbent	CA	ES	....	....	....
Arlington, VA..........	Director for Investment.......................................	Career Incumbent	CA	ES	....	....	....
Arlington, VA..........	Director for Military Personnel and Construction.	Career Incumbent	CA	ES	....	....	....
Arlington, VA..........	Director for Operations (Program/Budget)........	Career Incumbent	CA	ES	....	....	....
Arlington, VA..........	Director for Program and Financial Control	Career Incumbent	CA	ES	....	....	....

DEPARTMENT OF DEFENSE—Continued

OFFICE OF THE SECRETARY OF DEFENSE—Continued

Location	Position Title	Name of Incumbent	Type of Appt.	Pay Plan	Level, Grade, or Pay	Tenure	Expires
Arlington, VA...........	Assistant Deputy Comptroller (Budget and Appropriations Affairs).	Career Incumbent	CA	ES	....	....	....
Arlington, VA...........	Associate Director for Contingency and International Programs (Program/Budget).	Vacant	....	ES	....	....	....
Arlington, VA...........	Associate Director for Defense-Wide Programs.	Career Incumbent	CA	ES	....	....	....
Arlington, VA...........	Associate Director, Military Construction (Program/Budget).	Career Incumbent	CA	ES	....	....	....
Arlington, VA...........	Associate Director for Military Operations	Career Incumbent	CA	ES	....	....	....
Arlington, VA...........	Associate Director for Military Personnel and Health Care.	Career Incumbent	CA	ES	....	....	....
Arlington, VA...........	Associate Director for Investment (Program/Budget).	Career Incumbent	CA	ES	....	....	....
Arlington, VA...........	Director for Financial Improvement and Audit Remediation.	Career Incumbent	CA	ES	....	....	....
Arlington, VA...........	Deputy Director, Program and Financial Control.	Career Incumbent	CA	ES	....	....	....
Arlington, VA...........	Chief of Staff to the Under Secretary of Defense (Comptroller).	Yousra Fazili	NA	ES	....	....	....
Arlington, VA...........	Special Assistant...	Miriam Sefami.....................	SC	GS	12	....	....
Arlington, VA...........	Special Assistant...	John Bradley Allen..............	SC	GS	15	....	....
	OFFICE OF THE UNDER SECRETARY OF DEFENSE (PERSONNEL AND READINESS)						
Arlington, VA...........	Under Secretary of Defense (Personnel and Readiness).	Vacant	....	EX	....	....	....
Arlington, VA...........	Deputy Under Secretary of Defense (Personnel and Readiness).	Ashish Vazirani	PAS	EX	IV	....	....
Arlington, VA...........	Executive Director..	Career Incumbent	CA	ES	....	....	....
Arlington, VA...........	Director, Department of Defense/Veterans Affairs Collaboration Office.	Career Incumbent	CA	ES	....	....	....
Arlington, VA...........	Director, Office for Civil Rights and Equal Opportunity Policy.	Career Incumbent	CA	ES	....	....	....
Arlington, VA...........	Senior Advisor to the Under Secretary of Defense (Personnel and Readiness).	Emma Norvell	NA	ES	....	....	....
Arlington, VA...........	Special Assistant...	Joseph Costa........................	SC	GS	15	....	....
Arlington, VA...........	Special Assistant...	Brian Collins	SC	GS	14	....	....
Arlington, VA...........	Special Assistant...	Dori Susan Friedberg............	SC	GS	15	....	....
	Office of the Assistant Secretary of Defense (Health Affairs)						
Arlington, VA...........	Assistant Secretary of Defense (Health Affairs).	Lester Martinez-Lopez.........	PAS	EX	IV	....	....
Arlington, VA...........	Principal Deputy Assistant Secretary of Defense (Health Affairs).	Seileen M Mullen	NA	ES	....	....	....
Arlington, VA...........	Deputy Assistant Secretary of Defense (Health Readiness Policy and Oversight).	Career Incumbent	CA	ES	....	....	....
Arlington, VA...........	Deputy Assistant Secretary of Defense (Health Services Policy and Oversight).	Career Incumbent	CA	ES	....	....	....
Falls Church, VA	Deputy Assistant Secretary of Defense (Health Resources Management and Policy).	Career Incumbent	CA	ES	....	....	....
	Office of the Assistant Secretary of Defense (Manpower and Reserve Affairs)						
Arlington, VA...........	Assistant Secretary of Defense (Manpower and Reserve Affairs).	Ronald T Keohane................	PAS	EX	IV	....	....
Arlington, VA...........	Principal Deputy Assistant Secretary of Defense (Manpower and Reserve Affairs).	Career Incumbent	CA	ES	....	....	....
Arlington, VA...........	Deputy Assistant Secretary of Defense (Civilian Personnel Policy).	Vacant	....	ES	....	....	....
Arlington, VA...........	Deputy Assistant Secretary of Defense (Military Community and Family Policy).	Patricia Montes Barron	NA	ES	....	....	....
Arlington, VA...........	Deputy Assistant Secretary of Defense (Military Personnel Policy).	Career Incumbent	CA	ES	....	....	....
Arlington, VA...........	Deputy Assistant Secretary of Defense (Reserve Integration).	Vacant	....	ES	....	....	....
Arlington, VA...........	Principal Director, Civilian Personnel Policy.....	Career Incumbent	CA	ES	....	....	....
Arlington, VA...........	Principal Director, Military Community and Family Policy.	Career Incumbent	CA	ES	....	....	....
Arlington, VA...........	Principal Director, Military Personnel Policy	Career Incumbent	CA	ES	....	....	....
Arlington, VA...........	Director, Military Compensation	Career Incumbent	CA	ES	....	....	....
Arlington, VA...........	Senior Advisor to the Assistant Secretary of Defense (Manpower and Reserve Affairs).	Vacant	....	ES	....	....	....

DEPARTMENT OF DEFENSE—Continued

Office of the Secretary of Defense—Continued

Location	Position Title	Name of Incumbent	Type of Appt.	Pay Plan	Level, Grade, or Pay	Tenure	Expires
Arlington, VA............	Director, Accession Policy.....................................	Career Incumbent	CA	ES	....	....	....
Arlington, VA............	Director, Officer and Enlisted Personnel Mgmt.	Career Incumbent	CA	ES	....	....	....
	Office of the Assistant Secretary of Defense (Readiness)						
Arlington, VA............	Assistant Secretary of Defense (Readiness)	Shawn G Skelly....................	PAS	EX	IV	....	....
Arlington, VA............	Principal Deputy Assistant Secretary of Defense (Readiness).	Career Incumbent	CA	ES	....	....	....
Arlington, VA............	Deputy Assistant Secretary of Defense (Force Education and Training).	Vacant	....	ES	....	....	....
Arlington, VA............	Deputy Assistant Secretary of Defense (Force Readiness).	Judson A Crane....................	NA	ES	....	....	....
Arlington, VA............	Executive Director for Force Resiliency.............	Elizabeth Foster	NA	ES	....	....	....
Arlington, VA............	Deputy Director for Force Resiliency	Career Incumbent	CA	ES	....	....	....
Arlington, VA............	Special Assistant to the Executive Director, Force Resiliency.	Hailey Lawrence...................	SC	GS	12	....	....
	OFFICE OF THE UNDER SECRETARY OF DEFENSE (INTELLIGENCE AND SECURITY)						
Arlington, VA............	Under Secretary of Defense (Intelligence and Security).	Vacant	....	EX	....	....	....
Arlington, VA............	Deputy Under Secretary of Defense (Intelligence and Security).	Milancy Harris	PAS	EX	IV	....	....
Arlington, VA............	Special Advisor..	Meagen M Manning............	SC	GS	15	....	....
Arlington, VA............	Special Assistant..	Sameer P Punyani	SC	GS	15	....	....
Arlington, VA............	Special Assistant..	James Tingle........................	SC	GS	14	....	....
	OFFICE OF THE GENERAL COUNSEL						
Arlington, VA............	General Counsel of the Department of Defense.	Caroline D Krass..................	PAS	EX	IV	....	....
Arlington, VA............	Principal Deputy General Counsel....................	Vacant	....	ES	....	....	....
Arlington, VA............	Deputy General Counsel (Acquisition and Logistics).	Career Incumbent	CA	ES	....	....	....
Arlington, VA............	Deputy General Counsel (Environment and Installations).	Taylor N Ferrell....................	NA	ES	....	....	....
Arlington, VA............	Deputy General Counsel (Fiscal)........................	Career Incumbent	CA	ES	....	....	....
Arlington, VA............	Deputy General Counsel (International Affairs).	Career Incumbent	CA	ES	....	....	....
Arlington, VA............	Deputy General Counsel (Legal Counsel).........	Rita Davis	NA	ES	....	....	....
Arlington, VA............	Deputy General Counsel (Legislation, Investigations and Oversight).	Sheila Menz.........................	NA	ES	....	....	....
Arlington, VA............	Deputy General Counsel (Personnel and Health Policy).	Career Incumbent	CA	ES	....	....	....
Arlington, VA............	Chief of Staff to the General Counsel...............	Yaara Barnoon......................	NA	ES	....	....	....
	OFFICE OF THE DIRECTOR (COST ASSESSMENT AND PROGRAM EVALUATION)						
Arlington, VA............	Director, Cost Assessment and Program Evaluation.	Susanna V Blume.................	PAS	EX	IV	....	....
Arlington, VA............	Principal Deputy Director...................................	Career Incumbent	CA	ES	....	....	....
Arlington, VA............	Deputy Director, Analysis and Innovation........	Career Incumbent	CA	ES	....	....	....
Arlington, VA............	Deputy Director, Capability Enablers................	Career Incumbent	CA	ES	....	....	....
Arlington, VA............	Deputy Director, Cost Assessment	Career Incumbent	CA	ES	....	....	....
Arlington, VA............	Deputy Director, Program Evaluation	Career Incumbent	CA	ES	....	....	....
Arlington, VA............	Director, Land Forces Division	Career Incumbent	CA	ES	....	....	....
Arlington, VA............	Director, Tactical Air Forces Division................	Career Incumbent	CA	ES	....	....	....
Arlington, VA............	Director, Advanced Systems Cost Analysis Division.	Career Incumbent	CA	ES	....	....	....
Arlington, VA............	Director, Irregular Warfare Division	Career Incumbent	CA	ES	....	....	....
Arlington, VA............	Director, Command, Control, Communications, Computers (C4) and Information Programs Division.	Career Incumbent	CA	ES	....	....	....
Arlington, VA............	Director, Program Resources and Information Systems Management Division.	Career Incumbent	CA	ES	....	....	....
Arlington, VA............	Director, Program Analysis Division	Career Incumbent	CA	ES	....	....	....
Arlington, VA............	Director, Naval Forces Division	Career Incumbent	CA	ES	....	....	....
Arlington, VA............	Director, Economic and Manpower Analysis Division.	Career Incumbent	CA	ES	....	....	....
Arlington, VA............	Director, Strategic, Defensive and Science/Technology Division.	Career Incumbent	CA	ES	....	....	....

DEPARTMENT OF DEFENSE—Continued

OFFICE OF THE SECRETARY OF DEFENSE—Continued

Location	Position Title	Name of Incumbent	Type of Appt.	Pay Plan	Level, Grade, or Pay	Tenure	Expires
Arlington, VA..........	Director, Strategic Analysis and Analytic Innovation Division.	Career Incumbent	CA	ES	....	....	....
Arlington, VA..........	Director, Readiness and Force Employment Division.	Career Incumbent	CA	ES	....	....	....
Arlington, VA..........	Director, Space and Intelligence Division..........	Career Incumbent	CA	ES	....	....	....
Arlington, VA..........	Director, Land and Naval Warfare Cost Analysis Division.	Career Incumbent	CA	ES	....	....	....
Arlington, VA..........	Chief of Staff..........	Walter Rue	SC	GS	15	....	....
	OFFICE OF THE DIRECTOR, OPERATIONAL TEST AND EVALUATION						
Arlington, VA..........	Director, Operational Test and Evaluation........	Douglas Schmidt	PAS	EX	IV	....	....
Arlington, VA..........	Principal Deputy Director, Operational Test and Evaluation.	Career Incumbent	CA	ES	....	....	....
Arlington, VA..........	Deputy Director, Air Warfare..............................	Career Incumbent	CA	ES	....	....	....
Arlington, VA..........	Deputy Director, Net-Centric Space and Missile Defense Systems.	Career Incumbent	CA	ES	....	....	....
	OFFICE OF THE DEPARTMENT OF DEFENSE CHIEF INFORMATION OFFICER						
Arlington, VA..........	Chief Information Officer of the Department of Defense.	Vacant	....	EX	....	....	....
Arlington, VA..........	Principal Deputy Chief Information Officer......	Career Incumbent	CA	ES	....	....	....
Arlington, VA..........	Deputy Chief Information Officer for Command, Control and Communications.	Career Incumbent	CA	ES	....	....	....
Arlington, VA..........	Deputy Chief Information Officer for Cybersecurity.	Career Incumbent	CA	ES	....	....	....
Arlington, VA..........	Deputy Chief Information Officer for Information Enterprise.	Vacant	....	ES	....	....	....
Arlington, VA..........	Deputy Chief Information Officer for Resources and Analysis.	Career Incumbent	CA	ES	....	....	....
Arlington, VA..........	Principal Director to the Deputy Chief Information Officer for Command, Control and Communications.	Career Incumbent	CA	ES	....	....	....
Arlington, VA..........	Principal Director to the Deputy Chief Information Officer for Information Enterprise.	Career Incumbent	CA	ES	....	....	....
Arlington, VA..........	Principal Director to the Deputy Chief Information Officer for Resources and Analysis.	Career Incumbent	CA	ES	....	....	....
Arlington, VA..........	Cybersecurity Chief Operations Officer............	Career Incumbent	CA	ES	....	....	....
Arlington, VA..........	Director, Spectrum Policy and Programs..........	Career Incumbent	CA	ES	....	....	....
Arlington, VA..........	Director, Command, Control and Communications Infrastructure.	Career Incumbent	CA	ES	....	....	....
Arlington, VA..........	Director of Strategic Engagements	Ahmad Khan	NA	ES	....	....	....
Arlington, VA..........	Senior Advisor, Zero Trust Portfolio Management Office.	Randy Resnick.....................	TA	ES	....	....	01/30/25
	OFFICE OF THE ASSISTANT SECRETARY OF DEFENSE (LEGISLATIVE AFFAIRS)						
Arlington, VA..........	Assistant Secretary of Defense (Legislative Affairs).	Rheanne Wirkkala	PAS	EX	IV	....	....
Arlington, VA..........	Principal Deputy Assistant Secretary of Defense (Legislative Affairs).	Thomas Mancinelli..............	NA	ES	....	....	....
Arlington, VA..........	Deputy Assistant Secretary of Defense (House Affairs).	Jennifer Perrino	NA	ES	....	....	....
Arlington, VA..........	Deputy Assistant Secretary of Defense (Senate Affairs).	Lane Bodian	NA	ES	....	....	....
Arlington, VA..........	Director of Intergovernmental Affairs	Karim Farishta....................	SC	GS	15	....	....
Arlington, VA..........	Special Assistant to the Assistant Secretary of Defense (Legislative Affairs).	Jonah Glick-Unterman	SC	GS	12	....	....
Arlington, VA..........	Special Assistant to the Assistant Secretary of Defense (Legislative Affairs).	Serena Li	SC	GS	13	....	....
Arlington, VA..........	Special Assistant to the Assistant Secretary of Defense (Legislative Affairs).	Alex Davidson......................	SC	GS	13	....	....
Arlington, VA..........	Special Assistant to the Assistant Secretary of Defense (Legislative Affairs).	Anthony C Robinson	SC	GS	15	....	....
Arlington, VA..........	Special Assistant to the Assistant Secretary of Defense (Legislative Affairs).	Kelsey Lax	SC	GS	15	....	....
Arlington, VA..........	Special Assistant to the Assistant Secretary of Defense (Legislative Affairs).	Joshua Altman	SC	GS	14	....	....

DEPARTMENT OF DEFENSE—Continued

OFFICE OF THE SECRETARY OF DEFENSE—Continued

Location	Position Title	Name of Incumbent	Type of Appt.	Pay Plan	Level, Grade, or Pay	Tenure	Expires
Arlington, VA............	Special Assistant to the Assistant Secretary of Defense (Legislative Affairs).	Grant Saunders....................	SC	GS	12	....	....
Arlington, VA............	Special Assistant to the Assistant Secretary of Defense (Legislative Affairs).	Justin Maturo.......................	SC	GS	14	....	....
Arlington, VA............	Special Assistant to the Assistant Secretary of Defense (Legislative Affairs).	Barron Youngsmith..............	SC	GS	15	....	....
Arlington, VA............	Special Assistant to the Assistant Secretary of Defense (Legislative Affairs).	Won Yong Shim	SC	GS	14	....	....
	OFFICE OF THE ASSISTANT SECRETARY OF DEFENSE (SPECIAL OPERATIONS/LOW INTENSITY CONFLICT)						
Arlington, VA............	Assistant Secretary of Defense (Special Operations/Low Intensity Conflict).	Christopher P Maier	PAS	EX	IV	....	....
Arlington, VA............	Principal Deputy Assistant Secretary of Defense (Special Operations/Low Intensity Conflict).	Career Incumbent	CA	ES	....	....	....
Arlington, VA............	Deputy Assistant Secretary of Defense (Special Operations Policy and Programs).	Erin M Logan	NA	ES	....	....	....
Arlington, VA............	Deputy Assistant Secretary of Defense (Irregular Warfare and Counterterrorism).	Maren Brooks	NA	ES	....	....	....
Arlington, VA............	Deputy Assistant Secretary of Defense (Counternarcotics and Stabilization Policy).	James Saenz	NA	ES	....	....	....
Arlington, VA............	Principal Director, Counternarcotics and Global Threats.	Career Incumbent	CA	ES	....	....	....
Arlington, VA............	Principal Director, Secretariat for Special Operations Policy and Programs.	Career Incumbent	CA	ES	....	....	....
Arlington, VA............	Deputy Principal Information Operations Advisor.	Career Incumbent	CA	ES	....	....	....
Alexandria, VA	Director, Irregular Warfare Technical Support Directorate.	Career Incumbent	CA	ES	....	....	....
Arlington, VA............	Special Assistant......................................	Ryan Doherty	SC	GS	15	....	....
Arlington, VA............	Chief of Staff for Assistant Secretary of Defense (Special Operations/Low-Intensity Conflict).	Ariane M Tabatabai	SC	GS	15	....	....
	OFFICE OF THE ASSISTANT TO THE SECRETARY OF DEFENSE (PRIVACY, CIVIL LIBERTIES, AND TRANSPARENCY)						
Arlington, VA............	Assistant to the Secretary of Defense for Privacy Civil Liberties and Transparency.	Career Incumbent	CA	ES	....	....	....
	OFFICE OF THE ASSISTANT TO THE SECRETARY OF DEFENSE (PUBLIC AFFAIRS)						
Arlington, VA............	Assistant to the Secretary of Defense for Public Affairs.	Christopher Michael Meagher.	NA	ES	....	....	....
Arlington, VA............	Principal Deputy Assistant to the Secretary of Defense for Public Affairs.	Carlie Waibel	NA	ES	....	....	....
Arlington, VA............	Deputy Assistant to the Secretary of Defense for Strategic Engagement.	Melanie Kaye........................	NA	ES	....	....	....
Arlington, VA............	Speechwriter	Ezra Stoller..........................	SC	GS	11	....	....
Arlington, VA............	Deputy Press Secretary........................	Sabrina Singh......................	SC	GS	15	....	....
Fort Meade, MD	Director, Defense Media Activity......................	Career Incumbent	CA	ES	....	....	....
Arlington, VA............	Speechwriter	Aaron Benjamin Sherman....	SC	GS	15	....	....
Arlington, VA............	Speechwriter	Ashley Mitchell....................	SC	GS	15	....	....
Arlington, VA............	Special Assistant.................................	Joshua Schroeder	SC	GS	12	....	....
Arlington, VA............	Speechwriter	Patrick Kelly.......................	SC	GS	15	....	....
Arlington, VA............	Speechwriter	Caleb Gibson.......................	SC	GS	15	....	....
Arlington, VA............	Director, Digital Media........................	Jennifer Min	SC	GS	13	....	....
Arlington, VA............	Special Assistant.................................	Jessica Kosmider.................	SC	GS	15	....	....
	OFFICE OF THE CHIEF DIGITAL AND ARTIFICIAL INTELLIGENCE OFFICER						
Arlington, VA............	Chief Digital and Artificial Intelligence Officer.	Radha Plumb.......................	NA	ES	....	....	....
Arlington, VA............	Deputy Chief Digital and Artificial Intelligence Officer.	Career Incumbent	CA	ES	....	....	....
Arlington, VA............	Executive Director, Resource Management Office.	Career Incumbent	CA	ES	....	....	....

DEPARTMENT OF DEFENSE—Continued

OFFICE OF THE SECRETARY OF DEFENSE—Continued

Location	Position Title	Name of Incumbent	Type of Appt.	Pay Plan	Level, Grade, or Pay	Tenure	Expires
	OFFICE OF THE DIRECTOR OF ADMINISTRATION AND MANAGEMENT						
Arlington, VA..........	Performance Improvement Officer and Director, Administration and Management.	Career Incumbent	CA	ES	....	....	....
Arlington, VA..........	Deputy Director, Administration and Management.	Career Incumbent	CA	ES	....	....	....
Arlington, VA..........	Military Commission Appellate Judge.............	Lisa Schenck........................	PAS	AD	....	....	....
Arlington, VA..........	Military Commission Appellate Judge.............	William Pollard	PAS	AD	....	....	....
	OFFICE OF THE DIRECTOR, NET ASSESSMENT						
Arlington, VA..........	Director of Net Assessment	Career Incumbent	CA	ES	....	....	....
Arlington, VA..........	Deputy Director for Net Assessment	Career Incumbent	CA	ES	....	....	....
Arlington, VA..........	Associate Director for Net Assessment.............	Career Incumbent	CA	ES	....	....	....
	DEFENSE ADVANCED RESEARCH PROJECTS AGENCY						
Arlington, VA..........	Director, Defense Advanced Research Project Agency.	Stefanie Tompkins................	NA	ES	....	....	....
Arlington, VA..........	Comptroller	Career Incumbent	CA	ES	....	....	....
	DEFENSE COMMISSARY AGENCY						
Petersburg, VA........	Director/Chief Executive Officer, Defense Commissary Agency.	Career Incumbent	CA	ES	....	....	....
Petersburg, VA........	Deputy Director / Chief Operating Officer	Vacant	....	ES	....	....	....
Petersburg, VA........	Executive Director, Information Technology......	Career Incumbent	CA	ES	....	....	....
Petersburg, VA........	Executive Director, Sales Marketing and Logistics.	Career Incumbent	CA	ES	....	....	....
Petersburg, VA........	Executive Director, Store Operations................	Career Incumbent	CA	ES	....	....	....
	DEFENSE FINANCE AND ACCOUNTING SERVICE						
Alexandria, VA	Director, Defense Finance and Accounting Service.	Career Incumbent	CA	ES	....	....	....
Alexandria, VA	Principal Deputy Director, Defense Finance and Accounting Service.	Career Incumbent	CA	ES	....	....	....
Whitehall, OH	Deputy Director, Operations	Career Incumbent	CA	ES	....	....	....
Indianapolis, IN	Deputy Director, Strategy and Support	Career Incumbent	CA	ES	....	....	....
Cleveland, OH	Director, Enterprise Accounting and Audit Support.	Career Incumbent	CA	ES	....	....	....
Whitehall, OH	Director, Enterprise Solutions and Standards ..	Career Incumbent	CA	ES	....	....	....
Alexandria, VA	Director, Information and Technology...............	Career Incumbent	CA	ES	....	....	....
Indianapolis, IN	General Counsel	Career Incumbent	CA	ES	....	....	....
Alexandria, VA	Director, Internal Review.................................	Career Incumbent	CA	ES	....	....	....
Cleveland, OH	Site Director - Cleveland.................................	Career Incumbent	CA	ES	....	....	....
Whitehall, OH	Site Director - Columbus.................................	Career Incumbent	CA	ES	....	....	....
Indianapolis, IN	Site Director - Indianapolis	Career Incumbent	CA	ES	....	....	....
Rome, NY................	Site Director - Rome..	Career Incumbent	CA	ES	....	....	....
Indianapolis, IN	Chief Financial Officer	Career Incumbent	CA	ES	....	....	....
Alexandria, VA	Deputy Director, Information and Technology...	Career Incumbent	CA	ES	....	....	....
Cleveland, OH	Deputy Site Director - Cleveland	Career Incumbent	CA	ES	....	....	....
Whitehall, OH	Deputy Site Director - Columbus......................	Career Incumbent	CA	ES	....	....	....
Indianapolis, IN	Deputy Site Director - Indianapolis	Career Incumbent	CA	ES	....	....	....
Indianapolis, IN	Director, Emerging Capabilities and Systems...	Career Incumbent	CA	ES	....	....	....
Indianapolis, IN	Director, Enterprise Management Services.......	Career Incumbent	CA	ES	....	....	....
Indianapolis, IN	Director, Finance Standards and Customer Services.	Career Incumbent	CA	ES	....	....	....
Indianapolis, IN	Director, Strategy, Policy, and Requirements.....	Career Incumbent	CA	ES	....	....	....
	DEFENSE HEALTH AGENCY						
Falls Church, VA.....	Deputy Director, Defense Health Agency	Career Incumbent	CA	ES	....	....	....
Falls Church, VA.....	Assistant Director, Health Care Administration.	Career Incumbent	CA	ES	....	....	....
Falls Church, VA.....	Assistant Director, Support / Component Acquisition Executive.	Vacant	....	ES	....	....	....
Arlington, VA..........	Director, Federal Electronic Health Record Modernization.	Career Incumbent	CA	ES	....	....	....
Falls Church, VA.....	Deputy Assistant Director, Financial Operations.	Career Incumbent	CA	ES	....	....	....
Falls Church, VA.....	Deputy Assistant Director, Health Care Operations.	Career Incumbent	CA	ES	....	....	....
Falls Church, VA.....	Deputy Assistant Director, Information Operations / Military Health Systems Chief Information Officer.	Career Incumbent	CA	ES	....	....	....

DEPARTMENT OF DEFENSE—Continued

OFFICE OF THE SECRETARY OF DEFENSE—Continued

Location	Position Title	Name of Incumbent	Type of Appt.	Pay Plan	Level, Grade, or Pay	Tenure	Expires
Falls Church, VA.....	Deputy Assistant Director, Medical Affairs.......	Career Incumbent................	CA	ES	....	....	....
Falls Church, VA.....	Program Executive Officer, Defense Healthcare Mgmt Systems.	Career Incumbent................	CA	ES	....	....	....
Falls Church, VA.....	Director, Federal and Commercial Interoperability.	Career Incumbent................	CA	ES	....	....	....
Falls Church, VA.....	Deputy Assistant Director, Pricing and Contracting.	Career Incumbent................	CA	ES	....	....	....
	DEFENSE HUMAN RESOURCES ACTIVITY						
Alexandria, VA	Director, Defense Human Resources Activity....	Career Incumbent................	CA	ES	....	....	....
Alexandria, VA	Deputy Director, Defense Human Resources Activity.	Career Incumbent................	CA	ES	....	....	....
Alexandria, VA	Director, Defense Civilian Personnel Advisory Service.	Career Incumbent................	CA	ES	....	....	....
Arlington, VA...........	Director, Defense Manpower Data Center........	Career Incumbent................	CA	ES	....	....	....
Alexandria, VA	Director, Defense Personnel Analytics Center...	Career Incumbent................	CA	ES	....	....	....
Alexandria, VA	Director, Defense Support Service Center	Career Incumbent................	CA	ES	....	....	....
Alexandria, VA	Deputy Director, Defense Civilian Personnel Advisory Services.	Career Incumbent................	CA	ES	....	....	....
Seaside, CA..............	Deputy Director, Defense Manpower Data Center.	Career Incumbent................	CA	ES	....	....	....
Arlington, VA...........	Deputy Director, Defense Support Service Center.	Vacant	....	ES	....	....	....
Alexandria, VA	Director, Defense Suicide Prevention Office......	Career Incumbent................	CA	ES	....	....	....
Alexandria, VA	Director, Sexual Assault Prevention and Response Office.	Career Incumbent................	CA	ES	....	....	....
	DEFENSE INFORMATION SYSTEMS AGENCY						
Arlington, VA...........	General Counsel	Career Incumbent................	CA	ES	....	....	....
	DEFENSE LEGAL SERVICES AGENCY						
Arlington, VA...........	Director, Standards of Conduct Office...............	Career Incumbent................	CA	ES	....	....	....
	DEFENSE POW/MIA ACCOUNTING AGENCY						
Arlington, VA...........	Director, Defense Prisoner of War/Missing in Action Accounting Agency.	Career Incumbent................	CA	ES	....	....	....
Arlington, VA...........	Principal Deputy Director, Defense Pow/Mia Accounting Agency.	Career Incumbent................	CA	ES	....	....	....
	DEFENSE SECURITY COOPERATION AGENCY						
Arlington, VA...........	Director, Defense Security Cooperation Agency.	Career Incumbent................	CA	ES	....	....	....
Arlington, VA...........	Deputy Director, Defense Security Cooperation Agency.	Career Incumbent................	CA	ES	....	....	....
Arlington, VA...........	Assistant Director for Business Operations	Career Incumbent................	CA	ES	....	....	....
	DEFENSE TECHNOLOGY SECURITY ADMINISTRATION						
Alexandria, VA	Director, Defense Technology Security Administration.	Career Incumbent................	CA	ES	....	....	....
Arlington, VA...........	Deputy Director, Defense Technology Security Administration.	Career Incumbent................	CA	ES	....	....	....
	DEFENSE THREAT REDUCTION AGENCY						
Fort Belvoir, VA.......	Director, Defense Threat Reduction Agency......	Rebecca Kc Hersman	NA	ES	....	....	....
	DEPARTMENT OF DEFENSE EDUCATION ACTIVITY						
Alexandria, VA	Director, Department of Defense Education Activity.	Career Incumbent................	CA	ES	....	....	....
Alexandria, VA	Chief Academic Officer...	Vacant	....	ES	....	....	....
Sembach AB, Germany.	Director for Student Excellence - Dodea Europe.	Career Incumbent................	CA	ES	....	....	....
Peachtree City, GA..	Director for Student Excellence - Dodea Americas.	Career Incumbent................	CA	ES	....	....	....
Okinawa Island, Japan.	Director for Student Excellence - Dodea Pacific.	Career Incumbent................	CA	ES	....	....	....
Alexandria, VA	Chief Operating Officer...	Career Incumbent................	CA	ES	....	....	....
	MISSILE DEFENSE AGENCY						
Fort Belvoir, VA.......	General Counsel, Missile Defense Agency.........	Career Incumbent................	CA	ES	....	....	....

DEPARTMENT OF DEFENSE—Continued

OFFICE OF THE SECRETARY OF DEFENSE—Continued

Location	Position Title	Name of Incumbent	Type of Appt.	Pay Plan	Level, Grade, or Pay	Tenure	Expires
Redstone Arsenal, AL.	Director for Mission Support	Vacant		ES			
	NATIONAL RECONNAISSANCE OFFICE						
Chantilly, VA	Director, National Reconnaissance Office	Christopher Scolese	PAS	EX			
Chantilly, VA	Inspector General	Terrence Edwards	PAS	EX			
	OFFICE OF THE JOINT CHIEFS OF STAFF						
Suffolk, VA	Deputy Director for Cyber and Command Control Communications and Computers (C5) Integration.	Career Incumbent	CA	ES			
Arlington, VA	Deputy Director for Strategic Stability	Career Incumbent	CA	ES			
Arlington, VA	Deputy Director for Studies and Analysis	Career Incumbent	CA	ES			
Arlington, VA	Director, Directorate of Management	Career Incumbent	CA	ES			
Arlington, VA	Director for Joint History	Career Incumbent	CA	ES			
Arlington, VA	Principal Deputy Director for Logistics	Vacant		ES			
Arlington, VA	Principal Deputy Director for Strategic Plans and Policy.	Career Incumbent	CA	ES			
	UNITED STATES COURT OF APPEALS FOR THE ARMED FORCES						
Washington, DC	Chief Judge, United States Court of Appeals for the Armed Forces.	Kevin A Ohlson	PAS	OT			
Washington, DC	Associate Judge, United States Court of Appeals for the Armed Forces.	Liam Hardy	PAS	OT			
Washington, DC	Associate Judge, United States Court of Appeals for the Armed Forces.	John E Sparks	PAS	OT			
Washington, DC	Associate Judge, United States Court of Appeals for the Armed Forces.	Gregory Maggs	PAS	OT			
Washington, DC	Associate Judge, United States Court of Appeals for the Armed Forces.	Musetta Tia Johnson	PAS	OT			
Washington, DC	Clerk of the Court	Career Incumbent	CA	ES			
Washington, DC	Chief Deputy Clerk of the Court	Career Incumbent	CA	ES			
	WASHINGTON HEADQUARTERS SERVICES						
Arlington, VA	Director, Washington Headquarters Services	Career Incumbent	CA	ES			
Arlington, VA	Deputy Director, Washington Headquarters Services.	Career Incumbent	CA	ES			
Arlington, VA	General Counsel, Washington Headquarters Services and Pentagon Force Protection Agency.	Career Incumbent	CA	ES			
Arlington, VA	Director, Executive Services Directorate	Career Incumbent	CA	ES			
Arlington, VA	Director, Financial Management Directorate and Chief Financial Executive.	Career Incumbent	CA	ES			
Arlington, VA	Deputy General Counsel, Washington Headquarters Services and Pentagon Force Protection Agency.	Career Incumbent	CA	ES			
Washington, DC	Deputy Director, White House Military Office	Katherine Dickerson	NA	ES			
Arlington, VA	General Counsel, National Guard Bureau (Ngb).	Career Incumbent	CA	ES			
Arlington, VA	Director, Programs and Resources/Comptroller - Ngb.	Career Incumbent	CA	ES			
Arlington, VA	Vice Director, Manpower and Personnel - Ngb.	Career Incumbent	CA	ES			
Arlington, VA	Chief Information Officer and Director, J6 - Ngb.	Career Incumbent	CA	ES			
Arlington, VA	Us Chairman of the Us-Russia Joint Commission on Pow/Mia.	Robert Foglesong	PA	AD			
Arlington, VA	Senior Director for Technology and National Security.	Tarun Chhabra	SC	GS	15		
Arlington, VA	Senior Director for Strategic Planning	Thomas Wright	SC	GS	15		
Arlington, VA	Senior Advisor / Director for Integration and Optimization.	Gary G Coleman	TA	ES			04/08/25
Arlington, VA	Deputy Transition Director	Rayford Nichols	TA	ES			
Arlington, VA	Defense Fellow	Deema Sara Homsi	SC	GS	12		
Arlington, VA	Defense Fellow	Celina Maria Pouchet	SC	GS	9		
Arlington, VA	Defense Fellow	Karuna Chambless Nandkumar.	SC	GS	9		
Arlington, VA	Defense Fellow	Daribel Roman Torres	SC	GS	9		
Arlington, VA	Defense Fellow	Carmen Bretthauer	SC	GS	11		
Washington, DC	Ceo and Chief Strategist for Facility Modernization and Fiscal Reform.	Stephen Rippe	TA	ES			

DEPARTMENT OF DEFENSE—Continued

OFFICE OF THE SECRETARY OF DEFENSE—Continued

Location	Position Title	Name of Incumbent	Type of Appt.	Pay Plan	Level, Grade, or Pay	Tenure	Expires
Arlington, VA	Senior Advisor, United States of America Vietnam War Commemoration.	Edward Chrystal	TA	ES	....	....	01/28/26
Arlington, VA	Special Assistant to the Assistant Secretary of Defense (International Security Affairs).	Matthew Keating	SC	GS	12	....	....
Arlington, VA	Senior Advisor	Ilan Goldenberg	SC	GS	15	....	....
Washington, DC	Special Assistant to the White House Military Office.	Kaelynn Marie Crawford	SC	GS	9	....	....
Washington, DC	Chief Usher	Juan Dromgoole	SC	GS	13	....	....
Arlington, VA	Senior Advisor	Lindsey W Ford	SC	GS	15	....	....

DEPARTMENT OF DEFENSE—Continued

DEPARTMENT OF THE AIR FORCE

Location	Position Title	Name of Incumbent	Type of Appt.	Pay Plan	Level, Grade, or Pay	Tenure	Expires
	OFFICE OF THE SECRETARY						
Arlington, VA............	Secretary of the Air Force..................................	Frank Kendall	PAS	EX	II	....	....
Arlington, VA............	Special Assistant/Chief of Staff to the Secretary of the Air Force.	Vacant		ES		....	....
Arlington, VA............	Special Assistant to the Secretary of the Air Force.	Ashley Borneo.....................	SC	GS	11	....	....
Arlington, VA............	Deputy General Counsel (Fiscal, Ethics and Administrative Law).	Career Incumbent	CA	ES		....	....
Washington, DC	Chief of Staff to the Secretary of the Air Force.	Matthew Williams...............	NA	....		....	....
	UNITED STATES SPECIAL OPERATIONS COMMAND						
Macdill Air Force Base, FL.	Deputy Chief Financial Officer..........................	Vacant		ES		....	....
	DEPARTMENT OF THE AIR FORCE						
Arlington, VA............	Assistant Deputy Chief of Staff, Logistics, Engineering and Force Protection.	Vacant		ES		....	....
Arlington, VA............	Senior Advisor to the Secretary and Under Secretary of the Air Force.	Vacant		ES		....	....
Washington, DC	Senior Advisor for Strategic Action...................	Aron Axe	NA	....		....	....
	OFFICE OF ASSISTANT SECRETARY AIR FORCE FOR ACQUISITION						
Arlington, VA............	Assistant Secretary of the Air Force (Acquisition).	Andrew P Hunter.................	PAS	EX	IV	....	....
Arlington, VA............	Principal Deputy Assistant Secretary (Acquisition, Technology and Logistics).	Vacant		ES		....	....
Arlington, VA............	Special Assistant..	Jocelyn Yin.........................	SC	GS	14	....	....
	OFFICE OF ASSISTANT SECRETARY AIR FORCE FOR FINANCIAL MANAGEMENT AND COMPTROLLER						
Arlington, VA............	Assistant Secretary of the Air Force (Financial Management and Comptroller).	Vacant		EX		....	....
Arlington, VA............	Principal Deputy Assistant Secretary Financial Management and Comptroller.	Vacant		ES		....	....
Arlington, VA............	Special Assistant..	Wendy Jordan......................	SC	GS	15	....	....
	OFFICE OF THE UNDER SECRETARY						
Arlington, VA............	Under Secretary of the Air Force	Melissa G Dalton..................	PAS	EX	III	....	....
Washington, DC	Headquarters Air Force Chief Data Officer.......	Career Incumbent	CA	ES		....	....
	OFFICE OF THE GENERAL COUNSEL						
Arlington, VA............	Deputy General Counsel (Contractor Responsibility).	Career Incumbent	CA	ES		....	....
Arlington, VA............	Principal Deputy General Counsel.....................	Career Incumbent	CA	ES		....	....
Arlington, VA............	Deputy General Counsel (Intelligence, International and Military Affairs).	Vacant		ES		....	....
Washington, DC	Deputy General Counsel (Acquisition)..............	Career Incumbent	CA	ES		....	....
Arlington, VA............	General Counsel	Peter Beshar.......................	PAS	EX	IV	....	....
Washington, DC	Deputy General Counsel (Installations, Energy and Environment).	Career Incumbent	CA	ES		....	....
Arlington, VA............	Special Assistant..	Peri Tenenbaum	SC	GS	15	....	....
	OFFICE OF ASSISTANT SECRETARY AIR FORCE, INSTALLATIONS, ENVIRONMENT, AND ENERGY						
Arlington, VA............	Deputy Assistant Secretary (Environment, Safety and Occupational Health).	Vacant		ES		....	....
Arlington, VA............	Deputy Assistant Secretary (Energy)................	Career Incumbent	CA	ES		....	....
Arlington, VA............	Assistant Secretary of the Air Force (Installations, Environment and Energy).	Ravi Chaudhary	PAS	EX	IV	....	....
Arlington, VA............	Principal Deputy Assistant Secretary (Installations, Environment and Logistics).	Career Incumbent	CA	ES		....	....
	OFFICE OF ASSISTANT SECRETARY OF THE AIR FORCE FOR MANPOWER AND RESERVE AFFAIRS						
Arlington, VA............	Assistant Secretary of the Air Force (Manpower and Reserve Affairs).	Alex Wagner.........................	PAS	EX	IV	....	....
Arlington, VA............	Deputy Assistant Secretary for Force Management and Integration.	Vacant		ES		....	....
Arlington, VA............	Deputy Assistant Secretary for Force Management and Integration.	Career Incumbent	CA	ES		....	....

DEPARTMENT OF DEFENSE—Continued

DEPARTMENT OF THE AIR FORCE—Continued

Location	Position Title	Name of Incumbent	Type of Appt.	Pay Plan	Level, Grade, or Pay	Tenure	Expires
Arlington, VA..........	Deputy Assistant Secretary for Strategic Diversity Integration.	Vacant	....	ES	....	....	....
Arlington, VA..........	Special Assistant...	Bhavana Kodira	SC	GS	13	....	....
	DEPUTY CHIEF OF STAFF, PERSONNEL						
Arlington, VA..........	Program Manager, National Security Personnel System (Nsps) Program Management Office.	Vacant	....	ES			
	OFFICE DEPUTY ASSISTANT SECRETARY INSTALLATIONS						
Washington, DC	Deputy Assistant Secretary (Installations)	Career Incumbent	CA	ES	....	....	....
	DEPUTY UNDER SECRETARY (SPACE)						
Arlington, VA..........	Director, Principal Dod Space Advisor Staff......	Vacant	....	ES	....	....	....
	OFFICE OF THE ASSISTANT SECRETARY OF THE AIR FORCE FOR SPACE ACQUISITION AND INTEGRATION						
Arlington, VA..........	Assistant Secretary of the Air Force for Space Acquisition and Integration.	Frank Calvelli........................	PAS	EX	IV	....	....
Arlington, VA..........	Special Assistant...	Ramsey Smith	SC	GS	15	....	....
	DEPUTY UNDER SECRETARY (INTERNATIONAL AFFAIRS)						
Washington, DC	Deputy Under Secretary (International Affairs).	Career Incumbent	CA	ES	....	....	....

DEPARTMENT OF DEFENSE—Continued

DEPARTMENT OF THE ARMY

Location	Position Title	Name of Incumbent	Type of Appt.	Pay Plan	Level, Grade, or Pay	Tenure	Expires
	OFFICE OF THE SECRETARY						
Arlington, VA..........	Secretary of the Army	Christine Wormuth	PAS	EX	II	....	....
Arlington, VA..........	Chief of Staff to the Secretary of the Army.......	Jacob M Freedman..............	NA	ES	....	....	....
Arlington, VA..........	Principal Cyber Advisor to Secretary of the Army.	Michael L Sulmeyer..............	TA	ES	....	....	....
	OFFICE OF THE UNDER SECRETARY						
Arlington, VA..........	Under Secretary of the Army	Gabriel O Camarillo..............	PAS	EX	III	....	....
Arlington, VA..........	Chief, Strategic Staff Advisor	Vacant	....	ES	....	....	....
	OFFICE DEPUTY UNDER SECRETARY OF ARMY						
Arlington, VA..........	Deputy Under Secretary of the Army	Mario A Diaz	NA	ES	....	....	....
	OFFICE OF THE GENERAL COUNSEL						
Arlington, VA..........	Principal Deputy General Counsel......................	Denise A Council-Ross	NA	ES	....	....	....
Arlington, VA..........	Deputy General Counsel (Acquisition)..............	Career Incumbent	CA	ES	....	....	....
Arlington, VA..........	Deputy General Counsel (Ethics and Fiscal)	Career Incumbent	CA	ES	....	....	....
Arlington, VA..........	Deputy General Counsel (Operations and Personnel).	Career Incumbent	CA	ES	....	....	....
Arlington, VA..........	Deputy General Counsel (Installations, Environment and Civil Works).	Career Incumbent	CA	ES	....	....	....
Arlington, VA..........	General Counsel	Carrie Ricci..........................	PAS	EX	IV	....	....
Arlington, VA..........	Senior Intellectual Property Law Attorney	Charles H Harris	XS	SL	....	....	....
Arlington, VA..........	Attorney Advisor to the Army General Counsel.	Jessica Adair Adair Brinich..	SC	GS	15	....	....
	OFFICE OF SMALL AND DISADVANTAGED BUSINESS UTILITILIZATION						
Arlington, VA..........	Director of Small Business Programs	Career Incumbent	CA	ES	....	....	....
	OFFICE ASSISTANT SECRETARY ARMY (CIVIL WORKS)						
Arlington, VA..........	Assistant Secretary of the Army (Civil Works) ..	Michael L Connor................	PAS	EX	IV	....	....
Arlington, VA..........	Deputy Assistant Secretary of the Army (Project Planning and Review).	Career Incumbent	CA	ES	....	....	....
Arlington, VA..........	Principal Deputy Assistant Secretary of the Army (Civil Works).	Jaime A Pinkham..................	NA	ES	....	....	....
Arlington, VA..........	Special Assistant to the Assistant Secretary of the Army (Civil Works).	Jay Francis Shannon	SC	GS	13	....	....
	OFFICE ASSISTANT SECRETARY ARMY (FINANCIAL MANAGEMENT AND COMPTROLLER)						
Arlington, VA..........	Principal Deputy Assistant Secretary of the Army (Financial Management and Comptroller).	Robert T Cook......................	NA	ES	....	....	....
Arlington, VA..........	Assistant Secretary of the Army (Financial Management and Comptroller).	Caral E Spangler..................	PAS	EX	IV	....	....
Arlington, VA..........	Special Assistant to the Assistant Secretary of the Army (Financial Management and Comptroller).	Hae Jean Kwon	SC	GS	15	....	....
	OFFICE ASSISTANT SECRETARY ARMY (INSTALLATIONS, ENERGY AND ENVIRONMENT)						
Arlington, VA..........	Principal Deputy Assistant Secretary of the Army (Installations, Energy and Environment).	Paul W Farnan	NA	ES	....	....	....
Arlington, VA..........	Assistant Secretary of the Army (Installations and Environment).	Rachel L Jacobson................	PAS	EX	IV	....	....
Arlington, VA..........	Special Assistant to the Assistant Secretary of the Army (Installation, Energy and Environment).	William M Rogers	SC	GS	15	....	....
	OFFICE ASSISTANT SECRETARY ARMY (MANPOWER AND RESERVE AFFAIRS)						
Arlington, VA..........	Assistant Secretary of the Army (Manpower and Reserve Affairs).	Agnes Schaefer	PAS	EX	IV	....	....
Arlington, VA..........	Principal Deputy to the Assistant Secretary of the Army (Manpower and Reserve Affairs).	Yvette K W Bourcicot	NA	ES	....	....	....
Arlington, VA..........	Special Assistant to the Assistant Secretary of the Army (Manpower and Reserve Affairs).	Ana Paula Velasco................	SC	GS	11	....	....
Arlington, VA..........	Special Assistant to the Assistant Secretary of the Army (Manpower and Reserve Affairs).	Faiq S Raza........................	SC	GS	13	....	....

DEPARTMENT OF DEFENSE—Continued

DEPARTMENT OF THE ARMY—CONTINUED

Location	Position Title	Name of Incumbent	Type of Appt.	Pay Plan	Level, Grade, or Pay	Tenure	Expires
Arlington, VA..........	Sr Advisor for Equity and Inclusion/Dasa (Equity and Inclusion).	Career Incumbent	CA	ES	....	....	....
	OFFICE ASSISTANT SECRETARY ARMY (ACQUISITION, LOGISTICS AND TECHNOLOGY)						
Arlington, VA..........	Assistant Secretary of the Army (Acquisition, Logistics and Technology).	Douglas R Bush....................	PAS	EX	IV	....	....
Arlington, VA..........	Deputy Assistant Secretary of the Army (Strategy Acquisition Reform).	Margaret Boatner................	NA	ES	....	....	....
Arlington, VA..........	Principal Deputy Assist Secretary of the Army (Acquisition, Logistics and Technology).	Young J Bang	NA	ES	....	....	....
	CHIEF INFORMATION OFFICER						
Arlington, VA..........	Chief Information Officer....................................	Leonel Garciga	TA	ES	....	....	07/15/26
Arlington, VA..........	Director of Architecture, Data and Standards ..	Career Incumbent	CA	ES	....	....	....
	OFFICE OF LEGISLATIVE LIAISON						
Arlington, VA..........	Principal Deputy Chief of Legislative Liaison ..	Career Incumbent	CA	ES	....	....	....
	OFFICE, CHIEF OF STAFF						
Washington, DC	Director of Management/Vice Director of the Army Staff.	Career Incumbent	CA	ES	....	....	....
	CENTER FOR ARMY ANALYSIS (CENTER FOR ARMY ANALYSIS)						
Fort Belvoir, VA.......	Technical Director....................................	Career Incumbent	CA	ES	....	....	....
Fort Belvoir, VA.......	Director, Center for Army Analysis....................	Career Incumbent	CA	ES	....	....	....
	U.S. ARMY TEST AND EVALUATION COMMAND						
Falls Church, VA.....	Executive Technical Director/Deputy to the Commander.	Career Incumbent	CA	ES	....	....	....
White Sands Msl Rge, NM.	Executive Technical Director, Army Test and Evaluation Command.	Vincent Liddiard	TA	ES	....	....	07/29/26
Aberdeen, MD	Atec Hq – Chief Data Officer.............................	Joseph Kelly	XS	ST	....	....	....
	OFFICE, DEPUTY CHIEF OF STAFF, G-9						
Arlington, VA..........	Director, Quality of Life Task Force	Dolores Geise........................	TA	ES	....	....	....
	OFFICE OF THE JUDGE ADVOCATE GENERAL						
Arlington, VA..........	Director, Civilian Personnel, Labor and Employment Law.	Career Incumbent	CA	ES	....	....	....
Rosslyn, VA..............	Director, Soldier and Family Legal Services......	Career Incumbent	CA	ES	....	....	....
	UNITED STATES ARMY CORPS OF ENGINEERS						
Washington, DC	Chief Counsel...	Career Incumbent	CA	ES	....	....	....
Washington, DC	Deputy Chief Counsel	Career Incumbent	CA	ES	....	....	....
	OFFICE OF COMMAND COUNSEL						
Redstone Arsenal, AL.	Command Counsel...	Career Incumbent	CA	ES	....	....	....
Redstone Arsenal, AL.	Deputy Command Counsel	Career Incumbent	CA	ES	....	....	....
	UNITED STATES ARMY SUSTAINMENT COMMAND						
Rock Island, IL........	Chief Counsel...	Career Incumbent	CA	ES	....	....	....
	U.S. ARMY COMMUNICATIONS ELECTRONICS COMMAND						
Aberdeen, MD	Chief Counsel...	Career Incumbent	CA	ES	....	....	....
	UNITED STATES ARMY AVIATION AND MISSILE COMMAND (ARMY MATERIEL COMMAND)						
Redstone Arsenal, AL.	Chief Counsel...	Career Incumbent	CA	ES	....	....	....
	TANK-AUTOMOTIVE AND ARMAMENTS COMMAND (TANK-AUTOMOTIVE AND ARMAMENTS COMMAND)						
Warren, MI	Chief Counsel...	Career Incumbent	CA	ES	....	....	....
	HEADQUARTERS, UNITED STATES ARMY, EUROPE						
Wiesbaden, Germany.	Assistant Chief of Staff, Strategy and Plans U.S. Army Europe.	Career Incumbent	CA	ES	....	....	....

DEPARTMENT OF DEFENSE—Continued

DEPARTMENT OF THE ARMY—CONTINUED

Location	Position Title	Name of Incumbent	Type of Appt.	Pay Plan	Level, Grade, or Pay	Tenure	Expires
	UNITED STATES ARMY SPACE AND MISSILE DEFENSE COMMAND						
Huntsville, AL	Director, Space and Missile Defense Center of Excellence.	Career Incumbent	CA	ES	....	....	....
	OFFICE, DEPUTY CHIEF OF STAFF, G-8						
Arlington, VA...........	Deputy Director, Program Analysis and Evaluation Directorate.	Vacant	....	ES	....	....	....
	UNITED STATES EUROPEAN COMMAND						
Stuttgart, Germany.	Civilian Deputy / Foreign Policy Advisory to the Commander European Command.	Vacant	....	ES	....	....	....
	UNITED STATES AFRICA COMMAND						
Stuttgart, Germany.	Deputy to the Commander for Civil-Military Activities, U.S. Africa Command.	Vacant	....	ES	....	....	....
Stuttgart, Germany.	Advisor, Development and Humanitarian Assistance, U.S. Africa Command.	Maura Barry Boyle	TA	ES	....	....	....
	NORTH ATLANTIC TREATY ORGANIZATION						
Brussels, Belg..........	Director, Defense Policy and Planning.............	Vacant	....	ES	....	....	....
Brussels, Belg..........	Administrative Advisor to United States Ambassador to North Atlantic Treaty Organization.	Career Incumbent	CA	ES	....	....	....
Brussels, Belg..........	Director, Resources and Logistics......................	Career Incumbent	CA	ES	....	....	....
Brussels, Belg..........	Managing Director Defense Armaments, Communications Electronics and Investments Division.	Career Incumbent	CA	ES	....	....	....
Rome, Italy	Dean, North Atlantic Treaty Organization Defense College.	Christopher M Schnaubelt ..	TA	ES	....	3	....
	UNITED STATES ARMY CONTRACTING COMMAND						
Redstone Arsenal, AL.	Chief Counsel, Army Contracting Command	Career Incumbent	CA	ES	....	....	....
	OFFICE OF THE PROVOST MARSHALL GENERAL						
Arlington, VA...........	Director, Forensics and Biometrics Field Operating.	Vacant	....	ES	....	....	....
	U.S. ARMY FUTURES COMMAND						
Austin, TX................	Senior Advisor for Science and Technology	Keith Aliberti........................	XS	SL			
	AFC, COMBAT CAPABILITIES DEVELOPMENT CMD, ARMY RESEARCH LABORATORY						
Adelphi, MD	Senior Research Scientist (Quantum Sciences), ARL.	Fatemi Fredrik	XS	ST	....	....	....

DEPARTMENT OF DEFENSE—Continued

DEPARTMENT OF THE NAVY

Location	Position Title	Name of Incumbent	Type of Appt.	Pay Plan	Level, Grade, or Pay	Tenure	Expires
	DEPARTMENT OF THE NAVY						
Arlington, VA............	Senior Advisor, Department of the Navy..........	Vacant	....	ES	....	....	....
Arlington, VA............	Deputy Under Secretary of the Navy, Intelligence and Security.	Career Incumbent	CA	ES	....	....	....
	OFFICE OF THE SECRETARY OF THE NAVY						
Arlington, VA............	Special Assistant to the Secretary of the Navy.	Roger Huffstetler Jr.	SC	GS	15	....	....
Arlington, VA............	Special Advisor to Don Secnav	Vacant	....	ES	....	....	....
Arlington, VA............	Secretary of the Navy....................................	Carlos Del Toro....................	PAS	EX	II	....	....
Arlington, VA............	Special Assistant to the Secretary of the Navy.	Roger Dean Huffstetler.......	NA	ES	....	....	....
Arlington, VA............	Deputy Chief of Staff...................................	Theresa Roosevelt	SC	GS	15	....	....
Washington, DC	Special Assistant to the Secretary for Information Management/Chief Information Officer.	Career Incumbent	CA	ES	....	....	....
Washington, DC	Principal Cyber Advisor	Career Incumbent	CA	ES	....	....	....
Arlington, VA............	Chief of Staff to the Under Secretary of the Navy.	Robin Fortner	SC	GS	15	....	....
Arlington, VA............	Special Advisor to Secretary of the Navy	Vacant	....	ES	....	....	....
Arlington, VA............	Chief of Staff to the Secretary of the Navy	Christopher E Diaz..............	NA	ES	....	....	....
Arlington, VA............	Senior Advisor to the Secretary of the Navy.....	Steve Brock.........................	NA	ES	....	....	....
Arlington, VA............	Director of External Engagements....................	Marjorie Steiner	SC	GS	13	....	....
	OFFICE OF THE UNDER SECRETARY OF THE NAVY						
Arlington, VA............	Deputy Under Secretary of the Navy - Policy ...	Career Incumbent	CA	ES	....	....	....
Arlington, VA............	Under Secretary of the Navy............................	Erik K Raven.......................	PAS	EX	III	....	....
Washington, DC	Deputy Under Secretary of the Navy (Management).	Career Incumbent	CA	ES	....	....	....
Washington, DC	Director, Small Business Programs....................	Career Incumbent	CA	ES	....	....	....
Washington, DC	Residential Manager and Social Secretary for the Vice President.	Storm Horncastle	SC	GS	14	....	....
	OFFICE OF THE ASSISTANT SECRETARY OF NAVY (MANPOWER AND RESERVE AFFAIRS)						
Arlington, VA............	Deputy Assistant Secretary of the Navy (Analytics).	Career Incumbent	CA	ES	....	....	....
Arlington, VA............	Assistant Secretary of the Navy (Manpower and Reserve Affairs).	Franklin R Parker................	PAS	EX	IV	....	....
Arlington, VA............	Special Assistant to the Assistant Secretary of the Navy (Manpower and Reserve Affairs).	Mohammed Zahir Al-Gailany.	SC	GS	13	....	....
	OFFICE OF THE ASSISTANT SECRETARY OF NAVY (ENERGY, INSTALLATIONS AND ENVIRONMENT)						
Arlington, VA............	Assistant Secretary of the Navy (Energy, Installations and Environment).	Meredith A Berger	PAS	EX	IV	....	....
Washington, DC	Deputy Assistant Secretary of the Navy (Safety).	Career Incumbent	CA	ES	....	....	....
Arlington, VA............	Deputy Assistant Secretary of the Navy (Energy).	Vacant	....	ES	....	....	....
Arlington, VA............	Senior Advisor to the Secretary of the Navy (Climate).	Deborah Loomis	SC	GS	15	....	....
	OFFICE OF THE ASSISTANT SECRETARY OF THE NAVY (RESEARCH, DEVELOPMENT AND ACQUISITION)						
Arlington, VA............	Assistant Secretary of the Navy (Research Development and Acquisition).	Nickolas Guertin	PAS	EX	IV	....	....
	OFFICE OF THE ASSISTANT SECRETARY OF NAVY (FINANCIAL MANAGEMENT AND COMPTROLLER)						
Arlington, VA............	Assistant Secretary of the Navy (Financial Management and Comptroller).	Ralph Russell Rumbaugh	PAS	EX	IV	....	....
	OFFICE OF THE GENERAL COUNSEL						
Arlington, VA............	General Counsel	John Coffey...........................	PAS	EX	IV	....	....
Arlington, VA............	Attorney-Advisor (General).................................	Louise Vitale.......................	XS	SL	....	....	....
	CHIEF OF NAVAL OPERATIONS						
Washington, DC	Director, Installations Division...........................	Career Incumbent	CA	ES	....	....	....
Arlington, VA............	Director, Logistics and Shore Integration Division (N4Z).	Career Incumbent	CA	ES	....	....	....
Arlington, VA............	Deputy Director, Logistics Divisions (N4lb).......	Career Incumbent	CA	ES	....	....	....

DEPARTMENT OF DEFENSE—Continued

DEPARTMENT OF THE NAVY—Continued

Location	Position Title	Name of Incumbent	Type of Appt.	Pay Plan	Level, Grade, or Pay	Tenure	Expires
Naples, Italy............	**OFFICE OF COMMANDER, UNITED STATES FLEET FORCES COMMAND** Executive Director, Commander U.S. Naval Forces/Africa.	Career Incumbent................	CA	ES	....	....	....
Camp Hm Smith M Corp B, HI.	**OFFICE OF THE COMMANDER, UNITED STATES PACIFIC COMMAND** Director, Center for Excellence...........................	Career Incumbent................	CA	ES	....	....	....
Arlington, VA...........	**UNITED STATES MARINE CORPS HEADQUARTERS OFFICE** Assistant Director...	Vacant......................................	....	ES	....	....	....
Virginia Beach, VA..	**COMMANDER, NAVAL EXPEDITIONARY COMBAT COMMAND** Executive Director, Navy Expeditionary Combat Command.	Career Incumbent................	CA	ES	....	....	....

DEPARTMENT OF EDUCATION

Location	Position Title	Name of Incumbent	Type of Appt.	Pay Plan	Level, Grade, or Pay	Tenure	Expires
	OFFICE OF THE SECRETARY						
Washington, DC	Secretary	Miguel Cardona....................	PAS	EX	I	....	....
Washington, DC	Chief of Staff..	Alexis S Barrett....................	NA	ES	....	....	....
Washington, DC	Deputy Chief of Staff for Policy and Programs.	Scott E Sargrad....................	NA	ES	....	....	....
Washington, DC	Deputy Chief of Staff for Strategy	Blanchi Roblero	NA	ES	....	....	....
Washington, DC	Director, Executive Secretariat........................	Career Incumbent	CA	ES	....	....	....
Washington, DC	Director, Strategic Partnerships	Shital Shah..........................	SC	GS	15	....	....
Washington, DC	Chief Freedom of Information Act Officer	Career Incumbent	CA	ES	....	....	....
Washington, DC	Director, Executive Management Staff	Vacant	....	ES	....	....	....
Washington, DC	Deputy Assistant Secretary for Management and Planning.	Career Incumbent	CA	ES	....	....	....
Washington, DC	Executive Director, White House Initiative on Advancing Educational Equity, Excellence, and Economic Opportunity for Black Americans.	Alexis Holmes......................	SC	GS	15	....	....
Washington, DC	Executive Director, White House Initiative for Historically Black Colleges and Universities.	Dietra Trent........................	SC	GS	15	....	....
Washington, DC	Executive Director for the White House Initiative on Advancing Educational Equity, Excellence, and Economic Opportunity for Hispanics.	Melody Gonzales	SC	GS	15	....	....
Washington, DC	Executive Director, White House Initiative on Advancing Educational Equity, Excellence, and Economic Opportunity for Native Americans and Strengthening Tribal Colleges and Universities.	Naomi Miguel	SC	GS	15	....	....
Washington, DC	Deputy Director, White House Initiative on Advancing Educational Equity, Excellence, and Economic Opportunity for Black Americans.	Larry Bowden	SC	GS	14	....	....
Washington, DC	Deputy Director, White House Initiative on Advancing Educational Equity, Excellence, and Economic Opportunity for Hispanics.	Kevin Lima	SC	GS	14	....	....
Washington, DC	Deputy Director, White House Initiative on Advancing Educational Equity, Excellence, and Economic Opportunity Through Historically Black Colleges and Universities.	Naeem Jenkins-Nixon..........	SC	GS	14	....	....
Washington, DC	Director, Center for Faith Based and Neighborhood Partnerships.	Margaret Mitchell	SC	GS	15	....	....
Washington, DC	Deputy Director, Center for Faith-Based and Neighborhood Partnerships.	Kathryn Joseph	SC	GS	14	....	....
Washington, DC	Director, Scheduling and Advance......................	Madeline Douglas................	SC	GS	15	....	....
Washington, DC	White House Liaison	Jacob Larson Dana Brett-Turner.	SC	GS	14	....	....
Washington, DC	Special Assistant to the White House Liaison ..	Andrea Piccardo	SC	GS	12	....	....
Washington, DC	Senior Advisor, Labor Relations	Maralyn O'Brien..................	SC	GS	15	....	....
Washington, DC	Senior Advisor...	Kalila Winters	SC	GS	15	....	....
Washington, DC	Special Advisor..	Amanda Delgiudice..............	SC	GS	14	....	....
Washington, DC	Senior Advisor...	Vacant	....	ES	....	....	....
Washington, DC	Senior Advisor...	Christian Soto	SC	GS	15	....	....
Washington, DC	Special Assistant..	Chase Moore	SC	GS	12	....	....
Washington, DC	Confidential Assistant, White House Initiatives.	Salome Daniel	SC	GS	11	....	....
Washington, DC	Confidential Assistant..	Nisa Danitz..........................	SC	GS	9	....	....
Washington, DC	Confidential Assistant..	Troi Dixon............................	SC	GS	11	....	....
Washington, DC	Deputy Chief of Staff for Strategic Communications and Partnerships.	LaWanda Toney....................	NA		....	....	....
Washington, DC	Senior Advisor...	Rachel Levitan	SC	GS	15	....	....
Washington, DC	Senior Advisor...	Melissa Castillo	SC	GS	15	....	....
Washington, DC	Director of Scheduling..	Jessica Butherus	SC	GS	14	....	....
Washington, DC	Deputy Director, White House Liaison	Kaushika Soundararajan.....	SC	GS	13	....	....
Washington, DC	Deputy Director of Advance...............................	Jordan Johnson	SC	GS	13	....	....
Washington, DC	Executive Assistant..	Fabiola Yanez	SC	GS	13	....	....
Washington, DC	Special Assistant, Advance	Elizabeth Silvia-Chandley ...	SC	GS	12	....	....
Washington, DC	Scheduler...	Mericel Mirabal...................	SC	GS	11	....	....
Washington, DC	Confidential Assistant..	Jessica Simmons	SC	GS	9	....	....
	OFFICE OF THE DEPUTY SECRETARY						
Washington, DC	Deputy Secretary..	Cynthia Marten....................	PAS	EX	II	....	....
Washington, DC	Chief of Staff..	Jillian Doody........................	NA	ES	....	....	....
Washington, DC	Deputy Chief of Staff..	Ramon Carranza	SC	GS	14	....	....
Washington, DC	Confidential Assistant..	Alexandra Smith Macias	SC	GS	11	....	....
Washington, DC	Special Assistant..	Robert Morissette................	SC	GS	11	....	....

DEPARTMENT OF EDUCATION—Continued

Location	Position Title	Name of Incumbent	Type of Appt.	Pay Plan	Level, Grade, or Pay	Tenure	Expires
Washington, DC	Senior Policy Advisor	Mekka Smith	SC	GS	15		
Washington, DC	Special Assistant	Taylor DuBard	SC	GS	11		
	OFFICE OF THE UNDER SECRETARY						
Washington, DC	Under Secretary	James Richard Kvaal	PAS	EX	IV		
Washington, DC	Principal Deputy Under Secretary	Benjamin L Miller	NA	ES			
Washington, DC	Deputy Under Secretary	Juliana Rinz	NA	ES			
Washington, DC	Chief of Staff	Melanie M Muenzer	NA	ES			
Washington, DC	Senior Advisor	Richard Williams	SC	GS	15		
Washington, DC	Policy Advisor	Wesley Whistle	SC	GS	15		
Washington, DC	Policy Advisor	Jenna Sablan	SC	GS	14		
Washington, DC	Special Assistant	Jack Hurley	SC	GS	12		
Washington, DC	Special Assistant	Latricia Hardman	SC	GS	12		
Washington, DC	Special Advisor	Heather Ward	SC	GS	14		
Washington, DC	Confidential Assistant	Carlos Vivaldi Lanauze	SC	GS	11		
	OFFICE OF THE GENERAL COUNSEL						
Washington, DC	General Counsel	Elizabeth M Brown	PAS	EX	IV		
Washington, DC	Principal Deputy General Counsel	Vacant		ES			
Washington, DC	Principal Deputy General Counsel	Lynn Eisenberg	NA	ES			
Washington, DC	Deputy General Counsel for Program Service	Career Incumbent	CA	ES			
Washington, DC	Deputy General Counsel, Postsecondary Service.	Vacant		ES			
Washington, DC	Deputy General Counsel	Toby Merrill	NA	ES			
Washington, DC	Assistant General Counsel for Legislative Counsel Division.	Career Incumbent	CA	ES			
Washington, DC	Assistant General Counsel Ethics	Career Incumbent	CA	ES			
Washington, DC	Assistant General Counsel for Regulatory Services.	Career Incumbent	CA	ES			
Warren, RI	Assistant General Counsel, Division of Elementary, Secondary, Adult and Vocational Education.	Career Incumbent	CA	ES			
Washington, DC	Assistant General Counsel for Regulatory Services.	Career Incumbent	CA	ES			
Washington, DC	Assistant General Counsel for Business and Administrative Law.	Career Incumbent	CA	ES			
Washington, DC	Chief of Staff	Rachel Homer	SC	GS	15		
Washington, DC	Senior Counsel, Oversight	Matthew Robinson	SC	GS	15		
Washington, DC	Senior Counsel	Genevieve Torres	SC	GS	15		
Washington, DC	Senior Counsel	John Bailey	SC	GS	15		
Washington, DC	Senior Counsel	William Desmond	SC	GS	15		
Washington, DC	Senior Counsel	Ariel Warner	SC	GS	15		
Washington, DC	Senior Counsel	Laura Booth	SC		15		
Washington, DC	Special Assistant	Jennifer Rodriguez	SC	GS	12		
	OFFICE FOR CIVIL RIGHTS						
Washington, DC	Assistant Secretary for Civil Rights	Catherine Lhamon	PAS	EX	IV		
Washington, DC	Deputy Assistant Secretary for Management and Planning.	Career Incumbent	CA	ES			
Washington, DC	Deputy Assistant Secretary for Strategic Operations and Outreach.	Vacant		ES			
Washington, DC	Deputy Assistant Secretary for Policy	Vacant		ES			
Washington, DC	Deputy Assistant Secretary for Policy	Rukku Singla	SC	GS	15		
Washington, DC	Deputy Assistant Secretary	Mathew S Nosanchuk	SC	GS	15		
Washington, DC	Senior Legal Advisor	Vacant		ES			
Washington, DC	Senior Counsel	Adaku Onyeka-Crawford	SC	GS	15		
Washington, DC	Confidential Assistant	Sandrien Mekany	SC	GS	9		
Washington, DC	Principal Deputy Assistant Secretary	Seth Galanter	NA	ES			
Washington, DC	Special Assistant	Hannah Zack	SC	GS	12		
	OFFICE OF LEGISLATION AND CONGRESSIONAL AFFAIRS						
Washington, DC	Assistant Secretary for Office of Legislation and Congressional Affairs.	Gwendolyn Graham	PAS	EX	IV		
Washington, DC	Principal Advisor for Legislative Affairs	Melissa Bellin	SC	GS	14		
Washington, DC	Senior Advisor, Oversight	Joann A Martinez-Shriver	SC	GS	15		
Washington, DC	Special Advisor	Stephen Cekuta	SC	GS	13		
Washington, DC	Special Advisor	Marco Sanchez	SC	GS	13		
Washington, DC	Special Assistant	Jacob Blaut	SC	GS	12		
Washington, DC	Confidential Assistant	Taron Henton, Jr.	SC	GS	9		
Washington, DC	Principal Deputy Assistant Secretary	Rachel Niebling	NA	ES			
	OFFICE OF FINANCIAL OPERATIONS						
Washington, DC	Principal Deputy Assistant Secretary	Career Incumbent	CA	ES			
Washington, DC	Deputy Assistant Secretary for Business Support Services.	Career Incumbent	CA	ES			

DEPARTMENT OF EDUCATION—Continued

Location	Position Title	Name of Incumbent	Type of Appt.	Pay Plan	Level, Grade, or Pay	Tenure	Expires
Washington, DC	Deputy Assistant Secretary for Grants Management.	Career Incumbent	CA	ES	....	....	....
Washington, DC	Director, Office of Small and Disadvantaged Business Utilization.	Vacant	....	ES	....	....	....
Washington, DC	Director, Hearings and Appeals..........................	Career Incumbent	CA	ES	....	....	....
Washington, DC	Senior Advisor to the Assistant Secretary..........	Vacant	....	ES	....	....	....
	OFFICE OF ELEMENTARY AND SECONDARY EDUCATION						
Washington, DC	Assistant Secretary for Office of Elementary and Secondary Education.	Vacant	....	EX	....	....	....
Washington, DC	Principal Deputy Assistant Secretary................	Adam Schott	NA	ES	....	....	....
Washington, DC	Deputy Assistant Secretary for Management and Planning.	Career Incumbent	CA	ES	....	....	....
Washington, DC	Deputy Assistant Secretary for Policy and Programs.	Career Incumbent	CA	ES	....	....	....
Washington, DC	Deputy Assistant Secretary for Policy and Programs.	Daniel Carlson......................	SC	GS	15	....	....
Washington, DC	Deputy Assistant Secretary, Policy and Early Learning.	Swati Adarkar	SC	GS	15	....	....
Washington, DC	Deputy Assistant Secretary, Equity and Discretionary Grants and Support Services.	Bernadine Pearson Futrell ..	NA	ES	....	....	....
Washington, DC	Chief of Staff...	Brenda Calderon	SC	GS	15	....	....
Washington, DC	Senior Advisor...	Laura Magali Jimenez.........	SC	GS	15	....	....
Washington, DC	Senior Advisor...	Kortne Edogun	SC	GS	15	....	....
Washington, DC	Policy Advisor...	Sarah Mehrotra....................	SC	GS	14	....	....
Washington, DC	Confidential Assistant...	Alex Turney	SC	GS	11	....	....
	OFFICE OF POSTSECONDARY EDUCATION						
Washington, DC	Assistant Secretary for Office of Postsecondary Education.	Nasser Paydar	PAS	EX	IV	....	....
Washington, DC	Deputy Assistant Secretary for Policy, Planning, and Innovation.	Antoinette Flores.................	NA	ES	....	....	....
Washington, DC	Deputy Assistant Secretary, Higher Education Programs.	Amanda Lauren Miller........	NA	ES	....	....	....
Washington, DC	Senior Director, Student Services......................	Career Incumbent	CA	ES	....	....	....
Washington, DC	Chief of Staff...	Roxanne Garza	SC	GS	15	....	....
Washington, DC	Senior Advisor...	Jennifer Engle	SC	GS	15	....	....
Washington, DC	Policy Advisor...	Lindsey Tepe........................	SC	GS	14	....	....
Washington, DC	Special Assistant..	Stephen Lamb	SC	GS	12	....	....
Washington, DC	Confidential Assistant...	Ruben Cedillo Orozco..........	SC	GS	9	....	....
	OFFICE OF COMMUNICATIONS AND OUTREACH						
Washington, DC	Assistant Secretary, Office of Communications and Outreach.	Vacant	....	EX	....	....	....
Washington, DC	Deputy Assistant Secretary for State and Local Outreach.	Lauren Mendoza	NA	ES	....	....	....
Washington, DC	Deputy Assistant Secretary, Communications...	Shinichi Inouye	NA	ES	....	....	....
Washington, DC	Deputy Assistant Secretary for Management and Planning.	Career Incumbent	CA	ES	....	....	....
Washington, DC	Director of Speechwriting and Editorial Content.	Tiffany Taber	SC	GS	15	....	....
Washington, DC	Director, Rural Engagement	Julia Cunningham	SC	GS	15	....	....
Washington, DC	Director, Media Strategies	Vanessa Harmoush	SC	GS	15	....	....
Washington, DC	Senior Digital Director..	Chelsea Daley.......................	SC	GS	14	....	....
Washington, DC	Chief Speechwriter	Mintaro Oba	SC	GS	15	....	....
Washington, DC	Press Secretary, Higher Education....................	Johanny Adames	SC	GS	15	....	....
Washington, DC	Deputy Press Secretary.......................................	Colleen May..........................	SC	GS	11	....	....
Washington, DC	Deputy Chief of Staff...	Chauncey Alexander	SC	GS	14	....	....
Washington, DC	Senior Speechwriter	Ashley Lauren Mushnick	SC	GS	15	....	....
Washington, DC	Senior Advisor...	Rachel R Thomas	SC	GS	15	....	....
Washington, DC	Press Assistant	Shahzeb Malik......................	SC	GS	11	....	....
Washington, DC	Special Assistant..	Megan Romero......................	SC	GS	11	....	....
Washington, DC	Director, Family Outreach..................................	Cecily Adams	SC	GS	14	....	....
	OFFICE OF SPECIAL EDUCATION AND REHABILITATIVE SERVICES						
Washington, DC	Assistant Secretary for Special Education and Rehabilitative Services.	Glenna Wright-Gallo............	PAS	EX	IV	....	....
Washington, DC	Commissioner, Rehabilitation Services Administration.	Dante Quintin Allen	PAS	EX	V	....	....
Washington, DC	Deputy Commissioner for the Rehabilitation Services Administration.	Career Incumbent	CA	ES	....	....	....
Washington, DC	Deputy Director, Special Education Programs ..	Career Incumbent	CA	ES	....	....	....

DEPARTMENT OF EDUCATION—Continued

Location	Position Title	Name of Incumbent	Type of Appt.	Pay Plan	Level, Grade, or Pay	Tenure	Expires
Washington, DC	Deputy Assistant Secretary for Management and Planning.	Career Incumbent	CA	ES			
Washington, DC	Deputy Assistant Secretary	Vacant		ES			
Washington, DC	Director, Office of Special Education Programs.	Valerie Williams	NA	ES			
Washington, DC	Chief of Staff	Eric Gutshall	SC	GS	15		
Washington, DC	Policy Advisor	Meghan Whittaker	SC	GS	15		
Washington, DC	Confidential Assistant	Daniel Dela Cruz	SC	GS	11		
	OFFICE OF CAREER TECHNICAL AND ADULT EDUCATION						
Washington, DC	Assistant Secretary for Career, Technical and Adult Education.	Amy Loyd	PAS	EX	IV		
Washington, DC	Deputy Assistant Secretary on Community Colleges.	Vacant		ES			
Washington, DC	Deputy Assistant Secretary	Jennifer M Mishory	SC	GS	15		
Washington, DC	Deputy Assistant Secretary	Luke Rhine	SC	GS	15		
Washington, DC	Deputy Assistant Secretary for Management and Planning.	Career Incumbent	CA	ES			
Washington, DC	Deputy Assistant Secretary	Vacant		ES			
Washington, DC	Chief of Staff	Deandre Jones	SC	GS	15		
Washington, DC	Senior Advisor	Jacob Brown	SC	GS	15		
Washington, DC	Policy Advisor	Emily Lamont	SC	GS	15		
Washington, DC	Policy Advisor	Catherine McConnell	SC	GS	15		
Washington, DC	Confidential Assistant	Vikram Chaudhuri	SC	GS	9		
	INSTITUTE OF EDUCATION SCIENCES						
Washington, DC	Director of the Institute of Education Sciences.	Vacant		WC			
Washington, DC	Commissioner of Education Statistics	Peggy G Carr	PA	EX	IV		
Washington, DC	Commissioner, National Center for Education Evaluation.	Matthew Soldner	XS	AD			
Washington, DC	Associate Commissioner, Sample Survey	Career Incumbent	CA	ES			
Washington, DC	Deputy Director for Administration and Policy.	Vacant		ES			
	OFFICE OF PLANNING, EVALUATION AND POLICY DEVELOPMENT						
Washington, DC	Assistant Secretary for Planning, Evaluation, and Policy Development.	Roberto Rodriguez	PAS	EX	IV		
Washington, DC	Principal Deputy Assistant Secretary	Vacant		ES			
Washington, DC	Deputy Assistant Secretary, P-12 Education	Mary Catherine Wall	NA	ES			
Washington, DC	Director, Elementary, Secondary, and Vocational Analysis Division.	Career Incumbent	CA	ES			
Washington, DC	Director, Budget Services	Career Incumbent	CA	ES			
Washington, DC	Deputy Director Budget Service	Career Incumbent	CA	ES			
Washington, DC	Director, Cost Estimation and Analysis Division.	Career Incumbent	CA	ES			
Washington, DC	Chief Data Officer	Career Incumbent	CA	ES			
Washington, DC	Chief of Staff	Anil Hurkadli	SC	GS	15		
Washington, DC	Senior Advisor	Maureen Tracey-Mooney	SC	GS	15		
Washington, DC	Senior Advisor	Johnny Garcia	SC	GS	15		
Washington, DC	Policy Advisor	Loredana Valtierra	SC	GS	15		
Washington, DC	Policy Advisor	Kayla Patrick	SC	GS	15		
Washington, DC	Policy Advisor	Jessica Gall	SC	GS	15		
Washington, DC	Policy Advisor	Julia Sproul	SC	GS	14		
Washington, DC	Special Assistant	Heather Shuttleworth	SC	GS	12		
Washington, DC	Confidential Assistant	Eliza McCarron	SC	GS	9		
	OFFICE OF POLICY						
Washington, DC	Special Assistant	Lino Pena-Martinez	SC		12		
	OFFICE OF MANAGEMENT						
Washington, DC	Director of Scheduling and Advance	Cambria Hayashino	SC		15		
Washington, DC	Deputy Director of Scheduling and Advance	Cassidy Ballard	SC		13		
Washington, DC	Scheduler	Deion Lemelle	SC		13		
	OFFICE OF PUBLIC AFFAIRS						
Washington, DC	Digital Director and Senior Communications Advisor.	Anthony Martinez	SC	GS	15		
	FEDERAL STUDENT AID						
Washington, DC	Chief Operating Officer	Vacant		OT			
Washington, DC	Principal Deputy Chief Operating Officer	Career Incumbent	CA	ES			
Washington, DC	Principal Deputy Chief Operating Officer, Partner Participation and Oversight.	Career Incumbent	CA	ES			
Washington, DC	Director, Financial Management Group	Career Incumbent	CA	ES			

DEPARTMENT OF EDUCATION—Continued

Location	Position Title	Name of Incumbent	Type of Appt.	Pay Plan	Level, Grade, or Pay	Tenure	Expires
Washington, DC	Director, Budget Group	Career Incumbent	CA	ES	....	....	....
Washington, DC	Director, Strategy and Performance..................	Career Incumbent	CA	ES	....	....	....
Washington, DC	Director, Enterprise Assessment and Design	Career Incumbent	CA	ES	....	....	....
Washington, DC	Senior Advisor..	Career Incumbent	CA	ES	....	....	....
	OFFICE OF THE CHIEF INFORMATION OFFICER						
Washington, DC	Deputy Chief Information Officer	Career Incumbent	CA	ES	....	....	....
Washington, DC	Director, Enterprise Technology Services	Career Incumbent	CA	ES	....	....	....
Washington, DC	Director, Information Technology and Program Services.	Career Incumbent	CA	ES	....	....	....
	OFFICE OF ENGLISH LANGUAGE ACQUISITION, LANGUAGE ENHANCEMENT, AND ACADEMIC ACHIEVEMENT FOR LIMITED ENGLISH PROFICIENT STUDENTS						
Washington, DC	Assistant Deputy Secretary and Director..........	Montserrat Garibay	NA	ES	....	....	....
Washington, DC	Deputy Assistant Secretary	Career Incumbent	CA	ES	....	....	....
Washington, DC	Confidential Assistant..	Sheila Janet Gomez Matias.	SC	GS	9	....	....
	OFFICE OF THE CHIEF FINANCIAL OFFICER						
Washington, DC	Chief Financial Officer...	Vacant	....	WC	....	....	....
Washington, DC	Director, Financial Management Operations	Career Incumbent	CA	ES	....	....	....

DEPARTMENT OF EDUCATION OFFICE OF THE INSPECTOR GENERAL

Location	Position Title	Name of Incumbent	Type of Appt.	Pay Plan	Level, Grade, or Pay	Tenure	Expires
Washington, DC	Inspector General	Sandra D Bruce....................	PAS	EX	IV	....	....

DEPARTMENT OF ENERGY

Location	Position Title	Name of Incumbent	Type of Appt.	Pay Plan	Level, Grade, or Pay	Tenure	Expires
	OFFICE OF THE SECRETARY						
Washington, DC	Secretary, Department of Energy	Jennifer Granholm...............	PAS	EX	I	....	....
Washington, DC	Chief of Staff..	Christopher E Davis	NA	ES	....	....	....
Washington, DC	Deputy Chief of Staff...	Jasmine Dimitriou	NA	ES	....	....	....
Washington, DC	Deputy Chief of Staff...	Bridget Versteegden Bartol .	NA	ES	....	....	....
Washington, DC	Senior Advisor..	Vacant	....	ES	....	....	....
Washington, DC	Senior Advisor..	Vacant	....	ES	....	....	....
Washington, DC	Senior Advisor to the Secretary........................	Vacant	....	ES	....	....	....
Washington, DC	Senior Advisor to the Secretary........................	Vacant	....	ES	....	....	....
Washington, DC	Senior Policy Advisor...	Vacant	....	ES	....	....	....
Washington, DC	Director of Energy Jobs.......................................	Vacant	....	ES	....	....	....
Washington, DC	White House Liaison	Elizabeth Berliant...............	SC	GS	14	....	....
Washington, DC	Deputy White House Liaison	Vanessa Elyse Alderete.......	SC	GS	13	....	....
Washington, DC	Advisor to the Secretary	Narayan Swamy Subramanian.	SC	GS	15	....	....
Washington, DC	Special Assistant to the Secretary	Paige Nygaard......................	SC	GS	14	....	....
Washington, DC	Special Assistant to the Secretary	Christiana Ho.......................	SC	GS	13	....	....
Washington, DC	Special Advisor to the Chief of Staff of the Secretary.	Arjun Jacob Krishnaswami .	SC	GS	13	....	....
Washington, DC	Special Assistant to the Chief of Staff..............	Claire Gibbs........................	SC	GS	10	....	....
Washington, DC	Special Assistant..	Tylor Collier.........................	SC	GS	9	....	....
Washington, DC	Strategic Engagement Coordinator....................	Chloe Parrish........................	SC	GS	11	....	....
	OFFICE OF THE DEPUTY SECRETARY						
Washington, DC	Deputy Secretary of Energy...............................	David M Turk.......................	PAS	EX	II	....	....
Washington, DC	Chief of Staff..	Gregory Ryan Degen............	SC	GS	15	....	....
Washington, DC	Special Advisor...	Arianna Menzelos	SC	GS	12	....	....
	UNDER SECRETARY OF ENERGY						
Washington, DC	Under Secretary of Energy	David Crane..........................	PAS	EX	III	....	....
Washington, DC	Director of National Laboratory Operations Board.	Vacant	....	ES	....	....	....

DEPARTMENT OF ENERGY—Continued

Location	Position Title	Name of Incumbent	Type of Appt.	Pay Plan	Level, Grade, or Pay	Tenure	Expires
Washington, DC	Chief Operating Officer for Research Management Operations.	Vacant	....	ES	....	....	....
Washington, DC	Chief of Staff.................................	Caroline Rachel Lee Grey....	NA	ES	....	....	....
Washington, DC	Special Advisor.................................	Frances Hannah Swanson...	SC	GS	13	....	....
Morgantown, WV	Senior Advisor.................................	Career Incumbent	CA	ES	....	....	....
Washington, DC	Senior Advisor, Director of Policy and Implementation.	Jeremiah David Baumann...	NA	ES	....	....	....
	UNDER SECRETARY FOR SCIENCE						
Washington, DC	Under Secretary for Science	Geraldine Richmond	PAS	EX	III	....	....
Washington, DC	Associate Deputy Under Secretary for Science and Energy.	Vacant	....	ES	....	....	....
Washington, DC	Principal Deputy Under Secretary....................	Career Incumbent	CA	ES	....	....	....
Washington, DC	Director, Office of Clean Energy Demonstrations.	Vacant	....	ES	....	....	....
Washington, DC	Chief of Staff.....................	Ariel Marshall	NA	ES	....	....	....
Washington, DC	Senior Advisor.................................	Vacant	....	ES	....	....	....
Washington, DC	Senior Advisor.................................	Henry McKoy......................	NA	ES	....	....	....
	OFFICE OF THE CHIEF FINANCIAL OFFICER						
Washington, DC	Chief Financial Officer.................................	Vacant	....	EX	....	....	....
Washington, DC	Chief Risk Officer	Career Incumbent	CA	ES	....	....	....
	DEPUTY ADMINISTRATOR FOR DEFENSE PROGRAMS						
Washington, DC	Senior Advisor.................................	Vacant	....	ES	....	....	....
	NATIONAL NUCLEAR SECURITY ADMINISTRATION						
Washington, DC	Under Secretary for Nuclear Security/Administrator for Nuclear Security.	Jill Marie Hruby	PAS	EX	III	....	....
Washington, DC	Principal Deputy Administrator for National Nuclear Security.	Vacant	....	EX	....	....	....
Washington, DC	Deputy Administrator for Defense Programs, National Nuclear Security Administration.	Marvin Adams	PAS	EX	IV	....	....
Washington, DC	Deputy Administrator for Defense Nuclear Nonproliferation.	Corey Hinderstein................	PAS	EX	IV	....	....
Washington, DC	Associate Administrator for External Affairs....	Vacant	....	ES	....	....	....
Washington, DC	Associate Administrator for Congressional and Intergovernmental Affairs.	Jessica J Lee......................	SC	GS	15	....	....
Washington, DC	Chief of Staff.................................	Career Incumbent	CA	ES	....	....	....
Washington, DC	Director, Office of Policy	Career Incumbent	CA	ES	....	....	....
Washington, DC	Director of Public Affairs	Anna Newby	SC	GS	15	....	....
Washington, DC	Senior Advisor.................................	Career Incumbent	CA	ES	....	....	....
Washington, DC	Special Assistant.................................	Sneha Nair...........................	SC	GS	11	....	....
	ADVANCED RESEARCH PROJECTS AGENCY - ENERGY						
Washington, DC	Director, Advanced Research Project Agency - Energy.	Evelyn Wang......................	PAS	EX	III	....	....
Washington, DC	Senior Advisor.................................	Alexander Bok......................	SC	GS	15	....	....
	ASSISTANT SECRETARY FOR CONGRESSIONAL AND INTERGOVERNMENTAL AFFAIRS						
Washington, DC	Principal Deputy Assistant Secretary................	Jennifer Bumgarner............	NA	ES	....	....	....
Washington, DC	Deputy Assistant Secretary for Intergovernmental and External Affairs.	Spencer Thibodeau..............	SC	GS	15	....	....
Washington, DC	Deputy Assistant Secretary for Senate Affairs .	Brian Christopher Eiler.......	SC	GS	15	....	....
Washington, DC	Deputy Assistant Secretary for House Affairs ..	Eric Delaney	SC	GS	14	....	....
Washington, DC	Senior Advisor.................................	Jane Catherine Wise Thompson.	SC	GS	15	....	....
Washington, DC	Deputy Assistant Secretary, Public Engagement.	Stephanie Klein....................	SC	GS	14	....	....
Washington, DC	Advisor, Congressional Affairs	Adrian Culea	SC	GS	14	....	....
Washington, DC	Senior Regional Intergovernmental and External Affairs Specialist.	Christian Bato....................	SC	GS	14	....	....
Washington, DC	Senior Regional Advisor, Intergovernmental and External Affairs.	Crystal Kay Perkins.............	SC	GS	14	....	....
Washington, DC	Senior Tribal Liaison.................................	Matthew Dannenberg..........	SC	GS	15	....	....
Washington, DC	Senior Legislative Affairs Advisor, Senate........	Danisha Craig	SC	GS	13	....	....
Washington, DC	Legislative Affairs Advisor, House....................	Alexa Bishopric	SC	GS	11	....	....
Washington, DC	Regional Intergovernmental and External Affairs Specialist for the Midwest.	Ruby Goldberg......................	SC	GS	13	....	....
Washington, DC	Regional and Intergovernmental Affairs Specialist for the Mid-Atlantic.	Chakeia Blocker	SC	GS	12	....	....

DEPARTMENT OF ENERGY—Continued

Location	Position Title	Name of Incumbent	Type of Appt.	Pay Plan	Level, Grade, or Pay	Tenure	Expires
Washington, DC	Regional Intergovernmental and External Affairs Specialist.	Christina Nunez Cohen	SC	GS	12	....	....
Washington, DC	Regional Intergovernmental and External Affairs Specialist.	Royce Kim	SC	GS	13	....	....
Washington, DC	Special Advisor..	Derrick Bhole	SC	GS	11	....	....
	ASSISTANT SECRETARY FOR ENERGY EFFICIENCY AND RENEWABLE ENERGY						
Washington, DC	Assistant Secretary (Energy Efficiency and Renewable Energy).	Vacant	....	EX		....	....
Washington, DC	Principal Deputy Assistant Secretary................	Jeffrey Matthew Marootian.	NA	ES		....	....
Washington, DC	Deputy Assistant Secretary for Sustainable Transportation and Fuels.	Career Incumbent	CA	ES		....	....
Washington, DC	Executive Director, Joint Office of Energy and Transportation.	Career Incumbent	CA	ES		....	....
Washington, DC	Director, Hydrogen and Fuel Cell Technologies Office.	Career Incumbent	CA	ES		....	....
Washington, DC	Director, Vehicle Technologies Office.................	Career Incumbent	CA	ES		....	....
Washington, DC	Deputy Director, Vehicle Technologies Office.....	Career Incumbent	CA	ES		....	....
Washington, DC	Deputy Assistant Secretary for Buildings and Industry.	Career Incumbent	CA	ES		....	....
Washington, DC	Director, Building Technologies Office	Vacant	....	ES		....	....
Washington, DC	Director, Advanced Materials and Manufacturing Technologies Office.	Career Incumbent	CA	ES		....	....
Washington, DC	Director, Industrial Efficiency and Decarbonization Office.	Career Incumbent	CA	ES		....	....
Washington, DC	Deputy Assistant Secretary for Operations.......	Career Incumbent	CA	ES		....	....
Lakewood, CO	Director, Golden Field Office...............................	Vacant	....	ES		....	....
Golden, CO	Deputy Director, Golden Field Office	Career Incumbent	CA	ES		....	....
Washington, DC	Director, Office of Budget....................................	Career Incumbent	CA	ES		....	....
Washington, DC	Deputy Assistant Secretary for Renewable Energy.	Vacant	....	ES		....	....
Washington, DC	Director, Bioenergy Technology Office................	Career Incumbent	CA	ES		....	....
Washington, DC	Director, Geothermal Technologies Office	Career Incumbent	CA	ES		....	....
Washington, DC	Director, Solar Energy Technologies Office........	Career Incumbent	CA	ES		....	....
Washington, DC	Director, Water Power Technologies Office	Vacant	....	ES		....	....
Washington, DC	Director, Wind Energy Technologies Office........	Career Incumbent	CA	ES		....	....
Washington, DC	Senior Advisor..	Jalonne White-Newsome......	SC	GS	15	....	....
	U.S. ENERGY INFORMATION ADMINISTRATION						
Washington, DC	Administrator-Energy Information Administration.	Joseph Decarolis...................	PAS	EX	IV	....	....
	OFFICE OF ENERGY JUSTICE AND EQUITY						
Washington, DC	Director of the Office of Minority Economic Impact.	Vacant	....	EX		....	....
Washington, DC	Deputy Director, Office of Civil Rights and Equal Employment Opportunity.	Career Incumbent	CA	ES		....	....
Washington, DC	Deputy Director for Energy Justice	Career Incumbent	CA	ES		....	....
Washington, DC	Senior Advisor..	Vacant	....	ES		....	....
Washington, DC	Special Advisor for Stakeholder Engagement ...	Sonrisa Lucero......................	SC	GS	14	....	....
	ASSISTANT SECRETARY FOR ENVIRONMENTAL MANAGEMENT						
Washington, DC	Assistant Secretary of Energy (Environmental Management).	Vacant	....	EX		....	....
Washington, DC	Associate Principal Deputy Assistant Secretary for Regulatory and Policy Affairs.	Career Incumbent	CA	ES		....	....
Washington, DC	Deputy Assistant Secretary for Resource Management.	Career Incumbent	CA	ES		....	....
Washington, DC	Director for Budget and Planning......................	Vacant	....	ES		....	....
Washington, DC	Director for Information Systems.......................	Career Incumbent	CA	ES		....	....
Washington, DC	Director for Communications..............................	Vacant	....	ES		....	....
Aiken, SC.................	Special Projects Senior Advisor	Career Incumbent	CA	ES		....	....
Washington, DC	Senior Advisor..	Career Incumbent	CA	ES		....	....
	ASSISTANT SECRETARY FOR FOSSIL ENERGY AND CARBON MANAGEMENT						
Washington, DC	Assistant Secretary for Fossil Energy...............	Bradford Crabtree................	PAS	EX	IV	....	....
Washington, DC	Principal Deputy Assistant Secretary................	Jennifer Wilcox....................	NA	ES		....	....
Bruceton, PA............	Director National Energy Technology Laboratory.	Career Incumbent	CA	ES		....	....

DEPARTMENT OF ENERGY—Continued

Location	Position Title	Name of Incumbent	Type of Appt.	Pay Plan	Level, Grade, or Pay	Tenure	Expires
Washington, DC	Deputy Assistant Secretary for Clean Coal and Carbon Management.	Vacant	....	ES	....	....	....
Washington, DC	Deputy Assistant Secretary for the Office of Resource Sustainability.	Career Incumbent	CA	ES	....	....	....
Washington, DC	Chief of Staff..	Priyanka Hooghan	SC	GS	15	....	....
Washington, DC	Chief of Staff..	Kathryn Hendrickson	SC	GS	15	....	....
Washington, DC	Special Advisor.......................................	Gabriel Hernandez..............	SC	GS	12	....	....
	OFFICE OF GENERAL COUNSEL						
Washington, DC	General Counsel	Samuel Taylor Walsh	PAS	EX	IV	....	....
Washington, DC	Principal Deputy General Counsel...................	Vacant	....	ES	....	....	....
Washington, DC	Deputy General Counsel for Litigation Regulation and Enforcement.	Vacant	....	ES	....	....	....
Washington, DC	Deputy General Counsel for Energy Policy	Vacant	....	ES	....	....	....
Washington, DC	Deputy General Counsel for Energy Policy	Paul Tiao..............................	NA	ES	....	....	....
Washington, DC	Deputy General Counsel for Environment and Litigation.	Career Incumbent	CA	ES	....	....	....
Washington, DC	Deputy General Counsel for Energy Efficiency and Clean Energy Demonstrations.	Alexandra Elizabeth Teitz ...	NA	ES	....	....	....
Washington, DC	Deputy General Counsel for Agency Operations.	Vacant	....	ES	....	....	....
Washington, DC	Assistant General Counsel, Federal Litigation .	Career Incumbent	CA	ES	....	....	....
Washington, DC	Assistant General Counsel, Civilian Nuclear Programs.	Career Incumbent	CA	ES	....	....	....
Washington, DC	Assistant General Counsel for Ethics and Personal Law.	Vacant	....	ES	....	....	....
Washington, DC	Assistant General Counsel for International and National Security Programs.	Career Incumbent	CA	ES	....	....	....
Washington, DC	Assistant General Counsel for Legislation, Regulation and Energy Efficiency.	Career Incumbent	CA	ES	....	....	....
Washington, DC	Assistant General Counsel for Electricity	Career Incumbent	CA	ES	....	....	....
Washington, DC	Assistant General Counsel for Environment.....	Career Incumbent	CA	ES	....	....	....
Washington, DC	Director, Office of Standard Contract Management.	Career Incumbent	CA	ES	....	....	....
Washington, DC	Attorney-Advisor (General)...............................	Frederick Pfaeffle................	SC	GS	15	....	....
Washington, DC	Attorney-Advisor (General)...............................	Lila Nojima.........................	SC	GS	14	....	....
	ASSISTANT SECRETARY FOR INTERNATIONAL AFFAIRS						
Washington, DC	Assistant Secretary for International Affairs....	Andrew Eilperin Light.........	PAS	EX	IV	....	....
Washington, DC	Principal Deputy Assistant Secretary for International Affairs.	Julie Cerqueira....................	NA	ES	....	....	....
Washington, DC	Senior Advisor and Non-Federal Liaison..........	Career Incumbent	CA	ES	....	....	....
Washington, DC	Deputy Assistant Secretary for Multilateral Engagement, Climate and Market Development.	Isabel Munilla	NA	ES	....	....	....
Washington, DC	Chief of Staff..	Matthew Baca	SC	GS	15	....	....
Washington, DC	Special Advisor.......................................	Hayley Emerson	SC	GS	12	....	....
	ASSISTANT SECRETARY FOR NUCLEAR ENERGY						
Washington, DC	Assistant Secretary for Energy (Nuclear Energy).	Vacant	....	EX	....	....	....
Washington, DC	Principal Deputy Assistant Secretary...............	Career Incumbent	CA	ES	....	....	....
Germantown, MD....	Deputy Assistant Secretary for Nuclear Infrastructure Programs.	Career Incumbent	CA	ES	....	....	....
Washington, DC	Deputy Assistant Secretary for Nuclear Reactors.	Vacant	....	ES	....	....	....
Germantown, MD....	Deputy Assistant Secretary for Nuclear Fuel Cycle.	Career Incumbent	CA	ES	....	....	....
Washington, DC	Deputy Asst Secretary for Int'l Nuclear Energy Policy and Cooperation.	Career Incumbent	CA	ES	....	....	....
Washington, DC	Deputy Assistance Secretary for Strategic Crosscuts.	Career Incumbent	CA	ES	....	....	....
Washington, DC	Chief of Staff..	Rory Stanley........................	SC	GS	15	....	....
Washington, DC	Special Assistant.....................................	Krystal Milam	SC	GS	11	....	....
	ASSISTANT SECRETARY FOR ELECTRICITY						
Washington, DC	Assistant Secretary Office of Electricity............	Gene Rodrigues	PAS	EX	IV	....	....
Washington, DC	Principal Deputy Assistant Secretary...............	Career Incumbent	CA	ES	....	....	....
Washington, DC	Deputy Assistant Secretary for Advanced Grid Research and Development.	Career Incumbent	CA	ES	....	....	....
Washington, DC	Deputy Assistant Secretary for the Energy Storage.	Career Incumbent	CA	ES	....	....	....

DEPARTMENT OF ENERGY—Continued

Location	Position Title	Name of Incumbent	Type of Appt.	Pay Plan	Level, Grade, or Pay	Tenure	Expires
Washington, DC	Deputy Assistant Secretary for the Grid Controls and Communications.	Career Incumbent	CA	ES	....	....	....
Phoenix, AZ	Senior Advisor..	Vacant	....	ES	....	....	....
Washington, DC	Chief of Staff...	Michael Mendoza Fernandez.	SC	GS	15	....	....
Washington, DC	Special Assistant......................................	Megan Husted	SC	GS	9	....	....
	OFFICE OF SCIENCE						
Washington, DC	Director, Office of Science	Vacant	....	EX	....	....	....
Washington, DC	Principal Deputy Director, Office of Science......	Vacant	....	ES	....	....	....
Germantown, MD....	Associate Deputy Director for Operations.........	Career Incumbent	CA	ES	....	....	....
Germantown, MD....	Associate Deputy Director for Science Programs.	Career Incumbent	CA	ES	....	....	....
Germantown, MD....	Director, Biological Systems Sciences Division .	Career Incumbent	CA	ES	....	....	....
Germantown, MD....	Director, Earth and Environmental System Sciences Division.	Career Incumbent	CA	ES	....	....	....
Germantown, MD....	Director, Computational Science Research and Partnership Division.	Career Incumbent	CA	ES	....	....	....
Germantown, MD....	Director, Facilities Division............................	Career Incumbent	CA	ES	....	....	....
Germantown, MD....	Director Facilities Operations and Projects.......	Career Incumbent	CA	ES	....	....	....
Germantown, MD....	Director, Facility and Project Management Division.	Career Incumbent	CA	ES	....	....	....
Germantown, MD....	Director, High Energy Research and Technology Division.	Career Incumbent	CA	ES	....	....	....
Germantown, MD....	Director, Material Sciences and Engineering Division.	Career Incumbent	CA	ES	....	....	....
Germantown, MD....	Director, Office of Basic Energy Sciences, Chemical Sciences, Geosciences.	Career Incumbent	CA	ES	....	....	....
Germantown, MD....	Director, Office of Budget...............................	Career Incumbent	CA	ES	....	....	....
Washington, DC	Director, Office of Engineering and Technology.	Vacant	....	ES	....	....	....
Germantown, MD....	Director, Office of Isotope RandD and Production.	Career Incumbent	CA	ES	....	....	....
Germantown, MD....	Director, Office of Project Assessment	Career Incumbent	CA	ES	....	....	....
Germantown, MD....	Director, Office of Safety and Security..............	Career Incumbent	CA	ES	....	....	....
Washington, DC	Director Office of Science Laboratories Infrastructure.	Career Incumbent	CA	ES	....	....	....
Germantown, MD....	Director, Physics Research Division....................	Career Incumbent	CA	ES	....	....	....
Germantown, MD....	Director Research Division	Career Incumbent	CA	ES	....	....	....
Germantown, MD....	Director, Scientific User Facilities......................	Vacant	....	ES	....	....	....
Germantown, MD....	Assistant Director Information Technology Services Division.	Career Incumbent	CA	ES	....	....	....
Germantown, MD....	Associate Director, Office of Advanced Scientific Computing Research.	Career Incumbent	CA	ES	....	....	....
Germantown, MD....	Associate Director, Office of Basic Energy Sciences.	Vacant	....	ES	....	....	....
Germantown, MD....	Associate Director, Office of Biological and Environmental Research.	Career Incumbent	CA	ES	....	....	....
Germantown, MD....	Associate Director, Office of Fusion Energy Sciences.	Vacant	....	ES	....	....	....
Germantown, MD....	Associate Director, Office of High Energy Physics.	Career Incumbent	CA	ES	....	....	....
Germantown, MD....	Associate Director, Office of Nuclear Physics....	Career Incumbent	CA	ES	....	....	....
Oak Ridge, TN.........	Manager, Consolidated Service Center	Career Incumbent	CA	ES	....	....	....
Washington, DC	Senior Advisor...	Joshua Shiode......................	NA	ES	....	....	....
Washington, DC	Special Assistant..	Chloe Koseff.........................	SC	GS	13	....	....
	ASSOCIATE ADMINISTRATOR FOR ENVIRONMENT, SAFETY AND HEALTH						
Washington, DC	Employee Workplace Programs Director	Career Incumbent	CA	ES	....	....	....
	ASSOCIATE ADMINISTRATOR FOR INFORMATION MANAGEMENT AND CHIEF INFORMATION OFFICER						
Washington, DC	Associate Administrator for Information Management and Chief Information Officer.	Career Incumbent	CA	ES	....	....	....
	ASSOCIATE UNDER SECRETARY FOR ENVIRONMENT, HEALTH, SAFETY AND SECURITY						
Washington, DC	Director Office of the Departmental Representative to the Defense Nuclear Facilities Safety Board.	Career Incumbent	CA	ES	....	....	....
Germantown, MD....	Director, Office of Classification	Career Incumbent	CA	ES	....	....	....
Washington, DC	Director, Office of Corporate Security Strategy, Analysis and Special Operations.	Career Incumbent	CA	ES	....	....	....

DEPARTMENT OF ENERGY—Continued

Location	Position Title	Name of Incumbent	Type of Appt.	Pay Plan	Level, Grade, or Pay	Tenure	Expires
Washington, DC	Director, Office of Health and Safety	Career Incumbent	CA	ES	....	....	....
Germantown, MD....	Director, Office of Resource Management........	Vacant	....	ES	....	....	....
Germantown, MD....	Director, Office of Security.....................	Career Incumbent	CA	ES	....	....	....
GRID DEPLOYMENT OFFICE							
Washington, DC	Director, Grid Deployment Office	Maria Robinson	NA	ES	....	....	....
Washington, DC	Senior Advisor...	Whitney Yvette Muse	SC	GS	15	....	....
Washington, DC	Chief of Staff..	Emily Anne Doran	SC	GS	14	....	....
Washington, DC	Special Advisor...	Joshua Inaba	SC	GS	13	....	....
LOAN PROGRAMS OFFICE							
Washington, DC	Director, Loan Programs Office	Jigar Shah	NA	ES	....	....	....
New York, NY..........	Chief Investment Officer...................................	Christopher Creed...............	TA	ES	....	....	....
Washington, DC	Chief Operating Officer...................................	Career Incumbent	CA	ES	....	....	....
Washington, DC	Director, Outreach and Business Development.	Career Incumbent	CA	ES	....	....	....
Washington, DC	Director, Technical and Project Management Division.	Career Incumbent	CA	ES	....	....	....
Washington, DC	Director, Management and Operations Division.	Career Incumbent	CA	ES	....	....	....
Washington, DC	Senior Advisor, Chief Climate Officer	Vacant	....	ES	....	....	....
Washington, DC	Chief of Staff..	Rebecca Kasper	SC	GS	15	....	....
OFFICE OF THE CHIEF INFORMATION OFFICER							
Washington, DC	Chief Information Officer.................................	Ann Dunkin.........................	NA	ES	....	....	....
Washington, DC	Deputy Chief Information Officer for Cybersecurity and Ciso.	Career Incumbent	CA	ES	....	....	....
Germantown, MD....	Deputy Chief Information Officer for Enterprise Operations and Shared Services.	Career Incumbent	CA	ES	....	....	....
Washington, DC	Deputy Chief Information Officer for Architecture, Engineering, Technology and Innovation.	Career Incumbent	CA	ES	....	....	....
Washington, DC	Deputy Chief Information Officer for Resources Management.	Career Incumbent	CA	ES	....	....	....
Washington, DC	Deputy Chief Information Officer for Enterprise Records Management, Privacy and Compliance.	Career Incumbent	CA	ES	....	....	....
Washington, DC	Deputy Chief Information Officer for Enterprise It Policy and Governance.	Career Incumbent	CA	ES	....	....	....
Washington, DC	Chief Data Officer....................................	Career Incumbent	CA	ES	....	....	....
OFFICE OF MANAGEMENT							
Washington, DC	Director, Office of Executive Secretariat............	Sarah Butler........................	SC	GS	15	....	....
Washington, DC	Senior Advisor..	Vacant	....	ES	....	....	....
Washington, DC	Director of Advance	Miranda Dixon	SC	GS	14	....	....
Washington, DC	Advance Lead..	Mikael Hasan Rafiqi............	SC	GS	11	....	....
Washington, DC	Special Assistant for Advance...........................	Rafael Cestero	SC	GS	11	....	....
Washington, DC	International Trip Lead	Jordan Morales....................	SC	GS	13	....	....
Washington, DC	Special Assistant..	Jessica Harding....................	SC	GS	10	....	....
Washington, DC	Special Assistant for Briefing Book....................	Alayna Jenkins....................	SC	GS	9	....	....
OFFICE OF PUBLIC AFFAIRS							
Washington, DC	Director of Public Affairs	Amanda Finney....................	NA	ES	....	....	....
Washington, DC	Digital Content Manager	Juaquin Robles....................	SC	GS	11	....	....
Washington, DC	Deputy Press Secretary.................................	Samah Shaiq	SC	GS	12	....	....
Washington, DC	Digital Content Manager	Kerri Ebanks	SC	GS	12	....	....
Washington, DC	Deputy Press Secretary.................................	Christopher Ford.................	SC	GS	13	....	....
Washington, DC	Deputy Director and Chief Spokesperson...........	Charisma Luetece Troiano ..	SC	GS	15	....	....
Washington, DC	Deputy Speechwriter..................................	Andrew Sacks......................	SC	GS	11	....	....
Washington, DC	Chief Speechwriter	Usha Sahay..........................	SC	GS	15	....	....
Washington, DC	Deputy Press Secretary.................................	Jeremy Ortiz........................	SC	GS	13	....	....
Washington, DC	Press Assistant..	Allie Peck	SC	GS	11	....	....
Washington, DC	Principal Deputy Speech Writer........................	Cate Yuriko Hurley	SC	GS	13	....	....
OFFICE OF TECHNOLOGY TRANSITION							
Washington, DC	Director (Chief Commercialization Officer).......	Vanessa Zee-Haye Chan	NA	ES	....	....	....
Washington, DC	Principal Deputy Director..............................	Career Incumbent	CA	ES	....	....	....
Washington, DC	Chief of Staff..	Julius Goldberg-Lewis	SC	GS	14	....	....
OFFICE OF CLEAN ENERGY DEMONSTRATIONS							
Washington, DC	Director...	Vacant	....	ES	....	....	....
Washington, DC	Chief of Staff..	Raylene Kay Yung................	SC	GS	15	....	....
Washington, DC	Special Advisor...	Jacob Matthew Smith..........	SC	GS	14	....	....

DEPARTMENT OF ENERGY—Continued

Location	Position Title	Name of Incumbent	Type of Appt.	Pay Plan	Level, Grade, or Pay	Tenure	Expires
	OFFICE OF CYBERSECURITY, ENERGY SECURITY AND EMERGENCY RESPONSE						
Washington, DC	Deputy Director for Petroleum Reserves	Career Incumbent	CA	ES	....	....	....
Washington, DC	Senior National Security Advisor......................	Career Incumbent	CA	ES	....	....	....
	OFFICE OF INDIAN ENERGY POLICY AND PROGRAMS						
Washington, DC	Director Office of Indian Energy Policy and Programs.	Wahleah Suzanne Johns......	XS	AD	....	....	....
	OFFICE OF MANUFACTURING AND ENERGY SUPPLY CHAINS						
Washington, DC	Director...	Giulia Siccardo	NA	ES	....	....	....
Washington, DC	Chief of Staff..	Rebecca Claire Ward	SC	GS	15	....	....
Washington, DC	Advisor...	Zachary Valdez	SC	GS	14	....	....
	OFFICE OF POLICY						
Washington, DC	Chief of Staff..	Vanessa Marie Grisko..........	SC	GS	13	....	....
Washington, DC	Special Advisor......................................	Jay Vaingankar.....................	SC	GS	12	....	....
	OFFICE OF SMALL AND DISADVANTAGED BUSINESS UTILIZATION						
Washington, DC	Director Office of Small and Disadvantaged Business Utilization.	Ron Pierce.............................	NA	ES	....	....	....
	STATE AND COMMUNITY ENERGY PROGRAMS						
Washington, DC	Director...	Vacant	....	ES	....	....	....
Washington, DC	Principal Deputy Director of State and Community Energy Programs.	Vacant	....	ES	....	....	....
Washington, DC	Associate Director, Director of Community Engagement.	Rose Dady	SC	GS	15	....	....
Washington, DC	Chief of Staff..	Christopher Castro..............	SC	GS	14	....	....
Washington, DC	Special Assistant...................................	Jessica Hernandez...............	SC	GS	10	....	....
	OFFICE OF ARTIFICIAL INTELLIGENCE AND TECHNOLOGY						
Washington, DC	Director, Office of Artificial Intelligence and Technology.	Vacant	....	ES	....	....	....

DEPARTMENT OF ENERGY OFFICE OF THE INSPECTOR GENERAL

Location	Position Title	Name of Incumbent	Type of Appt.	Pay Plan	Level, Grade, or Pay	Tenure	Expires
Washington, DC	Inspector General	Teri L Donaldson..................	PAS	EX	III	....	....

DEPARTMENT OF HEALTH AND HUMAN SERVICES

Location	Position Title	Name of Incumbent	Type of Appt.	Pay Plan	Level, Grade, or Pay	Tenure	Expires
	OFFICE OF THE SECRETARY						
Washington, DC	Secretary, Health and Human Services............	Xavier Becerra......................	PAS	EX	I	....	....
Washington, DC	Chief of Staff..	Sean Edward McCluskie	NA	ES	....	....	....
Washington, DC	Deputy Chief of Staff..............................	Angela Karina Ramirez......	NA	ES	....	....	....
Washington, DC	Counselor to the Secretary	Stephen Sung-Ki Cha	NA	ES	....	....	....
Washington, DC	Counselor to the Secretary	Stacy Jane Sanders..............	NA	ES	....	....	....
Washington, DC	Counselor to the Secretary	Lynn Sha	NA	ES	....	....	....
Washington, DC	Counselor to the Secretary	Katharine Cooper Wulff......	NA	ES	....	....	....
Washington, DC	Counselor for Public Health and Science	Sarah Despres	NA	ES	....	....	....
Washington, DC	Counselor for Health Policy	Rachel Celia Pryor	NA	ES	....	....	....
Washington, DC	Counselor to the Secretary on Strategic Communications.	Vacant	....	ES	....	....	....
Washington, DC	Senior Advisor......................................	Vacant	....	ES	....	....	....
Washington, DC	Senior Policy Advisor.............................	Martine Sadarangani Gordon.	SC	GS	15	....	....
Washington, DC	Senior Policy Advisor.............................	Samantha Nicole Satchell ...	SC	GS	15	....	....
Washington, DC	Senior Advisor......................................	Brian Daniel Kaplun	SC	GS	13	....	....

DEPARTMENT OF HEALTH AND HUMAN SERVICES—Continued

Location	Position Title	Name of Incumbent	Type of Appt.	Pay Plan	Level, Grade, or Pay	Tenure	Expires
Washington, DC	Policy Advisor..	Sabah Qutbuddin Ghulamali.	SC	GS	15	....	....
Washington, DC	Policy Advisor..	Joshua Harris Kramer........	SC	GS	13	....	....
Washington, DC	Special Advisor......................................	Maria Isabel Rangel Ramirez.	SC	GS	13	....	....
Washington, DC	White House Liaison	Manuel Joe Carrillo	NA	ES	....	....	....
Washington, DC	Deputy White House Liaison....................	Jose Manuel Garibay-Medrano.	SC	GS	13	....	....
Washington, DC	Special Assistant....................................	Mathieu Douceur................	SC	GS	9	....	....
Washington, DC	Executive Secretary to the Department	Elizabeth Joy Gramling......	NA	ES	....	....	....
Washington, DC	Deputy Executive Secretary for Operations......	Career Incumbent	CA	ES	....	....	....
Washington, DC	Senior Advisor to the Executive Secretary	Kemba Ayanna Hendrix	SC	GS	15	....	....
Washington, DC	Special Assistant and Briefing Book Coordinator.	Joseph Nolan	SC	GS	11	....	....
Washington, DC	Director of Scheduling and Advance................	Cynthia Michelle Palafox.....	SC	GS	15	....	....
Washington, DC	Deputy Director of Advance...........................	Lizeth Zardeneta................	SC	GS	13	....	....
Washington, DC	Special Assistant for Scheduling and Advance .	Marc Alexander Gonzales....	SC	GS	9	....	....
Washington, DC	Scheduler..	Makana Demetriades Meyer.	SC	GS	11	....	....
Washington, DC	Advance Representative..............................	José Pablo Rojas	SC	GS	9	....	....
Washington, DC	Advance Representative..............................	Hannah Lynn Salazar........	SC	GS	12	....	....
	OFFICE OF THE DEPUTY SECRETARY						
Washington, DC	Deputy Secretary, Health and Human Services.	Andrea J Palm....................	PAS	EX	II	....	....
Washington, DC	Chief of Staff to the Deputy Secretary	Angela Nichole Botticella	NA	ES	....	....	....
Washington, DC	Counselor to the Deputy Secretary..................	Erin R Szulman..................	NA	ES	....	....	....
Washington, DC	Counselor to the Deputy Secretary..................	Vacant	....	ES	....	....	....
Washington, DC	Counselor..	Kathryn Elizabeth Wessel...	NA	ES	....	....	....
Washington, DC	Senior Counsel for Oversight........................	Pilar Gabrielle Mendez........	SC	GS	15	....	....
Washington, DC	Senior Advisor for Technology and Delivery......	Sarah Edwards Esty	NA	ES	....	....	....
Washington, DC	Advisor..	Naava Gabriela Ellenberg...	SC	GS	12	....	....
Washington, DC	Advisor..	Akshay Venugopalan...........	SC	GS	12	....	....
Washington, DC	Special Assistant....................................	Monica Isabel Aponte Rodriguez.	SC	GS	9	....	....
Washington, DC	Special Assistant....................................	Darnelle Stinfort	SC	GS	9	....	....
	OFFICE OF INTERGOVERNMENTAL AND EXTERNAL AFFAIRS						
Washington, DC	Director, Office of Intergovernmental and External Affairs.	Bertha Alisia Guerrero	NA	ES	....	....	....
Washington, DC	Principal Deputy Director, Office of Intergovernmental and External Affairs.	Jessica Smith......................	NA	ES	....	....	....
Washington, DC	Senior Advisor to the Director........................	Zachary Lee Kahan..............	SC	GS	13	....	....
Washington, DC	Special Assistant....................................	Saynab Dahir Jama	SC	GS	11	....	....
Washington, DC	Special Assistant....................................	Kathya Xiomara Meza........	SC	GS	9	....	....
Washington, DC	Director of External Affairs	Eduardo Cisneros...............	SC	GS	15	....	....
Boston, MA	Regional Director, Boston, Massachusetts, Region I.	Everett Legrone Handford...	SC	GS	15	....	....
Philadelphia, PA	Regional Director Philadelphia Region III	Melissa Ann Herd	SC	GS	15	....	....
Atlanta, GA	Regional Director, Atlanta,Georgia, Region IV..	Antrell Dernard Tyson.........	SC	GS	15	....	....
Chicago, IL	Regional Director, Chicago, Illinois-Region V....	Michael Mario Cabonargi	SC	GS	15	....	....
Kansas City, MO	Regional Director, Kansas City, Missouri, Region VII.	Joseph Salvador Palm..........	SC	GS	15	....	....
Denver, CO	Regional Director, Denver, Colorado, Region VIII.	Lily Yvonne Romero Griego.	SC	GS	15	....	....
San Francisco, CA...	Regional Director, San Francisco, California, Region IX.	Jeffrey Reynoso	SC	GS	15	....	....
Washington, DC	Director, Center for Faith-Based and Neighborhood Partnerships.	Que English	SC	GS	15	....	....
Washington, DC	Executive Director, White House Initiative on Asian Americans, Native Hawaiians, and Pacific Islanders.	Krystal Chieko Kuuipo Ka'ai.	SC	GS	15	....	....
Washington, DC	Senior Advisor..	Helen Hyunjung Beaudreau.	SC	GS	15	....	....
Washington, DC	Senior Advisor..	Erika Ninoyu......................	SC	GS	14	....	....
Washington, DC	Senior Advisor..	Judith Aiko Teruya	SC	GS	14	....	....
	OFFICE OF THE ASSISTANT SECRETARY FOR ADMINISTRATION						
Washington, DC	Assistant Secretary for Administration	Cheryl Romaine Campbell...	NA	ES	....	....	....
Washington, DC	Senior Advisor for Strategic Initiatives	Samantha Olivas Stiles	SC	GS	15	....	....
Washington, DC	Special Assistant....................................	Thomas Martin Berry..........	SC	GS	9	....	....
Washington, DC	Chief of Staff...	Career Incumbent	CA	ES	....	....	....
Washington, DC	Executive Financial Officer............................	Christopher M O'Connell.....	TA	ES	....	....	02/10/27

DEPARTMENT OF HEALTH AND HUMAN SERVICES—Continued

Location	Position Title	Name of Incumbent	Type of Appt.	Pay Plan	Level, Grade, or Pay	Tenure	Expires
Bethesda, MD..........	Director, Federal Occupational Health..............	Career Incumbent	CA	ES	....	....	....
	OFFICE OF THE ASSISTANT SECRETARY FOR FINANCIAL RESOURCES						
Washington, DC	Assistant Secretary for Financial Resources.....	Vacant	....	EX	....	....	....
Washington, DC	Principal Deputy Assistant Secretary for Financial Resources.	Lisa Zweig Molyneux...........	NA	ES	....	....	....
Washington, DC	Senior Advisor...	Emily Sarah Ianacone	SC	GS	15	....	....
	OFFICE OF THE DEPUTY ASSISTANT SECRETARY FOR BUDGET						
Washington, DC	Director, Division of Discretionary Programs....	Career Incumbent	CA	ES	....	....	....
	OFFICE OF THE ASSISTANT SECRETARY FOR HEALTH						
Washington, DC	Assistant Secretary, Health	Rachel Leland Levine	PAS	EX	IV	....	....
Washington, DC	Principal Deputy Assistant Secretary for Health.	Sarah Newman Boateng......	NA	ES	....	....	....
Washington, DC	Surgeon General..	Vivek Hallegere Murthy	PAS	EX	IV	....	....
Washington, DC	Chief Strategy Officer	Max S Lesko	NA	ES	....	....	....
Washington, DC	Chief of Staff, Office of the Surgeon General....	Melea Crockin Atkins	SC	GS	15	....	....
Rockville, MD	Deputy Assistant Secretary for Population Affairs.	Vacant	....	ES	....	....	....
Washington, DC	Deputy Assistant Secretary for Women's Health and Director.	Career Incumbent	CA	ES	....	....	....
Washington, DC	Director, Office of Infectious Disease and HIV/AIDS Policy.	Career Incumbent	CA	ES	....	....	....
Washington, DC	Director of Sexual and Gender-Based Violence.	Sarah Lynn Rosenthal........	NA	ES	....	....	....
Washington, DC	Senior Advisor, LGBTQ Health	Adrian Edward Shanker......	SC	GS	15	....	....
Washington, DC	Senior Advisor on Environmental Justice and Climate Change.	Ana Delgado Mascareñas	SC	GS	15	....	....
Washington, DC	Director of Communications	Adam Cory Sarvana.............	SC	GS	15	....	....
Washington, DC	Policy Advisor...	Jonathan Riley Moore..........	SC	GS	15	....	....
Washington, DC	Special Advisor...	Madeline Kelly Triggs Anscombe.	SC	GS	11	....	....
Washington, DC	Special Advisor...	Career Incumbent	CA	ES	....	....	....
Washington, DC	Executive Director, Presidents Council on Sports, Fitness, and Nutrition.	Rayhaan Habib Merani	SC	GS	14	....	....
	OFFICE OF THE ASSISTANT SECRETARY FOR LEGISLATION						
Washington, DC	Assistant Secretary for Legislation....................	Melanie Anne Egorin	PAS	EX	IV	....	....
Washington, DC	Principal Deputy Assistant Secretary for Legislation.	Kelsey Crowley Mellette......	NA	ES	....	....	....
Washington, DC	Chief of Staff..	Ernesto Rodriguez...............	NA	ES	....	....	....
Washington, DC	Deputy Assistant Secretary for Legislation (Human Services).	Madeline Viola Daly.............	NA	ES	....	....	....
Washington, DC	Deputy Assistant Secretary for Legislation (Mandatory Health Programs).	Alexander Carl Graf	NA	ES	....	....	....
Washington, DC	Deputy Assistant Secretary for Legislation (Discretionary Health).	Kimberly Ryan Miller-Tolbert.	NA	ES	....	....	....
Washington, DC	Deputy Assistant Secretary for Legislation (Oversight).	Peter James Rechter............	NA	ES	....	....	....
Washington, DC	Deputy Assistant Secretary	Vacant	....	ES	....	....	....
Washington, DC	Senior Advisor and Congressional Liaison	Kevin James Klinkenberg ..	SC	GS	13	....	....
Washington, DC	Policy Advisor...	Erin Michelle Lunsford.......	SC	GS	12	....	....
Washington, DC	Special Assistant..	Noah Wood Emanuel............	SC	GS	7	....	....
	OFFICE OF THE ASSISTANT SECRETARY FOR PLANNING AND EVALUATION						
Washington, DC	Assistant Secretary for Planning and Evaluation.	Vacant	....	EX	....	....	....
Washington, DC	Principal Deputy Assistant Secretary for Planning and Evaluation.	Rebecca Lee Haffajee...........	NA	ES	....	....	....
Washington, DC	Deputy Assistant Secretary for Planning and Evaluation (Office of Behavioral Health, Disability and Aging Policy).	Tisamarie Bose Sherry	NA	ES	....	....	....
Washington, DC	Associate Deputy Assistant Secretary for Planning and Evaluation (Disability, Aging, and Long-Term Care Policy).	Career Incumbent	CA	ES	....	....	....
Washington, DC	Deputy Assistant Secretary Planning and Evaluation (Health Policy).	Thomas Carl Buchmueller ..	NA	ES	....	....	....
Washington, DC	Associate Deputy Assistant Secretary for Planning and Evaluation (Health Policy).	Career Incumbent	CA	ES	....	....	....

DEPARTMENT OF HEALTH AND HUMAN SERVICES—Continued

Location	Position Title	Name of Incumbent	Type of Appt.	Pay Plan	Level, Grade, or Pay	Tenure	Expires
Washington, DC	Deputy Assistant Secretary for Planning and Evaluation (Human Services Policy).	Miranda Clara Lynch-Smith.	NA	ES	....	....	....
Washington, DC	Deputy Assistant Secretary for Planning and Evaluation (Science and Data Policy).	Career Incumbent	CA	ES	....	....	....
Washington, DC	Associate Deputy Assistant Secretary for Planning and Evaluation (Science and Data Policy).	Vacant	....	ES	....	....	....
	OFFICE OF THE ASSISTANT SECRETARY FOR PUBLIC AFFAIRS						
Washington, DC	Assistant Secretary for Public Affairs..............	Jeffrey Asher Nesbit	PA	EX	IV	....	....
Washington, DC	Principal Deputy Assistant Secretary for Public Affairs.	Samira Jali Burns................	NA	ES	....	....	....
Washington, DC	Deputy Assistant Secretary for Public Affairs (Human Services).	Rafael Benavides................	NA	ES	....	....	....
Washington, DC	Deputy Assistant Secretary for Public Affairs (Health Care).	Sara Elizabeth Rose Lonardo.	NA	ES	....	....	....
Washington, DC	Deputy Assistant Secretary for Public Affairs (Public Health).	Heather Bettina Purcell	NA	ES	....	....	....
Washington, DC	Senior Advisor to the Assistant Secretary........	Vacant	....	ES	....	....	....
Washington, DC	Senior Advisor.......................	Anne Elizabeth Feldman	SC	GS	15	....	....
Washington, DC	Senior Advisor.......................	Maysoon Mirghani Malik	SC	GS	15	....	....
Washington, DC	Advisor for Strategic Planning	Jorge Luis Zurita-Coronado.	SC	GS	12	....	....
Washington, DC	Director of Speechwriting	Brian Alexander Reich........	SC	GS	15	....	....
Washington, DC	Online Communications Director......................	Kelly Marie Langford..........	SC	GS	15	....	....
Washington, DC	Online Communications Manager.....................	Destiny Makayla Gregg.......	SC	GS	11	....	....
Washington, DC	National Press Secretary	Paola Laryssa Amador........	SC	GS	14	....	....
Washington, DC	National Press Secretary	McKenzie Alcott Wilson.......	SC	GS	14	....	....
Washington, DC	Press Secretary (Health Care)..........................	Renata Marguerite Miller ...	SC	GS	12	....	....
Washington, DC	Press Assistant	Conner Mather Coles..........	SC	GS	12	....	....
Washington, DC	Special Assistant..	Kyle Michael McCarthy.......	SC	GS	11	....	....
	OFFICE FOR CIVIL RIGHTS						
Washington, DC	Director Office for Civil Rights.......................	Melanie Fontes Rainer........	NA	ES	....	....	....
Washington, DC	Principal Deputy Director................................	Jenny Suhjin Ma................	NA	ES	....	....	....
Washington, DC	Chief of Staff...	Dennis James Gonzalez......	NA	ES	....	....	....
Washington, DC	Senior Advisor...	Leah Ford.......................	SC	GS	15	....	....
Washington, DC	Senior Advisor...	Clark Tien Jan Lee	SC	GS	15	....	....
Washington, DC	Special Assistant..	Johanna Marquez Diaz.......	SC	GS	11	....	....
	OFFICE OF THE GENERAL COUNSEL						
Washington, DC	General Counsel	Samuel Robert Bagenstos....	PAS	EX	IV	....	....
Washington, DC	Deputy General Counsel	Stephanie Oluchukwu Akpa.	NA	ES	....	....	....
Washington, DC	Deputy General Counsel	Mark Howard Greenberg.....	NA	ES	....	....	....
Washington, DC	Deputy General Counsel	Paul Richard Rodriguez.......	NA	ES	....	....	....
Washington, DC	Deputy General Counsel	Karuna Seshasai................	NA	ES	....	....	....
Washington, DC	Deputy General Counsel	Patricia Jolene Zettler	NA	ES	....	....	....
Washington, DC	Deputy General Counsel	Vacant	....	ES	....	....	....
Washington, DC	Senior Counsel, Oversight	Perrin Cooke....................	SC	GS	15	....	....
Washington, DC	Senior Counsel, Oversight	Nicole Walton...................	SC	GS	15	....	....
Washington, DC	Director, Office of Legal Resources...................	Career Incumbent	CA	ES	....	....	....
Washington, DC	Associate General Counsel - Children, Families and Aging Division.	Career Incumbent	CA	ES	....	....	....
Washington, DC	Deputy Associate General Counsel for Claims and Employment Law.	Career Incumbent	CA	ES	....	....	....
Washington, DC	Associate General Counsel, Civil Rights Division.	Career Incumbent	CA	ES	....	....	....
Washington, DC	Deputy Associate General Counsel for Public Health (National Institutes of Health).	Career Incumbent	CA	ES	....	....	....
Washington, DC	Deputy Program Integrity	Career Incumbent	CA	ES	....	....	....
	Chief Counsels						
Boston, MA..............	Chief Counsel, Region I...................................	Career Incumbent	CA	ES	....	....	....
New York, NY..........	Chief Counsel, Region II..................................	Career Incumbent	CA	ES	....	....	....
Philadelphia, PA	Chief Counsel, Region III.................................	Career Incumbent	CA	ES	....	....	....
Atlanta, GA	Chief Counsel, Region IV.................................	Career Incumbent	CA	ES	....	....	....
Chicago, IL	Chief Counsel, Region V..................................	Career Incumbent	CA	ES	....	....	....
Dallas, TX	Chief Counsel, Region VI.................................	Career Incumbent	CA	ES	....	....	....
Kansas City, MO	Chief Counsel, Region VII................................	Career Incumbent	CA	ES	....	....	....
Denver, CO	Chief Counsel, Region VIII	Career Incumbent	CA	ES	....	....	....
San Francisco, CA...	Chief Counsel, Region IX	Career Incumbent	CA	ES	....	....	....
Seattle, WA..............	Chief Counsel, Region X..................................	Career Incumbent	CA	ES	....	....	....

DEPARTMENT OF HEALTH AND HUMAN SERVICES—Continued

Location	Position Title	Name of Incumbent	Type of Appt.	Pay Plan	Level, Grade, or Pay	Tenure	Expires
	Associate General Counsel Divisions						
Washington, DC	Associate General Counsel, Legislation Division.	Career Incumbent	CA	ES	....	....	....
Rockville, MD	Associate General Counsel, Public Health	Career Incumbent	CA	ES	....	....	....
Washington, DC	Associate General Counsel, Centers for Medicaid and Medicare Services.	Career Incumbent	CA	ES	....	....	....
Washington, DC	Deputy Associate General Counsel, Centers for Medicare and Medicaid Services Division.	Career Incumbent	CA	ES	....	....	....
Woodlawn, MD	Deputy Associate General Counsel for Litigation, Centers for Medicare and Medicaid Services Division.	Career Incumbent	CA	ES	....	....	....
Washington, DC	Associate General Counsel.................................	Career Incumbent	CA	ES	....	....	....
Atlanta, GA	Deputy Associate General Counsel	Career Incumbent	CA	ES	....	....	....
Washington, DC	Deputy Associate General Counsel for Public Health Division.	Career Incumbent	CA	ES	....	....	....
Rockville, MD	Deputy Associate General Counsel for Public Health.	Vacant	....	ES	....	....	....
Washington, DC	Deputy Associate General Counsel for Procurement and Fiscal Information Law.	Career Incumbent	CA	ES	....	....	....
	OFFICE OF GLOBAL AFFAIRS						
Washington, DC	Assistant Secretary for Global Affairs	Loyce Lashawndra Pace	NA	ES	....	....	....
Washington, DC	Principal Deputy Assistant Secretary for Global Affairs.	Susan Chong Kim	NA	ES	....	....	....
Washington, DC	Chief of Staff...	Michael Joseph Beard..........	NA	ES	....	....	....
Washington, DC	Chief Advisor for Policy and Strategy................	Caya Lewis Atkins	NA	ES	....	....	....
San Francisco, CA...	Pandemic Instrument Negotiator for the United States.	Pamela Kiyomi Hamamoto..	NA	ES	....	....	....
Washington, DC	Senior Advisor, Human Rights and Gender Equity.	Stephanie Robin Psaki.........	SC	GS	15	....	....
Washington, DC	Special Assistant..	Kevin Becerra Segura..........	SC	GS	12	....	....
Washington, DC	Director, Office of Pandemics and Emerging Threats.	Career Incumbent	CA	ES	....	....	....
	OFFICE OF THE NATIONAL COORDINATOR FOR HEALTH INFORMATION TECHNOLOGY						
Washington, DC	National Health Information Technology Coordinator.	Suhas Tripathi......................	NA	ES	....	....	....
	ADMINISTRATION FOR CHILDREN AND FAMILIES						
Washington, DC	Assistant Secretary for Children and Families.	Vacant	....	EX	....	....	....
Washington, DC	Principal Deputy Assistant Secretary Administration for Children and Families.	Steven Jeffrey Hild	NA	ES	....	....	....
Washington, DC	Deputy Assistant Secretary for Management ...	Lawrence James Handerhan.	NA	ES	....	....	....
Washington, DC	Chief of Staff...	Larry Levi Sandigo	NA	ES	....	....	....
Washington, DC	Counselor..	Meg Shannon Sullivan	NA	ES	....	....	....
Washington, DC	Deputy Assistant Secretary for Policy	Jennifer M Cannistra	NA	ES	....	....	....
Washington, DC	Director, Office of Head Start	Khari Marcus Garvin...........	NA	ES	....	....	....
Washington, DC	Director, Office of Child Care............................	Ruth Jennifer Friedman......	NA	ES	....	....	....
Washington, DC	Deputy Assistant Secretary for Early Childhood Development.	Kathleen Daly Hamm..........	NA	ES	....	....	....
Washington, DC	Deputy Assistant Secretary, Office of Planning, Research, and Evaluation.	Career Incumbent	CA	ES	....	....	....
Washington, DC	Deputy Assistant Secretary for External Affairs.	Debra Nicole Johnson	NA	ES	....	....	....
Washington, DC	Director of Communications	Stacie Bernette Burgess	SC	GS	15	....	....
Washington, DC	Press Secretary	Claudia Paloma Alarco Alarco.	SC	GS	14	....	....
Washington, DC	Senior Advisor, Oversight...................................	Jesseca Lane Boyer..............	SC	GS	15	....	....
Washington, DC	Senior Advisor..	Jermatic Rushing Chambers.	SC	GS	13	....	....
Washington, DC	Senior Advisor..	Mari Patricia Dorn-Lopez....	SC	GS	15	....	....
Washington, DC	Senior Advisor..	Anna Esther Fogel	SC	GS	15	....	....
Washington, DC	Senior Advisor..	David Laurence Gonzalez Rice.	SC	GS	15	....	....
Washington, DC	Special Advisor...	Shoshana Kaplan	SC	GS	13	....	....
Washington, DC	Special Advisor...	Jasmin Coral Palomares......	SC	GS	13	....	....
Washington, DC	Director, Unaccompanied Children Program.....	Career Incumbent	CA	ES	....	....	....
Washington, DC	Director, Office of Regional Operations.............	Vacant	....	ES	....	....	....
Washington, DC	Director, Office of Legislative Affairs and Budget.	Career Incumbent	CA	ES	....	....	....

DEPARTMENT OF HEALTH AND HUMAN SERVICES—Continued

Location	Position Title	Name of Incumbent	Type of Appt.	Pay Plan	Level, Grade, or Pay	Tenure	Expires
Washington, DC	Director, Refugee Program	Career Incumbent	CA	ES	....	....	....
	Administration for Children, Youth and Families / Office of Commissioner						
Washington, DC	Commissioner Administration for Children Youth and Families.	Rebecca Ellen Jones Gaston.	PAS	EX	V	....	....
	Office of Family Assistance / Office of the Director						
Washington, DC	Director, Office of Family Assistance	Ann Clark Flagg..................	NA	ES	....	....	....
	Office of Child Support Enforcement / Office of the Director						
Washington, DC	Director Office of Child Support Enforcement ..	Tanguler Roulette Summia Gray.	NA	ES	....	....	....
	Office of Refugee Resettlement / Office of the Director						
Washington, DC	Deputy Assistant Secretary for Humanitarian Services and Director for the Office of Refugee Resettlement.	Robin Lynn Dunn Marcos ...	NA	ES	....	....	....
Washington, DC	Deputy Director, Office of Refugee Resettlement.	Jenifer Susan Smyers..........	NA	ES	....	....	....
Washington, DC	Senior Advisor..	Miriam Abaya Maigadi........	SC	GS	14	....	....
	Office of Community Services / Office of the Director						
Washington, DC	Director, Office of Community Services	Lanikque Laquiel Howard...	NA	ES	....	....	....
	Administration for Native Americans / Office of Commissioner						
Washington, DC	Commissioner, Administration for Native Americans.	Patrice Helen Kunesh..........	PAS	EX	V	....	....
	Administration for Community Living						
Washington, DC	Assistant Secretary for Aging and Administrator, Administration for Community Living.	Vacant	....	EX	....	....	....
Washington, DC	Principal Deputy Administrator.........................	Alison Barkoff......................	NA	ES	....	....	....
Washington, DC	Deputy Assistant Secretary for Programs	Maura Dalton Calsyn	NA	ES	....	....	....
Washington, DC	Advisor..	Jennifer Leigh Baker...........	SC	GS	13	....	....
Washington, DC	Deputy Assistant Secretary for Aging...............	Career Incumbent	CA	ES	....	....	....
Washington, DC	Deputy Administrator for Policy and Evaluation.	Career Incumbent	CA	ES	....	....	....
Washington, DC	Senior Advisor to the Administrator/Chief of Staff.	Career Incumbent	CA	ES	....	....	....
	ADMINISTRATION FOR STRATEGIC PREPAREDNESS AND RESPONSE						
Washington, DC	Administrator and Assistant Secretary for Preparedness and Response.	Dawn Christianne O'Connell.	PAS	EX	IV	....	....
Washington, DC	Chief of Staff..	Kathryn Marie Alvarez........	NA	ES	....	....	....
Washington, DC	Chief Strategy Officer	Kimberly Lorraine Espinosa.	NA	ES	....	....	....
Washington, DC	Senior Advisor..	Jessica Zahira Porras...........	SC	GS	15	....	....
Washington, DC	Strategic Advisor for Communications	Zachary Weatherby Dembner.	SC	GS	12	....	....
Washington, DC	Principal Deputy and Chief Operating Officer..	Career Incumbent	CA	ES	....	....	....
Washington, DC	Director, Office of Executive Management	Career Incumbent	CA	ES	....	....	....
Washington, DC	Deputy Assistant Secretary for Incident Command and Control.	Career Incumbent	CA	ES	....	....	....
Washington, DC	Director of Resource Planning and Evaluation.	Career Incumbent	CA	ES	....	....	....
Washington, DC	Director, Office of Strategy, Planning, Policy, Requirements.	Career Incumbent	CA	ES	....	....	....
	AGENCY FOR HEALTHCARE RESEARCH AND QUALITY						
Rockville, MD	Director..	Robert O Valdez....................	NA	ES	....	....	....
Rockville, MD	Senior Advisor..	Sean Patrick Bruna..............	SC	GS	14	....	....
Rockville, MD	Director, Office of Communications...................	Career Incumbent	CA	ES	....	....	....
	CENTERS FOR DISEASE CONTROL AND PREVENTION						
Atlanta, GA	Director, Center for Disease Control and Prevention and Administrator Agency for Toxic Substances and Disease Registry.	Mandy Krauthamer Cohen..	NA	ES	....	....	....
Atlanta, GA	Chief of Staff..	Kathryn Lea Wolff...............	NA	ES	....	....	....
Atlanta, GA	Special Advisor to Chief of Staff........................	Tiffany J Brown	TA	ES	....	....	03/25/25
Atlanta, GA	Covid Implementation and Evaluation Manager.	Sara Patterson......................	TA	ES	....	....	10/08/25

DEPARTMENT OF HEALTH AND HUMAN SERVICES—Continued

Location	Position Title	Name of Incumbent	Type of Appt.	Pay Plan	Level, Grade, or Pay	Tenure	Expires
Washington, DC	Deputy Director for Policy, Communication and Legislative Affairs.	Andrea Samuel Lipstein Fristedt.	NA	ES	....	....	....
Atlanta, GA	Special Assistant................	Casey Lyn Garay................	SC	GS	12	....	....
Atlanta, GA	Associate Director for Communications.............	Career Incumbent	CA	ES	....	....	....
Washington, DC	Director, Centers for Disease Control and Prevention, Washington Office.	Career Incumbent	CA	ES	....	....	....
Atlanta, GA	Director, Covid and Health Equity Initiative	Stacey Mattison Jenkins	TA	ES	....	....	09/10/25
	CENTERS FOR MEDICARE AND MEDICAID SERVICES						
Washington, DC	Administrator Centers for Medicare and Medicaid Services.	Chiquita White Brooks-Lasure.	PAS	EX	III	....	....
Baltimore, MD........	Principal Deputy Administrator and Chief Operating Officer.	Jonathan D Blum................	NA	ES	....	....	....
Baltimore, MD........	Chief of Staff, Centers for Medicare and Medicaid Services.	Erin Elizabeth Richardson ..	NA	ES	....	....	....
Washington, DC	Senior Advisor........................	Hannah Ruth Katch............	SC	GS	15	....	....
Washington, DC	Senior Advisor........................	Eden Tesfaye........................	SC	GS	13	....	....
Baltimore, MD........	Deputy Administrator and Director, Center for Medicare.	Meena Seshamani................	NA	ES	....	....	....
Washington, DC	Deputy Chief of Staff and Director for the Office of Legislation.	Arielle Victoria Woronoff	NA	ES	....	....	....
Baltimore, MD........	Senior Communications Outreach Liaison........	Bruce Carlton Alexander	SC	GS	15	....	....
Woodlawn, MD	Director, Office of Strategy, Performance and Results.	Career Incumbent	CA	ES	....	....	....
Baltimore, MD........	Director, Office of Minority Health....................	Career Incumbent	CA	ES	....	....	....
Woodlawn, MD	Deputy Chief Operating Officer	Career Incumbent	CA	ES	....	....	....
	Office of Communications						
Washington, DC	Deputy Director, Office of Communications	Career Incumbent	CA	ES	....	....	....
Woodlawn, MD	Deputy Director for Operations........................	Career Incumbent	CA	ES	....	....	....
	Office of Legislation						
Washington, DC	Deputy Director, Office of Legislation................	Career Incumbent	CA	ES	....	....	....
	Center for Medicare						
Baltimore, MD........	Policy Advisor........................	Molly Thornton Turco	SC	GS	15	....	....
	Center for Medicaid and Chip Services						
Baltimore, MD........	Deputy Administrator and Director, Center for Medicaid and CHIP Services.	Daniel Weihen Tsai.............	NA	ES	....	....	....
Baltimore, MD........	Senior Advisor........................	Perrie Tracy Briskin	SC	GS	15	....	....
Baltimore, MD........	Policy Advisor........................	Kirsten Kessler Beronio	SC	GS	15	....	....
	Center for Medicare and Medicaid Innovation						
Baltimore, MD........	Deputy Administrator and Director, Center for Medicare and Medicaid Innovation.	Elizabeth Jean Fowler	NA	ES	....	....	....
	Center for Consumer Information and Insurance Oversight						
Baltimore, MD........	Deputy Administrator and Director, Center for Consumer Information and Insurance Oversight.	Ellen Janine Montz..............	NA	ES	....	....	....
	Food and Drug Administration						
Rockville, MD	Commissioner of Food and Drugs	Robert Califf	PAS	EX	IV	....	....
White Oak, MD	Associate Commissioner for External Affairs....	Leah Rose Hunter	NA	ES	....	....	....
Washington, DC	Deputy General Counsel and Chief Counsel.....	Career Incumbent	CA	ES	....	....	....
Washington, DC	Deputy General Counsel for Program Review ..	Career Incumbent	CA	ES	....	....	....
Washington, DC	Deputy Associate General Counsel for Program Review.	Career Incumbent	CA	ES	....	....	....
Silver Spring, MD ...	Deputy Associate General Counsel for Litigation.	Career Incumbent	CA	ES	....	....	....
Silver Spring, MD ...	Associate Commissioner for Legislative Affairs.	Vacant	....	ES	....	....	....
Silver Spring, MD ...	Deputy Director, Office of Policy, Legislation and International Affairs.	Career Incumbent	CA	ES	....	....	....
Rockville, MD	Associate Commissioner for Policy....................	Career Incumbent	CA	ES	....	....	....
Silver Spring, MD ...	Associate Commissioner for Global Policy and Strategy.	Career Incumbent	CA	ES	....	....	....
Rockville, MD	Director, Office of Communications and Project Management.	Vacant	....	ES	....	....	....
Silver Spring, MD ...	Program Director, Office of Medical Device and Radiological Health Operations.	Vacant	....	ES	....	....	....
Rockville, MD	Deputy Director for Import Operations Enforcement.	Vacant	....	ES	....	....	....

DEPARTMENT OF HEALTH AND HUMAN SERVICES—Continued

Location	Position Title	Name of Incumbent	Type of Appt.	Pay Plan	Level, Grade, or Pay	Tenure	Expires
	Office of the Commissioner						
Silver Spring, MD ...	Deputy Commissioner for Policy, Legislation, and International Affairs.	Kimberlee Trzeciak	NA	ES	....	....	....
Silver Spring, MD ...	Associate Commissioner for Congressional Appropriations.	Vacant	....	ES	....	....	....
	Office of External Relations						
Silver Spring, MD ...	Assistant Commissioner for Media Affairs	Career Incumbent	CA	ES	....	....	....
	Office of External Affairs						
Rockville, MD	Deputy Associate Commissioner for External Affairs.	Career Incumbent	CA	ES	....	....	....
	Office of Regulatory Affairs						
Silver Spring, MD ...	Director, Office of Strategic Planning and Operational Policy.	Vacant	....	ES	....	....	....
	HEALTH RESOURCES AND SERVICES ADMINISTRATION						
Rockville, MD	Administrator, Health Resources and Services Administration.	Carole Anne Johnson	NA	ES	....	....	....
Rockville, MD	Deputy Administrator	Jordan M Grossman.............	NA	ES	....	....	....
Rockville, MD	Chief of Staff...	Garrett Paul Devenney........	SC	GS	15	....	....
Rockville, MD	Director of Strategic Communications...............	Brenda Davis Jones	SC	GS	15	....	....
Rockville, MD	Senior Advisor, Immediate Office of the Administrator.	Career Incumbent	CA	ES	....	....	....
Rockville, MD	Director, Office of Communications...................	Vacant	....	ES	....	....	....
Rockville, MD	Director, Office of Legislation	Career Incumbent	CA	ES	....	....	....
Rockville, MD	Director, Office of Planning, Analysis and Evaluation.	Vacant	....	ES	....	....	....
Rockville, MD	Special Assistant to the Associate Administrator, Health Systems Bureau.	Hanock John.....................	TA	ES	....	....	06/17/26
Rockville, MD	Deputy Associate Administrator, Provider Relief Bureau.	Alexandra Huttinger............	TA	ES	....	....	05/17/25
	INDIAN HEALTH SERVICE						
Rockville, MD	Director, Indian Health Service.........................	Roselyn Tso......................	PAS	EX	V	....	....
Washington, DC	Senior Advisor to the Director..........................	Joshuah Cole Marshall........	SC	GS	14	....	....
	NATIONAL INSTITUTES OF HEALTH						
Bethesda, MD	Director, National Institutes of Health.............	Monica Marie Bertagnolli....	PAS	EX	IV	....	....
Washington, DC	Senior Director..	Danielle Marie Carnival......	NA	ES	....	....	....
Bethesda, MD	Associate Director for Legislative Policy Analysis.	Career Incumbent	CA	ES	....	....	....
Bethesda, MD..........	Associate Director for Communications and Public Liaison.	Vacant	....	ES	....	....	....
Bethesda, MD..........	Director, Office of Communications and Government Relations.	Career Incumbent	CA	ES	....	....	....
	Office of the Director						
Bethesda, MD..........	Chief of Staff...	Career Incumbent	CA	ES	....	....	....
	National Cancer Institute						
Bethesda, MD.........	Director, National Cancer Institute...................	Wendy Kimryn Rathmell.....	PA	OT	....	....	....
Bethesda, MD..........	Assistant Director, Cancer Moonshot Engagement.	Anabella Aspiras	SC	GS	15	....	....
	Advanced Research Projects Agency for Health						
Bethesda, MD..........	Director, Advanced Research Projects Agency for Health.	Renee Diane Wegrzyn	PA	OT	....	....	....
Bethesda, MD..........	Director, Legislative and Governmental Affairs Office.	Career Incumbent	CA	ES	....	....	....
	SUBSTANCE ABUSE AND MENTAL HEALTH SERVICES ADMINISTRATION						
Rockville, MD	Director, Center for Behavioral Health Statistics and Quality.	Career Incumbent	CA	ES	....	....	....
Rockville, MD	Assistant Secretary for Mental Health and Substance Use.	Miriam Elizabeth Delphin-Rittmon.	PAS	EX	IV	....	....
Rockville, MD	Principal Deputy Assistant Secretary...............	Career Incumbent	CA	ES	....	....	....
Rockville, MD	Deputy Assistant Secretary	Sonia Gotsch Chessen..........	NA	ES	....	....	....
Rockville, MD	Chief of Staff...	Trina Dutta.......................	NA	ES	....	....	....
Rockville, MD	Senior Advisor...	Career Incumbent	CA	ES	....	....	....
Washington, DC	Senior Advisor...	Shalini Wickramatilake.......	SC	GS	15	....	....
Rockville, MD	Director, 988 and Behavioral Health Crisis	Career Incumbent	CA	ES	....	....	....

DEPARTMENT OF HEALTH AND HUMAN SERVICES OFFICE OF THE INSPECTOR GENERAL

Location	Position Title	Name of Incumbent	Type of Appt.	Pay Plan	Level, Grade, or Pay	Tenure	Expires
Washington, DC	Inspector General	Christi A Grimm	PAS	EX	III	....	....

DEPARTMENT OF HOMELAND SECURITY

Location	Position Title	Name of Incumbent	Type of Appt.	Pay Plan	Level, Grade, or Pay	Tenure	Expires
	OFFICE OF THE SECRETARY						
Washington, DC	Secretary of the Department of Homeland Security.	Alejandro Mayorkas.............	PAS	EX	I	....	....
Washington, DC	Deputy Secretary of the Department of Homeland Security.	Vacant	....	EX	....	....	....
Washington, DC	Principal Senior Counselor	Kristie Canegallo..................	NA	ES	....	....	....
Washington, DC	Chief of Staff..	Jonathan Clements Davidson.	NA	ES	....	....	....
Washington, DC	Chief of Staff to the Deputy Secretary	Bryn McDonough	NA	ES	....	....	....
Washington, DC	Deputy Chief of Staff (Operations)....................	Vacant	....	ES	....	....	....
Washington, DC	Deputy Chief of Staff (Policy)	Sharmistha Das....................	NA	ES	....	....	....
Washington, DC	Senior Counselor..	Ricki Seidman	NA	ES	....	....	....
Washington, DC	Senior Counselor (Immigration and Border Security).	Charanya Krishnaswami.....	NA	ES	....	....	....
Washington, DC	Senior Counselor..	Vacant	....	ES	....	....	....
Washington, DC	Assistant Secretary for State and Local Law Enforcement.	Heather Jeanne Fong...........	NA	ES	....	....	....
Washington, DC	White House Liaison	Michell Figueroa	NA	ES	....	....	....
Washington, DC	Counselor..	Alexandra Schmitt	SC	GS	15	....	....
Washington, DC	Counselor..	Carole House	SC	GS	15	....	....
Washington, DC	Director of Scheduling and Advance	Michael Carey......................	SC	GS	15	....	....
Washington, DC	Deputy White House Liaison	Amit Jani..............................	SC	GS	15	....	....
Washington, DC	Senior Advance Officer..	D'Andre Carter.....................	SC	GS	12	....	....
Washington, DC	Senior Advance Officer..	Emily Varady	SC	GS	11	....	....
Washington, DC	Special Assistant to the Secretary	Justine Liebenson	SC	GS	13	....	....
Washington, DC	Special Assistant to the Secretary	Evelyn Chang	SC	GS	13	....	....
Washington, DC	Special Assistant to the Secretary	Ashly Estevez-Perez...........	SC	GS	11	....	....
Washington, DC	Special Assistant to the Deputy Secretary	Christopher Dimuro.............	SC	GS	12	....	....
Washington, DC	Special Assistant, White House Liaison	Kayla Green..........................	SC	GS	11	....	....
Washington, DC	Executive Secretary..	Deborah Fleischaker	NA	ES	....	....	....
Washington, DC	Briefing Book Coordinator	Gabrielle Sigler	SC	GS	11	....	....
Washington, DC	Briefing Book Coordinator	Joseph Quillin	SC	GS	11	....	....
Washington, DC	Special Assistant...	Olive Kinga...........................	SC	GS	11	....	....
Washington, DC	Briefing Book Coordinator	Meshulam Ungar	SC	GS	9	....	....
Washington, DC	Family Reunification Task Force	Vacant	....	ES	....	....	....
Washington, DC	Director, Joint Requirements Council	Career Incumbent	CA	ES	....	....	....
Washington, DC	Deputy Counterterrorism Coordinator	Career Incumbent	CA	ES	....	....	....
Washington, DC	Senior Transition Advisor	Career Incumbent	CA	ES	....	....	....
	MANAGEMENT DIRECTORATE						
Washington, DC	Under Secretary for Management.......................	Vacant	....	EX	....	....	....
Washington, DC	Deputy Under Secretary for Management	Career Incumbent	CA	ES	....	....	....
Washington, DC	Associate Deputy Under Secretary for Management.	Career Incumbent	CA	ES	....	....	....
Washington, DC	Chief of Staff...	Career Incumbent	CA	ES	....	....	....
Washington, DC	Chief Creative Officer	Career Incumbent	CA	ES	....	....	....
Washington, DC	Chief Financial Officer	Vacant	....	EX	....	....	....
Washington, DC	Deputy Chief Financial Officer..........................	Career Incumbent	CA	ES	....	....	....
Washington, DC	Director, Financial Operations...........................	Vacant	....	ES	....	....	....
Washington, DC	Director, Financial Systems Modernization......	Vacant	....	ES	....	....	....
Washington, DC	Director, Program Analysis and Evaluation	Vacant	....	ES	....	....	....
Washington, DC	Deputy Director, Office of Program Analysis and Evaluation.	Career Incumbent	CA	ES	....	....	....
Washington, DC	Chief Information Officer....................................	Eric N Hysen	PA	OT	....	....	....
Washington, DC	Customer Experience Advisor for Program Development.	Dana Chisnell......................	TA	ES	....	....	....
Washington, DC	Deputy Chief Technology Officer........................	Career Incumbent	CA	ES	....	....	....
Washington, DC	Senior Advisor...	David Ceasar	SC	GS	15	....	....
Washington, DC	Senior Advisor...	Abby Deift.............................	SC	GS	15	....	....
San Francisco, CA...	Senior Advisor...	Anil Dewan	SC	GS	15	....	....
Washington, DC	Chief Human Capital Officer..............................	Career Incumbent	CA	ES	....	....	....

DEPARTMENT OF HOMELAND SECURITY—Continued

Location	Position Title	Name of Incumbent	Type of Appt.	Pay Plan	Level, Grade, or Pay	Tenure	Expires
Washington, DC	Chief Learning Officer (CLO) and Executive Director, Learning, Education, and Development Strategy (LEADS).	Career Incumbent	CA	ES	....	....	....
Washington, DC	Executive Director, Cybersecurity and Intelligence Talent Experience.	Career Incumbent	CA	ES	....	....	....
Washington, DC	Chief Readiness Support Officer	Career Incumbent	CA	ES	....	....	....
Washington, DC	Executive Director Future of Work (FoW)	Margaret Hartigan..............	TA	ES	....	....	....
Washington, DC	Director, Office of Biometric Identity Management.	Career Incumbent	CA	ES	....	....	....
Washington, DC	Homeland Advanced Recognition Technology (HART) Executive Program Manager.	Timothy Murray...................	TA	ES	....	....	....
Washington, DC	Executive Director, Office of Small and Disadvantaged Business Utilization.	Career Incumbent	CA	ES	....	....	....
Washington, DC	Director, Office of Selective Acquisitions	Career Incumbent	CA	ES	....	....	....
Washington, DC	Executive Director, Office of Acquisition Workforce.	Career Incumbent	CA	ES	....	....	....
	SCIENCE AND TECHNOLOGY DIRECTORATE						
Washington, DC	Under Secretary for Science and Technology	Dimitri F Kusnezov..............	PAS	EX	III	....	....
Washington, DC	Deputy Under Secretary for Science and Technology.	Career Incumbent	CA	ES	....	....	....
Washington, DC	Chief of Staff..	Steven Feder........................	NA	ES	....	....	....
Washington, DC	Executive Director, Office of Enterprise Services.	Career Incumbent	CA	ES	....	....	....
Washington, DC	Executive Director, Office of Innovation and Collaboration.	Career Incumbent	CA	ES	....	....	....
Washington, DC	Executive Director, Office of Science and Engineering.	Career Incumbent	CA	ES	....	....	....
Washington, DC	Director, Office of National Laboratories...........	Career Incumbent	CA	ES	....	....	....
Washington, DC	Director, Plum Island Animal Disease Center ..	Career Incumbent	CA	ES	....	....	....
Washington, DC	Special Assistant.....................................	Padmavathi Ganduri............	SC	GS	12	....	....
Washington, DC	Special Assistant.....................................	Adeline Tolle	SC	GS	12	....	....
Washington, DC	Director, Compliance	Vacant	....	ES	....	....	....
Washington, DC	Executive Director, Office of Mission Capability and Support.	Career Incumbent	CA	ES	....	....	....
	OFFICE OF STRATEGY, POLICY, AND PLANS						
Washington, DC	Under Secretary for Strategy, Policy, and Plans.	Robert P Silvers	PAS	EX	III	....	....
Washington, DC	Deputy Under Secretary for Strategy, Policy, and Plans.	Career Incumbent	CA	ES	....	....	....
Washington, DC	Chief of Staff..	Hannah Edwards	NA	ES	....	....	....
Washington, DC	Senior Advisor.......................................	Alexandra Carnes	NA	ES	....	....	....
Washington, DC	Special Advisor......................................	Jared Lang..........................	SC	GS	12	....	....
Washington, DC	Special Assistant....................................	Quristin Walker...................	SC	GS	11	....	....
Washington, DC	Assistant Secretary, Counterterrorism, Threat Prevention, and Law Enforcement Policy.	Jeohn Favors........................	NA	ES	....	....	....
Washington, DC	Principal Deputy Assistant Secretary for Counterterrorism, Threat Prevention, and Law Enforcement.	Lucian Sikorskyj	NA	ES	....	....	....
Washington, DC	Deputy Assistant Secretary for Screening and Vetting.	Career Incumbent	CA	ES	....	....	....
Washington, DC	Deputy Assistant Secretary for Countering Transnational Organized Crime.	Career Incumbent	CA	ES	....	....	....
Washington, DC	Deputy Assistant Secretary for Law Enforcement.	Career Incumbent	CA	ES	....	....	....
Washington, DC	Director, Targeted Violence and Terrorism Prevention.	Career Incumbent	CA	ES	....	....	....
Washington, DC	Assistant Secretary for International Affairs....	Vacant	....	ES	....	....	....
Washington, DC	Deputy Assistant Secretary for International Affairs (Eastern Hemisphere).	Career Incumbent	CA	ES	....	....	....
Washington, DC	Special Assistant....................................	Nathan Williams	SC	GS	15	....	....
Washington, DC	Executive Director, International Affairs...........	Career Incumbent	CA	ES	....	....	....
London, Unit	Department of Homeland Security Attaché to European Union.	Vacant	....	ES	....	....	....
Washington, DC	Assistant Secretary for Border Security and Immigration.	Royce Murray	NA	ES	....	....	....
Washington, DC	Deputy Assistant Secretary for Immigration Policy.	Adam Hunter........................	NA	ES	....	....	....
Washington, DC	Deputy Assistant Secretary for Border Policy...	Career Incumbent	CA	ES	....	....	....
Washington, DC	Special Assistant (Border and Immigration).....	John Pratt...........................	SC	GS	11	....	....
Washington, DC	Assistant Secretary for Cyber, Infrastructure, Risk, and Resilience.	Iranga Kahangama	NA	ES	....	....	....

DEPARTMENT OF HOMELAND SECURITY—Continued

Location	Position Title	Name of Incumbent	Type of Appt.	Pay Plan	Level, Grade, or Pay	Tenure	Expires
Washington, DC	Senior Advisor...	Uttara Sivaram	SC	GS	15	....	....
Washington, DC	Policy Advisor...	William Bishop	SC	GS	13	....	....
Washington, DC	Special Advisor...	Sina Nemazi	SC	GS	12	....	....
Washington, DC	Assistant Secretary for Trade and Economic Security.	Christa Brzozowski	PA	OT	....	....	....
Washington, DC	Deputy Assistant Secretary for Trade Policy	Career Incumbent	CA	ES	....	....	....
Washington, DC	Policy Advisor...	Laura Murphy	SC	GS	15	....	....
Washington, DC	Policy Advisor...	Victoria Murrieta	SC	GS	14	....	....
Washington, DC	Senior Policy Analyst................................	Andrew Dolan......................	SC	GS	14	....	....
Washington, DC	Deputy Assistant Secretary, Strategic Integration and Policy Planning.	Daniel White........................	NA	ES	....	....	....
Washington, DC	Senior Counselor......................................	Jennifer C Daskal	NA	ES	....	....	....
Washington, DC	Senior Counselor......................................	Tracy Pakulniewicz..............	NA	ES	....	....	....
Washington, DC	Senior Advisor...	Alejandro Rosenkranz..........	SC	GS	15	....	....
Washington, DC	Policy Advisor...	Wells Bennett	SC	GS	15	....	....
	OFFICE OF INTELLIGENCE AND ANALYSIS						
Washington, DC	Under Secretary for Intelligence and Analysis .	Kenneth L Wainstein	PAS	EX	III	....	....
Washington, DC	Director, Counterterrorism Center....................	Vacant	....	ES		....	....
	OFFICE OF THE GENERAL COUNSEL						
Washington, DC	General Counsel	Jonathan E Meyer................	PAS	EX	IV	....	....
Washington, DC	Principal Deputy General Counsel....................	Career Incumbent	CA	ES		....	....
Washington, DC	Deputy General Counsel............................	Joseph Jackson Eaton..........	NA	ES		....	....
Washington, DC	Counselor to the General Counsel....................	Vacant	....	ES		....	....
Washington, DC	Senior Advisor to the General Counsel..............	Stephen Jonas	NA	ES		....	....
Washington, DC	Senior Advisor to the General Counsel..............	Vacant	....	ES		....	....
Washington, DC	Deputy General Counsel (Regulatory, Oversight, and Litigation).	Vacant	....	ES		....	....
Washington, DC	Deputy General Counsel (Immigration)	Kara Lynum	NA	ES		....	....
Washington, DC	Special Assistant..	Brianna Smith......................	SC	GS	11	....	....
Washington, DC	Oversight Counsel	Victoria Clark	SC	GS	14	....	....
Washington, DC	Oversight Counsel	Jonathan Parnes	SC	GS	15	....	....
Washington, DC	Associate General Counsel for General Law	Career Incumbent	CA	ES		....	....
Washington, DC	Associate General Counsel for Legal Counsel...	Career Incumbent	CA	ES		....	....
Washington, DC	Associate General Counsel for Intelligence	Career Incumbent	CA	ES		....	....
Washington, DC	Associate General Counsel for Regulatory Affairs.	Career Incumbent	CA	ES		....	....
Washington, DC	Associate General Counsel for Operations and Enforcement.	Vacant	....	ES		....	....
Washington, DC	Associate General Counsel for Technology Programs.	Career Incumbent	CA	ES		....	....
Washington, DC	Associate General Counsel for Immigration......	Career Incumbent	CA	ES		....	....
Washington, DC	Deputy General Counsel (Cyber and Technology).	Vacant	....	ES		....	....
	OFFICE OF PUBLIC AFFAIRS						
Washington, DC	Assistant Secretary for Public Affairs............	Daniel Watson	PA	EX	IV	....	....
Washington, DC	Principal Deputy Assistant Secretary for Communications.	Luis Miranda........................	NA	ES		....	....
Washington, DC	Principal Deputy Assistant Secretary for Public Affairs.	Vacant	....	ES		....	....
Washington, DC	Deputy Assistant Secretary for Strategic Communications.	Jeff Solnet............................	NA	ES		....	....
Washington, DC	Special Assistant..	Beatrice Brawer	SC	GS	11	....	....
Washington, DC	Chief of Staff...	Career Incumbent	CA	ES		....	....
Washington, DC	Deputy Assistant Secretary for Media Relations.	Sarah Schakow	NA	ES		....	....
Washington, DC	Director of Strategic Communications and Speechwriting.	John Davies	SC	GS	15	....	....
Washington, DC	Manager for Communications and Outreach	Anna McMahon	SC	GS	12	....	....
Washington, DC	Social Media Director....................................	Jennifer Tyre	SC	GS	13	....	....
Washington, DC	Deputy Director for Social Media....................	Christopher Ryan..................	SC	GS	12	....	....
Washington, DC	Deputy Press Secretary................................	Erin Heeter..........................	SC	GS	13	....	....
Washington, DC	Deputy Press Secretary................................	Nareetorn Ketudat..............	SC	GS	13	....	....
Washington, DC	Assistant Press Secretary	Dana Gallagher....................	SC	GS	12	....	....
Washington, DC	Assistant Press Secretary	Patrick McGovern	SC	GS	11	....	....
Washington, DC	Assistant Press Secretary	Mayra Rodriguez..................	SC	GS	12	....	....
Washington, DC	Assistant Press Secretary	Alexander Howard	SC	GS	12	....	....
Washington, DC	Press Assistant	Jazmin Sellars......................	SC	GS	12	....	....
	OFFICE OF LEGISLATIVE AFFAIRS						
Washington, DC	Assistant Secretary for Legislative Affairs........	Zephranie Buetow	PA	EX	IV	....	....

DEPARTMENT OF HOMELAND SECURITY—Continued

Location	Position Title	Name of Incumbent	Type of Appt.	Pay Plan	Level, Grade, or Pay	Tenure	Expires
Washington, DC	Deputy Assistant Secretary for Legislative Affairs (Senate).	Stephanie Doherty	NA	ES	....	....	....
Washington, DC	Deputy Assistant Secretary for Legislative Affairs (House Liaison).	Vacant	....	ES	....	....	....
Washington, DC	Chief of Staff....................	Chloe I Himmel	SC	GS	15	....	....
Washington, DC	Senior Advisor to the Assistant Secretary........	Shaeda Ahmadi	SC	GS	14	....	....
Washington, DC	Director of Legislative Affairs	Aimee Collins-Mandeville....	SC	GS	15	....	....
Washington, DC	Senior Advisor for Legislative Affairs (Oversight).	Jacob Marx	SC	GS	15	....	....
Washington, DC	Director of Legislative Affairs, Oversight	Koushik Pal	SC	GS	15	....	....
	OFFICE OF HEALTH SECURITY						
Washington, DC	Chief Medical Officer....................	Vacant	....	EX	....	....	....
	OFFICE FOR CIVIL RIGHTS AND CIVIL LIBERTIES						
Washington, DC	Officer for Civil Rights and Civil Liberties	Shoba Wadhia..................	PA	OT	....	....	....
Washington, DC	Senior Advisor...........................	Lauren Skompinski..............	SC	GS	15	....	....
	COUNTERING WEAPONS OF MASS DESTRUCTION OFFICE						
Washington, DC	Assistant Secretary of Countering Weapons of Mass Destruction.	Mary Ellen Callahan	PA	OT	....	....	....
Washington, DC	Principal Deputy Assistant Secretary...............	Career Incumbent	CA	ES	....	....	....
Washington, DC	Deputy Assistant Secretary for Systems Support.	Career Incumbent	CA	ES	....	30	....
Washington, DC	Deputy Assistant Secretary for Enterprise Services.	Career Incumbent	CA	ES	....	....	....
Washington, DC	Senior Advisor...........................	Christopher Ramos	SC	GS	15	....	....
Washington, DC	Special Advisor...........................	Edward Haver	SC	GS	12	....	....
	OFFICE OF HOMELAND SECURITY SITUATIONAL AWARENESS (OSA)						
Washington, DC	Director, Office of Homeland Security Situational Awareness.	Career Incumbent	CA	ES	....	....	....
Washington, DC	Deputy Director, Office of Homeland Security Situational Awareness.	Career Incumbent	CA	ES	....	....	....
Washington, DC	Chief of Staff...........................	Career Incumbent	CA	ES	....	....	....
Washington, DC	Director, Integration Division	Career Incumbent	CA	ES	....	....	....
Washington, DC	Director, National Operations Center...............	Career Incumbent	CA	ES	....	....	....
Washington, DC	Director, Operations Coordination Division.......	Vacant	....	ES	....	....	....
	OFFICE OF PARTNERSHIP AND ENGAGEMENT						
Washington, DC	Assistant Secretary, Office of Partnership and Engagement.	Fayrouz F Saad	NA	ES	....	....	....
Washington, DC	Principal Deputy Assistant Secretary, Office of Partnership and Engagement.	Rebecca Sternhell................	NA	ES	....	....	....
Washington, DC	Chief of Staff...........................	Nathaniel L Snyder	SC	GS	15	....	....
Washington, DC	Partnership and Engagement Specialist	Erika Amaya........................	SC	GS	14	....	....
Washington, DC	Partnership and Engagement Specialist	Edgar Estrada	SC	GS	14	....	....
Washington, DC	Deputy Assistant Secretary for Intergovernmental Affairs.	Vacant	....	ES	....	....	....
Washington, DC	Intergovernmental Affairs Associate Director...	Scott Genzink	SC	GS	14	....	....
Washington, DC	Intergovernmental Affairs Associate Director...	Cedric McMinn	SC	GS	14	....	....
Washington, DC	Intergovernmental Affairs Associate Director...	Marcella Richardson	SC	GS	14	....	....
Washington, DC	Deputy Assistant Secretary for Private Sector Office.	Vacant	....	ES	....	....	....
	PRIVACY OFFICE						
Washington, DC	Chief Privacy Officer and Chief Freedom of Information Act Officer.	Mason Clutter	NA	ES	....	....	....
Washington, DC	Deputy Chief Privacy Officer..........................	Career Incumbent	CA	ES	....	....	....
Washington, DC	Deputy Chief Freedom of Information Act Officer.	Career Incumbent	CA	ES	....	....	....
Washington, DC	Senior Advisor...........................	Annan Mortensen	SC	GS	15	....	....
Washington, DC	Special Policy Advisor and Director for Strategy and Integration.	Brent A Robinson	SC	GS	15	....	....
Washington, DC	Special Assistant...........................	Heavin Hunter	SC	GS	12	....	....
	OFFICE OF THE OMBUDSMAN FOR IMMIGRATION DETENTION						
Washington, DC	Immigration Detention Ombudsman.................	Michelle Brané	NA	ES	....	....	....
Washington, DC	Deputy Ombudsman, Office of Immigration Detention Ombudsman.	Career Incumbent	CA	ES	....	....	....
Washington, DC	Senior Advisor...........................	Christopher Brundage	TA	ES	....	....	....

DEPARTMENT OF HOMELAND SECURITY—Continued

Location	Position Title	Name of Incumbent	Type of Appt.	Pay Plan	Level, Grade, or Pay	Tenure	Expires
	OFFICE OF CITIZENSHIP AND IMMIGRATION SERVICES OMBUDSMAN						
Washington, DC	Citizenship and Immigration Services Ombudsman.	Vacant	....	ES	....	....	....
Washington, DC	Deputy Director, Office of Citizenship and Immigration Services Ombudsman.	Career Incumbent	CA	ES	....	....	....
	U.S. CITIZENSHIP AND IMMIGRATION SERVICES						
Camp Springs, MD .	Director, United States Citizenship and Immigration Services.	Ur Mendoza Jaddou............	PAS	EX	III	....	....
Washington, DC	Deputy Director, Citizenship and Immigration Services.	Career Incumbent	CA	ES	....	....	....
Camp Springs, MD .	Chief of Staff...	Felicia A Escobar Carrillo....	NA	ES	....	....	....
Camp Springs, MD .	Senior Counselor and Strategic Policy Advisor to the Director (USCIS).	Emilie R Hyams	NA	ES	....	....	....
Washington, DC	Associate Director, External Affairs...................	Career Incumbent	CA	ES	....	....	....
Camp Springs, MD .	Chief, Office of Legislative Affairs....................	Luz Mendez	NA	ES	....	....	....
Camp Springs, MD .	Chief, Office of Public Affairs	Brenda Gonzalez	NA	ES	....	....	....
Washington, DC	Chief, Citizenship and Applicant Information Services.	Career Incumbent	CA	ES	....	....	....
Camp Springs, MD .	Chief, Office of Citizenship, Partnership and Engagement.	Eva A Millona.......................	NA	ES	....	....	....
Camp Springs, MD .	Chief Counsel..	Afsaneh Tabaddor	NA	ES	....	....	....
Washington, DC	Principal Deputy Chief Counsel	Career Incumbent	CA	ES	....	....	....
Camp Springs, MD .	Chief, Office of Policy and Strategy...................	Avideh Moussavian	NA	ES	....	....	....
Camp Springs, MD .	Senior Advisor...	Blas Nunez-Neto	NA	ES	....	....	....
Camp Springs, MD .	Deputy Chief Human Capital Officer for Talent Management and Employee Experience.	Career Incumbent	CA	ES	....	....	....
Washington, DC	Deputy Chief Human Capital Office for Talent Acquisition and Stakeholder Services.	Career Incumbent	CA	ES	....	....	....
Camp Springs, MD .	Deputy Chief of Staff....................................	Joshua Wodka......................	SC	GS	15	....	....
Camp Springs, MD .	Senior Advisor for Customer Experience...........	Bitta Mostofi........................	SC	GS	15	....	....
Camp Springs, MD .	Senior Advisor..	Douglas Rand	SC	GS	15	....	....
New York, NY..........	Policy and Regulatory Advisor to the Director..	Huma Shah..........................	SC	GS	14	....	....
	UNITED STATES COAST GUARD						
Washington, DC	Director for Civil Rights...............................	Career Incumbent	CA	ES	....	....	....
Washington, DC	Director of Civilian Human Resources	Career Incumbent	CA	ES	....	....	....
Washington, DC	Director of Commercial Regulations and Standards.	Career Incumbent	CA	ES	....	....	....
Washington, DC	Deputy Judge Advocate General and Deputy Chief Counsel.	Career Incumbent	CA	ES	....	....	....
Washington, DC	Deputy Assistant Commandant for Engineering and Logistics.	Career Incumbent	CA	ES	....	....	....
Washington, DC	Director, Shore Infrastructure Bill Execution Program.	Robert J Thomas	TA	ES	....	....	....
Norfolk, VA	Deputy, Director Operational Logistics Command.	Career Incumbent	CA	ES	....	....	....
Washington, DC	Deputy, Force Readiness Command	Career Incumbent	CA	ES	....	....	....
Washington, DC	Director, International Affairs and Foreign Policy Advisor.	Career Incumbent	CA	ES	....	....	....
	U.S. CUSTOMS AND BORDER PROTECTION						
Washington, DC	Commissioner, United States Customs and Border Protection.	Vacant	....	EX	....	....	....
Washington, DC	Chief of Staff..	Nathaniel Kaine....................	NA	ES	....	....	....
Washington, DC	Chief Counsel...	Career Incumbent	CA	ES	....	....	....
Washington, DC	Assistant Commissioner, Office of Public Affairs.	Erin M Waters.......................	NA	ES	....	....	....
Washington, DC	Assistant Commissioner for Congressional Affairs.	Vacant	....	ES	....	....	....
Washington, DC	Executive Director, Trade Relations..................	Felicia Pullam......................	NA	ES	....	....	....
Washington, DC	Executive Director of Policy and Planning........	Vacant	....	ES	....	....	....
Washington, DC	Counselor to the Commissioner......................	Abigail Shenkle	NA	ES	....	....	....
Washington, DC	Deputy Chief of Staff....................................	Kenneth Syring	SC	GS	15	....	....
Washington, DC	Senior Advisor..	Kevin Flores	SC	GS	15	....	....
Washington, DC	Senior Advisor to the Commissioner (Technology, Strategy and Delivery).	Manuel Tehan-Menendez	SC	GS	15	....	....
Washington, DC	Advisor to Commissioner	Sigrid Gonzalez	SC	GS	15	....	....
Washington, DC	Senior Advisor, Public Affairs	Vanessa Velasquez................	SC	GS	15	....	....
Washington, DC	Policy Advisor...	Robert Maes.........................	SC	GS	14	....	....

DEPARTMENT OF HOMELAND SECURITY—Continued

Location	Position Title	Name of Incumbent	Type of Appt.	Pay Plan	Level, Grade, or Pay	Tenure	Expires
	CYBERSECURITY AND INFRASTRUCTURE SECURITY AGENCY						
Washington, DC	Director, Cybersecurity and Infrastructure Security Agency.	Jennie Easterly	PAS	EX	II	....	....
Washington, DC	Deputy Director, Cybersecurity and Infrastructure Security Agency.	Nitin Natarajan...................	NA	ES	....	....	....
Washington, DC	Executive Assistant Director for Cybersecurity.	Jeffrey Greene	PA	OT	....	....	....
Washington, DC	Executive Assistant Director for Infrastructure Security.	Brian D A Mussington.........	PA	OT	....	....	....
Washington, DC	Senior Election Security Advisor......................	Caitlin Conley......................	NA	ES	....	....	....
Washington, DC	Chief of Staff...	Career Incumbent	CA	ES	....	....	....
Washington, DC	Director of Legislative Affairs	Vacant	....	ES	....	....	....
Washington, DC	Chief External Affairs Officer........................	Vacant	....	ES	....	....	....
Washington, DC	Chief Learning Officer	Career Incumbent	CA	ES	....	....	....
Washington, DC	Chief Counsel for Cybersecurity and Infrastructure Security Agency.	Career Incumbent	CA	ES	....	....	....
Washington, DC	Deputy Chief Counsel	Career Incumbent	CA	ES	....	....	....
Washington, DC	Chief, Workforce Engagement...........................	Michael Widomski	TA	ES	....	....	....
Arlington, VA...........	Executive Director for Intelligence Operations.	Zandreia Keys	TA	ES	....	....	....
Washington, DC	Associate Director for Exercise........................	Career Incumbent	CA	ES	....	....	....
Arlington, VA...........	Associate Director Bombing Prevention	Career Incumbent	CA	ES	....	....	....
Arlington, VA...........	Senior Technical Advisor................................	Leisel Bogan	SC	GS	15	....	....
Washington, DC	Senior Advisor for Strategic Communications and Operations.	Elizabeth A Murray	SC	GS	15	....	....
Washington, DC	Senior Advisor..	Cassandra Wilcox................	SC	GS	15	....	....
Washington, DC	Senior Advisor..	Vacant	....	ES	....	....	....
Washington, DC	Senior Advisor to the Director of Legislative Affairs.	Robert Bacon	SC	GS	15	....	....
Washington, DC	Director of Public Affairs	Michael C Feldman.............	SC	GS	14	....	....
Washington, DC	Policy Coordinator	Aaron Arriaga.....................	SC	GS	12	....	....
Washington, DC	Senior Advisor..	Vacant	....	ES	....	....	....
Washington, DC	Director, Strategy, Policy and Plans	Vacant	....	ES	....	....	....
Washington, DC	Senior Advisor..	Lauren Boas Hayes..............	SC	GS	15	....	....
Washington, DC	Senior Advisor..	Andrew Seiffert	SC	GS	15	....	....
Washington, DC	Senior Advisor for Public Affairs......................	Ronald Eckstein	SC	GS	14	....	....
	FEDERAL EMERGENCY MANAGEMENT AGENCY						
Washington, DC	Administrator for Federal Emergency Management Agency.	Deanne B Criswell	PAS	EX	II	....	....
Washington, DC	Deputy Administrator for Federal Emergency Management Agency.	Erik Hooks...........................	PAS	EX	III	....	....
Washington, DC	Chief of Staff...	Michael A Coen Jr...............	NA	ES	....	....	....
Washington, DC	Deputy Chief of Staff...................................	Jenna R Peters	NA	ES	....	....	....
Washington, DC	Deputy Administrator for Resilience................	Vacant	....	EX	....	....	....
Washington, DC	Associate Administrator for Resilience	Victoria Salinas	NA	ES	....	....	....
Washington, DC	Chief Counsel..	Career Incumbent	CA	ES	....	....	....
Washington, DC	Director, Law Enforcement Engagement and Integration.	Career Incumbent	CA	ES	....	....	....
Washington, DC	Associate Administrator for Policy, Program Analysis, and International Affairs.	Career Incumbent	CA	ES	....	....	....
Washington, DC	Associate Administrator for External Affairs....	Justin Knighten	NA	ES	....	....	....
Washington, DC	Director, Center for Faith-Based and Neighborhood Partnerships.	Vacant	....	ES	....	....	....
Washington, DC	Associate Administrator for the Office of National Continuity Programs.	Michael George.....................	NA	ES	....	....	....
Washington, DC	Deputy Associate Administrator, National Continuity Programs.	Career Incumbent	CA	ES	....	....	....
Bluemont, VA	Executive Administrator, Mount Weather Emergency Operations Center.	Career Incumbent	CA	ES	....	....	....
Washington, DC	Director, Continuity Division	Career Incumbent	CA	ES	....	....	....
Washington, DC	Assistant Administrator, Grants Programs	Pamela Williams..................	PA	EX	IV	....	....
Boston, MA	Regional Administrator, Region I	Lori Ehrlich	NA	ES	....	....	....
New York, NY.........	Regional Administrator, Region II.....................	David Warrington................	NA	ES	....	....	....
San Juan, PR...........	Federal Disaster Recovery Coordinator, San Juan, PR.	Career Incumbent	CA	ES	....	....	....
Philadelphia, PA	Regional Administrator, Region III	Career Incumbent	CA	ES	....	....	....
Atlanta, GA	Regional Administrator, Region IV....................	Career Incumbent	CA	ES	....	....	....
Chicago, IL	Regional Administrator, Region V	Thomas Sivak.......................	NA	ES	....	....	....
Denton, TX..............	Regional Administrator, Region VI....................	Career Incumbent	CA	ES	....	....	....
Kansas City, MO	Regional Administrator, Region VII	Andrea Spillars	NA	ES	....	....	....
Denver, CO	Regional Administrator, Region VIII.................	Nancy Dragani	NA	ES	....	....	....

DEPARTMENT OF HOMELAND SECURITY—Continued

Location	Position Title	Name of Incumbent	Type of Appt.	Pay Plan	Level, Grade, or Pay	Tenure	Expires
San Francisco, CA...	Regional Administrator, Region IX	Career Incumbent	CA	ES			
Seattle, WA	Regional Administrator, Region X	Willie Nunn	NA	ES			
Washington, DC	Administrator, United States Fire Administration.	Lori Moore-Merrell	PA	EX	IV		
Emmitsburg, MD	Deputy Assistant Administrator, U.S. Fire Administration.	Career Incumbent	CA	ES			
Emmitsburg, MD	Superintendent, National Fire Academy	Career Incumbent	CA	ES			
Washington, DC	Associate Administrator for Response and Recovery.	Vacant		ES			
Washington, DC	Deputy Associate Administrator for Response and Recovery.	Career Incumbent	CA	ES			
Washington, DC	Assistant Administrator for Response	Career Incumbent	CA	ES			
Washington, DC	Assistant Administrator for Recovery	Career Incumbent	CA	ES			
Washington, DC	Deputy Assistant Administrator for Recovery	Career Incumbent	CA	ES			
Washington, DC	Assistant Administrator, Logistics	Career Incumbent	CA	ES			
Washington, DC	Deputy Assistant Administrator, Logistics Support.	Career Incumbent	CA	ES			
Washington, DC	Deputy Assistant Administrator for Logistics Operations.	Career Incumbent	CA	ES			
Washington, DC	Chief Information Officer	Career Incumbent	CA	ES			
Washington, DC	Chief Human Capital Officer	Career Incumbent	CA	ES			
Washington, DC	Counselor to the Administrator (Technology, Strategy, and Delivery).	Christopher Frommann	SC	GS	15		
Washington, DC	Director of Legislative Affairs	Margarita Varela-Rosa	SC	GS	15		
Washington, DC	Director, Public Affairs and Planning Division	Jaclyn Rothenberg	SC	GS	15		
Washington, DC	Assistant Administrator, Environmental Planning and Historic Preservation.	Career Incumbent	CA	ES			
Washington, DC	National Incident Management Assistance Team Leader (Non-Stafford).	Career Incumbent	CA	ES			
Sacramento, CA	National Incident Management Assistance Team Leader, West.	Career Incumbent	CA	ES			
Herndon, VA	National Incident Management Assistance Team Leader, East.	Vacant		ES			
Washington, DC	National Incident Management Assistance Team Leader (Central).	Career Incumbent	CA	ES			
Washington, DC	Advisor	Emily Dunn	SC	GS	13		
Washington, DC	Special Assistant	Sarah Eskra	SC	GS	12		
Washington, DC	Special Assistant	Keihysha Cenord	SC	GS	11		
Washington, DC	Special Assistant	Aaron Chan	SC	GS	11		
Washington, DC	Senior Tribal Nations Advisor	Kelbie Kennedy	SC	GS	14		
	U.S. IMMIGRATION AND CUSTOMS ENFORCEMENT						
Washington, DC	Director, Immigration and Customs Enforcement.	Vacant		EX			
Washington, DC	Assistant Director, Office of Regulatory Affairs and Policy.	Scott Shuchart	NA	ES			
Washington, DC	Chief of Staff	Michael Lumpkin	NA	ES			
Washington, DC	Senior Advisor	Vacant		ES			
Washington, DC	Associate Director for External Affairs	Jonathon Bertran-Harris	NA	ES			
Washington, DC	Principal Legal Advisor	Kerry Doyle	NA	ES			
Washington, DC	Assistant Director, Office of Public Affairs	Vacant		ES			
Washington, DC	Assistant Director, Office of Detention Policy and Planning.	Claire R Trickler-McNulty	NA	ES			
Washington, DC	Assistant Director for Office of Partnership and Engagement.	Francey L Youngberg	NA	ES			
Washington, DC	Deputy Assistant Director of Public Affairs	Julian E Perez Melendez	SC	GS	15		
Washington, DC	Deputy Chief of Staff	Daniel Marquith	SC	GS	15		
Washington, DC	Advisor for External Affairs	Hamza Rahman	SC	GS	12		
	TRANSPORTATION SECURITY ADMINISTRATION						
Springfield, VA	Administrator, Transportation Security Administration.	David P Pekoske	PAS	EX	II		
Springfield, VA	Deputy Administrator, Transportation Security Administration.	Holly E Canevari	PA	EX	III		
Springfield, VA	Assistant Administrator of Legislative Affairs	Charles M Makings	XS	OT			
Springfield, VA	Assistant Administrator for Strategic Communications and Public Affairs.	Alexa Lopez	XS	OT			
Springfield, VA	Chief of Staff	Vacant		OT			
Springfield, VA	Executive Director for Strategy, Policy Coordination, and Innovation.	Harlan C Geer	XS	OT			
Springfield, VA	Senior Counselor for Industry Engagement	Vacant		OT			
Springfield, VA	Senior Counselor	Riki Parikh	XS	OT			

DEPARTMENT OF HOMELAND SECURITY—Continued

Location	Position Title	Name of Incumbent	Type of Appt.	Pay Plan	Level, Grade, or Pay	Tenure	Expires
Springfield, VA	Senior Counselor..	Michael S Herman	NA	ES	....	....	....
Springfield, VA	Counselor..	Faiza Khan	SC	OT	....	....	....
Springfield, VA	Speechwriter	Christopher Peleo-Lazar......	SC	OT	....	....	....
Springfield, VA	Advisor for Strategy, Policy Coordination and Innovation.	Ethan Tan	SC	OT	....	....	....
Springfield, VA	Executive Assistant Administrator for Enterprise Support.	Julie A Scanlon...................	XS	OT	....	....	....
Springfield, VA	Executive Assistant Administrator for Operations Support.	Vacant	....	OT	....	....	....
Springfield, VA	Executive Assistant Administrator for Security Operations.	Melanie Harvey....................	XS	OT	....	....	....
Springfield, VA	Executive Assistant Administrator for Law Enforcement/Federal Air Marshals.	Brian C Belcher....................	XS	OT	....	....	....
Springfield, VA	Deputy Executive Assistant Administrator for Enterprise Support.	Kimberly Hutchinson...........	XS	OT	....	....	....
Springfield, VA	Deputy Executive Assistant Administrator for Operations Support.	Chad Gorman	XS	OT	....	....	....
Springfield, VA	Deputy Executive Assistant Administrator for Security Operations.	Steve C Lorincz	XS	OT	....	....	....
Springfield, VA	Deputy Executive Assistant Administrator/Deputy Director, Office of Law Enforcement/Federal Air Marshal Service.	Vacant	....	OT	....	....	....
Springfield, VA	Assistant Administrator for Acquisitions Program Management.	Mario Wilson	XS	OT	....	....	....
Springfield, VA	Assistant Administrator, Civil Rights and Liberties Ombudsman/Traveler Engagement.	Christine Griggs..................	XS	OT	....	....	....
Springfield, VA	Assistant Administrator, Compliance.................	Kevin Frederick....................	XS	OT	....	....	....
Springfield, VA	Assistant Administrator, Office of Contracting and Procurement.	Dina Thompson	XS	OT	....	....	....
Springfield, VA	Assistant Administrator, Domestic Aviation Operations.	Michael C Morgan-Rottman.	XS	OT	....	....	....
Springfield, VA	Assistant Administrator, Enrollment Services and Vetting Programs.	John N Latta	XS	OT	....	....	....
Springfield, VA	Assistant Administrator, Field Operations Division.	William R Aupperlee............	XS	OT	....	....	....
Springfield, VA	Assistant Administrator, Flight Operations Division.	Vacant	....	OT	....	....	....
Springfield, VA	Assistant Administrator for Human Capital.....	Jason L Nelson.....................	XS	OT	....	....	....
Springfield, VA	Assistant Administrator for Inspections............	Susan M Tashiro	XS	OT	....	....	....
Springfield, VA	Assistant Administrator, Office of Intelligence and Analysis.	Nancy Nykamp.....................	XS	OT	....	....	....
Springfield, VA	Assistant Administrator, Office of International Operations.	Gary O Renfrow	XS	OT	....	....	....
Springfield, VA	Assistant Administrator, Investigations	Kimberley Thompson	XS	OT	....	....	....
Springfield, VA	Assistant Administrator, Operations Management.	Brett A Gunter	XS	OT	....	....	....
Springfield, VA	Assistant Administrator, Operations Management.	Rana Khan...........................	XS	OT	....	....	....
Springfield, VA	Assistant Administrator, Operations Management.	Karen R Shelton-Waters......	XS	OT	....	....	....
Springfield, VA	Assistant Administrator for Policy, Plans and Engagement.	Eddie D Mayenschein	XS	OT	....	....	....
Springfield, VA	Assistant Administrator, Office of Requirements and Capabilities Analysis.	Austin Gould	XS	OT	....	....	....
Springfield, VA	Assistant Administrator, Security and Administrative Services.	Larry Smith..........................	XS	OT	....	....	....
Springfield, VA	Assistant Administrator, Surface Operations....	Sonya T Proctor...................	XS	OT	....	....	....
Springfield, VA	Assistant Administrator, Office of Training and Development.	Tina Cariola.........................	XS	OT	....	....	....
Springfield, VA	Assistant Administrator/Chief Financial Officer.	Holly C Mehringer	XS	OT	....	....	....
Springfield, VA	Assistant Administrator/Chief Information Officer.	Opeyemi Oshinnaiye............	XS	OT	....	....	....
Springfield, VA	Chief Counsel..	Francine J Kerner................	XS	OT	....	....	....
Springfield, VA	Chief Diversity, Equity, Inclusion, and Accessibility Officer.	Vernell Sutherland...............	XS	OT	....	....	....
Springfield, VA	Chief Innovation Officer....................................	Steven R Parker	XS	OT	....	....	....
Springfield, VA	Chief Technology Officer/Chief Data Officer	James Gilkeson	XS	OT	....	....	....
Springfield, VA	Deputy Assistant Administrator for Acquisitions Program Management.	Kenneth Lee	XS	OT	....	....	....

DEPARTMENT OF HOMELAND SECURITY—Continued

Location	Position Title	Name of Incumbent	Type of Appt.	Pay Plan	Level, Grade, or Pay	Tenure	Expires
Springfield, VA	Deputy Assistant Administrator, Civil Rights and Liberties, Ombudsman/Traveler Engagement.	Seena Foster	XS	OT			
Springfield, VA	Deputy Assistant Administrator, Compliance ...	Nikki R Harding	XS	OT			
Springfield, VA	Deputy Assistant Administrator, Office of Contracting and Procurement.	Vacant		OT			
Springfield, VA	Deputy Assistant Administrator, Domestic Aviation Operations.	Michael D Turner	XS	OT			
Springfield, VA	Deputy Assistant Administrator, Enrollment Services and Vetting Programs.	Donald Lombardo	XS	OT			
Springfield, VA	Deputy Assistant Administrator for Human Capital.	Linwood T Smith	XS	OT			
Springfield, VA	Deputy Assistant Administrator for Intelligence and Analysis.	Hao-y Froemling	XS	OT			
Springfield, VA	Deputy Assistant Administrator, Office of International Operations.	Anthony Monreal	XS	OT			
Springfield, VA	Deputy Assistant Administrator for Policy, Plans and Engagement.	Robert P Vente	XS	OT			
Springfield, VA	Deputy Assistant Administrator, Office of Requirements and Capabilities Analysis.	Christina L Peach	XS	OT			
Springfield, VA	Deputy Assistant Administrator, Strategic Communications and Public Affairs.	Amelia L Roberson	XS	OT			
Springfield, VA	Deputy Assistant Administrator, Surface Operations.	Ronald A Pavlik	XS	OT			
Springfield, VA	Deputy Assistant Administrator, Office of Training and Development.	Jason P DePasquale	XS	OT			
Springfield, VA	Deputy Assistant Administrator/Chief Security Officer.	Clifford McCoy	XS	OT			
Springfield, VA	Deputy Assistant Administrator/Deputy Chief Financial Officer.	Christopher W Toms	XS	OT			
Springfield, VA	Deputy Assistant Administrator/Deputy Chief Information Officer.	Kristin Ruiz	XS	OT			
Springfield, VA	Deputy Chief Counsel for Enforcement and Incident Management.	Vacant		OT			
Springfield, VA	Deputy Chief Counsel for Field Operations	Michael Feikes	XS	OT			
Springfield, VA	Deputy Chief Counsel (General Law)	Jennifer Ellison	XS	OT			
Springfield, VA	Deputy Chief Counsel (Legislation and Authorities).	John A Wasowicz	XS	OT			
Springfield, VA	Deputy Chief Counsel for Litigation	Michael R Gaches	XS	OT			
Springfield, VA	Deputy Chief Counsel (Operations)	Mary Kate Whalen	XS	OT			
Springfield, VA	Deputy Chief Counsel for Procurement	Ross W Dembling	XS	OT			
Springfield, VA	Deputy Chief Counsel for Regulations and Security Standards.	Susan M Prosnitz	XS	OT			
Springfield, VA	Deputy Chief of Staff	Myung H Kim	XS	OT			
Queens, NY	Deputy Federal Security Director (DFSD) – Operations, John F Kennedy International Airport.	Valerie Doyle	XS	OT			
Newark, NJ	Deputy Federal Security Director (Operations), Newark Liberty International Airport; Newark, New Jersey.	Alicia R Elsetinow	XS	OT			
Newark, NJ	Deputy Federal Security Director (Security), Newark Liberty International Airport; Newark, New Jersey.	Vacant		OT			
Queens, NY	Deputy Federal Security Director (Security), John F Kennedy Airport; New York.	Przemyslaw Smolinski	XS	OT			
Los Angeles, CA	Deputy Federal Security Director (Security), Los Angeles International Airport; Los Angeles, California.	Vacant		OT			
Los Angeles, CA	Deputy Federal Security Director – Security (Spokes and Hubs), Los Angeles International Airport.	Cheri N Baez	XS	OT			
Boston, MA	Deputy Federal Security Director, Boston Logan International Airport; Boston, Massachusetts.	Marcy Donnelly	XS	OT			
Chicago, IL	Deputy Federal Security Director, O'Hare International Airport; Chicago, Illinois.	Brian E Moses	XS	OT			
Las Vegas, NV	Deputy Federal Security Director, McCarran International Airport; Las Vegas, Nevada.	Daniel Wyllie	XS	OT			
Miami, FL	Deputy Federal Security Director, Miami International Airport; Miami, Florida.	John T Lewis	XS	OT			
Phoenix, AZ	Deputy Federal Security Director, Phoenix International Airport; Phoenix, Arizona.	Lisa B Christenson	XS	OT			
Arlington, VA	Deputy Federal Security Director, Reagan National Airport; Washington, DC.	Ron Mildiner	XS	OT			

DEPARTMENT OF HOMELAND SECURITY—Continued

Location	Position Title	Name of Incumbent	Type of Appt.	Pay Plan	Level, Grade, or Pay	Tenure	Expires
Dulles Airport, VA...	Deputy Federal Security Director; Washington-Dulles International Airport; Fairfax, Virginia.	Eric A Beane	XS	OT			
Springfield, VA	Executive Director, Administrative Services	Kimberly R Harrison	XS	OT			
Springfield, VA	Executive Director, Administrative Services	Jon Kessmeier	XS	OT			
Springfield, VA	Executive Director, Administrative Services, Security Division.	David H Wilkinson	XS	OT			
Springfield, VA	Executive Director, Administrative Services	Talin Zarookian	XS	OT			
Springfield, VA	Executive Director, Air Cargo Division	Benjamin Currier	XS	OT			
Springfield, VA	Executive Director, Analysis and Engineering	Erick J Rekstad	XS	OT			
Springfield, VA	Executive Director, Aviation Division	Robert M Rottman	XS	OT			
Springfield, VA	Executive Director, Budget Division	Annemarie Juhlin	XS	OT			
Springfield, VA	Executive Director, Capability Management and Innovation.	Melissa D Conley	XS	OT			
Springfield, VA	Executive Director, Coordination and Analysis Division.	Dennis G Scarborough	XS	OT			
Springfield, VA	Executive Director, Equal Opportunity and Civil Liberties.	Cyrus Salazar	XS	OT			
Springfield, VA	Executive Director, Financial Management Division.	Hee Kwon Song	XS	OT			
Springfield, VA	Executive Director, Human Capital Operations.	Natasha Sikorsky	XS	OT			
Springfield, VA	Executive Director, Information Assurance and Cyber Security Division.	Darryl Gingles	XS	OT			
Springfield, VA	Executive Director, Information Technology (IT) Delivery.	Balaji Subramaniam	XS	OT			
Springfield, VA	Executive Director, Information Technology (IT) Operations.	Robert Vojtik	XS	OT			
Springfield, VA	Executive Director, Intelligence	Mary Quinn	XS	OT			
Springfield, VA	Executive Director, International Policies and Programs.	Eric Yatar	XS	OT			
Springfield, VA	Executive Director, Large Hubs	Jenel L Chang	XS	OT			
Springfield, VA	Executive Director, Medium Hubs	Julian Williams	XS	OT			
Springfield, VA	Executive Director, Real Property Division	Peter McVey Jr	XS	OT			
Springfield, VA	Executive Director, Screening Systems	Adam P Caughran	XS	OT			
Springfield, VA	Executive Director, Small Hubs	Carolyn Dorgham	XS	OT			
Springfield, VA	Executive Director, Surface Operations	Kerwin Phillip Wilson	XS	OT			
Springfield, VA	Executive Director, Surface Policy	Scott Gorton	XS	OT			
Springfield, VA	Executive Director, Test and Evaluation	Thomas Tomaiko	XS	OT			
Springfield, VA	Executive Director, Training Centers Division	Vacant		OT			
Springfield, VA	Executive Director, Traveler Engagement	Jose Bonilla	XS	OT			
Springfield, VA	Executive Director, Vetting	Erinn L Wagner	XS	OT			
Baltimore, MD	Federal Security Director, Baltimore-Washington International Airport; Baltimore, Maryland.	Christopher Murgia	XS	OT			
Boston, MA	Federal Security Director, Boston Logan International Airport; Boston, Massachusetts.	Robert P Allison	XS	OT			
Chicago, IL	Federal Security Director, O'Hare International Airport; Chicago, Illinois.	James M Spriggs	XS	OT			
Dallas, TX	Federal Security Director, Dallas/Fort Worth International Airport; Dallas, Texas.	Kriste M Jordan	XS	OT			
Honolulu, HI	Federal Security Director, Honolulu International Airport, Honolulu, Hawaii.	Nanea G Vasta	XS	OT			
Denver, CO	Federal Security Director, Denver International Airport; Aurora, Colorado.	Douglas Cruz	XS	OT			
Detroit, MI	Federal Security Director, Detroit Airport; Detroit, Michigan.	Reginald L Stephens	XS	OT			
Fort Lauderdale, FL.	Federal Security Director, Fort Lauderdale-Hollywood International Airport; Fort Lauderdale, Florida.	Jason Martin	XS	OT			
Houston, TX	Federal Security Director, George Bush International Airport; Houston, Texas.	Juan Sanchez Jr	XS	OT			
Las Vegas, NV	Federal Security Director, McCarrin International Airport; Las Vegas, Nevada.	Karen Burke	XS	OT			
Atlanta, GA	Federal Security Director, Atlanta International Airport; Atlanta, Georgia.	Robert Spinden	XS	OT			
Queens, NY	Federal Security Director, John F Kennedy Airport; New York.	John Essig	XS	OT			
Queens, NY	Federal Security Director, La Guardia International Airport; New York.	Robert A Duffy	XS	OT			
Los Angeles, CA	Federal Security Director, Los Angeles International Airport; Los Angeles, California.	Jason G Pantages	XS	OT			

DEPARTMENT OF HOMELAND SECURITY—Continued

Location	Position Title	Name of Incumbent	Type of Appt.	Pay Plan	Level, Grade, or Pay	Tenure	Expires
San Juan, PR..........	Federal Security Director, Luis Munoz Marin International Airport; San Juan, Puerto Rico.	Mariely Loperena Moure.....	XS	OT	....	....	....
Miami, FL...............	Federal Security Director, Miami International Airport; Miami, Florida.	Stephen G Taber	XS	OT	....	....	....
Minneapolis, MN.....	Federal Security Director, Minneapolis/St Paul International Airport; Minneapolis, Minnesota.	Martin W Robinson..............	XS	OT	....	....	....
Nashville, TN	Federal Security Director, Nashville International Airport, Nashville, Tennessee.	Stephen Wood	XS	OT	....	....	....
Newark, NJ	Federal Security Director, Newark International Airport; Newark, New Jersey.	Thomas J Carter	XS	OT	....	....	....
Philadelphia, PA	Federal Security Director, Philadelphia International Airport; Philadelphia, PA.	Gerardo J Spero	XS	OT	....	....	....
Phoenix, AZ	Federal Security Director, Phoenix International Airport; Phoenix, Arizona.	Jerry W Agnew	XS	OT	....	....	....
Arlington, VA...........	Federal Security Director, Reagan National Airport; Washington, DC.	John Busch	XS	OT	....	....	....
Salt Lake City, UT..	Federal Security Director, Salt Lake City International Airport; Salt Lake City, Utah.	Ryan M Davis......................	XS	OT	....	....	....
San Francisco, CA...	Federal Security Director, San Francisco International Airport; San Francisco, California.	Fred H Lau	XS	OT	....	....	....
Seattle, WA.............	Federal Security Director, Seattle-Tacoma International Airport; Seattle, Washington.	Gregory Hawko....................	XS	OT	....	....	....
Dulles, VA	Federal Security Director, Washington-Dulles International Airport; Fairfax, Virginia.	Scott T Johnson	XS	OT	....	....	....
Orlando, FL	Federal Security Director; Orlando International Airport; Orlando, Florida.	Pete R Garcia	XS	OT	....	....	....
San Diego, CA	Federal Security Director; San Diego International Airport; San Diego, California.	Kathleen A Connon..............	XS	OT	....	....	....
Singapore.................	Regional Director (Asia-Pacific Region), Singapore.	Stephanie L Metzger............	XS	OT	....	....	....
Germany	Regional Director (Europe)	Demetrios Lambropoulos.....	XS	OT	....	....	....
Ethiopia	Regional Director (Middle East/Africa)..............	Jason E Schwabel................	XS	OT	....	....	....
Miami, FL................	Regional Director (Western Hemisphere/Miami).	Dwaine Antonio Murray	XS	OT	....	....	....
Queens, NY..............	Regional Director, Region 1 (Northeast Region).	Marisa M Maola	XS	OT	....	....	....
Atlanta, GA	Regional Security Director, Atlanta, Georgia	Mary Leftridge-Byrd	XS	OT	....	....	....
Chicago, IL	Regional Security Director, Chicago, Illinois	Fredrick Stein......................	XS	OT	....	....	....
Dallas, TX	Regional Director, Region 4 (South Central Region).	Melvin J Carraway	XS	OT	....	....	....
Seattle, WA..............	Regional Director, Region 5 (Northwest Region).	James G Duncan	XS	OT	....	....	....
Springfield, VA	Senior Advisor, Workforce Relations	Vacant	....	OT	....	....	....
Springfield, VA	Senior Liaison Officer..	Julie Carrigan	XS	OT	....	....	....
Springfield, VA	Senior Liaison Officer..	Paul Fujimura	XS	OT	....	....	....
Springfield, VA	Senior Liaison Officer..	Carissa A Vandermey...........	XS	OT	....	....	....
Atlanta, GA	Supervisory Federal Air Marshal (Field), Atlanta Field Office.	Stanley L Lee	XS	OT	....	....	....
Boston, MA	Supervisory Air Marshal (Field), Boston Field Office.	David F Bassett....................	XS	OT	....	....	....
Chicago, IL	Supervisory Federal Air Marshal (Field), Chicago Field Office.	Robert Duerr	XS	OT	....	....	....
Dallas, TX	Supervisory Federal Air Marshal (Field), Dallas Field Office.	Thomas Aguilera	XS	OT	....	....	....
Houston, TX.............	Supervisory Federal Air Marshal (Field), Houston Field Office.	Noel C Curtin	XS	OT	....	....	....
Los Angeles, CA	Supervisory Federal Air Marshal (Field), Los Angeles Field Office.	Daniel Babor........................	XS	OT	....	....	....
Miami, FL................	Supervisory Federal Air Marshal (Field), Miami Field Office.	Adam Nikaj.........................	XS	OT	....	....	....
Queens, NY..............	Supervisory Federal Air Marshal (Field), New York Field Office.	Kevin F Honore	XS	OT	....	....	....
Newark, NJ	Supervisory Federal Air Marshal(Field), Newark Field Office.	Jared Addorisio....................	XS	OT	....	....	....
Philadelphia, PA	Supervisory Federal Air Marshal (Field) Philadelphia Field Office.	Michael V Lafrance..............	XS	OT	....	....	....
Chantilly, VA	Supervisory Federal Air Marshal(Field), Washington Field Office.	Eric Sarandrea	XS	OT	....	....	....
Springfield, VA	Supervisory Federal Air Marshal (Executive Director, Flight Operations).	Scott Carpender	XS	OT	....	....	....

DEPARTMENT OF HOMELAND SECURITY—Continued

Location	Position Title	Name of Incumbent	Type of Appt.	Pay Plan	Level, Grade, or Pay	Tenure	Expires
Springfield, VA	Supervisory Federal Air Marshal (Executive Director, Flight Programs).	Serge V Potapov	XS	OT	....	....	....
Springfield, VA	Supervisory Federal Air Marshal (Regional Director), Northeast Region, Field Operations (Region 1).	David C Park	XS	OT	....	....	....
Springfield, VA	Supervisory Federal Air Marshal (Regional Director), Southwest Region, Field Operations (Region 2).	John Muth	XS	OT	....	....	....
Springfield, VA	Executive Advisor	Vacant	....	OT	....	....	....

DEPARTMENT OF HOMELAND SECURITY OFFICE OF THE INSPECTOR GENERAL

Location	Position Title	Name of Incumbent	Type of Appt.	Pay Plan	Level, Grade, or Pay	Tenure	Expires
Washington, DC	Inspector General	Joseph Cuffari	PAS	EX	II	....	....

DEPARTMENT OF HOUSING AND URBAN DEVELOPMENT

Location	Position Title	Name of Incumbent	Type of Appt.	Pay Plan	Level, Grade, or Pay	Tenure	Expires
	OFFICE OF THE SECRETARY						
Washington, DC	Secretary, Housing and Urban Development	Vacant	....	EX	....	....	....
Washington, DC	Chief of Staff	Eugenia Metrakas	NA	ES	....	....	....
Washington, DC	Senior Advisor for Housing and Services	Richard Cho	NA	ES	....	....	....
Washington, DC	Deputy Chief of Staff..........................	Patrice Taylor	NA	ES	....	....	....
Washington, DC	Deputy Chief of Staff..........................	Vacant	....	ES	....	....	....
Washington, DC	Senior Advisor for Racial Equity	Adjoa B Asamoah	NA	ES	....	....	....
Washington, DC	Senior Advisor for Climate	Alexis Pelosi.......................	NA	ES	....	....	....
Washington, DC	Chief Operations Officer	Vacant	....	ES	....	....	....
Washington, DC	Senior Counselor	Julienne Joseph	NA	ES	....	....	....
Washington, DC	Director of Domestic Violence	Karlo Ng	SC	GS	15	....	....
Washington, DC	White House Liaison	David Charles Jones	SC	GS	15	....	....
Washington, DC	Deputy White House Liaison	Bryan Raymond Moose.......	SC	GS	13	....	....
Washington, DC	Policy Advisor.....................................	Zachary McRae....................	SC	GS	13	....	....
Washington, DC	Policy Advisor.....................................	Wendy Gomez.....................	SC	GS	12	....	....
Washington, DC	Special Assistant and Briefing Book Coordinator.	Aryiana Jada Hill.................	SC	GS	11	....	....
Washington, DC	Executive Assistant	Michaela West	SC	GS	11	....	....
	Office of the Deputy Secretary						
Washington, DC	Deputy Secretary, Housing and Urban Development.	Adrianne Todman................	PAS	EX	II	....	....
Washington, DC	Senior Advisor for Disaster Management..........	Elizabeth Niblock	NA	ES	....	....	....
Washington, DC	Senior Advisor.....................................	Faith A Rogers....................	NA	ES	....	....	....
Washington, DC	Senior Policy Advisor............................	Richard A Reffett	NA	ES	....	....	....
Washington, DC	Director, Executive Secretariat..........................	Career Incumbent	CA	ES	....	....	....
Washington, DC	Special Advisor....................................	Bertram Welton Pride..........	SC	GS	13	....	....
Washington, DC	Special Advisor....................................	Kailynn Cummings	SC	GS	13	....	....
	Office of the General Counsel						
Washington, DC	General Counsel	Damon Y Smith...................	PAS	EX	IV	....	....
Washington, DC	Principal Deputy General Counsel...................	Benjamin Klubes................	NA	ES	....	....	....
Washington, DC	Deputy General Counsel for Enforcement........	Sasha Samberg-Champion ..	NA	ES	....	....	....
Washington, DC	Associate General Counsel for Assistant Housing and Community Development.	Career Incumbent	CA	ES	....	....	....
Washington, DC	Associate Gen Counsel for Insured Housing and Urban Development.	Career Incumbent	CA	ES	....	....	....
Washington, DC	Associate Gen Counsel for Finance, Procurement, and Administrative Law.	Career Incumbent	CA	ES	....	....	....
Washington, DC	Associate General Counsel Legislation and Regulations.	Career Incumbent	CA	ES	....	....	....
Washington, DC	Associate General Counsel for Fair Housing.....	Career Incumbent	CA	ES	....	....	....
Washington, DC	Deputy General Counsel for Housing Programs.	Career Incumbent	CA	ES	....	....	....
Washington, DC	Senior Counsel.....................................	Corey Minor Smith	SC	GS	15	....	....
Washington, DC	Senior Counsel for Oversight...........................	Jordan H Blumenthal..........	SC	GS	15	....	....

DEPARTMENT OF HOUSING AND URBAN DEVELOPMENT—Continued

Location	Position Title	Name of Incumbent	Type of Appt.	Pay Plan	Level, Grade, or Pay	Tenure	Expires
	Office of the Chief Financial Officer						
Washington, DC	Chief Financial Officer	Vinay Vijay Singh	PAS	EX	IV	....	....
	Office of Public Affairs						
Washington, DC	Assistant Secretary for Public Affairs...............	Natalia Vanegas	PA	EX	....	....	....
Washington, DC	Deputy Assistant Secretary for Strategic Communications.	Sondra Denise Roberts	SC	GS	15	....	....
Washington, DC	Deputy Assistant Secretary for Public Engagement.	Cynthia Denise Goode	SC	GS	15	....	....
Washington, DC	Press Secretary	Niambe Tomlinson	SC	GS	14	....	....
Washington, DC	Digital Strategist	Kaleena Maureen Dwyer.....	SC	GS	11	....	....
Washington, DC	Deputy Press Secretary..	Zachary Berger Nosanchuk.	SC	GS	11	....	....
Washington, DC	Senior Advisor for Public Affairs......................	Ramzey Smith	SC	....	....	....	....
	Office of the Administration						
Washington, DC	Assistant Secretary for Administration	Elizabeth de Leon Bhargava.	PAS	EX	IV	....	....
Washington, DC	Chief Administrative Officer..............................	Career Incumbent	CA	ES		....	....
Washington, DC	Deputy Chief Administrative Officer	Career Incumbent	CA	ES		....	....
Washington, DC	Senior Advisor..	Juven Jacob	SC	GS	15	....	....
Washington, DC	Senior Advisor..	Brandon Chaderton..............	SC	GS	15	....	....
Washington, DC	Senior Advisor..	Brandon Thaler	SC	GS	14	....	....
Washington, DC	Special Assistant..	Cameron Jirbaud Whitaker.	SC	GS	12	....	....
Washington, DC	Advance Coordinator	Christina Simon	SC	GS	11	....	....
Washington, DC	Advance Coordinator	Tiffany Ruth McIver	SC	GS	11	....	....
	Office of Congressional and Intergovernmental Relations						
Washington, DC	Assistant Secretary for Congressional and Intergovernmental Relations.	Kimberly A McClain	PAS	EX	IV	....	....
Washington, DC	Deputy Assistant Secretary for Intergovernmental Relations.	Patrick Byrne	SC	GS	15	....	....
Washington, DC	Senior Advisor for Intergovernmental Relations.	Chiekezie Onyekwere Chukwuka.	SC	GS	14	....	....
Washington, DC	Special Advisor...	Blaike Ashley Bibbs	SC	GS	13	....	....
Washington, DC	Congressional Relations Specialist....................	Paul Matthew Nicholas	SC	GS	13	....	....
Washington, DC	Congressional Relations Specialist....................	Emily Jenette Nunez	SC	GS	13	....	....
Washington, DC	Congressional Relations Specialist....................	Alexander Caleb Molina	SC	GS	13	....	....
	Office of Policy Development and Research						
Washington, DC	Assistant Secretary for Policy Development and Research.	Vacant	....	EX	....	....	....
Washington, DC	Deputy Assistant Secretary for Policy Development.	Vacant	....	ES	....	....	....
Washington, DC	Principal Deputy Assistant Secretary................	Solomon Jeffrey Greene.......	NA	ES	....	....	....
Washington, DC	Deputy Assistant Secretary for Economic Affairs.	Career Incumbent	CA	ES	....	....	....
Washington, DC	Deputy Assistant Secretary for the Office of Research, Evaluation and Monitoring.	Career Incumbent	CA	ES	....	....	....
Washington, DC	Senior Advisor for Innovation............................	Tanaya Srinivasakrishnan ..	SC	GS	14	....	....
Washington, DC	Senior Advisor for Outreach and Engagement .	Sahian Valladares	SC	GS	14	....	....
	Office of Housing						
Washington, DC	Assistant Secretary for Housing, Federal Housing Commissioner.	Julia Ruth Gordon	PAS	EX	IV	....	....
Washington, DC	Chief of Staff..	Nathan Shultz......................	NA	ES	....	....	....
Washington, DC	Deputy Assistant Secretary for Single Family ..	Sarah Jane Edelman.............	NA	ES	....	....	....
Washington, DC	Deputy Assistant Secretary for Risk Management and Regulatory Affairs.	Mia Pittman	NA	ES	....	....	....
Washington, DC	Deputy Assistant Secretary for Multifamily Housing.	Ethan Handelman.................	NA	ES	....	....	....
Washington, DC	Principal Deputy Assistant Secretary for Housing.	Vacant	....	ES	....	....	....
Washington, DC	Senior Advisor..	Eric Sears Stein	NA	ES	....	....	....
Washington, DC	Director, Office of Multifamily Production.........	Career Incumbent	CA	ES	....	....	....
Washington, DC	Deputy Assistant Secretary for Office of Housing Counseling.	Career Incumbent	CA	ES	....	....	....
Washington, DC	Director, Office of Single Family Asset Management.	Career Incumbent	CA	ES	....	....	....
Washington, DC	Associate General Deputy Assistant Secretary for Housing.	Career Incumbent	CA	ES	....	....	....
Washington, DC	Associate Deputy Assistant Secretary Multifamily Housing Programs.	Career Incumbent	CA	ES	....	....	....
Washington, DC	Director, Office of Recapitalization....................	Career Incumbent	CA	ES	....	....	....
Washington, DC	Director, Office of Single Family Program Development.	Career Incumbent	CA	ES	....	....	....

DEPARTMENT OF HOUSING AND URBAN DEVELOPMENT—Continued

Location	Position Title	Name of Incumbent	Type of Appt.	Pay Plan	Level, Grade, or Pay	Tenure	Expires
Washington, DC	Director, Office of Lender Activities and Program Compliance.	Career Incumbent	CA	ES	....	....	....
Washington, DC	Associate Deputy Assistant Secretary for Single Family Housing.	Career Incumbent	CA	ES	....	....	....
Washington, DC	Director, Office of Asset Management and Portfolio Oversight.	Career Incumbent	CA	ES	....	....	....
Washington, DC	Deputy Assistant Secretary for Operations.......	Career Incumbent	CA	ES	....	....	....
Washington, DC	Senior Policy Advisor..	David Victor Sanchez...........	SC	GS	15	....	....
Washington, DC	Senior Policy Advisor..	Elayne Weiss.........................	SC	GS	15	....	....
Washington, DC	Policy Advisor..	Daniel Hardcastle	SC	GS	14	....	....
Washington, DC	Special Assistant..	Alexander Goldman	SC	GS	12	....	....
	Office of Fair Housing and Equal Opportunity						
Washington, DC	Principal Deputy Assistant Secretary for Fair Housing and Equal Opportunity.	Diane Shelley	NA	ES	....	....	....
Washington, DC	Assistant Secretary for Fair Housing and Equal Opportunity.	Vacant	....	EX	....	....	....
Washington, DC	Deputy Assistant Secretary for Operations.......	Vacant	....	ES	....	....	....
Washington, DC	Senior Advisor...	Vacant	....	ES	....	....	....
Washington, DC	Deputy Assistant Secretary, Office of Policy, Legislative Initiatives and Outreach.	Career Incumbent	CA	ES	....	....	....
Washington, DC	Deputy Assistant Secretary for Enforcement....	Career Incumbent	CA	ES	....	....	....
Washington, DC	Chief of Staff...	Sinchang Chiu	SC	GS	15	....	....
Washington, DC	Special Advisor..	Kidus Moges	SC	GS	13	....	....
	Office of Community Planning and Development						
Washington, DC	Assistant Secretary for Community Planning and Development.	Vacant	....	EX	....	....	....
Washington, DC	Principal Deputy Assistant Secretary for Community Planning and Development.	Marion M McFadden...........	NA	ES	....	....	....
Washington, DC	Deputy Assistant Secretary for Economic Development.	Vacant	....	ES	....	....	....
Washington, DC	Deputy Assistant Secretary for Grant Programs.	Vacant	....	ES	....	....	....
Washington, DC	Senior Advisor for Economic Development.......	Robin Keegan	NA	ES	....	....	....
Washington, DC	Director Office of Affordable Housing Programs.	Career Incumbent	CA	ES	....	....	....
Washington, DC	Deputy Assistant Secretary for Field Operations.	Vacant	....	ES	....	....	....
Washington, DC	Director, Office of Block Grant Assistance........	Vacant	....	ES	....	....	....
Washington, DC	Director, Disaster Recovery and Special Issues Division.	Career Incumbent	CA	ES	....	....	....
Washington, DC	Director, Environment and Energy	Career Incumbent	CA	ES	....	....	....
Washington, DC	Senior Advisor for Disaster Recovery	Patrick Forbes	SC	GS	15	....	....
Washington, DC	Chief of Staff...	Kera Package	SC	GS	15	....	....
Washington, DC	Special Advisor..	Elena Taeyaerts....................	SC	GS	13	....	....
Washington, DC	Special Advisor..	Leonard Ayala	SC	GS	12	....	....
	Government National Mortgage Association						
Washington, DC	President, Government National Mortgage Association.	Vacant	....	EX	....	....	....
Washington, DC	Executive Vice President and Chief Operating Officer.	Vacant	....	ES	....	....	....
Washington, DC	Principal Executive Vice President	Sam Valverde.......................	NA	ES	....	....	....
Washington, DC	Chief of Staff...	Vacant	....	ES	....	....	....
Washington, DC	Senior Vice President of Administration and Senior Advisor to the Office of the President.	Career Incumbent	CA	ES	....	....	....
Washington, DC	Senior Vice President of Strategic Planning and Policy.	Vacant	....	ES	....	....	....
Washington, DC	Senior Advisor...	Laura Kenney.......................	TA	ES	....	....	....
Washington, DC	Senior Advisor for Communications and Stakeholder Relations.	Alejandro Aviles	SC	GS	15	....	....
Washington, DC	Senior Advisor...	Brittany Michele Van..........	SC	GS	14	....	....
Washington, DC	Special Advisor..	Caitlyn Grady.......................	SC	GS	14	....	....
	Office of Public and Indian Housing						
Washington, DC	Assistant Secretary for Public and Indian Housing.	Vacant	....	EX	....	....	....
Washington, DC	Principal Deputy Assistant Secretary..............	Richard Monocchio..............	NA	ES	....	....	....
Washington, DC	Associate Deputy Assistant Secretary for Field Operations.	Vacant	....	ES	....	....	....
Washington, DC	Deputy Assistant Secretary for Public Housing and Voucher Programs.	Career Incumbent	CA	ES	....	....	....

DEPARTMENT OF HOUSING AND URBAN DEVELOPMENT—Continued

Location	Position Title	Name of Incumbent	Type of Appt.	Pay Plan	Level, Grade, or Pay	Tenure	Expires
Washington, DC	Deputy Assistant Secretary for Native American Programs.	Career Incumbent	CA	ES	....	....	....
Washington, DC	Deputy Assistant Secretary for Operations.......	Career Incumbent	CA	ES	....	....	....
Washington, DC	Deputy Assistant Secretary for Field Operations.	Career Incumbent	CA	ES	....	....	....
Washington, DC	Associate Deputy Assistant Secretary for Office of Native American Programs.	Career Incumbent	CA	ES	....	....	....
Washington, DC	Chief of Staff......................................	Stephen Lucas	SC	GS	15	....	....
Washington, DC	Senior Advisor....................................	Vacant	....	ES	....	....	....
Washington, DC	Policy Advisor....................................	James Crawford	SC	GS	13	....	....
Washington, DC	Special Advisor....................................	Michaela Jane Inman Amos.	SC	GS	12	....	....
Washington, DC	Special Assistant....................................	Jordan Harris	SC	GS	12	....	....
	Office of Field Policy and Management						
Washington, DC	Assistant Deputy Secretary for Field Policy and Management.	Peter Hunter.........................	NA	ES	....	....	....
Washington, DC	Director, Field Policy and Management.............	Career Incumbent	CA	ES	....	....	....
Washington, DC	Deputy Director, Office of Field Policy and Management.	Career Incumbent	CA	ES	....	....	....
Washington, DC	Director of Stakeholder Engagement.................	Career Incumbent	CA	ES	....	....	....
Boston, MA..............	Regional Administrator Region 1	Juana Matias......................	SC	GS	15	....	....
New York, NY.........	Regional Administrator Region 2	Alicka Ampry-Samuel..........	SC	GS	15	....	....
Philadelphia, PA	Regional Administrator Region 3	Matthew Heckles..................	SC	GS	15	....	....
Atlanta, GA	Regional Administrator Region 4	Jennifer Alicia Riley Collins.	SC	GS	15	....	....
Fort Worth, TX	Regional Administrator Region 6	Candace Valenzuela	SC	GS	15	....	....
Kansas City, MO	Regional Administrator Region 7	Ulysses Clayborn..................	SC	GS	15	....	....
Denver, CO	Regional Administrator Region 8	Dominique Jackson	SC	GS	15	....	....
Los Angeles, CA	Regional Administrator Region 9	Jason Pu	SC	GS	15	....	....
Seattle, WA.............	Regional Administrator Region 10	Andrew James Lofton	SC	GS	15	....	....
Washington, DC	Senior Advisor....................................	Alan Williams	SC	GS	15	....	....
	Office of the Chief Information Officer						
Washington, DC	Business Change and Integration Officer	Career Incumbent	CA	ES	....	....	....
Washington, DC	Senior Advisor to the Principal Deputy Chief Information Officer.	Career Incumbent	CA	ES	....	....	....
Washington, DC	Special Assistant....................................	Vianne Singh	SC	GS	11	....	....
	Office of the Chief Human Capital Officer						
Washington, DC	Chief Performance Officer.................................	Career Incumbent	CA	ES	....	....	....

DEPARTMENT OF HOUSING AND URBAN DEVELOPMENT OFFICE OF THE INSPECTOR GENERAL

Location	Position Title	Name of Incumbent	Type of Appt.	Pay Plan	Level, Grade, or Pay	Tenure	Expires
Washington, DC	Inspector General	Rae Oliver Davis	PAS	EX	III	....	....

DEPARTMENT OF THE INTERIOR

Location	Position Title	Name of Incumbent	Type of Appt.	Pay Plan	Level, Grade, or Pay	Tenure	Expires
	DEPARTMENT OF THE INTERIOR						
Washington, DC	Secretary	Debra Haaland	PAS	EX	I		
	SECRETARY'S IMMEDIATE OFFICE						
Washington, DC	Chief of Staff	Rachael Taylor......................	NA	ES	....	....	....
Washington, DC	Deputy Chief of Staff - Policy	Katherine P Kelly	NA	ES	....	....	....
Washington, DC	Deputy Chief of Staff - Operations....................	Mili Gosar	NA	ES	....	....	....
Washington, DC	Senior Counselor to the Secretary	Lynn Trujillo.........................	NA	ES	....	....	....
Washington, DC	Senior Counselor to the Secretary	Laura Daniel-Davis..............	NA	ES	....	....	....
Washington, DC	Senior Advisor to the Secretary.........................	Heidi Todacheene	NA	ES	....	....	....
Washington, DC	Senior Advisor for Native Hawaiian Affairs......	Summer Sylva	NA	ES	....	....	....
Washington, DC	Senior Advisor for Alaskan Affairs and Strategic Priorities.	Raina Thiele	NA	ES	....	....	....
Washington, DC	Senior Advisor and Infrastructure Coordinator.	Cynthia Stachelberg.............	NA	ES	....	....	....

DEPARTMENT OF THE INTERIOR—Continued

Location	Position Title	Name of Incumbent	Type of Appt.	Pay Plan	Level, Grade, or Pay	Tenure	Expires
Washington, DC	Deputy Infrastructure Coordinator	Katherine P Currie	NA	ES	....	....	....
Washington, DC	Senior Advisor for Infrastructure Equity	Philip Burton........................	SC	GS	15	....	....
Washington, DC	Senior Advisor for Infrastructure Strategy	Torend Collins	SC	GS	15	....	....
Washington, DC	Special Assistant to the Senior Counselor........	Hadeel Shadid	SC	GS	12	....	....
Washington, DC	Advisor..	Matthew Dutko	SC	GS	12	....	....
Washington, DC	Briefing Book Coordinator..............................	Emma Powell........................	SC	GS	11	....	....
Washington, DC	Chief Information Officer................................	Career Incumbent	CA	ES	....	....	....
Washington, DC	Director of Executive Secretariat and Office of Regulatory Affairs.	Career Incumbent	CA	ES	....	....	....
Washington, DC	Communications Director	Vacant	....	ES	....	....	....
Washington, DC	Senior Communications Advisor for Infrastructure.	Sally Tucker........................	SC	GS	15	....	....
Washington, DC	Press Secretary	Giovanni Rocco	SC	GS	14	....	....
Washington, DC	Speechwriter	Michelle Gullett...................	SC	GS	13	....	....
Washington, DC	Advisor..	John Grandy	SC	GS	13	....	....
Washington, DC	Deputy Press Secretary.................................	Justin Horn..........................	SC	GS	12	....	....
Washington, DC	Director, Intergovernmental and External Affairs.	Shantha Alonso	SC	GS	15	....	....
Washington, DC	Deputy Director, Office of Intergovernmental and External Affairs.	Thomas Franco.....................	SC	GS	14	....	....
Washington, DC	Advisor to the Director of Intergovernmental and External Affairs.	Cristina Villa	SC	GS	14	....	....
Washington, DC	White House Liaison	Amber Gaither......................	SC	GS	14	....	....
Washington, DC	Special Advisor to the Secretary	Naomie Germain	SC	GS	13	....	....
Washington, DC	Director, Office of Scheduling and Advance......	Amanda Kules	SC	GS	15	....	....
Washington, DC	Deputy Director for Advance	Brendan Jackson..................	SC	GS	14	....	....
Washington, DC	Scheduler..	Catherine Ming	SC	GS	13	....	....
	OFFICE OF THE DEPUTY SECRETARY						
Washington, DC	Deputy Secretary of the Interior	Vacant	....	EX	....	....	....
Washington, DC	Associate Deputy Secretary	Sarah Devins Greenberger..	NA	ES	....	....	....
Washington, DC	Senior Counselor to the Secretary and Chief of Staff to the Deputy Secretary.	Melissa Schwartz	NA	ES	....	....	....
Washington, DC	Director, Office of Small and Disadvantaged Business Utilization.	Career Incumbent	CA	ES	....	....	....
Washington, DC	Senior Advisor to the Deputy Secretary	Mackenzie Landa	SC	GS	15	....	....
	OFFICE OF CONGRESSIONAL AND LEGISLATIVE AFFAIRS						
Washington, DC	Director, Office of Congressional and Legislative Affairs.	Vacant	....	ES	....	....	....
Washington, DC	Deputy Director, Office of Congressional and Legislative Affairs.	Paniz Rezaeerod	SC	GS	15	....	....
Washington, DC	Deputy Director of Congressional Affairs - Senate.	Leslie Gray	SC	GS	15	....	....
Washington, DC	Oversight Counsel	Christopher Martinez	SC	GS	15	....	....
Washington, DC	Advisor..	Alejandro Oms......................	SC	GS	13	....	....
	NATIONAL INDIAN GAMING COMMISSION						
Washington, DC	Chairman, National Indian Gaming Commission.	Vacant	....	EX	....	....	....
Washington, DC	Associate Member, National Indian Gaming Commission.	Sharon Avery........................	XS	OT	....	....	06/03/27
Washington, DC	Associate Member, National Indian Gaming Commission.	Jean Hovland........................	XS	OT	....	....	....
	OFFICE OF THE SOLICITOR						
Washington, DC	Solicitor..	Robert T Anderson	PAS	EX	IV	....	....
Washington, DC	Principal Deputy Solicitor...............................	Ann Marie Bledsoe Downes.	NA	ES	....	....	....
Washington, DC	Senior Advisor to the Solicitor.........................	Laura Bloomer......................	SC	GS	15	....	....
Washington, DC	Senior Advisor for Oversight	Zaheer Tajani.......................	SC	GS	15	....	....
Washington, DC	Deputy Solicitor for Land Resources.................	Natalie Landreth..................	NA	ES	....	....	....
Washington, DC	Deputy Solicitor for Water Resources	Vacant	....	ES	....	....	....
Washington, DC	Deputy Solicitor for Indian Affairs....................	Joel Williams	NA	ES	....	....	....
Washington, DC	Deputy Solicitor for Parks and Wildlife.............	Sarah Krakoff......................	NA	ES	....	....	....
Washington, DC	Deputy Solicitor for Energy and Mineral Resources.	Travis Annatoyn...................	NA	ES	....	....	....
Washington, DC	Deputy Solicitor - General Law	Jacek Pruski	NA	ES	....	....	....
Washington, DC	Associate Solicitor for Indian Affairs	Career Incumbent	CA	ES	....	....	....
Washington, DC	Associate Solicitor for Parks and Wildlife	Career Incumbent	CA	ES	....	....	....
Washington, DC	Associate Solicitor for Mineral Resources..........	Career Incumbent	CA	ES	....	....	....
Washington, DC	Associate Solicitor - General Law	Vacant	....	ES	....	....	....
Washington, DC	Senior Ethics Advisor....................................	Monica Garcia	XS	SL	....	....	....

DEPARTMENT OF THE INTERIOR—Continued

Location	Position Title	Name of Incumbent	Type of Appt.	Pay Plan	Level, Grade, or Pay	Tenure	Expires
	ASSISTANT SECRETARY - POLICY, MANAGEMENT AND BUDGET						
Washington, DC	Assistant Secretary - Policy Management and Budget.	Vacant	....	EX	....	....	....
Washington, DC	Principal Deputy Assistant Secretary - Policy, Management and Budget.	Joan M Mooney	NA	ES	....	....	....
Washington, DC	Director, Bipartisan Infrastructure Law Program Management Office.	Career Incumbent	CA	ES	....	....	....
Long Beach, CA......	Orphan Wells Director	Career Incumbent	CA	ES	....	....	....
Washington, DC	Senior Advisor, Orphan Wells	Peter Gallagher	SC	GS	15	....	....
Washington, DC	Director, Great American Outdoors Program Office.	Career Incumbent	CA	ES	....	....	....
Washington, DC	Deputy Assistant Secretary - Policy, Budget and Management.	Eric Werwa	NA	ES	....	....	....
Washington, DC	Deputy Assistant Secretary - Administrative Services.	Career Incumbent	CA	ES	....	....	....
Washington, DC	Director, Gulf of Mexico Restoration	Career Incumbent	CA	ES	....	....	....
Washington, DC	Director, Office of Environmental Policy and Compliance.	Career Incumbent	CA	ES	....	....	....
Washington, DC	Director, Office of Policy Analysis......................	Career Incumbent	CA	ES	....	....	....
Washington, DC	Associate Director - Asset Management	Career Incumbent	CA	ES	....	....	....
Washington, DC	Deputy Director, Business Integration Office....	Career Incumbent	CA	ES	....	....	....
Washington, DC	Director, Office of Wildland Fire........................	Career Incumbent	CA	ES	....	....	....
Boise, ID	Director, Office of Aviation Services..................	Career Incumbent	CA	ES	....	....	....
Washington, DC	Director, Office of Facilities and Administrative Services.	Career Incumbent	CA	ES	....	....	....
Washington, DC	Deputy Chief Information Officer - Resource Management.	Career Incumbent	CA	ES	....	....	....
Washington, DC	Director, Office of Planning and Performance Management.	Career Incumbent	CA	ES	....	....	....
Washington, DC	Director, Office of Restoration and Damage Assessment.	Career Incumbent	CA	ES	....	....	....
Lakewood, CO	Director, Business Integration Office	Career Incumbent	CA	ES	....	....	....
Washington, DC	Advisor..	Rebecca Anne Jablonski-Diehl.	SC	GS	15	....	....
	Interior Business Center						
Washington, DC	Director, Interior Business Center	Career Incumbent	CA	ES	....	....	....
Washington, DC	Deputy Director, Interior Business Center........	Vacant	....	ES	....	....	....
	Office of Natural Resources Revenue Management						
Lakewood, CO	Director, Office of Natural Resources Revenue Management.	Career Incumbent	CA	ES	....	....	....
	ASSISTANT SECRETARY - FISH AND WILDLIFE AND PARKS						
Washington, DC	Assistant Secretary - Fish and Wildlife and Parks.	Shannon A Estenoz.............	PAS	EX	IV	....	....
Washington, DC	Deputy Assistant Secretary - Fish and Wildlife and Parks.	Matthew Strickler	NA	ES	....	....	....
Washington, DC	Deputy Assistant Secretary - Fish and Wildlife and Parks.	Michael Martinez	NA	ES	....	....	....
Miami, FL................	Director Everglades Restoration Initiatives/Executive Director South Florida Ecosystem Restoration Task Force.	Career Incumbent	CA	ES	....	....	....
Washington, DC	Senior Advisor..	Margrette K Thompson........	SC	GS	15	....	....
Washington, DC	Senior Advisor..	Courtney Fogwell	SC	GS	15	....	....
Washington, DC	Special Assistant..	Maria Camila Gomez Osorio.	SC	GS	12	....	....
	National Park Service						
Washington, DC	Director, National Park Service...........................	Charles Sams.......................	PAS	EX	V	....	....
Washington, DC	Deputy Director for Congressional and External Relations.	Vacant	....	ES	....	....	....
Washington, DC	Associate Director, Business Services	Career Incumbent	CA	ES	....	....	....
Washington, DC	Associate Director, Natural Resource Stewardship and Science.	Career Incumbent	CA	ES	....	....	....
Washington, DC	Associate Director for Partnerships and Civic Engagement.	Career Incumbent	CA	ES	....	....	....
Washington, DC	Senior Advisor	Malcolm McGeary	NA	ES	....	....	....
Washington, DC	Policy Associate..	Maria Castro	SC	GS	11	....	....
	Field Offices - NPS						
Washington, DC	Regional Director, National Capitol Region.......	Career Incumbent	CA	ES	....	....	....
Omaha, NE..............	Regional Director, Midwest Region	Career Incumbent	CA	ES	....	....	....

DEPARTMENT OF THE INTERIOR—Continued

Location	Position Title	Name of Incumbent	Type of Appt.	Pay Plan	Level, Grade, or Pay	Tenure	Expires
	United States Fish and Wildlife Service						
Washington, DC	Director, United States Fish and Wildlife Service.	Martha Macgill Colhoun Williams.	PAS	EX	V	....	....
Washington, DC	Deputy Director	Siva Sundaresan	NA	ES		....	....
Washington, DC	Assistant Director - Fish and Aquatic Conservation.	Career Incumbent	CA	ES		....	....
Baileys Crossroads, VA.	Assistant Director - Migratory Bird Programs .	Career Incumbent	CA	ES		....	....
Washington, DC	Assistant Director - Office of Communications.	Career Incumbent	CA	ES		....	....
Washington, DC	Assistant Director - Wildlife and Sportfish Restoration Programs.	Career Incumbent	CA	ES		....	....
Washington, DC	Assistant Director - Management and Administration.	Career Incumbent	CA	ES		....	....
Shepherdstown, WV.	Director, National Conservation Training Center.	Career Incumbent	CA	ES		....	....
Washington, DC	Senior Advisor - Energy Policy	Career Incumbent	CA	ES		....	....
Washington, DC	Senior Advisor to the Director for Fish and Wildlife Service.	James Guthrie	NA	ES		....	....
Washington, DC	Special Assistant to Director, Fish and Wildlife Service.	Chloe Leaverton	SC	GS	9	....	....
	ASSISTANT SECRETARY - WATER AND SCIENCE						
Washington, DC	Assistant Secretary - Water and Science...........	Vacant	....	EX		....	....
Washington, DC	Principal Deputy Assistant Secretary - Water and Science.	Michael Brain	NA	ES		....	....
Washington, DC	Deputy Assistant Secretary - Water and Science.	Annalise Blum	NA	ES		....	....
Washington, DC	Deputy Assistant Secretary - Water and Science.	Gary Gold	NA	ES		....	....
Washington, DC	Advisor..	Joseph Younkle	SC	GS	12	....	....
	Bureau of Reclamation						
Washington, DC	Commissioner Bureau of Reclamation..............	M Camille Calimlim Touton.	PAS	EX	V	....	....
Washington, DC	Deputy Commissioner	Roque Sanchez....................	NA	ES		....	....
Washington, DC	Deputy Commissioner - Operations	Career Incumbent	CA	ES		....	....
Washington, DC	Deputy Commissioner - Program, Administration and Budget.	Career Incumbent	CA	ES		....	....
Washington, DC	Director, Program and Budget.....................	Vacant	....	ES		....	....
Washington, DC	Director, Office of Communications................	Career Incumbent	CA	ES		....	....
Washington, DC	Senior Counselor	John Watts	NA	ES		....	....
Washington, DC	Policy Associate	James Langhenry.................	SC	GS	11	....	....
	Field Offices - Bureau of Reclamation						
Sacramento, CA.......	Regional Director, California-Great Basin Region.	Career Incumbent	CA	ES		....	....
	United States Geological Survey						
Reston, VA	Director, U.S. Geological Survey	David Applegate	PAS	EX	V	....	....
Washington, DC	Special Advisor..................................	Alexx Diera......................	SC	GS	13	....	....
	ASSISTANT SECRETARY - LAND AND MINERALS MANAGEMENT						
Washington, DC	Assistant Secretary-Land and Minerals Management.	Vacant	....	EX		....	....
Washington, DC	Principal Deputy Assistant Secretary - Land and Minerals Management.	Steven H Feldgus	NA	ES		....	....
Washington, DC	Deputy Assistant Secretary - Land and Minerals Management.	Kathryn Kovacs....................	NA	ES		....	....
Sacramento, CA.......	Counselor to the Assistant Secretary for Land and Minerals Management.	Vacant	....	ES		....	....
Washington, DC	Advisor to the Assistant Secretary - Land and Minerals Management.	Alexandra Sanchez...............	SC	GS	14	....	....
	Bureau of Land Management						
Washington, DC	Director Bureau of Land Management..............	Tracy Stone-Manning	PAS	EX	V	....	....
New York, NY..........	Principal Deputy Director.......................	Nada Culver	NA	ES		....	....
Washington, DC	Deputy Director for State Operations...............	Career Incumbent	CA	ES		....	....
Washington, DC	Deputy Director for Administration and Programs.	Career Incumbent	CA	ES		....	....
Grand Junction, CO.	Assistant Director, Resources and Planning	Career Incumbent	CA	ES		....	....
Grand Junction, CO.	Assistant Director, Energy, Minerals and Realty Management.	Career Incumbent	CA	ES		....	....
Grand Junction, CO.	Assistant Director, Business and Administration.	Career Incumbent	CA	ES		....	....

DEPARTMENT OF THE INTERIOR—Continued

Location	Position Title	Name of Incumbent	Type of Appt.	Pay Plan	Level, Grade, or Pay	Tenure	Expires
Grand Junction, CO.	Assistant Director, Communications and Public Relations.	Career Incumbent	CA	ES	....	....	....
Boise, ID	Assistant Director, Fire and Aviation................	Career Incumbent	CA	ES	....	....	....
Grand Junction, CO.	Assistant Director, National Conservation Lands and Community Partnerships.	Career Incumbent	CA	ES	....	....	....
Grand Junction, CO.	Program Executive for Intergovernmental and External Affairs.	Career Incumbent	CA	ES	....	....	....
Washington, DC	Senior Advisor..	Career Incumbent	CA	ES	....	....	....
Washington, DC	Senior Advisor..	Sara Moffat........................	SC	GS	15	....	....
Washington, DC	Advisor..	Henry Wykowski	SC	GS	13	....	....
	Office of Surface Mining						
Washington, DC	Director Office of Surface Mining Reclamation and Enforcement.	Vacant	....	EX	....	....	....
Washington, DC	Deputy Director...	Career Incumbent	CA	ES	....	....	....
Washington, DC	Principal Deputy Director...............................	Sharon Buccino	NA	ES	....	....	....
Washington, DC	Assistant Director, Program Support................	Career Incumbent	CA	ES	....	....	....
Washington, DC	Senior Advisor..	Sara Cawley........................	SC	GS	15	....	....
	Bureau of Safety and Environmental Enforcement						
Washington, DC	Director, Bureau of Safety and Environmental Enforcement.	Kevin Sligh	NA	ES	....	....	....
Washington, DC	Deputy Director...	Career Incumbent	CA	ES	....	....	....
Sterling, VA	Associate Director for Administration	Career Incumbent	CA	ES	....	....	....
Washington, DC	Regulatory Programs Chief	Career Incumbent	CA	ES	....	....	....
Washington, DC	Senior Advisor to the Director	Iqra Nasir	SC	GS	14	....	....
	Bureau of Ocean Energy Management						
Washington, DC	Director, Bureau of Ocean Energy Management.	Elizabeth Anne Klein..........	NA	ES	....	....	....
Washington, DC	Deputy Director...	Career Incumbent	CA	ES	....	....	....
Washington, DC	Chief Environmental Officer...........................	Vacant	....	ES	....	....	....
Washington, DC	Program Manager, Office of Budget and Program Coordination.	Career Incumbent	CA	ES	....	....	....
Washington, DC	Chief, Office of Renewable Energy	Career Incumbent	CA	ES	....	....	....
Washington, DC	Senior Advisor..	Marissa Knodel	SC	GS	15	....	....
Washington, DC	Advisor..	Manuokalani Tupper	SC	GS	13	....	....
	Field Offices—Bureau of Ocean Energy Management						
Anchorage, AK........	Regional Director, Alaska Region	Career Incumbent	CA	ES	....	....	....
	ASSISTANT SECRETARY - INDIAN AFFAIRS						
Washington, DC	Assistant Secretary - Indian Affairs	Bryan T Newland................	PAS	EX	IV	....	....
Brimley, MI..............	Principal Deputy Assistant Secretary - Indian Affairs.	Wizipan Garriott	NA	ES	....	....	....
Washington, DC	Deputy Assistant Secretary - Indian Affairs	Kathryn C Isom-Clause	NA	ES	....	....	....
Washington, DC	Deputy Assistant Secretary - Indian Affairs (Management).	Career Incumbent	CA	ES	....	....	....
Washington, DC	Director, Office of Indian Gaming Management.	Career Incumbent	CA	ES	....	....	....
Reston, VA	Director, Facilities, Property and Safety Management.	Career Incumbent	CA	ES	....	....	....
Washington, DC	Director, Office of Self-Governance...................	Career Incumbent	CA	ES	....	....	....
Reston, VA	Associate Chief Information Officer.................	Career Incumbent	CA	ES	....	....	....
Washington, DC	Senior Advisor to the Assistant Secretary—Indian Affairs.	Tracy Goodluck....................	SC	GS	15	....	....
Washington, DC	Advisor..	Joaquin Gallegos	SC	GS	14	....	....
	Bureau of Indian Education						
Washington, DC	Director - Bureau of Indian Education	Career Incumbent	CA	ES	....	....	....
	Bureau of Indian Affairs						
Billings, MT.............	Director, Bureau of Indian Affairs....................	Career Incumbent	CA	ES	....	....	....
Albuquerque, NM....	Deputy Director, Field Operations	Career Incumbent	CA	ES	....	....	....
Washington, DC	Deputy Director, Trust Services	Career Incumbent	CA	ES	....	....	....
Washington, DC	Deputy Bureau Director, Indian Services..........	Career Incumbent	CA	ES	....	....	....
	Bureau of Trust Funds Administration						
Washington, DC	Director Bureau of Trust Funds Administration.	Career Incumbent	CA	ES	....	....	....
Albuquerque, NM....	Principal Deputy Bureau Director, Trust Operations.	Career Incumbent	CA	ES	....	....	....
Albuquerque, NM....	Deputy Bureau Director Trust Operations-Field.	Career Incumbent	CA	ES	....	....	....

DEPARTMENT OF THE INTERIOR—Continued

Location	Position Title	Name of Incumbent	Type of Appt.	Pay Plan	Level, Grade, or Pay	Tenure	Expires
Albuquerque, NM....	Director, Office of Trust Risk, Evaluation and Compliance.	Career Incumbent	CA	ES	....	....	....
Arlee, MT...............	Regional Trust Director..	Career Incumbent	CA	ES	....	....	....
Albuquerque, NM....	Regional Trust Director..	Career Incumbent	CA	ES	....	....	....
Albuquerque, NM....	Senior Advisor..	Career Incumbent	CA	ES	....	....	....
	ASSISTANT SECRETARY - INSULAR AFFAIRS						
Washington, DC	Assistant Secretary - Insular Areas...................	Carmen G Cantor.................	PAS	EX	IV	....	....
Washington, DC	Deputy Assistant Secretary- Insular and International Affairs.	Keone Nakoa	NA	ES	....	....	....
Washington, DC	Director, Office of Insular Affairs	Career Incumbent	CA	ES	....	....	....
Washington, DC	Policy Associate..	Abdiel Razo..........................	SC	GS	12	....	....

DEPARTMENT OF THE INTERIOR OFFICE OF THE INSPECTOR GENERAL

Location	Position Title	Name of Incumbent	Type of Appt.	Pay Plan	Level, Grade, or Pay	Tenure	Expires
Washington, DC	Inspector General	Mark Lee Greenblatt	PAS	EX	III	....	....

DEPARTMENT OF JUSTICE

Location	Position Title	Name of Incumbent	Type of Appt.	Pay Plan	Level, Grade, or Pay	Tenure	Expires
	OFFICE OF THE ATTORNEY GENERAL						
Washington, DC	Attorney General	Merrick B Garland...............	PAS	EX	I	....	....
Washington, DC	Chief of Staff and Senior Counselor to the Attorney General.	Matthew Bennett Klapper...	NA	ES	....	....	....
Washington, DC	Deputy Chief of Staff and Senior Counselor to the Attorney General.	Christine Ku Berger	NA	ES	....	....	....
Washington, DC	Deputy Chief of Staff and Counselor	Elena Satten-Lopez..............	NA	ES	....	....	....
Washington, DC	Senior Counselor to the Attorney General	Susan M Pelletier	NA	ES	....	....	....
Washington, DC	Senior Counselor to the Attorney General	Shaylyn Capri Cochran	NA	ES	....	....	....
Washington, DC	Counselor to the Attorney General	Michael Qian	NA	ES	....	....	....
Washington, DC	Confidential Assistant	Marcia Davidson	SC	GS	14	....	....
Washington, DC	Deputy Director of Scheduling and Advance for Trips and Engagements.	Sofia Greco-Byrne	SC	GS	13	....	....
	OFFICE OF THE DEPUTY ATTORNEY GENERAL						
Washington, DC	Deputy Attorney General.....................................	Lisa Monaco..........................	PAS	EX	II	....	....
Washington, DC	Principal Associate Deputy Attorney General...	Marshall Leigh Miller..........	NA	ES	....	....	....
Washington, DC	Chief of Staff and Associate Deputy Attorney General.	Andrew Joseph Bruck..........	NA	ES	....	....	....
Washington, DC	Associate Deputy Attorney General....................	Career Incumbent	CA	ES	....	....	....
Washington, DC	Associate Deputy Attorney General....................	Vacant	....	ES	....	....	....
Washington, DC	Associate Deputy Attorney General....................	Myesha Kiana Braden	NA	ES	....	....	....
Washington, DC	Associate Deputy Attorney General....................	Austin Ridgely Evers	NA	ES	....	....	....
Washington, DC	Associate Deputy Attorney General....................	Shankar Duraiswamy..........	NA	ES	....	....	....
Washington, DC	National Criminal Discovery Coordinator	Career Incumbent	CA	ES	....	....	....
Washington, DC	Senior Counsel	Carlton Eliot Forbes.............	SC	GS	15	....	....
Washington, DC	Senior Counsel	Adrienne Benson	SC	GS	15	....	....
Washington, DC	Counsel	Bradley Darren Pough.........	SC	GS	14	....	....
Washington, DC	Counsel	Danielle A Schulkin	SC	GS	14	....	....
Washington, DC	Special Assistant...	Benjamin Martel	SC	GS	12	....	....
Washington, DC	Special Assistant...	Khira Jitendra Mistry	SC	GS	7	....	....
	Office of Privacy and Civil Liberties						
Washington, DC	Chief Privacy and Civil Liberties Officer	Vacant	....	ES	....	....	....
Washington, DC	Director, Office of Privacy and Civil Liberties...	Career Incumbent	CA	ES	....	....	....
	Office of the Executive Secretariat						
Washington, DC	Executive Secretary..	Emily Ross............................	NA	ES	....	....	....
	Criminal Division						
Washington, DC	Assistant Attorney General Criminal Division .	Vacant	....	EX	....	....	....
Washington, DC	Principal Deputy Assistant Attorney General...	Nicole Marie Argentieri	NA	ES	....	....	....
Washington, DC	Chief of Staff and Counselor...............................	Vacant	....	ES	....	....	....
Washington, DC	Deputy Assistant Attorney General	Lisa Miller	NA	ES	....	....	....

DEPARTMENT OF JUSTICE—Continued

Location	Position Title	Name of Incumbent	Type of Appt.	Pay Plan	Level, Grade, or Pay	Tenure	Expires
Washington, DC	Deputy Assistant Attorney General	Vacant	....	ES	....	....	....
Washington, DC	Deputy Assistant Attorney General	Career Incumbent	CA	ES	....	....	....
Washington, DC	Deputy Assistant Attorney General	Career Incumbent	CA	ES	....	....	....
Washington, DC	Deputy Assistant Attorney General	Career Incumbent	CA	ES	....	....	....
Washington, DC	Counselor Narc and Transntl Org Crime	Career Incumbent	CA	ES	....	....	....
Washington, DC	Deputy Director for International Policy..........	Career Incumbent	CA	ES	....	....	....
Washington, DC	Counselor for Transnational and Organized Crime and International Affairs.	Career Incumbent	CA	ES	....	....	....
Washington, DC	Director, Office of Policy and Legislation..........	Vacant	....	ES	....	....	....
Washington, DC	Senior Counsel..	Vacant	....	ES	....	....	....
Baghdad, Iraq..........	Justice Attache, Iraq............................	Ellen V Endrizzi..................	TA	ES	....	....	02/08/25
	National Security Division						
Washington, DC	Assistant Attorney General	Matthew G Olsen	PAS	EX	IV	....	....
Washington, DC	Principal Deputy Assistant Attorney General...	David Aubrey Newman........	NA	ES	....	....	....
Washington, DC	Chief of Staff..	Susan Julia Klein Hennessey.	NA	ES	....	....	....
Washington, DC	Deputy Assistant Attorney General	Career Incumbent	CA	ES	....	....	....
Washington, DC	Deputy Assistant Attorney General	Career Incumbent	CA	ES	....	....	....
Washington, DC	Deputy Assistant Attorney General	Career Incumbent	CA	ES	....	....	....
Washington, DC	Chief, Counterintelligence, Export Control, and Economic Espionage.	Career Incumbent	CA	ES	....	....	....
Washington, DC	Chief, Policy, Office of Law and Policy	Career Incumbent	CA	ES	....	....	....
Washington, DC	Chief, Counterterrorism Section........................	Career Incumbent	CA	ES	....	....	....
Washington, DC	Executive Deputy Chief, Counterintelligence Export Control.	Jennifer K Gellie..................	TA	ES	....	360	01/10/27
Washington, DC	Counsel...	Margot Benedict....................	SC	GS	15	....	....
Washington, DC	Counsel...	Hilary Anne Hurd	SC	GS	14	....	....
	Justice Management Division						
Washington, DC	Director, Office of Small and Disadvantaged Business.	Career Incumbent	CA	ES	....	....	....
Washington, DC	Director, Office of Small and Disadvantaged Business Utilization.	Career Incumbent	CA	ES	....	....	....
Washington, DC	Deputy Director, Operations and Infrastructure.	Career Incumbent	CA	ES	....	....	....
Washington, DC	Director, Strategic Planning and Performance..	Career Incumbent	CA	ES	....	....	....
	Office of Public Affairs						
Washington, DC	Director, Office of Public Affairs........................	Xochitl Hinojosa	NA	ES	....	....	....
Washington, DC	Principal Deputy Director..................................	Dena Iverson Debonis..........	NA	ES	....	....	....
Washington, DC	Associate Director for Speechwriting.................	Marissa Brogger....................	SC	GS	15	....	....
Washington, DC	Deputy Director for Public Engagement.............	Kelsey Pietranton.................	SC	GS	15	....	....
Washington, DC	Senior Communications Advisor	Terrence Clark.....................	SC	GS	15	....	....
Washington, DC	Senior Communications Advisor	Aryele N Bradford...............	SC	GS	15	....	....
Washington, DC	Press Secretary..	Emmalynn Moriah Dulaney.	SC	GS	14	....	....
Washington, DC	Deputy Speechwriter................................	Charlie Stanton.....................	SC	GS	13	....	....
Washington, DC	Speechwriter..	Sarah Muller........................	SC	GS	13	....	....
Washington, DC	Special Advisor for Public Engagement.............	Jordan Rachel Shub............	SC	GS	11	....	....
Washington, DC	Press Assistant	Sophie Dubow Ulin	SC	GS	9	....	....
Washington, DC	Press Assistant	Julia Hartnett	SC	GS	9	....	....
Washington, DC	Special Assistant to the Director and Press Advance.	Catherine Morris.................	SC	GS	9	....	....
	Office of Legislative Affairs						
Washington, DC	Assistant Attorney General (Legislative Affairs).	Carlos F Uriarte....................	PAS	EX	IV	....	....
Washington, DC	Deputy Assistant Attorney General	Sara Schofield Zdeb	NA	ES	....	....	....
Washington, DC	Deputy Assistant Attorney General	Nelson Slade Bond	NA	ES	....	....	....
Washington, DC	Deputy Assistant Attorney General	Matthew Blake Hanson.......	NA	ES	....	....	....
Washington, DC	Senior Counselor.....................................	Career Incumbent	CA	ES	....	....	....
Washington, DC	Chief of Staff and Senior Counsel......................	Abigail Kohlman	SC	GS	15	....	....
Washington, DC	Senior Counsel.......................................	Greta Gao............................	SC	GS	15	....	....
Washington, DC	Senior Counsel.......................................	Rayshon Jamil Payton	SC	GS	15	....	....
Washington, DC	Senior Counsel.......................................	Reyna Simone Walters-Morgan.	SC	GS	15	....	....
Washington, DC	Senior Counsel.......................................	Corey Linehan......................	SC	GS	15	....	....
Washington, DC	Counsel...	Miranda Hernandez.............	SC	GS	14	....	....
Washington, DC	Counsel...	Joshua Langley Mogil..........	SC	GS	14	....	....
Washington, DC	Attorney Advisor....................................	Taylor Burnett......................	SC	GS	14	....	....
Washington, DC	Special Assistant....................................	Christian Ryan Rubio..........	SC	GS	11	....	....
	Office of Legal Counsel						
Washington, DC	Assistant Attorney General Legal Counsel	Christopher Fonzone............	PAS	EX	IV	....	....
Washington, DC	Principal Deputy Assistant Attorney General...	Dawn E Johnsen	NA	ES	....	....	....

DEPARTMENT OF JUSTICE—Continued

Location	Position Title	Name of Incumbent	Type of Appt.	Pay Plan	Level, Grade, or Pay	Tenure	Expires
Washington, DC	Deputy Assistant Attorney General	Zachary Schauf......................	NA	ES	....	....	....
Washington, DC	Deputy Assistant Attorney General	Trisha B Anderson	NA	ES	....	....	....
Washington, DC	Deputy Assistant Attorney General	Jamal Kwame Greene..........	NA	ES	....	....	....
Washington, DC	Deputy Assistant Attorney General	Gillian Elizabeth Metzger ...	NA	ES	....	....	....
Washington, DC	Deputy Assistant Attorney General	Vacant	....	ES	....	....	....
Washington, DC	Special Counsel................................	Career Incumbent	CA	ES	....	....	....
Washington, DC	Counsel	Nicholas Aleaxander Nasrallah.	SC	GS	15	....	....
Washington, DC	Senior Counselor........................	Neil Kinkopf	SC	GS	15	....	....
	Office of Legal Policy						
Washington, DC	Assistant Attorney General, Office of Legal Policy.	Vacant	....	EX	....	....	....
Washington, DC	Principal Deputy Assistant Attorney General...	Susan Marie Davies.............	NA	ES	....	....	....
Washington, DC	Deputy Assistant Attorney General	Michael Zubrensky................	NA	ES	....	....	....
Washington, DC	Deputy Assistant Attorney General	Career Incumbent	CA	ES	....	....	....
Washington, DC	Deputy Assistant Attorney General	Career Incumbent	CA	ES	....	....	....
Washington, DC	Senior Counsel.......................................	Brian Farnkoff......................	SC	GS	15	....	....
Washington, DC	Senior Counsel.......................................	Tina Thomas........................	SC	GS	15	....	....
Washington, DC	Senior Counsel.......................................	Zachary Michael Spiegel Blau.	SC	GS	15	....	....
Washington, DC	Senior Counsel.......................................	Deanna Elizabeth Evans	SC	GS	15	....	....
Washington, DC	Senior Counsel.......................................	Rahel Boghossian................	SC	GS	15	....	....
Washington, DC	Senior Counsel.......................................	Keagan D Buchanan............	SC	GS	15	....	....
Washington, DC	Counsel and Advisor to the Assistant Attorney General.	Hector Gustavo Ruiz............	SC	GS	14	....	....
Washington, DC	Counsel	Grant Lerner Tanenbaum ...	SC	GS	13	....	....
	United States Parole Commission						
Washington, DC	Chairman	Vacant	....	EX	....	....	....
Washington, DC	Parole Commissioner............................	Vacant	....	EX	....	....	....
Washington, DC	Parole Commissioner............................	Charles Thomas Massarone.	PAS	EX	V	....	....
Washington, DC	Parole Commissioner............................	Patricia K Cushwa	PAS	EX	V	....	....
Washington, DC	Parole Commissioner............................	Vacant	....	EX	....	....	....
	Executive Office for United States Attorneys						
Washington, DC	Director..	Vacant	....	ES	....	....	....
Washington, DC	Principal Deputy Director	Career Incumbent	CA	ES	....	....	....
Montgomery, AL	United States Attorney, Alabama, Middle District.	Jonathan Ross	PAS	AD	....	....	....
Huntsville, AL	United States Attorney, Alabama, Northern District.	Vacant	....	AD	....	....	....
Mobile, AL	United States Attorney, Alabama, Southern District.	Vacant	....	AD	....	....	....
Anchorage, AK........	United States Attorney, Alaska	Shelley Lane Tucker	PAS	AD	....	....	....
Phoenix, AZ	United States Attorney, Arizona................	Gary Restaino......................	PAS	AD	....	....	....
Little Rock, AR........	United States Attorney, Arkansas, Eastern District.	Vacant	....	AD	....	....	....
Fort Smith, AR........	United States Attorney, Arkansas Western District.	Vacant	....	AD	....	....	....
Los Angeles, CA	United States Attorney, California, Central District.	Estaban Estrada	PAS	AD	....	....	....
Sacramento, CA.......	United States Attorney, California, Eastern District.	Phillip Talbert	PAS	AD	....	....	....
San Francisco, CA...	United States Attorney, California, Northern District.	Ismail Ramsey......................	PAS	AD	....	....	....
San Diego, CA	United States Attorney, California, Southern District.	Tara McGrath.......................	PAS	AD	....	....	....
New Haven, CT.......	United States Attorney, Connecticut................	Vanessa Avery	PAS	AD	....	....	....
Denver, CO	United States Attorney, Colorado......................	Vacant	....	AD	....	....	....
Wilmington, DE.......	United States Attorney, Delaware.....................	David Charles Weiss	PAS	AD	....	....	....
Washington, DC	United States Attorney, District of Columbia....	Matthew Graves.................	PAS	AD	....	....	....
Tampa, FL	United States Attorney, Florida, Middle District.	Roger Handberg III.............	PAS	AD	....	....	....
Tallahassee, FL	United States Attorney, Florida, Northern District.	Vacant	....	AD	....	....	....
Miami, FL................	United States Attorney, Florida, Southern District.	Markenzy Lapointe	PAS	AD	....	....	....
Macon, GA	United States Attorney, Georgia, Middle District.	Peter Leary	PAS	AD	....	....	....
Atlanta, GA	United States Attorney, Georgia, Northern District.	Ryan Buchanan....................	PAS	AD	....	....	....
Savannah, GA	United States Attorney, Georgia, Southern District.	Jill E Steinberg	PAS	AD	....	....	....

DEPARTMENT OF JUSTICE—Continued

Location	Position Title	Name of Incumbent	Type of Appt.	Pay Plan	Level, Grade, or Pay	Tenure	Expires
Agana, Guam..........	United States Attorney, Guam...........................	Vacant	....	AD	....	....	....
Honolulu, HI...........	United States Attorney, Hawaii.........................	Clare Connors....................	PAS	AD	....	....	....
Boise, ID	United States Attorney, Idaho	Joshua Hurwit....................	PAS	AD	....	....	....
Springfield, IL	United States Attorney, Illinois, Central District.	Gregory Keith Harris..........	PAS	AD	....	....	....
Chicago, IL	United States Attorney, Illinois, Northern District.	Vacant	....	AD	....	....	....
Fairview Heights, IL.	United States Attorney, Southern District, Illinois.	Rachelle Crowe....................	PAS	AD	....	....	....
Hammond, IN.........	United States Attorney, Indiana, Northern District.	Clifford Johnson	PAS	AD	....	....	....
Indianapolis, IN	United States Attorney, Indiana, Southern District.	Zachary Myers.....................	PAS	AD	....	....	....
Cedar Rapids, IA.....	United States Attorney, Iowa, Northern District.	Vacant	....	AD	....	....	....
Des Moines, IA........	United States Attorney, Iowa, Southern District.	Vacant	....	AD	....	....	....
Kansas City, KS	United States Attorney, Kansas	Kate Brubacher	PAS	AD	....	....	....
Lexington, KY	United States Attorney, Kentucky, Eastern District.	Vacant	....	AD	....	....	....
Louisville, KY..........	United States Attorney, Kentucky, Western District.	Vacant	....	AD	....	....	....
New Orleans, LA.....	United States Attorney, Louisiana, Eastern District.	Vacant	....	AD	....	....	....
Shreveport, LA........	United States Attorney, Louisiana, Western District.	Brandon Brown	PAS	AD	....	....	....
Baton Rouge, LA.....	United States Attorney, Louisiana, Middle District.	Ronald Gathe......................	PAS	AD	....	....	....
Portland, ME	United States Attorney, Maine	Darcie Leighton	PAS	AD	....	....	....
Baltimore, MD........	United States Attorney, Maryland	Erek Lawrence Barron	PAS	AD	....	....	....
Boston, MA	United States Attorney, Massachusetts	Joshua Levy........................	PAS	AD	....	....	....
Detroit, MI.............	United States Attorney, Michigan, Eastern District.	Dawn Ison..........................	PAS	AD	....	....	....
Grand Rapids, MI ...	United States Attorney, Michigan, Western District.	Mark Allan Totten...............	PAS	AD	....	....	....
Minneapolis, MN.....	United States Attorney, Minnesota	Andrew M Luger	PAS	AD	....	....	....
Oxford, MS	United States Attorney, Mississippi, Northern District.	Vacant	....	AD	....	....	....
Jackson, MS............	United States Attorney, Mississippi, Southern District.	Todd Gee	PAS	AD	....	....	....
St Louis, MO	United States Attorney, Missouri, Eastern District.	Vacant	....	AD	....	....	....
Kansas City, MO	United States Attorney, Missouri, Western District.	Teresa Moore	PAS	AD	....	....	....
Billings, MT............	United States Attorney, Montana......................	Jesse Laslovich	PAS	AD	....	....	....
Omaha, NE.............	United States Attorney, Nebraska.....................	Vacant	....	AD	....	....	....
Las Vegas, NV	United States Attorney, Nevada	Jason Frierson.....................	PAS	AD	....	....	....
Concord, NH	United States Attorney, New Hampshire	Jane Ellen Young.................	PAS	AD	....	....	....
Newark, NJ	United States Attorney, New Jersey	Philip Sellinger..................	PAS	AD	....	....	....
Albuquerque, NM....	United States Attorney, New Mexico	Alexander Uballez...............	PAS	AD	....	....	....
New York-Kings, NY.	United States Attorney, New York, Eastern District.	Breon Peace	PAS	AD	....	....	....
Syracuse, NY...........	United States Attorney, New York, Northern District.	Carla Freedman	PAS	AD	....	....	....
New York, NY..........	United States Attorney, New York, Southern District.	Andre Damian Williams	PAS	AD	....	....	....
Buffalo, NY	United States Attorney, New York, Western District.	Trini Ross	PAS	AD	....	....	....
Raleigh, NC	United States Attorney, North Carolina, Eastern District.	Michael Francis Easley........	PAS	AD	....	....	....
Greensboro, NC.......	United States Attorney, North Carolina, Middle District.	Sandra Hairston..................	PAS	AD	....	....	....
Charlotte, NC	United States Attorney, North Carolina, Western District.	Dena Janae King.................	PAS	AD	....	....	....
Fargo, ND	United States Attorney, North Dakota	McLain Schneider	PAS	AD	....	....	....
Cleveland, OH.........	United States Attorney, Ohio, Northern District.	Vacant	....	AD	....	....	....
Columbus, OH.........	United States Attorney, Ohio, Southern District.	Kenneth Parker	PAS	AD	....	....	....
Muskogee, OK	United States Attorney, Oklahoma, Eastern District.	Vacant	....	AD	....	....	....
Tulsa, OK.................	United States Attorney, Oklahoma, Northern District.	Clinton Johnson	PAS	AD	....	....	....

DEPARTMENT OF JUSTICE—Continued

Location	Position Title	Name of Incumbent	Type of Appt.	Pay Plan	Level, Grade, or Pay	Tenure	Expires
Oklahoma City, OK.	United States Attorney, Oklahoma, Western District.	Vacant		AD			
Portland, OR	United States Attorney, Oregon	Natalie Wight	PAS	AD			
Philadelphia, PA	United States Attorney, Pennsylvania, Eastern District.	Jacqueline C Romero	PAS	AD			
Harrisburg, PA	United States Attorney, Pennsylvania, Middle District.	Gerard Karam	PAS	AD			
Pittsburgh, PA	United States Attorney, Pennsylvania, Western District.	Eric Olshan	PAS	AD			
Hato Rey, Puer	United States Attorney, Puerto Rico	William S Muldrow	PAS	AD			
Providence, RI	United States Attorney, Rhode Island	Zachary Cunha	PAS	AD			
Columbia, SC	United States Attorney, South Carolina	Adair Boroughs	PAS	AD			
Sioux Falls, SD	United States Attorney, South Dakota	Vacant		AD			
Chattanooga, TN	United States Attorney, Tennessee, Eastern District.	Vacant		AD			
Nashville, TN	United States Attorney, Tennessee, Middle District.	Henry Leventis	PAS	AD			
Memphis, TN	United States Attorney, Western District, Tennessee.	Kevin Ritz	PAS	AD			
Beaumont, TX	United States Attorney, Texas, Eastern District.	Diggs Damian	PAS	AD			
Dallas, TX	United States Attorney, Texas, Northern District.	Leigha Simonton Horan	PAS	AD			
Houston, TX	United States Attorney, Texas, Southern District.	Alamdar Hamdani	PAS	AD			
San Antonio, TX	United States Attorney, Texas, Western District.	Jaime Esparza	PAS	AD			
Salt Lake City, UT..	United States Attorney, Utah	Trina Arline Higgins	PAS	AD			
Burlington, VT	United States Attorney, Vermont	Nikolas Kerest	PAS	AD			
St Croix, Virg	United States Attorney, Virgin Islands	Delia Laverne Smith	PAS	AD			
Alexandria, VA	United States Attorney, Virginia, Eastern District.	Jessica Diane Aber	PAS	AD			
Roanoke, VA	United States Attorney, Virginia, Western District.	Christopher Kavanaugh	PAS	AD			
Spokane, WA	United States Attorney, Washington, Eastern District.	Vanessa Ruth Waldref	PAS	AD			
Seattle, WA	United States Attorney, Washington, Western District.	Vacant		AD			
Wheeling, WV	United States Attorney, West Virginia, Northern District.	William Ihlenfeld	PAS	AD			
Charleston, WV	United States Attorney, West Virginia, Southern District.	William Thompson	PAS	AD			
Milwaukee, WI	United States Attorney, Wisconsin, Eastern District.	Gregory Haanstad	PAS	AD			
Madison, WI	United States Attorney, Wisconsin, Western District.	Vacant		AD			
Cheyenne, WY	United States Attorney, Wyoming	Vacant		AD			
Scranton, PA	Confidential Assistant	Mari E Burke	SC	GS	11		
Concord, NH	Confidential Assistant	Kathryn A Desrochers	SC	GS	9		
Miami, FL	Confidential Assistant	Tina Sutton	SC	GS	9		
Washington, DC	Confidential Assistant	Delaney Hewitt	SC	GS	9		
	Executive Office for Immigration Review						
Falls Church, VA	Director	Vacant		ES			
Falls Church, VA	Deputy Director	Career Incumbent	CA	ES			
Falls Church, VA	Chief Information Officer	Career Incumbent	CA	ES			
Falls Church, VA	Chief Management Officer	Vacant		ES			
Washington, DC	Regional Deputy Chief Immigration Judge	Career Incumbent	CA	ES			
	Office of the Pardon Attorney						
Washington, DC	Pardon Attorney	Career Incumbent	CA	ES			
	Office of Professional Responsibility						
Washington, DC	Senior Counselor	Vacant		ES			
	EXECUTIVE OFFICE FOR ORGANIZED CRIME DRUG ENFORCEMENT TASK FORCES						
Washington, DC	Director, Organized Crime Drug Enforcement Task Forces, Fusion Center.	Vacant		ES			
Washington, DC	Deputy Director, Organized Crime Drug Enforcement Task Forces.	Career Incumbent	CA	ES			
	Federal Bureau of Investigation						
Washington, DC	Director, Federal Bureau of Investigation	Christopher A Wray	PAS	EX	II		02/02/27

DEPARTMENT OF JUSTICE—Continued

Location	Position Title	Name of Incumbent	Type of Appt.	Pay Plan	Level, Grade, or Pay	Tenure	Expires
	Drug Enforcement Administration						
Washington, DC	Administrator, Drug Enforcement Administration.	Anne Melissa Milgram	PAS	EX	III	....	....
Washington, DC	Deputy Administrator, Drug Enforcement Administration.	Vacant	....	EX	....	....	....
	Bureau of Alcohol, Tobacco, Firearms and Explosives						
Washington, DC	Director, Bureau of Alcohol, Tobacco, Firearms, and Explosives.	Steven Dettelbach	PAS	EX	III	....	....
Washington, DC	Chief Counsel..	Career Incumbent	CA	ES	....	....	....
Washington, DC	Deputy Chief Counsel	Career Incumbent	CA	ES	....	....	....
Washington, DC	Executive Assistant Director for Administration.	Career Incumbent	CA	ES	....	....	....
Washington, DC	Chief, Firearms Operations Division.................	Vacant	....	ES	....	....	....
Washington, DC	Associate Assistant Director, Industry Operations.	Career Incumbent	CA	ES	....	....	....
Washington, DC	Deputy Assistant Director, Office of Enforcement Programs and Services.	Career Incumbent	CA	ES	....	....	....
	United States Marshals Service						
Arlington, VA..........	Director..	Ronald Davis	PAS	EX	IV	....	....
Arlington, VA..........	General Counsel	Career Incumbent	CA	ES	....	....	....
Montgomery, AL	United States Marshall, Middle District, Alabama.	Jesse Seroyer	PAS	GS	15	....	....
Birmingham, AL	United States Marshal, Northern District, Alabama.	Chester M Keely...................	PAS	GS	15	....	....
Mobile, AL	United States Marshal, Southern District, Alabama.	Mark F Sloke........................	PAS	GS	15	....	....
Anchorage, AK........	United States Marshal, Alaska	Robert W Heun.....................	PAS	GS	15	....	....
Phoenix, AZ	United States Marshal, District of Arizona (Phoenix).	Vacant	....	SL	....	....	....
Little Rock, AR........	United States Marshal, Eastern District, Arkansas.	Vacant	....	GS	....	....	....
Fort Smith, AR........	United States Marshal, Western District, Arkansas.	Vacant	....	GS	....	....	....
Los Angeles, CA	United States Marshal, Central District of California (Los Angeles).	David Singer	PAS	SL	....	....	....
Sacramento, CA.......	United States Marshal, Eastern District of California (Sacramento).	Vacant	....	SL	....	....	....
San Francisco, CA...	United States Marshal, Northern District of California (San Francisco).	Vacant	....	SL	....	....	....
San Diego, CA	United States Marshal, Southern District of California (San Diego).	Steven C Stafford	PAS	SL	....	....	....
Denver, CO	United States Marshal, Colorado (Denver)	Kirk M Taylor......................	PAS	SL	....	....	....
New Haven, CT.......	United States Marshal, Connecticut	Vacant	....	GS	....	....	....
Wilmington, DE.......	United States Marshal, Delaware	Michael C McGowan	PAS	GS	15	....	....
Tampa, FL	United States Marshal, Middle District of Florida (Tampa).	William B Berger	PAS	SL	....	....	....
Tallahassee, FL	United States Marshal, Northern District of Florida (Tallahassee).	Vacant	....	SL	....	....	....
Miami, FL................	United States Marshal, Southern District of Florida (Miami).	Gadyaces S Serralta............	PAS	SL	....	....	....
Macon, GA	United States Marshal, Middle District, Georgia.	Stephen D Lynn	PAS	GS	15	....	....
Atlanta, GA	United States Marshal, Northern District of Georgia (Atlanta).	Thomas Brown	PAS	SL	....	....	....
Savannah, GA	United States Marshal, Southern District, Georgia.	David L Lyons	PAS	GS	15	....	....
Agana, Guam...........	United States Marshal, Guam/Northern Mariana Islands.	Fernando Lg Sablan.............	PAS	GS	15	....	....
Honolulu, HI...........	United States Marshal, Hawaii	Vacant	....	GS	....	....	....
Boise, ID	United States Marshal, Idaho	Brent R Bunn	PAS	GS	15	....	....
Springfield, IL	United States Marshal, Central District, Illinois.	Brendan O Heffner	PAS	GS	15	....	....
Chicago, IL	United States Marshal, Northern District of Illinois (Chicago).	Ladon A Reynolds	PAS	SL	....	....	....
East St Louis, IL.....	United States Marshal, Southern District, Illinois.	David C Davis	PAS	GS	15	....	....
Hammond, IN..........	United States Marshal, Northern District, Indiana.	Todd L Nukes	PAS	GS	15	....	....
Indianapolis, IN	United States Marshal, Southern District, Indiana.	Joseph D McClain	PAS	GS	15	....	....

DEPARTMENT OF JUSTICE—Continued

Location	Position Title	Name of Incumbent	Type of Appt.	Pay Plan	Level, Grade, or Pay	Tenure	Expires
Cedar Rapids, IA.....	United States Marshal, Northern District, Iowa.	Vacant	....	GS	....	....	....
Des Moines, IA........	United States Marshal, Southern District, Iowa.	Theoharris G Kamatchus	PAS	GS	15	....	....
Kansas City, KS	United States Marshal, Kansas.........................	Ronald Miller.......................	PAS	GS	15	....	....
Lexington, KY	United States Marshal, Eastern District, Kentucky.	Vacant	....	GS	....	....	....
Louisville, KY..........	United States Marshal, Western District, Kentucky.	Gary B Burman....................	PAS	GS	15	....	....
New Orleans, LA.....	United States Marshal, Eastern District, Louisiana.	Enix Smith...........................	PAS	GS	15	....	....
Baton Rouge, LA.....	United States Marshal, Middle District, Louisiana.	William T Brown	PAS	GS	15	....	....
Shreveport, LA........	United States Marshal, Western District, Louisiana.	Vacant	....	GS	....	....	....
Portland, ME..........	United States Marshal, Maine	Vacant	....	GS	....	....	....
Baltimore, MD........	United States Marshal District of Maryland (Baltimore).	Vacant	....	SL	....	....	....
Boston, MA..............	United States Marshal, Massachusetts	Brian A Kyes	PAS	SL	....	....	....
Detroit, MI..............	United States Marshal, Eastern District of Michigan (Detroit).	Owen Cypher.......................	PAS	SL	....	....	....
Grand Rapids, MI ...	United States Marshal, Western District, Michigan.	Vacant	....	GS	....	....	....
Minneapolis, MN.....	United States Marshal, District of Minnesota (Minneapolis).	Eddie Frizell	PAS	SL	....	....	....
Oxford, MS	United States Marshal, Northern District, Mississippi.	Daniel R McKittrick.............	PAS	GS	15	....	....
Jackson, MS............	United States Marshal, Southern District, Mississippi.	Mark B Shepherd.................	PAS	GS	15	....	....
St Louis, MO	United States Marshal, Eastern District, Missouri (St Louis).	Jonathan D Jordan	PAS	SL	....	....	....
Kansas City, MO	United States Marshal, Western District, Missouri.	Vacant	....	GS	....	....	....
Billings, MT............	United States Marshal, Montana.......................	Craig Anderson....................	PAS	GS	15	....	....
Omaha, NE..............	United States Marshal, Nebraska......................	Scott E Kracl	PAS	GS	15	....	....
Las Vegas, NV..........	United States Marshal, Nevada (Las Vegas).....	Gary G Schofield	PAS	SL	....	....	....
Concord, NH...........	United States Marshal, New Hampshire..........	William R Hart....................	PAS	GS	15	....	....
Newark, NJ	United States Marshal, District of New Jersey (Newark).	Juan Mattos.........................	PAS	SL	....	....	....
Albuquerque, NM....	United States Marshal District New Mexico (Albuquerque).	Vacant	....	SL	....	....	....
New York-Kings, NY.	United States Marshal Eastern District of New York (Kings).	Vincent F Demarco	PAS	SL	....	....	....
Syracuse, NY	United States Marshal, Northern District, New York.	David L McNulty.................	PAS	GS	15	....	....
New York, NY.........	United States Marshal, Southern District of New York (New York).	Ralph Sozio	PAS	SL	....	....	....
Buffalo, NY..............	United States Marshal, Western District, New York.	Vacant	....	GS	....	....	....
Buffalo, NY..............	United States Marshal, Western District, New York.	Charles F Salina	PAS	GS	15	....	....
Raleigh, NC	United States Marshal, Eastern District, North Carolina.	Glenn M McNeill.................	PAS	GS	15	....	....
Greensboro, NC.......	United States Marshal, Middle District, North Carolina.	Catrina A Thompson...........	PAS	GS	15	....	....
Charlotte, NC	United States Marshal, Western District, North Carolina.	Terry J Burgin.....................	PAS	GS	15	....	....
Fargo, ND	United States Marshal, North Dakota..............	Dallas L Carlson	PAS	GS	15	....	....
Cleveland, OH........	United States Marshal, Northern District of Ohio (Cleveland).	Peter J Elliott.....................	PAS	SL	....	....	....
Cincinnati, OH.......	United States Marshal, Southern District, Ohio (Cincinnati).	Michael Black	PAS	SL	....	....	....
Muskogee, OK.........	United States Marshal, Eastern District, Oklahoma.	Kerry L Pettingill.................	PAS	GS	15	....	....
Tulsa, OK................	United States Marshal, Northern District, Oklahoma.	Clayton D Johnson...............	PAS	GS	15	....	....
Oklahoma City, OK.	United States Marshal, Western District, Oklahoma.	Johnny Lee Kuhlman...........	PAS	GS	15	....	....
Portland, OR...........	United States Marshal, Oregon (Portland)........	Vacant	....	SL	....	....	....
Philadelphia, PA	United States Marshal, Eastern District of Pennsylvania (Philadelphia).	Eric S Gartner.....................	PAS	SL	....	....	....
Scranton, PA............	United States Marshal, Middle District, Pennsylvania.	Vacant	....	SL	....	....	....

DEPARTMENT OF JUSTICE—Continued

Location	Position Title	Name of Incumbent	Type of Appt.	Pay Plan	Level, Grade, or Pay	Tenure	Expires
Pittsburgh, PA.........	United States Marshal, Western District, Pennsylvania.	Stephen Eberle......................	PAS	GS	15	....	....
San Juan, PR...........	United States Marshal, Puerto Rico	Wilmer Ocasio	PAS	SL	....	....	....
Providence, RI	United States Marshal, Rhode Island...............	Wing Chau..........................	PAS	GS	15	....	....
Columbia, SC...........	United States Marshal, District of South Carolina (Columbia).	Chrissie C Latimore.............	PAS	SL	....	....	....
Sioux Falls, SD	United States Marshal, South Dakota..............	Vacant	....	GS	....	....	....
Knoxville, TN...........	United States Marshal, Eastern District, Tennessee.	David G Jolley......................	PAS	GS	15	....	....
Nashville, TN	United States Marshal, Middle District, Tennessee.	Denny W King	PAS	GS	15	....	....
Memphis, TN...........	United States Marshal, Western District, Tennessee.	Tyreece L Miller..................	PAS	GS	15	....	....
Tyler, TX	United States Marshal, Eastern District, Texas (Tyler).	John W Garrison	PAS	SL	....	....	....
Dallas, TX	United States Marshal, Northern District of Texas (Dallas).	Vacant	....	SL	....	....	....
Houston, TX............	United States Marshal, Southern District of Texas (Houston).	Thomas M Oconnor..............	PAS	SL	....	....	....
San Antonio, TX	United States Marshal, Western District of Texas (San Antonio).	Susan L Pamerleau..............	PAS	SL	....	....	....
Salt Lake City, UT..	United States Marshal, Utah	Justin L Martinez	PAS	GS	15	....	....
Burlington, VT	United States Marshal, Vermont.....................	Vacant	....	GS	....	....	....
St Thomas, Virg.......	United States Marshal, Virgin Islands	Vacant	....	GS	....	....	....
Alexandria, VA	United States Marshal, Eastern District of Virginia (Alexandria).	Shannon Saylor	PAS	SL	....	....	....
Roanoke, VA	United States Marshal, Western District, Virginia.	Thomas Foster......................	PAS	GS	15	....	....
Washington, DC	United States Marshal, District of Columbia (Washington, District of Columbia).	Vacant	....	SL	....	....	....
Washington, DC	United States Marshal, Superior Court (Washington District of Columbia).	Robert A Dixon	PAS	SL	....	....	....
Spokane, WA	United States Marshal, Eastern District, Washington.	Craig E Thayer.....................	PAS	GS	15	....	....
Seattle, WA..............	United States Marshal, Western District, Washington (Seattle).	Vacant	....	SL	....	....	....
Clarksburg, WV........	United States Marshal, Northern District, West Virginia.	Vacant	....	GS	....	....	....
Charleston, WV	United States Marshal, Southern District, West Virginia.	Michael T Baylous................	PAS	GS	15	....	....
Milwaukee, WI	United States Marshal, Eastern District, Wisconsin.	Anna M Ruzinski	PAS	GS	15	....	....
Madison, WI	United States Marshal, Western District, Wisconsin.	Kim V Gaffney......................	PAS	GS	15	....	....
Cheyenne, WY	United States Marshal, Wyoming	Randall P Huff	PAS	GS	15	....	....
	Federal Bureau of Prisons						
Washington, DC	Director National Institute of Corrections	Vacant	CA	ES	....	....	....
Washington, DC	Director...	Career Incumbent	CA	ES	....	....	....
Washington, DC	Correctional Program Officer (Chief of Staff)....	Career Incumbent	CA	ES	....	....	....
Grand Prairie, TX ...	Correctional Program Officer	Career Incumbent	CA	ES	....	....	....
Washington, DC	Correctional Program Officer	Career Incumbent	CA	ES	....	....	....
Washington, DC	Associate Deputy Director	Career Incumbent	CA	ES	....	....	....
Washington, DC	Director of Communications and Government Relations.	Career Incumbent	CA	ES	....	....	....
	OFFICE OF THE ASSOCIATE ATTORNEY GENERAL						
Washington, DC	Associate Attorney General	Vacant	....	EX	....	....	....
Washington, DC	Principal Deputy Associate Attorney General...	Benjamin Mizer....................	NA	ES	....	....	....
Washington, DC	Chief of Staff and Deputy Associate Attorney General.	Mitchell Reich......................	NA	ES	....	....	....
Washington, DC	Deputy Associate Attorney General	Nicole Ndumele	NA	ES	....	....	....
Washington, DC	Deputy Associate Attorney General	Saeed A Mody	NA	ES	....	....	....
Washington, DC	Deputy Associate Attorney General	Paul Wolfson	NA	ES	....	....	....
Washington, DC	Deputy Associate Attorney General	Josephine Thacher Morse	NA	ES	....	....	....
Washington, DC	Deputy Chief of Staff and Senior Counsel........	Dahlia Dila Mignouna	SC	GS	15	....	....
	Access to Justice						
Washington, DC	Director, Access to Justice	Rachel Alexandra Rossi	NA	ES	....	....	....
Washington, DC	Deputy Director (Policy)..................................	Career Incumbent	CA	ES	....	....	....
	Antitrust Division						
Washington, DC	Assistant Attorney General Antitrust...............	Jonathan Kanter	PAS	EX	IV	....	....
Washington, DC	Principal Deputy Assistant Attorney General...	Doha G Mekki	NA	ES	....	....	....
Washington, DC	Deputy Assistant Attorney General	Andrew Joseph Forman	NA	ES	....	....	....

DEPARTMENT OF JUSTICE—Continued

Location	Position Title	Name of Incumbent	Type of Appt.	Pay Plan	Level, Grade, or Pay	Tenure	Expires
Washington, DC	Deputy Assistant Attorney General	Michael Kades	NA	ES	....	....	....
Washington, DC	Deputy Assistant Attorney General	Career Incumbent	CA	ES	....	....	....
Washington, DC	Deputy Assistant Attorney General	Hetal Doshi.........................	NA	ES	....	....	....
Washington, DC	Deputy Assistant Attorney General	John Elias	NA	ES	....	....	....
Washington, DC	Senior Counsel and Director of Risk Management.	Career Incumbent	CA	ES	....	....	....
Washington, DC	Chief, Appellate Section	Career Incumbent	CA	ES	....	....	....
New York, NY	Chief, New York Field Office...........................	Career Incumbent	CA	ES	....	....	....
Chicago, IL	Chief, Chicago Field Office............................	Career Incumbent	CA	ES	....	....	....
San Francisco, CA...	Chief, San Francisco Field Office	Career Incumbent	CA	ES	....	....	....
Washington, DC	Chief, Defense, Industrial and Aerospace..........	Career Incumbent	CA	ES	....	....	....
Washington, DC	Chief Economic Litigation Section	Career Incumbent	CA	ES	....	....	....
Washington, DC	Chief, Economic Regulatory Section...................	Career Incumbent	CA	ES	....	....	....
Washington, DC	Chief, Healthcare and Consumer Products	Career Incumbent	CA	ES	....	....	....
Washington, DC	Chief, Transportation/Energy/Agriculture Section.	Vacant	....	ES	....	....	....
Washington, DC	Chief, Washington Criminal I Section................	Career Incumbent	CA	ES	....	....	....
Washington, DC	Chief, Washington Criminal Ii Section...............	Career Incumbent	CA	ES	....	....	....
Washington, DC	Director of Civil Enforcement........................	Career Incumbent	CA	ES	....	....	....
Washington, DC	Director, Criminal Enforcement	Career Incumbent	CA	ES	....	....	....
Washington, DC	Director, Procurement Collusion Strike Force...	Career Incumbent	CA	ES	....	....	....
Washington, DC	Policy Director...	Career Incumbent	CA	ES	....	....	....
Washington, DC	Senior Counsel for International and Intergovernmental Engagement.	Vacant	....	ES	....	....	....
Washington, DC	Chief Competition Policy Section	Vacant	....	ES	....	....	....
Washington, DC	Chief, Foreign Commerce Section......................	Career Incumbent	CA	ES	....	....	....
Washington, DC	Chief, Media and Entertainment......................	Career Incumbent	CA	ES	....	....	....
Washington, DC	Chief, Networks and Technology Enforcement Section.	Career Incumbent	CA	ES	....	....	....
Washington, DC	Senior Director of Investigation and Litigation.	Vacant	....	ES	....	....	....
Washington, DC	Chief of Staff and Senior Counsel	Joshua Eric Tzuker	SC	GS	15	....	....
Washington, DC	Senior Counsel..	Perry Howard Apelbaum	SC	GS	15	....	....
Washington, DC	Senior Counsel..	Sarah Hubbard..................	SC	GS	15	....	....
	Civil Division						
Washington, DC	Assistant Attorney General Civil Division	Vacant	....	EX	....	....	....
Washington, DC	Principal Deputy Assistant Attorney General...	Brian Boynton	NA	ES	....	....	....
Washington, DC	Deputy Assistant Attorney General	Career Incumbent	CA	ES	....	....	....
Washington, DC	Deputy Assistant Attorney General	Sarah Harrington..................	NA	ES	....	....	....
Washington, DC	Deputy Assistant Attorney General	Arun G Rao.........................	NA	ES	....	....	....
Washington, DC	Deputy Assistant Attorney General	Brian Netter	NA	ES	....	....	....
Washington, DC	Deputy Assistant Attorney General	Vacant	....	ES	....	....	....
Washington, DC	Deputy Assistant Attorney General	Christopher Paul Tenorio	NA	ES	....	....	....
Washington, DC	Director, Appellate Staff...........................	Career Incumbent	CA	ES	....	....	....
Washington, DC	Director, Appellate Section	Career Incumbent	CA	ES	....	....	....
Washington, DC	Appellate Litigation Counsel	Career Incumbent	CA	ES	....	....	....
Washington, DC	Director, Commercial Litigation Branch, Corporate/Financial Section.	Career Incumbent	CA	ES	....	....	....
Washington, DC	Director, Commercial Litigation Branch, Civil Fraud Section.	Career Incumbent	CA	ES	....	....	....
Washington, DC	Director, Commercial Litigation Branch, Intellectual Property Section.	Career Incumbent	CA	ES	....	....	....
Washington, DC	Director, Commercial Litigation Branch, National Courts Section.	Career Incumbent	CA	ES	....	....	....
Washington, DC	Deputy Director, National Courts Section	Career Incumbent	CA	ES	....	....	....
Washington, DC	Branch Director, Federal Programs..................	Career Incumbent	CA	ES	....	....	....
Washington, DC	Branch Director, Federal Programs..................	Career Incumbent	CA	ES	....	....	....
Washington, DC	Branch Director, Federal Programs..................	Career Incumbent	CA	ES	....	....	....
Washington, DC	Special Litigation Counsel, Federal Programs ..	Career Incumbent	CA	ES	....	....	....
Washington, DC	Director, Torts Aviation, Space and Admiralty Litigation.	Career Incumbent	CA	ES	....	....	....
Washington, DC	Director, Constitutional and Specialized Tort Litigation Section.	Career Incumbent	CA	ES	....	....	....
Washington, DC	Deputy Director, Constitutional and Specialized Torts Litigation-Bivens.	Career Incumbent	CA	ES	....	....	....
Washington, DC	Director, Federal Tort Claims Act Section	Career Incumbent	CA	ES	....	....	....
Washington, DC	Director, Environmental Tort Litigation Section.	Career Incumbent	CA	ES	....	....	....
Washington, DC	Director, Office of Immigration Litigation (District Court Section).	Career Incumbent	CA	ES	....	....	....
Washington, DC	Special Master	Career Incumbent	CA	ES	....	....	....
Washington, DC	Senior Counsel...	Christopher Scott McAbee...	SC	GS	15	....	....

DEPARTMENT OF JUSTICE—Continued

Location	Position Title	Name of Incumbent	Type of Appt.	Pay Plan	Level, Grade, or Pay	Tenure	Expires
Washington, DC	Senior Counsel	Anjali Motgi...........................	SC	GS	15	....	....
Washington, DC	Counsel	Kathleen A Choi..................	SC	GS	15	....	....
Washington, DC	Counsel	Medha Gargeya	SC	GS	15	....	....
	Civil Rights Division						
Washington, DC	Assistant Attorney General Civil Rights	Kristen Clarke.....................	PAS	EX	IV	....	....
Washington, DC	Principal Deputy Assistant Attorney General...	Sparkle Leah Sooknanan	NA	ES		....	....
Washington, DC	Deputy Assistant Attorney General	Vacant	....	ES		....	....
Washington, DC	Deputy Assistant Attorney General	Jennifer Ellen Mathis	NA	ES		....	....
Washington, DC	Senior Counselor..	Vacant	....	ES		....	....
Washington, DC	Chief of Staff and Senior Counsel	Alexander Nathan Rias	SC	GS	15	....	....
Washington, DC	Senior Counsel	Robert Neil Weiner...............	SC	GS	15	....	....
Washington, DC	Senior Counsel	Harry Jay Hulings	SC	GS	15	....	....
Washington, DC	Senior Counsel	Omar Noureldin	SC	GS	15	....	....
Washington, DC	Senior Counsel	Mikael Andres Rojas	SC	GS	15	....	....
	Environment and Natural Resources Division						
Washington, DC	Assistant Attorney General Environment and Natural Resources.	Todd Sunhwae Kim..............	PAS	EX	IV	....	....
Washington, DC	Principal Deputy Assistant Attorney General...	Katherine E Konschnik	NA	ES		....	....
Washington, DC	Deputy Assistant Attorney General	Career Incumbent	CA	ES		....	....
Washington, DC	Deputy Assistant Attorney General	Vacant	....	ES		....	....
Washington, DC	Deputy Assistant Attorney General	Vacant	....	ES		....	....
Washington, DC	Deputy Assistant Attorney General	Career Incumbent	CA	ES		....	....
Washington, DC	Chief, Law and Policy Section	Vacant	....	ES		....	....
Washington, DC	Deputy Assistant Attorney General	Matthew Littleton	NA	ES		....	....
Washington, DC	Deputy Assistant Attorney General	Gina Louise Allery	NA	ES		....	....
	Tax Division						
Washington, DC	Assistant Attorney General Tax Division	Vacant	....	EX	IV	....	....
Washington, DC	Deputy Assistant Attorney General	Vacant	....	ES		....	....
Washington, DC	Deputy Assistant Attorney General	Vacant	....	ES		....	....
Washington, DC	Deputy Assistant Attorney General	Vacant	....	ES		....	....
Washington, DC	Senior Counselor to the Assistant Attorney General.	Career Incumbent	CA	ES		....	....
	OFFICE OF JUSTICE PROGRAMS						
Washington, DC	Assistant Attorney General, Office of Justice Programs.	Amy Solomon.......................	PAS	EX	IV	....	....
Washington, DC	Principal Deputy Assistant Attorney General...	Brent Cohen	NA	ES		....	....
Washington, DC	Chief of Staff	Vacant	....	ES		....	....
Washington, DC	Deputy Assistant Attorney General, Operations and Management.	Career Incumbent	CA	ES		....	....
Washington, DC	General Counsel	Career Incumbent	CA	ES		....	....
Washington, DC	Chief Information Officer	Career Incumbent	CA	ES		....	....
Washington, DC	Director, Office of Civil Rights (OCR)	Career Incumbent	CA	ES		....	....
Washington, DC	Deputy Administrator for Policy	Career Incumbent	CA	ES		....	....
Washington, DC	Senior Counselor..	Linda A Seabrook................	NA	ES		....	....
Washington, DC	Senior Policy Advisor..	Hayne Yoon.........................	SC	GS	15	....	....
Washington, DC	Policy Advisor..	Trelaine Ito.........................	SC	GS	13	....	....
Washington, DC	Director, Bureau of Justice Assistance...............	Karhlton Frederick Vanview Moore.	PA	EX	IV	....	....
Washington, DC	Director of Criminal Justice, Innovation, Development, and Engagement.	Karen Friedman...................	NA	ES		....	....
Washington, DC	Deputy Director for Planning, Bureau of Justice Assistance.	Career Incumbent	CA	ES		....	....
Washington, DC	Deputy Director for Programs, Bureau of Justice Assistance.	Career Incumbent	CA	ES		....	....
Washington, DC	Deputy Director, Policy..	Career Incumbent	CA	ES		....	....
Washington, DC	Director Office for Victims of Crime..................	Kristina Rose.......................	PA	EX	IV	....	....
Washington, DC	Director, Smart Office..	Helena Heath	PA	EX	IV	....	....
Washington, DC	Senior Counselor..	Vacant	....	ES		....	....
Washington, DC	Senior Counselor..	Vacant	....	ES		....	....
Washington, DC	Senior Advisor..	Vacant	....	ES		....	....
Washington, DC	Executive Director, Federal Interagency Council on Crime Prevention and Improving Reentry.	Vacant	....	ES		....	....
	Bureau of Justice Statistics						
Washington, DC	Director, Bureau of Justice Statistics................	Vacant	....	EX		....	....
Washington, DC	Principal Deputy Director..................................	Career Incumbent	CA	ES		....	....
	National Institute of Justice						
Washington, DC	Director, National Institute of Justice	Nancy La Vigne....................	PA	EX	IV	....	....
Washington, DC	Deputy Director, National Institute of Justice ..	Career Incumbent	CA	ES		....	....
Washington, DC	Executive Science Advisor...................................	Career Incumbent	CA	ES		....	....

DEPARTMENT OF JUSTICE—Continued

Location	Position Title	Name of Incumbent	Type of Appt.	Pay Plan	Level, Grade, or Pay	Tenure	Expires
	Office of Juvenile Justice and Delinquency Prevention						
Washington, DC	Administrator, Office of Juvenile Justice and Delinquency Prevention.	Elizabeth Ryan	PA	EX	IV		
Washington, DC	Deputy Administrator	Career Incumbent	CA	ES			
Washington, DC	Principal Deputy Administrator	Vacant		ES			
	Community Relations Service						
Washington, DC	Director, Community Relations Service	Vacant		EX			
Washington, DC	Deputy Director	Vacant		ES			
San Francisco, CA	Chief of Staff and Senior Advisor	Justin Lock	SC	GS	15		
Washington, DC	Senior Advisor	Meghann P Galloway	SC	GS	15		
Washington, DC	Senior Counsel	Margaret Lee Baskette	SC	GS	15		
Washington, DC	Director, Center for Faith-Based and Neighborhood Partnerships.	Simranjit Johnny Attariwala.	SC	GS	14		
Washington, DC	Policy Advisor	Jerron Hawkins	SC	GS	11		
	Foreign Claims Settlement Commission						
Washington, DC	Chairman	Vacant		EX			
Washington, DC	Member	Sylvia Becker	PAS	EX	V		
Washington, DC	Member	Patrick Hovakimian	PAS	EX	V		
	Office on Violence Against Women						
Washington, DC	Director, Office on Violence Against Women	Rosemarie Hidalgo	PAS	EX	V		
Washington, DC	Principal Deputy Director	Allison Land Randall	NA	ES			
Washington, DC	Deputy Director for Policy Development	Dieu Xuan Phan	SC	GS	14		
Washington, DC	Policy Advisor	Shilesha Bamberg	SC	GS	13		
	Executive Office for United States Trustees						
Washington, DC	Director	Career Incumbent	CA	ES			
Washington, DC	Deputy Director for Field Operations	Career Incumbent	CA	ES			
Washington, DC	Deputy Director (General Counsel)	Career Incumbent	CA	ES			
Washington, DC	Deputy Director (Management)	Career Incumbent	CA	ES			
	Community Oriented Policing Services						
Washington, DC	Director	Hugh T Clements	NA	ES			
Washington, DC	Principal Deputy Director	Vacant		ES			
Washington, DC	Senior Advisor	Career Incumbent	CA	ES			
	Office of Information Policy						
Washington, DC	Director, Office of Information Policy	Career Incumbent	CA	ES			
	Office of the Solicitor General						
Washington, DC	Solicitor General	Elizabeth Prelogar	PAS	EX	III		
Washington, DC	Principal Deputy Solicitor General	Brian Halligan Fletcher	NA	ES			
Washington, DC	Deputy Solicitor General	Career Incumbent	CA	ES			
Washington, DC	Deputy Solicitor General	Career Incumbent	CA	ES			
Washington, DC	Deputy Solicitor General	Career Incumbent	CA	ES			
Washington, DC	Deputy Solicitor General	Career Incumbent	CA	ES			

DEPARTMENT OF JUSTICE OFFICE OF THE INSPECTOR GENERAL

Location	Position Title	Name of Incumbent	Type of Appt.	Pay Plan	Level, Grade, or Pay	Tenure	Expires
Washington, DC	Inspector General	Michael E Horowitz	PAS	EX	III		

DEPARTMENT OF LABOR

Location	Position Title	Name of Incumbent	Type of Appt.	Pay Plan	Level, Grade, or Pay	Tenure	Expires
	OFFICE OF THE SECRETARY						
Washington, DC	Secretary of Labor	Vacant		EX			
Washington, DC	Chief of Staff	Allison L Zelman	NA	ES			
Washington, DC	Deputy Chief of Staff	John Towle	NA	ES			
Washington, DC	Chief Diversity and Equity Officer	Alaysia Hackett	NA	ES			
Washington, DC	Senior Counselor	Joshua Orton	SC	GS	15		
Washington, DC	Senior Counselor	Betty Hung	NA	ES			
Washington, DC	Executive Assistant to the Secretary	Sonja J Hoover	SC	GS	15		
Washington, DC	Senior Counselor to the Secretary	Mary Patricia Smith	SC	GS	15		

DEPARTMENT OF LABOR—Continued

Location	Position Title	Name of Incumbent	Type of Appt.	Pay Plan	Level, Grade, or Pay	Tenure	Expires
Washington, DC	Senior Advisor to the Secretary........................	Bartholomew John Sheard ..	SC	GS	15	....	....
Washington, DC	Senior Advisor..	Monica Sarah Weeks............	SC	GS	15	....	....
Washington, DC	Senior Advisor..	Christina Ellen Chen...........	SC	GS	15	....	....
Washington, DC	Chief Economist...	Sarah Glynn	SC	GS	15	....	....
Washington, DC	Senior Counselor..	Joseph Shantz	NA	ES	....	....	....
Washington, DC	Director of the Office of Public Engagement.....	Taylor Barnes	SC	GS	15	....	....
Washington, DC	Deputy Director for the Office of Public Engagement.	Valeria Treves......................	SC	GS	15	....	....
Washington, DC	Director of Scheduling and Advance	Adia Cherida Jordan...........	SC	GS	15	....	....
Washington, DC	Advisor for Private Sector Engagement	Fernando Ortiz	SC	GS	14	....	....
Washington, DC	White House Liaison	Dionne Jackson	SC	GS	14	....	....
Washington, DC	Deputy White House Liaison.............................	Nicola Wagner	SC	GS	13	....	....
Washington, DC	Advisor for Infrastructure and Climate Engagement.	John Laadt...........................	SC	GS	13	....	....
Washington, DC	Director of Advance	Claire Marie Frueauff..........	SC	GS	13	....	....
Washington, DC	Advance Associate	Madeline Valdez	SC	GS	12	....	....
Washington, DC	Event Director..	Nora Doherty.......................	SC	GS	13	....	....
Washington, DC	Advisor...	John Warner	SC	GS	13	....	....
Washington, DC	Advance Associate	Maia Renee Ito	SC	GS	12	....	....
	Office of the Deputy Secretary						
Washington, DC	Deputy Secretary of Labor...............................	Julie Su	PAS	EX	II	....	....
Washington, DC	Associate Deputy Secretary	Julia McKinney	NA	ES	....	....	....
Washington, DC	Senior Accountability Officer...........................	Career Incumbent	CA	ES	....	....	....
	OFFICE OF THE SOLICITOR						
Washington, DC	Solicitor of Labor	Seema Nanda	PAS	EX	IV	....	....
Washington, DC	Deputy Solicitor	Elena Goldstein	NA	ES	....	....	....
Washington, DC	Senior Counsel	Laura Huizar.......................	SC	GS	15	....	....
Washington, DC	Senior Counsel	Tanisha Raechelle Wilburn .	SC	GS	15	....	....
Washington, DC	Senior Counsel	Daniel Alexander McGrath .	SC	GS	15	....	....
Washington, DC	Associate Solicitor for Legislation and Legal Counsel.	Vacant	....	ES	....	....	....
Washington, DC	Associate Solicitor for Employment and Training Legal Services.	Career Incumbent	CA	ES	....	....	....
	OFFICE OF THE ASSISTANT SECRETARY FOR ADMINISTRATION AND MANAGEMENT						
Washington, DC	Assistant Secretary for Administration and Management.	Carolyn Buffie Angus-Hornbuckle.	PA	EX	IV	....	....
Washington, DC	Deputy Assistant Secretary for Policy	Surjeet Kaur Ahluwalia.......	NA	ES	....	....	....
Washington, DC	Special Advisor...	Thomas Murabito.................	SC	GS	13	....	....
Washington, DC	Director of Talent Transformation	Braye Cloud	TA	ES	....	....	....
Washington, DC	Chief Information Officer	Career Incumbent	CA	ES	....	....	....
Washington, DC	Deputy Chief Information Officer	Career Incumbent	CA	ES	....	....	....
	OFFICE OF THE ASSISTANT SECRETARY FOR POLICY						
Washington, DC	Assistant Secretary for Policy..........................	Vacant	....	EX	....	....	....
Washington, DC	Deputy Assistant Secretary for Policy	Katelyn Walker-Mooney.......	NA	ES	....	....	....
Washington, DC	Chief of Staff...	Diana Boesch........................	SC	GS	15	....	....
Washington, DC	Director of Workers and Tech Policy	Mary Beech..........................	SC	GS	15	....	....
Washington, DC	Deputy Director of the Good Jobs Initiative and Senior Policy Advisor.	Teresa Acuna	SC	GS	15	....	....
Washington, DC	Senior Policy Advisor and Director of Migrant Worker Policy.	Trudy Rebert	SC	GS	15	....	....
	OFFICE OF CONGRESSIONAL AND INTERGOVERNMENTAL AFFAIRS						
Washington, DC	Assistant Secretary for Congressional and Intergovernmental Affairs.	Elizabeth Schoff Watson	PAS	EX	IV	....	....
Washington, DC	Deputy Assistant Secretary for Congressional Affairs.	Jennifer Blair Waits............	NA	ES	....	....	....
Washington, DC	Associate Assistant Secretary for Budget and Appropriations.	Andria D Oliver...................	NA	ES	....	....	....
Washington, DC	Chief of Staff...	Catherine Rowley.................	SC	GS	15	....	....
Washington, DC	Secretary's Representative on Retirement and Pension Issues.	Kathleen Kennedy Townsend.	SC	GS	15	....	....
Washington, DC	Tribal Liaison..	Jack C Jackson	SC	GS	15	....	....
Washington, DC	Oversight Counsel	Edward Pierce Blue	SC	GS	15	....	....
Washington, DC	Senior Legislative Officer.................................	Sabrina Steel	SC	GS	15	....	....
Washington, DC	Senior Legislative Officer.................................	Joshua Mark Oppenheimer .	SC	GS	15	....	....
Washington, DC	Senior Legislative Officer.................................	Andrew Robert Fuentes.......	SC	GS	15	....	....
Washington, DC	Deputy Director of Intergovernmental Affairs ..	Nezly Emiret Silva...............	SC	GS	14	....	....
Washington, DC	Advisor to the Assistant Secretary....................	Malbert Smith	SC	GS	13	....	....

DEPARTMENT OF LABOR—Continued

Location	Position Title	Name of Incumbent	Type of Appt.	Pay Plan	Level, Grade, or Pay	Tenure	Expires
Washington, DC	Legislative Officer..	Wesley Harmon Crew	SC	GS	11	....	....
Washington, DC	Legislative Officer..	Jonathan Pekkala	SC	GS	12	....	....
Washington, DC	Senior Legislative Assistant	Kevin Wu	SC	GS	13	....	....
Washington, DC	Special Assistant...	Gillian Villarroel	SC	GS	7	....	....
	EMPLOYMENT AND TRAINING ADMINISTRATION						
Washington, DC	Assistant Secretary for Employment and Training.	Jose Alberto Rodriguez	PAS	EX	IV	....	....
Washington, DC	Deputy Assistant Secretary, Employment and Training Administration.	Vacant		ES		....	....
Washington, DC	Deputy Assistant Secretary	Career Incumbent	CA	ES		....	....
Washington, DC	Deputy Assistant Secretary	Manoach Lamarre	NA	ES		....	....
Washington, DC	Chief of Staff..	Ana Laura Hageage	SC	GS	15	....	....
Washington, DC	Director for Investing in Americas Workforce, Employment and Training Administration.	Brittany Anne Stich	SC	GS	15	....	....
Washington, DC	Senior Advisor and Director of Ui Modernization.	Andrew Stettner...................	SC	GS	15	....	....
Washington, DC	Senior Policy Advisor..	Renato Rocha.......................	SC	GS	14	....	....
Washington, DC	Senior Policy Advisor for Workforce Development.	Molly Bahin Bashay.............	SC	GS	14	....	....
Washington, DC	Special Assistant...	Marquis Antonio Hardy.......	SC	GS	9	....	....
Washington, DC	Administrator, Office of Management and Administrative Services.	Career Incumbent	CA	ES		....	....
Washington, DC	Administrator, Office of Workforce Investment.	Career Incumbent	CA	ES		....	....
	EMPLOYEE BENEFITS SECURITY ADMINISTRATION						
Washington, DC	Assistant Secretary for Employee Benefits Security.	Lisa Gomez	PAS	EX	IV	....	....
Washington, DC	Deputy Assistant Secretary, Employee Benefits Security Administration.	Ali Khawar	NA	ES		....	....
Washington, DC	Special Assistant...	Gwendolyn Marie McCullough.	SC	GS	11	....	....
Washington, DC	Administrative Officer......................................	Career Incumbent	CA	ES		....	....
	OCCUPATIONAL SAFETY AND HEALTH ADMINISTRATION						
Washington, DC	Assistant Secretary for Occupational Safety and Health.	Douglas Parker.....................	PAS	EX	IV	....	....
Washington, DC	Deputy Assistant Secretary, Occupational Safety and Health Administration.	James Frederick	NA	ES		....	....
Washington, DC	Chief of Staff..	Emily Hargrove	SC	GS	15	....	....
Washington, DC	Senior Policy Advisor..	Natalicia Tracy	SC	GS	15	....	....
Washington, DC	Special Advisor...	Riter Hoopes	SC	GS	12	....	....
Washington, DC	Deputy Assistant Secretary	Career Incumbent	CA	ES		....	....
Atlanta, GA	Regional Administrator - Atlanta.....................	Career Incumbent	CA	ES		....	....
Boston, MA	Regional Administrator - Boston.....................	Career Incumbent	CA	ES		....	....
Chicago, IL	Regional Administrator - Chicago....................	Career Incumbent	CA	ES		....	....
Dallas, TX	Regional Administrator - Dallas......................	Career Incumbent	CA	ES		....	....
Denver, CO	Regional Administrator - Denver.....................	Career Incumbent	CA	ES		....	....
New York, NY..........	Regional Administrator - New York	Career Incumbent	CA	ES		....	....
Philadelphia, PA	Regional Administrator - Philadelphia	Career Incumbent	CA	ES		....	....
San Francisco, CA...	Regional Administrator - San Francisco...........	Career Incumbent	CA	ES		....	....
Seattle, WA	Regional Administrator - Seattle......................	Career Incumbent	CA	ES		....	....
Washington, DC	Director, Directorate of Cooperative and State Programs.	Career Incumbent	CA	ES		....	....
Washington, DC	Director, Directorate of Enforcement Programs.	Vacant		ES		....	....
Washington, DC	Director, Directorate of Standards and Guidance.	Career Incumbent	CA	ES		....	....
Washington, DC	Director, Directorate of Whistleblower Protection Program.	Career Incumbent	CA	ES		....	....
Kansas City, MO	Safety and Health Administrator - Kansas City.	Career Incumbent	CA	ES		....	....
	MINE SAFETY AND HEALTH ADMINISTRATION						
Washington, DC	Assistant Secretary for Mine Safety and Health.	Christopher John Williamson.	PAS	EX	IV	....	....
Washington, DC	Director for Educational Policy and Development.	Career Incumbent	CA	ES		....	....
Washington, DC	Administrator, Mine Safety and Health Enforcement.	Career Incumbent	CA	ES		....	....
Denver, CO	Deputy Administrator for Regional Operations.	Career Incumbent	CA	ES		....	....

DEPARTMENT OF LABOR—Continued

Location	Position Title	Name of Incumbent	Type of Appt.	Pay Plan	Level, Grade, or Pay	Tenure	Expires
Arlington, VA..........	Deputy Assistant Secretary	Julie Ellen Aaronson............	NA	ES	....	....	....
Arlington, VA..........	Senior Advisor...	Sulaiman Balogun................	SC	GS	15	....	....
Arlington, VA..........	Senior Policy Advisor......................................	Amar Pandya........................	SC	GS	15	....	....
Washington, DC	Chief of Staff...	Mary Kathryn Fletcher........	SC	GS	15	....	....
	OFFICE OF PUBLIC AFFAIRS						
Washington, DC	Assistant Secretary for Public Affairs...............	Julie Downey	PA	EX	IV	....	....
Washington, DC	Deputy Assistant Secretary, Office of Public Affairs.	Jesse Lawder	NA	ES	....	....	....
Washington, DC	Deputy Assistant Secretary for Public Affairs ..	Career Incumbent	CA	ES	....	....	....
Washington, DC	Special Advisor...	Allison Barry	SC	GS	13	....	....
Washington, DC	Special Assistant..	Paloma Renteria....................	SC	....	9	....	....
Washington, DC	Press Advisor	Jacob Andrejat......................	SC	GS	12	....	....
Washington, DC	Deputy Press Secretary...................................	Grace Hagerty	SC	GS	12	....	....
Washington, DC	Deputy Director of Digital Engagement............	Justin Lee Karlins	SC	GS	11	....	....
Washington, DC	Deputy Speechwriter.......................................	Catherine Petersen	SC	GS	11	....	....
Washington, DC	Chief of Staff...	Amanda McClure	SC	GS	15	....	....
Washington, DC	Chief of Speechwriting	Israel Igualate......................	SC	GS	....	....	....
	OFFICE OF THE CHIEF FINANCIAL OFFICER						
Washington, DC	Associate Deputy Chief Financial Officer for Fiscal Integrity.	Career Incumbent	CA	ES	....	....	....
Washington, DC	Associate Deputy CFO for Financial Systems Integrity.	Vacant	....	ES	....	....	....
	WAGE AND HOUR DIVISION						
Washington, DC	Wage and Hour Administrator	Jessica Looman	PAS	EX	V	....	....
Washington, DC	Deputy Wage and Hour Administrator..............	Kristin Garcia......................	NA	ES	....	....	....
Washington, DC	Deputy Administrator	Career Incumbent	CA	ES	....	....	....
Washington, DC	Policy Advisor	Joseph Sweeney....................	SC	GS	14	....	....
Washington, DC	Advisor..	Augusto Goncalves...............	SC	GS	13	....	....
Chicago, IL	Regional Administrator for Wage and Hour......	Career Incumbent	CA	ES	....	....	....
Washington, DC	Assistant Administrator for Policy....................	Career Incumbent	CA	ES	....	....	....
Atlanta, GA	Regional Administrator for Wage and Hour......	Career Incumbent	CA	ES	....	....	....
Dallas, TX.................	Regional Administrator for Wage and Hour......	Career Incumbent	CA	ES	....	....	....
San Francisco, CA...	Regional Administrator for Wage and Hour......	Career Incumbent	CA	ES	....	....	....
Washington, DC	Assistant Administrator for Planning, Performance Evaluation and Training.	Career Incumbent	CA	ES	....	....	....
Philadelphia, PA	Regional Administrator for Wage and Hour......	Career Incumbent	CA	ES	....	....	....
	VETERANS EMPLOYMENT AND TRAINING SERVICE						
Washington, DC	Assistant Secretary for Veterans Employment and Training.	James D Rodriguez	PAS	EX	IV	....	....
Washington, DC	Deputy Assistant Secretary, Veterans Employment and Training Service.	Julian Purdy.........................	NA	ES	....	....	....
Washington, DC	Chief of Staff...	Karla Langham	SC	....	15	....	....
	OFFICE OF DISABILITY EMPLOYMENT POLICY						
Washington, DC	Assistant Secretary for Disability Employment Policy.	Taryn Williams.....................	PAS	EX	IV	....	....
Washington, DC	Chief of Staff...	Anupa Iyer Geevarghese	SC	GS	15	....	....
Washington, DC	Policy Advisor	Tyrec Grooms	SC	GS	14	....	....
	WOMEN'S BUREAU						
Washington, DC	Director of the Women's Bureau.......................	Wendy Chun Hoon	PA	SL	....	....	....
Washington, DC	Deputy Director, Women's Bureau	Gayle Goldin	NA	ES	....	....	....
Washington, DC	Chief of Staff...	Agatha Kotani	SC	GS	13	....	....
Washington, DC	Senior Advisor...	Anne Bailey Danhoffer	SC	GS	15	....	....
Washington, DC	Senior Advisor...	Sophia Christelle Kerby	SC	GS	15	....	....
	BUREAU OF LABOR STATISTICS						
Washington, DC	Commissioner of Labor Statistics......................	Erika McEntarfer.................	PAS	EX	IV	4	....
	OFFICE OF FEDERAL CONTRACT COMPLIANCE PROGRAMS						
Washington, DC	Deputy Director, Office of Federal Contract Compliance Program.	Career Incumbent	CA	ES	....	....	....
Washington, DC	Director, Division of Program Operations..........	Vacant	....	ES	....	....	....
Washington, DC	Director of Enforcement..................................	Career Incumbent	CA	ES	....	....	....
	OFFICE OF LABOR-MANAGEMENT STANDARDS						
Washington, DC	Director, Office of Labor-Management Standards.	Jeffrey Freund......................	NA	ES	....	....	....

DEPARTMENT OF LABOR—Continued

Location	Position Title	Name of Incumbent	Type of Appt.	Pay Plan	Level, Grade, or Pay	Tenure	Expires
	OFFICE OF WORKERS COMPENSATION PROGRAMS						
Washington, DC	Director, Office of Workers Compensation Programs.	Christopher J Godfrey	NA	ES	....	....	....
Washington, DC	Senior Advisor....................	Abdirahman Mahamud Muse.	SC	GS	15	....	....
Dallas, TX	National Admin of Field Operations, Division of Coal Mine Workers Compensation.	Vacant	....	ES	....	....	....
Washington, DC	Deputy Director, Division of Coal Mine Workers Compensation.	Career Incumbent	CA	ES	....	....	....
	BUREAU OF INTERNATIONAL LABOR AFFAIRS						
Washington, DC	Deputy Under Secretary for International Labor Affairs.	Thea Mei Lee.......................	NA	ES	....	....	....
Washington, DC	Associate Deputy Under Secretary for International Affairs.	Molly Ann McCoy	NA	ES	....	....	....
Washington, DC	Associate Deputy Undersecretary for International Affairs (Policy and Management).	Career Incumbent	CA	ES	....	....	....
Washington, DC	Director, Office of Child Labor, Forced Labor Human Trafficking.	Career Incumbent	CA	ES	....	....	....
Washington, DC	Director, Office of Trade and Labor Affairs	Career Incumbent	CA	ES	....	....	....
Washington, DC	Chief of Staff....................	Oliva Lopez..........................	SC	GS	15	....	....
Washington, DC	Senior Advisor....................	Caitlin Coyne Helfrich.........	SC	GS	14	....	....
Washington, DC	Advisor....................	Elizabeth Pena	SC	GS	13	....	....

DEPARTMENT OF LABOR OFFICE OF INSPECTOR GENERAL

Location	Position Title	Name of Incumbent	Type of Appt.	Pay Plan	Level, Grade, or Pay	Tenure	Expires
Washington, DC	Inspector General	Larry Delano Turner............	PAS	IG	....	....	....

DEPARTMENT OF STATE

Location	Position Title	Name of Incumbent	Type of Appt.	Pay Plan	Level, Grade, or Pay	Tenure	Expires
	OFFICE OF THE SECRETARY						
Washington, DC	Secretary of State	Antony J Blinken	PAS	EX	I	....	....
Washington, DC	Chief of Staff..................................	Suzanne A George...............	NA	ES	....	....	....
Washington, DC	Deputy Chief of Staff for Operations	Jessica Nicole Wright...........	NA	ES	....	....	....
Washington, DC	Counselor and Deputy Chief of Staff for Policy.	Thomas David Sullivan	NA	ES	....	....	....
Washington, DC	Special Presidential Envoy for Climate............	Vacant	....	ES	....	....	....
Washington, DC	Special Envoy for Iran	Robert Malley	NA	ES	....	....	....
Washington, DC	Special Presidential Envoy for Hostage Affairs.	Roger Carstens	PA	ES	....	....	....
Washington, DC	Senior Advisor for Outreach and Strategic Planning.	Melissa Toufanian	SC	GS	15	....	....
Washington, DC	Senior Advisor....................	Allison Claire Wong	SC	GS	15	....	....
Washington, DC	Senior Advisor....................	Vacant	....	ES	....	....	....
Washington, DC	Staff Assistant....................	Sarah Marie McCool	SC	GS	12	....	....
Washington, DC	Staff Assistant....................	Adele Malle...........................	SC	GS	11	....	....
Washington, DC	Special Assistant....................	Matthew Groum	SC	GS	13	....	....
Washington, DC	Special Advisor....................	Elena Lund	SC	GS	13	....	....
	Office of the Deputy Secretary						
Washington, DC	Deputy Secretary of State.......................	Kurt Campbell.......................	PAS	EX	II	....	....
Washington, DC	Senior Advisor (Speechwriter)............................	Anna Van Hollen	SC	GS	....	....	....
Washington, DC	Senior Advisor for Policy.......................	Nazih Hazem El-Khatib	SC	GS	15	....	....
Washington, DC	Deputy Assistant Secretary International Cyberspace Security.	Career Incumbent	CA	ES	....	....	....
	Office of the Deputy Secretary for Management and Resources						
Washington, DC	Deputy Secretary of State for Management and Resources.	Richard R Verma................	PAS	EX	II	....	....

DEPARTMENT OF STATE—Continued

Location	Position Title	Name of Incumbent	Type of Appt.	Pay Plan	Level, Grade, or Pay	Tenure	Expires
Washington, DC	Staff Assistant..	Abhinav Seetharaman	SC	GS	11	....	....
Washington, DC	Confidential Assistant....................................	Kennedy Murray	SC	GS	9	....	....
Washington, DC	Deputy Director	Career Incumbent	CA	ES	....	....	....
	Office of U.S. Foreign Assistance						
Washington, DC	Office Director..	Vacant	....	ES	....	....	....
Washington, DC	Director..	Career Incumbent	CA	ES	....	....	....
Washington, DC	Managing Director..	Career Incumbent	CA	ES	....	....	....
	Bureau of Cyberspace and Digital Policy						
Washington, DC	Ambassador At Large for Cyberspace and Digital Policy.	Nathaniel Fick......................	PAS	EX	IV	....	....
Washington, DC	Special Envoy and Coordinator for Digital Freedom.	Eileen Donahoe	NA	ES	....	....	....
Washington, DC	Senior Advisor	Gerard John Lumban...........	SC	GS	15	....	....
Washington, DC	Special Implementation Envoy for Critical and Emerging Technology.	Vacant	....	ES	....	....	12/31/26
	Office of Policy Planning						
Washington, DC	Director, Policy Planning................................	Salman S Ahmed..................	NA	ES	....	....	....
Washington, DC	Principal Deputy Director...............................	Matan Chorev.......................	NA	ES	....	....	....
Washington, DC	Senior Advisor (Speechwriter)	Shana Gabrielle Mansbach .	SC	GS	15	....	....
Washington, DC	Senior Advisor..	Aya R Ibrahim......................	SC	GS	15	....	....
Washington, DC	Senior Advisor (Speechwriter)	Zev Karlin-Neumann	SC	GS	15	....	....
Washington, DC	Senior Advisor..	Robert Nelson	SC	GS	15	....	....
Washington, DC	Senior Advisor..	Nikolaus S Steinberg...........	SC	GS	15	....	....
Washington, DC	Special Advisor...	Lalitha Adury	SC	GS	13	....	....
Washington, DC	Special Assistant..	Maria Laura Rodriguez Lopez.	SC	GS	13	....	....
Washington, DC	Special Advisor (Speech Writer)	Elena Souris	SC	GS	13	....	....
	United States Mission to United Nations						
New York, NY..........	Representative of the USA to the United Nations, With the Rank and Status of Ambassador Extraordinary and Plenipotentiary, and the Representative of the USA to the Security Council of the United Nations.	Linda Thomas-Greenfield	PAS	AD	2	....	....
New York, NY..........	Deputy Representative of the USA to the United Nations, With the Rank and Status of Ambassador Extraordinary and Plenipotentiary and the Deputy Representative of the USA in the Security Council of the United Nations.	Vacant	....	AD	....	....	....
New York, NY..........	Chief of Staff..	Jonathan Stahler..................	SC	AD	4	....	....
New York, NY..........	Representative of the USA to the United Nations for UN Management and Reform, With the Rank of Ambassador.	Christopher P Lu	PAS	AD	4	....	....
New York, NY..........	Alternate Representative of the USA for Special Political Affairs in the United Nations, With the Rank of Ambassador.	Robert A Wood	PAS	AD	4	....	....
New York, NY..........	Representative of the USA on the Economic and Social Council of the UN, With the Rank of Ambassador.	Lisa Carty	PAS	AD	4	....	....
Washington, DC	Deputy to the Representative of the USA to the United Nations.	Edward Price	PA	AD	IV	....	....
Washington, DC	Counselor, International Legal Affairs...............	Career Incumbent	CA	ES	....	....	....
New York, NY..........	Deputy Chief of Staff......................................	Nabila Baptiste	XS	OT	....	....	....
Washington, DC	Senior Policy Advisor......................................	Alexandra S Davis	SC	GG	15	....	....
New York, NY..........	Director of Communications	Nathan Evans	XS	OT	....	....	....
New York, NY..........	Policy Advisor	Aditi Gorur	SC	OT	....	....	....
New York, NY..........	Director of Speechwriting	Sarah Gruen	XS	OT	....	....	....
New York, NY..........	Senior Policy Advisor......................................	Shiouyu Lou	XS	OT	....	....	....
New York, NY..........	Senior Policy Advisor......................................	Sean Misko	XS	OT	....	....	....
Washington, DC	Senior Policy Advisor (Legislative Affairs and Global Issues) (W).	Kevin Lawson	XS	....	....	....	....
New York, NY..........	Deputy Chief of Staff, and XS Appointment Type.	Jasmine Wyatt......................	SC	OT	....	....	....
New York, NY..........	Special Advisor...	Alejandra Gonzalez	XS	OT	....	....	....
New York, NY..........	Staff Assistant..	Austin Sams	XS	OT	....	....	....
New York, NY..........	Policy Advisor	Matthew Finkel....................	SC	OT	....	....	....
	Office of the Chief of Protocol						
Washington, DC	Chief of Protocol and to have rank of Ambassador during tenure of service.	Vacant	....	EX	....	....	....
Washington, DC	Deputy Chief of Protocol	Sharon E Weber	SC	GS	15	....	....

DEPARTMENT OF STATE—Continued

Location	Position Title	Name of Incumbent	Type of Appt.	Pay Plan	Level, Grade, or Pay	Tenure	Expires
Washington, DC	Deputy Chief of Protocol	Maya Rao...............................	SC	GS	15	....	....
Washington, DC	Assistant Chief of Protocol (Ceremonials)........	Eleanor Warner	SC	GS	15	....	....
Washington, DC	Assistant Chief of Protocol (Visits)...................	Margaret Freshwater...........	SC	GS	15	....	....
Washington, DC	Senior Protocol Officer (Ceremonials)...............	Nancy Orloff........................	SC	GS	15	....	....
Washington, DC	Assistant Chief of Protocol (Diplomatic Partnerships).	Sally Marx	SC	GS	15	....	....
Washington, DC	Senior Protocol Officer (Visits)	Reid Fitzgerald.....................	SC	GS	15	....	....
Washington, DC	Senior Protocol Officer (Visits)	Cristina Flores......................	SC	GS	15	....	....
Washington, DC	Senior Protocol Officer (Major Events)	Timothy S Hartz	SC	GS	15	....	....
Washington, DC	Protocol Officer (Gifts).......................................	Candace Johnson...................	SC	GS	14	....	....
Washington, DC	Director of Events and Hospitality	Shannon Ricchetti	SC	GS	13	....	....
Washington, DC	Protocol Officer	Adonna Biel..........................	SC	GS	13	....	....
Washington, DC	Protocol Officer	Esther K Ongeri	SC	GS	13	....	....
Washington, DC	Protocol Officer (Ceremonials)...........................	Elizabeth Hascher................	SC	GS	12	....	....
Washington, DC	Protocol Officer (Visits)	Amijah C Townsend-Holmes.	SC	GS	12	....	....
Washington, DC	Protocol Officer (Visits)	Tyler Brumfield...................	SC	GS	12	....	....
Washington, DC	Senior Advisor..	Evan Glover..........................	SC	GS	....	....	....
	Bureau of Global Health Security and Diplomacy						
Washington, DC	Ambassador At Large and Coordinator of United States Government Activities to Combat HIV/AIDS Globally.	John Nkengasong.................	PAS	EX	IV	....	....
Washington, DC	Principal Deputy Coordinator............................	Vacant	....	ES	....	....	....
Washington, DC	Deputy Coordinator...	Career Incumbent	CA	ES	....	....	....
Washington, DC	Deputy Coordinator for Health Diplomacy........	Career Incumbent	CA	ES	....	....	....
Washington, DC	Deputy Coordinator for Health Security	Career Incumbent	CA	ES	....	....	....
	Office of Diversity and Inclusion (ODI)						
Washington, DC	Senior Adviser..	Constance M Mayer	TA	ES	....	....	....
Washington, DC	Chief Diversity and Inclusion Officer	Zakiya Carr Johnson............	NA	ES	....	....	....
	Office of China Coordination						
Washington, DC	Deputy Coordinator for Global Affairs..............	Henrietta Levin....................	SC	GS	15	....	....
Washington, DC	Advisor for Strategic Communications	Ashley Wood	SC	GS	12	....	....
	Office of Global Womens Issues						
Washington, DC	Senior Advisor..	Varina J Winder	SC	GS	15	....	....
Washington, DC	Ambassador At Large for Global Womens Issues.	Geeta R Gupta......................	PAS	EX	IV	....	....
New York, NY..........	Special Envoy for Afghanistan Women, Inclusion, and Minorities.	Rina Amiri	NA	ES	....	....	....
Washington, DC	Congressional Advisor	Michelle Schein	SC	GS	13	....	....
Washington, DC	Staff Assistant..	Efe Oboh-Idahosa.................	SC	GS	7	....	....
	Office of Sanctions Coordination						
Washington, DC	Head of the Office of Sanctions Coordination, with the rank of Ambassador.	Vacant	....	EX	....	....	....
Washington, DC	Senior Advisor..	Sumona Guha......................	NA	ES	....	....	....
	Office of Civil Rights						
Washington, DC	Director (Assistant Secretary Equivalent).........	Career Incumbent	CA	ES	....	....	....
	Office of the Legal Adviser						
Washington, DC	Legal Adviser of the Department of State........	Vacant	....	EX	....	....	....
Washington, DC	Principal Deputy Legal Adviser	Career Incumbent	CA	ES	....	....	....
Washington, DC	Deputy Legal Adviser	Career Incumbent	CA	ES	....	....	....
Washington, DC	Deputy Legal Adviser	Career Incumbent	CA	ES	....	....	....
Washington, DC	Assistant Legal Adviser	Career Incumbent	CA	ES	....	....	....
Washington, DC	Assistant Legal Adviser	Career Incumbent	CA	ES	....	....	....
Washington, DC	Deputy Assistant Legal Adviser	Career Incumbent	CA	ES	....	....	....
Washington, DC	Assistant Legal Adviser	Career Incumbent	CA	ES	....	....	....
Washington, DC	Assistant Legal Adviser	Career Incumbent	CA	ES	....	....	....
Washington, DC	Deputy Legal Adviser	Career Incumbent	CA	ES	....	....	....
Washington, DC	Assistant Legal Adviser	Career Incumbent	CA	ES	....	....	....
Washington, DC	Assistant Legal Adviser	Career Incumbent	CA	ES	....	....	....
Washington, DC	Assistant Legal Adviser	Career Incumbent	CA	ES	....	....	....
Washington, DC	Assistant Legal Adviser	Career Incumbent	CA	ES	....	....	....
Washington, DC	Assistant Legal Adviser	Career Incumbent	CA	ES	....	....	....
Washington, DC	Assistant Legal Adviser	Career Incumbent	CA	ES	....	....	....
Washington, DC	Assistant Legal Adviser	Career Incumbent	CA	ES	....	....	....
Washington, DC	Assistant Legal Adviser	Career Incumbent	CA	ES	....	....	....
Washington, DC	Assistant Legal Adviser	Career Incumbent	CA	ES	....	....	....
Washington, DC	Assistant Legal Adviser	Career Incumbent	CA	ES	....	....	....

DEPARTMENT OF STATE—Continued

Location	Position Title	Name of Incumbent	Type of Appt.	Pay Plan	Level, Grade, or Pay	Tenure	Expires
Washington, DC	Assistant Legal Adviser	Career Incumbent	CA	ES	....	....	....
Washington, DC	Assistant Legal Adviser	Career Incumbent	CA	ES	....	....	....
Washington, DC	Executive Director...	Career Incumbent	CA	ES	....	....	....
Washington, DC	Assistant Legal Adviser	Career Incumbent	CA	ES	....	....	....
Washington, DC	Assistant Legal Adviser	Career Incumbent	CA	ES	....	....	....
Washington, DC	Assistant Legal Adviser	Career Incumbent	CA	ES	....	....	....
Washington, DC	Assistant Legal Adviser	Career Incumbent	CA	ES	....	....	....
Washington, DC	Assistant Legal Adviser	Career Incumbent	CA	ES	....	....	....
	Bureau of Legislative Affairs						
Washington, DC	Assistant Secretary of State (Legislative Affairs).	Naz Durakoglu	PAS	EX	IV	....	....
Washington, DC	Deputy Assistant Secretary	Vacant	....	ES	....	....	....
Washington, DC	Senior Advisor...	Career Incumbent	CA	ES	....	....	....
Washington, DC	Deputy Assistant Secretary (House)..................	Stacy Thompson	SC	GS	15	....	....
Washington, DC	Deputy Assistant Secretary (Senate).................	Roy Awabdeh	SC	GS	15	....	....
Washington, DC	House Director..	Nicholas Johnson	SC	GS	14	....	....
Washington, DC	Senior Advisor...	Edward Edney......................	SC	GS	15	....	....
Washington, DC	Senate Director	Saadia Khan	SC	GS	14	....	....
Washington, DC	Senior Advisor (House Affairs)	Elya Taichman.....................	SC	GS	14	....	....
	Bureau of Intelligence and Research						
Washington, DC	Assistant Secretary of State (Intelligence and Research).	Brett Holmgren	....	EX	....	....	....
Washington, DC	Geographer..	Vacant	....	ES	....	....	....
Washington, DC	Office Director...	Career Incumbent	CA	ES	....	....	....
Washington, DC	Office Director...	Career Incumbent	CA	ES	....	....	....
Washington, DC	Deputy Assistant Secretary	Vacant	....	ES	....	....	....
Washington, DC	Executive Director...	Career Incumbent	CA	ES	....	....	....
Washington, DC	Office Director...	Career Incumbent	CA	ES	....	....	....
Washington, DC	Office Director...	Career Incumbent	CA	ES	....	....	....
Washington, DC	Deputy Assistant Secretary	Career Incumbent	CA	ES	....	....	....
Washington, DC	Senior Advisor...	Philip McDaniel..................	SC	GS	15	....	....
	Office of the Presidential Coordinator for the Partnership for Global Infrastructure and Investment						
Washington, DC	Special Presidential Coordinator........................	Amos J Hochstein	NA	ES	....	....	....
Washington, DC	Policy Advisor..	Connor Goddard	SC	GS	15	....	....
Washington, DC	Senior Advisor...	Kathryn Pauli......................	SC	GS	15	....	....
Washington, DC	Policy Advisor..	Joseph Scheidler..................	SC	GS	13	....	....
	Office of the Special Envoy to Monitor and Combat Anti-Semitism						
Washington, DC	Special Envoy to Monitor and Combat Anti-Semitism, with the rank of Ambassador.	Deborah Lipstadt	PAS	EX	IV	....	....
	Special Presidential Envoy for Climate Change						
Washington, DC	Lead Negotiations Team	Sue Biniaz............................	XS	....	....	....	....
Washington, DC	Liaison to White House Climate Team	Rick Duke	XS	....	....	....	....
Washington, DC	Senior Advisor...	Elan Strait............................	XS	....	....	....	....
Washington, DC	Senior Advisor...	Leonardo Martinez-Diaz......	XS	....	....	....	....
	Office for the Under Secretary of Political Affairs						
Washington, DC	Permanent Representative of the USA to the Organization of American States, With the Rank of Ambassador.	Francisco Mora.....................	PAS	FA	....	....	....
International	Under Secretary of State (Political Affairs)......	Vacant	....	EX	....	....	....
International	Afghanistan—Ambassador to the Islamic Republic of.	Vacant	....	FA	....	....	....
International	Albania—Ambassador to the Republic of	Vacant	....	FA	....	....	....
International	Algeria—Ambassador to the People'S Democratic Republic of.	Elizabeth Moore Aubin	PAS	FA	14	....	....
International	Angola—Ambassador to the Republic Of; Sao Tome and Principe, Democratic Republic of.	Tulinabo S Mushingi	PAS	FA	14	....	....
International	Argentina—Ambassador to the Argentine Republic.	Marc R Stanley.....................	PAS	FA	14	....	....
International	Armenia—Ambassador to the Republic of.........	Kristina A Kvien	PAS	FA	14	....	....
International	Australia—Ambassador to the Commonwealth of.	Caroline Kennedy.................	PAS	FA	13	....	....
International	Austria—Ambassador to the Republic of...........	Victoria Reggie Kennedy	PAS	FA	14	....	....
International	Azerbaijan—Ambassador to the Republic of	Mark W Libby	PAS	FA	14	....	....
International	Bahamas—Ambassador to the Commonwealth of the.	Vacant	....	FA	....	....	....
International	Bahrain—Ambassador to the Kingdom of.........	Steven C Bondy....................	PAS	FA	14	....	....

DEPARTMENT OF STATE—Continued

Location	Position Title	Name of Incumbent	Type of Appt.	Pay Plan	Level, Grade, or Pay	Tenure	Expires
International	Bangladesh—Ambassador to the People'S Republic of.	Peter D Haas	PAS	FA	13		
International	Barbados—Ambassador To; Antigua and Barbuda, Dominica, Commonwealth Of, Grenada, Saint Kitts and Nevis, Federation Of, Saint Lucia, Saint Vincent and the Grenadines.	Roger Nyhus	PAS	FA	14		
International	Belarus—Ambassador to the Republic of	Vacant		FA			
International	Belgium—Ambassador to the Kingdom of	Michael Adler	PAS	FA	14		
International	Belize—Ambassador to	Michelle Kwan	PAS	FA	14		
International	Benin—Ambassador to the Republic of	Brian Wesley Shukan	PAS	FA	14		
International	Bolivia—Ambassador to the Plurinational State of.	Vacant		FA			
International	Bosnia—Ambassador to Bosnia and Herzegovina.	Michael J Murphy	PAS	FA	14		
International	Botswana—Ambassador to the Republic of	Howard A Van Vranken	PAS	FA	14		
International	Brazil—Ambassador to the Federative Republic of.	Elizabeth Frawley Bagley	PAS	FA	13		
International	Brunei—Ambassador to Brunei Darussalam	Caryn R McClelland	PAS	FA	14		
International	Bulgaria—Ambassador to the Republic of	Kenneth Merten	PAS	FA	14		
International	Burkina Faso—Ambassador to	Joann Lockard	PAS	FA	14		
International	Burma—Ambassador to the Union of	Vacant		FA			
International	Burundi—Ambassador to the Republic of	Lisa Peterson	PAS	FA	14		
International	Cabo Verde—Ambassador to the Republic of	Jennifer Adams	PAS	FA	14		
International	Cambodia—Ambassador to the Kingdom of	Vacant		FA			
International	Cameroon—Ambassador to the Republic of	Christopher John Lamora	PAS	FA	14		
International	Canada—Ambassador to	David L Cohen	PAS	FA	13		
International	Central African Republic—Ambassador to the .	Patricia Mahoney	PAS	FA	14		
International	Chad—Ambassador to the Republic of	Alexander Mark Laskaris	PAS	FA	14		
International	Chile—Ambassador to the Republic of	Bernadette M Meehan	PAS	FA	14		
International	China—Ambassador to the People'S Republic of.	R Nicholas Burns	PAS	FA	13		
International	Colombia—Ambassador to the Republic of	Vacant		FA			
International	Congo—Ambassador to the Democratic Republic of the (Kinshasa).	Lucy Tamlyn	PAS	FA	14		
International	Congo—Ambassador to the Republic of the (Brazzaville).	Eugene S Young	PAS	FA	14		
International	Costa Rica—Ambassador to the Republic of	Cynthia Ann Telles	PAS	FA	14		
International	Cote D'Ivoire—Ambassador to the Republic of .	Jessica Davis Ba	PAS	FA	14		
International	Croatia—Ambassador to the Republic of	Nathalie Rayes	PAS	FA	14		
International	Cuba—Ambassador to the Republic of	Vacant		FA			
International	Cyprus—Ambassador to the Republic of	Julie D Fisher	PAS	FA	14		
International	Czech Republic—Ambassador to the	Bijan Sabet	PAS	FA	14		
International	Denmark—Ambassador to the Kingdom of	Alan M Leventhal	PAS	FA	14		
International	Djibouti—Ambassador to the Republic of	Cynthia Kierscht	PAS	FA	14		
International	Dominican Republic—Ambassador to	Vacant		FA			
International	Ecuador—Ambassador to the Republic of	Arthur Brown	PAS	FA	14		
International	Egypt—Ambassador to the Arab Republic of	Herro Mustafa Garg	PAS	FA	13		
International	El Salvador—Ambassador to To Republic of	William H Duncan	PAS	FA	14		
International	Equatorial Guinea—Ambassador to the Republic of.	David R Gilmour	PAS	FA	14		
International	Eritrea—Ambassador to the State of	Vacant		FA			
International	Estonia—Ambassador to the Republic of	George P Kent	PAS	FA	14		
International	Eswatini—Ambassador to the Kingdom of	Vacant		FA			
International	Ethiopia—Ambassador to the Federal Democratic Republic of.	Ervin Jose Massinga	PAS	FA	13		
International	FAO—U.S. Representative to the United Nations Agencies for Food and Agriculture, With the Rank of Ambassador.	Jeffrey Prescott	PAS	FA	14		
International	Fiji—Ambassador to the Republic Of; Kiribati, Republic Of, Nauru, Republic Of, Tonga, Kingdom Of, Tuvalu.	Marie C Damour	PAS	FA	14		
International	Finland—Ambassador to the Republic of	Douglas T Hickey	PAS	FA	14		
International	France—Ambassador to the French Republic; Monaco, Principality of.	Denise Campbell Bauer	PAS	FA	13		
International	Gabon—Ambassador to the Gabonese Republic.	Vernelle Trim Fitzpatrick	PAS	FA	14		
International	Gambia—Ambassador to the Republic of the	Sharon L Cromer	PAS	FA	14		
International	Georgia—Ambassador to	Robin Dunnigan	PAS	FA	14		
International	Germany—Ambassador to the Federal Republic of.	Vacant		FA			
International	Ghana—Ambassador to the Republic of	Virginia E Palmer	PAS	FA	14		

DEPARTMENT OF STATE—Continued

Location	Position Title	Name of Incumbent	Type of Appt.	Pay Plan	Level, Grade, or Pay	Tenure	Expires
International	Greece—Ambassador to (The Hellenic Republic).	George J Tsunis	PAS	FA	14		
International	Guatemala—Ambassador to the Republic of	Tobin Bradley	PAS	FA	13		
International	Guinea—Ambassador to the Republic of	Troy Damian Fitrell	PAS	FA	14		
International	Guyana—Ambassador to the Co-Operative Republic of.	Nicole D Theriot	PAS	FA	14		
International	Haiti—Ambassador to the Republic of	Dennis Hankins	PAS	FA	14		
International	Holy See—Ambassador to the	Vacant		FA			
International	Honduras—Ambassador to the Republic of	Laura Farnsworth Dogu	PAS	FA	13		
International	Hungary—Ambassador to	David Pressman	PAS	FA	14		
International	Iaea—Representative of the U.S. to the International Atomic Energy Agency, With the Rank of Ambassador.	Laura S H Holgate	PAS	FA	14		
International	Icao—Representative of the U.S. on the Council of the International Civil Aviation Organization, With the Rank of Ambassador.	Vacant		FA			
International	Iceland—Ambassador to the Republic of	Carrin F Patman	PAS	FA	14		
International	India—Ambassador to the Republic of	Eric M Garcetti	PAS	FA	13		
International	Indonesia—Ambassador to the Republic of	Kamala Lakhdhir	PAS	FA	13		
International	Iraq—Ambassador to the Republic of	Alina L Romanowski	PAS	FA	13		
International	Ireland—Ambassador to	Claire D Cronin	PAS	FA	14		
International	Israel—Ambassador to the State of	Jacob J Lew	PAS	FA	13		
International	Italy—Ambassador to the Italian Republic; San Marino, Republic of.	Jack A Markell	PAS	FA	13		
International	Jamaica—Ambassador to	N Nickolas Perry	PAS	FA	14		
International	Japan—Ambassador to	Rahm Emanuel	PAS	FA	13		
International	Jordan—Ambassador to the Hashemite Kingdom of.	Yael Lempert	PAS	FA	13		
International	Kazakhstan—Ambassador to the Republic of	Daniel N Rosenblum	PAS	FA	14		
International	Kenya—Ambassador to the Republic of	Margaret C Whitman	PAS	FA	13		
International	Korea—Ambassador to the Republic of Korea	Philip S Goldberg	PAS	FA	13		
International	Kosovo—Ambassador to the Republic of	Jeffrey M Hovenier	PAS	FA	14		
International	Kuwait—Ambassador to the State of	Karen Sasahara	PAS	FA	14		
International	Kyrgyz Republic—Ambassador to the	Lesslie Viguerie	PAS	FA	14		
International	Laos—Ambassador to the Lao People'S Democratic Republic.	Heather Roach Variava	PAS	FA	14		
International	Latvia—Ambassador to the Republic of	Christopher T Robinson	PAS	FA	14		
International	Lebanon—Ambassador to the Lebanese Republic.	Lisa A Johnson	PAS	FA	14		
International	Lesotho—Ambassador to the Kingdom of	Vacant		FA			
International	Liberia—Ambassador to the Republic of	Mark Toner	PAS	FA	14		
International	Libya—Ambassador to	Vacant		FA			
International	Lithuania—Ambassador to the Republic of	Kara C McDonald	PAS	FA	14		
International	Luxembourg—Ambassador to the Grand Duchy of.	Thomas Barrett	PAS	FA	14		
International	Madagascar—Ambassador to the Republic Of; Comoros, Union of the.	Claire A Pierangelo	PAS	FA	14		
International	Malawi—Ambassador to the Republic of	Vacant		FA			
International	Malaysia—Ambassador to	Edgard D Kagan	PAS	FA	14		
International	Maldives—Ambassador to the Republic of	Hugo Yue-Ho Yon	PAS	FA	14		
International	Mali—Ambassador to the Republic of	Rachna Sachdeva Korhonen.	PAS	FA	14		
International	Malta—Ambassador to the Republic of	Constance J Milstein	PAS	FA	14		
International	Marshall Islands—Ambassador to the Republic of the.	Laura Stone	PAS	FA	14		
International	Mauritania—Ambassador to the Islamic Republic of.	Vacant		FA			
International	Mauritius—Ambassador to the Republic Of; Seychelles, Republic of.	Henry V Jardine	PAS	FA	14		
International	Mexico—Ambassador to the United Mexican States.	Kenneth Lee Salazar	PAS	FA	13		
International	Micronesia—Ambassador to the Federated States of.	Jennifer L Johnson	PAS	FA	14		
International	Moldova—Ambassador to the Republic of	Vacant		FA			
International	Mongolia—Ambassador to	Richard Lee Buangan	PAS	FA	14		
International	Montenegro—Ambassador to	Judy Rising Reinke	PAS	FA	14		
International	Morocco—Ambassador to the Kingdom of	Puneet Talwar	PAS	FA	13		
International	Mozambique—Ambassador to the Republic of	Peter Hendrick Vrooman	PAS	FA	14		
International	Namibia—Ambassador to the Republic of	Randy W Berry	PAS	FA	14		

DEPARTMENT OF STATE—Continued

Location	Position Title	Name of Incumbent	Type of Appt.	Pay Plan	Level, Grade, or Pay	Tenure	Expires
International	Nato—U.S. Permanent Representative on the Council of the North Atlantic Treaty Organization, With the Rank and Status of Ambassador.	Julianne Smith	PAS	FA	13		
International	Nepal—Ambassador to	Dean R Thompson	PAS	FA	14		
International	Netherlands—Ambassador to the Kingdom of the.	Shefali Razdan Duggal	PAS	FA	14		
International	New Zealand—Ambassador To; Samoa, Independent State of.	Tom Udall	PAS	FA	14		
International	Nicaragua—Ambassador to the Republic of	Vacant		FA			
International	Niger—Ambassador to the Republic of	Kathleen A Fitzgibbon	PAS	FA	14		
International	Nigeria—Ambassador to the Federal Republic of.	Richard Mills, Jr	PAS	FA	13		
International	North Macedonia—Ambassador to the Republic of.	Angela Price Aggeler	PAS	FA	14		
International	Norway—Ambassador to the Kingdom of	Vacant		FA			
International	OECD—Representative of the United States of America to the Organization for Economic Cooperation and Development, With the Rank of Ambassador.	Sean P Maloney	PAS	FA	13		
International	Oman—Ambassador to the Sultanate of	Ana A Escrogima	PAS	FA	14		
International	OSCE—U.S. Representative to the Organization for Security and Cooperation in Europe, With the Rank of Ambassador.	Vacant		FA			
International	Pakistan—Ambassador to the Islamic Republic of.	Donald Armin Blome	PAS	FA	13		
International	Palau—Ambassador to the Republic of	Joel Ehrendreich	PAS	FA	14		
International	Panama—Ambassador to the Republic of	Mari Carmen Aponte	PAS	FA	13		
International	Papua New Guinea—Ambassador to the Independent State Of; Solomon Islands, Vanuatu, Republic of.	Ann Marie Yastishock	PAS	FA	14		
International	Paraguay—Ambassador to the Republic of	Marc Ostfield	PAS	FA	14		
International	Peru—Ambassador to the Republic of	Stephanie Syptak Ramnath.	PAS	FA	13		
International	Philippines—Ambassador to the Republic of the.	Marykay Loss Carlson	PAS	FA	13		
International	Poland—Ambassador to the Republic of	Mark Brzezinski	PAS	FA	13		
International	Portugal—Ambassador to the Portuguese Republic.	Randi Charno Levine	PAS	FA	14		
International	Qatar—Ambassador to the State of	Timmy Davis	PAS	FA	13		
International	Romania—Ambassador to	Kathleen Ann Kavalec	PAS	FA	14		
International	Russia—Ambassador to the Russian Federation.	Lynne M Tracy	PAS	FA	13		
International	Rwanda—Ambassador to the Republic of	Eric W Kneedler	PAS	FA	14		
International	Saudi Arabia—Ambassador to the Kingdom of.	Michael Alan Ratney	PAS	FA	13		
International	Senegal—Ambassador to the Republic Of; Guinea-Bissau, Republic of.	Michael Raynor	PAS	FA	14		
International	Serbia—Ambassador to the Republic of	Christopher R Hill	PAS	FA	14		
International	Sierra Leone—Ambassador to the Republic of.	Bryan David Hunt	PAS	FA	14		
International	Singapore—Ambassador to the Republic of	Jonathan Eric Kaplan	PAS	FA	13		
International	Slovak Republic—Ambassador to the	Gautam A Rana	PAS	FA	14		
International	Slovenia—Ambassador to the Republic of	Jamie L Harpootlian	PAS	FA	14		
International	Somalia—Ambassador to the Federal Republic of.	Richard Riley IV	PAS	FA	14		
International	South Africa—Ambassador to the Republic of	Reuben E Brigety Ii	PAS	FA	13		
International	South Sudan—Ambassador to the Republic of	Michael M Adler	PAS	FA	14		
International	Spain—Ambassador to the Kingdom Of; Andorra, Principality of.	Vacant		FA			
International	Sri Lanka—Ambassador to the Democratic Socialist Republic of.	Julie Chung	PAS	FA	14		
International	Sudan—Ambassador to the Republic of the	Vacant		FA			
International	Suriname—Ambassador to the Republic of	Robert J Faucher	PAS	FA	14		
International	Sweden—Ambassador to the Kingdom of	Erik D Ramanathan	PAS	FA	14		
International	Swiss Confederation—Ambassador to The; Liechtenstein, Principality of.	Scott Miller	PAS	FA	14		
International	Syria—Ambassador to the Syrian Arab Republic.	Vacant		FA			
International	Tajikistan—Ambassador to the Republic of	Manuel P Micaller, Jr.	PAS	FA	14		
International	Tanzania—Ambassador to the United Republic of.	Michael Battle	PAS	FA	14		
International	Timor-Leste—Ambassador to the Democratic Republic of.	Donna Welton	PAS	FA	14		
International	Thailand—Ambassador to the Kingdom of	Robert F Godec	PAS	FA	13		

DEPARTMENT OF STATE—Continued

Location	Position Title	Name of Incumbent	Type of Appt.	Pay Plan	Level, Grade, or Pay	Tenure	Expires
International	Togo—Lese Republic—Ambassador to	Vacant	....	FA	....	....	....
International	Trinidad and Tobago—Ambassador to the Republic of.	Candace A Bond	PAS	FA	14	....	....
International	Tunisia—Ambassador to the Republic of...........	Joey R Hood..........................	PAS	FA	14	....	....
International	Turkey—Ambassador to the Republic of	Jeffry Lane Flake	PAS	FA	13	....	....
International	Turkmenistan—Ambassador to..........................	Elizabeth Rood	PAS	FA	14	....	....
International	Uganda—Ambassador to the Republic of	William W Popp...................	PAS	FA	14	....	....
International	UNESCO—United States Permanent Representative to the United Nations Educational, Scientific, and Cultural Organization, With the Rank of Ambassador.	Courtney O'Donnell.............	PAS	FA	14	....	....
International	United Arab Emirates—Ambassador to	Martina Anna Tkadlec Strong.	PAS	FA	13	....	....
International	United Kingdom—Ambassador to the United Kingdom of Great Britain and Northern Ireland.	Jane Hartley.........................	PAS	FA	13	....	....
International	Un Geneva—Representative of the U.S. to the Office of the United Nations and Other International Organizations in Geneva, With the Rank of Ambassador.	Bathsheba Nell Crocker.......	PAS	FA	13	....	....
International	Unhrc—United States Representative to the Un Human Rights Council, With the Rank of Ambassador.	Michèle Taylor	PAS	FA	14	....	....
International	Ukraine—Ambassador to..................................	Bridget A Brink...................	PAS	FA	13	....	....
International	Unvie—Representative of the United States of America to the Vienna Office of the United Nations, With the Rank of Ambassador.	Laura S H Holgate...............	PAS	FA	14	....	....
International	Uruguay—Ambassador to the Oriental Republic of.	Heide B Fulton	PAS	FA	14	....	....
International	USASEAN—Representative of the U.S. to the Association of the Southeast Asian Nations, With the Rank and Status of Ambassador Extraordinary and Plenipotentiary.	Yohannes Abraham	PAS	FA	14	....	....
International	USAU—Representative of the U.S. to the African Union, With the Rank and Status of Ambassador Extraordinary and Plenipotentiary.	Stephanie Sanders Sullivan.	PAS	FA	14	....	....
International	USEU—Representative of the U.S. to the European Union, With the Rank and Status of Ambassador Extraordinary and Plenipotentiary.	Mark Gitenstein	PAS	FA	13	....	....
International	Uzbekistan—Ambassador to the Republic of	Jonathan Henick	PAS	FA	14	....	....
International	Venezuela—Ambassador to the Bolivarian Republic of.	Vacant	....	FA	....	....	....
International	Vietnam—Ambassador to the Socialist Republic of.	Marc Evans Knapper...........	PAS	FA	13	....	....
International	Yemen—Ambassador to the Republic of............	Steven H Fagin.....................	PAS	FA	14	....	....
International	Zambia—Ambassador to the Republic of...........	Michael C Gonzales.............	PAS	FA	14	....	....
International	Zimbabwe—Ambassador to the Republic of	Pamela Tremont...................	PAS	FA	14	....	....
Washington, DC	U.S. Coordinator for International Communications and Information Policy, with the rank of Ambassador.	Stephan Lang	PAS	....	....	....	....
	Bureau of African Affairs						
Washington, DC	Assistant Secretary of State (African Affairs)...	Mary Catherine Phee...........	PAS	EX	IV	....	....
Washington, DC	Special Envoy for Sudan	Thomas Stuart Price Perriello.	PA	ES	....	....	....
Washington, DC	Deputy Assistant Secretary	Joyatee Basu.........................	NA	ES	....	....	....
Washington, DC	Special Advisor..	Taylor Redick.......................	SC	GS	14	....	....
	Bureau of East Asian and Pacific Affairs						
Washington, DC	Assistant Secretary of State (East Asian and Pacific Affairs).	Daniel J Kritenbrink	PAS	EX	IV	....	....
Washington, DC	United States Senior Official for the Asia-Pacific Economic Corporat.	Matthew Murray	PAS	....	....	....	....
Washington, DC	Special Envoy on North Korean Human Rights Issues, With the Rank of Ambassador.	Julie E Turner	PAS	EX	IV	....	....
Washington, DC	Deputy Assistant Secretary	Vacant	....	ES	....	....	....
Washington, DC	Senior Advisor..	Ellison Laskowski	SC	GS	15	....	....
	Bureau of European and Eurasian Affairs						
Washington, DC	Assistant Secretary of State (European and Eurasian Affairs).	James C O'Brien	PAS	EX	IV	....	....

DEPARTMENT OF STATE—Continued

Location	Position Title	Name of Incumbent	Type of Appt.	Pay Plan	Level, Grade, or Pay	Tenure	Expires
Washington, DC	Coordinator for Overall Assistance and Economic Cooperation Strategy for the Independent States of the Former Soviet Union and Coordinator of the Support for East European Democracy (SEED) Program.	Career Incumbent	CA	ES	....	....	....
Washington, DC	Office Director................	Career Incumbent	CA	ES	....	....	....
Washington, DC	Deputy Assistant Secretary	Dorian Jacqueline Ramos....	NA	ES	....	....	....
Washington, DC	Chief of Staff for Special Representative for Ukraine's Economic Recovery.	Jeremy Bernton....................	NA	ES	....	....	....
Washington, DC	Special Representative for Ukraine's Economic Recovery.	Penny Pritzker	PA	OT	....	....	....
Washington, DC	Senior Advisor................	Michael Carpenter	SC	GS	....	....	....
Washington, DC	Senior Advisor................	Tyson Barker........................	SC	GS	15	....	....
	Bureau of Near Eastern Affairs						
Washington, DC	Assistant Secretary of State (Near Eastern Affairs).	Barbara Leaf	PAS	EX	IV	....	....
Washington, DC	Special Envoy for Middle East Humanitarian Issues.	Lise Grande	NA	ES	....	....	....
Washington, DC	Deputy Assistant Secretary	Career Incumbent	CA	ES	....	....	....
Washington, DC	Office Director................	Career Incumbent	CA	ES	....	....	....
Washington, DC	Deputy Assistant Secretary	Daniel Paul Benaim............	NA	ES	....	....	....
Washington, DC	Special Representative for Palestinian Affairs..	Hady A Amr........................	NA	ES	....	....	....
Washington, DC	Senior Policy Advisor to Special Envoy to Yemen.	Yousef Farsakh	SC	GS	15	....	....
	Bureau of South and Central Asian Affairs						
Washington, DC	Assistant Secretary of State for South Asian Affairs.	Donald Lu	PAS	EX	IV	....	....
Washington, DC	Deputy Assistant Secretary	Afreen Akhter......................	SC	GS	15	....	....
Washington, DC	Special Representative for Afghanistan and Deputy Assistant Secretary.	Thomas Wilkins West	NA	ES	....	....	....
	Bureau of Western Hemisphere Affairs						
Washington, DC	Assistant Secretary of State (Western Hemisphere Affairs).	Brian A Nichols	PAS	EX	IV	....	....
Washington, DC	Deputy Assistant Secretary	Eric Jacobstein	SC	GS	15	....	....
Washington, DC	Office Director................	Career Incumbent	CA	ES	....	....	....
Washington, DC	Deputy Assistant Secretary	Career Incumbent	CA	ES	....	....	....
Washington, DC	Senior Advisor................	Laura M Jimenez................	SC	GS	15	....	....
	Bureau of International Organizational Affairs						
Washington, DC	Assistant Secretary of State (International Organization Affairs).	Michele Jeanne Sison	PAS	EX	IV	....	....
Washington, DC	Deputy Assistant Secretary	Career Incumbent	CA	ES	....	....	....
Washington, DC	Office Director................	Career Incumbent	CA	ES	....	....	....
Washington, DC	Deputy Assistant Secretary	Allison K Lombardo	NA	ES	....	....	....
Washington, DC	Deputy Assistant Secretary	Ella Lipin	SC	GS	15	....	....
	Bureau of Counterterrorism						
Washington, DC	Coordinator for Counterterrorism, With the Rank and Status of Ambassador At Large.	Elizabeth H Richard	PAS	EX	IV	....	....
Washington, DC	Deputy Coordinator................	Career Incumbent	CA	ES	....	....	....
Washington, DC	Deputy Coordinator................	Ian Creft Moss....................	SC	GS	15	....	....
	Office of the Under Secretary for Economic Growth, Energy, and the Environment						
Washington, DC	Under Secretary of State (Economic Growth, Energy, and the Environment).	Jose W Fernandez	PAS	EX	III	....	....
Washington, DC	Deputy Assistant Secretary	Mahlet Mesfin	NA	ES	....	....	....
Washington, DC	Senior Advisor................	Melanie Marie Hart............	SC	GS	15	....	....
Washington, DC	Senior Advisor................	Nelson Cunningham	NA	ES	....	....	....
Washington, DC	Senior Advisor................	Isabel Malowany	SC	GS	15	....	....
Washington, DC	Senior Advisor................	Natalia Cote-Munoz	SC	GS	14	....	....
Washington, DC	Special Advisor................	Douglas Levinson	SC	GS	13	....	....
	Bureau of Economic and Business Affairs						
Washington, DC	Assistant Secretary of State (Economic and Business Affairs).	Vacant	....	EX	....	....	....
Washington, DC	Deputy Assistant Secretary	Career Incumbent	CA	ES	....	....	....
Washington, DC	Deputy Assistant Secretary	Vacant	....	ES	....	....	....
Washington, DC	Office Director................	Career Incumbent	CA	ES	....	....	....
Washington, DC	Special Representative for Commercial and Business Affairs.	Sarah Morgenthau	NA	ES	....	....	....
Washington, DC	Senior Advisor................	Francine Rachel Harris	SC	GS	15	....	....

DEPARTMENT OF STATE—Continued

Location	Position Title	Name of Incumbent	Type of Appt.	Pay Plan	Level, Grade, or Pay	Tenure	Expires
	Bureau of Energy Resources						
Washington, DC	Assistant Secretary of State (Energy Resources).	Geoffrey R Pyatt..................	PAS	EX	IV	....	....
Washington, DC	Deputy Assistant Secretary	Anna Shpitsberg..................	SC	GS	15	....	....
Washington, DC	Special Advisor..	Tyler Andrew Sady-Kennedy.	SC	GS	12	....	....
	Office of the Chief Economist						
Washington, DC	Chief Economist......................	Chad Bown	NA	ES	....	....	....
Washington, DC	Deputy Chief Economist	Philip A Luck......................	SC	GS	....	....	....
	Office of Global Partnership						
Washington, DC	Special Representative for Global Partnerships.	Dorothy McAuliffe...............	NA	ES	....	....	....
Washington, DC	Partnerships and Outreach Officer	Tomas Kloosterman	SC	GS	13	....	....
	Bureau of Oceans and International Environmental and Scientific Affairs						
Washington, DC	Assistant Secretary of State for Oceans and International Environmental and Scientific Affairs.	Vacant	....	EX	....	....	....
Washington, DC	Director..................................	Career Incumbent	CA	ES	....	....	....
Washington, DC	Executive Director...	Career Incumbent	CA	ES	....	....	....
Washington, DC	Office Director...	Career Incumbent	CA	ES	....	....	....
Washington, DC	Office Director...	Career Incumbent	CA	ES	....	....	....
Washington, DC	Office Director...	Career Incumbent	CA	ES	....	....	....
Washington, DC	Office Director...	Career Incumbent	CA	ES	....	....	....
Washington, DC	Senior Advisor..	Kaitlyn Guy	SC	GS	15	....	....
Washington, DC	Special Advisor..	Jonathan Gillibrand.............	SC	GS	13	....	....
	Office of Global Food Security						
Washington, DC	Special Envoy for Global Food Security.............	Morgan Carrington Fowler..	SC	GS	15	....	....
	Office of the Under Secretary for Arms Control and International Security Affairs						
Washington, DC	Under Secretary of State for Arms Control and International Security.	Bonnie Denise Jenkins	PAS	EX	III	....	....
International	CD—U.S. Representative to the Conference on Disarmament, With the Rank of Ambassador.	Bruce I Turner.....................	PAS	FA	14	....	....
International	OPCW—United States Representative to the Organization for the Prohibition of Chemical Weapons, With the Rank of Ambassador.	Nicole Shampaine	PAS	FA	14	....	....
Washington, DC	Senior Advisor...	Jane Kim Coloseus...............	SC	GS	15	....	....
Washington, DC	Senior Adviser...	Career Incumbent	CA	ES	....	....	....
	Bureau of Arms Control, Deterrence, and Stability						
Washington, DC	Assistant Secretary of State (Verification and Compliance).	Mallory Anne Stewart..........	PAS	EX	IV	....	....
Washington, DC	Principal Deputy Assistant Secretary................	Career Incumbent	CA	ES	....	....	....
Washington, DC	Deputy Assistant Secretary	Alexandra F Bell.................	SC	GS	15	....	....
Washington, DC	Office Director...	Career Incumbent	CA	ES	....	....	....
Washington, DC	Office Director...	Vacant	....	ES	....	....	....
Washington, DC	Office Director...	Career Incumbent	CA	ES	....	....	....
Washington, DC	Office Director...	Career Incumbent	CA	ES	....	....	....
Washington, DC	Staff Assistant...	Isabel Martinez	SC	GS	11	....	....
	Bureau of International Security and Nonproliferation						
Washington, DC	Assistant Secretary of State (International Security and Non-Proliferation).	C.S Eliot Kang......................	PAS	EX	IV	....	....
Washington, DC	Special Representative of the President for Nuclear Nonproliferation, With the Rank of Ambassador.	Adam M Scheinman.............	PAS	EX	IV	....	....
Washington, DC	Principal Deputy Assistant Secretary................	Career Incumbent	CA	ES	....	....	....
Washington, DC	Deputy Assistant Secretary	Lowell Hays Schwartz	NA	ES	....	....	....
Washington, DC	Special Representative for Biological Weapons Convention.	Career Incumbent	CA	ES	....	....	....
Washington, DC	Executive Director...	Career Incumbent	CA	ES	....	....	....
Washington, DC	Office Director...	Career Incumbent	CA	ES	....	....	....
Washington, DC	Office Director...	Career Incumbent	CA	ES	....	....	....
Washington, DC	Office Director...	Career Incumbent	CA	ES	....	....	....
	Bureau of Political-Military Affairs						
Washington, DC	Assistant Secretary of State (Political-Military Affairs).	Vacant	....	EX	....	....	....

DEPARTMENT OF STATE—Continued

Location	Position Title	Name of Incumbent	Type of Appt.	Pay Plan	Level, Grade, or Pay	Tenure	Expires
Washington, DC	Principal Deputy Assistant Secretary...............	Career Incumbent	CA	ES	....	....	....
Washington, DC	Deputy Assistant Secretary	Mira Kogen Resnick............	NA	ES	....	....	....
Washington, DC	Deputy Assistant Secretary	Career Incumbent	CA	ES	....	....	....
Washington, DC	Office Director..	Career Incumbent	CA	ES	....	....	....
Washington, DC	Office Director..	Career Incumbent	CA	ES	....	....	....
	Office of the Under Secretary for Public Diplomacy and Public Affairs						
Washington, DC	Under Secretary of State for Public Diplomacy.	Elizabeth M Allen	PAS	EX	III	....	....
Washington, DC	Special Envoy for Global Youth	Abby Finkenauer.................	NA	ES	....	....	....
Washington, DC	Supervisory Senior Advisor...............................	Stephanie C Sutton............	SC	GS	15	....	....
Washington, DC	Advisor for Strategic Communications	Ankita Verma	SC	GS	13	....	....
Washington, DC	Special Assistant...	Hoor Qureshi	SC	GS	12	....	....
	Bureau of Educational and Cultural Affairs						
Washington, DC	Assistant Secretary of State (Educational and Cultural Affairs).	Lee Satterfield	PAS	EX	IV	....	....
Washington, DC	Deputy Assistant Secretary	Ethan Rosenzweig................	SC	GS	15	....	....
Washington, DC	Executive Director..	Career Incumbent	CA	ES	....	....	....
Washington, DC	Deputy Assistant Secretary	Nicole Louise Elkon	NA	ES	....	....	....
Washington, DC	Supervisory Public Affairs Specialist................	Rebekah T Sergent..............	SC	GS	15	....	....
Washington, DC	Special Assistant...	Sreyashe Dhar	SC	GS	13	....	....
Washington, DC	Program Officer	Taylor Emerson	SC	GS	12	....	....
	Bureau of Global Public Affairs						
Washington, DC	Assistant Secretary of State (Global Public Affairs).	Vacant	....	EX	....	....	....
Washington, DC	Spokesperson..	Matthew Alan Miller	NA	ES	....	....	....
Washington, DC	Principal Deputy Spokesperson.........................	Vedant Patel	SC	GS	15	....	....
Washington, DC	Executive Director..	Career Incumbent	CA	ES	....	....	....
Washington, DC	Senior Advisor (Strategic Communications and Outreach).	Lauren French.....................	SC	GS	15	....	....
Washington, DC	Chief Content Strategist	Hannah Flom.......................	SC	GS	15	....	....
Washington, DC	Senior Advisor..	Charles Kennedy.................	SC	GS	15	....	....
Washington, DC	Special Advisor..	Connor Coughlan	SC	GS	12	....	....
Washington, DC	Special Advisor..	Asjia Garner	SC	GS	12	....	....
Washington, DC	Special Advisor..	Muhammad Rasheed	SC	GS	12	....	....
Washington, DC	Special Advisor..	Darcy Hai Fei Palder	SC	GS	12	....	....
	Global Engagement Center						
Washington, DC	Special Envoy and Coordinator for Global Engagement Center.	James P Rubin	PA	AD	....	....	....
Washington, DC	Senior Advisor..	Carissa Goux	SC	GS	....	....	....
	Subnational Diplomacy Unit						
Los Angeles, CA	Special Representative for City and State Diplomacy.	Nina Hachigian	NA	ES	....	....	....
Washington, DC	Deputy Special Representative...........................	Daniel Ricchetti..................	SC	GS	15	....	....
	Office of the Under Secretary for Management						
Washington, DC	Under Secretary of State (Management)..........	John R Bass........................	PAS	EX	III	....	....
Washington, DC	Office Director..	Career Incumbent	CA	ES	....	....	....
Washington, DC	White House Liaison	Joshua Romero	NA	ES	....	....	....
Washington, DC	Senior Advisor..	Sean Stephan Bartlett.........	SC	GS	15	....	....
Washington, DC	Deputy White House Liaison	Shawn Hall..........................	SC	GS	14	....	....
Washington, DC	Special Advisor..	Farah Sabir.........................	SC	GS	12	....	....
	Bureau of Administration						
Washington, DC	Assistant Secretary of State (Administration)..	Alaina B Teplitz	PA	EX	IV	....	....
Washington, DC	Office Director..	Career Incumbent	CA	ES	....	....	....
Washington, DC	Director, Small and Disadvantaged Business Utilization.	Career Incumbent	CA	ES	....	....	....
Washington, DC	Office Director, Office of Program Management and Policy.	Career Incumbent	CA	ES	....	....	....
Washington, DC	Chief Privacy Officer...	Career Incumbent	CA	ES	....	....	....
Washington, DC	Executive Director..	Career Incumbent	CA	ES	....	....	....
Washington, DC	Managing Director..	Career Incumbent	CA	ES	....	....	....
Washington, DC	Office Director, Information Resource Management Programs and Services.	Career Incumbent	CA	ES	....	....	....
Washington, DC	Officer Director..	Career Incumbent	CA	ES	....	....	....
Washington, DC	Chief Technology Transition Officer..................	Andrea Nichole Villalba.......	TA	ES	....	....	....
Washington, DC	Director, Office of Acquisitions Management	Career Incumbent	CA	ES	....	....	....
	Bureau of Budget and Planning						
Washington, DC	Director...	Career Incumbent	CA	ES	....	....	....
Washington, DC	Deputy Director..	Career Incumbent	CA	ES	....	....	....

DEPARTMENT OF STATE—Continued

Location	Position Title	Name of Incumbent	Type of Appt.	Pay Plan	Level, Grade, or Pay	Tenure	Expires
Washington, DC	Deputy Director, Resource Planning and Budget Information.	Career Incumbent	CA	ES			
	Bureau of the Comptroller and Global Financial Services						
Washington, DC	Chief Financial Officer	Vacant		EX			
Charleston, SC	Comptroller	Career Incumbent	CA	ES			
Charleston, SC	Deputy Comptroller	Career Incumbent	CA	ES			
Washington, DC	Deputy Comptroller	Career Incumbent	CA	ES			
Washington, DC	Executive Director	Vacant		ES			
Charleston, SC	Managing Director, Global Compensation	Career Incumbent	CA	ES			
Charleston, SC	Managing Director	Career Incumbent	CA	ES			
Washington, DC	Managing Director	Career Incumbent	CA	ES			
Washington, DC	Managing Director	Career Incumbent	CA	ES			
	Bureau of Consular Affairs						
Washington, DC	Assistant Secretary of State (Consular Affairs).	Rena Bitter	PAS	EX	IV		
Washington, DC	Deputy Assistant Secretary	Vacant		ES			
Washington, DC	Managing Director, Passport Support Services	Career Incumbent	CA	ES			
Washington, DC	Managing Director	Career Incumbent	CA	ES			
Washington, DC	Comptroller	Career Incumbent	CA	ES			
Washington, DC	Chief Information Officer for Ca	Career Incumbent	CA	ES			
Washington, DC	Managing Director	Career Incumbent	CA	ES			
Washington, DC	Senior Policy Adviser	Career Incumbent	CA	ES			
Washington, DC	Chief Technology Officer	Raphael Jamshid Majma	NA	ES			
	Bureau of Diplomatic Security						
Washington, DC	Assistant Secretary of State (Diplomatic Security).	Gentry Smith	PAS	EX	IV		
Washington, DC	Executive Director	Career Incumbent	CA	ES			
Washington, DC	Senior Coordinator	Career Incumbent	CA	ES			
Washington, DC	Comptroller	Career Incumbent	CA	ES			
Washington, DC	Supvy Mgmt and Program Analyst	Career Incumbent	CA	ES			
Washington, DC	Senior Coordinator	Vacant		ES			
	Office of Foreign Missions						
Washington, DC	Director of the Office of Foreign Missions, with the rank of Ambassador.	Rebecca Eliza Gonzales	PAS	EX	IV		
Washington, DC	Principal Deputy Director	Career Incumbent	CA	ES			
	Foreign Service Institute						
Washington, DC	Executive Director	Career Incumbent	CA	ES			
Washington, DC	Associate Dean	Career Incumbent	CA	ES			
Washington, DC	Associate Dean	Career Incumbent	CA	ES			
Washington, DC	Associate Dean	Career Incumbent	CA	ES			
Washington, DC	Office Director, Education Programs	Career Incumbent	CA	ES			
Washington, DC	Director	Career Incumbent	CA	ES			
	Bureau of Diplomatic Technology						
Washington, DC	Chief Information Officer	Career Incumbent	CA	ES			
Washington, DC	Deputy Chief Information Officer	Career Incumbent	CA	ES			
Washington, DC	Deputy Chief Information Officer	Vacant		ES			
Washington, DC	Chief Technology Officer	Career Incumbent	CA	ES			
Washington, DC	Enterprise Chief Information Security Officer	Career Incumbent	CA	ES			
Washington, DC	Office Director, Strategic Planning Office	Career Incumbent	CA	ES			
Washington, DC	Director, It Acquisitions Office	Career Incumbent	CA	ES			
Washington, DC	Office Director	Career Incumbent	CA	ES			
Washington, DC	Office Director	Career Incumbent	CA	ES			
	Bureau of Global Talent Management						
Washington, DC	Director, Resource Management and Organization Analysis.	Vacant		ES			
Washington, DC	Senior Adviser	Career Incumbent	CA	ES			
Washington, DC	Director General of the Foreign Service	Marcia Bernicat	PAS	EX	IV		
Washington, DC	Deputy Assistant Secretary	Career Incumbent	CA	ES			
Washington, DC	Deputy Assistant Secretary	Career Incumbent	CA	ES			
Washington, DC	Office Director	Career Incumbent	CA	ES			
Washington, DC	Office Director	Career Incumbent	CA	ES			
Washington, DC	Office Director	Career Incumbent	CA	ES			
Washington, DC	Office Director	Career Incumbent	CA	ES			
	Bureau of Overseas Buildings Operations						
Washington, DC	Managing Director	Career Incumbent	CA	ES			
Washington, DC	Office Director	Career Incumbent	CA	ES			
Washington, DC	Supervisory General Engineer	Career Incumbent	CA	ES			
Washington, DC	Office Director	Career Incumbent	CA	ES			

DEPARTMENT OF STATE—Continued

Location	Position Title	Name of Incumbent	Type of Appt.	Pay Plan	Level, Grade, or Pay	Tenure	Expires
Washington, DC	Managing Director..	Career Incumbent	CA	ES	....	....	....
Washington, DC	Supervisory Museum Curator (Arts).................	Beyer Carroll Megan............	SC	GS	15	....	....
Washington, DC	Director of Arts in the Embassies	Megan Beyer..........................	SC	....	15	....	....
	Office of the Under Secretary for Civilian Security, Democracy, and Human Rights						
Washington, DC	Under Secretary of State (Civilian Security, Democracy, and Human Rights).	Uzra Zeya	PAS	EX	III	....	....
Washington, DC	Coordinator for Democratic Renewal	Career Incumbent	CA	ES	....	3	09/11/24
Washington, DC	Special Advisor for International Disability Rights.	Sara Minkara	NA	ES	....	....	....
Washington, DC	Deputy Special Envoy to Monitor and Combat Anti-Semitism.	Aaron Keyak..........................	SC	GS	15	....	....
Washington, DC	Deputy Special Envoy for Guantanamo Issues.	Daniel Schneiderman...........	SC	GS	15	....	....
Washington, DC	Deputy Special Representative for Racial Equity and Justice.	Amber Greene	SC	GS	15	....	....
Washington, DC	Senior Advisor...	Hannah Suh	SC	GS	14	....	....
	Bureau of Conflict and Stabilization Operations						
Washington, DC	Assistant Secretary of State (Conflict and Stabilization Operations).	Anne A Witkowsky...............	PAS	EX	IV	....	....
Washington, DC	Deputy Assistant Secretary	Career Incumbent	CA	ES	....	....	....
Washington, DC	Deputy Assistant Secretary	Mark Iozzi............................	NA	ES	....	....	....
	Bureau of Democracy, Human Rights and Labor						
Washington, DC	Assistant Secretary of State for Democracy, Human Rights, and Labor.	Vacant	....	EX	....	....	....
Washington, DC	Deputy Assistant Secretary	Vacant	....	ES	....	....	....
Washington, DC	Deputy Assistant Secretary	Christopher J Le Mon..........	NA	ES	....	....	....
Washington, DC	Deputy Assistant Secretary	Enrique Roig........................	SC	GS	15	....	....
Washington, DC	Special Envoy to Advance the Human Rights of Lesbian, Gay, Bisexual, Transgender, Queer and Intersex (LGBTQI+) Persons.	Jessica Stern........................	NA	ES	....	....	....
Washington, DC	Special Representative for Racial Equity and Justice.	Desiree Cormier Smith........	NA	ES	....	....	....
Washington, DC	Special Representative for International Labor Affairs.	Kelly Fay Rodriguez.............	NA	ES	....	....	....
Washington, DC	Office Director...	Career Incumbent	CA	ES	....	....	....
Washington, DC	Senior Advisor...	Allison L Peters....................	SC	GS	15	....	....
Washington, DC	Senior Advisor...	Suzanne Goldberg	SC	GS	15	....	....
Washington, DC	Special Envoy International LGBTQ+ Rights...	Reginald Greer	SC	GS	15	....	....
	Office of Global Criminal Justice						
Washington, DC	Ambassador At Large for Global Criminal Justice.	Elizabeth Maria Van Schaack.	PAS	EX	IV	....	....
Washington, DC	Senior Advisor...	Nema Milaninia	SC	GS	15	....	....
Washington, DC	Senior Advisor...	Pratima Tejaswini Narayan.	SC	GS	15	....	....
	Bureau of International Narcotics and Law Enforcement Affairs						
Washington, DC	Assistant Secretary of State (International Narcotics and Law Enforcement Affairs).	Todd Robinson	PAS	EX	IV	....	....
Washington, DC	Controller/Executive Director...........................	Vacant	....	ES	....	....	....
Washington, DC	Office Director...	Career Incumbent	CA	ES	....	....	....
Washington, DC	Deputy Assistant Secretary	Career Incumbent	CA	ES	....	....	....
Washington, DC	Office Director...	Career Incumbent	CA	ES	....	....	....
Washington, DC	Coordinator on Global Anti-Corruption	Vacant	....	ES	....	....	....
Washington, DC	Deputy Assistant Secretary	Brandon P Yoder	SC	GS	15	....	....
	Office To Monitor and Combat Trafficking in Persons						
Washington, DC	Director of the Office to Monitor and Combat Trafficking, With Rank of Ambassador At Large.	Cynthia Diane Dyer.............	PAS	EX	IV	....	....
Washington, DC	Principal Deputy Director.................................	Vacant	....	ES	....	....	....
	Office of International Religious Freedom						
Washington, DC	Ambassador At Large for International Religious Freedom.	Rashad Hussain	PAS	EX	IV	....	....
Washington, DC	Principal Deputy..	Career Incumbent	CA	ES	....	....	....
	Bureau of Population, Refugees and Migration						
Washington, DC	Assistant Secretary of State (Population, Refugees, and Migration).	Julieta Noyes........................	PAS	EX	IV	....	....
Washington, DC	Deputy Assistant Secretary	Career Incumbent	CA	ES	....	....	....

DEPARTMENT OF STATE—Continued

Location	Position Title	Name of Incumbent	Type of Appt.	Pay Plan	Level, Grade, or Pay	Tenure	Expires
Washington, DC	Office Director	Vacant		ES			
Washington, DC	Office Director	Vacant		ES			
Washington, DC	Comptroller	Career Incumbent	CA	ES			
Washington, DC	Office Director	Vacant		ES			
Washington, DC	Deputy Assistant Secretary	Sarah Rebecca Cross	NA	ES			
Washington, DC	Deputy Assistant Secretary	Elizabeth Campbell	NA	ES			
Washington, DC	Deputy Assistant Secretary	Career Incumbent	CA	ES			
Washington, DC	Senior Adviser	Career Incumbent	CA	ES			
Washington, DC	Senior Advisor	Rosanna Boyoung Kim	SC	GS	14		
Washington, DC	Senior Advisor	Lindsay Marie Jenkins	SC	GS	15		

DEPARTMENT OF STATE OFFICE OF THE INSPECTOR GENERAL

Location	Position Title	Name of Incumbent	Type of Appt.	Pay Plan	Level, Grade, or Pay	Tenure	Expires
Washington, DC	Inspector General	Cardell Richardson	PAS	EX	III		

DEPARTMENT OF TRANSPORTATION

Location	Position Title	Name of Incumbent	Type of Appt.	Pay Plan	Level, Grade, or Pay	Tenure	Expires
	OFFICE OF THE SECRETARY						
Washington, DC	Secretary	Peter Paul Montgomery Buttigieg.	PAS	EX	I		
Washington, DC	Chief of Staff	Mohsin Raza Syed	NA	ES			
Washington, DC	Deputy Chief of Staff	Kara Lynn Fischer	NA	ES			
	Secretary						
Washington, DC	Senior Advisor	Michael Mackay Halle	NA	ES			
Washington, DC	Senior Advisor	Marcus J Switzer	NA	ES			
Washington, DC	Special Advisor to the Secretary of Transportation.	Alexis Christina Gonzaludo.	SC	GS	13		
Washington, DC	Deputy Chief of Staff for Operations	Vacant		ES			
Washington, DC	White House Liaison	Sarah Murphy	SC	GS	15		
Washington, DC	Director of Scheduling and Advance	Leah Beth Seigle	SC	GS	15		
Washington, DC	Director of Advance and Trip Operations	Roy Sherman	SC	GS	15		
Washington, DC	Director for Strategy and Operations	Lisa Zhang	SC	GS	14		
Washington, DC	Director of Scheduling	Casey Michael Clemmons	SC	GS	13		
Washington, DC	Policy Advisor	Derrek Aaran Chung	SC	GS	13		
Washington, DC	Special Assistant for Scheduling	Kebra Baako	SC	GS	9		
Washington, DC	Special Assistant for Advance	Sophia Elizabeth McGrath	SC	GS	11		
Washington, DC	Special Assistant for Advance	Emilie Erzsebet Karolyi	SC	GS	11		
	Office of the Deputy Secretary						
Washington, DC	Deputy Secretary	Polly E Trottenberg	PAS	EX	II		
Washington, DC	Chief of Staff to the Deputy Secretary	Sabrina Sanam Sussman	NA	ES			
Washington, DC	Policy Advisor to the Deputy Secretary	Leeann Sinpatanasakul	SC	GS	12		
	Office of the Under Secretary of Transportation for Policy						
Washington, DC	Under Secretary of Transportation for Policy	Vacant		EX			
Washington, DC	Senior Advisor to the Under Secretary of Transportation for Policy.	Coral A Torres Cruz	SC	GS	15		
Washington, DC	Director of Bipartisan Infrastructure Law Implementation.	Vacant		ES			
Washington, DC	Deputy Director of Bipartisan Infrastructure Law Implementation.	Stephen Michael Goepfert	SC	GS	15		
Washington, DC	Bipartisan Infrastructure Law Media Advisor	Paige Eleanor Sterling	SC	GS	13		
Washington, DC	Chief Competition Officer	Jennifer Marguerite Howard.	NA	ES			
Washington, DC	Principal Deputy Assistant Secretary for Multimodal Freight Infrastructure and Policy.	Allison Lee Dane Camden	NA	ES			
Washington, DC	Deputy Assistant Secretary for Multimodal Freight Infrastructure and Policy.	Andrew Ryan Petrisin	NA	ES			
Washington, DC	Director, Office of Credit Programs	Career Incumbent	CA	ES			

DEPARTMENT OF TRANSPORTATION—Continued

Location	Position Title	Name of Incumbent	Type of Appt.	Pay Plan	Level, Grade, or Pay	Tenure	Expires
Washington, DC	Director, Office of Outreach and Project Development.	Vacant	....	ES	....	....	....
	Executive Secretariat						
Washington, DC	Director...	Claris Jarren Chang	SC	GS	15	....	....
Washington, DC	Advisor to the Director.............................	Margaret Katharine Horgan Travis.	SC	GS	11	....	....
Washington, DC	Special Assistant.............................	Kellen McLaughlin...............	SC	GS	9	....	....
	Office of Civil Rights						
Washington, DC	Director, Office of Civil Rights.............................	Irene Bianca Marion	NA	ES	....	....	....
Washington, DC	Deputy Director, Office of Civil Rights	Career Incumbent	CA	ES	....	....	....
Washington, DC	Senior Advisor..................................	Angela Roberson...................	NA	ES	....	....	....
Washington, DC	Policy Advisor.......................................	Warner Alyssa Jade Dixon ..	SC	GS	12	....	....
	Small and Disadvantaged Business Utilization						
Washington, DC	Director, Office of Small and Disadvantaged Business Utilization.	Tyra Latrice Redus	NA	ES	....	....	....
	Office of the Chief Information Officer						
Washington, DC	Chief Information Officer.............................	Cordell Schachter...............	NA	ES	....	....	....
Washington, DC	Assistant Chief Information Officer for Strategic Portfolio Management.	Career Incumbent	CA	ES	....	....	....
Washington, DC	Associate Chief Information Officer for Resources Management.	Career Incumbent	CA	ES	....	....	....
Washington, DC	Associate CIO for Applications and Digital Solutions.	Vacant	....	ES	....	....	....
Washington, DC	Associate Chief Information Officer for Infrastructure and Operations.	Vacant	....	ES	....	....	....
	Office of Public Affairs and Public Engagement						
Washington, DC	Assistant to the Secretary and Director of Public Affairs.	Kerry Elizabeth Garro........	NA	ES	....	....	....
Washington, DC	Deputy Director for Public Affairs	Elizabeth Lopez-Sandoval ...	SC	GS	15	....	....
Washington, DC	Traveling Press Secretary................................	Alexandra Devon Caffrey	SC	GS	12	....	....
Washington, DC	Press Assistant	Katherine Ann Poltrack.......	SC	GS	9	....	....
Washington, DC	Senior Speechwriter	Daniel Rogan Kadishson	SC	GS	14	....	....
Washington, DC	Speechwriter..	Margaret Mallon	SC	GS	13	....	....
Washington, DC	Digital Director...	Brenna Marie Parker...........	SC	GS	14	....	....
Washington, DC	Media Advisor	Sean Manning	SC	GS	12	....	....
Washington, DC	Social Media Manager.................................	Samuel Martin Aleman	SC	GS	11	....	....
Washington, DC	Director of Public Engagement.........................	Kala Sadiq Wright	NA	ES	....	....	....
Washington, DC	Principal Deputy Director of Public Engagement.	Rafael Martin Freedman-Gurspan.	SC	GS	15	....	....
Washington, DC	Associate Director for Public Engagement	Justin Luis Ramirez............	SC	GS	14	....	....
Washington, DC	Special Assistant for Public Engagement..........	Kristina Grace Benjamin.....	SC	GS	11	....	....
Washington, DC	Content Producer.......................................	Emma Simon	SC	GS	12	....	....
	Assistant Secretary for Budget and Programs						
Washington, DC	Chief Financial Officer and Assistant Secretary for Budget and Programs.	Victoria B Wassmer..............	PAS	EX	IV	....	....
Washington, DC	Principal Deputy Assistant Secretary for Finance and Budget.	Joseph Humphrey Jarrin.....	NA	ES	....	....	....
	Office of Budget and Program Performance						
Washington, DC	Deputy Director, Office of Budget and Program Performance.	Career Incumbent	CA	ES	....	....	....
	Office of Financial Management						
Washington, DC	Director, Office of Financial Management.........	Career Incumbent	CA	ES	....	....	....
	Office of the General Counsel						
Washington, DC	General Counsel	Vacant	NA	EX	....	....	....
Washington, DC	Principal Deputy General Counsel....................	Sarah Elizabeth Baker	NA	ES	....	....	....
Washington, DC	Deputy General Counsel.............................	Career Incumbent	CA	ES	....	....	....
Washington, DC	Deputy General Counsel.............................	Brian Thomas Stansbury.....	NA	ES	....	....	....
Washington, DC	Senior Counsel for Oversight............................	Brian M Castro	NA	ES	....	....	....
Washington, DC	Senior Counsel..	Meeran Ahn.........................	SC	GS	15	....	....
Washington, DC	Special Counsel.......................................	Vacant	....	ES	....	....	....
	Office of Operations						
Washington, DC	Assistant General Counsel for Operations	Career Incumbent	CA	ES	....	....	....
	Office of General Law						
Washington, DC	Assistant General Counsel for General Law	Vacant	....	ES	....	....	....
	Immediate Office of the General Counsel						
Washington, DC	Senior Counsel for Oversight............................	Career Incumbent	CA	ES	....	....	....

DEPARTMENT OF TRANSPORTATION—Continued

Location	Position Title	Name of Incumbent	Type of Appt.	Pay Plan	Level, Grade, or Pay	Tenure	Expires
	Office of Federal Financial Assistance, Acquisition, and Fiscal Law						
Washington, DC	Assistant General Counsel for Federal Financial Assistance, Acquisition, and Fiscal Law.	Career Incumbent	CA	ES			
	Office of Regulation and Legislation						
Washington, DC	Assistant General Counsel for Regulation and Enforcement.	Career Incumbent	CA	ES			
	Office of International and Aviation Economic Law						
Washington, DC	Assistant General Counsel for International and Aviation Economic Law.	Career Incumbent	CA	ES			
	Office of Aviation and Consumer Protection						
Washington, DC	Assistant General Counsel for Aviation and Consumer Protection.	Career Incumbent	CA	ES			
	Assistant Secretary for Governmental Affairs						
Washington, DC	Assistant Secretary for Governmental Affairs	Vacant		EX			
Washington, DC	Principal Deputy Assistant Secretary for Governmental Affairs.	Craig Link	SC	GS	15		
Washington, DC	Deputy Assistant Secretary for Congressional Affairs (House).	Jean Hall Roehrenbeck	SC	GS	15		
Washington, DC	Deputy Assistant Secretary for Congressional Affairs (Senate).	Seth Caleb Gainer	SC	GS	15		
Washington, DC	Deputy Assistant Secretary for Intergovernmental Affairs.	Evan H Wessel	SC	GS	15		
Washington, DC	Advisor for Governmental Affairs	Tyler Scott Ricchetti	SC	GS	12		
Washington, DC	Advisor for Intergovernmental Affairs	Landon David Bailey	SC	GS	12		
	Assistant Secretary for Tribal Government Affairs						
Washington, DC	Assistant Secretary for Tribal Government Affairs.	Arlando Teller	PA	EX	IV		
	Assistant Secretary for Administration						
Washington, DC	Assistant Secretary for Administration	Philip A McNamara	NA	ES			
Washington, DC	Director of Management Services	Vacant		ES			
Washington, DC	Director, Office of Grants and Financial Assistance.	Career Incumbent	CA	ES			
	Departmental Office of Human Resource Management						
Washington, DC	Director, Departmental Office of Human Resource Management.	Career Incumbent	CA	ES			
Washington, DC	Deputy Director, Departmental Office of Human Resource Management.	Career Incumbent	CA	ES			
	Office of Security						
Washington, DC	Director, Office of Security	Career Incumbent	CA	ES			
	Office of Financial Management						
Washington, DC	Director, Office of Financial Management and Transit Benefits Programs.	Career Incumbent	CA	ES			
Washington, DC	Deputy Director, Office of Financial Management and Transit Benefit Programs.	Career Incumbent	CA	ES			
	Office of Facilities, Information and Asset Management						
Washington, DC	Director, Office of Facilities, Information and Asset Management.	Career Incumbent	CA	ES			
	Assistant Secretary for Transportation Policy						
Washington, DC	Assistant Secretary for Transportation Policy	Christopher Alexander Coes.	PAS	EX	IV		
Washington, DC	Principal Deputy Assistant Secretary for Transportation Policy.	Mariia Vicarius Zimmerman.	NA	ES			
Washington, DC	Deputy Assistant Secretary for Transportation Policy.	Ann M Shikany	NA	ES			
Washington, DC	Deputy Assistant Secretary for Transportation Policy.	Veronica Perry McBeth	NA	ES			
Washington, DC	Deputy Assistant Secretary and Advisor for Transportation Policy.	Scott Ross Goldstein	NA	ES			
Washington, DC	Disability Policy Advisor	Kelly Jay Buckland	SC	GS	15		
Washington, DC	Labor Policy Advisor	Ross Templeton	SC	GS	15		
Washington, DC	Policy Advisor	Ryckesha Wells	SC	GS	13		
Washington, DC	Advisor for Policy and Program Implementation.	Lindsey Sherrill Teel	SC	GS	14		

DEPARTMENT OF TRANSPORTATION—Continued

Location	Position Title	Name of Incumbent	Type of Appt.	Pay Plan	Level, Grade, or Pay	Tenure	Expires
Washington, DC	Advisor for Policy and Program Implementation.	Julianne Rhinebeck..............	SC	GS	14	....	....
	Office of Infrastructure Finance and Innovation						
Washington, DC	Director, Office of Infrastructure Finance and Innovation.	Career Incumbent	CA	ES	....	....	....
	Office of the Chief Economist						
Washington, DC	Chief Economist..	Career Incumbent	CA	ES	....	....	....
	Assistant Secretary for Research and Technology						
Washington, DC	Assistant Secretary for Research and Technology.	Vacant	....	EX	....	....	....
Washington, DC	Principal Deputy Assistant Secretary for Research and Technology.	Robert Cornelius Hampshire.	NA	ES	....	....	....
Cambridge, MA	Director, Center for Safety Management and Human Factors.	Career Incumbent	CA	ES	....	....	....
Washington, DC	Director of Strategic Initiatives...........................	Benjamin Ross Levine	SC	GS	15	....	....
	Office of Research, Development and Technology						
Washington, DC	Director, Office of Research Development and Technology.	Career Incumbent	CA	ES	....	....	....
Washington, DC	Director, National Space-Based Positioning, Navigation, and Timing Coordination Office.	Career Incumbent	CA	ES	....	....	....
	Bureau of Transportation Statistics						
Washington, DC	Director, Bureau of Transportation Statistics ...	Career Incumbent	CA	ES	....	....	....
Washington, DC	Deputy Director, Bureau of Transportation Statistics.	Career Incumbent	CA	ES	....	....	....
	Volpe National Transportation Systems Center						
Cambridge, MA	Director, Volpe National Transportation Systems Center.	Career Incumbent	CA	ES	....	....	....
	Office of the Deputy Associate Administrator for Operations						
Cambridge, MA	Deputy Director for Operations........................	Vacant	....	ES	....	....	....
	Office of the Deputy Associate Administrator for Research and Innovative Technology						
Cambridge, MA	Director for Research and Innovative Technology.	Career Incumbent	CA	ES	....	....	....
Cambridge, MA	Director for Policy, Planning, and Environment.	Career Incumbent	CA	ES	....	....	....
Cambridge, MA	Director for Infrastructure Systems and Technology.	Career Incumbent	CA	ES	....	....	....
Cambridge, MA	Director, Center for Communications, Navigation, Surveillance Systems, and Engineering.	Career Incumbent	CA	ES	....	....	....
	Assistant Secretary for Aviation and International Affairs						
Washington, DC	Assistant Secretary for Aviation and International Affairs.	Carol Annette Petsonk.........	PAS	EX	IV	....	....
Washington, DC	Principal Deputy Assistant Secretary for Aviation and International Affairs.	Vacant	....	ES	....	....	....
Washington, DC	Deputy Assistant Secretary for Aviation and International Affairs.	Career Incumbent	CA	ES	....	....	....
	Office of International Transportation and Trade						
Washington, DC	Director, Office of International Transportation and Trade.	Career Incumbent	CA	ES	....	....	....
	Office of International Aviation						
Washington, DC	Director, Office of International Aviation	Career Incumbent	CA	ES	....	....	....
	Office of Aviation Analysis						
Washington, DC	Director, Office of Aviation Analysis.................	Career Incumbent	CA	ES	....	....	....
Washington, DC	Deputy Director, Office of Aviation Analysis	Career Incumbent	CA	ES	....	....	....
	FEDERAL AVIATION ADMINISTRATION						
	Immediate Office of the Administrator						
Washington, DC	Administrator..	Michael G Whitaker.............	PAS	EX	II	....	....
Washington, DC	Deputy Administrator	Kathryn Thomson	PA	EX	IV	....	....
	Federal Aviation Administration						
Washington, DC	FAA Chief Counsel	Marc Anthony Nichols	NA	ES	....	....	....
Washington, DC	Associate Admin for Airports............................	Shannetta Rosay Griffin......	XS	OT	....	....	....

DEPARTMENT OF TRANSPORTATION—Continued

Location	Position Title	Name of Incumbent	Type of Appt.	Pay Plan	Level, Grade, or Pay	Tenure	Expires
Washington, DC	Assistant Administrator for Communications...	Bridgett Dowling Frey	XS	OT	....	....	....
Washington, DC	Assistant Administrator for Government and Industry Affairs.	Lauren Rochon Dudley	NA	ES	....	....	....
	Assistant Administrator for Aviation Policy, International Affairs, and Environment						
Washington, DC	Assistant Administrator for Policy, International Affairs, and Environment.	Laurence SS Wildgoose........	XS	OT	....	....	....
	FEDERAL HIGHWAY ADMINISTRATION						
	Immediate Office of the Administrator						
Washington, DC	Administrator...................................	Shailen Bhatt	PAS	EX	II	....	....
Washington, DC	Deputy Administrator	Kristin Rae White	NA	ES	....	....	....
Washington, DC	Program Director, Intelligent Transportation Systems Joint Program Office.	Career Incumbent	CA	ES	....	....	....
	Federal Highway Administration						
Harrisburg, PA........	Senior Field Coordinator for Bipartisan Infrastructure Law Project Delivery.	Robert Arnold	TA	ES	....	....	....
Washington, DC	Director of Public Affairs	Samantha Keitt...................	SC	GS	15	....	....
	Office of the Chief Counsel						
Washington, DC	FHWA Chief Counsel	Jennifer Ayanna Butler	NA	ES	....	....	....
Washington, DC	Deputy Chief Counsel	Career Incumbent	CA	ES	....	....	....
Washington, DC	Assistant Chief Counsel for Legislation and Regulations and General Law Division.	Career Incumbent	CA	ES	....	....	....
	Office of Technical Services						
Baltimore, MD.........	Director, Office of Innovation Implementation..	Career Incumbent	CA	ES	....	....	....
	Associate Administrator for Planning, Environment and Realty						
Washington, DC	Associate Administrator for Planning, Environment, and Realty.	Career Incumbent	CA	ES	....	....	....
Washington, DC	Director, Office of Human Environment............	Career Incumbent	CA	ES	....	....	....
Washington, DC	Director, Office of Project Development and Environmental Review.	Career Incumbent	CA	ES	....	....	....
Washington, DC	Director, Office of Natural Environment	Career Incumbent	CA	ES	....	....	....
Washington, DC	Director, Office of Planning........................	Career Incumbent	CA	ES	....	....	....
	Associate Administrator for Safety						
Washington, DC	Director, Office of Safety Technologies...............	Vacant	....	ES	....	....	....
Washington, DC	Director, Office of Safety Programs....................	Career Incumbent	CA	ES	....	....	....
	Associate Administrator for Infrastructure						
Lakewood, CO	Associate Administrator for Infrastructure.......	Career Incumbent	CA	ES	....	....	....
Washington, DC	Director, Office of Stewardship, Oversight, and Management.	Career Incumbent	CA	ES	....	....	....
Washington, DC	Director, Office of Bridges and Structures.........	Career Incumbent	CA	ES	....	....	....
	Associate Administrator for Federal Lands Highway Programs						
Washington, DC	Associate Administrator for Federal Lands Highway.	Career Incumbent	CA	ES	....	....	....
Sterling, VA	Federal Lands Highway Division Engineer, Eastern.	Vacant	....	ES	....	....	....
Lakewood, CO	Federal Lands Highway Division Engineer, Central.	Career Incumbent	CA	ES	....	....	....
Vancouver, WA.........	Federal Lands Highway Division Engineer, Western.	Career Incumbent	CA	ES	....	....	....
	Associate Administrator for Operations						
Washington, DC	Associate Administrator for Operations	Career Incumbent	CA	ES	....	....	....
Washington, DC	Director, Office of Freight Management and Operations.	Career Incumbent	CA	ES	....	....	....
Washington, DC	Director, Office of Transportation Management.	Career Incumbent	CA	ES	....	....	....
Washington, DC	Director, Office of Transportation Operations ...	Career Incumbent	CA	ES	....	....	....
	Associate Administrator for Highway Policy and External Affairs						
Washington, DC	Associate Administrator for Highway Policy and External Affairs.	Randall Keith Benjamin......	NA	ES	....	....	....
Washington, DC	Deputy Associate Administrator for Highway Policy and External Affairs.	Career Incumbent	CA	ES	....	....	....
Washington, DC	Director, Office of International Programs	Career Incumbent	CA	ES	....	....	....
Washington, DC	Director, Office of Highway Policy Information.	Career Incumbent	CA	ES	....	....	....
Washington, DC	Director, Office of Transportation Policy Studies.	Career Incumbent	CA	ES	....	....	....

DEPARTMENT OF TRANSPORTATION—Continued

Location	Position Title	Name of Incumbent	Type of Appt.	Pay Plan	Level, Grade, or Pay	Tenure	Expires
Washington, DC	Director, Office of Legislative Affairs and Policy Communications.	Career Incumbent	CA	ES	....	....	....
	Associate Administrator for Administration						
Washington, DC	FHWA Associate Administrator for Administration.	Career Incumbent	CA	ES	....	....	....
Washington, DC	Director, Office of Innovation and Data Services/Chief Technology Officer.	Career Incumbent	CA	ES	....	....	....
Washington, DC	Director, Office of Human Resources	Career Incumbent	CA	ES	....	....	....
	Associate Administrator for Research, Development and Technology						
Washington, DC	Associate Administrator for Research, Development and Technology.	Career Incumbent	CA	ES	....	....	....
Washington, DC	Director, Office of Infrastructure Research, and Development.	Career Incumbent	CA	ES	....	....	....
Washington, DC	Director, Office of Safety and Operations Research, Development and Technology.	Vacant	....	ES	....	....	....
	Associate Administrator for Civil Rights						
Washington, DC	Associate Administrator for Civil Rights...........	Career Incumbent	CA	ES	....	....	....
	Field Services						
Atlanta, GA	Director of Field Services—South	Vacant	....	ES	....	....	....
Baltimore, MD.........	Director of Field Services—North	Career Incumbent	CA	ES	....	....	....
Lakewood, CO	Director of Field Services—West	Career Incumbent	CA	ES	....	....	....
Sacramento, CA......	Division Administrator, California	Career Incumbent	CA	ES	....	....	....
Washington, DC	Division Administrator, Florida	Career Incumbent	CA	ES	....	....	....
Austin, TX.............	Division Administrator, Austin, Texas	Career Incumbent	CA	ES	....	....	....
Albany, NY..............	Division Administrator, New York.....................	Career Incumbent	CA	ES	....	....	....
Matteson, IL............	Director of Field Services - Mid-America	Career Incumbent	CA	ES	....	....	....
	FEDERAL MOTOR CARRIER SAFETY ADMINISTRATION						
	Federal Motor Carrier Safety Administration						
Washington, DC	Administrator..	Vacant	....	EX	....	....	....
Washington, DC	Deputy Administrator	Vincent Gerard White..........	NA	ES	....	....	....
Washington, DC	Chief Technology Officer	Career Incumbent	CA	ES	....	....	....
Washington, DC	Advisor for External Affairs	Oriella Mejia.......................	SC	GS	12	....	....
Washington, DC	Associate Administrator for Governmental and External Affairs.	Brenna Kay Marron.............	NA	ES	....	....	....
	Office of the Chief Counsel						
Washington, DC	FMCSA Chief Counsel	Melody Nichole Drummond Hansen.	NA	ES	....	....	....
Washington, DC	Deputy Chief Counsel	Career Incumbent	CA	ES	....	....	....
	Associate Administrator for Administration						
Washington, DC	FMCSA Associate Administrator for Administration.	Vacant	....	ES	....	....	....
	Federal Motor Carrier Safety Administration						
Washington, DC	Deputy Associate Administrator for Safety	Career Incumbent	CA	ES	....	....	....
Baltimore, MD.........	Regional Field Administrator, Eastern Region..	Career Incumbent	CA	ES	....	....	....
Lakewood, CO	Regional Field Administrator, Western Region .	Career Incumbent	CA	ES	....	....	....
	Associate Administrator for Research and Registration						
Washington, DC	Associate Administrator for Research and Registration.	Career Incumbent	CA	ES	....	....	....
	Office of Analysis, Research and Technology						
Washington, DC	Director, Office of Innovation Safety Management.	Vacant	....	ES	....	....	....
	Office of Motor Carrier Safety Programs						
Washington, DC	Director, Office of Safety Programs....................	Career Incumbent	CA	ES	....	....	....
	Associate Administrator for Policy and Program Development						
Washington, DC	Associate Administrator for Policy and Program Development.	Career Incumbent	CA	ES	....	....	....
	Office of Policy, Plans and Regulations						
Washington, DC	Director, Office of Policy, Strategic Planning and Regulations.	Career Incumbent	CA	ES	....	....	....
	FEDERAL RAILROAD ADMINISTRATION						
	Immediate Office of the Administrator						
Washington, DC	Administrator..	Amit Bose	PAS	EX	III	....	....

DEPARTMENT OF TRANSPORTATION—Continued

Location	Position Title	Name of Incumbent	Type of Appt.	Pay Plan	Level, Grade, or Pay	Tenure	Expires
Washington, DC	Deputy Administrator	Jennifer Mitchell	NA	ES	....	....	....
	Office of the Chief Counsel						
Washington, DC	FRA Chief Counsel	Allison Ishihara Fultz..........	NA	ES	....	....	....
Washington, DC	Deputy Chief Counsel	Career Incumbent	CA	ES	....	....	....
	Federal Railroad Administration						
Washington, DC	Senior Advisor to the Administrator..................	Andrea Nicole Wohleber	SC	GS	15	....	....
Washington, DC	Director of Communications and External Affairs.	Daniel S Griffin....................	SC	GS	14	....	....
	Associate Administrator for Administration						
Washington, DC	FRA Associate Administrator for Administration.	Career Incumbent	CA	ES	....	....	....
	Associate Administrator for Railroad Safety						
Washington, DC	Director, Office of Railroad Infrastructure and Mechanical.	Vacant	....	ES	....	....	....
Washington, DC	Director, Office of Railroad Systems, Technology and Innovation.	Career Incumbent	CA	ES	....	....	....
Washington, DC	Director, Office of Program Management	Career Incumbent	CA	ES	....	....	....
Washington, DC	Director, Office of Regional Operations and Outreach.	Career Incumbent	CA	ES	....	....	....
	Associate Administrator for Research, Data Solutions, and Innovation						
Washington, DC	Associate Administrator for Research, Data Solutions and Innovation.	Career Incumbent	CA	ES	....	....	....
Washington, DC	Director, Office of Research and Development..	Career Incumbent	CA	ES	....	....	....
Washington, DC	Director, Industry Data and Economic Analysis.	Career Incumbent	CA	ES	....	....	....
	Associate Administrator for Railroad Development						
Washington, DC	Associate Administrator for Railroad Development.	Career Incumbent	CA	ES	....	....	....
Washington, DC	Director, Office of Environmental Program Management.	Career Incumbent	CA	ES	....	....	....
Washington, DC	Director, Office of Railroad Program Development.	Career Incumbent	CA	ES	....	....	....
Washington, DC	Director, Office of Railroad Planning and Engineering.	Career Incumbent	CA	ES	....	....	....
Washington, DC	Director, Office of Regional Outreach and Project Delivery.	Career Incumbent	CA	ES	....	....	....
New York, NY..........	Director, Amtrak and Northeast Corridor	Career Incumbent	CA	ES	....	....	....
	FEDERAL TRANSIT ADMINISTRATION						
	Immediate Office of the Administrator						
Washington, DC	Administrator..	Vacant	....	EX	....	....	....
Washington, DC	Deputy Administrator	Veronica Maria Vanterpool..	NA	ES	....	....	....
Washington, DC	Executive Director..	Career Incumbent	CA	ES	....	....	....
	Office of the Chief Counsel						
Washington, DC	FTA Chief Counsel	Subash Subramanian Iyer...	NA	ES	....	....	....
Washington, DC	Deputy Chief Counsel	Career Incumbent	CA	ES	....	....	....
	Federal Transit Administration						
Washington, DC	Associate Administrator for Communications and Legislative Affairs.	Paul S Kincaid......................	SC	GS	15	....	....
Washington, DC	Advisor for Policy and Program Implementation.	Catherine Monique Teebay..	SC	GS	14	....	....
	Associate Administrator for Safety and Oversight						
Washington, DC	Associate Administrator for Safety and Oversight.	Career Incumbent	CA	ES	....	....	....
	Associate Administrator for Planning and Environment						
Washington, DC	Associate Administrator for Planning and Environment.	Career Incumbent	CA	ES	....	....	....
	Associate Administrator for Program Management						
Washington, DC	Associate Administrator for Program Management.	Career Incumbent	CA	ES	....	....	....
	Associate Administrator for Administration						
Washington, DC	FTA Associate Administrator for Administration.	Career Incumbent	CA	ES	....	....	....

DEPARTMENT OF TRANSPORTATION—Continued

Location	Position Title	Name of Incumbent	Type of Appt.	Pay Plan	Level, Grade, or Pay	Tenure	Expires
	Associate Administrator for Research, Demonstration and Innovation						
Washington, DC	Associate Administrator for Research, Demonstration and Innovation.	Career Incumbent	CA	ES	....	....	....
	Associate Administrator for Budget and Policy						
Washington, DC	Associate Administrator for Budget and Policy.	Career Incumbent	CA	ES	....	....	....
	Associate Administrator for Civil Rights						
Washington, DC	Associate Administrator for Civil Rights...........	Career Incumbent	CA	ES	....	....	....
	Associate Administrator for Regional Operations and Program Delivery						
Washington, DC	Associate Administrator for Regional Services .	Career Incumbent	CA	ES	....	....	....
	Regional Administrator						
Cambridge, MA	Regional Administrator, Region 1......................	Career Incumbent	CA	ES	....	....	....
New York, NY..........	Regional Administrator, Region 2......................	Career Incumbent	CA	ES	....	....	....
Philadelphia, PA	Regional Administrator, Region 3......................	Career Incumbent	CA	ES	....	....	....
Atlanta, GA	Regional Administrator, Region 4......................	Career Incumbent	CA	ES	....	....	....
Chicago, IL	Regional Administrator, Region 5......................	Career Incumbent	CA	ES	....	....	....
Fort Worth, TX	Regional Administrator, Region 6......................	Career Incumbent	CA	ES	....	....	....
Kansas City, MO	Regional Administrator, Region 7......................	Vacant	....	ES	....	....	....
Denver, CO	Regional Administrator, Region 8......................	Career Incumbent	CA	ES	....	....	....
San Francisco, CA...	Regional Administrator, Region 9......................	Career Incumbent	CA	ES	....	....	....
Seattle, WA..............	Regional Administrator, Region 10....................	Career Incumbent	CA	ES	....	....	....
	GREAT LAKES ST LAWRENCE SEAWAY DEVELOPMENT CORPORATION						
	Immediate Office of the Administrator						
Washington, DC	Administrator................	Adam Michael Tindall-Schlicht.	PA	EX	IV	....	....
Washington, DC	Deputy Administrator	Career Incumbent	CA	ES	....	....	....
Massena, NY	Associate Administrator/Resident Manager	Career Incumbent	CA	ES	....	....	....
	MARITIME ADMINISTRATION						
	Immediate Office of the Administrator						
Washington, DC	Administrator................	Ann Claire Phillips	PAS	EX	III	....	....
Washington, DC	Deputy Administrator	Vacant	....	ES	....	....	....
	Maritime Administration						
Washington, DC	Advisor to the Administrator............................	Celeste Zumwalt................	SC	GS	12	....	....
Newport, RI	Faculty Liaison Officer...................................	Career Incumbent	CA	ES	....	....	....
	Office of the Chief Counsel						
Washington, DC	MARAD Chief Counsel....................................	Jeffrey Hardin Lewis	NA	ES	....	....	....
	Office of the Chief Financial Officer						
Washington, DC	Associate Administrator for Budget and Programs/Chief Financial Officer.	Career Incumbent	CA	ES	....	....	....
	Associate Administrator for Ports and Inland Waterways						
Washington, DC	Associate Administrator for Ports and Inland Waterways.	Career Incumbent	CA	ES	....	....	....
	Associate Administrator for Administration						
Washington, DC	MARAD Associate Administrator for Administration.	Career Incumbent	CA	ES	....	....	....
	Associate Administrator for Business and Finance Development						
Washington, DC	Associate Administrator for Business and Finance Development.	Career Incumbent	CA	ES	....	....	....
	Associate Administrator for Strategic Sealift						
Washington, DC	Associate Administrator for Strategic Sealift....	Vacant	....	ES	....	....	....
Washington, DC	Deputy Associate Administrator for Commercial Sealift.	Career Incumbent	CA	ES	....	....	....
	Merchant Marine Academy						
Kings Point, NY	Superintendent	Career Incumbent	CA	ES	....	....	....
Kings Point, NY	Deputy Superintendent......................................	Career Incumbent	CA	ES	....	....	....
Kings Point, NY	Academic Dean/Provost.....................................	Vacant	....	ES	....	....	....
Kings Point, NY	Director, Office of Facilities and Infrastructure Management.	Vacant	....	ES	....	....	....

DEPARTMENT OF TRANSPORTATION—Continued

Location	Position Title	Name of Incumbent	Type of Appt.	Pay Plan	Level, Grade, or Pay	Tenure	Expires
	NATIONAL HIGHWAY TRAFFIC SAFETY ADMINISTRATION						
	Immediate Office of the Administrator						
Washington, DC	Administrator...	Vacant	....	EX	....	....	....
Washington, DC	Deputy Administrator	Sophie Mikhal Shulman	NA	ES	....	....	....
	National Highway Traffic Safety Administration						
Washington, DC	Director of the Office of Governmental Affairs, Policy and Strategic Planning.	Jason K Levine....................	SC	GS	15	....	....
	Office of the Chief Counsel						
Washington, DC	NHTSA Chief Counsel	Adam Raviv	NA	ES	....	....	....
Washington, DC	Assistant Chief Counsel (Vehicle Safety Standards and Harmonization).	Career Incumbent	CA	ES	....	....	....
Washington, DC	Assistant Chief Counsel (Litigation and Enforcement).	Career Incumbent	CA	ES	....	....	....
Washington, DC	Assistant Chief Counsel (Legislation and General Law).	Career Incumbent	CA	ES	....	....	....
	Associate Administrator for Research and Program Development						
Washington, DC	Associate Administrator for Research and Program Development.	Career Incumbent	CA	ES	....	....	....
Washington, DC	Director, Office of Impaired Driving and Occupant Protection.	Career Incumbent	CA	ES	....	....	....
Washington, DC	Director, Office of Safety Programs....................	Career Incumbent	CA	ES	....	....	....
	Office of the Chief Financial Officer						
Washington, DC	Chief Financial Officer............................	Career Incumbent	CA	ES	....	....	....
	Associate Administrator for Administration						
Washington, DC	NHTSA Associate Administrator for Administration.	Career Incumbent	CA	ES	....	....	....
	Associate Administrator for Communications and Consumer Information						
Washington, DC	Associate Administrator for Communications and Consumer Information.	Career Incumbent	CA	ES	....	....	....
Washington, DC	Chief Technology Officer	Career Incumbent	CA	ES	....	....	....
	Associate Administrator for Rulemaking						
Washington, DC	Associate Administrator for Rulemaking..........	Career Incumbent	CA	ES	....	....	....
Washington, DC	Director, Office of Crash Avoidance Standards .	Career Incumbent	CA	ES	....	....	....
Washington, DC	Director, Office of International Policy, Fuel, Economy and Consumer Programs.	Career Incumbent	CA	ES	....	....	....
Washington, DC	Director Office of Automation Safety................	Career Incumbent	CA	ES	....	....	....
	Associate Administrator for Vehicle Safety Research						
Washington, DC	Associate Administrator for Vehicle Safety Research.	Career Incumbent	CA	ES	....	....	....
Ohio, OH.................	Director, Vehicle Research and Test Center (Ohio).	Career Incumbent	CA	ES	....	....	....
Washington, DC	Director, Office of Crash Avoidance and Electronic Controls Research.	Career Incumbent	CA	ES	....	....	....
	Associate Administrator for the National Center for Statistics and Analysis						
Washington, DC	Associate Administrator for the National Center for Statistics and Analysis.	Career Incumbent	CA	ES	....	....	....
Washington, DC	Director, Office of Regulatory Analysis and Evaluation.	Career Incumbent	CA	ES	....	....	....
	PIPELINE AND HAZARDOUS MATERIALS SAFETY ADMINISTRATION						
Washington, DC	Administrator...	Vacant	....	EX	....	....	....
Washington, DC	Deputy Administrator	Tristan Brown	NA	ES	....	....	....
Washington, DC	Senior Advisor...	Adil Syed Ahmed.................	SC	GS	15	....	....
	Office of the Chief Counsel						
Washington, DC	PHMSA Chief Counsel	Vacant	....	ES	....	....	....
Washington, DC	Deputy Chief Counsel	Career Incumbent	CA	ES	....	....	....
	Associate Administrator for Planning and Analytics						
Washington, DC	Associate Administrator for Planning and Analytics.	Vacant	....	ES	....	....	....

DEPARTMENT OF TRANSPORTATION—Continued

Location	Position Title	Name of Incumbent	Type of Appt.	Pay Plan	Level, Grade, or Pay	Tenure	Expires
	Office of Hazardous Materials Safety						
Washington, DC	Deputy Associate Administrator for Policy and Programs.	Career Incumbent	CA	ES	....	....	....
Washington, DC	Deputy Associate Administrator for Field Operations.	Career Incumbent	CA	ES	....	....	....
	Associate Administrator for Administration						
Washington, DC	PHMSA Associate Administrator for Administration.	Career Incumbent	CA	ES	....	....	....

DEPARTMENT OF TRANSPORTATION OFFICE OF THE INSPECTOR GENERAL

Location	Position Title	Name of Incumbent	Type of Appt.	Pay Plan	Level, Grade, or Pay	Tenure	Expires
Washington, DC	Inspector General	Eric Soskin............................	PAS	EX	IV	....	....

DEPARTMENT OF THE TREASURY

Location	Position Title	Name of Incumbent	Type of Appt.	Pay Plan	Level, Grade, or Pay	Tenure	Expires
	SECRETARY OF TREASURY						
Washington, DC	Secretary	Janet L Yellen........................	PAS	EX	I	....	....
Washington, DC	Deputy Secretary of the Treasury	Adewale Olabimeji Adeyemo.	PAS	EX	II	....	....
Washington, DC	Chief of Staff...	Didem A Nisanci	NA	ES		....	
Washington, DC	Deputy Chief of Staff....................................	Vacant		ES		....	
Washington, DC	Deputy Chief of Staff....................................	Wishcha Ngarmboonanant ..	SC	GS	15	....	
Washington, DC	Executive Secretary......................................	Kayla Arslanian	NA	ES		....	
Washington, DC	Principal Deputy Executive Secretary..............	Nicole Lindler........................	SC	GS	15	....	
Washington, DC	Deputy Executive Secretary	Matthew Brandon Ellison ...	SC	GS	15	....	
Washington, DC	Director of Strategic Planning and Protocol......	Ari Benjamin Krupkin...........	NA	ES		....	
Washington, DC	White House Liaison	Raymond Minhtri Pham......	SC	GS	15	....	
Washington, DC	Deputy White House Liaison............................	Sebastian Rozo	SC	GS	14	....	
Washington, DC	Chief Speechwriter	Talya Lockman-Fine	SC	GS	15	....	
Washington, DC	Counselor to the Secretary	Alvin Isaac Rosenblum	SC	GS	15	....	
Washington, DC	Associate Director of Scheduling and Advance .	Carly Shayna Edlin..............	SC	GS	11	....	
Washington, DC	Senior Scheduling and Advance Associate	Vincy Mandy Fok	SC	GS	11	....	
Washington, DC	Scheduling and Advance Associate	Emmanuel Brantley.............	SC	GS	9	....	
Washington, DC	Special Assistant...	Anna Brozycki	SC	GS	7	....	
Washington, DC	Special Assistant...	Allen Xiang Li	SC	GS	7	....	
Washington, DC	Special Assistant...	Alexander Jarin....................	SC	GS	9	....	
Washington, DC	Climate Counselor	Ethan Zindler	NA	ES		....	
Washington, DC	Special Assistant...	Phoebe Sara Hering.............	SC	GS	9	....	
Washington, DC	Chief Implementation Officer for the Inflation Reduction Act.	Laurel Blatchford.................	NA	ES		....	
Washington, DC	Policy Advisor for IRA Implementation.............	Genevieve Duncan	SC	GS	14	....	
Washington, DC	Counselor for Racial Equity............................	Janis Lee Bowdler...............	NA	ES		....	
Washington, DC	Senior Advisor..	Laura Burr Gerrard.............	SC	GS	15	....	
Washington, DC	Policy Advisor...	Samarth Gupta.....................	SC	GS	13	....	
Washington, DC	Special Assistant...	Faith Goetzke	SC	GS	7	....	
Washington, DC	Special Assistant (Exec Sec)	Virginia Lo...........................	SC	GS	7	....	
Washington, DC	Chief Diversity Equity Inclusion Accessibility Officer.	Career Incumbent	CA	ES		....	
Washington, DC	Senior Advisor...	Sourav Bhowmick	SC	GS	15	....	
Washington, DC	Director of Policy and Program Impact.	Luke Harbour Bassett	SC	GS	15	....	
Washington, DC	Policy Advisor for Inflation Reduction Act Implementation.	Pablo Ivan McConnie-Saad .	SC	GS	13	....	
Washington, DC	Special Advisor for Inflation Reduction Act Implementation.	Daisy Buenrostro-Avila........	SC	GS	12	....	
Washington, DC	Special Assistant for Inflation Reduction Act Implementation.	Adam Shaw...........................	SC	GS	11	....	
Washington, DC	Special Assistant for Inflation Reduction Act Implementation.	Jissel Marie Aceves..............	SC	GS	9	....	
Washington, DC	Director, Treasury Equity Hub	Career Incumbent	CA	ES		....	
Washington, DC	Senior Advisor...	Nicole Elyse Gore-Hayes	SC	GS	15	....	
Washington, DC	Special Advisor for Racial Equity.....................	Samantha Chu Jun Ng........	SC	GS	13	....	

DEPARTMENT OF THE TREASURY—Continued

Location	Position Title	Name of Incumbent	Type of Appt.	Pay Plan	Level, Grade, or Pay	Tenure	Expires
Washington, DC	Special Advisor for Racial Equity......................	Kriss Ascanio Gomez	SC	GS	11	....	....
Washington, DC	Chief Program Officer	Jessica A Milano..................	TA	ES	....	....	....
Washington, DC	Deputy Chief Program Officer for State and Local Programs.	Career Incumbent	CA	ES	....	....	....
Washington, DC	Deputy Chief Operating Officer, Office of Recovery Programs.	Career Incumbent	CA	ES	....	....	....
Washington, DC	Deputy Chief Program Officer Small Business and Community Investment Program.	Career Incumbent	CA	ES	....	....	....
	GENERAL COUNSEL						
Washington, DC	General Counsel	Vacant	....	EX	....	....	....
Washington, DC	Principal Deputy General Counsel....................	Addar Levi	NA	ES	....	....	....
Washington, DC	Deputy General Counsel	Eric Scott Nguyen	NA	ES	....	....	....
Washington, DC	Deputy General Counsel	Vacant	....	ES	....	....	....
Washington, DC	Assistant General Counsel (General Law, Ethics and Regulations).	Career Incumbent	CA	ES	....	....	....
Washington, DC	Deputy Assistant General Counsel (General Law and Regulation).	Career Incumbent	CA	ES	....	....	....
Washington, DC	Deputy Assistant General Counsel (Ethics)	Career Incumbent	CA	ES	....	....	....
Washington, DC	Assistant General Counsel (Banking and Finance).	Career Incumbent	CA	ES	....	....	....
Washington, DC	Deputy Assistant General Counsel (Banking and Finance).	Career Incumbent	CA	ES	....	....	....
Washington, DC	Assistant General Counsel (International Affairs).	Career Incumbent	CA	ES	....	....	....
Washington, DC	Deputy Assistant General Counsel (International Affairs).	Vacant	....	ES	....	....	....
Washington, DC	Deputy Assistant General Counsel (International Affairs).	Career Incumbent	CA	ES	....	....	....
Washington, DC	Deputy Assistant General Counsel (International Affairs).	Career Incumbent	CA	ES	....	....	....
Washington, DC	Principal Deputy Assistant Attorney General (Enforcement and Intelligence).	Career Incumbent	CA	ES	....	....	....
Washington, DC	Assistant General Counsel (Enforcement and Intelligence).	Career Incumbent	CA	ES	....	....	....
Washington, DC	Deputy Assistant General Counsel (Enforcement and Intelligence).	Career Incumbent	CA	ES	....	....	....
Washington, DC	Deputy Assistant General Counsel for Oversight and Litigation.	Career Incumbent	CA	ES	....	....	....
Washington, DC	International Tax Counsel	Career Incumbent	CA	ES	....	....	....
Washington, DC	Deputy International Tax Counsel....................	Career Incumbent	CA	ES	....	....	....
Washington, DC	Benefits Tax Counsel..	Career Incumbent	CA	ES	....	....	....
Washington, DC	Deputy Benefits Tax Counsel	Career Incumbent	CA	ES	....	....	....
Washington, DC	Tax Legislative Counsel	Career Incumbent	CA	ES	....	....	....
Washington, DC	Deputy Tax Legislative Counsel (Climate)	Career Incumbent	CA	ES	....	....	....
Washington, DC	Special Advisor..	Bernadine Vassor	SC	GS	9	....	....
Washington, DC	Chief Counsel, (Alcohol and Tobacco, Tax and Trade Bureau).	Career Incumbent	CA	ES	....	....	....
Washington, DC	Chief Counsel, Bureau of the Fiscal Service	Career Incumbent	CA	ES	....	....	....
Washington, DC	Chief Counsel, United States Mint	Career Incumbent	CA	ES	....	....	....
Washington, DC	Chief Counsel, Bureau of Engraving and Printing.	Career Incumbent	CA	ES	....	....	....
Washington, DC	Chief Counsel, Office of Foreign Assets Control.	Career Incumbent	CA	ES	....	....	....
	UNDER SECRETARY FOR INTERNATIONAL AFFAIRS						
Washington, DC	Under Secretary for International Affairs	Jay C Shambaugh	PAS	EX	III	....	....
Washington, DC	Counselor to the Secretary	Vacant	....	ES	....	....	....
Washington, DC	Counselor..	Vacant	....	ES	....	....	....
Washington, DC	Counselor..	Vacant	....	ES	....	....	....
Washington, DC	Special Advisor..	Lily Anna McGrail	SC	GS	11	....	....
Washington, DC	Special Advisor..	Samin Mirfakhrai	SC	GS	12	....	....
Washington, DC	Special Assistant...	Isabel Rose Kurtovich...........	SC	GS	9	....	....
	UNDER SECRETARY FOR DOMESTIC FINANCE						
Washington, DC	Under Secretary for Domestic Finance.............	J Nellie Liang......................	PAS	EX	III	....	....
Washington, DC	Counselor to the Under Secretary for Domestic Finance.	John Patrick McGrail...........	SC	GS	15	....	....
Washington, DC	Member, Financial Stability Oversight Council.	Thomas Eldon Workman	PAS	EX	III	6	....
Washington, DC	Member, Financial Stability Oversight Council.	Robert Tobias........................	PAS	....	....	....	....

DEPARTMENT OF THE TREASURY—Continued

Location	Position Title	Name of Incumbent	Type of Appt.	Pay Plan	Level, Grade, or Pay	Tenure	Expires
Washington, DC	Deputy Assistant Secretary, Financial Stability Oversight Council.	Vacant	....	ES	....	....	....
Washington, DC	Director of Policy	Career Incumbent	CA	ES	....	....	....
Washington, DC	Senior Policy Advisor...............................	Devin O'Connor	SC	....	....	....	....
Washington, DC	Director of Analysis.................................	Career Incumbent	CA	ES	....	....	....
Washington, DC	Deputy Assistant Secretary for Financial Institutions Policy.	Jeanette Quick......................	NA	ES	....	....	....
Washington, DC	Senior Advisor for Financial Institutions	Chastity Murphy	SC	GS	15	....	....
Washington, DC	Director, Office of Financial Research...............	Vacant	....	EX	....	6	....
Washington, DC	Director Community Development Financial Institutions Fund.	Career Incumbent	CA	ES	....	....	....
Washington, DC	Deputy Assistant Secretary for Consumer Policy.	Suzanna Marie Fritzberg	NA	ES	....	....	....
Washington, DC	Deputy Director for Policy and Programs..........	Career Incumbent	CA	ES	....	....	....
Washington, DC	Deputy Director for Finance and Operations....	Vacant	....	ES	....	....	....
Washington, DC	Advisor..	Jeffrey Joseph Ricchetti.......	SC	GS	11	....	....
Washington, DC	Special Advisor..	Kasandra Negrete	SC	GS	11	....	....
	UNDER SECRETARY FOR TERRORISM AND FINANCIAL INTELLIGENCE						
Washington, DC	Under Secretary for Terrorism and Financial Intelligence.	Brian Eddie Nelson.............	PAS	EX	III	....	....
Washington, DC	Deputy Director, Treasury Executive Office for Asset Forfeiture.	Career Incumbent	CA	ES	....	....	....
Washington, DC	Director, Foreign Assets Control.........................	Career Incumbent	CA	ES	....	....	....
Washington, DC	Deputy Director, Office of Foreign Assets Control.	Career Incumbent	CA	ES	....	....	....
Washington, DC	Associate Director, Resource Management........	Career Incumbent	CA	ES	....	....	....
Washington, DC	Associate Director, Program Policy and Implementation.	Vacant	....	ES	....	....	....
Washington, DC	Associate Director, Office of Global Targeting...	Career Incumbent	CA	ES	....	....	....
Washington, DC	Deputy Associate Director, Office of Global Targeting.	Career Incumbent	CA	ES	....	....	....
Washington, DC	Associate Director, Office of Compliance and Enforcement.	Career Incumbent	CA	ES	....	....	....
Washington, DC	Advisor for Strategic Planning	Evan Seltzer	SC	GS	13	....	....
Washington, DC	Special Assistant.......................................	Jordan Alexander Ceasar	SC	GS	9	....	....
	ASSISTANT SECRETARY (LEGISLATIVE AFFAIRS)						
Washington, DC	Assistant Secretary (Deputy Under Secretary) for Legislative Affairs.	Vacant	....	EX	....	....	....
Washington, DC	Principal Deputy Assistant Secretary for Legislative Affairs.	Corey Anne Tellez	NA	ES	....	....	....
Washington, DC	Deputy Assistant Secretary for Legislative Affairs (Tax and Budget).	Alice Lin...............................	NA	ES	....	....	....
Washington, DC	Deputy Assistant Secretary for Legislative Affairs (Appropriations and Management).	Angel Luis Nigaglioni	NA	ES	....	....	....
Washington, DC	Deputy Assistant Secretary, Legislative Affairs (Terrorism and Financial Intelligence).	Career Incumbent	CA	ES	....	....	....
Washington, DC	Deputy Assistant Secretary for Legislative Affairs (Oversight).	Isabella Michelle More.........	NA	ES	....	....	....
Washington, DC	Deputy Assistant Secretary for Legislative Affairs (International Affairs).	Diana Pilipenko....................	NA	ES	....	....	....
Washington, DC	Deputy Assistant Secretary for Legislative Affairs (Financial Institution Policy).	Alexandra T Victor May	NA	ES	....	....	....
Washington, DC	Senior Advisor..	Namrata Mujumdar.............	SC	GS	15	....	....
Washington, DC	Senior Advisor (Tax)	Tommy Brown	SC	GS	15	....	....
Washington, DC	Legislative Advisor	Emma Grace Nix Coughlan.	SC	GS	11	....	....
Washington, DC	Special Assistant.......................................	Araoluwa Omotowa.............	SC	GS	11	....	....
Washington, DC	Special Assistant.......................................	Austin Tyree	SC	GS	7	....	....
Washington, DC	Special Assistant.......................................	Rebecca Navarro	SC	GS	7	....	....
	ASSISTANT SECRETARY (PUBLIC AFFAIRS)						
Washington, DC	Assistant Secretary (Public Affairs)....................	Lily Anna Adams.................	PA	EX	IV	....	....
Washington, DC	Principal Deputy Assistant Secretary for Public Affairs.	Michael James Gwin............	NA	ES	....	....	....
Washington, DC	Digital Specialist	Donovan Harris...................	SC	GS	11	....	....
Washington, DC	Deputy Assistant Secretary Public Affairs	Vacant	....	ES	....	....	....
Washington, DC	Deputy Assistant Secretary, Public Affairs (Terrorism and Financial Intelligence).	Vacant	....	ES	....	....	....
Washington, DC	Deputy Assistant Secretary for Public Engagement.	Scott B Arceneaux................	NA	ES	....	....	....

DEPARTMENT OF THE TREASURY—Continued

Location	Position Title	Name of Incumbent	Type of Appt.	Pay Plan	Level, Grade, or Pay	Tenure	Expires
Washington, DC	Senior Spokesperson...	Ashley Schapitl......................	SC	GS	15	....	....
Washington, DC	Senior Spokesperson...	Megan Ashely Apper............	SC	GS	15	....	....
Washington, DC	Senior Spokesperson...	Christopher Hayden..............	SC	GS	15	....	....
Washington, DC	Senior Spokesperson...	Morgan Finkelstein...............	SC	GS	15	....	....
Washington, DC	Spokesperson..	Yoatzin Ruby Robles Perez..	SC	GS	13	....	....
Washington, DC	Spokesperson..	Michael Martinez..................	SC	GS	13	....	....
Washington, DC	Spokesperson..	Haris Talwar.........................	SC	GS	13	....	....
Washington, DC	Press Assistant	Tyla Evans	SC	GS	9	....	....
Washington, DC	Senior Advisor for Community Engagement.....	Jessica Argelia Mejia	SC	GS	15	....	....
Washington, DC	Senior Advisor..	Subhan Cheema	SC	GS	15	....	....
Washington, DC	Special Assistant for Public Engagement..........	Elizabeth Plasencia..............	SC	GS	11	....	....
Washington, DC	Special Assistant..	Grady Robert Thomson........	SC	GS	7	....	....
	ASSISTANT SECRETARY (ECONOMIC POLICY)						
Washington, DC	Assistant Secretary (Economic Policy).............	Vacant	....	EX	....	....	....
Washington, DC	Deputy Assistant Secretary (Macroeconomic Analysis).	Vacant	....	ES	....	....	....
Washington, DC	Director, Office of Macroeconomic Analysis.......	Career Incumbent	CA	ES	....	....	....
Washington, DC	Deputy Assistant Secretary (Microeconomic Analysis).	Vacant	....	ES	....	....	....
Washington, DC	Director, Office of Microeconomic Analysis........	Career Incumbent	CA	ES	....	....	....
Washington, DC	Deputy Assistant Secretary, Climate and Energy Economics.	Vacant	....	ES	....	....	....
Washington, DC	Deputy Assistant Secretary for Financial Economics.	Eric Andrew Van Nostrand .	NA	ES	....	....	....
	ASSISTANT SECRETARY (TAX POLICY)						
Washington, DC	Assistant Secretary (Tax Policy)........................	Vacant	....	EX	....	....	....
Washington, DC	Deputy Assistant Secretary (Tax Policy)	Aviva Ronit Aron-Dine........	NA	ES	....	....	....
Washington, DC	Deputy Assistant Secretary (Tax Policy and Delivery).	Theodore Lee	NA	ES	....	....	....
Washington, DC	Deputy Assistant Secretary (Tax Analysis).......	Gregory Quick Leiserson	NA	ES	....	....	....
Washington, DC	Director, Office of Tax Analysis	Career Incumbent	CA	ES	....	....	....
Washington, DC	Deputy Assistant Secretary (International Tax Affairs).	Vacant	....	ES	....	....	....
Washington, DC	Deputy Assistant Secretary for Tax and Climate Policy.	Seth David Hanlon..............	NA	ES	....	....	....
Washington, DC	Director for International Tax	Scott Marshall Levine..........	SC	GS	15	....	....
Washington, DC	Director for Business and International Taxation.	Career Incumbent	CA	ES	....	....	....
Washington, DC	Director for Business Revenue	Career Incumbent	CA	ES	....	....	....
Washington, DC	Director for Individual Taxation	Career Incumbent	CA	ES	....	....	....
Washington, DC	Director for Receipts Forecasting	Career Incumbent	CA	ES	....	....	....
Washington, DC	Associate Benefits Tax Counsel	Kurt Lawson.........................	XS	SL	....	....	....
Washington, DC	Director, Health Economics and Taxation	Career Incumbent	CA	ES	....	....	....
Washington, DC	Advisor..	Danielle Seong Suh..............	SC	GS	13	....	....
Washington, DC	Special Assistant..	Eshika Kaul..........................	SC	GS	7	....	....
Washington, DC	Special Assistant..	Noah Ball-Burack.................	SC	GS	7	....	....
	ASSISTANT SECRETARY FOR MANAGEMENT						
Washington, DC	Assistant Secretary (Management)...................	Aditi Hardikar......................	PA	EX	IV	....	....
Washington, DC	Deputy Assistant Secretary for Privacy, Transparency, and Records.	Career Incumbent	CA	ES	....	....	....
Washington, DC	Deputy Assistant Secretary for Management and Budget.	Career Incumbent	CA	ES	....	....	....
Washington, DC	Counselor to the Assistant Secretary for Management.	Career Incumbent	CA	ES	....	....	....
Washington, DC	Director, Office of Financial Management.........	Career Incumbent	CA	ES	....	....	....
Washington, DC	Deputy Assistant Secretary for Planning and Performance Improvement.	Career Incumbent	CA	ES	....	....	....
Washington, DC	Director, Financial Reporting, Policy and Operations.	Career Incumbent	CA	ES	....	....	....
Washington, DC	Departmental Budget Director...........................	Vacant	....	ES	....	....	....
Washington, DC	Deputy Assistant Secretary (Human Resources) and Chief Human Capital Officer.	Career Incumbent	CA	ES	....	....	....
Washington, DC	Associate Chco for Executive and Human Capital Services.	Career Incumbent	CA	ES	....	....	....
Washington, DC	Director, Office of District of Columbia Pensions.	Career Incumbent	CA	ES	....	....	....
Washington, DC	Deputy Chief Human Capital Officer	Vacant	....	ES	....	....	....
Washington, DC	Deputy Assistant Secretary for Treasury Operations.	Vacant	....	ES	....	....	....

DEPARTMENT OF THE TREASURY—Continued

Location	Position Title	Name of Incumbent	Type of Appt.	Pay Plan	Level, Grade, or Pay	Tenure	Expires
Washington, DC	Deputy Assistant Secretary, Information Systems and Chief Information Officer.	Career Incumbent	CA	ES	....	....	....
Washington, DC	Associate Chief Information Officer for Enterprise Infrastructure Operations Services.	Career Incumbent	CA	ES	....	....	....
Washington, DC	Chief Data Officer................................	Career Incumbent	CA	ES	....	....	....
Washington, DC	Chief Technology Officer	Career Incumbent	CA	ES	....	....	....
Washington, DC	Bureau Chief Information Officer for Do..........	Career Incumbent	CA	ES	....	....	....
Washington, DC	Deputy Chief Information Officer	Career Incumbent	CA	ES	....	....	....
Washington, DC	Associate CIO for Human Resources (HR) Systems.	Career Incumbent	CA	ES	....	....	....
Washington, DC	Chief of Operations/Deputy to the Das for Operations.	Career Incumbent	CA	ES	....	....	....
Washington, DC	Information Technology Transformation Lead Inflation Reduction Act.	Matthew Scott Burton	TA	ES	....	....	....
Washington, DC	Director Shared Services....................	Career Incumbent	CA	ES	....	....	....
Washington, DC	Associate Chief Information Officer for Cyber Security.	Vacant	....	ES	....	....	....
Washington, DC	Associate Chief Information Officer for Enterprise Application Services.	Career Incumbent	CA	ES	....	....	....
Washington, DC	Deputy Assistant Secretary for Acquisition......	Career Incumbent	CA	ES	....	....	....
Washington, DC	Assistant Administrator for Data Analytics - Chief Data Officer.	Career Incumbent	CA	ES	....	....	....
Washington, DC	Counselor to the Director, District of Columbia Pensions.	Vacant	....	ES	....	....	....
ASSISTANT SECRETARY FOR FINANCIAL INSTITUTIONS							
Washington, DC	Assistant Secretary (Financial Institutions)	Vacant	....	EX	....	....	....
Washington, DC	Principal Deputy Assistant Secretary Financial Institutions.	Laurie Stephanie Schaffer...	NA	ES	....	....	....
Washington, DC	Director, Office of Financial Institutions Policy.	Career Incumbent	CA	ES	....	....	....
Washington, DC	Deputy Assistant Secretary, Cybersecurity and Critical Infrastructure Protection.	Career Incumbent	CA	ES	....	....	....
Washington, DC	Director of Cyber Policy, Preparedness and Response.	Vacant	....	ES	....	....	....
Washington, DC	Director of International Coordination and Mission Support.	Career Incumbent	CA	ES	....	....	....
Washington, DC	Deputy Assistant Secretary for Community and Economic Development.	Noel Poyo	NA	ES	....	....	....
Washington, DC	Director, Office of Community and Economic Development.	Career Incumbent	CA	ES	....	....	....
Washington, DC	Deputy Assistant Secretary for Consumer Policy.	Vacant	....	ES	....	....	....
Washington, DC	Director, Office of Consumer Policy....................	Career Incumbent	CA	ES	....	....	....
Washington, DC	Senior Advisor....................	Jeffrey Joseph Rapp............	SC	GS	15	....	....
ASSISTANT SECRETARY FOR FINANCIAL MARKETS							
Washington, DC	Assistant Secretary for Financial Markets.......	Joshua Frost	PAS	EX	IV	....	....
Washington, DC	Deputy Assistant Secretary (Federal Finance)..	Career Incumbent	CA	ES	....	....	....
Washington, DC	Deputy Assistant Secretary Public Finance	Career Incumbent	CA	ES	....	....	....
Washington, DC	Director of Federal Program Finance	Career Incumbent	CA	ES	....	....	....
Washington, DC	Director, Office of State and Local Finance	Career Incumbent	CA	ES	....	....	....
Washington, DC	Director, Office of Debt Management..................	Career Incumbent	CA	ES	....	....	....
Washington, DC	Deputy Assistant Secretary for Capital Markets.	Nandini Ajmani	NA	ES	....	....	....
Washington, DC	Director, Capital Markets	Career Incumbent	CA	ES	....	....	....
Washington, DC	Senior Advisor for Capital Markets	Laura Thrift........................	SC	GS	15	....	....
ASSISTANT SECRETARY FOR INTELLIGENCE AND ANALYSIS							
Washington, DC	Assistant Secretary (Intelligence and Analysis).	Shannon H R Corless...........	PAS	EX	IV	....	....
Washington, DC	Deputy Assistant Secretary for Intelligence......	Career Incumbent	CA	ES	....	....	....
Washington, DC	Principal Deputy Assistant Secretary Support and Technology.	Career Incumbent	CA	ES	....	....	....
Washington, DC	Deputy Assistant Secretary, Support and Technology.	Career Incumbent	CA	ES	....	....	....
Washington, DC	Deputy Assistant Secretary for Analysis and Production.	Vacant	....	ES	....	....	....
Washington, DC	Director, Office of Security Programs................	Career Incumbent	CA	ES	....	....	....
Washington, DC	Director, Civil Liberties, Privacy Protection and Transparency.	Career Incumbent	CA	ES	....	....	....

DEPARTMENT OF THE TREASURY—Continued

Location	Position Title	Name of Incumbent	Type of Appt.	Pay Plan	Level, Grade, or Pay	Tenure	Expires
Washington, DC	Chief Information Officer for Treasury Intelligence Capabilities.	Career Incumbent	CA	ES	....	....	....
Washington, DC	Special Advisor..	Milton Roland Patch	SC	GS	13	....	....
	ASSISTANT SECRETARY FOR INTERNATIONAL FINANCE						
Washington, DC	Deputy Under Secretary/Designated Assistant Secretary for International Finance.	Brent Isaac Neiman..............	PAS	EX	IV	....	....
Washington, DC	Principal Deputy Assistant Secretary International Monetary Policy.	Vacant	....	ES	....	....	....
Washington, DC	Deputy Assistant Secretary (International Monetary and Financial Policy).	Career Incumbent	CA	ES	....	....	....
Washington, DC	Deputy Assistant Secretary Europe and Eurasia.	Career Incumbent	CA	ES	....	....	....
Washington, DC	Deputy Assistant Secretary (Western Hemisphere and South Asia.	Career Incumbent	CA	ES	....	....	....
Washington, DC	Director Western Hemisphere	Career Incumbent	CA	ES	....	....	....
Washington, DC	Deputy Assistant Secretary (South and East Asia).	Career Incumbent	CA	ES	....	....	....
Washington, DC	Director, East Asia...	Career Incumbent	CA	ES	....	....	....
Washington, DC	Deputy Assistant Secretary International Development Finance and Policy.	Career Incumbent	CA	ES	....	....	....
Washington, DC	Director Office of International Monetary Policy.	Vacant	....	ES	....	....	....
Washington, DC	Director, Office of Development Results and Accountability.	Career Incumbent	CA	ES	....	....	....
Washington, DC	Director,Office of International Trade Policy.....	Career Incumbent	CA	ES	....	....	....
Washington, DC	Director, Markets Room	Career Incumbent	CA	ES	....	....	....
Washington, DC	Senior Advisor..	Career Incumbent	CA	ES	....	....	....
	ASSISTANT SECRETARY FOR INTERNATIONAL MARKETS AND DEVELOPMENT						
Washington, DC	Assistant Secretary for International Trade and Development.	Alexia Latortue	PAS	EX	IV	....	....
Washington, DC	Deputy Assistant Secretary for Trade and Investment Policy.	Career Incumbent	CA	ES	....	....	....
Washington, DC	Deputy Assistant Secretary (Technical Assistance Policy).	Luyen D Tran	NA	ES	....	....	....
Washington, DC	Director, Office of Technical Assistance	Career Incumbent	CA	ES	....	....	....
Washington, DC	Das, International Financial Markets	Career Incumbent	CA	ES	....	....	....
Washington, DC	Deputy Assistant Secretary, Africa and Middle East.	Career Incumbent	CA	ES	....	....	....
Washington, DC	Director, African Nations	Vacant	....	ES	....	....	....
Washington, DC	Director, Multilateral Development Banks........	Career Incumbent	CA	ES	....	....	....
Washington, DC	Deputy Assistant Secretary for Climate, Energy, Infrastructure.	Adam Wang-Levine	NA	ES	....	....	....
Washington, DC	Director, Energy and Infrastructure	Career Incumbent	CA	ES	....	....	....
Austria, Aust	Treasury Attache Austria..................................	Career Incumbent	CA	ES	....	....	....
Washington, DC	Senior Advisor..	Career Incumbent	CA	ES	....	....	....
	ASSISTANT SECRETARY FOR TERRORIST FINANCING						
Washington, DC	Assistant Secretary (Terrorist Financing).........	Vacant	....	EX	....	....	....
Washington, DC	Counselor to the Under Secretary (Terrorism and Financial Intelligence)).	Career Incumbent	CA	ES	....	....	....
Washington, DC	Deputy Assistant Secretary, Office of Strategic Policy.	Career Incumbent	CA	ES	....	....	....
Washington, DC	Deputy Assistant Secretary, Office of Global Affairs Asia,/Africa/Latin America.	Career Incumbent	CA	ES	....	....	....
Washington, DC	Deputy Assistant Secretary, Global Affairs (Europe and Middle East).	Career Incumbent	CA	ES	....	....	....
	ASSISTANT SECRETARY INVESTMENT SECURITY						
Washington, DC	Assistant Secretary Investment Security	Paul Michael Rosen..............	PAS	EX	....	....	....
Washington, DC	Deputy Assistant Secretary Investment Security Policy.	Career Incumbent	CA	ES	....	....	....
Washington, DC	Deputy Assistant Secretary Investment Security Operations.	Career Incumbent	CA	ES	....	....	....
Washington, DC	Director of Monitoring and Enforcement...........	Career Incumbent	CA	ES	....	....	....
	Counselor to the Assistant Secretary Investment Security						
Washington, DC	Counselor to the Assistant Secretary for Investment Policy.	Vacant	....	ES	....	....	....

DEPARTMENT OF THE TREASURY—Continued

Location	Position Title	Name of Incumbent	Type of Appt.	Pay Plan	Level, Grade, or Pay	Tenure	Expires
	BUREAU OF ENGRAVING AND PRINTING						
Washington, DC	Director, Bureau of Engraving and Printing	Career Incumbent	CA	ES	....	....	....
Washington, DC	Deputy Director, Chief Administrative Officer ..	Vacant	....	ES	....	....	....
Washington, DC	Deputy Director, Chief Operating Officer	Vacant	....	ES	....	....	....
Washington, DC	Associate Director (Management)	Career Incumbent	CA	ES	....	....	....
Washington, DC	Associate Director (Chief Financial Officer)......	Career Incumbent	CA	ES	....	....	....
Washington, DC	Associate Director (Chief Information Officer)..	Career Incumbent	CA	ES	....	....	....
Washington, DC	Associate Director, D.C Replacement Facility Program.	Career Incumbent	CA	ES	....	....	....
Fort Worth, TX	Associate Director, Manufacturing (Wcf)	Career Incumbent	CA	ES	....	....	....
Washington, DC	Associate Director, Manufacturing (Dcf)............	Career Incumbent	CA	ES	....	....	....
Washington, DC	Associate Director (Product Design and Development).	Career Incumbent	CA	ES	....	....	....
Washington, DC	Associate Director, Quality..................................	Career Incumbent	CA	ES	....	....	....
	BUREAU OF THE FISCAL SERVICE						
Washington, DC	Deputy Assistant Commissioner and Chief Information Security Officer.	Vacant	....	ES	....	....	....
Washington, DC	Deputy Assistant Commissioner and Business Transformation Executive.	Career Incumbent	CA	ES	....	....	....
Washington, DC	Executive Director, Transforming Tax Collections.	Vacant	....	ES	....	....	....
	COMMISSION ON SOCIAL IMPACT PARTNERSHIPS						
Washington, DC	Chair...	Orin Kramer.........................	PA		....	....	....
	NORTH AMERICAN DEVELOPMENT BANK						
Washington, DC	U.S. Border State Representative......................	Mary Gonzalez......................	PA		....	....	....
	FINANCIAL CRIMES ENFORCEMENT NETWORK						
Washington, DC	Counselor to the Financial Crimes Enforcement Network Director.	Vacant	....	ES	....	....	....
Vienna, VA...............	Deputy Associate Director, Chief Technology Officer.	Career Incumbent	CA	ES	....	....	....
	FISCAL ASSISTANT SECRETARY						
Washington, DC	Director, Office of Fiscal Projections	Career Incumbent	CA	ES	....	....	....
	INSPECTOR GENERAL						
Washington, DC	Inspector General	Vacant	....	EX	....	....	....
	INTERNAL REVENUE SERVICE CHIEF COUNSEL						
Washington, DC	Chief Counsel, Internal Revenue Service	Marjorie Anne Rollinson......	PAS	EX	V	....	....
	TREASURY INSPECTOR GENERAL FOR TAX ADMINISTRATION						
Washington, DC	Treasury Inspector General for Tax Administration.	Vacant	....	EX	....	....	....
	UNITED STATES MINT						
Washington, DC	Director of the Mint...	Ventris C Gibson	PAS	SL	....	5	....
Washington, DC	Deputy Director of the Mint	Career Incumbent	CA	ES	....	....	....
	TREASURER OF THE UNITED STATES						
Washington, DC	Treasurer of the United States	Marilynn Roberge Malerba .	PA	SL	....	....	....
Washington, DC	Policy Advisor..	Emery Real Bird	SC	GS	13	....	....
	COMPTROLLER OF THE CURRENCY						
Washington, DC	Comptroller of the Currency...............................	Vacant	....	EX	....	5	....
Washington, DC	Deputy Chief of Staff..	Lauren Oppenheimer...........	XS	OT	....	....	....
	INTERNAL REVENUE SERVICE						
Washington, DC	Commissioner of Internal Revenue....................	Daniel I Werfel	PAS	EX	III	5	11/12/27
Washington, DC	Transformation Coordination Officer................	Vacant	....	ES	....	....	....

DEPARTMENT OF THE TREASURY OFFICE OF THE INSPECTOR GENERAL

Location	Position Title	Name of Incumbent	Type of Appt.	Pay Plan	Level, Grade, or Pay	Tenure	Expires
	DEPARTMENT OF THE TREASURY OFFICE OF THE INSPECTOR GENERAL						
Washington, DC	Inspector General	Vacant	....	EX	....	....	....
Washington, DC	Special Inspector General for Pandemic Recovery (SIGPR).	Brian Miller	PAS	....	....	....	....
	OFFICE OF AUDIT						
Washington, DC	Deputy Assistant Inspector General for Audit (Coronavirus Relief Fund and Air Carriers Audit).	Lisa Deangelis	TA	ES	....	....	....
Washington, DC	Executive Advisor for Audit	Career Incumbent	CA	ES	....	....	....
Washington, DC	Executive Advisor for Audit	Career Incumbent	CA	ES	....	....	....
	OFFICE OF INVESTIGATIONS						
Washington, DC	Executive Special Agent in Charge (Esac).........	Vacant	....	ES	....	....	....

DEPARTMENT OF THE TREASURY TAX ADMINISTRATION OFFICE OF THE INSPECTOR GENERAL

Location	Position Title	Name of Incumbent	Type of Appt.	Pay Plan	Level, Grade, or Pay	Tenure	Expires
Washington, DC	Inspector General	Vacant	....	EX	....	....	....

DEPARTMENT OF VETERANS AFFAIRS

Location	Position Title	Name of Incumbent	Type of Appt.	Pay Plan	Level, Grade, or Pay	Tenure	Expires
	DEPARTMENT OF VETERANS AFFAIRS						
	Office of the Secretary and Deputy						
Washington, DC	Secretary of Veterans Affairs	Denis R McDonough	PAS	EX	I	....	....
Washington, DC	Deputy Secretary of Veterans Affairs................	Tanya J Bradsher................	PAS	EX	II	....	....
Washington, DC	Deputy Secretary and White House Liaison	Jennifer Esparza	NA	ES	....	....	....
Washington, DC	Chief of Staff..	Margaret Kabat....................	NA	ES	....	....	....
Washington, DC	Deputy Chief of Staff..	Career Incumbent	CA	ES	....	....	....
Washington, DC	Deputy Chief of Staff..	Vacant	....	ES	....	....	....
Washington, DC	Executive Secretary to the Department	Career Incumbent	CA	ES	....	....	....
Washington, DC	Principal Senior Advisor	Vacant	....	ES	....	....	....
Washington, DC	Senior Advisor for Policy	Julia Louisa Cardozo	NA	ES	....	....	....
Washington, DC	Vso Liaison..	Kimberly Mae Mitchell........	NA	ES	....	....	....
Washington, DC	Chief Diversity Officer	Vacant	....	ES	....	....	....
Washington, DC	Senior Advisor for Benefits	Career Incumbent	CA	ES	....	....	....
Washington, DC	Senior Advisor, Strategic Engagement..............	Vacant	....	ES	....	....	....
Washington, DC	Deputy Director Federal Electronic Health Records Modernization.	Career Incumbent	CA	ES	....	....	....
Bend, OR	Senior Executive Agent, Homelessness Coordinator, Greater Los Angeles.	Keith W Harris	TA	ES	....	....	12/04/24
Washington, DC	Transitional Executive Director Promise to Address Comprehensive Toxics Act Epmo.	Steven M Miska	TA	ES	....	....	12/04/25
Washington, DC	Advisor to the Chief of Staff.............................	Kristin M Lein......................	SC	GS	15	....	....
Washington, DC	Chief Speechwriter	Alberto J Ramos..................	SC	GS	15	....	....
Washington, DC	Director, Center for Minority Veterans	James Albino	NA	ES	....	....	....
Washington, DC	Director, Center for Women Veterans................	Maria Lourdes Tiglao...........	NA	ES	....	....	....
Washington, DC	Executive Director, Office of Electronic Health Record Modernization.	Vacant	....	ES	....	....	....
Atlanta, GA	Deputy Chief Information Officer	Career Incumbent	CA	ES	....	....	....
Washington, DC	Executive Director, Program Management Office.	Career Incumbent	CA	ES	....	....	....
Washington, DC	Deputy Executive Director, Program Management.	Career Incumbent	CA	ES	....	....	....
Washington, DC	Chief Technology Officer	Vacant	....	ES	....	....	....
Washington, DC	Assistant Deputy Chief Information Officer	Career Incumbent	CA	ES	....	....	....
	Office of Acquisition, Logistics and Construction						
Washington, DC	Principal Executive Director..............................	Michael David Parrish.........	NA	ES	....	....	....
Washington, DC	Senior Advisor..	Career Incumbent	CA	ES	....	....	....

DEPARTMENT OF VETERANS AFFAIRS—Continued

Location	Position Title	Name of Incumbent	Type of Appt.	Pay Plan	Level, Grade, or Pay	Tenure	Expires
Washington, DC	Associate Executive Director, Strategic Acquisition Management Initiatives.	Career Incumbent	CA	ES			
Frederick, MD	Chancellor, Veterans Affairs Acquisition Academy.	Career Incumbent	CA	ES			
Washington, DC	Deputy Executive Director, Office of Construction and Facilities Management.	Career Incumbent	CA	ES			
Washington, DC	Associate Executive Director	Career Incumbent	CA	ES			
Washington, DC	Chief Facilities Strategy Officer	John Becker	TA	ES			05/07/25
	Board of Veterans' Appeals						
Washington, DC	Chairman, Board of Veterans Appeals	Jaime A Areizaga-Soto	PAS	EX	IV		
Washington, DC	Executive Director, Appeals Support	Career Incumbent	CA	ES			
	Office of Human Resources Management						
Washington, DC	Chief Human Capitol Officer	Career Incumbent	CA	ES			
Brunswick, GA	Executive Director Human Capital Programs	Career Incumbent	CA	ES			
Washington, DC	Executive Director, Management, Planning, and Analysis.	Vacant		ES			
Washington, DC	Senior Advisor Human Capital Services Center.	Vacant		ES			
	Office of the General Counsel						
Washington, DC	General Counsel	Vacant		EX			
Washington, DC	Special Counsel	Gabriel Podesta	NA	ES			
Washington, DC	Special Counsel	Michael L Waldman	NA	ES			
	Office of the Assistant Secretary for Management						
Washington, DC	Assistant Secretary for Management and Chief Financial Officer.	Vacant		EX			
Washington, DC	Executive Director, Programming Analysis and Evaluation.	Career Incumbent	CA	ES			
Washington, DC	Executive Director, Revolving Fund	Career Incumbent	CA	ES			
	Office of Finance						
Washington, DC	Deputy Executive Director, Financial Services Center.	Career Incumbent	CA	ES			
	Regional Office Directors						
Atlanta, GA	Executive Director, Atlanta Regional Office	Career Incumbent	CA	ES			
Columbia, SC	Executive Director, Columbia Regional Office	Career Incumbent	CA	ES			
Muskogee, OK	Executive Director, Muskogee Regional Office	Career Incumbent	CA	ES			
St Paul, MN	Executive Director, Saint Paul Regional Office	Career Incumbent	CA	ES			
Seattle, WA	Executive Director, Seattle Regional Office	Vacant		ES			08/04/24
St Louis, MO	Executive Director, St Louis Regional Office	Career Incumbent	CA	ES			
St Petersburg, FL	Executive Director, St Petersburg Regional Office.	Career Incumbent	CA	ES			
Winston Salem, NC.	Executive Director, Winston-Salem Regional Office.	Career Incumbent	CA	ES			
Waco, TX	Executive Director, Waco Regional Office	Career Incumbent	CA	ES			
Baltimore, MD	Executive Director, Baltimore Regional Office	Career Incumbent	CA	ES			
Boston, MA	Executive Director, Boston Regional Office	Career Incumbent	CA	ES			
Buffalo, NY	Executive Director, Buffalo Regional Office	Career Incumbent	CA	ES			
Chicago, IL	Executive Director, Chicago Regional Office	Vacant		ES			07/21/24
Cleveland, OH	Executive Director, Cleveland Regional Office	Career Incumbent	CA	ES			
Lakewood, CO	Executive Director, Denver Regional Office	Career Incumbent	CA	ES			
Detroit, MI	Executive Director, Detroit Regional Office	Career Incumbent	CA	ES			
Houston, TX	Executive Director, Houston Regional Office	Career Incumbent	CA	ES			
Indianapolis, IN	Executive Director, Indianapolis Regional Office.	Career Incumbent	CA	ES			
Jackson, MS	Executive Director, Jackson Regional Office	Career Incumbent	CA	ES			
Lincoln, NE	Executive Director, Lincoln Regional Office	Career Incumbent	CA	ES			
Little Rock, AR	Executive Director, Little Rock Regional Office.	Career Incumbent	CA	ES			
Los Angeles, CA	Executive Director, Los Angeles Regional Office.	Career Incumbent	CA	ES			
Louisville, KY	Executive Director, Louisville Regional Office	Career Incumbent	CA	ES			
Milwaukee, WI	Executive Director, Milwaukee Regional Office.	Career Incumbent	CA	ES			
Montgomery, AL	Executive Director, Montgomery Regional Office.	Career Incumbent	CA	ES			
Nashville, TN	Executive Director, Nashville Regional Office	Career Incumbent	CA	ES			
New Orleans, LA	Executive Director, New Orleans Regional Office.	Career Incumbent	CA	ES			
New York, NY	Executive Director, New York Regional Office	Career Incumbent	CA	ES			
Oakland, CA	Executive Director, Oakland Regional Office	Career Incumbent	CA	ES			

DEPARTMENT OF VETERANS AFFAIRS—Continued

Location	Position Title	Name of Incumbent	Type of Appt.	Pay Plan	Level, Grade, or Pay	Tenure	Expires
Philadelphia, PA	Executive Director, Philadelphia Regional Office.	Career Incumbent	CA	ES	....	....	....
Phoenix, AZ	Executive Director, Phoenix Regional Office	Career Incumbent	CA	ES	....	....	....
Pittsburgh, PA.........	Executive Director, Pittsburgh Regional Office.	Career Incumbent	CA	ES	....	....	....
Portland, OR............	Executive Director, Portland Regional Office	Vacant	....	ES	....	....	07/21/24
Providence, RI	Executive Director Providence Regional Office.	Career Incumbent	CA	ES	....	....	....
Roanoke, VA	Executive Director, Roanoke Regional Office	Career Incumbent	CA	ES	....	....	....
Salt Lake City, UT ..	Executive Director, Salt Lake City Regional Office.	Career Incumbent	CA	ES	....	....	....
San Diego, CA	Executive Director San Diego Regional Office ..	Career Incumbent	CA	ES	....	....	....
San Juan, PR...........	Executive Director, San Juan Regional Office...	Vacant	....	ES	....	....	....
Togus, ME................	Executive Director, Togus Regional Office	Career Incumbent	CA	ES	....	....	....
	Office of the Assistant Secretary for Enterprise Integration						
Washington, DC	Assistant Secretary for Enterprise Integration.	Guy T Kiyokawa...................	PAS	EX	IV	....	....
Washington, DC	Principal Deputy Assistant Secretary...............	Career Incumbent	CA	ES	....	....	....
Washington, DC	Deputy Assistant Secretary	Vacant	....	ES	....	....	....
Washington, DC	Executive Director, Data Governance and Analysis.	Career Incumbent	CA	ES	....	....	....
Washington, DC	Deputy Executive Director, Data Governance and Analytics, Office of Enterprise Integration.	Vacant	....	ES	....	....	....
Washington, DC	Executive Director, Enterprise Governance and Policy Management.	Career Incumbent	CA	ES	....	....	....
Washington, DC	Executive Director, Enterprise Integration Program Office.	Vacant	....	ES	....	....	....
Washington, DC	Deputy Executive Director, Enterprise Program Integration O.	Career Incumbent	CA	ES	....	....	....
Washington, DC	Associate Deputy Assistant Secretary for Planning and Performance Management.	Career Incumbent	CA	ES	....	....	....
Washington, DC	Director, Enterprise Access and Integration......	Vacant	....	ES	....	....	....
Washington, DC	Senior Advisor..	Vacant	....	ES	....	....	....
Washington, DC	Senior Call Center Advisor, Architecture and Design.	Vacant	....	ES	....	....	....
Washington, DC	Senior Advisor, Health Care Integration	Vacant	....	ES	....	....	....
Washington, DC	Strategic Advisor	Henry H Montalbano............	SC	GS	15	....	....
	Office of Policy						
Washington, DC	Deputy Assistant Secretary for Planning and Performance Management.	Vacant	....	ES	....	....	....
Washington, DC	Executive Director	Vacant	....	ES	....	....	....
	Office of the Assistant Secretary for Human Resources and Administration/operations, Security, and Preparedness						
Washington, DC	Assistant Secretary for Human Resources and Administration/Operations, Security, and Preparedness.	Cassandra Law......................	PA	EX	IV	....	....
Washington, DC	Principal Deputy Assistant Secretary for Human Resources and Administration.	Vacant	....	ES	....	....	....
Washington, DC	Chief of Staff..	Career Incumbent	CA	ES	....	....	....
Washington, DC	Associate Deputy Assistant Secretary for Human Resources, Information Technology Systems and Analytics.	Career Incumbent	CA	ES	....	....	....
Washington, DC	Chief Learning Officer/ Executive Director, Human Resource Enterprise Center.	Career Incumbent	CA	ES	....	....	....
Washington, DC	Executive Director, Human Capital Policies......	Career Incumbent	CA	ES	....	....	....
Washington, DC	Senior Advisor..	Vacant	....	ES	....	....	....
	Office of Administration						
Washington, DC	Deputy Assistant Secretary	Career Incumbent	CA	ES	....	....	....
Washington, DC	Associate Deputy Assistant Secretary for Administration.	Career Incumbent	CA	ES	....	....	....
	Office of the Assistant Secretary for Public and Intergovernmental Affairs						
Washington, DC	Assistant Secretary for Public and Intergovernmental Affairs.	Adam Slater Farina	PA	EX	IV	....	....
Washington, DC	Principal Deputy Assistant Secretary...............	Career Incumbent	CA	ES	....	....	....
Washington, DC	Executive Director, Strategic Planning and Veterans Outreach.	Vacant	....	ES	....	....	....
Washington, DC	Senior Advisor..	Joseph Todd Breasseale.......	NA	ES		....	....
Washington, DC	Special Advisor for Oversight............................	Mara Sloan Boroughs	SC	GS	15	....	....
Washington, DC	Strategic Communications Advisor	John L Santos.......................	SC	GS	13	....	....

DEPARTMENT OF VETERANS AFFAIRS—Continued

Location	Position Title	Name of Incumbent	Type of Appt.	Pay Plan	Level, Grade, or Pay	Tenure	Expires
	Office of Intergovernmental Affairs						
Washington, DC	Deputy Assistant Secretary for Intergovernmental Affairs.	Zaneta I Adams	NA	ES	....	....	....
Washington, DC	Executive Director, Tribal Government Relations.	Vacant	....	ES	....	....	....
Washington, DC	Senior Advisor	Vacant	....	ES	....	....	....
	Office of Public Affairs						
Washington, DC	Deputy Assistant Secretary, Office of Public Affairs.	Terrence Lamar Hayes	NA	ES	....	....	....
	Office of the Assistant Secretary for Congressional and Legislative Affairs						
Washington, DC	Assistant Secretary for Congressional and Legislative Affairs.	Patricia L Ross	PAS	EX	IV	....	....
Washington, DC	Principal Deputy Assistant Secretary for Congressional and Legislative Affairs.	Career Incumbent	CA	ES	....	....	....
Washington, DC	Deputy Assistant Secretary for Congressional Affairs.	Aaron Joseph Scheinberg	NA	ES	....	....	....
Washington, DC	Special Counsel Oversight	David Michael Tucker	NA	ES	....	....	....
Washington, DC	Special Assistant	Lauren Calmet	SC	GS	14	....	....
	Office of the Assistant Secretary for Information and Technology						
Washington, DC	Assistant Secretary for Information and Technology.	Kurt Davis Delbene	PAS	EX	IV	....	....
Pittsburgh, PA	Principal Deputy Assistant Secretary for Information and Technology.	Career Incumbent	CA	ES	....	....	....
Washington, DC	Chief of Staff	Career Incumbent	CA	ES	....	....	....
Washington, DC	Chief Technology Officer	Career Incumbent	CA	ES	....	....	....
Long Beach, CA.......	Chief Architect	Career Incumbent	CA	ES	....	....	....
Washington, DC	Deputy Chief Risk Officer	Career Incumbent	CA	ES	....	....	....
Washington, DC	Deputy Chief Information Officer, Freedom of Information Act.	Career Incumbent	CA	ES	....	....	....
Austin, TX...............	Chief People Officer	Career Incumbent	CA	ES	....	....	....
Washington, DC	Deputy Chief Information Officer, Strategic Sourcing.	Career Incumbent	CA	ES	....	....	....
Denver, CO	Executive Director, Acquisition Strategy and Category Management.	Career Incumbent	CA	ES	....	....	....
Washington, DC	Executive Director Contract and Operations Management.	Career Incumbent	CA	ES	....	....	....
Austin, TX................	Deputy Assistant Secretary, Chief Information Security Officer.	Career Incumbent	CA	ES	....	....	....
Savannah, GA	Deputy Chief Information Security Officer, Cybersecurity Integration, Logistics and Planning.	Career Incumbent	CA	ES	....	....	....
Port Charlotte, FL...	Deputy Chief Information Security Officer, Information Security Operations.	Career Incumbent	CA	ES	....	....	....
Washington, DC	Deputy Chief Information Security Officer/Executive Director.	Career Incumbent	CA	ES	....	....	....
Albany, NY...............	Deputy Chief Information Officer, End User Services.	Career Incumbent	CA	ES	....	....	....
Washington, DC	Executive Director, End User Operations..........	Career Incumbent	CA	ES	....	....	....
Washington, DC	Executive Director, Enterprise Command Operations.	Career Incumbent	CA	ES	....	....	....
Austin, TX................	Deputy Chief Information Officer for Business Integration and Outcome Services.	Career Incumbent	CA	ES	....	....	....
Washington, DC	Deputy Chief Information Officer, Business Integration and Outcome Services Corporate.	Career Incumbent	CA	ES	....	....	....
Washington, DC	Deputy Chief Information Officer Account Manager.	Career Incumbent	CA	ES	....	....	....
Lebanon, PA	Deputy Chief Information Officer Strategic Integration for Emerging Concepts.	Career Incumbent	CA	ES	....	....	....
Washington, DC	Deputy Chief Information Officer, Business Integration and Outcome Services/Health.	Career Incumbent	CA	ES	....	....	....
Washington, DC	Executive Director, Office of Technical Integration.	Career Incumbent	CA	ES	....	....	....
Columbia, SC...........	Chief Interoperability and Veteran Access Officer.	Career Incumbent	CA	ES	....	....	....
Virgin Islands..........	Deputy Chief Information Officer, Connectivity and Collaboration Services.	Career Incumbent	CA	ES	....	....	....
Washington, DC	Deputy Chief Information Officer, Software Product Management.	Vacant	....	ES	....	....	....

DEPARTMENT OF VETERANS AFFAIRS—Continued

Location	Position Title	Name of Incumbent	Type of Appt.	Pay Plan	Level, Grade, or Pay	Tenure	Expires
Washington, DC	Executive Director, Portfolio Management (Bam).	Vacant	....	ES	....	....	....
Trumbull, CT..........	Executive Director, Portfolio Management for Health.	Career Incumbent	CA	ES	....	....	....
Austin, TX................	Executive Director Information Technology Products and Services.	Career Incumbent	CA	ES	....	....	....
Austin, TX................	Deputy Chief Information Officer, Infrastructure Operations.	Career Incumbent	CA	ES	....	....	....
Austin, TX................	Executive Director, Production Services	Career Incumbent	CA	ES	....	....	....
Washington, DC	Deputy Chief Information Officer, Product Engineering Service.	Career Incumbent	CA	ES	....	....	....
	National Cemetery Administration						
Washington, DC	Under Secretary for Memorial Affairs	Vacant	....	EX	....	....	....
Washington, DC	Chief of Staff...	Career Incumbent	CA	ES	....	....	....
Washington, DC	Principal Deputy Under Secretary for Memorial Affairs.	Career Incumbent	CA	ES	....	....	....
Washington, DC	Deputy Under Secretary for Management	Career Incumbent	CA	ES	....	....	....
Washington, DC	Executive Director, Strategy and Analysis	Career Incumbent	CA	ES	....	....	....
Washington, DC	Executive Director, Human Capital Management.	Career Incumbent	CA	ES	....	....	....
Washington, DC	Deputy Under Secretary for Field Programs and Cemetery.	Career Incumbent	CA	ES	....	....	....
Washington, DC	Associate Director, Office of Field Programs	Career Incumbent	CA	ES	....	....	....
Philadelphia, PA	Executive Director, North Atlantic District.......	Career Incumbent	CA	ES	....	....	....
Oakland, CA	Executive Director, Pacific District...................	Career Incumbent	CA	ES	....	....	....
Decatur, GA	Executive Director, Southeast District...............	Career Incumbent	CA	ES	....	....	....
Lakewood, CO	Memorial Service Network Director	Career Incumbent	CA	ES	....	....	....
Indianapolis, IN	Executive Director, Midwest District................	Career Incumbent	CA	ES	....	....	....
Washington, DC	Executive Director, Cemetery Operations..........	Career Incumbent	CA	ES	....	....	....
Riverside, CA..........	Executive Director, Riverside National Cemetery.	Career Incumbent	CA	ES	....	....	....
Florida, FL..............	Executive Director, Florida National Cemetery.	Career Incumbent	CA	ES	....	....	....
Minneapolis, MN.....	Executive Director, Ft Snelling National Cemetery.	Career Incumbent	CA	ES	....	....	....
Washington, DC	Executive Director, Engagement and Memorial Innovations.	Career Incumbent	CA	ES	....	....	....
St Louis, MO	Executive Director, Jefferson Barracks National Cemetery.	Career Incumbent	CA	ES	....	....	....
Calverton, NY..........	Executive Director Calverton National Cemetery.	Career Incumbent	CA	ES	....	....	....
Washington, DC	Senior Advisor Information Technology Modernization and Automation.	Deyo Johnson......................	XS	SL	....	....	....
	Veterans Benefits Administration						
Washington, DC	Under Secretary for Benefits.............................	Joshua David Jacobs............	PAS	EX	III	....	....
Washington, DC	Principal Deputy Under Secretary for Benefits.	Career Incumbent	CA	ES	....	....	....
Washington, DC	Chief of Staff..	Career Incumbent	CA	ES	....	....	....
Washington, DC	Deputy Under Secretary, Automated Benefits Delivery.	Career Incumbent	CA	ES	....	....	....
Washington, DC	Deputy Under Secretary for Benefits, Policy and Oversight.	Career Incumbent	CA	ES	....	....	....
Washington, DC	Deputy Under Secretary for Field Operations ..	Career Incumbent	CA	ES	....	....	....
Denver, CO	District Executive Director, Continental District.	Career Incumbent	CA	ES	....	....	....
St Louis, MO	District Executive Director, Northeast District.	Career Incumbent	CA	ES	....	....	....
Phoenix, AZ	District Executive Director, Pacific District.......	Career Incumbent	CA	ES	....	....	....
Atlanta, GA	District Executive Director, Southeast District.	Career Incumbent	CA	ES	....	....	....
Washington, DC	Executive Director, Compensation Service	Career Incumbent	CA	ES	....	....	....
Washington, DC	Executive Director Education Service...............	Career Incumbent	CA	ES	....	....	....
Washington, DC	Executive Director, Equity Assurance...............	Career Incumbent	CA	ES	....	....	....
Washington, DC	Executive Director, Office of Human Capital Services.	Career Incumbent	CA	ES	....	....	....
Washington, DC	Executive Director, Pension and Fiduciary Service.	Career Incumbent	CA	ES	....	....	....
Washington, DC	Executive Director, Office of Transition and Economic Development.	Career Incumbent	CA	ES	....	....	....
Washington, DC	Executive Director Veteran Readiness and Employment Service.	Career Incumbent	CA	ES	....	....	....
Washington, DC	Senior Advisor for Benefits.................................	Maureen Michele Elias........	NA	ES	....	....	....
Washington, DC	Assistant Deputy Under Secretary for Policy and Oversight.	Career Incumbent	CA	ES	....	....	....

DEPARTMENT OF VETERANS AFFAIRS—Continued

Location	Position Title	Name of Incumbent	Type of Appt.	Pay Plan	Level, Grade, or Pay	Tenure	Expires
Washington, DC	Asst Deputy Under Secretary, Automated Benefits Delivery.	Career Incumbent	CA	ES	....	....	....
Washington, DC	Assistant Deputy Under Secretary for Field Operations, Operations Management.	Career Incumbent	CA	ES	....	....	....
Washington, DC	Deputy Chief of Staff Operations	Career Incumbent	CA	ES	....	....	....
Washington, DC	Deputy Executive Director, Operations, Office Human Capital Services.	Career Incumbent	CA	ES	....	....	....
Washington, DC	Deputy Executive Director Outreach Transition and Economic Development.	Vacant	....	ES	....	....	09/09/24
Washington, DC	Deputy Executive Director, Program Administration, Human Capital Services.	Career Incumbent	CA	ES	....	....	....
Washington, DC	Executive Director, Office of Administrative Review.	Vacant	....	ES	....	....	....
Philadelphia, PA	Executive Director Insurance Service	Career Incumbent	CA	ES	....	....	....
Washington, DC	Executive Director, Strategic Program Management Office.	Career Incumbent	CA	ES	....	....	....
Washington, DC	Senior Advisor, Strategic Change Management.	Vacant	....	ES	....	....	....
Washington, DC	Assistant Deputy Under Secretary for Field Operations Contact Operations.	Career Incumbent	CA	ES	....	....	....
Washington, DC	Chief Administrative Officer	Vacant	....	ES	....	....	10/13/24
Washington, DC	Deputy Executive Director, Office of Mission Support.	Career Incumbent	CA	ES	....	....	....
Washington, DC	Executive Director Business Integration	Career Incumbent	CA	ES	....	....	....
Washington, DC	Senior Advisor Enterprise Communications	David A Lapan	TA	ES	....	....	07/05/26
Washington, DC	Benefits Advisor to the Under Secretary for Benefits.	Maria Carolina Gonzalez Prats.	SC	GS	14	....	....
Veterans Health Administration							
Washington, DC	Under Secretary for Health	Shereef Elnahal	PAS	EX	III	....	....
Washington, DC	Deputy Under Secretary for Health	Steven Lieberman	XS	OT	....	....	....
Washington, DC	Chief of Staff, Veterans Health Administration.	Ryung Suh	XS	OT	....	....	....
Long Beach, CA	Assistant Under Secretary for Health for Dentistry.	Christine Lamarre	XS	OT	....	....	....
Washington, DC	Assistant Under Secretary for Health for Discovery, Education, Affiliates and Network.	Carolyn M Clancy	XS	OT	....	....	....
Washington, DC	Assistant Under Secretary for Health for Integrated Veteran Care.	Miguel H Lapuz	XS	OT	....	....	....
Salt Lake City, UT ..	Assistant Under Secretary for Health for Operations.	Career Incumbent	CA	ES	....	....	....
Gulfport, MS	Assistant Under Secretary for Health for Patient Care Services / Chief Nursing Officer.	Mark Saslo	XS	OT	....	....	....
Washington, DC	Assistant Deputy Under Secretary for Health for Clinical Services.	Erica Scavella	XS	OT	....	....	....
Washington, DC	Associate Deputy Under Secretary for Health for Quality and Patient Safety.	Gerard R Cox	XS	OT	....	....	....
Washington, DC	Deputy Assistant Under Secretary for Health for Discovery, Education and Affiliate Network.	Susan Riga Kirsh	XS	OT	....	....	....
Washington, DC	Deputy Assistant Under Secretary for Health for Patient Care Services.	Antoinette V Shappell	XS	OT	....	....	....
Washington, DC	Deputy Chief of Staff Veterans Health Administration.	Career Incumbent	CA	ES	....	....	....
Upper Arlington, OH.	Deputy to the Assistant Under Secretary for Health for Clinical Services.	Elizabeth Brill	XS	OT	....	....	....
Providence, RI	Deputy to the Assistant Under Secretary Health for Clinical Services Quality and Field Operations.	Thomas Otoole	XS	OT	....	....	....
Washington, DC	Deputy to the Assistant Under Secretary for Health for Integrated Veterans Care.	Hillary Peabody	XS	OT	....	....	....
Storrs, CT	Deputy to the Assistant Under Secretary for Health for Operations.	Career Incumbent	CA	ES	....	....	....
Phoenix, AZ	Deputy to the Assistant Under Secretary for Health for Operations for Redesign.	Michelle Dorsey	XS	OT	....	....	....
Washington, DC	Deputy to the Assistant Under Secretary for Health for Patient Care Service.	Maria Llorente	XS	OT	....	....	....
Washington, DC	Deputy to the Assistant Under Secretary for Health for Support.	Career Incumbent	CA	ES	....	....	....
Washington, DC	Deputy to the Assistant Under Secretary for Health for Support Services.	Vacant	....	OT	....	....	....

DEPARTMENT OF VETERANS AFFAIRS—Continued

Location	Position Title	Name of Incumbent	Type of Appt.	Pay Plan	Level, Grade, or Pay	Tenure	Expires
Washington, DC	Deputy to the Deputy Under Secretary for Health.	Mark Upton	XS	OT	....	....	....
Washington, DC	Chief Academic Affiliations Officer	Marjorie Bowman.................	XS	OT	....	....	....
Washington, DC	Chief Audit Executive	Vacant	....	ES	....	....	....
San Antonio, TX	Chief Consultant to the Deputy Under Secretary for Health.	Lisa Kearney	XS	OT	....	....	....
Washington, DC	Chief Consultant to the Deputy Under Secretary for Health.	Career Incumbent	CA	ES	....	....	....
Santa Cruz, CA	Chief Health Informatics Officer, Federal Electronic Health Record Modernization.	Francisco Rhein....................	XS	OT	....	....	....
Washington, DC	Chief Human Capital Management..................	Career Incumbent	CA	ES	....	....	....
Washington, DC	Chief Informatics Officer	Charles C Hume...................	XS	OT	....	....	....
Springboro, OH	Chief Learning Officer, Employee Education System.	Career Incumbent	CA	ES	....	....	....
St Cloud, FL............	Chief Medical Informatics Officer	Donald Kowalewski.............	XS	OT	....	....	....
Pittsburgh, PA.........	Chief Medical Officer, Integrated Veterans Care.	Sachin Yende	XS	OT	....	....	....
Greenville, VA	Chief Nursing Informatics Officer......................	Sheila Ochylski....................	XS	OT	....	....	....
Houston, TX.............	Chief Officer, Disability and Medical Assessment.	Career Incumbent	CA	ES	....	....	....
Atlanta, GA	Chief Officer for Specialty Care Services	Ajay K Dhawan	XS	OT	....	....	....
Washington, DC	Chief Officer, Office of Connected Care	Neil Evans	XS	OT	....	....	....
Washington, DC	Chief Officer, Readjustment Counseling Service.	Career Incumbent	CA	ES	....	....	....
Washington, DC	Chief Officer, Womens Health Services.............	Vacant	....	OT	....	....	....
Oklahoma City, OK.	Chief Officer, Workforce Management and Consulting.	Career Incumbent	CA	ES	....	....	....
Boston, MA.............	Chief Research and Development Officer..........	Rachel B Ramoni.................	XS	OT	....	....	....
Washington, DC	Chief Strategy Officer	Career Incumbent	CA	ES	....	....	....
Alexandria, VA	Chief Transformation Officer.............................	Career Incumbent	CA	ES	....	....	....
Minneapolis, MN.....	Deputy Chief Academic Affiliations Officer.......	Ezgi Tiryaki	XS	OT	....	....	....
Sumterville, FL	Deputy Chief Learning Officer, Employee Education System.	Career Incumbent	CA	ES	....	....	....
Salt Lake City, UT ..	Deputy Chief Officer, Specialty Care Services ..	Vacant	....	OT	....	....	....
Opelousas, LA	Deputy Chief Officer, Workforce Management and Consulting.	Career Incumbent	CA	ES	....	....	....
Washington, DC	Deputy Chief Readjustment Counselor.............	Pedro Ortiz	XS	OT	....	....	....
Washington, DC	Deputy Chief Research and Development Officer, Enterprise Optimization.	Grant Huang	XS	OT	....	....	....
Washington, DC	Deputy Chief Research and Development Officer for Enterprise Protections Regulatory, Outreach and Systems.	Mary Klote..........................	XS	OT	....	....	....
Washington, DC	Deputy Chief Research and Development Officer for Operations and Workplace Culture.	Wendy N Tenhula.................	XS	OT	....	....	....
Washington, DC	Deputy Chief Research and Development Officer for Strategic Priorities, Outreach, and Communications.	Marc A Wynne	XS	OT	....	....	....
Washington, DC	Deputy Chief Research and Development Officer, Program and Services.	Vacant	....	OT	....	....	....
Washington, DC	Deputy Chief Strategy Officer..........................	Career Incumbent	CA	ES	....	....	....
Denver, CO	Deputy Chief Transformation Officer	Career Incumbent	CA	ES	....	....	....
Washington, DC	Deputy Director, Office of Mental Health Operations.	Clifford Smith......................	XS	OT	....	....	....
Washington, DC	Deputy Director, Office of Patient Care Services and Cultural Transformation.	Cynthia Gantt	XS	OT	....	....	....
Menlo Park, CA.......	Deputy Executive Director...............................	Ilse Wiechers	XS	OT	....	....	....
Moore, OK...............	Deputy Executive Director...............................	Kyle Inhofe	XS	OT	....	....	....
Lebanon, OR...........	Deputy Executive Director, Clinical Operation .	Tracy Weistreich..................	XS	OT	....	....	....
Prairie Du Sac, WI..	Deputy Executive Director Diagnostic Services.	Jeffrey Chenoweth	XS	OT	....	....	....
Richmond, VA..........	Deputy Executive Director, Geriatrics and Extended Care.	Catherine Kelso...................	XS	OT	....	....	....
Washington, DC	Deputy Executive Director, Home and Community Based Purchase Care and Business Operations.	Cheryl Schmitz.....................	XS	OT	....	....	....
North Plainfield, NJ.	Deputy Executive Director, Human Resources Operations.	Career Incumbent	CA	ES	....	....	....
Topeka, KS	Deputy Executive Director, Member Services ...	Career Incumbent	CA	ES	....	....	....
Cincinnati, OH	Deputy Executive Director, National Center for Organizational Development.	Career Incumbent	CA	ES	....	....	....
Washington, DC	Deputy Executive Director, National Center for Patient Safety.	Greta Krapohl	XS	OT	....	....	....

DEPARTMENT OF VETERANS AFFAIRS—Continued

Location	Position Title	Name of Incumbent	Type of Appt.	Pay Plan	Level, Grade, or Pay	Tenure	Expires
Washington, DC	Deputy Executive Director, Quality Management.	Susan Roberts	XS	OT	....	....	....
Seminole, FL	Deputy Executive Director, Rehabilitation and Prosthetic Services.	Rachel A McArdle..............	XS	OT	....	....	....
Westminster, CO	Deputy Executive Director, Reporting, Analytics, Performance and Development.	Tamara Box	XS	OT	....	....	....
Washington, DC	Deputy Executive Director Research Oversight.	Peter N Poon........................	XS	OT	....	....	....
Lexington, KY	Deputy Executive Director Surgery	Erik Ballert........................	XS	OT	....	....	....
Biloxi, MS	Deputy Functional Champion............................	Paul Veregge	XS	OT	....	....	....
Washington, DC	Director, Biomedical Laboratory Research and Development Services.	Christopher T Bever	XS	OT	....	....	....
Washington, DC	Director Clinical Science Research and Development Service.	Vacant	....	OT	....	....	....
Washington, DC	Director, Continuum of Care and General Mental Health.	Marsden H McGuire	XS	OT	....	....	....
Ann Arbor, MI	Director Health Systems Research Portfolio	Amy Kilbourne	XS	OT	....	....	....
Washington, DC	Director Physician Assistant Services	Scot Burroughs	XS	OT	....	....	....
Washington, DC	Executive Advisor, Strategic Forecast	Mark Koeniger	XS	OT	....	....	....
Washington, DC	Executive Director, Acquisition Technology and Logistics.	Career Incumbent	CA	ES	....	....	....
Wilmington, DE.......	Executive Director, Analytics and Performance Integration.	Joseph Francis.....................	XS	OT	....	....	....
Washington, DC	Executive Director, Bioinformatics....................	Vacant	....	OT	....	....	....
Midlothian, TX	Executive Director, Caregiver Support Program.	Colleen Richardson	XS	OT	....	....	....
Savannah, GA	Executive Director, Care Management and Social Work.	Jill Debord	XS	OT	....	....	....
Cincinnati, OH	Executive Director Change Management..........	Jill Draime..........................	XS	OT	....	....	....
Washington, DC	Executive Director, Chief Financial Officer Operations.	Career Incumbent	CA	ES	....	....	....
Washington, DC	Executive Director, Clinical Care	Career Incumbent	CA	ES	....	....	....
Salt Lake City, UT..	Executive Director Clinical Informatics.............	Jonathan Nebeker	XS	OT	....	....	....
Washington, DC	Executive Director, Communication..................	Career Incumbent	CA	ES	....	....	....
Boston, MA..............	Executive Director, Diagnostic Services............	William Arndt......................	XS	OT	....	....	....
Washington, DC	Executive Director, Diversity Equity Inclusion Assault and Harassment Prevention.	Career Incumbent	CA	ES	....	....	....
Martinsburg, WV	Executive Director, Emergency Management....	Career Incumbent	CA	ES	....	....	....
Philadelphia, PA	Executive Director, End User Engagement Adoption.	Francine Sandrow	XS	OT	....	....	....
Washington, DC	Executive Director for Connected Care	Meredith Josephs	XS	OT	....	....	....
San Antonio, TX	Executive Director, Geriatrics and Extended Care.	Scotte Hartronft	XS	OT	....	....	....
Washington, DC	Executive Director, Healthcare Environment and Facilities and Programs.	Career Incumbent	CA	ES	....	....	....
Washington, DC	Executive Director Healthcare Operations........	Yemi Arunsi	XS	OT	....	....	....
Washington, DC	Executive Director Health Information Governance.	Marcia Insley.......................	XS	OT	....	....	....
Washington, DC	Executive Director Health Professions Education.	Vacant	....	OT	....	....	....
Palo Alto, CA	Executive Director, Health Solutions	Lisa Backus	XS	OT	....	....	....
Orlando, FL	Executive Director, Homeless Program.............	Career Incumbent	CA	ES	....	....	....
Oklahoma City, OK.	Executive Director, Human Capital Management.	Career Incumbent	CA	ES	....	....	....
Lawrenceville, GA...	Executive Director, Human Resources Operations.	Career Incumbent	CA	ES	....	....	....
Bradenton, FL.........	Executive Director, Human Resources Strategy and Programs.	Career Incumbent	CA	ES	....	....	....
Ann Arbor, MI	Executive Director, Integrated Access, Integrated Veteran Care.	Mark Hausman	XS	OT	....	....	....
Pensacola, FL	Executive Director, Integrated External Network.	Career Incumbent	CA	ES	....	....	....
Richfield, OH	Executive Director, Integrated Field Operations.	Lisa Arfons.........................	XS	OT	....	....	....
Louisville, KY.........	Executive Director Integrated Informatics and Analytics.	Mary J Fields	XS	OT	....	....	....
Houston, TX.............	Executive Director, Lesbian, Gay, Bisexual, Transgender, and Queer Health.	Michael Kauth......................	XS	OT	....	....	....
Washington, DC	Executive Director, Logistics............................	Career Incumbent	CA	ES	....	....	....
Atlanta, GA	Executive Director, Member Services................	Career Incumbent	CA	ES	....	....	....
Liberty, OH	Executive Director Mental Health and Suicide Prevention.	Tamara Campbell.................	XS	OT	....	....	....

DEPARTMENT OF VETERANS AFFAIRS—Continued

Location	Position Title	Name of Incumbent	Type of Appt.	Pay Plan	Level, Grade, or Pay	Tenure	Expires
Washington, DC	Executive Director, National Center for Ethics in Healthcare.	Career Incumbent	CA	ES	....	....	....
Cincinnati, OH	Executive Director, National Center for Organizational Development.	Career Incumbent	CA	ES	....	....	....
Washington, DC	Executive Director National Center for Patient Safety.	Edward Yackel....................	XS	OT	....	....	....
Washington, DC	Executive Director National Chaplain Service .	Kimberly Willis....................	XS	OT	....	....	....
Cincinnati, OH	Executive Director, National Infectious Disease Services.	Gary Roselle	XS	OT	....	....	....
Washington, DC	Executive Director National Pathology and Laboratory Medicine Service.	Jessica Wang Rodriguez.......	XS	OT	....	....	....
Providence, RI	Executive Director, National Radiology Program.	Patrick Malloy	XS	OT	....	....	....
Washington, DC	Executive Director, National Teleradiology Program.	Vacant	....	OT	....	....	....
Washington, DC	Executive Director Neurology............................	Sharyl Martini.....................	XS	OT	....	....	....
Washington, DC	Executive Director Nuclear Medicine and Radiation Safety Service.	David Bushnell.....................	XS	OT	....	....	....
Birmingham, AL	Executive Director Nursing Services, Deputy Chief Nursing Officer.	Jennifer Strawn....................	XS	OT	....	....	....
Beaverton, OR	Executive Director of Operations, Oncology and Precision Medicine.	Career Incumbent	CA	ES	....	....	....
Washington, DC	Executive Director, Office of Health Equity	Ernest Moy	XS	OT	....	....	....
Washington, DC	Executive Director, Office of Patient Advocacy .	Ann E Doran	XS	OT	....	....	....
Washington, DC	Executive Director Optometry.........................	Vacant	....	OT	....	....	....
Washington, DC	Executive Director, Patient Centered Care.......	Benjamin Kligler..................	XS	OT	....	....	....
Bellaire, TX..............	Executive Director, Payment Operations...........	Career Incumbent	CA	ES	....	....	....
Washington, DC	Executive Director Pharmacy Benefits Management Services.	Thomas Emmendorfer	XS	OT	....	....	....
Washington, DC	Executive Director, Policy and Strategic Planning.	Vacant	....	ES	....	....	....
Washington, DC	Executive Director, Post Deployment Health Services.	Patricia Hastings..................	XS	OT	....	....	....
Durham, NC	Executive Director, Preventive Medicine	Jane Kim..............................	XS	OT	....	....	....
Athens, TN..............	Executive Director, Primary Care	Angela Denietolis	XS	OT	....	....	....
Washington, DC	Executive Director, Prosthetic and Sensory Aids Service.	Penny L Nechanicky	XS	OT	....	....	....
Pensacola, FL	Executive Director, Quality Management..........	Kristine Groves	XS	OT	....	....	....
South Amboy, NJ.....	Executive Director Radiation Oncology Program.	Maria Kelly..........................	XS	OT	....	....	....
Washington, DC	Executive Director, Regulatory and Administrative Affairs.	Career Incumbent	CA	ES	....	....	....
Lyons, NJ.................	Executive Director, Rehabilitation and Prosthetic.	Ajit Pai	XS	OT	....	....	....
Washington, DC	Executive Director, Rehabilitation Research and Development Services.	Patricia Dorn	XS	OT	....	....	....
Washington, DC	Executive Director, Research Oversight	Douglas Bannerman	XS	OT	....	....	....
Washington, DC	Executive Director, Revenue Operations	Career Incumbent	CA	ES	....	....	....
Iowa City, IA............	Executive Director, Rural Health	Peter Kaboli	XS	OT	....	....	....
Washington, DC	Executive Director, Spinal Cord Injuries and Disorders Services.	Itala Wickremasinghe..........	XS	OT	....	....	....
Washington, DC	Executive Director Sterile Process Services	Alan Bernstein	XS	OT	....	....	....
Washington, DC	Executive Director, Strategic Investment Management.	Career Incumbent	CA	ES	....	....	....
Washington, DC	Executive Director, Strategic Planning and Analysis.	Career Incumbent	CA	ES	....	....	....
Washington, DC	Executive Director, Strategy and Integration ...	Vacant	....	ES	....	....	....
Washington, DC	Executive Director, Strategy and Operations....	Career Incumbent	CA	ES	....	....	....
Saginaw, MI............	Executive Director, Suicide Prevention.............	Matthew Alan Miller	XS	OT	....	....	....
Atlanta, ID..............	Executive Director, Telehealth Services.............	Kevin Galpin	XS	OT	....	....	....
Washington, DC	Executive Director Veterans Affairs / Department of Defense Health Affairs.	Career Incumbent	CA	ES	....	....	....
Washington, DC	Executive Director, Veterans Affairs Logistics Redesign Program Office.	Career Incumbent	CA	ES	....	....	....
Denver, CO	Executive Director, Veterans Crisis Line	Christopher Watson	XS	OT	....	....	....
Washington, DC	Medical Inspector	Frederick Kotler....................	XS	OT	....	....	....
Washington, DC	National Director for Surgery............................	Mark Wilson	XS	OT	....	....	....
Houston, TX............	National Director, Nutrition and Food Services.	Anne Utech	XS	OT	....	....	....
Washington, DC	National Director, Physical Medicine and Rehabilitation Services.	Joel Scholten........................	XS	OT	....	....	....
Washington, DC	National Program Director, Ophthalmology......	Glenn Cockerham..................	XS	OT	....	....	....
Washington, DC	National Program Executive Director................	David B Ross	XS	OT	....	....	....

DEPARTMENT OF VETERANS AFFAIRS—Continued

Location	Position Title	Name of Incumbent	Type of Appt.	Pay Plan	Level, Grade, or Pay	Tenure	Expires
Cleveland, OH	Podiatric Medical Director	Jeffrey M Robbins	XS	OT			
Washington, DC	Senior Advisor	Career Incumbent	CA	ES			
Washington, DC	Senior Advisor	Caitlin A O'Brien	XS	OT			
Washington, DC	Senior Advisor	Reena Duseja	XS	OT			
Phoenix, AZ	Senior Advisor	Leslie Lockridge	XS	OT			
South Kingstown, RI.	Senior Advisor, Food Security Office	Christine Going	XS	OT			
Washington, DC	Senior Advisor Healthcare Operations to the Veterans Health Administration Chief of Staff.	Harrison Hines	XS	OT			
Washington, DC	Senior Advisor to the Chief of Staff, Veterans Health Administration.	Career Incumbent	CA	ES			
Washington, DC	Senior Advisor to the Deputy Under Secretary for Health.	Latriece R Prince-Wheeler	XS	OT			
Cleveland, OH	Senior Advisor to the Deputy Under Secretary for Health.	Susan M Fuehrer	XS	OT			
Washington, DC	Senior Advisor to the Deputy Under Secretary for Health.	Elizabeth Ragan	XS	OT			
Washington, DC	Senior Advisor to the Deputy Under Secretary for Health.	Vacant		ES			
Washington, DC	Senior Advisor to the Under Secretary for Health, Digital Health.	Nadia A Smith	XS	OT			
Washington, DC	Senior Advisor to the Under Secretary for Health Innovation.	Gregory J Downing	XS	OT			
Washington, DC	Senior Advisor to the Under Secretary for Health, Strategic Engagement.	Mark H Chichester	XS	OT			
Wilmington, DE	Senior Clinical Advisor	Joann Seppelt	XS	OT			
Washington, DC	Senior Health Technology Officer	Career Incumbent	CA	ES			
Franklin, TN	Senior Medical Advisor, Functional Champion	David Massaro	XS	OT			
Orlando, FL	Senior Nursing Advisor	Traci Solt	XS	OT			
Bedford, MA	Executive Director, Veterans Integrated Systems Network (VISN 1).	Career Incumbent	CA	ES			
Bedford, MA	Chief Medical Officer (VISN 1)	Latha Sivaprasad	XS	OT			
Manchester, NH	Executive Director, Medical Center (VISN 1)	Career Incumbent	CA	ES			
Bedford, MA	Executive Director, Medical Center (VISN 1)	Joan Clifford	XS	OT			
Boston, MA	Executive Director, Medical Center (VISN 1)	Career Incumbent	CA	ES			
Leeds, MA	Executive Director, Medical Center (VISN 1)	Vacant		ES			
Providence, RI	Executive Director, Medical Center (VISN 1)	Career Incumbent	CA	ES			
White River Junction, VT.	Executive Director, Medical Center (VISN 1)	Brett Rusch	XS	OT			
West Haven, CT	Executive Director, Medical Center (VISN 1)	Career Incumbent	CA	ES			
Togus, ME	Executive Director, Medical Center (VISN 1)	Career Incumbent	CA	ES			
Boston, MA	Deputy Executive Director, Medical Center (VISN 1).	Career Incumbent	CA	ES			
West Haven, CT	Deputy Executive Director, Medical Center (VISN 1).	Vacant		ES			
Albany, NY	Executive Director, Veterans Integrated Service Network (VISN 2).	Vacant		ES			
Bronx, NY	Chief Medical Officer (VISN 2)	Curt Dill	XS	OT			
Montrose, NY	Executive Director, Medical Center (VISN 2)	Career Incumbent	CA	ES			
New York, NY	Executive Director, Medical Center (VISN 2)	Career Incumbent	CA	ES			
Northport, NY	Executive Director, Medical Center (VISN 2)	Antonio Sanchez	XS	OT			
Syracuse, NY	Executive Director, Medical Center (VISN 2)	Career Incumbent	CA	ES			
Bath, NY	Executive Director, Medical Center (VISN 2)	Career Incumbent	CA	ES			
East Orange, NJ	Executive Director, Medical Center (VISN 2)	Career Incumbent	CA	ES			
Bronx, NY	Executive Director, Medical Center (VISN 2)	Balavenkatesh Kanna	XS	OT			
Albany, NY	Executive Director, Medical Center (VISN 2)	Career Incumbent	CA	ES			
Buffalo, NY	Executive Director, Medical Center (VISN 2)	Career Incumbent	CA	ES			
New York, NY	Deputy Executive Director, Medical Center (VISN 2).	Career Incumbent	CA	ES			
Pittsburgh, PA	Executive Director, Veterans Integrated Service Network (VISN 4).	Career Incumbent	CA	ES			
Pittsburgh, PA	Chief Medical Officer (VISN 4)	Timothy R Burke	XS	OT			
Altoona, PA	Executive Director, Medical Center (VISN 4)	Career Incumbent	CA	ES			
Butler, PA	Executive Director, Medical Center (VISN 4)	Career Incumbent	CA	ES			
Erie, PA	Executive Director, Medical Center (VISN 4)	Career Incumbent	CA	ES			
Coatesville, PA	Executive Director, Medical Center (VISN 4)	Jennifer Harkins	XS	OT			
Wilmington, DE	Executive Director, Medical Center (VISN 4)	Career Incumbent	CA	ES			
Lebanon, PA	Executive Director, Medical Center (VISN 4)	Career Incumbent	CA	ES			
Wilkes Barre, PA	Executive Director, Medical Center (VISN 4)	Career Incumbent	CA	ES			
Philadelphia, PA	Executive Director, Medical Center (VISN 4)	Career Incumbent	CA	ES			
Pittsburgh, PA	Executive Director, Medical Center (VISN 4)	Career Incumbent	CA	ES			

DEPARTMENT OF VETERANS AFFAIRS—Continued

Location	Position Title	Name of Incumbent	Type of Appt.	Pay Plan	Level, Grade, or Pay	Tenure	Expires
Pittsburgh, PA	Deputy Executive Director, Medical Center (VISN 4).	Career Incumbent	CA	ES			
Linthicum Hghts, MD.	Executive Director, Veterans Integrated Service Network (VISN 5).	Career Incumbent	CA	ES			
Linthicum Hghts, MD.	Chief Medical Officer (VISN 5)	Mark Kobelja	XS	OT			
Washington, DC	Executive Director, Medical Center (VISN 5)	Career Incumbent	CA	ES			
Beckley, WV	Executive Director, Medical Center (VISN 5)	Career Incumbent	CA	ES			
Huntington, WV	Executive Director, Medical Center (VISN 5)	Career Incumbent	CA	ES			
Clarksburg, WV	Executive Director, Medical Center (VISN 5)	Career Incumbent	CA	ES			
Martinsburg, WV	Executive Director, Medical Center (VISN 5)	Career Incumbent	CA	ES			
Baltimore, MD	Executive Director, Medical Center (VISN 5)	Career Incumbent	CA	ES			
Washington, DC	Deputy Executive Director, Medical Center (VISN 5).	Career Incumbent	CA	ES			
Durham, NC	Executive Director, Veterans Integrated Service Network (VISN 6).	Career Incumbent	CA	ES			
Washington, DC	Chief Medical Officer (VISN 6)	James Goff	XS	OT			
Asheville, NC	Executive Director, Medical Center (VISN 6)	Career Incumbent	CA	ES			
Durham, NC	Executive Director, Medical Center (VISN 6)	Career Incumbent	CA	ES			
Fayetteville, NC	Executive Director, Medical Center (VISN 6)	Career Incumbent	CA	ES			
Hampton, VA	Executive Director, Medical Center (VISN 6)	Taquisa Simmons	XS	OT			
Richmond, VA	Executive Director, Medical Center (VISN 6)	Career Incumbent	CA	ES			
Salisbury, NC	Executive Director, Medical Center (VISN 6)	Career Incumbent	CA	ES			
Salem, VA	Executive Director, Medical Center (VISN 6)	Career Incumbent	CA	ES			
Duluth, GA	Executive Director, Veterans Integrated Service Network (VISN 7).	David Walker	XS	OT			
Atlanta, GA	Chief Medical Officer (VISN 7)	Vacant		OT			
Atlanta, GA	Executive Director, Medical Center (VISN 7)	Career Incumbent	CA	ES			
Tuscaloosa, AL	Executive Director, Medical Center (VISN 7)	Career Incumbent	CA	ES			
Montgomery, AL	Executive Director, Medical Center (VISN 7)	Career Incumbent	CA	ES			
Charleston, SC	Executive Director, Medical Center (VISN 7)	Career Incumbent	CA	ES			
Augusta, GA	Executive Director, Medical Center (VISN 7)	Career Incumbent	CA	ES			
Birmingham, AL	Executive Director, Medical Center (VISN 7)	Oladipo Kukoyi	XS	OT			
Columbia, SC	Executive Director, Medical Center (VISN 7)	Career Incumbent	CA	ES			
Dublin, GA	Executive Director, Medical Center (VISN 7)	Career Incumbent	CA	ES			
Atlanta, GA	Deputy Executive Director, Medical Center (VISN 7).	Career Incumbent	CA	ES			
Augusta, GA	Deputy Executive Director, Medical Center (VISN 7).	Career Incumbent	CA	ES			
Bay Pines, FL	Executive Director, Veterans Integrated Service Network (VISN 8).	Career Incumbent	CA	ES			
Bay Pines, FL	Deputy Executive Director, Veterans Integrated Systems Network (VISN 8).	Career Incumbent	CA	ES			
Bay Pines, FL	Chief Medical Officer (VISN 8)	Edward Cutolo	XS	OT			
Tampa, FL	Executive Director, Medical Center (VISN 8)	Career Incumbent	CA	ES			
West Palm Beach, FL.	Executive Director, Medical Center (VISN 8)	Career Incumbent	CA	ES			
Gainesville, FL	Executive Director, Medical Center (VISN 8)	Career Incumbent	CA	ES			
Bay Pines, FL	Executive Director, Medical Center (VISN 8)	Vacant		ES			
San Juan, PR	Executive Director, Medical Center (VISN 8)	Vacant		ES			
Orlando, FL	Executive Director, Medical Center (VISN 8)	Career Incumbent	CA	ES			
Miami, FL	Executive Director, Medical Center (VISN 8)	Career Incumbent	CA	ES			
Gainesville, FL	Deputy Executive Director, Medical Center (VISN 8).	Career Incumbent	CA	ES			
Nashville, TN	Executive Director, Veterans Integrated Service Network (VISN 9).	Career Incumbent	CA	ES			
Nashville, TN	Chief Medical Officer (VISN 9)	Anthony Stazzone	XS	OT			
Lexington, KY	Executive Director, Medical Center (VISN 9)	Career Incumbent	CA	ES			
Memphis, TN	Executive Director, Medical Center (VISN 9)	Career Incumbent	CA	ES			
Louisville, KY	Executive Director, Medical Center (VISN 9)	Career Incumbent	CA	ES			
Nashville, TN	Executive Director, Medical Center (VISN 9)	Career Incumbent	CA	ES			
Johnson City, TN	Executive Director, Medical Center (VISN 9)	Career Incumbent	CA	ES			
Nashville, TN	Deputy Executive Director, Medical Center (VISN 9).	Career Incumbent	CA	ES			
Cincinnati, OH	Executive Director, Veterans Integrated Systems Network (VISN 10).	Career Incumbent	CA	ES			
Cincinnati, OH	Chief Medical Officer (VISN 10)	Anthony Restuccio	XS	OT			
Fort Wayne, IN	Executive Director, Medical Center (VISN 10)	Career Incumbent	CA	ES			
Saginaw, MI	Executive Director, Medical Center (VISN 10)	Career Incumbent	CA	ES			
Ann Arbor, MI	Executive Director, Medical Center (VISN 10)	Career Incumbent	CA	ES			
Indianapolis, IN	Executive Director, Medical Center (VISN 10)	Career Incumbent	CA	ES			
Cincinnati, OH	Executive Director, Medical Center (VISN 10)	Career Incumbent	CA	ES			
Chillicothe, OH	Executive Director, Medical Center (VISN 10)	Career Incumbent	CA	ES			

DEPARTMENT OF VETERANS AFFAIRS—Continued

Location	Position Title	Name of Incumbent	Type of Appt.	Pay Plan	Level, Grade, or Pay	Tenure	Expires
Battle Creek, MI	Executive Director, Medical Center (VISN 10)..	Career Incumbent	CA	ES			
Columbus, OH	Executive Director, Medical Center (VISN 10)..	Vacant		OT			
Dayton, OH..............	Executive Director, Medical Center (VISN 10)..	Career Incumbent	CA	ES			
Cleveland, OH	Executive Director, Medical Center (VISN 10)..	Career Incumbent	CA	ES			
Detroit, MI..............	Executive Director, Medical Center (VISN 10)..	Career Incumbent	CA	ES			
Hines, IL.................	Executive Director, Veterans Integrated Service Network (VISN 12).	Career Incumbent	CA	ES			
Hines, IL.................	Chief Medical Officer (VISN 12)........................	Gregg Meekins	XS	OT			
Milwaukee, WI	Executive Director, Medical Center (VISN 12)..	Career Incumbent	CA	ES			
Tomah, WI	Executive Director, Medical Center (VISN 12)..	Career Incumbent	CA	ES			
Danville, IL.............	Executive Director, Medical Center (VISN 12)..	Career Incumbent	CA	ES			
Iron Mountain, MI ..	Executive Director, Medical Center (VISN 12)..	Career Incumbent	CA	ES			
Hines, IL.................	Executive Director, Medical Center (VISN 12)..	Career Incumbent	CA	ES			
Madison, WI	Executive Director, Medical Center (VISN 12)..	Christine Kleckner..............	XS	OT			
North Chicago, IL ...	Executive Director, Medical Center (VISN 12)..	Robert Buckley	XS	OT			
Chicago, IL	Executive Director, Medical Center (VISN 12)..	Vacant		ES			
Kansas City, MO	Executive Director, Veterans Integrated Service Network (VISN 15).	Career Incumbent	CA	ES			
Kansas City, MO	Chief Medical Officer (VISN 15)........................	Ahmad Batrash	XS	OT			
Columbia, MO	Executive Director, Medical Center (VISN 15)..	Career Incumbent	CA	ES			
Kansas City, MO	Executive Director, Medical Center (VISN 15)..	Career Incumbent	CA	ES			
Marion, IL...............	Executive Director, Medical Center (VISN 15)..	Career Incumbent	CA	ES			
St Louis, MO	Executive Director, Medical Center (VISN 15)..	Career Incumbent	CA	ES			
Topeka, KS	Executive Director, Medical Center (VISN 15)..	Career Incumbent	CA	ES			
Poplar Bluff, MO	Executive Director, Medical Center (VISN 15)..	Vacant		ES			
Wichita, KS.............	Executive Director, Medical Center (VISN 15)..	Career Incumbent	CA	ES			
St Louis, MO	Deputy Executive Director, Medical Center (VISN 15).	Career Incumbent	CA	ES			
Jackson, MS.............	Executive Director, Veterans Integrated Service Network (VISN 16).	Career Incumbent	CA	ES			
Jackson, MS.............	Chief Medical Officer (VISN 16)........................	John Areno........................	XS	OT			
Houston, TX............	Executive Director, Medical Center (VISN 16)..	Career Incumbent	CA	ES			
New Orleans, LA.....	Executive Director, Medical Center (VISN 16)..	Career Incumbent	CA	ES			
Jackson, MS.............	Executive Director, Medical Center (VISN 16)..	Vacant		ES			
Alexandria, LA........	Executive Director, Medical Center (VISN 16)..	Career Incumbent	CA	ES			
Biloxi, MS	Executive Director, Medical Center (VISN 16)..	Career Incumbent	CA	ES			
Little Rock, AR.......	Executive Director, Medical Center (VISN 16)..	Margie A Scott....................	XS	OT			
Fayetteville, AR......	Executive Director, Medical Center (VISN 16)..	Career Incumbent	CA	ES			
Shreveport, LA........	Executive Director, Medical Center (VISN 16)..	Richard Crockett	XS	OT			
Little Rock, AR.......	Deputy Executive Director, Medical Center (VISN 16).	Career Incumbent	CA	ES			
Dallas, TX	Executive Director, Veterans Integrated Service Network (VISN 17).	Wendell E Jones	XS	OT			
Arlington, TX..........	Chief Medical Officer (VISN 17)........................	Stephen R Holt....................	XS	OT			
Temple, TX..............	Executive Director, Medical Center (VISN 17)..	Career Incumbent	CA	ES			
El Paso, TX	Executive Director, Medical Center (VISN 17)..	Career Incumbent	CA	ES			
Big Spring, TX.........	Executive Director, Medical Center (VISN 17)..	Career Incumbent	CA	ES			
Harlingen, TX..........	Executive Director, Medical Center (VISN 17)..	Career Incumbent	CA	ES			
Amarillo, TX	Executive Director, Medical Center (VISN 17)..	Rodney Gonzalez..................	XS	OT			
Dallas, TX	Executive Director, Medical Center (VISN 17)..	Career Incumbent	CA	ES			
San Antonio, TX	Executive Director, Medical Center (VISN 17)..	Julianne Flynn	XS	OT			
Dallas, TX	Deputy Executive Director, Medical Center (VISN 17).	Career Incumbent	CA	ES			
Temple, TX..............	Deputy Executive Director, Medical Center (VISN 17).	Career Incumbent	CA	ES			
San Antonio, TX	Deputy Executive Director, Medical Center (VISN 17).	Career Incumbent	CA	ES			
Denver, CO	Executive Director, Veterans Integrated Service Network (VISN 19).	Career Incumbent	CA	ES			
Glendale, CO	Chief Medical Officer (VISN 19)........................	Susan Bray Hall..................	XS	OT			
Fort Harrison, MT...	Executive Director, Medical Center (VISN 19)..	Career Incumbent	CA	ES			
Grand Junction, CO.	Executive Director, Medical Center (VISN 19)..	Career Incumbent	CA	ES			
Cheyenne, WY........	Executive Director, Medical Center (VISN 19)..	Career Incumbent	CA	ES			
Denver, CO	Executive Director, Medical Center (VISN 19)..	Career Incumbent	CA	ES			
Sheridan, WY	Executive Director, Medical Center (VISN 19)..	Career Incumbent	CA	ES			
Muskogee, OK	Executive Director, Medical Center (VISN 19)..	Career Incumbent	CA	ES			
Salt Lake City, UT..	Executive Director, Medical Center (VISN 19)..	Career Incumbent	CA	ES			
Oklahoma City, OK.	Executive Director, Medical Center (VISN 19)..	Career Incumbent	CA	ES			
Portland, OR...........	Executive Director, Veterans Integrated Service Network (VISN 20).	Teresa D Boyd	XS	OT			
Vancouver, WA........	Chief Medical Officer (VISN 20)........................	Brian Yee	XS	OT			

DEPARTMENT OF VETERANS AFFAIRS—Continued

Location	Position Title	Name of Incumbent	Type of Appt.	Pay Plan	Level, Grade, or Pay	Tenure	Expires
Boise, ID	Executive Director, Medical Center (VISN 20)	Career Incumbent	CA	ES			
Anchorage, AK	Executive Director, Medical Center (VISN 20)	Career Incumbent	CA	ES			
Spokane, WA	Executive Director, Medical Center (VISN 20)	Robert Fischer	XS	OT			
Roseburg, OR	Executive Director, Medical Center (VISN 20)	Career Incumbent	CA	ES			
Portland, OR	Executive Director, Medical Center (VISN 20)	Career Incumbent	CA	ES			
Seattle, WA	Executive Director, Medical Center (VISN 20)	Career Incumbent	CA	ES			
White City, OR	Executive Director, Medical Center (VISN 20)	Christina Cellura	XS	OT			
Walla Walla, WA	Executive Director Medical Center (VISN 20)	Scott Kelter	XS	OT			
Portland, OR	Deputy Executive Director, Medical Center (VISN 20).	Career Incumbent	CA	ES			
Seattle, WA	Deputy Executive Director, Medical Center (VISN 20).	Career Incumbent	CA	ES			
Mare Island(Nav Shipyd), CA.	Executive Director, Veterans Integrated Service Network (VISN 21).	Career Incumbent	CA	ES			
Mare Island(Nav Shipyd), CA.	Chief Medical Officer (VISN 21)	Regina Godbout	XS	OT			
Fresno, CA	Executive Director, Medical Center (VISN 21)	Vacant		ES			
Las Vegas, NV	Executive Director, Medical Center (VISN 21)	Career Incumbent	CA	ES			
Honolulu, HI	Executive Director, Medical Center (VISN 21)	Adam M Robinson	XS	OT			
Palo Alto, CA	Executive Director, Medical Center (VISN 21)	Career Incumbent	CA	ES			
Martinez, CA	Executive Director, Medical Center (VISN 21)	Career Incumbent	CA	ES			
Reno, NV	Executive Director, Medical Center (VISN 21)	Vacant		ES			
San Francisco, CA	Executive Director, Medical Center (VISN 21)	Career Incumbent	CA	ES			
Palo Alto, CA	Deputy Executive Director, Medical Center (VISN 21).	Vacant		ES			
Long Beach, CA	Executive Director, Veterans Integrated Service Network (VISN 22).	Steven Braverman	XS	OT			
Long Beach, CA	Chief Medical Officer (VISN 22)	Ayyasamy Selvam	XS	OT			
Albuquerque, NM	Executive Director, Medical Center (VISN 22)	Brenton Weintraub	XS	OT			
Loma Linda, CA	Executive Director, Medical Center (VISN 22)	Career Incumbent	CA	ES			
Prescott, AZ	Executive Director, Medical Center (VISN 22)	Career Incumbent	CA	ES			
San Diego, CA	Executive Director, Medical Center (VISN 22)	Career Incumbent	CA	ES			
Tucson, AZ	Executive Director, Medical Center (VISN 22)	Career Incumbent	CA	ES			
Long Beach, CA	Executive Director, Medical Center (VISN 22)	Career Incumbent	CA	ES			
Phoenix, AZ	Executive Director, Medical Center (VISN 22)	Career Incumbent	CA	ES			
Los Angeles, CA	Executive Director Medical Center (VISN 22)	Vacant		OT			
Phoenix, AZ	Deputy Executive Director, Medical Center (VISN 22).	Vacant		ES			
Los Angeles, CA	Deputy Executive Director, Medical Center (VISN 22).	Career Incumbent	CA	ES			
Minneapolis, MN	Executive Director, Veterans Integrated Systems Network (VISN 23).	Career Incumbent	CA	ES			
Minneapolis, MN	Chief Medical Officer (VISN 23)	Larry Brown	XS	OT			
Des Moines, IA	Executive Director, Medical Center (VISN 23)	Career Incumbent	CA	ES			
Fort Meade, SD	Executive Director, Medical Center (VISN 23)	Career Incumbent	CA	ES			
Omaha, NE	Executive Director, Medical Center (VISN 23)	Career Incumbent	CA	ES			
Sioux Falls, SD	Executive Director, Medical Center (VISN 23)	Career Incumbent	CA	ES			
Fargo, ND	Executive Director, Medical Center (VISN 23)	Vacant		OT			
Minneapolis, MN	Executive Director, Medical Center (VISN 23)	Career Incumbent	CA	ES			
St Cloud, MN	Executive Director, Medical Center (VISN 23)	Career Incumbent	CA	ES			
Iowa City, IA	Executive Director, Medical Center (VISN 23)	Career Incumbent	CA	ES			
	OFFICE OF EMERGENCY MANAGEMENT						
Washington, DC	Senior Advisor for Mission Support	Career Incumbent	CA	ES			
	VETERANS EXPERIENCE OFFICE						
Washington, DC	Senior Advisor/Chief Veteran Experience Officer.	John William Boerstler	NA	ES			
Washington, DC	Deputy Chief Veterans Experience Officer	Career Incumbent	CA	ES			
Washington, DC	Strategic Advisor to Chief Veterans Experience Officer.	Tahina Lee Montoya	SC	GS	14		
Washington, DC	Executive Director, Employee Experience and Organizational Management.	Vacant		ES			07/16/24
Washington, DC	Executive Director Enterprise Measurement and Design.	Career Incumbent	CA	ES			
Washington, DC	Executive Director, Multi-Channel Technology	Vacant		ES			
Alpena, AR	Executive Director, Tools and Implementation	Career Incumbent	CA	ES			
Oviedo, FL	Executive Director Veterans Family and Community Engagement.	Career Incumbent	CA	ES			

DEPARTMENT OF VETERANS AFFAIRS—Continued

Location	Position Title	Name of Incumbent	Type of Appt.	Pay Plan	Level, Grade, or Pay	Tenure	Expires
	OFFICE OF THE ASSISTANT SECRETARY FOR ACCOUNTABILITY AND WHISTLEBLOWER PROTECTION						
Washington, DC	Assistant Secretary for Accountability and Whistleblower Protection.	Vacant	....	EX	....	....	....
Washington, DC	Chief of Staff..	Career Incumbent	CA	ES	....	....	....

DEPARTMENT OF VETERANS AFFAIRS OFFICE OF THE INSPECTOR GENERAL

Location	Position Title	Name of Incumbent	Type of Appt.	Pay Plan	Level, Grade, or Pay	Tenure	Expires
	Immediate Office of the Inspector General						
Washington, DC	Inspector General	Michael Joseph Missal.........	PAS	EX	III	....	....

INDEPENDENT AGENCIES AND GOVERNMENT CORPORATIONS

ADMINISTRATIVE CONFERENCE OF THE UNITED STATES

Location	Position Title	Name of Incumbent	Type of Appt.	Pay Plan	Level, Grade, or Pay	Tenure	Expires
Washington, DC	Chairman	Andrew Fois.........................	PAS	EX	II	5	05/26/27
Washington, DC	Special Assistant and Counsel to the Chair......	Conrad Dryland...................	SC	GS	12	....	....

ADVISORY COUNCIL ON HISTORIC PRESERVATION

Location	Position Title	Name of Incumbent	Type of Appt.	Pay Plan	Level, Grade, or Pay	Tenure	Expires
Washington, DC	Chairman	Sara C Bronin	PAS	EX	V	4	01/19/25
Fairfax, VA..............	Vice Chairman	Jordan E Tannenbaum	PA	EX	....	....	06/10/25
Ridgefield, CT.........	Council Member (General Public)	Jane Woodfin	PA	EX	....	....	06/10/28
Bear, DE	Council Member (General Public)	Carmen A Jordan-Cox.........	PA	EX	....	....	06/10/26
Los Angeles, CA	Council Member (Expert)...................................	Charles Ward.......................	PA	EX	....	....	06/10/27
Midlothian, TX	Council Member (Expert)...................................	Monica Rhodes	PA	EX	....	....	06/10/26
Charleston, SC	Council Member (Expert)...................................	Erica Avrami........................	PA	EX	....	....	06/10/28
Wilmington, DE.......	Council Member (Expert)...................................	Frank G Matero	PA	EX	....	....	06/10/27
Santa Rosa, CA	Council Member (Indian Tribe Member)	Amelia Marchand................	PA	EX	....	....	06/10/28
Wilmington, DE.......	Council Member (Governor)..............................	John C Carney.....................	PA	EX	....	....	06/10/25
Birmingham, AL	Council Member (Mayor)....................................	Randall L Woodfin...............	PA	EX	....	....	06/10/25

AFRICAN DEVELOPMENT FOUNDATION

Location	Position Title	Name of Incumbent	Type of Appt.	Pay Plan	Level, Grade, or Pay	Tenure	Expires
Greenwich, CT.........	Board of Directors, Private Member, Chair	Carol Moseley Braun	PAS	EX	....	6	....
Jacksonville, FL	Board of Directors, Private Member, Vice Chair.	John Agwunobi.....................	PAS	EX	....	6	....
Minneapolis, MN......	Board of Directors, Private Member	Edward W Brehm..................	PAS	EX	....	6	....
Los Angeles, CA	Board of Directors, Private Member	Morgan M Davis...................	PAS	EX	....	6	....
Jacksonville, FL	Board of Directors, Private Member	Vacant	....	EX	....	6	....

AFRICAN DEVELOPMENT BANK

Location	Position Title	Name of Incumbent	Type of Appt.	Pay Plan	Level, Grade, or Pay	Tenure	Expires
Washington, DC	United States Alt. Governor	Jose W. Fernandez................	PAS	EX	....	....	07/29/26

AMERICAN BATTLE MONUMENTS COMMISSION

Location	Position Title	Name of Incumbent	Type of Appt.	Pay Plan	Level, Grade, or Pay	Tenure	Expires
Arlington, VA..........	Chairman	Michael X Garrett	PA	WC	....	....	....
Arlington, VA..........	Vice Chairman	Daniel P Woodward..............	PA	WC	....	....	....
Arlington, VA..........	Secretary	Charles K Djou	PA	OT	....	....	....
Arlington, VA..........	Commission Member...	John L Estrada.....................	PA	WC	....	....	....
Arlington, VA..........	Commission Member...	Darrell L Dorgan..................	PA	WC	....	....	....
Arlington, VA..........	Commission Member...	Florent Groberg....................	PA	WC	....	....	....
Arlington, VA..........	Commission Member...	Amy Looney Heffernan........	PA	WC	....	....	....
Arlington, VA..........	Commission Member...	Matthew E Jones..................	PA	WC	....	....	....
Arlington, VA..........	Commission Member...	Raymond D Kemp................	PA	WC	....	....	....
Arlington, VA..........	Commission Member...	Bud Pettigrew......................	PA	WC	....	....	....

AMERICAN BATTLE MONUMENTS COMMISSION—Continued

Location	Position Title	Name of Incumbent	Type of Appt.	Pay Plan	Level, Grade, or Pay	Tenure	Expires
Arlington, VA..........	Commission Member..	Gail Berry West..................	PA	WC	....	....	....
Arlington, VA..........	Commission Member..	Michael E Smith	PA	WC	....	....	....
	EXECUTIVE DIRECTOR, OPERATIONS						
Washington, DC	Director of Special Projects...............................	Career Incumbent	CA	ES	....	....	....

AMTRAK

Location	Position Title	Name of Incumbent	Type of Appt.	Pay Plan	Level, Grade, or Pay	Tenure	Expires
	BOARD OF DIRECTORS						
Washington, DC	Member...	Joel Szabat............................	PAS	....	....	....	01/23/29
Washington, DC	Member...	Anthony Coscia....................	PAS	....	....	....	01/23/29
Washington, DC	Member...	Yvonne Burke........................	PAS	....	....	....	
Washington, DC	Member...	Christopher Koos..................	PAS	....	....	....	01/23/29
Washington, DC	Member...	Jeffrey Moreland	PAS	....	....	....	
Washington, DC	Member...	Albert DiClemente	PAS	....	....	....	

APPALACHIAN REGIONAL COMMISSION

Location	Position Title	Name of Incumbent	Type of Appt.	Pay Plan	Level, Grade, or Pay	Tenure	Expires
Washington, DC	Federal Co-Chairman	Gayle C Manchin..................	PAS	EX	III	....	....
Washington, DC	Alternate Federal Co-Chairman	Vacant	....	EX		....	....
Charleston, WV	Executive Assistant	Melissa Phalen	SC	GS	12	....	....

ARCTIC RESEARCH COMMISSION

Location	Position Title	Name of Incumbent	Type of Appt.	Pay Plan	Level, Grade, or Pay	Tenure	Expires
Washington, DC	Commission Chair	Michael F Sfraga..................	PA	PD	....	....	02/26/28
Washington, DC	Commission Member	Cayenne N Carlo..................	PA	PD	....	....	02/26/27
Washington, DC	Commission Member	David M Kennedy	PA	PD	....	....	02/26/25
Washington, DC	Commission Member	Jacqueline A Richter-Menge.	PA	PD	....	....	02/26/28
Washington, DC	Commission Member	Elizabeth A Cravalho...........	PA	PD	....	....	02/26/28
Washington, DC	Commission Member	Mark D Myers	PA	PD	....	....	07/29/27
Washington, DC	Commission Member	Deborah A Vo........................	PA	PD	....	....	02/26/25

ARMED FORCES RETIREMENT HOME

Location	Position Title	Name of Incumbent	Type of Appt.	Pay Plan	Level, Grade, or Pay	Tenure	Expires
Washington, DC	Chief Operating Officer......................................	John Spencer Riscassi..........	PA	EX	....	....	....

ASIAN DEVELOPMENT BANK

Location	Position Title	Name of Incumbent	Type of Appt.	Pay Plan	Level, Grade, or Pay	Tenure	Expires
Washington, DC	United States Director	Chantale Wong	PAS	EX	....	....	....

BARRY GOLDWATER SCHOLARSHIP AND EXCELLENCE IN EDUCATION FOUNDATION

Location	Position Title	Name of Incumbent	Type of Appt.	Pay Plan	Level, Grade, or Pay	Tenure	Expires
Alexandria, VA	Chair	John Yopp	PAS	WC	....	6	10/13/17
Alexandria, VA	Vice Chair	Maria Rengifo-Ruess	PAS	WC	....	6	02/04/14
Alexandria, VA	Member	Margaret Goldwater-Clay	PAS	WC	....	6	06/05/12
Alexandria, VA	Member	Stewart Desoto	PAS	WC	....	6	08/11/16
Alexandria, VA	Member	Charles Korsmo	PAS	WC	....	6	10/13/17
Alexandria, VA	Member	Dennis Deconcini	PAS	WC	....	6	04/17/26
Alexandria, VA	Member	Joseph Green	PAS	WC	....	6	03/03/28
Alexandria, VA	Member	Vacant	....	WC	....	6	....
Alexandria, VA	President/Executive Secretary	John F Mateja	NA	ES	....	....	....

CENTRAL INTELLIGENCE AGENCY

Location	Position Title	Name of Incumbent	Type of Appt.	Pay Plan	Level, Grade, or Pay	Tenure	Expires
	OFFICE OF THE DIRECTOR						
Washington, DC	Director, Central Intelligence Agency	William J Burns	PAS	EX	II	....	....
Washington, DC	Deputy Director, Central Intelligence Agency	David S Cohen	PA	EX	III	....	....
Washington, DC	Statutory Inspector General	Robin C Ashton	PAS	EX	IV	....	....
Washington, DC	General Counsel	Kate Heinzelman	PAS	EX	IV	....	....

CHEMICAL SAFETY AND HAZARD INVESTIGATION BOARD

Location	Position Title	Name of Incumbent	Type of Appt.	Pay Plan	Level, Grade, or Pay	Tenure	Expires
Flagstaff, AZ	Board Chairperson	Stephen Owens	PAS	EX	IV	....	01/15/28
Washington, DC	Board Member	Sylvia Johnson	PAS	EX	IV	....	02/03/27
Campbell, CA	Board Member	Catherine Kissee-Sandoval	PAS	EX	IV	....	02/02/28
Washington, DC	Board Member	Vacant	....	EX	....	....	....
Washington, DC	Board Member	Vacant	....	EX	....	....	....
Washington, DC	Executive Director, Office of Investigations and Recommendations.	Career Incumbent	CA	ES	....	....	....
Washington, DC	General Counsel	Vacant	....	ES	....	....	....
Washington, DC	Managing Director	Vacant	....	ES	....	....	....

CIVIL RIGHTS COLD CASE RECORDS REVIEW BOARD

Location	Position Title	Name of Incumbent	Type of Appt.	Pay Plan	Level, Grade, or Pay	Tenure	Expires
Washington, DC	Member	Brenda Stevenson	PAS	....	....	....	....
Washington, DC	Member	Henry (Hank) Klibanoff	PAS	....	....	....	....
Washington, DC	Member	Gabrielle Dudley	PAS	....	....	....	....
Washington, DC	Member	Margaret Burnham	PAS	....	....	....	....

COMMISSION OF FINE ARTS

Location	Position Title	Name of Incumbent	Type of Appt.	Pay Plan	Level, Grade, or Pay	Tenure	Expires
Washington, DC	Chairman	Billie Tsien	PA	WC	....	4	06/09/25
Washington, DC	Vice Chair	Hazel R Edwards	PA	WC	....	4	06/09/25
Washington, DC	Member	Justin G Moore	PA	WC	....	4	06/09/25
Washington, DC	Member	Peter D Cook	PA	WC	....	4	06/09/25
Washington, DC	Member	Lisa E Delplace	PA	WC	....	4	04/05/26
Washington, DC	Member	Bruce Redman Becker	PA	WC	....	4	....
Washington, DC	Member	William J. Lenihan	PA	WC	....	4	....
	OFFICE OF THE SECRETARY						
Washington, DC	Secretary to the Commission	Career Incumbent	CA	ES	....	....	....

COMMODITY FUTURES TRADING COMMISSION

Location	Position Title	Name of Incumbent	Type of Appt.	Pay Plan	Level, Grade, or Pay	Tenure	Expires
	OFFICE OF THE CHAIRPERSON						
Washington, DC	Chairperson....................................	Rostin Behnam......................	PAS	EX	III	5	....
Washington, DC	Commissioner....................................	Caroline D Pham.................	PAS	EX	IV	5	....
Washington, DC	Commissioner....................................	Christy Goldsmith Romero..	PAS	EX	IV	5	....
Washington, DC	Commissioner....................................	Summer Mersinger..............	PAS	EX	IV	....	....
Washington, DC	Commissioner....................................	Kristin N Johnson................	PAS	EX	IV	5	....
Washington, DC	Confidential Assistant....................	Rebecca Lewis	SC	OT	....	....	....
Washington, DC	Confidential Assistant....................	Nicholas Elliot....................	SC	OT	....	....	....
Washington, DC	Confidential Assistant....................	Zachary Coplan	SC	OT	....	....	....
Washington, DC	Confidential Assistant....................	Timothy Achinger................	SC	OT	....	....	....
Washington, DC	Senior Advisor....................................	Taylor Foy	SC	OT	....	....	....
New York, NY..........	Senior Advisor....................................	Harry Jung	SC	OT	....	....	....
	DIVISION OF CLEARING AND RISK						
Washington, DC	Director..	Clark Hutchison...................	SC	OT	....	....	....
	OFFICE OF PUBLIC AFFAIRS						
Washington, DC	Director..	Steven W Adamske	SC	OT	....	....	....

CONSUMER FINANCIAL PROTECTION BUREAU

Location	Position Title	Name of Incumbent	Type of Appt.	Pay Plan	Level, Grade, or Pay	Tenure	Expires
	OFFICE OF THE DIRECTOR						
Washington, DC	Director..	Rohit Chopra	PAS	EX	II	....	....
Washington, DC	Chief of Staff....................................	Jan Edwards Singelmann....	SC	OT	....	....	....
Washington, DC	Senior Advisor to the Director (Communications).	Allison Preiss......................	SC	OT	....	....	....
Washington, DC	Chief Technologist and Senior Advisor to the Director.	Erie K Meyer	SC	OT	....	....	....
Washington, DC	Senior Advisor for Congressional Affairs...........	Allie Rebecca Neill	SC	OT	....	....	....
Washington, DC	Management and Program Analyst	Maria Bazan........................	SC	OT	....	....	....
Washington, DC	Public Affairs Specialist	Alysa James........................	SC	OT	....	....	....
	CONSUMER FINANCIAL PROTECTION BUREAU						
Washington, DC	Associate Director, Research, Monitoring, and Regulations.	Julie Morgan........................	SC	OT	....	....	....
Washington, DC	Associate Director, External Affairs..................	Angela Hanks	SC	OT	....	....	....

CONSUMER PRODUCT SAFETY COMMISSION

Location	Position Title	Name of Incumbent	Type of Appt.	Pay Plan	Level, Grade, or Pay	Tenure	Expires
Bethesda, MD..........	Chairman, Consumer Product Safety Commission.	Alexander Dennis Hoehn-Saric.	PAS	EX	III	7	10/27/27
Bethesda, MD..........	Special Assistant....................	Anna Laitin	SC	GS	15	....	....
Bethesda, MD..........	Special Assistant (Legal)...................	Michele Viterise..................	SC	GS	15	....	....
Bethesda, MD..........	Chief of Staff....................................	Jana L Fong-Swamidoss	SC	GS	15	....	....
Bethesda, MD..........	Executive Assistant	Anne Campbell......................	SC	GS	13	....	....
	OFFICE OF COMMISSIONERS						
Bethesda, MD..........	Commissioner....................	Peter Feldman	PAS	EX	IV	7	10/27/26
Bethesda, MD..........	Special Assistant (Legal).................	Nicole Brightbill..................	SC	GS	15	....	....
Bethesda, MD..........	Special Assistant (Legal).................	Thomas Fuller	SC	GS	15	....	....
Bethesda, MD..........	Executive Assistant	John A Mitchell	SC	GS	12	....	....
Bethesda, MD..........	Commissioner....................	Richard L Trumka................	PAS	EX	IV	7	10/27/28
Bethesda, MD..........	Special Assistant (Legal).................	Kaiwon M Tresvant	SC	GS	14	....	....
Bethesda, MD..........	Special Assistant (Legal).................	Robin Lipp	SC	GS	15	....	....
Bethesda, MD..........	Executive Assistant	Isabella Maxey	SC	GS	12	....	....
Bethesda, MD..........	Commissioner....................	Mary T Boyle......................	PAS	EX	IV	7	10/27/25
Bethesda, MD..........	Special Assistant....................	Evagren O Caldera	SC	GS	15	....	....
Bethesda, MD..........	Commissioner....................	Douglas Dziak	PAS	EX	IV	7	10/27/24
Bethesda, MD..........	Special Assistant....................	Dana Smullen......................	SC	GS	15	....	....
Bethesda, MD..........	Director, Office of Legislative Affairs	Adam M Alpert....................	SC	GS	15	....	....
Bethesda, MD..........	General Counsel	Jessica Rich	NA	ES	....	....	....

CONSUMER PRODUCT SAFETY COMMISSION—Continued

Location	Position Title	Name of Incumbent	Type of Appt.	Pay Plan	Level, Grade, or Pay	Tenure	Expires
	Office of Communications						
Bethesda, MD..........	Supervisory Public Affairs Specialist.................	Pamela R Springs..................	NA	ES	....	....	....
	OFFICE OF EXECUTIVE DIRECTOR						
Bethesda, MD..........	Executive Director......................................	Austin C Schlick...................	NA	ES	....	....	....
Bethesda, MD..........	Deputy Executive Director for Safety Operations.	Career Incumbent................	CA	ES	....	....	....
Bethesda, MD..........	Chief Financial Officer..	Career Incumbent................	CA	ES	....	....	....
	Office of Compliance						
Bethesda, MD..........	Deputy Director, Office of Compliance..............	Career Incumbent................	CA	ES	....	....	....
	Office Of Hazard Identification And Reduction						
Rockville, MD..........	Associate Executive Director for Health Sciences.	Career Incumbent................	CA	ES	....	....	....
Rockville, MD..........	Associate Executive Director for Laboratory Sciences.	Career Incumbent................	CA	ES	....	....	....

CORPORATION FOR NATIONAL AND COMMUNITY SERVICE

Location	Position Title	Name of Incumbent	Type of Appt.	Pay Plan	Level, Grade, or Pay	Tenure	Expires
	BOARD OF DIRECTORS						
Washington, DC	Board Member - Chair	Catherine McLaughlin.........	PAS	WC	III	5	10/06/24
Washington, DC	Board Member	Alvin Warren	PAS	WC	....	5	10/06/23
Washington, DC	Board Member	Fagan Harris	PAS	WC	....	5	10/06/23
Washington, DC	Board Member	Flor Romero	PAS	WC	....	5	12/01/25
Washington, DC	Board Member	Lisette Nieves......................	PAS	WC	....	5	10/06/27
Washington, DC	Board Member	Leslie Bluhm........................	PAS	WC	....	5	10/06/23
Washington, DC	Board Member	Shirley S Sagawa	PAS	WC	....	5	10/06/24
Washington, DC	Board Member	Vacant	....	WC	....	5	....
Washington, DC	Board Member	Vacant	....	WC	....	5	....
Washington, DC	Board Member	Vacant	....	WC	....	5	....
Washington, DC	Board Member	Vacant	....	WC	....	5	....
Washington, DC	Board Member	Vacant	....	WC	....	5	....
Washington, DC	Board Member	Vacant	....	WC	....	5	....
Washington, DC	Board Member	Vacant	....	WC	....	5	....
	OFFICE OF THE CHIEF EXECUTIVE OFFICER						
Washington, DC	Chief Executive Officer	Michael Smith II	PAS	EX	III	....	....
Washington, DC	Chief of Staff..	Jennifer Mauk	XS	OT	....	....	....
Washington, DC	Senior Advisor for Strategic Partnerships........	Anna Hartge.........................	XS	OT	....	....	....
Washington, DC	Senior Advisor for the American Climate Corps.	Yasmeen Shaheen-McConnell.	XS	OT	....	....	....
Washington, DC	Assistant to the Board of Directors...................	Vacant	....	OT	....	....	....
Washington, DC	White House Liaison	Beatrix Evans.......................	XS	OT	....	....	....
Washington, DC	Special Assistant to the CEO	Diego Andrades	XS	OT	....	....	....
	OFFICE OF GENERAL COUNSEL						
Washington, DC	General Counsel	Vacant	....	OT	....	....	....
	OFFICE OF STRATEGIC ENGAGEMENT						
Washington, DC	Deputy Chief of Staff for Strategic Engagement.	Adrienne Andrews...............	XS	OT	....	....	....
	OFFICE OF COMMUNICATIONS AND MARKETING						
Washington, DC	Director of Marketing and Communications.....	Tonya Williams.....................	XS	OT	....	....	....
	OFFICE OF GOVERNMENT RELATIONS						
Washington, DC	Director, Government Relations	Tess Mason-Elder................	XS	OT	....	....	....
Washington, DC	Senior Legislative Assistant	Shahryar Baig	XS	OT	....	....	....
	OFFICE OF THE CHIEF OF PROGRAM OPERATIONS						
Washington, DC	Chief Program Officer	Vacant	....	OT	....	....	....
Washington, DC	Senior Advisor for Veterans, Wounded Warrior, and Military Families.	John Lira	XS	OT	....	....	....
	CORPORATION FOR NATIONAL AND COMMUNITY SERVICE						
Washington, DC	Senior Legislative Assistant	Priya Amilineni	XS	OT	....	....	....

CORPORATION FOR NATIONAL AND COMMUNITY SERVICE—Continued

Location	Position Title	Name of Incumbent	Type of Appt.	Pay Plan	Level, Grade, or Pay	Tenure	Expires
Washington, DC	**OFFICE OF AMERICORPS VISTA** Director, Americorps Vista	Vacant	....	OT	....	....	....
Washington, DC	**OFFICE OF AMERICORPS STATE AND NATIONAL** Director, Americorps State and National...........	Sonali Nijhawan..................	XS	OT	....	....	....
Washington, DC	**OFFICE OF AMERICORPS SENIORS** Director, Americorps Seniors	Atalaya Sergi.......................	XS	OT	....	....	....
Washington, DC	**OFFICE OF EXTERNAL AFFAIRS** Speechwriter to the CEO and Public Affairs Specialist.	Joseph Graham	XS	....	....	....	....
Washington, DC	**OFFICE OF THE INSPECTOR GENERAL** Inspector General	Vacant	....	EX	....	....	....

CORPORATION FOR PUBLIC BROADCASTING

Location	Position Title	Name of Incumbent	Type of Appt.	Pay Plan	Level, Grade, or Pay	Tenure	Expires
Washington, DC	**BOARD OF DIRECTORS** Member..	Diane Kaplan.......................	PAS	....	....	....	01/31/26
Washington, DC	Member..	Bruce Ramer.......................	PAS	....	....	....	....
Washington, DC	Member..	Tom Rothman.....................	PAS	....	....	....	01/31/26
Washington, DC	Member..	Elizabeth Sembler...............	PAS	....	....	....	01/31/26
Washington, DC	Member..	Kathy Im............................	PAS	....	....	....	01/31/24
Washington, DC	Member..	Janice Hellreich..................	PAS	....	....	....	....
Washington, DC	Member..	Rubydee Calvert..................	PAS	....	....	....	01/31/28
Washington, DC	Member..	Laura Ross.........................	PAS	....	....	....	01/31/28

COURT SERVICES AND OFFENDER SUPERVISION AGENCY FOR THE DISTRICT OF COLUMBIA

Location	Position Title	Name of Incumbent	Type of Appt.	Pay Plan	Level, Grade, or Pay	Tenure	Expires
Washington, DC	Director..	Richard S Tischner...............	PAS	EX	IV	....	....
Washington, DC	Attorney (General Counsel)............................	Career Incumbent	CA	ES		....	....

DEFENSE NUCLEAR FACILITIES SAFETY BOARD

Location	Position Title	Name of Incumbent	Type of Appt.	Pay Plan	Level, Grade, or Pay	Tenure	Expires
Washington, DC	Chairman	Joyce Louise Connery	PAS	EX	III	....	....
Washington, DC	Vice Chairman	Thomas Andrew Summers ..	PAS	EX	III	....	....
Washington, DC	Member..	Vacant	....	EX		....	....
Washington, DC	Member..	Vacant	....	EX		....	....
Washington, DC	Member..	Vacant	....	EX		....	....
Washington, DC	Senior Counsel for Nuclear Safety Engineering.	Vacant	....	SL		....	....
Washington, DC	General Counsel	Career Incumbent	CA	ES		....	....
Washington, DC	Executive Director of Operations	Career Incumbent	CA	ES		....	....

DELTA REGIONAL AUTHORITY

Location	Position Title	Name of Incumbent	Type of Appt.	Pay Plan	Level, Grade, or Pay	Tenure	Expires
Clarksdale, MS........	Federal Co-Chairman	Corey Wiggins.....................	PAS	EX	III	....	....
New Orleans, LA......	Senior Advisor..	Laura Veazey.......................	SC	GS	15	....	....

ENVIRONMENTAL PROTECTION AGENCY

Location	Position Title	Name of Incumbent	Type of Appt.	Pay Plan	Level, Grade, or Pay	Tenure	Expires
	OFFICE OF THE ADMINISTRATOR						
Washington, DC	Administrator...	Michael Regan.......................	PAS	EX	II	....	....
Washington, DC	Deputy Administrator	Janet Garvin McCabe..........	PAS	EX	III	....	....
Washington, DC	Assistant Deputy Administrator	Mark W Rupp........................	NA	ES	....	....	....
Washington, DC	Chief of Staff...	Dan G Utech.........................	NA	ES	....	....	....
Washington, DC	Deputy Chief of Staff for Management..............	Career Incumbent	CA	ES	....	....	....
Washington, DC	Deputy Chief of Staff for Operations	Kathleen Lance	NA	ES	....	....	....
Washington, DC	Deputy Chief of Staff for Strategy, Policy, and Strategic Engagement.	Rosemary Enobakhare..........	NA	ES	....	....	....
Washington, DC	Senior Advisor to the Administrator (Greenhouse Gas Reduction Fund).	Jahi Wise	NA	ES	....	....	....
Washington, DC	Senior Advisor to the Administrator (Environmental Justice).	Vacant	....	ES	....	....	....
Washington, DC	Senior Advisor to the Administrator (Implementation).	Zealan Hoover	NA	ES	....	....	....
Washington, DC	Senior Advisor for Agriculture.........................	Rodney Snyder	NA	ES	....	....	....
Washington, DC	Attorney-Adviser (General)..............................	Grant Cope	SC	GS	15	....	....
Washington, DC	Advisor...	Alexander Mechanick..........	SC	GS	15	....	....
Washington, DC	White House Liaison	Howard Ou	SC	GS	15	....	....
Washington, DC	Strategic Communications Advisor for Implementation.	Nathan Hitchings..................	SC	GS	14	....	....
Washington, DC	Senior Advisor to the Chief of Staff..................	Hieu Le	SC	GS	14	....	....
Washington, DC	Deputy White House Liaison............................	Rayshawn Dyson..................	SC	GS	14	....	....
Washington, DC	Director of Advance	Rachel Hegarty.....................	SC	GS	14	....	....
Washington, DC	Deputy Director of Scheduling	Megan Grosspietsch.............	SC	GS	13	....	....
Washington, DC	Senior Advance Specialist	Crystal Saavedra..................	SC	GS	13	....	....
Washington, DC	Senior Advance Specialist...............................	Andrew Hoffner....................	SC	GS	13	....	....
Washington, DC	Special Assistant to the Deputy Chief of Staff..	Thoren Perego.......................	SC	GS	13	....	....
Washington, DC	Special Assistant for Agriculture......................	Felipe Afanador Beltran	SC	GS	11	....	....
Washington, DC	Special Assistant to the White House Liaison ..	Kevin Trejos.........................	SC	GS	11	....	....
Washington, DC	Special Assistant to the White House Liaison ..	Gabriela Albavera	SC	GS	11	....	....
Washington, DC	Scheduler...	Jillian Griffin......................	SC	GS	9	....	....
	Office of the Associate Administrator for Policy						
Washington, DC	Director, Office of Community Revitalization....	Career Incumbent	CA	ES	....	....	....
	Office of Small Business Programs						
Washington, DC	Director, Office of Small Business Programs.....	Career Incumbent	CA	ES	....	....	....
	Office of Civil Rights						
Washington, DC	Director, Office of Civil Rights........................	Career Incumbent	CA	ES	....	....	....
	OFFICE OF THE EXECUTIVE SECRETARIAT						
Washington, DC	Director, Office of the Executive Secretariat.....	Eric E Wachter	NA	ES	....	....	....
Washington, DC	Special Assistant..	Dylan Garvin........................	SC	GS	7	....	....
	Office of the Associate Administrator For Congressional and Intergovernmental Relations						
Washington, DC	Associate Administrator for Congressional and Intergovernmental Relations.	Timothy James Del Monico.	NA	ES	....	....	....
Washington, DC	Deputy Associate Administrator for Management.	Career Incumbent	CA	ES	....	....	....
Washington, DC	Deputy Associate Administrator for Intergovernmental Affairs.	John Lucey...........................	SC	GS	15	....	....
Washington, DC	Senior Advisor for Intergovernmental Affairs...	Keylin S Rivera	SC	GS	15	....	....
Washington, DC	Deputy Associate Administrator for House Relations.	Emma L Tyler	SC	GS	15	....	....
Washington, DC	Senior Advisor for Congressional Affairs..........	Michael Harris	SC	GS	14	....	....
Washington, DC	Deputy Associate Administrator for Senate Relations.	Ashley Margaret Morgan	SC	GS	15	....	....
Washington, DC	Senior Advisor for Implementation...................	Jack Groarke	SC	GS	14	....	....
Washington, DC	Special Advisor for Senate Relations	Angela Hervig.......................	SC	GS	13	....	....
Washington, DC	Special Advisor for House Relations	Royce Chen	SC	GS	13	....	....
Washington, DC	Special Assistant..	Annie Nguyen.......................	SC	GS	11	....	....
	Office of Public Affairs						
Washington, DC	Associate Administrator for Public Affairs........	Nicholas Conger	NA	ES	....	....	....
Washington, DC	Principal Deputy Associate Administrator for Public Affairs.	Career Incumbent	CA	ES	....	....	....
Washington, DC	Deputy Associate Administrator for Public Affairs.	Timothy Carroll....................	SC	GS	15	....	....
Washington, DC	Senior Advisor for Digital Strategy and Content Development.	Sarah Galvez	SC	GS	15	....	....

ENVIRONMENTAL PROTECTION AGENCY—Continued

Location	Position Title	Name of Incumbent	Type of Appt.	Pay Plan	Level, Grade, or Pay	Tenure	Expires
Washington, DC	Senior Advisor for Media Relations	Ann Hunter-Pirtle...............	SC	GS	15	....	....
Washington, DC	Senior Advisor for Communications...................	Todd Zubatkin	SC	GS	15	....	....
Washington, DC	Senior Strategic Communications Advisor	Charissee Ridgeway.............	SC	GS	15	....	....
Washington, DC	Senior Creative Director	Julio Obscura.......................	SC	GS	15	....	....
Washington, DC	Press Secretary...	Remmington Belford............	SC	GS	15	....	....
Washington, DC	Senior Speechwriter	Desiree Allen	SC	GS	14	....	....
Washington, DC	Special Advisor for Digital Strategy	Jamie Green	SC	GS	14	....	....
Washington, DC	Communications Advisor	Khanya Brann......................	SC	GS	13	....	....
Washington, DC	Speechwriter	Ryan Linsey..........................	SC	GS	13	....	....
Washington, DC	Special Assistant..	Isabel Delgado-Betz	SC	GS	7	....	....
	Office of Public Engagement and Environmental Education						
Washington, DC	Associate Administrator for Public Engagement and Environmental Education.	Loni Russell..........................	NA	ES	....	....	....
Washington, DC	Deputy Associate Administrator for Public Engagement and Environmental Education.	Jessica Loya..........................	SC	GS	15	....	....
Washington, DC	Associate Deputy Director for Public Engagement and Environmental Education.	Vanessa Millan	SC	GS	15	....	....
Washington, DC	Senior Advisor for Environmental Education ...	Kim Noble.............................	SC	GS	14	....	....
Washington, DC	Public Engagement Specialist	Elias Romanos......................	SC	GS	13	....	....
Washington, DC	Public Engagement Specialist	Arielle Plavcan	SC	GS	12	....	....
Washington, DC	Special Assistant..	Bibiana Belknap Fernandez.	SC	GS	9	....	....
	Office of the Associate Administrator For Policy						
Washington, DC	Associate Administrator for Policy....................	Victoria Arroyo	NA	ES	....	....	....
Washington, DC	Principal Deputy Associate Administrator for Policy.	Adriana Hochberg...............	NA	ES	....	....	....
Washington, DC	Deputy Associate Administrator.........................	Career Incumbent	CA	ES	....	....	....
Washington, DC	Deputy Associate Administrator for Policy........	Navis Bermudez....................	SC	GS	15	....	....
Washington, DC	Special Advisor..	Ebadullah Ebadi...................	SC	GS	12	....	....
Washington, DC	Director, Office of Regulatory Policy and Management.	Career Incumbent	CA	ES	....	....	....
Washington, DC	Director, National Center for Environmental Economics.	Career Incumbent	CA	ES	....	....	....
Washington, DC	Director, Office of Federal Activities	Career Incumbent	CA	ES	....	....	....
	Office of Children's Health Protection						
Washington, DC	Director, Office of Children's Health Protection.	Career Incumbent	CA	ES	....	....	....
	Office of National Security						
Washington, DC	Associate Administrator for National Security .	Career Incumbent	CA	ES	....	....	....
	Office of Science Advisory Board						
Washington, DC	Director, Science Advisory Board.......................	Career Incumbent	CA	ES	....	....	....
	Office of the Greenhouse Gas Reduction Fund						
Washington, DC	Director, Office of the Greenhouse Gas Reduction Fund.	Career Incumbent	CA	ES	....	....	....
	OFFICE OF THE ASSISTANT ADMINISTRATOR FOR ENFORCEMENT AND COMPLIANCE ASSURANCE						
Washington, DC	Assistant Administrator for Enforcement and Compliance Assurance.	David M Uhlmann	PAS	EX	IV	....	....
Washington, DC	Principal Deputy Assistant Administrator for Enforcement and Compliance Assurance.	Career Incumbent	CA	ES	....	....	....
Washington, DC	Deputy Assistant Administrator for Enforcement and Compliance Assurance.	Stacey Geis	SC	GS	15	....	....
Washington, DC	Senior Advisor..	Vacant		ES	....	....	....
Washington, DC	Senior Advisor..	Mandy Warner......................	SC	GS	15	....	....
Washington, DC	Director, Office of Administration and Policy....	Vacant		ES	....	....	....
	OFFICE OF THE GENERAL COUNSEL						
Washington, DC	General Counsel	Jeffrey Michael Prieto..........	PAS	EX	IV	....	....
Washington, DC	Principal Deputy General Counsel.....................	Dimple Chaudhary...............	NA	ES	....	....	....
Washington, DC	Deputy General Counsel for Operations............	Career Incumbent	CA	ES	....	....	....
Washington, DC	Deputy General Counsel for Environmental Media and Regional Law Offices.	Career Incumbent	CA	ES	....	....	....
Washington, DC	Deputy General Counsel for Environmental Programs and Oversight.	Natalia Tania Sorgente........	NA	ES	....	....	....
Washington, DC	Deputy General Counsel for Nationwide Resource Protection Programs.	Susannah Weaver.................	NA	ES	....	....	....
Washington, DC	Associate Deputy General Counsel	Amanda Leiter	SC	GS	15	....	....

ENVIRONMENTAL PROTECTION AGENCY—Continued

Location	Position Title	Name of Incumbent	Type of Appt.	Pay Plan	Level, Grade, or Pay	Tenure	Expires
Washington, DC	Senior Legal Counsel...	Zachary Pilchen....................	SC	GS	15	....	....
Washington, DC	Attorney-Adviser (General)..............................	Meghan Greenfield..............	SC	GS	15	....	....
Washington, DC	Associate General Counsel (Cross-Cutting Issues Law Office).	Career Incumbent	CA	ES	....	....	....
Washington, DC	Associate General Counsel (Pesticides and Toxic Substances).	Career Incumbent	CA	ES	....	....	....
Washington, DC	Associate General Counsel (Air and Radiation Law Office).	Career Incumbent	CA	ES	....	....	....
Washington, DC	Associate General Counsel (Water)....................	Career Incumbent	CA	ES	....	....	....
Washington, DC	Associate General Counsel (Solid Waste and Emergency Response).	Career Incumbent	CA	ES	....	....	....
Washington, DC	Associate General Counsel (General Law Office).	Career Incumbent	CA	ES	....	....	....
Washington, DC	Associate General Counsel (Civil Rights and Finance Law Office).	Career Incumbent	CA	ES	....	....	....
Washington, DC	Associate General Counsel (National Freedom of Information Act Office).	Career Incumbent	CA	ES	....	....	....
	OFFICE OF THE ASSISTANT ADMINISTRATOR FOR INTERNATIONAL AND TRIBAL AFFAIRS						
Washington, DC	Assistant Administrator for International and Tribal Affairs.	Jane T Nishida	PAS	EX	IV	....	....
Washington, DC	Principal Deputy Assistant Administrator for International and Tribal Affairs.	Career Incumbent	CA	ES	....	....	....
Washington, DC	Director, Office of Management and International Services.	Career Incumbent	CA	ES	....	....	....
Washington, DC	Director, American Indian Environmental Office.	Kenneth P Martin.................	NA	ES	....	....	....
Washington, DC	Director, Office of International Affairs	Career Incumbent	CA	ES	....	....	....
	OFFICE OF THE CHIEF FINANCIAL OFFICER						
Washington, DC	Chief Financial Officer.......................................	Faisal Amin........................	PAS	EX	IV	....	....
Washington, DC	Senior Advisor to the Chief Financial Officer ...	Vacant	....	ES		....	....
Washington, DC	Senior Advisor for Implementation....................	Amanda Pizzuti....................	SC	GS	14	....	....
Washington, DC	Director, E-Enterprise for the Environment Program.	Career Incumbent	CA	ES	....	....	....
	OFFICE OF THE ASSISTANT ADMINISTRATOR FOR MISSION SUPPORT						
Washington, DC	Assistant Administrator for Mission Support ...	Vacant	....	EX		....	....
Washington, DC	Principal Deputy Assistant Administrator for Mission Support.	Career Incumbent	CA	ES	....	....	....
Washington, DC	Deputy Assistant Administrator for Infrastructure and Extramural Resources.	Career Incumbent	CA	ES	....	....	....
Washington, DC	Deputy Assistant Administrator for Workforce Solutions and Inclusive Excellence.	Career Incumbent	CA	ES	....	....	....
Washington, DC	Deputy Assistant Administrator for Information Technology and Information Management.	Career Incumbent	CA	ES	....	....	....
Washington, DC	Senior Advisor..	Career Incumbent	CA	ES	....	....	....
Washington, DC	Federal Chief Sustainability Officer	Andrew J Mayock................	NA	ES	....	....	....
Washington, DC	Director, Office of Records, Administrative Systems, and Ediscovery.	Career Incumbent	CA	ES	....	....	....
Washington, DC	Director, Office of Information Technology and Operations.	Career Incumbent	CA	ES	....	....	....
Washington, DC	Deputy Director, Office of Information Technology and Operations.	Vacant	....	ES		....	....
Washington, DC	Director, Office of Information Management.....	Career Incumbent	CA	ES	....	....	....
Washington, DC	Director, Office of Information Security and Privacy.	Career Incumbent	CA	ES	....	....	....
Washington, DC	Director, Office of Inclusive Excellence	Vacant	....	ES		....	....
	OFFICE OF THE ASSISTANT ADMINISTRATOR FOR WATER						
Washington, DC	Assistant Administrator for Water....................	Vacant	....	EX		....	....
Washington, DC	Principal Deputy Assistant Administrator for Water.	Vacant	....	ES		....	....
Washington, DC	Deputy Assistant Administrator for Management.	Career Incumbent	CA	ES	....	....	....
Washington, DC	Senior Advisor..	Career Incumbent	CA	ES	....	....	....
Washington, DC	Deputy Assistant Administrator for Strategic Initiatives.	Mae Wu	NA	ES	....	....	....

ENVIRONMENTAL PROTECTION AGENCY—Continued

Location	Position Title	Name of Incumbent	Type of Appt.	Pay Plan	Level, Grade, or Pay	Tenure	Expires
Washington, DC	Director of Special Projects for the Office of Water.	Zachary Schafer....................	SC	GS	15	....	....
Washington, DC	Director of Infrastructure Implementation for the Office of Water.	Wendi Wilkes........................	SC	GS	15	....	....
Washington, DC	Special Advisor..	Richard Figueroa..................	SC	GS	12	....	....
Washington, DC	Special Assistant..	Juan Sabater	SC	GS	9	....	....
Washington, DC	Director, Office of Wastewater Management	Career Incumbent	CA	ES	....	....	....
Washington, DC	Deputy Director, Office of Wastewater Management.	Career Incumbent	CA	ES	....	....	....
Washington, DC	Director, Office of Science and Technology	Career Incumbent	CA	ES	....	....	....
Washington, DC	Deputy Director, Office of Science and Technology.	Career Incumbent	CA	ES	....	....	....
Washington, DC	Director, Office of Wetlands, Oceans and Watersheds.	Career Incumbent	CA	ES	....	....	....
Washington, DC	Deputy Director, Office of Wetlands, Oceans and Watersheds.	Career Incumbent	CA	ES	....	....	....
Washington, DC	Director, Office of Ground Water and Drinking Water.	Career Incumbent	CA	ES	....	....	....
Washington, DC	Deputy Director, Office of Ground Water and Drinking Water.	Career Incumbent	CA	ES	....	....	....
	OFFICE OF THE ASSISTANT ADMINISTRATOR FOR LAND AND EMERGENCY MANAGEMENT						
Washington, DC	Assistant Administrator, Office of Solid Waste .	Vacant	....	EX	....	....	....
Washington, DC	Principal Deputy Assistant Administrator for Land and Emergency Management.	Career Incumbent	CA	ES	....	....	....
Washington, DC	Deputy Assistant Administrator for Land and Emergency Management.	Clifford Villa	NA	ES	....	....	....
Washington, DC	Senior Advisor for Implementation	Eric Kessler	NA	ES	....	....	....
Washington, DC	Special Advisor for Implementation..................	Sanjana Puskoor	SC	GS	14	....	....
Washington, DC	Senior Advisor..	Vacant	....	ES	....	....	....
Washington, DC	Director, Office of Program Management	Career Incumbent	CA	ES	....	....	....
Washington, DC	Senior Advisor for Workforce Development.......	Career Incumbent	CA	ES	....	....	....
Washington, DC	Director, Federal Facilities Restoration and Reuse Office.	Career Incumbent	CA	ES	....	....	....
Washington, DC	Director, Office of Superfund Remediation and Technology Innovation.	Career Incumbent	CA	ES	....	....	....
Washington, DC	Deputy Director, Office of Superfund Remediation and Technology Innovation.	Career Incumbent	CA	ES	....	....	....
Washington, DC	Director, Office of Resource Conservation and Recovery.	Career Incumbent	CA	ES	....	....	....
Washington, DC	Deputy Director, Office of Resource Conservation and Recovery.	Vacant	....	ES	....	....	....
Washington, DC	Director, Office of Underground Storage Tanks.	Career Incumbent	CA	ES	....	....	....
Washington, DC	Director, Office of Brownfields Cleanup and Redevelopment.	Career Incumbent	CA	ES	....	....	....
Washington, DC	Director, Office of Emergency Management	Career Incumbent	CA	ES	....	....	....
Washington, DC	Deputy Director, Office of Emergency Management.	Career Incumbent	CA	ES	....	....	....
	OFFICE OF THE ASSISTANT ADMINISTRATOR FOR AIR AND RADIATION						
Washington, DC	Assistant Administrator for Air and Radiation.	Joseph Matthew Goffman....	PAS	EX	IV	....	....
Washington, DC	Principal Deputy Assistant Administrator for Air and Radiation.	Alejandra Nunez	NA	ES	....	....	....
Washington, DC	Deputy Assistant Administrator for Air and Radiation.	Career Incumbent	CA	ES	....	....	....
Washington, DC	Deputy Assistant Administrator for Stationary Sources.	Tomas Carbonell..................	NA	ES	....	....	....
Washington, DC	Deputy Assistant Administrator for Implementation.	Jennifer Macedonia..............	NA	ES	....	....	....
Washington, DC	Deputy Assistant Administrator for Air Quality Implementation.	William Niebling	NA	ES	....	....	....
Washington, DC	Senior Advisor for Implementation.....................	Maria Laverdiere	SC	GS	15	....	....
Washington, DC	Special Assistant for Implementation and Climate Justice.	Ahmad Perez	SC	GS	7	....	....
Washington, DC	Special Assistant..	Evan Magallanes..................	SC	GS	9	....	....
Washington, DC	Director, Office of Atmospheric Protection.........	Career Incumbent	CA	ES	....	....	....
Durham, NC............	Director, Office of Air Quality Planning and Standards.	Career Incumbent	CA	ES	....	....	....
Durham, NC............	Deputy Director, Office of Air Quality Planning and Standards.	Career Incumbent	CA	ES	....	....	....

ENVIRONMENTAL PROTECTION AGENCY—Continued

Location	Position Title	Name of Incumbent	Type of Appt.	Pay Plan	Level, Grade, or Pay	Tenure	Expires
Washington, DC	Director, Office of Transportation and Air Quality.	Career Incumbent	CA	ES	....	....	....
Washington, DC	Deputy Director, Office of Transportation and Air Quality.	Career Incumbent	CA	ES	....	....	....
Washington, DC	Director, Office of Radiation and Indoor Air......	Career Incumbent	CA	ES	....	....	....
	OFFICE OF THE ASSISTANT ADMINISTRATOR FOR CHEMICAL SAFETY AND POLLUTION PREVENTION						
Washington, DC	Assistant Administrator for Toxic Substances ..	Michal Freedhoff	PAS	EX	IV	....	....
Washington, DC	Principal Deputy Assistant Administrator for Chemical Safety and Pollution Prevention.	Vacant	....	ES	....	....	....
Washington, DC	Deputy Assistant Administrator for Management.	Career Incumbent	CA	ES	....	....	....
Washington, DC	Deputy Assistant Administrator for Pesticide Programs.	Ya-Wei Li..............................	SC	GS	15	....	....
Washington, DC	Director, Office of Pollution Prevention and Toxics.	Career Incumbent	CA	ES	....	....	....
Washington, DC	Deputy Director for Programs, Office of Pollution Prevention and Toxics.	Career Incumbent	CA	ES	....	....	....
Washington, DC	Deputy Director for Management, Office of Pollution Prevention and Toxics.	Vacant	....	ES	....	....	....
Arlington, VA..........	Director, Office of Pesticides Programs..............	Career Incumbent	CA	ES	....	....	....
Washington, DC	Deputy Director for Programs, Opp	Vacant	....	ES	....	....	....
Washington, DC	Deputy Director for Management, Office of Pesticide Programs.	Career Incumbent	CA	ES	....	....	....
	OFFICE OF THE ASSISTANT ADMINISTRATOR FOR RESEARCH AND DEVELOPMENT						
Washington, DC	Assistant Administrator for Research and Development.	Henry Frey	PAS	EX	IV	....	....
Washington, DC	Principal Deputy Assistant Administrator for Research and Development.	Career Incumbent	CA	ES	....	....	....
Washington, DC	Deputy Assistant Administrator for Management.	Career Incumbent	CA	ES	....	....	....
Washington, DC	National Program Director for Sustainable and Healthy Communities Research Program.	Career Incumbent	CA	ES	....	....	....
Washington, DC	Environmental Protection Agency Laboratory Enterprise National Program Manager.	Career Incumbent	CA	ES	....	....	....
Washington, DC	Director, Office of Science Advisor, Policy and Engagement.	Vacant	....	ES	....	....	....
Washington, DC	Deputy Director, Office of Science Advisor, Policy and Engagement.	Career Incumbent	CA	ES	....	....	....
	OFFICE OF THE ASSISTANT ADMINISTRATOR FOR ENVIRONMENTAL JUSTICE AND EXTERNAL CIVIL RIGHTS						
Washington, DC	Principal Deputy Assistant Administrator for Environmental Justice and External Civil Rights.	Career Incumbent	CA	ES	....	....	....
Washington, DC	Deputy Assistant Administrator for Program Implementation.	Marianne Engelman-Lado...	NA	ES	....	....	....
Washington, DC	Deputy Assistant Administrator for Management.	Vacant	....	ES	....	....	....
Washington, DC	Senior Advisor..	Career Incumbent	CA	ES	....	....	....
Washington, DC	Deputy Assistant Administrator for Strategic Initiatives.	Alison Cassady	SC	GS	15	....	....
Washington, DC	Senior Advisor for Environmental Justice and External Civil Rights.	Karim Marshall	SC	GS	15	....	....
Washington, DC	Special Advisor..	Grace Yu Ying Smith	SC	GS	13	....	....
	REGIONAL OFFICES						
	Region 1 - Boston, Massachusetts						
Boston, MA	Regional Administrator................................	David Cash	NA	ES	....	....	....
Boston, MA	Deputy Regional Administrator........................	Career Incumbent	CA	ES	....	....	....
	Region 2 - New York, New York						
New York, NY..........	Regional Administrator...................................	Lisa Garcia	NA	ES	....	....	....
New York, NY..........	Deputy Regional Administrator................	Career Incumbent	CA	ES	....	....	....
New York, NY..........	Special Advisor for Implementation.................	Zaid Hassan.........................	SC	GS	15	....	....
	Region 3 - Philadelphia, Pennsylvania						
Philadelphia, PA	Regional Administrator......................................	Adam Ortiz	NA	ES	....	....	....

ENVIRONMENTAL PROTECTION AGENCY—Continued

Location	Position Title	Name of Incumbent	Type of Appt.	Pay Plan	Level, Grade, or Pay	Tenure	Expires
Philadelphia, PA	Deputy Regional Administrator...........................	Career Incumbent	CA	ES	....	....	....
	Region 4 - Atlanta, Georgia						
Atlanta, GA	Regional Administrator......................................	Vacant	....	ES	....	....	....
Atlanta, GA	Deputy Regional Administrator...........................	Career Incumbent	CA	ES	....	....	....
	Region 5 - Chicago, Illinois						
Chicago, IL	Regional Administrator......................................	Debra Shore.........................	NA	ES	....	....	....
Chicago, IL	Deputy Regional Administrator...........................	Career Incumbent	CA	ES	....	....	....
	Region 6 - Dallas, Texas						
Dallas, TX	Regional Administrator......................................	Earthea Nance......................	NA	ES	....	....	....
Dallas, TX	Deputy Regional Administrator...........................	Career Incumbent	CA	ES	....	....	....
Dallas, TX	Senior Advisor..	Career Incumbent	CA	ES	....	....	....
	Region 7 - Lenexa, Kansas						
Lenexa, KS	Regional Administrator......................................	Meghan McCollister.............	NA	ES	....	....	....
Lenexa, KS	Deputy Regional Administrator...........................	Career Incumbent	CA	ES	....	....	....
	Region 8 - Denver, Colorado						
Denver, CO	Regional Administrator......................................	Kathleen Becker...................	NA	ES	....	....	....
Denver, CO	Deputy Regional Administrator...........................	Career Incumbent	CA	ES	....	....	....
	Region 9 - San Francisco, California						
San Francisco, CA...	Regional Administrator......................................	Martha Aceves......................	NA	ES	....	....	....
San Francisco, CA...	Deputy Regional Administrator...........................	Career Incumbent	CA	ES	....	....	....
	Region 10 - Seattle, Washington						
Seattle, WA	Regional Administrator......................................	Casey Sixkiller	NA	ES	....	....	....
Seattle, WA	Deputy Regional Administrator...........................	Career Incumbent	CA	ES	....	....	....

ENVIRONMENTAL PROTECTION AGENCY OFFICE OF THE INSPECTOR GENERAL

Location	Position Title	Name of Incumbent	Type of Appt.	Pay Plan	Level, Grade, or Pay	Tenure	Expires
Washington, DC	Inspector General	Sean William O'Donnell.......	PAS	EX	III	....	....

EQUAL EMPLOYMENT OPPORTUNITY COMMISSION

Location	Position Title	Name of Incumbent	Type of Appt.	Pay Plan	Level, Grade, or Pay	Tenure	Expires
	OFFICE OF THE CHAIR						
Washington, DC	Chair, Equal Employment Opportunity Commission.	Charlotte A Burrows............	PAS	EX	III	5	07/01/28
Washington, DC	Chief Operating Officer......................................	Career Incumbent	CA	ES	....	....	....
Washington, DC	Senior Attorney-Advisor.....................................	Elizabeth Fox-Solomon	NA	ES	....	....	....
Washington, DC	Program Manager...	Vacant		ES	....	....	....
	OFFICE OF THE VICE CHAIR						
Washington, DC	Vice Chair, Equal Employment Opportunity Commission.	Jocelyn Samuels	PAS	EX	IV	5	07/01/26
	OFFICE OF COMMISSIONER						
Washington, DC	Member, Equal Employment Opportunity Commission.	Andrea Lucas.......................	PAS	EX	IV	5	07/01/25
Washington, DC	Member, Equal Employment Opportunity Commission.	Keith E Sonderling	PAS	EX	IV	5	07/01/24
Cincinnati, OH	Member Equal Employment Opportunity Commission.	Kalpana Kotagal	PAS	EX	IV	5	07/01/27
Washington, DC	Policy Analyst..	Yana Mayayeva	SC	GS	15	....	....
	OFFICE OF GENERAL COUNSEL						
Washington, DC	General Counsel	Karla A Gilbride..................	PAS	EX	V	4	10/18/27
Washington, DC	Deputy General Counsel	Career Incumbent	CA	ES	....	....	....
Washington, DC	Associate General Counsel for Litigation Management Services.	Career Incumbent	CA	ES	....	....	....
Washington, DC	Associate General Counsel for Appellate Services.	Career Incumbent	CA	ES	....	....	....

EQUAL EMPLOYMENT OPPORTUNITY COMMISSION—Continued

Location	Position Title	Name of Incumbent	Type of Appt.	Pay Plan	Level, Grade, or Pay	Tenure	Expires
	OFFICE OF COMMUNICATIONS AND LEGISLATIVE AFFAIRS						
Washington, DC	Director, Office of Communication and Legislative Affairs.	Jacinta Sandy Ma Chuang..	NA	ES	....	....	....
	OFFICE OF ENTERPRISE DATA AND ANALYTICS						
Washington, DC	Director, Office of Enterprise Data and Analytics.	Career Incumbent	CA	ES	....	....	....
	OFFICE OF INFORMATION TECHNOLOGY						
Washington, DC	Chief Information Officer....................	Career Incumbent	CA	ES	....	....	....
	OFFICE OF LEGAL COUNSEL						
Washington, DC	Legal Counsel....................................	Career Incumbent	CA	ES	....	....	....
Washington, DC	Associate Legal Counsel......................	Career Incumbent	CA	ES	....	....	....
Washington, DC	Associate Legal Counsel......................	Career Incumbent	CA	ES	....	....	....
	OFFICE OF FEDERAL OPERATIONS						
Washington, DC	Director, Office of Federal Operations...............	Career Incumbent	CA	ES	....	....	....
Washington, DC	Director, Federal Sector Programs	Career Incumbent	CA	ES	....	....	....
Washington, DC	Director, Appellate Review Programs	Vacant	....	ES	....	....	....
	OFFICE OF FIELD PROGRAMS						
Washington, DC	Director, Office of Field Programs	Vacant	....	ES	....	....	....
Washington, DC	Director, State, Local and Tribal Programs	Career Incumbent	CA	ES	....	....	....
Washington, DC	Chief Administrative Judge	Career Incumbent	CA	ES	....	....	....
Washington, DC	Program Manager...	Vacant	....	ES	....	....	....
	OFFICE OF THE CHIEF FINANCIAL OFFICER						
Washington, DC	Chief Financial Officer....................................	Career Incumbent	CA	ES	....	....	....

EXPORT-IMPORT BANK

Location	Position Title	Name of Incumbent	Type of Appt.	Pay Plan	Level, Grade, or Pay	Tenure	Expires
	BOARD OF DIRECTORS						
Washington, DC	First Vice President and Vice Chairman	Judith Pryor	PAS	EX	IV	4	....
Washington, DC	Member Board of Directors................................	Vacant	....	EX	....	....	....
Washington, DC	Member of the Board of Directors......................	Owen Herrnstadt	PAS	EX	IV	....	....
Washington, DC	Member of the Board of Directors......................	Vacant	....	EX	....	....	....
	Office of Communications						
Washington, DC	Press Secretary	Lucy E Herbert....................	SC	GS	13	....	....
Washington, DC	Senior Vice President for Communications	Elizabeth Lewis....................	SC	SL	....	....	....
	Office of the General Counsel						
Washington, DC	Deputy General Counsel	Lark Grier-Hapli	SC	GS	15	....	....
Washington, DC	Senior Vice President and General Counsel......	James Coughlan	SC	....	....	....	....
	Office of Congressional and Intergovernmental Affairs						
Washington, DC	Deputy Director for Congressional and Intergovernmental Affairs.	Derek L Kitchen...................	SC	GS	14	....	....
Washington, DC	Senior Vice President	Ben Widness	SC	OT	....	....	....
	OFFICE OF THE CHAIRMAN						
Washington, DC	President and Chairman....................................	Reta J Lewis	PAS	EX	III	4	....
Washington, DC	Executive Secretary...	Thomas Reynolds	SC	GS	15	....	....
Washington, DC	Senior Advisor, National Security	Sergio Fontanez....................	SC	GS	15	....	....
Washington, DC	Confidential Assistant to the Chairman............	Christopher Claude Organ ..	SC	GS	13	....	....
Washington, DC	Director of Scheduling.......................................	Andrew Martin Becht..........	SC	GS	14	....	....
Washington, DC	Special Assistant and Deputy Scheduler...........	Arrone Washington	SC	GS	13	....	....
Washington, DC	Special Advisor to the President and Chair	Laly Rivera Perez.................	SC	GS	14	....	....
	Office of the Chief of Staff						
Washington, DC	Senior Vice President and Chief of Staff...........	Brad Belzak	SC	SL	....	....	....
Washington, DC	Deputy Chief of Staff and White House Liaison.	Hazeen Ashby.......................	SC	SL	....	....	....
	Office of the Inspector General						
Washington, DC	Legal Counsel.......................................	Vacant	....	SL	....	....	....

EXPORT-IMPORT BANK—Continued

Location	Position Title	Name of Incumbent	Type of Appt.	Pay Plan	Level, Grade, or Pay	Tenure	Expires
Washington, DC	*Office of External Engagement* Senior Vice President for External Engagement.	Anastasia Dellaccio.............	SC	GS	15	....	....

EXPORT-IMPORT BANK OFFICE OF THE INSPECTOR GENERAL

Location	Position Title	Name of Incumbent	Type of Appt.	Pay Plan	Level, Grade, or Pay	Tenure	Expires
Washington, DC	Inspector General	Parisa Salehi	PAS	EX	III	....	....

FARM CREDIT ADMINISTRATION

Location	Position Title	Name of Incumbent	Type of Appt.	Pay Plan	Level, Grade, or Pay	Tenure	Expires
Mclean, VA...............	**OFFICE OF THE BOARD** Chairman, Farm Credit Administration Board.	Vincent G Logan	PAS	EX	III	6	05/21/26
Mclean, VA...............	Member, Farm Credit Administration Board	Jeffery Hall..........................	PAS	EX	IV	1	10/13/18
Mclean, VA...............	Member, Farm Credit Administration Board	Glen Smith...........................	PAS	EX	IV	6	05/21/22
Mclean, VA...............	Executive Assistant to Member.........................	Michael Alan Stokke............	SC	OT	42	....	....
Mclean, VA...............	**OFFICE OF CONGRESSIONAL AND PUBLIC AFFAIRS** Director..	Trevor Reuschel...................	SC	OT	44	....	....
Mclean, VA...............	**OFFICE OF THE CHIEF OF STAFF** Chief of Staff..	Maribel Duran......................	SC	OT	45	....	....

FEDERAL AGRICULTURAL MORTGAGE CORPORATION

Location	Position Title	Name of Incumbent	Type of Appt.	Pay Plan	Level, Grade, or Pay	Tenure	Expires
Washington, DC	**BOARD OF DIRECTORS** Member...	Chester Culver	PAS	....	....	....	....
Washington, DC	Member...	Sara Faivre-Davis	PAS	....	....	....	....
Washington, DC	Member...	Lowell Junkins	PAS	....	....	....	....
Washington, DC	Member...	LaJuana Wilcher	PAS	....	....	....	....

FEDERAL COMMUNICATIONS COMMISSION

Location	Position Title	Name of Incumbent	Type of Appt.	Pay Plan	Level, Grade, or Pay	Tenure	Expires
Washington, DC	**OFFICE OF THE CHAIRWOMAN** Chairwoman..	Jessica Rosenworcel.............	PAS	EX	III	....	06/30/25
Washington, DC	Commissioner..	Geoffrey Starks	PAS	EX	IV	....	06/30/27
Washington, DC	Commissioner..	Nathan A Simington...........	PAS	EX	IV	....	06/30/24
Washington, DC	Commissioner..	Anna M Gomez......................	PAS	EX	IV	....	06/30/26
Washington, DC	Commissioner..	Brendan T Carr...................	PAS	EX	IV	....	06/30/28
Washington, DC	Chief of Staff..	Narda Marisa Jones.............	NA	ES	....	....	....
Washington, DC	Senior Advisor to the Chairwoman...................	Vacant	....	SL	....	....	....
Washington, DC	**CONSUMER AND GOVERNMENTAL AFFAIRS BUREAU** Bureau Chief, Consumer and Governmental Affairs.	Alejandro Roark	NA	ES	....	....	....
Washington, DC	Deputy Bureau Chief	Career Incumbent	CA	ES	....	....	....
Washington, DC	**ENFORCEMENT BUREAU** Bureau Chief..	Career Incumbent	CA	ES	....	....	....
Washington, DC	Deputy Bureau Chief	Vacant	....	ES	....	....	....
Washington, DC	Deputy Bureau Chief	Peter Hyun	NA	ES	....	....	....

FEDERAL COMMUNICATIONS COMMISSION—Continued

Location	Position Title	Name of Incumbent	Type of Appt.	Pay Plan	Level, Grade, or Pay	Tenure	Expires
	MEDIA BUREAU						
Washington, DC	Bureau Chief....................................	Career Incumbent	CA	ES	....	....	....
Washington, DC	Deputy Bureau Chief	Career Incumbent	CA	ES	....	....	....
Washington, DC	Deputy Bureau Chief	Career Incumbent	CA	ES	....	....	....
Washington, DC	Deputy Bureau Chief	Career Incumbent	CA	ES	....	....	....
	OFFICE OF ECONOMICS AND ANALYTICS						
Washington, DC	Chief	Career Incumbent	CA	ES	....	....	....
Washington, DC	Deputy Chief....................................	Career Incumbent	CA	ES	....	....	....
Washington, DC	Deputy Chief....................................	Career Incumbent	CA	ES	....	....	....
Washington, DC	Deputy Chief....................................	Career Incumbent	CA	ES	....	....	....
	OFFICE OF ENGINEERING AND TECHNOLOGY						
Washington, DC	Chief	Career Incumbent	CA	ES	....	....	....
Washington, DC	Deputy Chief....................................	Career Incumbent	CA	ES	....	....	....
	OFFICE OF GENERAL COUNSEL						
Washington, DC	General Counsel	Career Incumbent	CA	ES	....	....	....
Washington, DC	Deputy General Counsel	Career Incumbent	CA	ES	....	....	....
Washington, DC	Deputy General Counsel.....................	Vacant	....	ES	....	....	....
Washington, DC	Deputy General Counsel for Fraud, Bankruptcy and Transactions.	Career Incumbent	CA	ES	....	....	....
Washington, DC	Associate General Counsel for Administrative Law.	Career Incumbent	CA	ES	....	....	....
Washington, DC	Associate General Counsel...................	Christopher R Day	NA	ES	....	....	....
	OFFICE OF INSPECTOR GENERAL						
Washington, DC	Inspector General	Fara Damelin......................	PAS	EX	III	....	....
Washington, DC	Assistant Inspector General for Investigations.	Career Incumbent	CA	ES	....	....	....
	OFFICE OF INTERNATIONAL AFFAIRS						
Washington, DC	Office Chief....................................	Vacant	....	ES	....	....	....
Washington, DC	Deputy Office Chief............................	Career Incumbent	CA	ES	....	....	....
Washington, DC	Deputy Office Chief............................	Career Incumbent	CA	ES	....	....	....
	OFFICE OF MEDIA RELATIONS						
Washington, DC	Director, Office of Media Relations....................	Paloma Isabel Villareyes Perez.	SC	GS	15	....	....
Washington, DC	Deputy Director, Office of Media Relations	Brian Phillips Jr...................	SC	GS	15	....	....
	OFFICE OF THE MANAGING DIRECTOR						
Washington, DC	Managing Director...............................	Career Incumbent	CA	ES	....	....	....
Washington, DC	Deputy Managing Director	Career Incumbent	CA	ES	....	....	....
Washington, DC	Deputy Managing Director	Vacant	....	ES	....	....	....
Washington, DC	Chief Financial Officer.........................	Career Incumbent	CA	ES	....	....	....
Washington, DC	Chief Human Capital Officer..........................	Career Incumbent	CA	ES	....	....	....
Washington, DC	Chief Administrative Officer...........................	Vacant	....	ES	....	....	....
Washington, DC	Chief Information Officer.......................	Career Incumbent	CA	ES	....	....	....
Washington, DC	Chief Information Security Officer..................	Career Incumbent	CA	ES	....	....	....
Washington, DC	Senior Procurement Executive	Career Incumbent	CA	ES	....	....	....
Washington, DC	Secretary	Career Incumbent	CA	ES	....	....	....
	OFFICE OF WORKPLACE DIVERSITY						
Washington, DC	Director........................	Career Incumbent	CA	ES	....	....	....
	PUBLIC SAFETY AND HOMELAND SECURITY BUREAU						
Washington, DC	Bureau Chief....................................	Career Incumbent	CA	ES	....	....	....
Washington, DC	Deputy Bureau Chief	Career Incumbent	CA	ES	....	....	....
Washington, DC	Deputy Bureau Chief	Career Incumbent	CA	ES	....	....	....
Washington, DC	Deputy Bureau Chief	Career Incumbent	CA	ES	....	....	....
Washington, DC	Deputy Bureau Chief	Career Incumbent	CA	ES	....	....	....
	SPACE BUREAU						
Washington, DC	Bureau Chief....................................	Career Incumbent	CA	ES	....	....	....
Washington, DC	Deputy Bureau Chief	Career Incumbent	CA	ES	....	....	....
Washington, DC	Deputy Bureau Chief	Career Incumbent	CA	ES	....	....	....
	WIRELINE COMPETITION BUREAU						
Washington, DC	Bureau Chief....................................	Career Incumbent	CA	ES	....	....	....
Washington, DC	Deputy Bureau Chief	Career Incumbent	CA	ES	....	....	....
	WIRELESS TELECOMMUNICATIONS BUREAU						
Washington, DC	Bureau Chief....................................	Career Incumbent	CA	ES	....	....	....
Washington, DC	Deputy Bureau Chief	Career Incumbent	CA	ES	....	....	....
Washington, DC	Deputy Bureau Chief	Career Incumbent	CA	ES	....	....	....

FEDERAL DEPOSIT INSURANCE CORPORATION

Location	Position Title	Name of Incumbent	Type of Appt.	Pay Plan	Level, Grade, or Pay	Tenure	Expires
Washington, DC	Chairman of the Board of Directors (Director).	Martin J Gruenberg............	PAS	EX	III	5	12/22/27
Washington, DC	Vice Chairman	Travis John Hill	PAS	EX	IV	6	12/22/28
Washington, DC	Member of the Board of Directors.....................	Jonathan Patrick McKernan.	PAS	EX	IV	6	12/22/28
	FEDERAL DEPOSIT INSURANCE CORPORATION, OFFICE OF THE INSPECTOR GENERAL						
Washington, DC	Inspector General	Jennifer Fain	PAS	EX	III	....	....

FEDERAL ELECTION COMMISSION

Location	Position Title	Name of Incumbent	Type of Appt.	Pay Plan	Level, Grade, or Pay	Tenure	Expires
Washington, DC	Commissioner Member....................................	Shana M Broussard	PAS	EX	IV	6	....
Washington, DC	Commissioner Member....................................	James Edwin Trainor..........	PAS	EX	IV	6	....
Washington, DC	Commissioner Member....................................	Ellen L Weintraub................	PAS	EX	IV	6	....
Washington, DC	Commissioner Member....................................	Dara Lindenbaum................	PAS	EX	IV	6	....
Washington, DC	Commissioner Member....................................	Allen Dickerson	PAS	EX	IV	6	....
Washington, DC	Commissioner Member....................................	Sean J Cooksey	PAS	EX	IV	6	....
Washington, DC	Staff Director	David A Palmer	XS	EX	IV	....	....
Washington, DC	General Counsel	Vacant	....	EX	....	....	....
Washington, DC	Deputy Staff Director for Management and Administration.	Dayna Brown......................	XS	SL	....	....	....
Washington, DC	Deputy General for General Law and Advice ...	Lisa Stevenson	XS	SL	....	....	....
Washington, DC	Associate General Counsel - Policy	Neven Stipanovic	XS	SL	....	....	....
Washington, DC	Chief Compliance Officer	Patricia C Orrock	XS	SL	....	....	....
Washington, DC	Deputy Staff Director for Communications......	Vacant	....	SL	....	....	....
Washington, DC	Deputy General Counsel for Administration.....	Gregory Baker	XS	SL	....	....	....
Washington, DC	Associate General Counsel for Enforcement	Charles Kitcher	XS	SL	....	....	....
Washington, DC	Associate General Counsel for Litigation	Vacant	....	SL	....	....	....
Washington, DC	Chief Information Officer.................................	David A Palmer	XS	SL	....	....	....
Washington, DC	Chief Financial Officer	John Quinlan......................	XS	SL	....	....	....
Washington, DC	Executive Assistant	Esther Gyory	XS	GS	15	....	....
Washington, DC	Executive Assistant	Phillip Olaya	XS	GS	15	....	....
Washington, DC	Executive Assistant (Chair/Vice Chair)	Amanda Gould......................	XS	GS	15	....	....
Washington, DC	Executive Assistant (Floater)	Elizabeth Kemp...................	XS	GS	15	....	....
Washington, DC	Executive Assistant	Ashley Stow	XS	GS	15	....	....
Washington, DC	Executive Assistant	Alyssa Specht	XS	GS	15	....	....
Washington, DC	Executive Assistant	Danna Seligman...................	XS	GS	15	....	....
Washington, DC	Executive Assistant	Dania Korkor......................	XS	GS	15	....	....
Washington, DC	Executive Assistant	Vacant	....	GS	....	....	....
Washington, DC	Executive Assistant	Nicholas Bamman................	XS	GS	15	....	....
Washington, DC	Executive Assistant (Chair/Vice Chair)	Vacant	....	GS	....	....	....
Washington, DC	Executive Assistant (Floater)	Vacant	....	GS	....	....	....
Washington, DC	Executive Assistant	Gabriela Fallon...................	XS	GS	15	....	....
Washington, DC	Executive Assistant	Richard Austin Graham	XS	GS	15	....	....
Washington, DC	Executive Assistant	Zachary Robert Morgan.......	XS	GS	15	....	....
Washington, DC	Executive Assistant	Jenna Kirsch........................	XS	GS	15	....	....

FEDERAL ELECTION COMMISSION OFFICE OF THE INSPECTOR GENERAL

Location	Position Title	Name of Incumbent	Type of Appt.	Pay Plan	Level, Grade, or Pay	Tenure	Expires
Washington, DC	Inspector General	Vacant	....	SL	....	....	....
Washington, DC	Deputy Inspector General...................................	Michael Mitchell..................	XS	SL	....	....	....

FEDERAL ENERGY REGULATORY COMMISSION

Location	Position Title	Name of Incumbent	Type of Appt.	Pay Plan	Level, Grade, or Pay	Tenure	Expires
	OFFICE OF THE CHAIRMAN						
Washington, DC	Chairman-Federal Energy Regulatory Commission.	Willie Phillips......................	PAS	EX	III	....	06/30/26
	Office of the Commissioner						
Washington, DC	Member-Federal Energy Regulatory Commission.	Mark Christie......................	PAS	EX	IV	....	06/30/25
Washington, DC	Member-Federal Energy Regulatory Commission.	David Rosner......................	PAS	EX	IV	....	06/30/27
Washington, DC	Member-Federal Energy Regulatory Commission.	Lindsay See	PAS	EX	IV	....	06/30/28
Washington, DC	Member-Federal Energy Regulatory Commission.	Judy W Chang.....................	PAS	EX	IV	....	....
Washington, DC	Economic Advisor...	Mannshya Grace Hu............	SC	GS	15	....	....
Washington, DC	Confidential Assistant......................................	Ashley Ingebrigtsen	SC	GS	12	....	....
	Office of General Counsel						
Washington, DC	General Counsel	Vacant	....	ES	....	....	....
Washington, DC	Associate General Counsel, Energy Projects.....	Career Incumbent	CA	ES	....	....	....
Washington, DC	Associate General Counsel, General and Administrative Law.	Career Incumbent	CA	ES	....	....	....
Washington, DC	Solicitor...	Career Incumbent	CA	ES	....	....	....
Washington, DC	Deputy Associate General Counsel, Energy Projects.	Career Incumbent	CA	ES	....	....	....
Washington, DC	Associate General Counsel...............................	Vacant	....	ES	....	....	....
Washington, DC	Associate General Counsel...............................	Career Incumbent	CA	ES	....	....	....
Washington, DC	Deputy General Counsel...................................	Career Incumbent	CA	ES	....	....	....
	Office of External Affairs						
Washington, DC	Senior Public Affairs Specialist	Benjamin Williams...............	SC	GS	15	....	....
	Office of Energy Projects						
Washington, DC	Director, Office of Energy Projects	Career Incumbent	CA	ES	....	....	....
Washington, DC	Deputy Director, Office of Energy Projects.......	Career Incumbent	CA	ES	....	....	....
Washington, DC	Director, Hydropower Administration and Compliance.	Career Incumbent	CA	ES	....	....	....
Washington, DC	Director, Gas Environment and Engineering....	Vacant	....	ES	....	....	....
Washington, DC	Director, Hydropower Licensing	Vacant	....	ES	....	....	....
Washington, DC	Director, Division of LNG Facility Review and Inspections.	Career Incumbent	CA	ES	....	....	....
Washington, DC	Director, Division of Pipeline Certificates..........	Career Incumbent	CA	ES	....	....	....
	Office of Administrative Litigation						
Washington, DC	Director, Office of Administrative Litigation	Career Incumbent	CA	ES	....	....	....
Washington, DC	Director, Technical Division	Career Incumbent	CA	ES	....	....	....
	Office of The Executive Director						
Washington, DC	Executive Director	Career Incumbent	CA	ES	....	....	....
Washington, DC	Chief Information Officer	Career Incumbent	CA	ES	....	....	....
Washington, DC	Chief Human Capital Officer............................	Career Incumbent	CA	ES	....	....	....
Washington, DC	Chief Financial Officer.....................................	Career Incumbent	CA	ES	....	....	....
Washington, DC	Chief Security Officer.......................................	Career Incumbent	CA	ES	....	....	....
	Office of Energy Market Regulation						
Washington, DC	Deputy Director, Office of Energy Market Regulation.	Career Incumbent	CA	ES	....	....	....
Washington, DC	Director, Division of Electric Power Regulation- West.	Career Incumbent	CA	ES	....	....	....
Washington, DC	Director, Division of Electric Power Regulation- Central.	Career Incumbent	CA	ES	....	....	....
Washington, DC	Director, Division of Electric Power Regulation- East.	Career Incumbent	CA	ES	....	....	....
Washington, DC	Director, Office of Energy Market Regulation...	Career Incumbent	CA	ES	....	....	....
Washington, DC	Director, Division of Pipeline Regulation...........	Career Incumbent	CA	ES	....	....	....
	Office of Enforcement						
Washington, DC	Director, Investigations	Career Incumbent	CA	ES	....	....	....
Washington, DC	Director, Office of Enforcement	Career Incumbent	CA	ES	....	....	....
Washington, DC	Deputy Director, Office of Enforcement	Career Incumbent	CA	ES	....	....	....
Washington, DC	Director, Division of Analytics and Surveillance.	Career Incumbent	CA	ES	....	....	....
	Office of Electric Reliability						
Washington, DC	Director, Office of Electric Reliability	Career Incumbent	CA	ES	....	....	....
Washington, DC	Deputy Director, Office of Electric Reliability ...	Career Incumbent	CA	ES	....	....	....
Washington, DC	Director, Division of Compliance	Career Incumbent	CA	ES	....	....	....
Washington, DC	Director, Division of Reliability Standards........	Career Incumbent	CA	ES	....	....	....

FEDERAL ENERGY REGULATORY COMMISSION—Continued

Location	Position Title	Name of Incumbent	Type of Appt.	Pay Plan	Level, Grade, or Pay	Tenure	Expires
Washington, DC	Director, Division of Engineering and Logistics.	Career Incumbent	CA	ES	....	....	....
Washington, DC	*Office of Energy Policy and Innovation* Deputy Director, Office of Energy Policy and Innovation.	Career Incumbent	CA	ES	....	....	....
Washington, DC	Director Office of Energy Policy and Innovation.	Career Incumbent	CA	ES	....	....	....
Washington, DC	Director, Economic and Technical Analysis	Career Incumbent	CA	ES	....	....	....
Washington, DC	Director, Policy Development	Career Incumbent	CA	ES	....	....	....
Washington, DC	Director, Division of Energy Market Assessments.	Career Incumbent	CA	ES	....	....	....
Washington, DC	*Office of the Secretary* Secretary of the Commission	Career Incumbent	....	ES	....	....	....
Washington, DC	*Office Of Energy Infrastructure Security* Director, Office of Energy Infrastructure Security.	Career Incumbent	CA	ES	....	....	....
Washington, DC	Deputy Director	Career Incumbent	CA	ES	....	....	....
Washington, DC	Senior Advisor	Career Incumbent	CA	ES	....	....	....
Washington, DC	*Office of Public Participation* Director, Office of Public Participation	Career Incumbent	CA	ES	....	....	....

FEDERAL HOUSING FINANCE AGENCY

Location	Position Title	Name of Incumbent	Type of Appt.	Pay Plan	Level, Grade, or Pay	Tenure	Expires
Washington, DC	**OFFICE OF DIRECTOR** Director	Sandra L Thompson	PAS	EX	II	....	....
Washington, DC	**INSPECTOR GENERAL** Inspector General	Brian Tomney	PAS	EX	....	....	02/01/26

FEDERAL LABOR RELATIONS AUTHORITY

Location	Position Title	Name of Incumbent	Type of Appt.	Pay Plan	Level, Grade, or Pay	Tenure	Expires
Washington, DC	**OFFICE OF THE CHAIRMAN** Chairman	Susan Tsui Grundmann	PAS	EX	IV	5	07/01/25
Washington, DC	*Foreign Services Labor Relations Board* Member, Foreign Service Labor Relations Board.	Thomas J Miller	XS	SL	....	....	10/06/24
Washington, DC	Member, Foreign Service Labor Relations Board.	Dennis Hays	XS	SL	....	....	10/06/24
Washington, DC	**OFFICE OF THE MEMBER** Member	Colleen D Kiko	PAS	EX	V	5	01/20/26
Washington, DC	**FEDERAL SERVICE IMPASSES PANEL** Chair, Federal Service Impasses Panel	Martin Howard Malin	PA	SL	....	....	01/22/25
Washington, DC	Member, Federal Service Impasses Panel	Marvin E Johnson	PA	SL	....	....	01/11/27
Washington, DC	Member, Federal Service Impasses Panel	Jeanne Charles	PA	SL	....	....	01/11/25
Washington, DC	Member, Federal Service Impasses Panel	Howard Friedman	PA	SL	....	....	01/10/29
Washington, DC	Member, Federal Service Impasses Panel	Pamela Schwartz	PA	SL	....	....	01/10/29
Washington, DC	Member, Federal Service Impasses Panel	Joseph Slater	PA	SL	....	....	01/10/27
Washington, DC	Member, Federal Service Impasses Panel	Mark Gaston Pearce	PA	SL	....	....	01/10/29
Washington, DC	Member, Federal Service Impasses Panel	Edward F Hartfield	PA	SL	....	....	10/02/24
Washington, DC	Member, Federal Service Impasses Panel	Wynter P Allen	PA	SL	....	....	01/11/25
Washington, DC	Member, Federal Service Impasses Panel	Martin Malin	PA	SL	....	....	....
Washington, DC	Member, Federal Service Impasses Panel	Tamiko Watkins	PA	GS	....	....	10/02/24
Washington, DC	**OFFICE OF THE GENERAL COUNSEL** General Counsel	Vacant	....	EX	....	5	....

FEDERAL MARITIME COMMISSION

Location	Position Title	Name of Incumbent	Type of Appt.	Pay Plan	Level, Grade, or Pay	Tenure	Expires
	OFFICE OF THE MEMBERS						
Washington, DC	Chairman	Daniel Benjamin Maffei	PAS	EX	III	5	06/30/27
Washington, DC	Member..	Louis Sola	PAS	EX	IV	5	06/30/23
Washington, DC	Member..	Max Vekich	PAS	EX	IV	5	06/30/26
Washington, DC	Member..	Carl Bentzel.........................	PAS	EX	IV	5	06/30/24
Washington, DC	Member..	Rebecca F Dye	PAS	EX	IV	5	06/30/25
Washington, DC	Chief of Staff..	Career Incumbent	CA	ES	....	....	....
Washington, DC	Counsel to Commissioner........................	John N Young	SC	GS	15	....	....
Washington, DC	Confidential Assistant............................	Anna N D Aprile	SC	GS	5	....	....
Washington, DC	Senior Legislative and Public Affairs Specialist.	John Kenneth Decrosta	SC	GS	15	....	....
	Office of the General Counsel						
Washington, DC	General Counsel	Career Incumbent	CA	ES	....	....	....

FEDERAL MEDIATION AND CONCILIATION SERVICE

Location	Position Title	Name of Incumbent	Type of Appt.	Pay Plan	Level, Grade, or Pay	Tenure	Expires
	OFFICE OF THE DIRECTOR						
Washington, DC	Director..	Vacant	....	EX	....	....	....
Chicago, IL	Deputy Director (Field Operations)...................	Career Incumbent	CA	ES	....	....	....
Washington, DC	Management and Program Analyst	Jourdan Smithwick	SC	GS	11	....	....
Indianola, IA	National Representative	Scot L Beckenbaugh............	XS	SL	....	....	....

FEDERAL MINE SAFETY AND HEALTH REVIEW COMMISSION

Location	Position Title	Name of Incumbent	Type of Appt.	Pay Plan	Level, Grade, or Pay	Tenure	Expires
	OFFICE OF THE COMMISSIONERS						
Washington, DC	Chairman	Mary L Jordan......................	PAS	EX	III	....	....
Washington, DC	Commissioner...	Marco M Rajkovich	PAS	EX	IV	....	....
Washington, DC	Commissioner...	Vacant	....	EX	....	6	....
Washington, DC	Commissioner...	William Ira Althen................	PAS	EX	IV	....	08/30/24
Washington, DC	Commissioner...	Timothy Baker	PAS	EX	IV	....	....
	OFFICE OF THE GENERAL COUNSEL						
Washington, DC	General Counsel	Vacant	....	ES	....	....	....
Washington, DC	General Counsel	Career Incumbent	CA	ES	....	....	....
	OFFICE OF THE CHAIRMAN						
Washington, DC	Chief Operating Officer...........................	Career Incumbent	CA	ES	....	....	....
Washington, DC	Senior Policy Advisor..............................	Vacant	....	ES	....	....	....
Washington, DC	Confidential Assistant............................	Rudolph Carlos Zepeda........	SC	GS	9	....	....

FEDERAL PERMITTING IMPROVEMENT STEERING COUNCIL

Location	Position Title	Name of Incumbent	Type of Appt.	Pay Plan	Level, Grade, or Pay	Tenure	Expires
Washington, DC	Executive Director...................................	Eric B Beightel	PA	ES	....	....	....
New Mexico, NM.....	Director of Tribal Affairs........................	Poqueen Rivera....................	SC	GS	14	....	....
Washington, DC	Chief of Staff..	Rebecca Higgins	SC	GS	15	....	....
Washington, DC	Director of Legislative and Intergovernmental Affairs.	Alexis Segal	SC	GS	15	....	....
San Francisco, CA...	Director of Public Engagement........................	Monica Sanchez....................	SC	GS	15	....	....

FEDERAL RESERVE SYSTEM

Location	Position Title	Name of Incumbent	Type of Appt.	Pay Plan	Level, Grade, or Pay	Tenure	Expires
Washington, DC	Chairman	Jerome H Powell	PAS	EX	I	4	
Washington, DC	Vice Chairman	Philip N Jefferson	PAS	EX	II	4	
Washington, DC	Board Member	Michelle W Bowman	PAS	EX	II	14	
Washington, DC	Board Member	Philip N Jefferson	PAS	EX	II	14	
Washington, DC	Board Member	Jerome H Powell	PAS	EX	II	14	
Washington, DC	Board Member	Michael Barr	PAS	EX	II	14	
Washington, DC	Board Member	Christopher Waller	PAS	EX	II	14	
Washington, DC	Vice Chair of Supervision	Michael S Barr	PAS	EX	II	14	
Washington, DC	Board Member	Adriana D Kugler	PAS	EX	II	14	
Washington, DC	Board Member	Lisa D Cook	PAS	EX	II	14	

FEDERAL RETIREMENT THRIFT INVESTMENT BOARD

Location	Position Title	Name of Incumbent	Type of Appt.	Pay Plan	Level, Grade, or Pay	Tenure	Expires
Washington, DC	Chairman of the Board	Michael Gerber	PAS	PD	IV	4	09/25/26
Washington, DC	Board Member	Dana Bilyeu	PAS	PD	IV	4	10/11/23
Washington, DC	Board Member	Leona Bridges	PAS	PD	IV	4	10/11/23
Washington, DC	Board Member	Stacie Olivares	PAS	PD	IV	4	09/25/24
Washington, DC	Board Member	Vacant		PD		4	
Washington, DC	Executive Director	Ravindra Deo	XS	EX	III		
Washington, DC	General Counsel	Career Incumbent	CA	ES			
Washington, DC	Chief Investment Officer	Career Incumbent	CA	ES			
Washington, DC	Director of Planning and Risk	Career Incumbent	CA	ES			
Washington, DC	Director of External Affairs	Career Incumbent	CA	ES			

FEDERAL TRADE COMMISSION

Location	Position Title	Name of Incumbent	Type of Appt.	Pay Plan	Level, Grade, or Pay	Tenure	Expires
	OFFICE OF THE CHAIR						
Washington, DC	Chair	Lina M Khan	PAS	EX	III	7	
Washington, DC	Chief of Staff	Sarah Beth Miller	NA	ES			
Washington, DC	Confidential Assistant	Caroline Siegel-Singh	SC	GS	11		
Washington, DC	Program Management (Special Advisor to the Chair).	Blake Narendra	SC	GS	15		
Washington, DC	Commissioner	Melissa Holyoak	PAS	EX	IV	7	
Washington, DC	Commissioner	Alvaro M Bedoya	PAS	EX	IV	7	
Washington, DC	Commissioner	Andrew Ferguson	PAS	EX	IV	7	
Washington, DC	Commissioner	Rebecca J Slaughter	PAS	EX	IV	7	
Washington, DC	Director, Office of Public Affairs	Douglas Farrar	SC	GS	15		
Washington, DC	Writer-Editor (Speechwriter)	Zehra Khan	SC	GS	13		
Washington, DC	Writer-Editor (Speechwriter)	Patrick Ross	SC	GS	13		
Washington, DC	Director, Office of Policy Planning	Hannah Garden-Monheit	NA	ES			
Washington, DC	Director, Office of Workplace Inclusivity and Opportunity.	Career Incumbent	CA	ES			
Washington, DC	Secretary	Career Incumbent	CA	ES			
	BUREAU OF COMPETITION						
Washington, DC	Director, Bureau of Competition	Henry Liu	NA	ES			
Seattle, WA	Deputy Director, Bureau of Competition	Rahul Rao	NA	ES			
San Francisco, CA	Deputy Director, Bureau of Competition	Kyle Mach	NA	ES			
Washington, DC	Deputy Director, Bureau of Competition	Laura Alexander	NA	ES			
Washington, DC	Assistant Director for Anticompetitive Practices I.	Career Incumbent	CA	ES			
Washington, DC	Assistant Director for Anticompetitive Practices II.	Career Incumbent	CA	ES			
Washington, DC	Assistant Director for Compliance	Career Incumbent	CA	ES			
Washington, DC	Assistant Director for Health Care	Vacant		ES			
Washington, DC	Assistant Director for Mergers I	Career Incumbent	CA	ES			
Washington, DC	Assistant Director for Mergers II	Career Incumbent	CA	ES			
Washington, DC	Assistant Director for Mergers III	Career Incumbent	CA	ES			
Washington, DC	Assistant Director for Mergers IV	Vacant		ES			
Washington, DC	Assistant Director for Technology Enforcement.	Career Incumbent	CA	ES			

FEDERAL TRADE COMMISSION—Continued

Location	Position Title	Name of Incumbent	Type of Appt.	Pay Plan	Level, Grade, or Pay	Tenure	Expires
	BUREAU OF CONSUMER PROTECTION						
Washington, DC	Director, Bureau of Consumer Protection..........	Samuel A Levine	NA	ES	....	....	....
Washington, DC	Deputy Director, Bureau of Consumer Protection.	Career Incumbent	CA	ES	....	....	....
Washington, DC	Deputy Director, Bureau of Consumer Protection.	Vacant	....	ES	....	....	....
Washington, DC	Associate Director for Advertising Practices	Career Incumbent	CA	ES	....	....	....
Washington, DC	Associate Director for Consumer and Business Education.	Career Incumbent	CA	ES	....	....	....
Washington, DC	Associate Director for Consumer Response and Operations.	Career Incumbent	CA	ES	....	....	....
Washington, DC	Associate Director for Enforcement	Career Incumbent	CA	ES	....	....	....
Washington, DC	Associate Director for Financial Practices.........	Career Incumbent	CA	ES	....	....	....
Washington, DC	Associate Director for Litigation Technology and Analysis.	Career Incumbent	CA	ES	....	....	....
Washington, DC	Associate Director for Marketing Practices.......	Career Incumbent	CA	ES	....	....	....
Washington, DC	Associate Director for Privacy and Identity Protection.	Career Incumbent	CA	ES	....	....	....
	BUREAU OF ECONOMICS						
Washington, DC	Deputy Director for Antitrust............................	Career Incumbent	CA	ES	....	....	....
Washington, DC	Deputy Director for Consumer Protection.........	Career Incumbent	CA	ES	....	....	....
Washington, DC	Assistant Director for Antitrust I......................	Career Incumbent	CA	ES	....	....	....
Washington, DC	Assistant Director for Antitrust II	Career Incumbent	CA	ES	....	....	....
Washington, DC	Assistant Director for Consumer Protection	Career Incumbent	CA	ES	....	....	....
	OFFICE OF EXECUTIVE DIRECTOR						
Washington, DC	Executive Director......................................	Career Incumbent	CA	ES	....	....	....
Washington, DC	Deputy Executive Director...............................	Career Incumbent	CA	ES	....	....	....
Washington, DC	Deputy Executive Director...............................	Career Incumbent	CA	ES	....	....	....
Washington, DC	Deputy Chief Information Officer	Vacant	....	ES	....	....	....
Washington, DC	Chief Administrative Services Officer...............	Career Incumbent	CA	ES	....	....	....
Washington, DC	Chief Financial Officer	Career Incumbent	CA	ES	....	....	....
Washington, DC	Chief Human Capital Officer............................	Vacant	....	ES	....	....	....
	OFFICE OF THE GENERAL COUNSEL						
Washington, DC	General Counsel	Anisha Sasheen Dasgupta...	NA	ES	....	....	....
Washington, DC	Deputy General Counsel for Litigation..............	Vacant	....	ES	....	....	....
Washington, DC	Deputy General Counsel for Legal Counsel	Vacant	....	ES	....	....	....
	OFFICE OF INTERNATIONAL AFFAIRS						
Washington, DC	Director, Office of International Affairs	Career Incumbent	CA	ES	....	....	....
Washington, DC	Deputy Director for International Consumer Protection.	Career Incumbent	CA	ES	....	....	....
	OFFICE OF TECHNOLOGY						
Washington, DC	Chief Technology Officer	Stephanie Nguyen................	NA	ES	....	....	....

GENERAL SERVICES ADMINISTRATION

Location	Position Title	Name of Incumbent	Type of Appt.	Pay Plan	Level, Grade, or Pay	Tenure	Expires
	OFFICE OF THE ADMINISTRATOR						
Washington, DC	Administrator of General Services.....................	Robin C Carnahan	PAS	EX	III	....	....
Washington, DC	Deputy Administrator	Katy A Kale	NA	ES	....	....	....
Washington, DC	Chief of Staff..	Brett J Prather.....................	NA	ES	....	....	....
Washington, DC	Deputy Chief of Staff for Policy	Jetta L Wong	SC	GS	15	....	....
Washington, DC	Deputy Chief of Staff for Operations	Trevor D Jones	SC	GS	15	....	....
Washington, DC	Senior Advisor to the Administrator (Delivery).	Michael P Flowers................	SC	GS	15	....	....
Washington, DC	Chief of Staff to the Deputy Administrator.......	Phuong-Quynh Tran	SC	GS	15	....	....
Washington, DC	Senior Advisor to the Deputy Administrator.....	Christine M Simpson	SC	GS	15	....	....
Washington, DC	Special Assistant...	Samuel A Herget..................	SC	GS	11	....	....
Washington, DC	Special Assistant...	James R Benner	SC	GS	9	....	....
Washington, DC	Executive Director, Technology Modernization Fund.	Career Incumbent	CA	ES	....	....	....
	FEDERAL ACQUISITION SERVICE						
Washington, DC	Commissioner..	Vacant	....	ES	....	....	....
Washington, DC	Deputy Commissioner	Career Incumbent	CA	ES	....	....	....
Washington, DC	Senior Advisor..	Kusai A Merchant................	SC	GS	15	....	....

GENERAL SERVICES ADMINISTRATION—Continued

Location	Position Title	Name of Incumbent	Type of Appt.	Pay Plan	Level, Grade, or Pay	Tenure	Expires
	TECHNOLOGY TRANSFORMATION SERVICES						
Washington, DC	Deputy Commissioner and Director of Technology Transformation Services.	Ann L Lewis	NA	ES	....	....	....
Portland, OR............	Deputy Director, Technology Transformation Services.	Career Incumbent	CA	ES	....	....	....
Washington, DC	Executive Director for Cloud Strategy...............	Eric R Mill	SC	SL	....	....	....
Washington, DC	Assistant Commissioner for Solutions	Career Incumbent	CA	ES	....	....	....
	PUBLIC BUILDINGS SERVICE						
Washington, DC	Commissioner...	Elliot D Doomes	NA	ES	....	....	....
Washington, DC	Deputy Commissioner	Career Incumbent	CA	ES	....	....	....
New York, NY.........	Director of Special Appropriations	Darin C Frost	TA	ES	....	....	04/22/26
	OFFICE OF GOVERNMENTWIDE POLICY						
Washington, DC	Associate Administrator for Governmentwide Policy.	Krystal Brumfield	NA	....	....	....	....
Washington, DC	Principal Deputy Associate Administrator for Governmentwide Policy.	Career Incumbent	CA	ES	....	....	....
	OFFICE OF ADMINISTRATIVE SERVICES						
Washington, DC	Chief Administrative Services Officer................	Career Incumbent	CA	ES	....	....	....
	OFFICE OF CIVIL RIGHTS						
Washington, DC	Associate Administrator for Civil Rights...........	Career Incumbent	CA	ES	....	....	....
	OFFICE OF STRATEGIC COMMUNICATION						
Washington, DC	Associate Administrator for Strategic Communication.	Channing A Grate...............	NA	ES	....	....	....
Washington, DC	Deputy Associate Administrator for Public Affairs.	Rachel L Davis Disbrow	SC	GS	15	....	....
Washington, DC	Speechwriter and Public Engagement Advisor .	Amelia Cohen-Levy..............	SC	GS	15	....	....
	OFFICE OF CONGRESSIONAL AND INTERGOVERNMENTAL AFFAIRS						
Washington, DC	Associate Administrator for Congressional and Intergovernmental Affairs.	Gianelle E Rivera................	NA	ES	....	....	....
Washington, DC	Policy Advisor...	Janay S Eyo.........................	SC	GS	13	....	....
Washington, DC	Policy Advisor...	Bryce C Causey	SC	GS	13	....	....
	OFFICE OF CUSTOMER EXPERIENCE						
Washington, DC	Chief Customer Officer	Vacant	....	ES	....	....	....
	OFFICE OF THE GENERAL COUNSEL						
Washington, DC	General Counsel	Alexander W Demots	NA	ES	....	....	....
Washington, DC	Deputy General Counsel	Fernando R Laguarda..........	NA	ES	....	....	....
Washington, DC	Oversight Attorney	Brandon T Faske..................	SC	GS	14	....	....
Washington, DC	Deputy General Counsel	Career Incumbent	CA	ES	....	....	....
Washington, DC	Associate General Counsel for Ethics Law........	Career Incumbent	CA	ES	....	....	....
Washington, DC	Associate General Counsel for General Law	Career Incumbent	CA	ES	....	....	....
Washington, DC	Associate General Counsel for Personal Property.	Career Incumbent	CA	ES	....	....	....
Washington, DC	Associate General Counsel for Real Property ...	Career Incumbent	CA	ES	....	....	....
Washington, DC	Associate General Counsel for Technology Law.	Career Incumbent	CA	ES	....	....	....
San Francisco, CA...	Regional Counsel, Pacific Rim Region	Career Incumbent	CA	ES	....	....	....
	OFFICE OF GSA IT						
Washington, DC	Chief Information Officer....................................	Career Incumbent	CA	ES	....	....	....
Washington, DC	Deputy Chief Information Officer	Vacant	....	ES	....	....	....
	OFFICE OF SMALL AND DISADVANTAGED BUSINESS UTILIZATION						
Washington, DC	Associate Administrator for Small and Disadvantaged Business Utilization.	Exodie C Roe III...................	NA	ES	....	....	....
	REGIONAL ADMINISTRATORS						
	National Capital Region						
Washington, DC	Regional Administrator..	Vacant	....	ES	....	....	....
Washington, DC	Special Assistant to the Regional Administrator.	Natasha S Syed....................	SC	GS	12	....	....
	Northeast And Caribbean Region						
New York, NY.........	Regional Administrator..	Francis A Thomas	NA	ES	....	....	....
Washington, DC	Special Assistant to the Regional Administrator.	Keonte A Lee	SC	GS	11	....	....

GENERAL SERVICES ADMINISTRATION—Continued

Location	Position Title	Name of Incumbent	Type of Appt.	Pay Plan	Level, Grade, or Pay	Tenure	Expires
Philadelphia, PA	*Mid-Atlantic Region* Regional Administrator..	Vacant	....	ES	....	....	....
Atlanta, GA	*Southeast Sunbelt Region* Regional Administrator..	Jason L Shelton...................	NA	ES	....	....	....
Washington, DC	Special Assistant to the Regional Administrator.	Nicolas D Valbuena.............	SC	GS	11	....	....
Lakewood, CO	*Rocky Mountain Region* Regional Administrator..	Denise S Maes......................	NA	ES	....	....	....
San Francisco, CA...	*Pacific Rim Region* Regional Administrator..	Sukhee Kang	NA	ES	....	....	....
Washington, DC	Special Assistant to the Regional Administrator.	Morgan N Carrico	SC	GS	11	....	....

GENERAL SERVICES ADMINISTRATION OFFICE OF THE INSPECTOR GENERAL

Location	Position Title	Name of Incumbent	Type of Appt.	Pay Plan	Level, Grade, or Pay	Tenure	Expires
Washington, DC	Inspector General	Vacant	....	EX	....	....	....

GREAT LAKES FISHERY COMMISSION

Location	Position Title	Name of Incumbent	Type of Appt.	Pay Plan	Level, Grade, or Pay	Tenure	Expires
Ann Arbor, MI	Commissioner..	Kendra Wecker	PA	WC	....	....	12/18/30
Ann Arbor, MI	Commissioner Member...	Ethan Baker	PA	WC	....	6	02/18/26
Ann Arbor, MI	Commissioner Member...	William Taylor	PA	WC	....	....	....
Ann Arbor, MI	Commissioner Member...	Karen Diver	PA	WC	....	6	04/11/28
Ann Arbor, MI	Commissioner Member...	Shannon Estenoz...................	PA	WC	....	....	....

GULF COAST ECOSYSTEM RESTORATION COUNCIL

Location	Position Title	Name of Incumbent	Type of Appt.	Pay Plan	Level, Grade, or Pay	Tenure	Expires
New Orleans, LA.....	Executive Director...	Career Incumbent	CA	ES	....	....	....

HARRY S TRUMAN SCHOLARSHIP FOUNDATION

Location	Position Title	Name of Incumbent	Type of Appt.	Pay Plan	Level, Grade, or Pay	Tenure	Expires
Washington, DC	**OFFICE OF EXECUTIVE SECRETARY** Executive Secretary..............................	Career Incumbent	CA	ES	....	....	....
Washington, DC	**BOARD OF TRUSTEES** Member, Board of Trustees	Stacey Brandenburg	PAS	WC	....	....	12/10/25
Washington, DC	Member, Board of Trustees	Audrey Schuster...................	PAS	WC	....	....	12/10/25
Washington, DC	Member, Board of Trustees	Todd Gloria	PAS	WC	....	....	....
Washington, DC	Member, Board of Trustees	Betty Jang	PAS	WC	....	....	....

INSTITUTE OF MUSEUM AND LIBRARY SERVICES

Location	Position Title	Name of Incumbent	Type of Appt.	Pay Plan	Level, Grade, or Pay	Tenure	Expires
Washington, DC	Director, Institute of Museum and Library Services.	Vacant	....	EX	....	4	01/23/24

INSTITUTE OF MUSEUM AND LIBRARY SERVICES—Continued

Location	Position Title	Name of Incumbent	Type of Appt.	Pay Plan	Level, Grade, or Pay	Tenure	Expires
Washington, DC	General Counsel	Vacant	....	ES	....	....	....
Washington, DC	Chief Operating Officer......	Career Incumbent	CA	ES	....	....	....
	NATIONAL MUSEUM AND LIBRARY SERVICES BOARD						
Washington, DC	Member......	William T Harris	PA	OT	....	....	12/06/25
Washington, DC	Member......	Brian T Allen......	PA	OT	....	....	12/06/26
Washington, DC	Member......	Allison Perkins	PA	OT	....	....	12/06/24
Washington, DC	Member......	Kelli A Mosteller	PA	OT	....	....	12/06/26
Washington, DC	Member......	Monica Ramirez-Montagut..	PA	OT	....	....	12/06/25
Washington, DC	Member......	Julius Jefferson	PA	OT	....	....	12/06/27
Washington, DC	Member......	Halona Norton-Westbrook ...	PA	OT	....	....	12/06/28
Washington, DC	Member......	Lisa R Hathaway	PA	OT	....	....	12/06/26
Washington, DC	Member......	Cameron Kitchin	PA	OT	....	....	12/06/27
Washington, DC	Member......	Annie Norman....................	PA	OT	....	....	12/06/24
Washington, DC	Member......	Amy Gilman	PA	OT	....	....	12/06/27
Washington, DC	Member......	Marylynn Mack	PA	OT	....	....	12/06/26
Washington, DC	Member......	Susan Lynn Gibbons...........	PA	OT	....	....	12/06/27
Washington, DC	Member......	Ashley Jordan......................	PA	OT	....	....	12/06/26
Washington, DC	Member......	Alan C Price	PA	OT	....	....	12/06/24
Washington, DC	Member......	Ramiro S Salazar	PA	OT	....	....	12/06/25
Washington, DC	Member......	Dipesh Navsaria..................	PA	OT	....	....	12/06/28
Washington, DC	Member......	James G Neal	PA	OT	....	....	12/06/28
Washington, DC	Member......	Timothy Murphy	PA	OT	....	....	12/06/28
Washington, DC	Member......	Joan Breier-Brodsky	PA	OT	....	....	12/06/24

INTERAGENCY COUNCIL ON THE HOMELESS

Location	Position Title	Name of Incumbent	Type of Appt.	Pay Plan	Level, Grade, or Pay	Tenure	Expires
Washington, DC	Executive Director	Jeffrey Olivet........................	XS	AD	....	....	....

INTER-AMERICAN FOUNDATION

Location	Position Title	Name of Incumbent	Type of Appt.	Pay Plan	Level, Grade, or Pay	Tenure	Expires
Washington, DC	Board Member (Chair)	Eduardo Arriola....................	PAS	WC	....	6	10/06/16
Washington, DC	Board Member (Vice Chair)......	Juan Carlos Iturregui	PAS	WC	....	6	06/26/20
Washington, DC	Board Member	Kelly J Ryan	PAS	WC	....	6	09/20/12
Washington, DC	Board Member	Luis A Viada	PAS	WC	....	6	09/20/18
Washington, DC	Board Member	Vacant	....	WC	....	6	....
Washington, DC	Board Member	Vacant	....	WC	....	6	....
Washington, DC	Board Member	Vacant	....	WC	....	6	....
Washington, DC	Board Member	Vacant	....	WC	....	6	....
Washington, DC	Board Member	Vacant	....	WC	....	6	....

INTER-AMERICAN DEVELOPMENT BANK

Location	Position Title	Name of Incumbent	Type of Appt.	Pay Plan	Level, Grade, or Pay	Tenure	Expires
Washington, DC	United States Alternate Executive Director......	Maria Fabiana Jorge............	PAS	EX	....	....	....

INTERNATIONAL BOUNDARY AND WATER COMMISSION

Location	Position Title	Name of Incumbent	Type of Appt.	Pay Plan	Level, Grade, or Pay	Tenure	Expires
Dallas, TX................	Commissioner......	Maria Elena Giner...............	PA	AD	....	....	....

INTERNATIONAL JOINT COMMISSION

Location	Position Title	Name of Incumbent	Type of Appt.	Pay Plan	Level, Grade, or Pay	Tenure	Expires
	OFFICE OF THE CHAIR						
Washington, DC	Commissioner (Chair)	Gerald Acker.........................	PAS	EX	....	....	....
	INTERNATIONAL JOINT COMMISSION						
Washington, DC	Commissioner...	Lance Virgil Yohe	PAS	EX	....	....	....
Washington, DC	Commissioner...	Robert Gioia..........................	PAS	EX	....	....	....

INTERSTATE COMMISSION ON THE POTOMAC RIVER BASIN

Location	Position Title	Name of Incumbent	Type of Appt.	Pay Plan	Level, Grade, or Pay	Tenure	Expires
	EMERGENCY MANAGEMENT EXTERNAL AFFAIRS ASSOCIATION						
Washington, DC	CFO...	Darryl J Madden..................	PA	WC	....	....	....
	SUSSMAN AND ASSOCIATES						
Washington, DC	Principal	Robert M Sussman...............	PA	WC	....	....	....
	U.S. ARMY CORPS OF ENGINEERS, NORTH ATLANTIC DIVISION						
Washington, DC	Commander...	John P. Lloyd	PA	WC	....	....	....

JAMES MADISON MEMORIAL FELLOWSHIP FOUNDATION

Location	Position Title	Name of Incumbent	Type of Appt.	Pay Plan	Level, Grade, or Pay	Tenure	Expires
Washington, DC	President	Lewis Larsen	XS	EX	III	....	....
Washington, DC	Board Member (U.S. Senator)............................	Joe Manchin	PA	OT	....	....	12/22/28
Washington, DC	Board Member (U.S. Senator)............................	Roger Wicker	PA	OT	....	....	12/22/28
Washington, DC	Board Member (Judiciary).................................	Terrence Berg......................	PA	OT	....	....	10/03/24
Washington, DC	Board Member (Public 1)..................................	Terrence Wright	PAS	OT	....	....	05/09/25
Washington, DC	Board Member	Bradford Wilson	PAS	....	....	....	09/27/26
Washington, DC	Board Member	Raymond Kethledge............	PA	....	....	....	11/14/27
Washington, DC	Board Member	Laura Dove	PAS	....	....	....	11/17/29

JAPAN-UNITED STATES FRIENDSHIP COMMISSION

Location	Position Title	Name of Incumbent	Type of Appt.	Pay Plan	Level, Grade, or Pay	Tenure	Expires
Washington, DC	Executive Director..	Career Incumbent	CA	ES	....	....	....

MARINE MAMMAL COMMISSION

Location	Position Title	Name of Incumbent	Type of Appt.	Pay Plan	Level, Grade, or Pay	Tenure	Expires
San Rafael, CA........	Chairman	Frances M Gulland	PAS	PD	....	....	05/13/12
Seattle, WA..............	Commissioner...	Sue Moore............................	PAS	PD	....	....	05/13/23
Beaufort, NC	Commissioner...	Andrew Read	PAS	PD	....	....	05/13/25

MEDICAID AND CHIP PAYMENT AND ACCESS COMMISSION

Location	Position Title	Name of Incumbent	Type of Appt.	Pay Plan	Level, Grade, or Pay	Tenure	Expires
Washington, DC	Executive Director..	Katherine Massey	XS	AD	....	....	....
Washington, DC	Policy Director...	Joanne Jee	XS	AD	....	....	....

MEDICAID AND CHIP PAYMENT AND ACCESS COMMISSION—Continued

Location	Position Title	Name of Incumbent	Type of Appt.	Pay Plan	Level, Grade, or Pay	Tenure	Expires
Washington, DC	Deputy Director for Operations, Finance and Management.	Vacant	....	AD	....	....	....
Washington, DC	Communications Director	Caroline Broder....................	XS	AD	....	....	....
Washington, DC	Policy Director...............................	Kirstin Blom........................	XS	AD	....	....	....
Washington, DC	Commissioner................................	Melanie Marie Bella	XS	PD	....	3	04/30/24
Washington, DC	Commissioner................................	Robert Duncan	XS	PD	....	3	....
Washington, DC	Commissioner................................	Katherine A Weno	XS	PD	....	3	04/30/21
Washington, DC	Commissioner................................	Angelo Giardino	XS	PD	....	3	04/30/25
Washington, DC	Commissioner................................	Jennifer L Gerstorff............	XS	PD	....	3	04/30/25
Washington, DC	Commissioner................................	Patricia Ann Brooks............	XS	PD	....	3	04/30/22
Washington, DC	Commissioner................................	Dennis Heaphy.....................	XS	PD	....	3	04/30/25
Washington, DC	Commissioner................................	Carolyn Ingram...................	XS	PD	....	3	04/30/26
Washington, DC	Commissioner................................	Patti Killingsworth..............	XS	PD	....	3	04/30/26
Washington, DC	Commissioner................................	John B McCarthy	XS	PD	....	3	04/30/24
Washington, DC	Commissioner................................	Rhonda Medows	XS	PD	....	3	04/30/25
Washington, DC	Commissioner................................	Jami Snyder........................	XS	PD	....	3	04/30/26
Washington, DC	Commissioner................................	Verlon Johnson	XS	PD	....	3	....
Washington, DC	Commissioner................................	Timothy B Hill	XS	PD	....	3	....
Washington, DC	Commissioner................................	Vacant	....	PD	....	3	....
Washington, DC	Commissioner................................	Heidi Allen..........................	XS	PD	....	3	04/30/24
Washington, DC	Commissioner................................	Sonja Bjork.........................	XS	PD	....	3	04/30/25

MEDICARE PAYMENT ADVISORY COMMISSION

Location	Position Title	Name of Incumbent	Type of Appt.	Pay Plan	Level, Grade, or Pay	Tenure	Expires
Washington, DC	Executive Director...............................	Paul Masi............................	XS	OT	....	....	....
Washington, DC	Chairman	Michael Chernew	XS	OT	....	....	....
Washington, DC	Vice Chairman	Amol Navathe......................	XS	OT	....	....	....

MERIT SYSTEMS PROTECTION BOARD

Location	Position Title	Name of Incumbent	Type of Appt.	Pay Plan	Level, Grade, or Pay	Tenure	Expires
	OFFICE OF THE BOARD, CHAIRMAN						
Washington, DC	Chairman	Cathy Ann Harris	PAS	EX	III	....	03/01/28
Washington, DC	Executive Director...............................	Career Incumbent	CA	ES	....	....	....
Washington, DC	Confidential Assistant to the Chairman...........	Alicia Horton	SC	GS	15	....	....
	Office of the Board, Vice Chairman						
Washington, DC	Vice Chairman	Raymond A Limon...............	PAS	EX	IV	....	03/01/25
Washington, DC	Confidential Assistant to the Vice Chairman....	Ann E Burroughs Sun	SC	GS	14	....	....
	Office of the Board, Member						
Washington, DC	Member..	Henry Kerner	PAS	EX	IV	....	03/01/30
	Office of Appeals Counsel						
Washington, DC	Director, Office of Appeals Counsel	Career Incumbent	CA	ES	....	....	....
	Office of the General Counsel						
Washington, DC	General Counsel	Allison J Boyle.....................	NA	ES	....	....	....

MILLENNIUM CHALLENGE CORPORATION

Location	Position Title	Name of Incumbent	Type of Appt.	Pay Plan	Level, Grade, or Pay	Tenure	Expires
	OFFICE OF THE CHIEF EXECUTIVE OFFICER						
Washington, DC	Chief Executive Officer	Alice P Albright....................	PAS	EX	II	....	....
Washington, DC	Deputy Chief Executive Officer.......................	Chidi Blyden........................	XS	OT	....	....	....
Washington, DC	Board Member	Vacant	....	OT	....	....	....
Washington, DC	Board Member	Alexander Crenshaw...........	PAS	OT	....	....	....
Washington, DC	Board Member	Vacant	....	OT	....	....	....
Washington, DC	Board Member	Vacant	....	OT	....	....	....

MILLENNIUM CHALLENGE CORPORATION—Continued

Location	Position Title	Name of Incumbent	Type of Appt.	Pay Plan	Level, Grade, or Pay	Tenure	Expires
Washington, DC	Senior Advisor	Maria Paula Garcia Tufro ...	XS	OT			
Washington, DC	Chief of Staff	Keri Marie Lowry	XS	OT			
Washington, DC	Special Advisor	Sierra K Rothermich	XS	OT			
Washington, DC	Special Assistant	Habebah Mounib	PA	OT			
Washington, DC	Special Assistant	Laila B Hawkins	XS	OT			
Washington, DC	Speechwriter and Communications Advisor	Lianna Havel	XS	OT			
	DEPARTMENT OF POLICY AND EVALUATION						
Washington, DC	Vice President	Alicia P Mandaville	XS	OT			
	OFFICE OF THE GENERAL COUNSEL						
Washington, DC	Vice President and General Counsel	Peter E Jaffe	XS	OT			
	DEPARTMENT OF ADMINISTRATION AND FINANCE						
Washington, DC	Vice President/Chief Financial Officer	Fouad Paul Saad	XS	OT			
	DEPARTMENT OF CONGRESSIONAL AND PUBLIC AFFAIRS						
Washington, DC	Vice President	Aysha R House	XS	OT			
	DEPARTMENT OF COMPACT OPERATIONS						
Washington, DC	Vice President	Cameron S Alford	XS	OT			

MORRIS K UDALL AND STEWART L UDALL FOUNDATION

Location	Position Title	Name of Incumbent	Type of Appt.	Pay Plan	Level, Grade, or Pay	Tenure	Expires
Seattle, WA	Trustee	Eric D Eberhard	PAS	WC		6	10/06/18
Portland, OR	Trustee	James L Huffman	PAS	WC		6	10/06/20
Maui, HI	Trustee	D Michael Rappoport	PAS	WC		6	10/06/08
Ada, OK	Trustee	Lisa L Johnson-Billy	PAS	WC		6	08/25/24
Suquamish, WA	Trustee	Rion Ramirez	PAS	WC		6	05/26/26
Duluth, MN	Trustee	Tadd M Johnson	PAS	WC		6	10/06/28
Berkeley, CA	Trustee	Denis Udall	PAS	WC		6	04/15/29
Boulder, CO	Trustee	Theresa A F Udall	PAS	WC		6	10/06/28
Tucson, AZ	Trustee	Vacant		WC		6	

NATIONAL AERONAUTICS AND SPACE ADMINISTRATION

Location	Position Title	Name of Incumbent	Type of Appt.	Pay Plan	Level, Grade, or Pay	Tenure	Expires
	OFFICE OF THE ADMINISTRATOR						
Washington, DC	Administrator	C William Nelson	PAS	EX	II		
Washington, DC	Deputy Administrator	Pamela A Melroy	PAS	EX	III		
Washington, DC	Chief of Staff	Roy Bale Dalton	NA	ES			
Washington, DC	Senior Advisor	Susan Perez Quinn	NA	ES			
Washington, DC	Senior Advisor for Engagement and Equity	Rashahra Teresa Lambert	NA	ES			
Washington, DC	Senior Policy Advisor	Thomas Zimmerman	NA	ES			
Washington, DC	Associate Administrator, Space Security Interests.	Career Incumbent	CA	ES			
Washington, DC	Counselor for Interagency and International Operations.	Amber Janay McIntyre	SC	GS	15		
Washington, DC	Administrative Director and Advisor	Alicia Orgera	SC	GS	15		
Washington, DC	White House Liaison	Ana Patchin	SC	GS	14		
Washington, DC	Special Assistant for Engagement	Helen Miller	SC	GS	14		
Washington, DC	Public Engagement Advisor	Sol Ortega	SC	GS	14		
Washington, DC	Policy Advisor	Reagan Hunter	SC	GS	14		
Washington, DC	Special Assistant to the Chief of Staff	Sunvy Yalamarthy	SC	GS	9		
	OFFICE OF THE CHIEF FINANCIAL OFFICER						
Washington, DC	Chief Financial Officer	Margaret Schaus	PAS	EX	IV		
	OFFICE OF COMMUNICATIONS						
Washington, DC	Associate Administrator for Communications	Marc Etkind	NA	ES			
Washington, DC	Senior Advisor for Strategic Communications and Guest Operations.	Bryan Fred Gulley	SC	GS	15		

NATIONAL AERONAUTICS AND SPACE ADMINISTRATION—Continued

Location	Position Title	Name of Incumbent	Type of Appt.	Pay Plan	Level, Grade, or Pay	Tenure	Expires
Washington, DC	Senior Advisor for Communications..................	Meira Bernstein	SC	GS	15	....	....
Washington, DC	Director of Speechwriting	Matthew Stone	SC	GS	14	....	....
Washington, DC	Press Secretary	Faith Dominique McKie.......	SC	GS	13	....	....
Washington, DC	Digital Manager..	Michael Ahn...........................	SC	GS	13	....	....
Washington, DC	Communications Manager	Luis Manuel Botello Faz......	SC	GS	11	....	....
	OFFICE OF LEGISLATIVE AND INTERGOVERNMENTAL AFFAIRS						
Washington, DC	Associate Administrator for Legislative and Intergovernmental Affairs.	Alicia Brown	NA	ES	....	....	....
Washington, DC	Senior Legislative Advisor	Sarah Russell Hanson	SC	GS	15	....	....
Washington, DC	Deputy Director of Congressional Affairs..........	Elizabeth A Ahrens	SC	GS	14	....	....
Washington, DC	Special Assistant for Legislative Affairs............	Jamara Noel Green..............	SC	GS	11	....	....
	OFFICE OF TECHNOLOGY, POLICY AND STRATEGY						
Washington, DC	Associate Administrator for Technology, Policy, and Strategy.	Charity Weeden	TA	ES	....	....	09/24/24
	OFFICE OF GENERAL COUNSEL						
Washington, DC	General Counsel	Career Incumbent	CA	ES	....	....	....
Washington, DC	Associate General Counsel, General Law	Career Incumbent	CA	ES	....	....	....
Washington, DC	Associate General Counsel, International Law Practice Group.	Career Incumbent	CA	ES	....	....	....
Washington, DC	Associate General Counsel, Commercial and Intellectual Property Law Practice Group.	Career Incumbent	CA	ES	....	....	....
	OFFICE INTERNATIONAL AND INTERAGENCY RELATIONS						
Washington, DC	Associate Administrator, Office of International and Interagency Relations.	Career Incumbent	CA	ES	....	....	....
	OFFICE OF THE CHIEF INFORMATION OFFICER						
Washington, DC	Chief Information Officer..................................	Career Incumbent	CA	ES	....	....	....
	OFFICE OF DIVERSITY AND EQUAL OPPORTUNITY						
Washington, DC	Associate Administrator, Office of Diversity and Equal Opportunity.	Career Incumbent	CA	ES	....	....	....
	OFFICE OF STEM ENGAGEMENT						
Washington, DC	Associate Administrator, Office of Stem Engagement.	Career Incumbent	CA	ES	....	....	....
	OFFICE OF SMALL BUSINESS PROGRAMS						
Washington, DC	Assistant Administrator, Office of Small Business Programs.	Career Incumbent	CA	ES	....	....	....
	AMES RESEARCH CENTER						
Moffett Field, CA	Director, Ames Research Center........................	Career Incumbent	CA	ES	....	....	....
Moffett Field, CA	Chief Counsel...	Career Incumbent	CA	ES	....	....	....
	ARMSTRONG FLIGHT RESEARCH CENTER						
Edwards Air Force Base, CA.	Director, Armstrong Flight Research Center.....	Career Incumbent	CA	ES	....	....	....
Edwards Air Force Base, CA.	Chief Counsel..	Career Incumbent	CA	ES	....	....	....
	GLENN RESEARCH CENTER						
Brook Park, OH.......	Director, Glenn Research Center........................	Career Incumbent	CA	ES	....	....	....
Brook Park, OH.......	Chief Counsel..	Career Incumbent	CA	ES	....	....	....
	GODDARD SPACE FLIGHT CENTER						
Greenbelt, MD.........	Director, Goddard Space Flight Center.............	Career Incumbent	CA	ES	....	....	....
Greenbelt, MD.........	Chief Counsel..	Career Incumbent	CA	ES	....	....	....
	JOHNSON SPACE CENTER						
Houston, TX............	Director, Johnson Space Center........................	Career Incumbent	CA	ES	....	....	....
Houston, TX............	Chief Counsel..	Vacant	....	ES	....	....	....
	KENNEDY SPACE CENTER						
Kennedy Space Center, FL.	Director, Kennedy Space Center........................	Career Incumbent	CA	ES	....	....	....
Kennedy Space Center, FL.	Chief Counsel..	Career Incumbent	CA	ES	....	....	....
	LANGLEY RESEARCH CENTER						
Hampton, VA...........	Director, Langley Research Center....................	Career Incumbent	CA	ES	....	....	....
Hampton, VA...........	Chief Counsel..	Career Incumbent	CA	ES	....	....	....

NATIONAL AERONAUTICS AND SPACE ADMINISTRATION—Continued

Location	Position Title	Name of Incumbent	Type of Appt.	Pay Plan	Level, Grade, or Pay	Tenure	Expires
	MARSHALL SPACE FLIGHT CENTER						
Huntsville, AL	Director, Marshall Space Flight Center	Career Incumbent	CA	ES	....	....	....
Huntsville, AL	Chief Counsel	Career Incumbent	CA	ES	....	....	....
	STENNIS SPACE CENTER						
Bay St Louis, MS	Director, Stennis Space Center	Career Incumbent	CA	ES	....	....	....
Bay St Louis, MS	Chief Counsel	Career Incumbent	CA	ES	....	....	....

NATIONAL AERONAUTICS AND SPACE ADMINISTRATION OFFICE OF THE INSPECTOR GENERAL

Location	Position Title	Name of Incumbent	Type of Appt.	Pay Plan	Level, Grade, or Pay	Tenure	Expires
Washington, DC	Inspector General	Vacant	....	EX	....	....	....

NATIONAL ARCHIVES AND RECORDS ADMINISTRATION

Location	Position Title	Name of Incumbent	Type of Appt.	Pay Plan	Level, Grade, or Pay	Tenure	Expires
	ARCHIVIST OF UNITED STATES AND DEPUTY ARCHIVIST OF THE UNITED STATES						
Washington, DC	Archivist of the United States	Colleen Shogan	PAS	EX	III	....	....
	OFFICE OF PRESIDENTIAL LIBRARIES						
Atlanta, GA	Director, Jimmy Carter Library	Meredith Rachelle Evans	XS	SL		....	....
College Station, TX ..	George Bush Presidential Library and Museum Director.	Dawn Hammatt	XS	SL		....	....
Boston, MA	Director, John F Kennedy Library	Alan Price	XS	SL		....	....
Simi Valley, CA	Ronald Reagan Presidential Library and Museum Director.	Janet Tran	XS	SL		....	....
Ann Arbor, MI	Director, Gerald R Ford Library	Brooke Clement	XS	SL		....	....
Austin, TX	Director, Lyndon B Johnson Library	Mark A Lawrence	XS	SL		....	....
Little Rock, AR	Director, William J Clinton Library	Walker Jay Barth	XS	SL		....	....
Yorba Linda, CA	Director, Richard Nixon Library	Tamara Martin	XS	SL		....	....
Lewisville, TX	George W Bush Presidential Library Director ..	Pearl Ponce	XS	SL		....	....
West Branch, IA	Director, Herbert Hoover Library	Thomas F Schwartz	XS	SL		....	....
Independence, MO ..	Director, Harry S Truman Library	Donald Kurt Graham	XS	SL		....	....
Abilene, KS	Director, Dwight D Eisenhower Library	Vacant	....	SL		....	....
Hyde Park, NY	Director, Franklin D Roosevelt Library	William Harris	XS	SL		....	....
Hoffman Estates, IL.	Barack H Obama Presidential Library Director.	Kenvi Phillips	XS	SL		....	....

NATIONAL CAPITAL PLANNING COMMISSION

Location	Position Title	Name of Incumbent	Type of Appt.	Pay Plan	Level, Grade, or Pay	Tenure	Expires
Washington, DC	Chairman	Therese H Goodmann	PA	OT	....	6	01/01/29
Washington, DC	Commission Member	Bryan Green	PA	OT	....	6	01/01/25
Washington, DC	Commission Member	Elizabeth Hewlett	PA	OT	....	....	01/01/27

NATIONAL COUNCIL ON DISABILITY

Location	Position Title	Name of Incumbent	Type of Appt.	Pay Plan	Level, Grade, or Pay	Tenure	Expires
Washington, DC	Chair, no longer Vice Chair	Claudia Gordon	PA	AD	....	3	09/17/25
Washington, DC	Council Member	Emily Voorde	PA	AD	....	3	09/17/25
Washington, DC	Council Member	Risa Rifkind	PA	AD	....	3	09/17/25
Washington, DC	Council Member	Theo Braddy	PA	AD	....	3	09/17/25

NATIONAL COUNCIL ON DISABILITY—Continued

Location	Position Title	Name of Incumbent	Type of Appt.	Pay Plan	Level, Grade, or Pay	Tenure	Expires
Washington, DC	Council Member..	Hoskie Benally	PA	AD	....	3	09/17/25

NATIONAL CREDIT UNION ADMINISTRATION

Location	Position Title	Name of Incumbent	Type of Appt.	Pay Plan	Level, Grade, or Pay	Tenure	Expires
	OFFICE OF THE CHAIRMAN						
Alexandria, VA	Chairman	Todd M Harper.....................	PAS	EX	III	6	....
Alexandria, VA	Confidential Assistant..	Jean Carroll..........................	SC	OT	....	....	....
Alexandria, VA	Chief of Staff..	Catherine Galicia	SC	OT	....	....	....
Alexandria, VA	Director, Office of External Affairs and Communications.	Elizabeth Anne Eurgubian..	SC	OT	....	....	....
Chattanooga, TN	Staff Assistant..	Hallie Elizabeth Haley	SC	OT	....	....	....
	OFFICE OF THE BOARD						
Alexandria, VA	Board Member	Kyle Stuart Hauptman........	PAS	EX	IV	....	....
Alexandria, VA	Board Member	Tanya F Otsuka....................	PAS	EX	IV	4	....
Las Vegas, NV	Senior Policy Advisor...	Sarah Catherine Bang........	SC	OT	....	....	....
Alexandria, VA	Senior Policy Advisor...	Renita Marcellin..................	SC	OT	....	....	....
Alexandria, VA	Executive Assistant	Gina Stuart..........................	SC	OT	....	....	....
Alexandria, VA	Special Assistant and Advisor	Natalie Elisabeth More........	SC	OT	....	....	....
	OFFICE OF EXTERNAL AFFAIRS AND COMMUNICATIONS						
Alexandria, VA	Deputy Director, Office of External Affairs and Communications.	Samuel Schumach................	SC	OT	....	....	....

NATIONAL ENDOWMENT FOR THE ARTS

Location	Position Title	Name of Incumbent	Type of Appt.	Pay Plan	Level, Grade, or Pay	Tenure	Expires
Washington, DC	Chair..	Maria Jackson	PAS	EX	....	....	01/01/29
Washington, DC	Council Member..	Kinan Azmeh........................	PAS	AD	....	....	....
Washington, DC	Council Member..	Deepa Gupta........................	PAS	AD	....	....	....
Washington, DC	Council Member..	Kamilah Forbes	PAS	AD	....	....	....
Washington, DC	Council Member..	Aaron Dworkin	PAS	AD	....	....	....
Washington, DC	Council Member..	Bidtah Becker......................	PAS	AD	....	....	....
Washington, DC	Council Member..	Bruce Carter........................	PAS	AD	....	....	....
Washington, DC	Council Member..	Ranee Ramaswamy..............	PAS	AD	....	....	....
Washington, DC	Council Member..	Jake Shimabukuro...............	PAS	AD	....	....	....
Washington, DC	Council Member..	Fiona Prine	PAS	AD	....	....	....
Washington, DC	Council Member..	Ismael Ahmed......................	PAS	AD	....	....	....
Washington, DC	Council Member..	Michael Lombardo...............	PAS	AD	....	....	....
Washington, DC	Council Member..	Huascar Medina	PAS	AD	....	....	....
Washington, DC	Council Member..	Paul Hodes	PAS	AD	....	....	....
Washington, DC	Council Member..	Emil Kang............................	PAS	AD	....	....	....
Washington, DC	Council Member..	Christopher Morgan............	PAS	AD	....	....	....
Washington, DC	Council Member..	Gretchen Gonzales Davidson.	PAS	AD	....	....	....
Washington, DC	Council Member..	Constance Williams.............	PAS	AD	....	....	....
Washington, DC	Council Member..	Maria Lopez De Leon...........	PAS	AD	....	....	....
Washington, DC	Senior Deputy Chairman	Ascala Sisk	NA	ES	....	....	....
Washington, DC	Chief of Staff..	Ra Joy	NA	ES	....	....	....
Washington, DC	White House Liaison and Senior Advisor to the Chair.	Jennifer Chang.....................	SC	GS	15	....	....
Washington, DC	Director of Congressional and Federal Affairs..	Ben Kessler..........................	SC	GS	15	....	....
Washington, DC	Director of Strategic Communications & Public Affairs.	Sonia Tower	SC	GS	15	....	....
Washington, DC	Special Assistant to the Chair...........................	Stephanie Scott-Melnyk.......	SC	GS	13	....	....
Washington, DC	Special Assistant for Chair Initiatives..............	Katherine Bray-Simons	SC	GS	13	....	....
Washington, DC	Senior Advisor and Envoy for Cultural Exchange.	Carla Canales.......................	SC	GS	15	....	....
Washington, DC	Speechwriter and Communications Specialist ..	Joseph Garcia	SC	GS	12	....	....
Washington, DC	Special Projects Manager and Assistant to the Senior Deputy Chair.	Tara Farwana	SC	GS	13	....	....
Washington, DC	Senior Advisor (Creative Forces Program)	William O Brien	SC	GS	15	....	....

NATIONAL ENDOWMENT FOR THE ARTS—Continued

Location	Position Title	Name of Incumbent	Type of Appt.	Pay Plan	Level, Grade, or Pay	Tenure	Expires
Washington, DC	Advisor to the Director of Event Management and Development.	Christine Gant......................	SC	GS	13	....	....
Washington, DC	Administrative Assistant to the Chief of Staff..	Tayler Troup	SC	GS	9	....	....

NATIONAL ENDOWMENT FOR THE HUMANITIES

Location	Position Title	Name of Incumbent	Type of Appt.	Pay Plan	Level, Grade, or Pay	Tenure	Expires
Washington, DC	Chairperson............................	Shelly C Lowe......................	PAS	EX	III	4	....
Washington, DC	Senior Deputy Chairperson	Anthony Howard Mitchell ...	NA	ES	....	....	....
Washington, DC	Chief of Staff........................	Kelsey Ayn Coates...............	NA	ES	....	....	....
Washington, DC	General Counsel	Career Incumbent	CA	ES	....	....	....
Washington, DC	Assistant Chairman for Programs	Career Incumbent	CA	ES	....	....	....
Washington, DC	Council Member......................	Kathe Ah Albrecht	PAS	AD	....	6	01/26/24
Washington, DC	Council Member......................	Russell Berman	PAS	AD	....	....	01/26/20
Washington, DC	Council Member......................	Claire M Griffin.................	PAS	AD	....	6	01/26/22
Washington, DC	Council Member......................	Vanessa Northington Gamble.	PAS	AD	....	6	01/26/25
Washington, DC	Council Member......................	Daryl Baldwin	PAS	AD	....	6	01/26/24
Washington, DC	Council Member......................	Francine Berman	PAS	AD	....	6	01/26/20
Washington, DC	Council Member......................	Allison Blakely	PAS	AD	....	....	01/26/16
Washington, DC	Council Member......................	Keegan Callanan	PAS	AD	....	....	01/26/24
Washington, DC	Council Member......................	Constance Carroll................	PAS	AD	....	....	01/26/16
Washington, DC	Council Member......................	Deborah Coen	PAS	AD	....	6	01/26/28
Washington, DC	Council Member......................	William English...................	PAS	AD	....	6	01/26/24
Washington, DC	Council Member......................	Genine Fidler......................	PAS	AD	....	6	01/26/22
Washington, DC	Council Member......................	David A Hajdu.....................	PAS	AD	....	6	02/26/26
Washington, DC	Council Member......................	Marjorie Fisher....................	PAS	AD	....	....	01/26/22
Washington, DC	Council Member......................	Beverly Gage	PAS	AD	....	....	01/26/26
Washington, DC	Council Member......................	Christine M Kim	PAS	AD	....	6	01/26/26
Washington, DC	Council Member......................	Dorothy Kosinski.................	PAS	AD	....	6	01/26/16
Washington, DC	Council Member......................	David Sing	PAS	AD	....	6	01/26/26
Washington, DC	Council Member......................	Kathryn K Matthew...........	PAS	AD	....	6	01/26/26
Washington, DC	Council Member......................	Lynnette Y Overby..............	PAS	AD	....	6	01/26/22
Washington, DC	Council Member......................	Matthew F Rose..................	PAS	AD	....	6	01/26/24
Washington, DC	Council Member......................	Ramon Saldivar...................	PAS	AD	....	6	01/26/18
Washington, DC	Council Member......................	Katherine H Tachau.............	PAS	AD	....	6	01/26/18
Washington, DC	Council Member......................	Karen A Stout......................	PAS	AD	....	6	01/26/26
Washington, DC	Chief Information Officer...................	Career Incumbent	CA	ES	....	....	....
Washington, DC	Director of Strategic Communications and Public Affairs.	Shelby Lopez.......................	SC	GS	15	....	....
Washington, DC	Director of Congressional Affairs	Alison L Share.....................	SC	GS	15	....	....
Washington, DC	White House Liaison	Ageliki Key	SC	GS	13	....	....
Washington, DC	Special Assistant to the Office of the Chair	Lauren Khawam...................	SC	GS	11	....	....
Washington, DC	Special Assistant for Congressional Affairs.......	Adriana Usmayo Macedonio.	SC	GS	12	....	....

NATIONAL ENDOWMENT FOR THE HUMANITIES OFFICE OF THE INSPECTOR GENERAL

Location	Position Title	Name of Incumbent	Type of Appt.	Pay Plan	Level, Grade, or Pay	Tenure	Expires
Washington, DC	Inspector General	Career Incumbent	CA	ES	....	....	....

NATIONAL INSTITUTE OF BUILDING SCIENCES

Location	Position Title	Name of Incumbent	Type of Appt.	Pay Plan	Level, Grade, or Pay	Tenure	Expires
Washington, DC	Member............................	William Holloway...............	PAS	....	....	....	9/7/2024
Washington, DC	Member............................	Evelyn Fujimoto...................	PAS	....	....	....	9/7/2022
Washington, DC	Member............................	Susan Maxman....................	PAS	....	....	....	....
Washington, DC	Member............................	Kimberly Jones...................	PAS	....	....	....	9/2/2023

NATIONAL INSTITUTE OF BUILDING SCIENCES—Continued

Location	Position Title	Name of Incumbent	Type of Appt.	Pay Plan	Level, Grade, or Pay	Tenure	Expires
Washington, DC	Member	Lori Peek	PAS				9/7/2022

NATIONAL LABOR RELATIONS BOARD

Location	Position Title	Name of Incumbent	Type of Appt.	Pay Plan	Level, Grade, or Pay	Tenure	Expires
	OFFICE OF THE BOARD MEMBERS						
Washington, DC	Chairman	Lauren M McFerran	PAS	EX	III		12/16/24
Washington, DC	Board Member	Marvin Kaplan	PAS	EX	IV		08/27/25
Washington, DC	Board Member	David Prouty	PAS	EX	IV		
Washington, DC	Board Member	Gwynne Wilcox	PAS	EX			
Washington, DC	Board Member	Vacant		EX			
Washington, DC	Executive Assistant to the Chairman	Career Incumbent	CA	ES			
Washington, DC	Chief Counsel to Board Member	Career Incumbent	CA	ES			
Washington, DC	Chief Counsel to Board Member	John F Colwell	NA	ES			
Washington, DC	Chief Counsel to Board Member	Amanda Jaret	NA	ES			
Washington, DC	Chief Counsel to Board Member	Vacant		ES			
Washington, DC	Chief Counsel to Board Member	David Goldman	NA	ES			
Washington, DC	Deputy Chief Counsel to Board Member	Career Incumbent	CA	ES			
Washington, DC	Deputy Chief Counsel to Board Member	Career Incumbent	CA	ES			
Washington, DC	Deputy Chief Counsel to Board Member	Career Incumbent	CA	ES			
Washington, DC	Director, Office Representation Appeals	Career Incumbent	CA	ES			
Washington, DC	Deputy Chief Counsel to Board Member	Career Incumbent	CA	ES			
Washington, DC	Solicitor	Career Incumbent	CA	ES			
Washington, DC	Special Advisor to the Deputy General Counsel.	Vacant		ES			
Washington, DC	Assistant General Counsel	Vacant		ES			
Washington, DC	Director Congressional and Public Affairs Officer.	Kayla Blado	SC	GS	15		
Washington, DC	Communications Specialist	Theodora Lederer	SC	GS	13		
Washington, DC	Congressional Liaison Specialist	Matthew Hayward	SC	GS	14		
	OFFICE OF THE GENERAL COUNSEL						
Washington, DC	General Counsel	Jennifer Abruzzo	PAS	EX	IV		
Washington, DC	Deputy General Counsel	Career Incumbent	CA	ES			
Washington, DC	Associate General Counsel	Career Incumbent	CA	ES			
Washington, DC	Associate General Counsel	Jessica Rutter	NA	ES			
	NATIONAL LABOR RELATIONS BOARD						
Washington, DC	Deputy Chief Counsel to Chairman	Career Incumbent	CA	ES			
Washington, DC	Chief Financial Officer	Career Incumbent	CA	ES			

NATIONAL MEDIATION BOARD

Location	Position Title	Name of Incumbent	Type of Appt.	Pay Plan	Level, Grade, or Pay	Tenure	Expires
Washington, DC	Chairman	Loren E Sweatt	PAS	EX	III		07/01/25
Washington, DC	Board Member	Deirdre Elizabeth Hamilton.	PAS	EX	IV		07/01/25
Washington, DC	Board Member	Linda A Puchala	PAS	EX	IV		07/01/27
Washington, DC	General Counsel	Career Incumbent	CA	ES			
Washington, DC	Confidential Assistant	Ernest Fleischer	SC	GS	12		

NATIONAL SCIENCE FOUNDATION

Location	Position Title	Name of Incumbent	Type of Appt.	Pay Plan	Level, Grade, or Pay	Tenure	Expires
	OFFICE OF THE DIRECTOR						
Alexandria, VA	Director	Sethuraman Panchanathan.	PAS	EX	II		06/21/26
Alexandria, VA	Deputy Director	Vacant		EX			
Alexandria, VA	Chief of Staff	Career Incumbent	CA	ES			
Alexandria, VA	Chief Officer for Research Facilities	Career Incumbent	CA	ES			

NATIONAL SCIENCE FOUNDATION—Continued

Location	Position Title	Name of Incumbent	Type of Appt.	Pay Plan	Level, Grade, or Pay	Tenure	Expires
Alexandria, VA	Chief of Research Security Strategy and Policy.	Career Incumbent	CA	ES	....	....	....
Alexandria, VA	Senior Advisor............................	Career Incumbent	CA	ES	....	....	....
Alexandria, VA	Senior Advisor............................	Career Incumbent	CA	ES	....	....	....
Alexandria, VA	Chief Diversity and Inclusion Officer	Career Incumbent	CA	ES	....	....	....
	OFFICE OF THE GENERAL COUNSEL						
Alexandria, VA	General Counsel	Career Incumbent	CA	ES	....	....	....
	OFFICE OF EQUITY AND CIVIL RIGHTS						
Alexandria, VA	Senior Advisor............................	Career Incumbent	CA	ES	....	....	....
	OFFICE OF LEGISLATIVE AND PUBLIC AFFAIRS						
Alexandria, VA	Office Head............................	Career Incumbent	CA	ES	....	....	....
Alexandria, VA	Deputy Office Head	Career Incumbent	CA	ES	....	....	....
	OFFICE OF INTEGRATIVE ACTIVITIES						
Alexandria, VA	Office Head............................	Career Incumbent	CA	ES	....	....	....
Alexandria, VA	Section Head, Integrative Activities Section	Career Incumbent	CA	ES	....	....	....
Alexandria, VA	Section Head, Established Program to Stimulate Competitive Research.	Sandra Richardson...............	TA	ES	....	....	....
Alexandria, VA	Senior Advisor............................	Career Incumbent	CA	ES	....	....	....
	OFFICE OF INTERNATIONAL SCIENCE AND ENGINEERING						
Alexandria, VA	Office Head............................	Vacant	....	ES	....	....	....
Alexandria, VA	Deputy Office Head	Career Incumbent	CA	ES	....	....	....
	NATIONAL SCIENCE BOARD						
Alexandria, VA	Executive Officer and Director, National Science Board Office.	Career Incumbent	CA	ES	....	....	....
Alexandria, VA	NSB Member............................	David Dominguez...............	PA	OT	....	....	05/10/26
Alexandria, VA	NSB Member............................	Roger Beachy........................	PA	OT	....	....	05/10/26
Alexandria, VA	NSB Member............................	Heather Wilson....................	PA	OT	....	....	05/10/26
Alexandria, VA	NSB Member............................	Matthew Malkan...................	PA	OT	....	....	05/10/26
Alexandria, VA	NSB Member............................	Melvyn Huff........................	PA	OT	....	....	05/10/26
Alexandria, VA	NSB Member............................	Julia Phillips	PA	OT	....	....	05/10/28
Alexandria, VA	NSB Member............................	Wanda Ward	PA	OT	....	....	05/10/28
Alexandria, VA	NSB Member............................	Dorota Grejner-Brzezinska..	PA	OT	....	....	05/10/28
Alexandria, VA	NSB Member............................	Marvi Matos Rodriguez	PA	OT	....	....	05/10/28
Alexandria, VA	NSB Member............................	Keivan Stassun	PA	OT	....	....	05/10/28
Alexandria, VA	NSB Member............................	Merlin Theodore	PA	OT	....	....	05/10/28
Alexandria, VA	NSB Member............................	Victor McCrary...................	PA	OT	....	....	05/10/28
Alexandria, VA	NSB Member............................	Bevlee Watford	PA	OT	....	....	05/10/28
Alexandria, VA	NSB Member............................	Dario Gil	PA	OT	....	....	05/10/26
Alexandria, VA	NSB Member............................	Sudarsanam Babu...............	PA	OT	....	....	05/10/26
Alexandria, VA	NSB Member............................	Scott Stanley	PA	OT	....	....	05/10/26
Alexandria, VA	NSB Member............................	Vacant	....	OT	....	....	....
Alexandria, VA	NSB Member............................	Vacant	....	OT	....	....	....
Alexandria, VA	NSB Member............................	Vacant	....	OT	....	....	....
Alexandria, VA	NSB Member............................	Vacant	....	OT	....	....	....
Alexandria, VA	NSB Member............................	Vacant	....	OT	....	....	....
Alexandria, VA	NSB Member............................	Vacant	....	OT	....	....	....
Alexandria, VA	NSB Member............................	Vacant	....	OT	....	....	....
	DIRECTORATE FOR BIOLOGICAL SCIENCES						
Alexandria, VA	Assistant Director............................	Vacant	....	ES	....	....	....
	Division of Integrative Organismal Systems						
Alexandria, VA	Deputy Division Director	Career Incumbent	CA	ES	....	....	....
	Division of Biological Infrastructure						
Alexandria, VA	Division Director............................	Vacant	....	ES	....	....	08/14/24
Alexandria, VA	Deputy Division Director	Career Incumbent	CA	ES	....	....	....
	Division of Molecular And Cellular Biosciences						
Alexandria, VA	Division Director............................	Career Incumbent	CA	ES	....	....	....
Alexandria, VA	Deputy Division Director	Career Incumbent	CA	ES	....	....	....
	Division of Environmental Biology						
Alexandria, VA	Deputy Division Director	Career Incumbent	CA	ES	....	....	....
	Division of Computer and Network Systems						
Alexandria, VA	Deputy Division Director	Career Incumbent	CA	ES	....	....	....

NATIONAL SCIENCE FOUNDATION—Continued

Location	Position Title	Name of Incumbent	Type of Appt.	Pay Plan	Level, Grade, or Pay	Tenure	Expires
	Division of Computing and Communication Foundations						
Alexandria, VA	Division Director................................	Vacant	....	ES	....	....	....
Alexandria, VA	Deputy Division Director	Career Incumbent	CA	ES	....	....	....
	Division of Information and Intelligent Systems						
Alexandria, VA	Deputy Division Director	Career Incumbent	CA	ES	....	....	....
	Office Of Advanced Cyberinfrastructure						
Alexandria, VA	Deputy Office Director	Career Incumbent	CA	ES	....	....	....
	DIRECTORATE FOR STEM EDUCATION						
Alexandria, VA	Deputy Assistant Director	Career Incumbent	CA	ES	....	....	....
Alexandria, VA	Senior Advisor................................	Career Incumbent	CA	ES	....	....	....
	Division of Graduate Education						
Alexandria, VA	Division Director................................	Vacant	....	ES	....	....	....
Alexandria, VA	Deputy Division Director	Career Incumbent	CA	ES	....	....	....
	Division of Equity and Excellence In Stem						
Alexandria, VA	Division Director................................	Vacant	....	ES	....	....	....
Alexandria, VA	Deputy Division Director	Vacant	....	ES	....	....	....
	Division of Research On Learning In Formal and Informal Settings						
Alexandria, VA	Division Director................................	Career Incumbent	CA	ES	....	....	....
Alexandria, VA	Deputy Division Director	Career Incumbent	CA	ES	....	....	....
	Division of Undergraduate Education						
Alexandria, VA	Deputy Division Director	Career Incumbent	CA	ES	....	....	....
	DIRECTORATE FOR ENGINEERING						
Alexandria, VA	Assistant Director................................	Vacant	....	ES	....	....	....
Alexandria, VA	Deputy Assistant Director	Career Incumbent	CA	ES	....	....	....
	Division of Chemical, Bioengineering, Environmental, and Transport Systems						
Alexandria, VA	Deputy Division Director	Career Incumbent	CA	ES	....	....	....
	Division of Civil, Mechanical, and Manufacturing Innovation						
Alexandria, VA	Division Director................................	Vacant	....	ES	....	....	....
Alexandria, VA	Deputy Division Director	Career Incumbent	CA	ES	....	....	....
	Division of Electrical, Communications and Cyber Systems						
Alexandria, VA	Deputy Division Director	Vacant	....	ES	....	....	....
	DIRECTORATE FOR GEOSCIENCES						
Alexandria, VA	Assistant Director................................	Career Incumbent	CA	ES	....	....	....
	Division of Atmospheric and Geospace Sciences						
Alexandria, VA	Division Director................................	Career Incumbent	CA	ES	....	....	....
	Division of Earth Sciences						
Alexandria, VA	Division Director................................	Career Incumbent	CA	ES	....	....	....
Alexandria, VA	Section Head, Disciplinary Programs Section...	Stephen Mackwell................	TA	ES	....	....	....
	Division of Ocean Sciences						
Alexandria, VA	Division Director................................	Career Incumbent	CA	ES	....	....	....
	Division of Research, Innovation, Synergies and Education						
Alexandria, VA	Deputy Division Director	Career Incumbent	CA	ES	....	....	....
	Office Of Polar Programs						
Alexandria, VA	Office Director................................	Vacant	....	ES	....	....	....
Alexandria, VA	Head, Section for Arctic Sciences	Career Incumbent	CA	ES	....	....	....
Alexandria, VA	Head, Section for Antarctic Sciences................	Career Incumbent	CA	ES	....	....	....
Alexandria, VA	Executive Officer................................	Vacant	....	ES	....	....	....
	DIRECTORATE FOR MATHEMATICAL AND PHYSICAL SCIENCES						
Alexandria, VA	Assistant Director................................	Vacant	....	ES	....	....	....
	Division of Astronomical Sciences						
Alexandria, VA	Division Director................................	Robert Christopher Smith ...	TA	ES	....	....	....
	Division of Chemistry						
Alexandria, VA	Division Director................................	Vacant	....	ES	....	....	....
Alexandria, VA	Deputy Division Director	Career Incumbent	CA	ES	....	....	....

NATIONAL SCIENCE FOUNDATION—Continued

Location	Position Title	Name of Incumbent	Type of Appt.	Pay Plan	Level, Grade, or Pay	Tenure	Expires
	Division of Materials Research						
Alexandria, VA	Division Director....................................	Vacant	....	ES	....	....	....
Alexandria, VA	Deputy Division Director	Vacant	....	ES	....	....	....
	Division of Mathematical Sciences						
Alexandria, VA	Deputy Division Director	Career Incumbent	CA	ES	....	....	....
	Division of Physics						
Alexandria, VA	Division Director....................................	Career Incumbent	CA	ES	....	....	....
Alexandria, VA	Deputy Division Director	Career Incumbent	CA	ES	....	....	....
Alexandria, VA	Senior Advisor.....................................	Vacant	....	ES	....	....	....
	DIRECTORATE FOR SOCIAL, BEHAVIORAL AND ECONOMIC SCIENCES						
Alexandria, VA	Assistant Director Social Behavioral and Economic Sciences.	Vacant	....	ES	....	....	....
	Division of Behavioral and Cognitive Sciences						
Alexandria, VA	Division Director....................................	Vacant	....	ES	....	....	....
Alexandria, VA	Deputy Division Director	Career Incumbent	CA	ES	....	....	....
	National Center For Science And Engineering Statistics						
Alexandria, VA	Deputy Division Director	Career Incumbent	CA	ES	....	....	....
	Division of Social and Economic Sciences						
Alexandria, VA	Division Director....................................	Vacant	....	ES	....	....	....
Alexandria, VA	Deputy Division Director	Career Incumbent	CA	ES	....	....	....
	DIRECTORATE FOR TECHNOLOGY, INNOVATION, AND PARTNERSHIPS						
Alexandria, VA	Assistant Director.....................................	Career Incumbent	CA	ES	....	....	....
Alexandria, VA	Deputy Assistant Director	Career Incumbent	CA	ES	....	....	....
	Division of Innovation and Technology Ecosystems						
Alexandria, VA	Division Director....................................	Career Incumbent	CA	ES	....	....	....
Alexandria, VA	Section Head for Convergence Accelerator........	Career Incumbent	CA	ES	....	....	....
	Division of Translational Impacts						
Alexandria, VA	Section Head for SBIR/STTR (SB)....................	Vacant	....	ES	....	....	....
Alexandria, VA	Section Head for Translational Programs	Career Incumbent	CA	ES	....	....	....
	OFFICE OF BUDGET, FINANCE AND AWARD MANAGEMENT						
Alexandria, VA	Deputy Director Large Facilities Projects	Career Incumbent	CA	ES	....	....	....
	OFFICE OF THE CHIEF INFORMATION OFFICER						
Alexandria, VA	Deputy Office Head and Deputy Chief Information Officer.	Career Incumbent	CA	ES	....	....	....
Alexandria, VA	Division Director and Chief Data Officer	Career Incumbent	CA	ES	....	....	....
Alexandria, VA	Division Director for Security and Operations..	Career Incumbent	CA	ES	....	....	....
Alexandria, VA	Division Director for Enterprise Services..........	Career Incumbent	CA	ES	....	....	....

NATIONAL TRANSPORTATION SAFETY BOARD

Location	Position Title	Name of Incumbent	Type of Appt.	Pay Plan	Level, Grade, or Pay	Tenure	Expires
	Office of the General Counsel						
Washington, DC	General Counsel	Career Incumbent	CA	ES	....	....	....
	Office of the Managing Director						
Washington, DC	Managing Director....................................	Career Incumbent	CA	ES	....	....	....
	Office of Safety Recommendations and Communications						
Washington, DC	Director, Office of Safety Recommendations and Communications.	Jennifer L Adler	NA	ES	....	....	....
	OFFICE OF BOARD MEMBERS						
Washington, DC	Chairman	Jennifer L Homendy	PAS	EX	III	....	....
Washington, DC	Vice Chairman	Vacant	....	EX		....	....
Washington, DC	Member..	Thomas B Chapman	PAS	EX	IV	....	....
Washington, DC	Member..	Alvin Brown..........................	PAS	EX	IV	....	....
Washington, DC	Member..	Michael E Graham................	PAS	EX	IV	....	....

NATIONAL TRANSPORTATION SAFETY BOARD—Continued

Location	Position Title	Name of Incumbent	Type of Appt.	Pay Plan	Level, Grade, or Pay	Tenure	Expires
Washington, DC	Member...............................	James Todd Inman...............	PAS	EX	IV	....	....
Washington, DC	Deputy Chief of Staff..	Kelly M Hessler.................	SC	GS	15	....	....
Washington, DC	Special Assistant................................	Michelle A Barth.................	SC	GS	15	....	....
Washington, DC	Special Assistant................................	Stephen A Stadius...............	SC	GS	14	....	....
Washington, DC	Confidential Assistant......................................	Anne Kerins......................	SC	GS	11	....	....
Washington, DC	Confidential Assistant......................................	Linda McGunigal	SC	GS	12	....	....
Washington, DC	Special Assistant................................	Ivan Cheung......................	SC	GS	15	....	....
Washington, DC	Special Assistant................................	Michael M Hampton	SC	GS	14	....	....
Washington, DC	Confidential Assistant......................................	Olivia G Marcus	SC	GS	11	....	....
Washington, DC	Confidential Assistant......................................	Braxton Coleman	SC	GS	9	....	....
Washington, DC	Special Assistant................................	Andrew F Giacini...............	SC	GS	15	....	....

NORTHERN BORDER REGIONAL COMMISSION

Location	Position Title	Name of Incumbent	Type of Appt.	Pay Plan	Level, Grade, or Pay	Tenure	Expires
Concord, NH............	Federal Co-Chairperson	Chris Saunders....................	PAS	EX	III	....	....

NUCLEAR REGULATORY COMMISSION

Location	Position Title	Name of Incumbent	Type of Appt.	Pay Plan	Level, Grade, or Pay	Tenure	Expires
	OFFICE OF THE CHAIRMAN						
Rockville, MD	Chairman	Christopher T Hanson	PAS	EX	II	5	....
Rockville, MD	Technical Assistant for Reactors	Tony Nakanishi	XS	OT	....	....	....
Rockville, MD	Deputy Chief of Staff.........................	Jessie Quintero....................	XS	OT	....	....	....
Rockville, MD	Materials Policy Advisor	Lisa Dimmick	XS	OT	....	....	....
Rockville, MD	Chief of Staff...............................	Molly B Marsh.....................	XS	OT	....	....	....
Rockville, MD	Budget Policy Advisor	Mauer Mandy	XS	OT	....	....	....
Rockville, MD	Legal Counsel............................	Olivia Mikula......................	XS	OT	....	....	....
	ADVISORY COMMITTEE ON REACTOR SAFEGUARDS						
Rockville, MD	Executive Director..................................	Career Incumbent	CA	ES	....	....	....
Rockville, MD	Senior Technical Advisor for Reactor Safety	Hossein P Nourbakhsh	XS	OT	....	....	....
	ATOMIC SAFETY AND LICENSING BOARD PANEL						
Bethesda, MD..........	Administrative Judge (Technical)......................	Nicholas G Trikouros	XS	OT	....	....	....
Bethesda, MD..........	Administrative Judge (Technical)......................	Vacant	....	OT	....	....	....
Rockville, MD	Chief Administrative Judge	Edward R Hawkens	XS	OT	....	....	....
Rockville, MD	Administrative Judge (Legal)	George P Bollwerk	XS	OT	....	....	....
Rockville, MD	Associate Chief Administrative Judge (Technical).	Vacant	....	OT	....	....	....
Rockville, MD	Administrative Judge (Legal)	Vacant	....	OT	....	....	....
Rockville, MD	Associate Chief Administrative Judge (Legal) ..	Paul S Ryerson	XS	OT	....	....	....
Rockville, MD	Administrative Judge (Legal)	Emily Krause.......................	XS	OT	....	....	....
Rockville, MD	Administrative Judge (Legal)	Michael M Gibson	XS	OT	....	....	....
Rockville, MD	Administrative Judge (Technical)......................	Gary S Arnold.....................	XS	OT	....	....	....
Rockville, MD	Administrative Judge (Technical)......................	Sue H Abreu	XS	OT	....	....	....
	OFFICE OF THE CHIEF FINANCIAL OFFICER						
Rockville, MD	Chief Financial Officer.......................................	Career Incumbent	CA	ES	....	....	....
	OFFICE OF THE SECRETARY						
Rockville, MD	Secretary of the Commission	Career Incumbent	CA	ES	....	....	....
Rockville, MD	Historian	Thomas R Wellock	XS	OT	....	....	....
	OFFICE OF THE GENERAL COUNSEL						
Rockville, MD	General Counsel	Career Incumbent	CA	ES	....	....	....
Rockville, MD	Special Counsel for Litigation	Sherwin E Turk....................	XS	OT	....	....	....
Rockville, MD	Special Counsel for Acquisitions	Robin A Baum	XS	OT	....	....	....
Rockville, MD	Special Counsel for New Reactor Licensing	Robert M Weisman...............	XS	OT	....	....	....
Rockville, MD	Deputy General Counsel for Licensing, Hearings, and Enforcement.	Career Incumbent	CA	ES	....	....	....
Rockville, MD	Assistant General Counsel for Materials, Fuel Cycle, and Waste Programs.	Career Incumbent	CA	ES	....	....	....

NUCLEAR REGULATORY COMMISSION—Continued

Location	Position Title	Name of Incumbent	Type of Appt.	Pay Plan	Level, Grade, or Pay	Tenure	Expires
Rockville, MD	Assistant General Counsel for Security and Enforcement.	Career Incumbent	CA	ES	....	....	....
Rockville, MD	Assistant General Counsel for Legislation, Ethics, and Administrative Law.	Career Incumbent	CA	ES	....	....	....
Rockville, MD	Assistant General Counsel for Labor, Employment, and Contract Law.	Career Incumbent	CA	ES	....	....	....
Rockville, MD	Assistant General Counsel for Rulemaking, Agreement States, and Fee Policy.	Career Incumbent	CA	ES	....	....	....
Rockville, MD	Assistant General Counsel for Reactor Programs.	Career Incumbent	CA	ES	....	....	....
Rockville, MD	Deputy General Counsel for Legislation, Rulemaking and Agency Administration.	Career Incumbent	CA	ES	....	....	....
	OFFICE OF CONGRESSIONAL AFFAIRS						
Rockville, MD	Director, Office of Congressional Affairs	Career Incumbent	CA	ES	....	....	....
	OFFICE OF INTERNATIONAL PROGRAMS						
Rockville, MD	Director, Office of International Programs	Career Incumbent	CA	ES	....	....	....
Rockville, MD	Deputy Director, Office of International Programs.	Career Incumbent	CA	ES	....	....	....
Rockville, MD	Senior Level Foreign Policy Advisor..................	Jennifer S Holzman	XS	OT	....	....	....
Rockville, MD	Senior Level Advisor for Non-Proliferation and International Nuclear Security.	Atanasia N Fragoyannis......	XS	OT	....	....	....
	OFFICE OF PUBLIC AFFAIRS						
Rockville, MD	Director, Office of Public Affairs	Vacant		ES	....	....	....
	OFFICE OF THE EXECUTIVE DIRECTOR FOR OPERATIONS						
Rockville, MD	Assistant for Operations	Career Incumbent	CA	ES	....	....	....
Rockville, MD	Executive Director for Operations	Career Incumbent	CA	ES	....	....	....
Rockville, MD	Deputy Executive Director for Materials, Waste, Research, State, Tribal, Compliance, Administration, and Human Capital.	Vacant		ES	....	....	....
Rockville, MD	Deputy Executive Director for Reactor and Preparedness Programs.	Career Incumbent	CA	ES	....	....	....
Rockville, MD	Director of Strategic Internal Communication..	Vacant		ES	....	....	....
	OFFICE OF ENFORCEMENT						
Rockville, MD	Director Office of Enforcement	Career Incumbent	CA	ES	....	....	....
Rockville, MD	Agency Allegations Advisor................................	Lisamarie Jarriel................	XS	OT	....	....	....
Rockville, MD	Senior Technical Advisor for Enforcement	Nicholas D Hilton................	XS	OT	....	....	....
	OFFICE OF ADMINISTRATION						
Bethesda, MD	Director of Transition..	Vacant		ES	....	....	....
Rockville, MD	Director, Office of Administration	Career Incumbent	CA	ES	....	....	....
	OFFICE OF THE CHIEF HUMAN CAPITAL OFFICER						
Rockville, MD	Chief Human Capital Officer...............................	Career Incumbent	CA	ES	....	....	....
Rockville, MD	Deputy Chief Human Capital Officer	Career Incumbent	CA	ES	....	....	....
Rockville, MD	Associate Director for Human Resources Training and Development/Chief Learning Officer.	Career Incumbent	CA	ES	....	....	....
Rockville, MD	Associate Director for Human Resources Operations and Policy.	Career Incumbent	CA	ES	....	....	....
Rockville, MD	Deputy Chief Human Capital Officer	Career Incumbent	CA	ES	....	....	....
Rockville, MD	Special Assistant to the Deputy Chief Human Capital Officer.	Vacant		ES	....	....	....
	OFFICE OF INVESTIGATIONS						
Rockville, MD	Director, Office of Investigations	Career Incumbent	CA	ES	....	....	....
	OFFICE OF NUCLEAR REACTOR REGULATION						
Rockville, MD	Director, Office of Nuclear Reactor Regulation .	Career Incumbent	CA	ES	....	....	....
Bethesda, MD..........	Sla for Probabilistic Assessment	Sunil D Weerakkody	XS	OT	....	....	....
Rockville, MD	Sla for Nuclear Material Power Plants..............	David L Rudland.................	XS	OT	....	....	....
Rockville, MD	Senior Level Advisor for Structural Mechanics.	Kamal A Manoly	XS	OT	....	....	....
Rockville, MD	Senior Technical Advisor for Systems and Fuels.	Benjamin T Parks	XS	OT	....	....	....
Rockville, MD	Senior Technical Advisor for Probabilistic Risk Assessment Technology.	Martin A Stutzke	XS	OT	....	....	....
Rockville, MD	Senior Technical Advisor for Human Factors Analysis and Performance Evaluation.	Brian Greene	XS	OT	....	....	....
Rockville, MD	Senior Technical Advisor for Reactor Fuel	Christopher N Van Wert......	XS	OT	....	....	....

NUCLEAR REGULATORY COMMISSION—Continued

Location	Position Title	Name of Incumbent	Type of Appt.	Pay Plan	Level, Grade, or Pay	Tenure	Expires
Rockville, MD	Senior Technical Advisor for License Renewal Aging Management.	John Wise	XS	OT			
Rockville, MD	Senior Technical Advisor for Advanced Reactor Research.	Vacant		OT			
Rockville, MD	Senior Technical Advisor for Nuclear Power Plant Siting.	Clifford G Munson	XS	OT			
	OFFICE OF NUCLEAR MATERIAL SAFETY AND SAFEGUARDS						
Rockville, MD	Director, Office of Nuclear Material Safety and Safeguards.	Career Incumbent	CA	ES			
Rockville, MD	Deputy Director, Office of Nuclear Material Safety and Safeguards.	Career Incumbent	CA	ES			
Rockville, MD	Director, Division of Fuel Management	Career Incumbent	CA	ES			
Rockville, MD	Senior Technical Advisor for Waste Management and Environmental Protection.	Rateb M Abu-Eid	XS	OT			
Rockville, MD	Senior Level Advisor for Health Physics	Eugene V Holahan	XS	OT			
Rockville, MD	Senior Level Advisor	Timothy J McCartin	XS	OT			
	OFFICE OF NUCLEAR REGULATORY RESEARCH						
Rockville, MD	Director, Office of Nuclear Regulatory Research.	Career Incumbent	CA	ES			
Rockville, MD	Deputy Director, Office of Nuclear Regulatory Research.	Career Incumbent	CA	ES			
Rockville, MD	Senior Technical Advisor for Earth Science and Geophysical Engineering.	Vacant		OT			
Rockville, MD	Senior Technical Advisor for Materials Engineering Issues.	Robert L Tregoning	XS	OT			
Rockville, MD	Senior Technical Advisor for Civil/Structural Engineering Issues.	Jose A Pires	XS	OT			
Rockville, MD	Senior Technical Advisor for Radionuclide Transport.	Vacant		OT			
Rockville, MD	Senior Technical Advisor for Thermal Hydraulics and Code Development.	Stephen M Bajorek	XS	OT			
Rockville, MD	Senior Technical Advisor for Probabilistic Risk Analysis.	Kevin Coyne	XS	OT			
Rockville, MD	Senior Technical Advisor for Structural and Seismic Analysis.	Vacant		OT			
Rockville, MD	Senior Technical Advisor for Computational Fluid Dynamics.	Christopher F Boyd	XS	OT			
Rockville, MD	Senior Technical Advisor for Computational Fluid Dynamics.	Abdelghani Zigh	XS	OT			
Rockville, MD	Senior Technical Advisor for Digital Instrumentation and Control.	Sushil K Birla	XS	OT			
Rockville, MD	Senior Advisor for Nuclear Safety	Anthony Ulses	XS	OT			
	REGION I						
King Of Prussia, PA.	Regional Administrator	Career Incumbent	CA	ES			
	REGION II						
Atlanta, GA	Regional Administrator	Career Incumbent	CA	ES			
	REGION III						
Lisle, IL	Regional Administrator	Career Incumbent	CA	ES			
	REGION IV						
Arlington, TX	Regional Administrator	Career Incumbent	CA	ES			
	OFFICE OF NUCLEAR SECURITY AND INCIDENT RESPONSE						
Rockville, MD	Director, Office of Nuclear Security and Incident Response.	Career Incumbent	CA	ES			
Rockville, MD	Senior Technical Advisor for Digital Instrumentation and Controls Cyber Security.	Ismael L Garcia	XS	OT			
Rockville, MD	Senior Level Advisor for Emergency Preparedness.	Todd Smith	XS	OT			
Rockville, MD	Senior Technical Advisor for Nuclear Security..	Vacant		OT			
	OFFICE OF THE CHIEF INFORMATION OFFICER						
Rockville, MD	Chief Information Officer	Career Incumbent	CA	ES			
Rockville, MD	Deputy Chief Information Officer	Career Incumbent	CA	ES			
Rockville, MD	Senior Level Advisor for Information Security	Kathy L Lyons-Burke	XS	OT			
	OFFICE OF COMMISSIONER CAPUTO						
Rockville, MD	Commissioner	Annie Caputo	PAS	EX	III	5	

NUCLEAR REGULATORY COMMISSION—Continued

Location	Position Title	Name of Incumbent	Type of Appt.	Pay Plan	Level, Grade, or Pay	Tenure	Expires
Rockville, MD	Chief of Staff	Vacant		OT			
Rockville, MD	Technical Assistant for Reactors	Eric Bowman	XS	OT			
Rockville, MD	Technical Assistant for Materials	Marilyn Diaz	XS	OT			
Rockville, MD	Legal Counsel	Julie Ezell	XS	OT			
Rockville, MD	Budget Advisor	Heather Dempsey	XS	OT			
	OFFICE OF COMMISSIONER WRIGHT						
Rockville, MD	Commissioner	David A Wright	PAS	EX	III	5	06/30/20
Rockville, MD	Chief of Staff	Christopher Fong	XS	OT			
Rockville, MD	Technical Assistant for Reactors	Shakur Walker	XS	OT			
Rockville, MD	Legal Counsel	Joe Ivy Gillespe	XS	OT			
Rockville, MD	Technical Assistant for Materials	Suzanne Dennis	XS	OT			
	OFFICE OF COMMISSIONER CROWELL						
Rockville, MD	Commissioner	Bradley R Crowell	PAS	EX	III	5	
Rockville, MD	Technical Assistant for Reactors	Thomas R Hipschman	XS	OT			
Rockville, MD	Technical Assistant for Materials	David D Brown	XS	OT			
Rockville, MD	Legal Counsel	Vacant		OT			
Rockville, MD	Senior Advisor	Amy Powell	XS	OT			
Rockville, IN	Chief of Staff	Maxine Keffe	XS	OT			

NUCLEAR REGULATORY COMMISSION OFFICE OF THE INSPECTOR GENERAL

Location	Position Title	Name of Incumbent	Type of Appt.	Pay Plan	Level, Grade, or Pay	Tenure	Expires
Rockville, MD	Inspector General	Robert J Feitel	PAS	OT			

NUCLEAR WASTE TECHNICAL REVIEW BOARD

Location	Position Title	Name of Incumbent	Type of Appt.	Pay Plan	Level, Grade, or Pay	Tenure	Expires
Arlington, VA	Executive Director	Career Incumbent	CA	ES			
Salem, OR	Member	Brian Woods	PA	AD		4	04/19/26
College Station, TX	Member	Kenneth Lee Peddicord	PA	AD		4	12/31/24
St Augustine, FL	Member	Allen G Croff	PA	AD		4	12/31/24
Potomac, MD	Member	Nathan O Siu	PA	AD		4	04/19/24
Boulder, CO	Member	Tissa H Illangasekare	PA	AD		4	12/31/24
Norfolk, VA	Member	Steven M Becker	PA	AD		4	12/31/24
Andover, MA	Member	Ronald Ballinger	PA	AD		4	04/19/26
Reno, NV	Member	Scott Tyler	PA	AD		4	12/31/24
	Member	Vacant		AD		4	
	Member	Vacant		AD		4	
	Member	Vacant		AD		4	

NATIONAL WOMEN'S BUSINESS COUNCIL

Location	Position Title	Name of Incumbent	Type of Appt.	Pay Plan	Level, Grade, or Pay	Tenure	Expires
Washington, DC	Chairperson	Sima Ladjevardian	PA				

OCCUPATIONAL SAFETY AND HEALTH REVIEW COMMISSION

Location	Position Title	Name of Incumbent	Type of Appt.	Pay Plan	Level, Grade, or Pay	Tenure	Expires
	OFFICE OF COMMISSIONERS						
Washington, DC	Commission Member (Chairman)	Cynthia L Attwood	PAS	EX	III		04/27/25
Washington, DC	Commission Member	Vacant		EX			
Washington, DC	Commission Member	Vacant		EX			
Washington, DC	Counsel to A Commissioner	Michael R Asplen	SC	GS	15		

OCCUPATIONAL SAFETY AND HEALTH REVIEW COMMISSION—Continued

Location	Position Title	Name of Incumbent	Type of Appt.	Pay Plan	Level, Grade, or Pay	Tenure	Expires
	OCCUPATIONAL SAFETY AND HEALTH REVIEW COMMISSION						
Washington, DC	Chief Counsel to the Chairman........................	Katherine A Tracy...............	NA	ES	....	....	....
Washington, DC	Special Assistant........................	Amanda Wood Laihow	TA	ES	....	....	04/26/25
	OFFICE OF THE GENERAL COUNSEL						
Washington, DC	General Counsel	Career Incumbent	CA	ES	....	....	....

OFFICE OF GOVERNMENT ETHICS

Location	Position Title	Name of Incumbent	Type of Appt.	Pay Plan	Level, Grade, or Pay	Tenure	Expires
Washington, DC	Director........................	Vacant	....	EX	....	5	....
Washington, DC	General Counsel	Career Incumbent	CA	ES	....	....	....

OFFICE OF THE DIRECTOR FOR NATIONAL INTELLIGENCE

Location	Position Title	Name of Incumbent	Type of Appt.	Pay Plan	Level, Grade, or Pay	Tenure	Expires
	OFFICE OF THE DIRECTOR						
Washington, DC	Director of National Intelligence........................	Avril D Haines......................	PAS	EX	I	3	....
Washington, DC	Principal Deputy Director of National Intelligence.	Stacey Dixon........................	PAS	EX	II	2.5	....
Washington, DC	Director of the National Counterterrorism Center.	Vacant	....	EX	....	0.2	02/11/25
Washington, DC	Intelligence Community Inspector General.......	Thomas A Monheim.............	PAS	EX	III	2	....
Washington, DC	Director of the National Counterintelligence and Security Center.	Michael Casey	PAS	EX	IV	....	....
Washington, DC	General Counsel	Vacant	....	EX	....	....	....

OFFICE OF PERSONNEL MANAGEMENT

Location	Position Title	Name of Incumbent	Type of Appt.	Pay Plan	Level, Grade, or Pay	Tenure	Expires
	OFFICE OF THE DIRECTOR						
Washington, DC	Director........................	Vacant	....	EX	....	....	....
Washington, DC	Deputy Director	Robert Harley Shriver, III ...	PAS	EX	III	....	....
Washington, DC	Chief of Staff........................	David Samuel Marsh	NA	ES	....	....	....
Washington, DC	Deputy Chief of Staff........................	Margot Conrad	NA	ES	....	....	....
Washington, DC	Deputy Chief of Staff........................	Ryan Uyehara	SC	GS	15	....	....
Washington, DC	Chief Transformation Officer...........................	Catherine Manfre................	NA	ES	....	....	....
Washington, DC	Senior Advisor to the Director........................	Jonathan Rockwell Foley.....	NA	ES	....	....	....
Washington, DC	Senior Advisor to the Director........................	Jane Y Lee	NA	ES	....	....	....
Washington, DC	Senior Advisor to the Director for Technology and Delivery.	Partha Teerdhala.................	NA	ES	....	....	....
Washington, DC	Executive Director, Chief Human Capital Officers Council.	Career Incumbent	CA	ES	....	....	....
Washington, DC	White House Liaison and Senior Advisor for Strategic Initiatives.	Jason Tengco........................	SC	GS	15	....	....
Washington, DC	Senior Advisor for Strategic Initiatives	Theodora Chang	SC	GS	15	....	....
Washington, DC	Senior Advisor for Digital Transformation.......	Erikka Knuti	SC	GS	15	....	....
Washington, DC	Senior Advisor for People Operations	Yahaira Enid Lopez............	SC	GS	15	....	....
Washington, DC	Senior Advisor for Leadership Development and Equity.	Tiffany Worthy	SC	GS	15	....	....
Washington, DC	Policy Advisor........................	Tiffany Avila	SC	GS	13	....	....
Washington, DC	Special Advisor........................	Gabriela Alvarado	SC	GS	12	....	....
Washington, DC	Special Advisor........................	Emily Stanley......................	SC	GS	12	....	....
Washington, DC	Confidential Assistant	Anna Martin........................	SC	GS	11	....	....
	FEDERAL PREVAILING RATE ADVISORY COMMITTEE						
Washington, DC	Chair, Federal Prevailing Rate Advisory Committee.	Janice R Lachance	NA	ES	....	....	....

OFFICE OF PERSONNEL MANAGEMENT—Continued

Location	Position Title	Name of Incumbent	Type of Appt.	Pay Plan	Level, Grade, or Pay	Tenure	Expires
	CONGRESSIONAL, LEGISLATIVE, AND INTERGOVERNMENTAL AFFAIRS						
Washington, DC	Director, Congressional, Legislative and Intergovernmental Affairs.	Eric Bursch............................	NA	ES	....	....	....
Washington, DC	Deputy Director, Congressional, Legislative and Intergovernmental Affairs.	Jacqueline Maffucci..............	SC	GS	15	....	....
Washington, DC	Senior Advisor...	Blake Davis...........................	SC	GS	15	....	....
Washington, DC	Senior Advisor...	Adam Tanga..........................	SC	GS	14	....	....
Washington, DC	Policy Advisor...	Sharon Kwon	SC	GS	13	....	....
	OFFICE OF COMMUNICATIONS						
Washington, DC	Director, Office of Communications....................	Jack Miller............................	NA	ES	....	....	....
Washington, DC	Deputy Director, Office of Communications	Viet Tran................................	SC	GS	15	....	....
Washington, DC	Chief Speechwriter and Senior Advisor for Communications.	Daniel Lindner	SC	GS	15	....	....
	OFFICE OF THE GENERAL COUNSEL						
Washington, DC	General Counsel	Webb Lyons...........................	NA	ES	....	....	....
Washington, DC	Deputy General Counsel......................................	Michael Ceja Martinez.........	NA	ES	....	....	....
Washington, DC	Senior Counsel for Oversight.............................	Laura O'Neill........................	NA	ES	....	....	....
Washington, DC	Special Counsel and Senior Advisor...................	Tanya Kansal Sehgal	SC	GS	15	....	....
	DIVERSITY, EQUITY, INCLUSION AND ACCESSIBILITY						
Washington, DC	Director, Office of Diversity, Equity, Inclusion and Accessibility.	Vacant	....	ES			
	PRESIDENTS COMMISSION ON WHITE HOUSE FELLOWSHIPS						
Washington, DC	Director, Presidents Commission on White House Fellowships.	Rosemarie Vela......................	NA	ES			
Washington, DC	Deputy Director, Presidents Commission on White House Fellowships.	Esteban Tapetillo	SC	GS	15	....	....
Washington, DC	Associate Director, Presidents Commission on White House Fellowships.	Kevin Lavery	SC	GS	12	....	....
	HUMAN CAPITAL DATA MANAGEMENT AND MODERNIZATION						
Washington, DC	Executive Director, Human Capital Data Management and Modernization.	Career Incumbent	CA	ES	....	....	....
Washington, DC	Senior Advisor, HR QSMO and HRLOB............	Steven Krauss	TA	ES	....	36	
	HEALTHCARE AND INSURANCE						
Washington, DC	Associate Director, Healthcare and Insurance ..	Career Incumbent	CA	ES	....	....	....
Washington, DC	Senior Advisor...	Career Incumbent	CA	ES	....	....	....
Washington, DC	Senior Advisor...	Luis Jose Vasquez	TA	ES	....	36	
	HUMAN RESOURCES SOLUTIONS						
Montgomery, PA......	Associate Director, Human Resources Solutions.	Career Incumbent	CA	ES	....	....	....
	WORKFORCE POLICY AND INNOVATION						
Washington, DC	Associate Director, Workforce Policy and Innovation.	Career Incumbent	CA	ES	....	....	....
Washington, DC	Deputy Associate Director, Federal Executive Boards.	Career Incumbent	CA	ES	....	....	....
	RETIREMENT SERVICES						
Washington, DC	Associate Director, Retirement Services	Career Incumbent	CA	ES	....	....	....
Washington, DC	Director for Strategic Initiatives	Career Incumbent	CA	ES	....	....	....
	SUITABILITY EXECUTIVE AGENT PROGRAMS						
Washington, DC	Suitability Director..	Career Incumbent	CA	ES	....	....	....
	SECURITY, SUITABILITY, AND CREDENTIALING LINE OF BUSINESS (SSCLOB)						
Aldie, VA..................	Director, Performance Accountability Council - Program Management Office.	Career Incumbent	CA	ES			
	OFFICE OF THE CHIEF INFORMATION OFFICER						
Washington, DC	Chief Information Officer....................................	Career Incumbent	CA	ES	....	....	....

OFFICE OF PERSONNEL MANAGEMENT OFFICE OF THE INSPECTOR GENERAL

Location	Position Title	Name of Incumbent	Type of Appt.	Pay Plan	Level, Grade, or Pay	Tenure	Expires
Washington, DC	**OFFICE OF THE INSPECTOR GENERAL** Inspector General	Krista Anne Boyd.................	PAS	EX	III	....	....

OFFICE OF SPECIAL COUNSEL

Location	Position Title	Name of Incumbent	Type of Appt.	Pay Plan	Level, Grade, or Pay	Tenure	Expires
Washington, DC	**HEADQUARTERS, OFFICE OF SPECIAL COUNSEL** Special Counsel..	Hampton Dellinger	PAS	EX	IV	5	02/28/29
Washington, DC	Principal Deputy Special Counsel.....................	Vacant	....	OT	....	5	....
Washington, DC	General Counsel	Susan Ullman......................	XS	SL	....	....	....
Oakland, CA	Associate Special Counsel for Investigation and Prosecution (Field Offices).	Career Incumbent	CA	ES	....	....	....
Washington, DC	Associate Special Counsel for Investigation and Prosecution.	Career Incumbent	CA	ES	....	....	....
Washington, DC	Associate Special Counsel for General Law Division.	Career Incumbent	CA	ES	....	....	....
Washington, DC	Chief Operating Officer....................................	Career Incumbent	CA	ES	....	....	....
Washington, DC	Public Affairs Specialist	Zachary S Kurz	XS	GS	15	....	....
Washington, DC	Legislative Affairs Director...............................	Corey Williams	XS	GS	14	....	....

OFFICE OF THE SECRETARY OF DEFENSE OFFICE OF THE INSPECTOR GENERAL

Location	Position Title	Name of Incumbent	Type of Appt.	Pay Plan	Level, Grade, or Pay	Tenure	Expires
Alexandria, VA	Inspector General	Robert P Storch....................	PAS	EX	IV	....	....

PEACE CORPS

Location	Position Title	Name of Incumbent	Type of Appt.	Pay Plan	Level, Grade, or Pay	Tenure	Expires
Washington, DC	**OFFICE OF THE DIRECTOR** Director of Peace Corps.....................................	Carol Spahn..........................	PAS	EX	III	5	....
Washington, DC	Deputy Director Peace Corps.............................	David E White Jr....................	PAS	EX	IV	5	....
Washington, DC	Chief of Staff...	Lauren Stephens	XS	OT	....	5	....
Washington, DC	Deputy Chief of Staff...	Jacklyn Dao Dinneen...........	XS	OT	....	5	....
Washington, DC	General Counsel	Ruchi Jain............................	XS	OT	....	5	....
Washington, DC	Chief of Operations and Administration...........	Vacant	....	OT	....	5	....
Washington, DC	Director, Strategic Partnership and Intergovernment Agencies (SPIGA).	Lila Jaafar	XS	OT	....	5	....
Washington, DC	White House Liaison	Karoun Rafi Tcholakian.......	XS	OT	....	5	....
Washington, DC	Senior Advisor to the Director...........................	Connolly Jean Keigher	XS	OT	....	5	....
Washington, DC	Senior Advisor to the Director...........................	Victor Sloan	XS	OT	....	5	....
Washington, DC	Special Advisor to the Director..........................	Vacant	....	OT	....	5	....
Washington, DC	Special Advisor for International Engagement.	Michaela Gaughan	XS	OT	....	5	....
Washington, DC	Speechwriter	Michael James McKiernan..	XS	OT	....	5	....
Washington, DC	Special Assistant to the Director.......................	Vacant	....	OT	....	5	....
Washington, DC	Special Assistant to Deputy Director................	Pablo Rasmussen	XS	OT	....	....	....
Washington, DC	Special Assistant to the Chief of Staff..............	Elizabeth Mariapen	XS	OT	....	5	....
Washington, DC	**OFFICE OF EXTERNAL AFFAIRS** Director of Congressional Relations...................	Clifford Stammerman	XS	OT	....	5	....
Washington, DC	Deputy Director of Congressional Relations	Vacant	....	OT	....	5	....
Washington, DC	Director of Communications	Charmion Nicole Kinder......	XS	OT	....	5	....
Washington, DC	Deputy Communications Director......................	Karen Mascarinas................	XS	OT	....	5	....
Washington, DC	Director of Press Relations	Vacant	....	OT	....	5	....
Washington, DC	Director of Gifts and Grants Management (GGM).	Lara M Fedorov....................	XS	OT	....	5	....
Washington, DC	Associate Director of External Affairs	Ruben Gonzalez....................	XS	OT	....	5	....
Washington, DC	Senior Advisor (National Service)	Erastus Bogonko Mong'are..	XS	OT	....	5	....

PEACE CORPS—Continued

Location	Position Title	Name of Incumbent	Type of Appt.	Pay Plan	Level, Grade, or Pay	Tenure	Expires
	AFRICA OPERATIONS						
Washington, DC	Regional Director....................................	Michelle Godette	XS	OT	....	5	....
	OFFICE OF GLOBAL OPERATION						
Washington, DC	Associate Director Office of Global Operations.	John Scott Beale...................	XS	OT	....	5	....
Washington, DC	Senior Advisor (Climate)......................................	Vacant	....	OT	....	5	....
	EUROPE, MEDITERRANEAN AND ASIA OPERATIONS (EMA)						
Washington, DC	Regional Director....................................	Paul Negley............................	XS	OT	....	5	....
	INTER-AMERICA AND THE PACIFIC OPERATIONS (IAP)						
Washington, DC	Regional Director....................................	Michael McCabe	XS	OT	....	5	....
	OFFICE OF VOLUNTEER RECRUITMENT AND SELECTION						
Washington, DC	Associate Director, Volunteer Recruitment and Selection (VRS).	Jennifer Brown.....................	XS	OT	....	5	....
	PEACE CORPS RESPONSE						
Washington, DC	Director of Peace Corps Response	Ryan Moore............................	XS	OT	....	5	....
	OFFICE OF HEALTH SERVICES						
Washington, DC	Director Office of Health Services......................	Vacant	....	OT	....	....	....
	OFFICE OF GLOBAL HEALTH AND HIV						
Washington, DC	Director Office of Global Health and HIV	Kechinyere Achebe...............	XS	OT	....	....	....
	OFFICE OF SAFETY AND SECURITY						
Washington, DC	Associate Director for Safety and Security........	Shawn Bardwell	XS	OT	....	....	....
	OFFICE OF THE CHIEF FINANCIAL OFFICER						
Washington, DC	Chief Financial Officer...............................	Allison Blotzer......................	XS	OT	....	5	....
	OFFICE OF THE CHIEF INFORMATION OFFICER						
Washington, DC	Chief Information Officer....................................	Michael J Terry III...............	XS	OT	....	....	....
Washington, DC	Deputy Chief Information Officer	Lara Bair	XS	OT	....	....	....
	OFFICE OF MANAGEMENT						
Washington, DC	Associate Director for Management...................	Francisco Reinoso.................	XS	OT	....	5	....
	OFFICE OF HUMAN RESOURCES						
Washington, DC	Chief Human Capital Officer.............................	Akoua Enow...........................	XS	OT	....	....	....
	INSPECTOR GENERAL						
Washington, DC	Inspector General	Joaquin Ferrao	XS	OT	....	....	....

PENSION BENEFIT GUARANTY CORPORATION

Location	Position Title	Name of Incumbent	Type of Appt.	Pay Plan	Level, Grade, or Pay	Tenure	Expires
	OFFICE OF THE EXECUTIVE DIRECTOR						
Washington, DC	Director....................................	Vacant	....	EX	....	....	....
Murray Hill NJ	Advisory Committee Member	Jeanmarie Grisi...................	PA	EX	IV	....	02/19/25
New York, NY.........	Advisory Committee Member	Joseph LoCicero...................	PA	EX	IV	....	02/19/25
Oak Park, IL............	Advisory Committee Member	Kweku Obed	PA	EX	IV	....	02/19/25
Varied......................	Advisory Committee Member	Vacant	....	EX	....	....	....
Varied......................	Advisory Committee Member	Vacant	....	EX	....	....	....
Varied......................	Advisory Committee Member	Vacant	....	EX	....	....	....
Varied......................	Advisory Committee Member	Vacant	....	EX	....	....	....
	OFFICE OF POLICY AND EXTERNAL AFFAIRS						
Washington, DC	Chief Policy Officer....................................	Ann Orr....................................	SC	SL	....	....	....

POSTAL REGULATORY COMMISSION

Location	Position Title	Name of Incumbent	Type of Appt.	Pay Plan	Level, Grade, or Pay	Tenure	Expires
	OFFICE OF THE COMMISSIONERS						
Washington, DC	Chairman	Michael M Kubayanda	PAS	EX	III	6	11/22/26
Washington, DC	Commissioner	Robert Taub	PAS	EX	IV	6	10/14/28
Washington, DC	Commissioner	Ann C Fisher	PAS	EX	IV	6	10/14/24
Washington, DC	Commissioner	Ashley J Poling	PAS	EX	IV	6	11/22/24
Washington, DC	Commissioner	Thomas Day	PAS	EX	IV	6	10/14/28
Washington, DC	Chief of Staff	Robert Borden	XS	OT			
Washington, DC	Special Assistant	April E Boston	XS	OT			
Washington, DC	Special Assistant	David A Cooper	XS	OT			
Washington, DC	Senior Economist and Economic Advisor	Viola B Stovall	XS	OT			
Washington, DC	Senior Economic Advisor	Mohammad Adra	XS	OT			
Washington, DC	Senior Economic and Public Policy Advisor	Virgil I Stanford	XS	OT			
Washington, DC	Confidential Assistant	Vacant		OT			
Washington, DC	Confidential Assistant	Sara Brandenburg	XS	OT			
Washington, DC	Confidential Assistant	Vacant		OT			
Washington, DC	Communications and Customer Experience Analyst/Confidential Assistant.	Michael McGuire	XS	OT			
	OFFICE OF THE GENERAL COUNSEL						
Washington, DC	General Counsel	David A Trissell	XS	OT			
Washington, DC	Deputy General Counsel	Christopher Laver	XS	OT			
Washington, DC	Deputy General Counsel	Lauren D'Agostino	XS	OT			
	OFFICE OF ACCOUNTABILITY AND COMPLIANCE						
Washington, DC	Director	Margaret Cigno	XS	OT			
Washington, DC	Deputy Director, Compliance	Jessica Raines	XS	OT			
Washington, DC	Deputy Director, Accountability	Matthew Robinson	XS	OT			
Washington, DC	Deputy Director, Analytic Division	Lyudmila Bzhilyanskaya	XS	OT			
	OFFICE OF SECRETARY AND ADMINISTRATION						
Washington, DC	Secretary and Chief Administrative Officer	Erica Barker	XS	OT			
	OFFICE OF PUBLIC AFFAIRS AND GOVERNMENT RELATIONS						
Washington, DC	Director	Jennifer Warburton	XS	OT			
	OFFICE OF BUDGET AND FINANCE						
Washington, DC	Director	Kellie King	XS	OT			

PRESIDENT'S COMMITTEE ON THE ARTS AND THE HUMANITIES

Location	Position Title	Name of Incumbent	Type of Appt.	Pay Plan	Level, Grade, or Pay	Tenure	Expires
Washington, DC	Executive Director	Tsione K Wolde-Michael	SC	GS	15		
Washington, DC	Member	Constance M Carroll	PA				
Washington, DC	Member	George Clooney	PA				
Washington, DC	Member	Bruce Lewis Cohen	PA				
Washington, DC	Member	Philip J Deloria	PA				
Washington, DC	Member	M Angélica Garcia	PA				
Washington, DC	Member	Jennifer Garner	PA				
Washington, DC	Member	Stefani Joanne Angelina Germanotta.	PA				
Washington, DC	Member	Nora Halpern	PA				
Washington, DC	Member	Steve Israel	PA				
Washington, DC	Member	Marta Kauffman	PA				
Washington, DC	Member	Ricky Kirshner	PA				
Washington, DC	Member	Troy Kotsur	PA				
Washington, DC	Member	Kathleen Anne McGrath	PA				
Washington, DC	Member	Laura Penn	PA				
Washington, DC	Member	Amanda Phingbodhipakkiya.	PA				
Washington, DC	Member	Shonda Lynn Rhimes	PA				
Washington, DC	Member	Kimberly Richter Shirley	PA				
Washington, DC	Member	Horacio Sierra	PA				
Washington, DC	Member	Anna Deavere Smith	PA				
Washington, DC	Member	Joe Walsh	PA				
Washington, DC	Member	Kerry Washington	PA				
Washington, DC	Member	Pauline Yu	PA				
Washington, DC	Member	Jon Batiste	PA				

PRESIDENT'S COMMITTEE ON THE ARTS AND THE HUMANITIES—Continued

Location	Position Title	Name of Incumbent	Type of Appt.	Pay Plan	Level, Grade, or Pay	Tenure	Expires
Washington, DC	Member	Vacant					
Washington, DC	Member	Vacant					
Washington, DC	Member	Vacant					
Washington, DC	Member	Vacant					
Washington, DC	Member	Vacant					
Washington, DC	Member	Vacant					

PRIVACY AND CIVIL LIBERTIES OVERSIGHT BOARD

Location	Position Title	Name of Incumbent	Type of Appt.	Pay Plan	Level, Grade, or Pay	Tenure	Expires
Washington, DC	Member	Ed Felten	PAS				
Washington, DC	Chair	Sharon Franklin	PAS				
Washington, DC	Member	Beth Williams	PAS				

PUBLIC BUILDINGS REFORM BOARD

Location	Position Title	Name of Incumbent	Type of Appt.	Pay Plan	Level, Grade, or Pay	Tenure	Expires
Washington, DC	Chairperson	Vacant		OT		6	
Washington, DC	Board Member	Jeffrey Gural	PA	OT		6	11/09/28
Washington, DC	Board Member	David T Hocker	PA	OT		6	08/14/24
Washington, DC	Board Member	David L Winstead	PA	OT		6	02/28/25
Washington, DC	Board Member	Nick J Rahall	PA	OT		6	08/14/24
Washington, DC	Board Member	Michael Capuano	PA	OT		6	11/09/28
Washington, DC	Board Member	Daniel Mathews	PA	OT		6	02/08/30

RAILROAD RETIREMENT BOARD

Location	Position Title	Name of Incumbent	Type of Appt.	Pay Plan	Level, Grade, or Pay	Tenure	Expires
	BOARD MEMBERS						
Chicago, IL	Chairman	Erhard R Chorle	PAS	EX	III		
Chicago, IL	Member of Board	Thomas R Jayne	PAS	EX	IV		
Chicago, IL	Member of Board	Johnathan D Bragg	PAS	EX	IV		

RAILROAD RETIREMENT BOARD OFFICE OF THE INSPECTOR GENERAL

Location	Position Title	Name of Incumbent	Type of Appt.	Pay Plan	Level, Grade, or Pay	Tenure	Expires
	OFFICE OF INSPECTOR GENERAL						
Chicago, IL	Inspector General	Vacant		EX			

SECURITIES AND EXCHANGE COMMISSION

Location	Position Title	Name of Incumbent	Type of Appt.	Pay Plan	Level, Grade, or Pay	Tenure	Expires
	OFFICE OF THE CHAIR						
Washington, DC	Chair	Gary Gensler	PAS	EX	III	5	06/05/26
Washington, DC	Chief of Staff	Amanda Fischer	SC	OT			
Washington, DC	Senior Advisor	Barbara Roper	SC	OT			
Washington, DC	Senior Advisor	Corey Frayer	SC	OT			
Washington, DC	Confidential Assistant	Lily Bailey	SC	OT			
Washington, DC	Confidential Assistant	Danielle Campbell	SC	OT			

SECURITIES AND EXCHANGE COMMISSION—Continued

Location	Position Title	Name of Incumbent	Type of Appt.	Pay Plan	Level, Grade, or Pay	Tenure	Expires
	OFFICE OF COMMISSIONER PEIRCE						
Washington, DC	Commissioner	Hester Peirce	PAS	EX	IV	5	06/05/25
Washington, DC	Confidential Assistant	Denene Dent	SC	OT			
	OFFICE OF COMMISSIONER UYEDA						
Washington, DC	Commissioner	Mark Uyeda	PAS	EX	IV	5	06/05/28
Washington, DC	Confidential Assistant	Taylor Asher	SC	OT			
	OFFICE OF COMMISSIONER LIZARRAGA						
Washington, DC	Commissioner	Jaime Lizarraga	PAS	EX	IV	5	06/05/27
	OFFICE OF COMMISSIONER CRENSHAW						
Washington, DC	Commissioner	Caroline Crenshaw	PAS	EX	IV	5	01/03/25
Washington, DC	Confidential Assistant	Kathleen Gallagher	SC	OT			
	OFFICE OF LEGISLATIVE AND INTERGOVERNMENTAL AFFAIRS						
Washington, DC	Legislative Affairs Specialist	David Fernandez	SC	OT			
	OFFICE OF PUBLIC AFFAIRS						
Washington, DC	Supervisory Public Affairs Specialist	Stephanie Allen	SC	OT			
Washington, DC	Digital Media Communication Specialist	Basmah Nada	SC	OT			
Washington, DC	Writer-Editor	Max Luong	SC	OT			

SECURITIES INVESTOR PROTECTION CORPORATION

Location	Position Title	Name of Incumbent	Type of Appt.	Pay Plan	Level, Grade, or Pay	Tenure	Expires
Washington, DC	Member	William Jasien	PAS				12/31/26
Washington, DC	Member	William (Bill) Brodsky	PAS	OT			12/31/26
Washington, DC	Member	Glen S. Fukushima	PAS	OT			12/31/24
Washington, DC	Member	Claudia Slacik	PAS	OT			12/31/26
Washington, DC	Member	Alan Patricof	PAS	OT			12/31/25

SELECTIVE SERVICE SYSTEM

Location	Position Title	Name of Incumbent	Type of Appt.	Pay Plan	Level, Grade, or Pay	Tenure	Expires
	OFFICE OF THE DIRECTOR						
Arlington, VA	Director Selective Service System	Vacant		EX			
Arlington, VA	Deputy Director	Joel Spangenberg	NA	ES			
Arlington, VA	Chief of Staff	Saif M Khan	SC	GS	15		

SMALL BUSINESS ADMINISTRATION

Location	Position Title	Name of Incumbent	Type of Appt.	Pay Plan	Level, Grade, or Pay	Tenure	Expires
	OFFICE OF THE ADMINISTRATOR						
Washington, DC	Administrator	Isabella Casillas Guzman	PAS	EX	III		
Washington, DC	Deputy Administrator	Dilawar Syed	PAS	EX	IV		
Washington, DC	Chief of Staff	Arthur Plews	NA	ES			
Washington, DC	Deputy Chief of Staff	Isabelle Paige James	NA	ES			
Washington, DC	Deputy Chief of Staff	Kendall L Corley	SC	GS	15		
Washington, DC	Director of Policy and Planning	George David Brown	NA	ES			
Washington, DC	Senior Advisor	Aditi Sharma Dussault	SC	GS	15		
Washington, DC	Senior Advisor	Diedra Henry-Spires	SC	GS	15		
Washington, DC	Senior Advisor	Mark Edward Ranneberger	SC	GS	15		
Washington, DC	Senior Advisor	Israel Nery	SC	GS	15		
Washington, DC	Senior Advisor	Thomas M Kerr	SC	GS	14		
Austin, TX	Director of Public Engagement	Jessica Reeves	SC	GS	15		
Washington, DC	Deputy White House Liaison	Remi R Roberts	SC	GS	13		
Washington, DC	Director of Advance	Cierra C Johnson	SC	GS	13		

SMALL BUSINESS ADMINISTRATION—Continued

Location	Position Title	Name of Incumbent	Type of Appt.	Pay Plan	Level, Grade, or Pay	Tenure	Expires
Washington, DC	Director of Scheduling	Brigid Campbell Gleason	SC	GS	13		
Washington, DC	Policy Advisor	Skye Bork	SC	GS	13		
Washington, DC	Special Advisor	Tyler Scott Robinson	SC	GS	12		
Washington, DC	Associate Director for Public Engagement	Frankie Lamar White	SC	GS	12		
Washington, DC	Confidential Assistant	Hannah Yoon Borison	SC	GS	11		
	Office of Advocacy						
Washington, DC	Chief Counsel for Advocacy	Vacant		EX			
	Office of Capital Access						
Washington, DC	Associate Administrator for Capital Access	Kathryn M Frost	NA	ES			
Washington, DC	Deputy Associate Administrator	Career Incumbent	CA	ES			
Washington, DC	Director of Credit Risk Management	Career Incumbent	CA	ES			
Washington, DC	Director of Financial Programs Operations	Career Incumbent	CA	ES			
Washington, DC	Director of Financial Assistance	Vacant		ES			
Washington, DC	Director of Performance and Systems Management.	Career Incumbent	CA	ES			
Fort Worth, TX	Director Processing Verification and Disbursement Center.	Career Incumbent	CA	ES			
Washington, DC	Senior Advisor	Sarah Koulogeorge	SC	GS	14		
Washington, DC	Senior Advisor	Stacie Posey	SC	GS	13		
	Office of Communications and Public Liaison						
Washington, DC	Associate Administrator	Han D Nguyen	NA	ES			
Washington, DC	Deputy Associate Administrator	Vacant		ES			
Washington, DC	Deputy Associate Administrator for Communications and Public Liaison.	Rachael Shackelford Dussuau.	SC	GS	15		
Washington, DC	Senior Advisor	Matthew Brady Sonneborn	SC	GS	14		
Washington, DC	Speechwriter	Peter L Clerkin	SC	GS	14		
Washington, DC	Press Secretary	Rebecca R Galanti	SC	GS	14		
Washington, DC	Deputy Press Secretary	Theodora Rose Lake	SC	GS	13		
Washington, DC	Press Assistant	Jessica Christina Evans	SC	GS	9		
	Office of Congressional and Legislative Affairs						
Washington, DC	Associate Administrator for Congressional and Legislative Affairs.	George F Holman	NA	ES			
Washington, DC	Senior Advisor	Jonathan S Alter	SC	GS	15		
Washington, DC	Deputy Associate Administrator (Senate)	Aneysha Bhat	SC	GS	14		
Washington, DC	Legislative Policy Advisor	Quinn Carrigan	SC	GS	12		
	Office of Disaster Recovery and Resilience						
Washington, DC	Associate Administrator for Disaster Assistance.	Francisco Sanchez	NA	ES			
Washington, DC	Deputy Associate Administrator	Career Incumbent	CA	ES			
Washington, DC	Director, Field Operations and Disaster Recovery.	Career Incumbent	CA	ES			
Washington, DC	Senior Advisor	Warren David Miller	SC	GS	15		
	Office of Entrepreneurial Development						
Washington, DC	Associate Administrator for Entrepreneurial Development.	Vacant		ES			
Washington, DC	Assistant Administrator for Women Business Ownership.	Christina Hale	NA	ES			
Washington, DC	Associate Administrator for Small Business Development Centers.	Career Incumbent	CA	ES			
Washington, DC	Chief of Policy, Analysis, and Evaluation	Career Incumbent	CA	ES			
Washington, DC	Assistant Administrator for Native American Affairs.	Jackson Brossy	SC	GS	15		
Washington, DC	Director of Rural Affairs	Anna Maria Lucas	SC	GS	15		
Washington, DC	Senior Advisor	Preston Hardge	SC	GS	14		
	Office of Diversity, Inclusion and Civil Rights						
Washington, DC	Assistant Administrator for the Office of Diversity, Inclusion and Civil Rights.	Career Incumbent	CA	ES			
	Office of Field Operations						
Washington, DC	Associate Administrator for the Office of Field Operations.	Jennifer Insil Kim	NA	ES			
Washington, DC	Deputy Associate Administrator for Field Operations.	Career Incumbent	CA	ES			
Washington, DC	Director of Field Ecosystems	Career Incumbent	CA	ES			
Washington, DC	Director of Field Policy	Career Incumbent	CA	ES			
Washington, DC	Director of Field Resources	Career Incumbent	CA	ES			
New York, NY	Regional Administrator, Region II	Marlene Cintron	SC	GS	15		
Wilmington, DE	Regional Administrator, Region III	John Francis Fleming	SC	GS	15		
Raleigh, NC	Regional Administrator, Region IV	Allen Thomas	SC	GS	15		
Chicago, IL	Regional Administrator, Region V	Geraldine Sanchez Aglipay	SC	GS	15		
Kansas City, MO	Regional Administrator, Region VII	Mindy Renae Brissey	SC	GS	15		

SMALL BUSINESS ADMINISTRATION—Continued

Location	Position Title	Name of Incumbent	Type of Appt.	Pay Plan	Level, Grade, or Pay	Tenure	Expires
Denver, CO	Regional Administrator, Region VIII	Aikta V Marcoulier	SC	GS	15		
San Francisco, CA	Regional Administrator, Region IX	Elmy A Bermejo	SC	GS	15		
Washington, DC	Regional Administrator, Region X	Beto Yarce	SC	GS	15		
Washington, DC	Senior Advisor	Chelsea Ann Goldinger	SC	GS	14		
	Office of Government Contracting and Business Development						
Washington, DC	Associate Administrator for Government Contracting and Business Development.	Jaqueline L Robinson-Burnette.	NA	ES			
Washington, DC	Associate Administrator for 8(A) Business Development.	Vacant		ES			
Washington, DC	Director of Government Contracting	Career Incumbent	CA	ES			
Washington, DC	Policy Advisor	Sarah Edwards	SC	GS	13		
	Office of International Trade						
Washington, DC	Associate Administrator for International Trade.	Daniel Krupnick	NA	ES			
	Office of Investment And Innovation						
Washington, DC	Associate Administrator for Investment and Innovation.	Bailey Geldermann Devries.	NA	ES			
Washington, DC	Director of Small Business Innovation Research and Technology Transfer.	Career Incumbent	CA	ES			
Washington, DC	Director of Patient Capital Investments	Career Incumbent	CA	ES			
	Office of the General Counsel						
Washington, DC	General Counsel	Therese Rohrbeck Meers	NA	ES			
Washington, DC	Deputy General Counsel	Juan Marcelo Sempertegui	SC	GS	15		
	Office of the Ombudsman						
Washington, DC	National Ombudsman and Assistant Administrator for Regulatory Enforcement Fairness.	Career Incumbent	CA	ES			
	Office of Veterans' Business Development						
Washington, DC	Associate Administrator for Veterans Business Development.	Vacant		ES			
Washington, DC	Assistant Administrator	Robert Anthony Yannuzzi	SC	GS	15		

SMALL BUSINESS ADMINISTRATION OFFICE OF THE INSPECTOR GENERAL

Location	Position Title	Name of Incumbent	Type of Appt.	Pay Plan	Level, Grade, or Pay	Tenure	Expires
Washington, DC	Inspector General	Hannibal Ware	PAS	EX	III		

SOCIAL SECURITY ADMINISTRATION

Location	Position Title	Name of Incumbent	Type of Appt.	Pay Plan	Level, Grade, or Pay	Tenure	Expires
	OFFICE OF THE COMMISSIONER						
Washington, DC	Commissioner	Martin J. O'Malley	PAS	EX	I		
Washington, DC	Deputy Commissioner of Social Security	Vacant		EX			
Woodlawn, MD	Chief of Staff	Scott L Frey	NA	ES			
Washington, DC	Deputy Chief of Staff	Vacant		ES			
Woodlawn, MD	Counselor to the Commissioner	Vacant		ES			
Washington, DC	Executive Secretary	Vacant		ES			
Washington, DC	Senior Advisor to the Commissioner	Carolyn W Colvin	TA	ES			
Woodlawn, MD	Senior Advisor to the Commissioner	Vacant		ES			
Woodlawn, MD	Senior Advisor to the Deputy Commissioner	Benidicto Feliciano Belton	NA	ES			
Woodlawn, MD	Senior Advisor	Lisa Allen	TA	ES			
Washington, DC	Director, Native American Partnerships	Career Incumbent	CA	ES			
Woodlawn, MD	Executive Assistant to the Commissioner	Michelle C Waller	SC	GS	13		
Washington, DC	Senior Advisor	Kristine Quinio	SC	GS	15		
Washington, DC	Senior Advisor	Abigail Zapote	SC	GS	15		
Washington, DC	Senior Advisor	Cortney Sanders	SC	GS	15		
Washington, DC	Senior Advisor for Communications and External Engagement.	Kathleen Dailey	SC	GS	15		
Washington, DC	Member, Social Security Advisory Board	Robert Joondeph	PAS	OT			
Washington, DC	Member, Social Security Advisory Board	Amy Gingrich	PAS	OT			

SOCIAL SECURITY ADMINISTRATION—Continued

Location	Position Title	Name of Incumbent	Type of Appt.	Pay Plan	Level, Grade, or Pay	Tenure	Expires
Washington, DC	Member, Social Security Advisory Board	Jagadeesh Gokhale	PAS	OT	....	....	....
Washington, DC	Member, Social Security Advisory Board	Nancy Altman.......................	PAS	OT	....	....	....
	OFFICE OF ANALYTICS, REVIEW AND OVERSIGHT						
Woodlawn, MD	Associate Commissioner for Analytics and Improvements.	Career Incumbent	CA	ES	....	....	....
Woodlawn, MD	Deputy Associate Commissioner for Analytics and Improvements.	Career Incumbent	CA	ES	....	....	....
Woodlawn, MD	Associate Commissioner for Quality Review	Career Incumbent	CA	ES	....	....	....
Woodlawn, MD	Deputy Associate Commissioner for Quality Review.	Career Incumbent	CA	ES	....	....	....
	OFFICE OF COMMUNICATIONS						
Woodlawn, MD	Deputy Commissioner for Communications	Nate Osburn	NA	ES	....	....	....
Woodlawn, MD	Assistant Deputy Commissioner for Communications.	Career Incumbent	CA	ES	....	....	....
Woodlawn, MD	Associate Commissioner for Public Inquiries and Communications Support.	Career Incumbent	CA	ES	....	....	....
Woodlawn, MD	Associate Commissioner for Strategic and Digital Communications.	Career Incumbent	CA	ES	....	....	....
	OFFICE OF THE GENERAL COUNSEL						
Woodlawn, MD	Senior Advisor to the General Counsel..............	Career Incumbent	CA	ES	....	....	....
Woodlawn, MD	Executive Advisor for Workforce Planning	Vacant	....	ES	....	....	....
Woodlawn, MD	Executive Director for Legal Operations	Career Incumbent	CA	ES	....	....	....
	OFFICE OF BUDGET, FINANCE, AND MANAGEMENT						
Woodlawn, MD	Deputy Commissioner for Budget, Finance, and Management.	Career Incumbent	CA	ES	....	....	....
Woodlawn, MD	Assistant Deputy Commissioner for Budget, Finance, and Management (Management).	Career Incumbent	CA	ES	....	....	....
Woodlawn, MD	Senior Advisor to the Deputy Commissioner for Budget, Finance, Quality and Management.	Career Incumbent	CA	ES	....	....	....
Woodlawn, MD	Associate Commissioner for Facilities and Logistics Management.	Career Incumbent	CA	ES	....	....	....
Woodlawn, MD	Deputy Associate Commissioner for Facilities and Logistics Management.	Career Incumbent	CA	ES	....	....	....
	OFFICE OF HEARINGS OPERATIONS						
Falls Church, VA	Associate Commissioner for Budget, Facilities and Security.	Career Incumbent	CA	ES	....	....	....
Falls Church, VA	Deputy Associate Commissioner for Budget, Facilities and Security.	Vacant	....	ES	....	....	....
Falls Church, VA	Deputy Associate Commissioner for Executive Operations and Strategic Management.	Vacant	....	ES	....	....	....
Woodlawn, MD	Senior Advisor..	Vacant	....	ES	....	....	....
Falls Church, VA	Associate Commissioner for Electronic Services and Strategic Information.	Career Incumbent	CA	ES	....	....	....
Falls Church, VA	Deputy Associate Commissioner for Electronic Services and Strategic Information.	Career Incumbent	CA	ES	....	....	....
Falls Church, VA	Associate Commissioner for Executive Operations and Strategic Management.	Career Incumbent	CA	ES	....	....	....
	OFFICE OF HUMAN RESOURCES						
Woodlawn, MD	Deputy Commissioner for Human Resources....	Career Incumbent	CA	ES	....	....	....
Woodlawn, MD	Assistant Deputy Commissioner for Human Resources.	Kristen N Medley-Proctor ...	....	ES	....	....	....
Woodlawn, MD	Senior Advisor to the Deputy Commissioner for Human Resources.	Career Incumbent	CA	ES	....	....	....
Woodlawn, MD	Associate Commissioner for Strategy, Learning, and Workforce Development.	Vacant	....	ES	....	....	....
Woodlawn, MD	Deputy Associate Commissioner for Strategy, Learning, and Workforce Development.	Career Incumbent	CA	ES	....	....	....
	OFFICE OF LEGISLATION AND CONGRESSIONAL AFFAIRS						
Washington, DC	Deputy Commissioner for Legislation and Congressional Affairs.	Tom Klouda	NA	ES	....	....	....
Washington, DC	Assistant Deputy Commissioner for Legislation and Congressional Affairs.	Vacant	....	ES	....	....	....
Woodlawn, MD	Associate Commissioner for Legislative Development and Operations.	Career Incumbent	CA	ES	....	....	....
Washington, DC	Senior Technical Advisor.....................................	Elisa Walker	SC	GS	15	....	....

SOCIAL SECURITY ADMINISTRATION—Continued

Location	Position Title	Name of Incumbent	Type of Appt.	Pay Plan	Level, Grade, or Pay	Tenure	Expires
	OFFICE OF OPERATIONS (HEADQUARTERS)						
Woodlawn, MD	Deputy Commissioner for Operations...............	Career Incumbent	CA	ES	....	....	....
Woodlawn, MD	Assistant Deputy Commissioner for Operations.	Career Incumbent	CA	ES	....	....	....
Woodlawn, MD	Assistant Deputy Commissioner for Operations.	Career Incumbent	CA	ES	....	....	....
Woodlawn, MD	Associate Commissioner for Public Service and Operations Support.	Career Incumbent	CA	ES	....	....	....
Woodlawn, MD	Deputy Associate Commissioner for Public Service and Operations Support.	Career Incumbent	CA	ES	....	....	....
Woodlawn, MD	Deputy Associate Commissioner for Public Service and Operations Support (Facilities and Security).	Vacant		ES	....	....	....
Woodlawn, MD	Associate Commissioner for Electronic Services and Technology.	Career Incumbent	CA	ES	....	....	....
Woodlawn, MD	Deputy Associate Commissioner for Electronic Services and Technology.	Career Incumbent	CA	ES	....	....	....
Woodlawn, MD	Associate Commissioner for Customer Service .	Career Incumbent	CA	ES	....	....	....
Woodlawn, MD	Deputy Associate Commissioner for Customer Service.	Career Incumbent	CA	ES	....	....	....
Woodlawn, MD	Deputy Associate Commissioner for Customer Service (Processing Centers).	Career Incumbent	CA	ES	....	....	....
Woodlawn, MD	Associate Commissioner for Central Operations.	Career Incumbent	CA	ES	....	....	....
Woodlawn, MD	Deputy Associate Commissioner for Central Operations.	Vacant		ES	....	....	....
Woodlawn, MD	Assistant Associate Commissioner for Management and Operations Support.	Career Incumbent	CA	ES	....	....	....
Woodlawn, MD	Assistant Associate Commissioner for Disability Operations.	Career Incumbent	CA	ES	....	....	....
Woodlawn, MD	Assistant Associate Commissioner for Earnings and International Operations.	Career Incumbent	CA	ES	....	....	....
Woodlawn, MD	Senior Advisor...	Career Incumbent	CA	ES	....	....	....
Woodlawn, MD	Executive Advisor for Agency Web Strategy......	Career Incumbent	CA	ES	....	....	....
Woodlawn, MD	Chief Business Officer (It Modernization).........	Vacant		ES	....	....	....
	OFFICE OF OPERATIONS (FIELD)						
Boston, MA	Regional Commissioner Region I....................	Career Incumbent	CA	ES	....	....	....
New York, NY..........	Regional Commissioner Region II....................	Career Incumbent	CA	ES	....	....	....
Philadelphia, PA	Regional Commissioner Region III...................	Career Incumbent	CA	ES	....	....	....
Atlanta, GA	Regional Commissioner Region IV...................	Career Incumbent	CA	ES	....	....	....
Chicago, IL	Regional Commissioner Region V	Career Incumbent	CA	ES	....	....	....
Kansas City, MO	Regional Commissioner Region VII..................	Career Incumbent	CA	ES	....	....	....
Dallas, TX	Regional Commissioner Region VI...................	Career Incumbent	CA	ES	....	....	....
San Francisco, CA...	Regional Commissioner Region IX...................	Career Incumbent	CA	ES	....	....	....
Seattle, WA.............	Regional Commissioner Region X	Career Incumbent	CA	ES	....	....	....
Philadelphia, PA	Deputy Regional Commissioner, Region III.......	Career Incumbent	CA	ES	....	....	....
Atlanta, GA	Deputy Regional Commissioner, Region IV.......	Career Incumbent	CA	ES	....	....	....
Chicago, IL	Deputy Regional Commissioner, Region V.........	Vacant		ES	....	....	....
Kansas City, MO	Deputy Regional Commissioner, Region VII......	Career Incumbent	CA	ES	....	....	....
San Francisco, CA...	Deputy Regional Commissioner, Region IX.......	Career Incumbent	CA	ES	....	....	....
New York, NY..........	Deputy Regional Commissioner, Region II........	Career Incumbent	CA	ES	....	....	....
New York, NY..........	Deputy Regional Commissioner, Region II........	Vacant		ES	....	....	....
Dallas, TX	Deputy Regional Commissioner, Region VI.......	Career Incumbent	CA	ES	....	....	....
Boston, MA	Deputy Regional Commissioner, Region I.........	Career Incumbent	CA	ES	....	....	....
Denver, CO	Deputy Regional Commissioner, Region VIII	Vacant		ES	....	....	....
Boston, MA	Assistant Regional Commissioner for Management and Operations Support.	Vacant		ES	....	....	....
Atlanta, GA	Assistant Regional Commissioner for Management and Operations Support.	Career Incumbent	CA	ES	....	....	....
Chicago, IL	Assistant Regional Commissioner for Management and Operations Support.	Career Incumbent	CA	ES	....	....	....
San Francisco, CA...	Assistant Regional Commissioner for Management and Operations Support.	Career Incumbent	CA	ES	....	....	....
New York, NY..........	Assistant Regional Commissioner for Management and Operations Support.	Vacant		ES	....	....	....
Philadelphia, PA	Assistant Regional Commissioner for Management and Operations Support.	Career Incumbent	CA	ES	....	....	....
Dallas, TX	Assistant Regional Commissioner for Management and Operations Support.	Vacant		ES	....	....	....
Seattle, WA.............	Assistant Regional Commissioner for Management and Operations Support.	Career Incumbent	CA	ES	....	....	....

SOCIAL SECURITY ADMINISTRATION—Continued

Location	Position Title	Name of Incumbent	Type of Appt.	Pay Plan	Level, Grade, or Pay	Tenure	Expires
New York, NY	Assistant Regional Commissioner for Processing Center Operations (New York).	Vacant	....	ES	....	....	....
Philadelphia, PA	Assistant Regional Commissioner for Processing Center Operations (Philadelphia).	Career Incumbent	CA	ES	....	....	....
Birmingham, AL	Assistant Regional Commissioner for Processing Center Operations (Atlanta).	Vacant	....	ES	....	....	....
Chicago, IL	Assistant Regional Commissioner for Processing Center Operations (Chicago).	Vacant	....	ES	....	....	....
Kansas City, MO	Assistant Regional Commissioner for Processing Center Operations (Kansas City).	Career Incumbent	CA	ES	....	....	....
San Francisco, CA...	Assistant Regional Commissioner for Processing Center Operations (San Francisco).	Vacant	....	ES	....	....	....
	OFFICE OF RETIREMENT AND DISABILITY POLICY						
Woodlawn, MD	Deputy Commissioner for Retirement and Disability Policy.	Kilolo Kijakazi......................	NA	ES	....	....	....
Woodlawn, MD	Assistant Deputy Commissioner for Retirement and Disability Policy.	Career Incumbent	CA	ES	....	....	....
Woodlawn, MD	Associate Commissioner for Data Exchange, Policy Publications, and International Negotiations.	Career Incumbent	CA	ES	....	....	....
Woodlawn, MD	Deputy Associate Commissioner for Data Exchange, Policy Publications, and International Negotiations.	Vacant	....	ES	....	....	....
Woodlawn, MD	Associate Commissioner for Disability Policy ...	Career Incumbent	CA	ES	....	....	....
Woodlawn, MD	Deputy Associate Commissioner for Disability Policy.	Career Incumbent	CA	ES	....	....	....
Woodlawn, MD	Associate Commissioner for Research, Demonstration, and Employment Support.	Career Incumbent	CA	ES	....	....	....
Woodlawn, MD	Associate Commissioner for Income Security Programs.	Career Incumbent	CA	ES	....	....	....
Woodlawn, MD	Deputy Associate Commissioner for Income Security Programs.	Vacant	....	ES	....	....	....
Washington, DC	Associate Commissioner for Research, Evaluation and Statistics.	Career Incumbent	CA	ES	....	....	....
Washington, DC	Deputy Associate Commissioner for Research, Evaluation, and Statistics.	Career Incumbent	CA	ES	....	....	....
	OFFICE OF THE CHIEF INFORMATION OFFICER						
Woodlawn, MD	Chief Information Officer....................................	Marcela Escobar-Alava	NA	ES	....	....	....
Woodlawn, MD	Deputy Chief Information Officer (Implementation and Delivery).	Career Incumbent	CA	ES	....	....	....
Woodlawn, MD	Deputy Chief Information Officer (Strategy)	Career Incumbent	CA	ES	....	....	....
Woodlawn, MD	Senior Advisor	Career Incumbent	CA	ES	....	....	....
Woodlawn, MD	Chief Program Officer, Benefits Modernization.	Career Incumbent	CA	ES	....	....	....
Woodlawn, MD	Deputy Chief Program Officer, Benefits Modernization.	Vacant	....	ES	....	....	....
Woodlawn, MD	Senior Advisor	Career Incumbent	CA	ES	....	....	....
Woodlawn, MD	Chief Technology Officer	Career Incumbent	CA	ES	....	....	....
Woodlawn, MD	Chief Architect	Vacant	....	ES	....	....	....
Woodlawn, MD	Deputy Associate Commissioner for Information Security (Security Operations).	Career Incumbent	CA	ES	....	....	....
Woodlawn, MD	Associate Commissioner for Benefit Information Systems.	Career Incumbent	CA	ES	....	....	....
Woodlawn, MD	Deputy Associate Commissioner for Benefit Information Systems.	Career Incumbent	CA	ES	....	....	....
Woodlawn, MD	Associate Commissioner for Enterprise Information Systems.	Career Incumbent	CA	ES	....	....	....
Woodlawn, MD	Deputy Associate Commissioner for Enterprise Information Systems.	Career Incumbent	CA	ES	....	....	....
Woodlawn, MD	Associate Commissioner for Disability Information Systems.	Career Incumbent	CA	ES	....	....	....
Woodlawn, MD	Deputy Associate Commissioner for Disability Information Systems.	Career Incumbent	CA	ES	....	....	....
Woodlawn, MD	Associate Commissioner for Systems Architecture.	Career Incumbent	CA	ES	....	....	....
Woodlawn, MD	Deputy Associate Commissioner for Systems Architecture.	Career Incumbent	CA	ES	....	....	....
Woodlawn, MD	Associate Commissioner for Digital Transformation.	Career Incumbent	CA	ES	....	....	....

SOCIAL SECURITY ADMINISTRATION—Continued

Location	Position Title	Name of Incumbent	Type of Appt.	Pay Plan	Level, Grade, or Pay	Tenure	Expires
Woodlawn, MD	Deputy Associate Commissioner for Digital Transformation.	Career Incumbent	CA	ES	....	....	....
Woodlawn, MD	**OFFICE OF INFORMATION SECURITY** Deputy Associate Commissioner for Information Security (Security Assurance).	Career Incumbent	CA	ES	....	....	....
Washington, DC	**OFFICE OF TRANSFORMATION** Chief Transformation Officer............................	Elizabeth G Beaumon..........	NA	ES	....	....	....
Woodlawn, MD	Customer Experience Officer.......................	Career Incumbent	CA	ES	....	....	....

SOCIAL SECURITY ADMINISTRATION OFFICE OF THE INSPECTOR GENERAL

Location	Position Title	Name of Incumbent	Type of Appt.	Pay Plan	Level, Grade, or Pay	Tenure	Expires
Woodlawn, MD	**IMMEDIATE OFFICE OF THE INSPECTOR GENERAL** Inspector General	Vacant	....	EX	....	....	....

SOUTHWEST BORDER REGIONAL COMMISSION

Location	Position Title	Name of Incumbent	Type of Appt.	Pay Plan	Level, Grade, or Pay	Tenure	Expires
Washington, DC	Federal Co-Chair	Juan Sanchez.......................	PAS	....	....	....	....
Washington, DC	Federal Co-Chair	Jennifer Clyburn Reed.........	PAS	....	....	....	....

SURFACE TRANSPORTATION BOARD

Location	Position Title	Name of Incumbent	Type of Appt.	Pay Plan	Level, Grade, or Pay	Tenure	Expires
Washington, DC	Chairman	Robert E Primus	PAS	EX	III	....	12/31/27
Washington, DC	Board Member	Karen J Hedlund.................	PAS	EX	IV	....	12/31/25
Washington, DC	Board Member	Vacant	....	EX	....	....	....
Washington, DC	Board Member	Patrick Fuchs.......................	PAS	EX	IV	....	01/14/29
Washington, DC	Board Member	Michelle Schultz	PAS	EX	IV	....	02/01/26

TENNESSEE VALLEY AUTHORITY

Location	Position Title	Name of Incumbent	Type of Appt.	Pay Plan	Level, Grade, or Pay	Tenure	Expires
Huntsville, AL	**BOARD OF DIRECTORS** Chair, Board of Directors	Joe Hale Ritch	PAS	OT	....	5	05/18/25
Nashville, TN	Director..	Beth Prichard Geer.............	PAS	OT	....	5	05/18/26
Nashville, TN	Director..	Beth Harwell	PAS	OT	....	5	05/18/24
Chattanooga, TN	Director..	Robert Preston Klein	PAS	OT	....	5	05/18/26
Midlothian, VA	Director..	Lori Michelle Moore.............	PAS	OT	....	5	05/18/26
Johnson City, TN.....	Director..	Brian Eugene Noland	PAS	OT	....	5	05/18/24
Ashland, MS............	Director..	William Jackson Renick.......	PAS	OT	....	5	05/18/27
Eddyville, KY	Director..	Adam Wade White...............	PAS	OT	....	5	05/18/27
....	Director..	Vacant	....	OT	....	5	05/18/27

TENNESSEE VALLEY AUTHORITY OFFICE OF THE INSPECTOR GENERAL

Location	Position Title	Name of Incumbent	Type of Appt.	Pay Plan	Level, Grade, or Pay	Tenure	Expires
Knoxville, TN..........	Inspector General	Ben R Wagner.......................	PAS	EX	III	....	....

TRADE AND DEVELOPMENT AGENCY

Location	Position Title	Name of Incumbent	Type of Appt.	Pay Plan	Level, Grade, or Pay	Tenure	Expires
	OFFICE OF THE DIRECTOR						
Arlington, VA..........	Director...	Enoh Titilayo Ebong	PAS	EX	III	....	....
Arlington, VA..........	Deputy Director and Chief Operating Officer ...	Eleanor Collinson.................	NA	ES	....	....	....
Arlington, VA..........	Chief of Staff...	Thamar E Harrigan.............	SC	GS	15	....	....
Arlington, VA..........	Director of Public Engagement.........................	Brandon Bradford	SC	GS	15	....	....
Arlington, VA..........	Congressional Affairs Director	Thomas J Woodburn	SC	GS	15	....	....

U.S. ABILITYONE COMMISSION

Location	Position Title	Name of Incumbent	Type of Appt.	Pay Plan	Level, Grade, or Pay	Tenure	Expires
	COMMITTEE FOR PURCHASE FROM PEOPLE WHO ARE BLIND OR SEVERELY DISABLED						
Winter Haven, FL ...	Member...	Bryan Bashin.......................	PA	PD	....	5	12/21/26
Arlington, VA..........	Member...	Christina Brandt.................	PA	PD	....	5	12/21/25
Washington, DC	Member...	Gabriel Cazares...................	PA	PD	....	....	....
Washington, DC	Member...	Chai Feldblum.....................	PA	PD	....	....	....

U.S. ADVISORY COMMISSION ON PUBLIC DIPLOMACY

Location	Position Title	Name of Incumbent	Type of Appt.	Pay Plan	Level, Grade, or Pay	Tenure	Expires
Washington, DC	Member...	Sim Farar.............................	PAS	....	....	....	....
Washington, DC	Member...	William Hybl	PAS	....	....	....	....

U.S. AGENCY FOR GLOBAL MEDIA

Location	Position Title	Name of Incumbent	Type of Appt.	Pay Plan	Level, Grade, or Pay	Tenure	Expires
Washington, DC	Chief Executive Officer	Amanda Bennett	PAS	EX	III	....	....
Washington, DC	Deputy Chief Executive Officer	Career Incumbent	CA	ES	....	....	....
Washington, DC	Senior Advisor..	Sandra Sugawara.................	SC	GS	15	....	....
Washington, DC	Strategic Transformation Officer for Government Relations.	Cheryl Johnson.....................	TA	ES	....	....	06/30/26
Washington, DC	Director of Public Affairs	Adriane Brown	SC	GS	15	....	....
Washington, DC	Sr Communications Advisor	Katrina A Martell	SC	GS	14	....	....
Washington, DC	Director, Office of Technology Services and Innovation.	Career Incumbent	CA	ES	....	....	....
Miami, FL...............	Director Office of Cuba Broadcasting	Sylvia Rosabal Stanley	NA	ES	....	....	....
Miami, FL...............	Senior Advisor for Cuba Broadcasting...............	Roberto Cespedes	SC	GS	15	....	....
	INTERNATIONAL BROADCASTING ADVISORY BOARD						
Washington, DC	Chair, International Broadcasting Advisory Board.	Kenneth Jarin	PAS	AD	....	....	01/01/27
Washington, DC	International Broadcasting Advisory Board Member.	Luis Botello............................	PAS	AD	....	....	01/01/25
Washington, DC	International Broadcasting Advisory Board Member.	Jamie M Fly.........................	PAS	AD	....	....	01/01/27
Washington, DC	International Broadcasting Advisory Board Member.	Jeffrey Gedmin	PAS	AD	....	....	01/01/25

U.S. AGENCY FOR GLOBAL MEDIA—Continued

Location	Position Title	Name of Incumbent	Type of Appt.	Pay Plan	Level, Grade, or Pay	Tenure	Expires
Washington, DC	International Broadcasting Advisory Board Member.	Michelle Giuda	PAS	AD	....	....	01/01/27
Washington, DC	International Broadcasting Advisory Board Member.	Kathleen Matthews..............	PAS	AD	....	....	01/01/27

U.S. ACCESS BOARD

Location	Position Title	Name of Incumbent	Type of Appt.	Pay Plan	Level, Grade, or Pay	Tenure	Expires
	PUBLIC BOARD						
Washington, DC	Member..	Elver Ariza-Silva	PA	AD	....	4	12/03/27
Washington, DC	Member..	Olivia Mae Asuncion	PA	AD	....	4	12/03/25
Washington, DC	Member..	Heather Gina Dowdy	PA	AD	....	4	12/03/27
Washington, DC	Member..	Stephanie L Enyart	PA	AD	....	4	12/03/24
Washington, DC	Member..	Gregory S Fehribach	PA	AD	....	4	12/03/24
Washington, DC	Member..	Mozhdeh A Hamraie	PA	AD	....	4	12/03/25
Washington, DC	Member..	Madeline Rode Ruvolo	PA	AD	....	4	12/03/24
Washington, DC	Member..	Tina G Pedersen	PA	AD	....	4	12/03/25
Washington, DC	Member..	Hannah Raissa Ibanez........	PA	AD	....	4	12/03/26
Washington, DC	Member..	Carmen D Jones...................	PA	AD	....	4	12/03/24
Washington, DC	Member..	Benjamin William Julian Nadolsky.	PA	AD	....	4	12/03/27
Washington, DC	Member..	Kristen Lynn Liu..................	PA	AD	....	4	12/03/26
Washington, DC	Member..	Alexis A Kashar	PA	AD	....	4	12/03/26
	OFFICE OF THE EXECUTIVE DIRECTOR						
Washington, DC	Attorney Advisor..	Christopher Kuczynski	XS	SL	....	....	....

UNITED STATES - CHINA ECONOMIC AND SECURITY REVIEW COMMISSION

Location	Position Title	Name of Incumbent	Type of Appt.	Pay Plan	Level, Grade, or Pay	Tenure	Expires
Washington, DC	Chairman	Vacant	....	PD	....	2	....
Washington, DC	Vice Chairman	Robin Cleveland	XS	PD	....	2	12/31/26
Washington, DC	Commissioner..	Aaron Friedberg	XS	PD	....	2	12/26/25
Washington, DC	Commissioner..	Jacob Helberg	XS	PD	....	2	12/31/24
Washington, DC	Commissioner..	Leland Miller......................	XS	PD	....	2	12/31/25
Washington, DC	Commissioner..	Vacant	....	PD	....	2	....
Washington, DC	Commissioner..	Reva Price...........................	XS	PD	....	2	12/31/24
Washington, DC	Commissioner..	Clifton Sims........................	XS	PD	....	2	12/31/25
Washington, DC	Commissioner..	Kimberly Thompson Glas	XS	PD	....	2	12/31/24
Washington, DC	Commissioner..	Vacant	....	PD	....	2	....
Washington, DC	Commissioner..	Vacant	....	PD	....	2	....
Washington, DC	Commissioner..	Michael Wessel	XS	PD	....	2	12/31/21

UNITED STATES AGENCY FOR INTERNATIONAL DEVELOPMENT

Location	Position Title	Name of Incumbent	Type of Appt.	Pay Plan	Level, Grade, or Pay	Tenure	Expires
	OFFICE OF THE ADMINISTRATOR						
Washington, DC	Administrator, Agency for International Development.	Samantha J Power	PAS	EX	II		
Washington, DC	Deputy Administrator (Policy and Programming), Agency for International Development.	Isobel Coleman	PAS	EX	IV		
Washington, DC	Chief of Staff	Rebecca Chalif	NA	ES			
	Deputy Chief of Staff	Adam Siegel		ES			
Washington, DC	Senior Advisor	Eric Postel	XS	AD			
Washington, DC	Senior Advisor	Robert Gardner Berschinski.	XS	AD			
Washington, DC	Senior Advisor	Sarah Rose	XS	AD			
Washington, DC	Deputy Assistant Administrator	Megan Doherty	XS	AD			
Washington, DC	Senior Advisor	Marcela Escobari	XS	AD			
Washington, DC	National Security Director	Colin Thomas-Jensen	XS	AD			
Washington, DC	Chief Diversity, Equity, Inclusion, and Accessibility Officer.	Neneh Diallo	XS	AD			
Washington, DC	Director, and Senior Coordinator Gender	Jamille Bigio	XS	AD			
Washington, DC	Special Assistant	Emily Green	XS	AD			
Washington, DC	Special Advisor	Rayden Llano	XS	AD			
Washington, DC	Senior Advisor	Kelly Razzouk	XS	AD			
Washington, DC	Special Advisor	Dennis Vega	XS	AD			
Washington, DC	Senior Policy Advisor	Kamal Essaheb	XS	AD			
Washington, DC	Senior Policy Advisor	Candace Zaidl	XS	AD			
Washington, DC	Senior Advisor	Hillary Schrenell	XS	AD			
Washington, DC	Senior Director for Strategy and Planning	Rebecca Wexler	XS	AD			
Washington, DC	Senior Director for Communications and Policy.	Maany N Peyvan	XS	AD			
Washington, DC	Senior Advisor	Sophia Lalani	XS	AD			
Washington, DC	Special Advisor	Jennifer Sosa	XS	AD			
Washington, DC	Trip Director	Ronalie De Alwis	XS	AD			
Washington, DC	Director of Operations	Blair Mallin	XS	AD			
Washington, DC	Special Advisor	Yasmin Faruki	XS	AD			
Washington, DC	White House Liaison	Elvir Klempic	XS	AD			
Washington, DC	Deputy White House Liaison	Heather Leinenbach	XS	AD			
Washington, DC	Special Advisor	Garrett Lam	XS	AD			
Washington, DC	Special Assistant to the Administrator	Molly Papermaster	XS	AD			
Washington, DC	Director of Scheduling	Amol Shalia	XS	AD			
Washington, DC	Special Assistant	Bayly Winder	XS	AD			
Washington, DC	Special Assistant	Noelle Carter	XS	AD			
Washington, DC	Special Assistant	Sedona Williams	XS	AD			
Washington, DC	General Counsel	Margaret Taylor	NA	ES			
Washington, DC	Senior Legal Advisor	Ozge Guzelsu	XS	AD			
Washington, DC	Senior Advisor	Career Incumbent	CA	ES			
	BUREAU FOR LEGISLATIVE AND PUBLIC AFFAIRS						
Washington, DC	Deputy Assistant Administrator	Career Incumbent	CA	ES			
Washington, DC	Deputy Assistant Administrator	Daphne McCurdy	XS	AD			
Washington, DC	Deputy Assistant Administrator & Chief Communications Officer.	Jessica Jennings	XS	AD			
Washington, DC	Director of Strategic Communications	Alexandria Gabrielle Phillips.	XS	AD			
Washington, DC	Director of Protocol	Adam Baron	XS	AD			
Washington, DC	Director of Policy and Strategic Initiatives	Tessa Wick	XS	AD			
Washington, DC	Director of Speechwriting	Elizabeth Schaack	XS	AD			
Washington, DC	Congressional Liaison Officer	Graham Markiewicz	XS	AD			
Washington, DC	Senior Advisor	Eliza Ramirez	XS	AD			
Washington, DC	Congressional Liaison Officer	Elisa Santana	XS	AD			
Washington, DC	Deputy Director of Public Engagement	Karen Vargas	XS	AD			
Washington, DC	Communication Advisor	Mariam Siddiqui	XS	AD			
Washington, DC	Digital Strategist	Melissa Cabezas Hevener	XS	AD			
Washington, DC	Public Engagement Advisor	Shea Elise Martinson	XS	AD			
Washington, DC	Communications Advisor	Lauren Miller	XS	AD			
Washington, DC	Speechwriter	Ramya Prabhakar	XS	AD			
	OFFICE OF CIVIL RIGHTS AND DIVERSITY						
Washington, DC	Equal Opportunity Officer	Career Incumbent	CA	ES			
	BUREAU FOR ASIA						
Washington, DC	Assistant Administrator for Asia	Rolfe M Schiffer	PAS	EX	IV		
Washington, DC	Deputy Assistant Administrator	Career Incumbent	CA	ES			
Washington, DC	Deputy Assistant Administrator	Sukhmeet Kaur	XS	AD			

UNITED STATES AGENCY FOR INTERNATIONAL DEVELOPMENT—Continued

Location	Position Title	Name of Incumbent	Type of Appt.	Pay Plan	Level, Grade, or Pay	Tenure	Expires
Washington, DC	Senior Advisor..	Ubong Akpaninyie...............	XS	AD	....	....	....
Washington, DC	Strategic Engagement Advisor	Hailey Becker	XS	AD	....	....	....
	BUREAU FOR DEMOCRACY, CONFLICT, AND HUMANITARIAN ASSISTANCE						
Washington, DC	Assistant to the Administrator..........................	Career Incumbent	CA	ES	....	....	....
	BUREAU FOR RESILIENCE, ENVIRONMENT, AND FOOD SECURITY						
Washington, DC	Deputy Assistant Administrator and Chief Climate Officer.	Gillian Caldwell	XS	AD	....	....	....
	BUREAU FOR GLOBAL HEALTH						
Washington, DC	Assistant Administrator for Global Health	Atul Gawande......................	PAS	EX	IV	....	....
Washington, DC	Deputy Assistant Administrator........................	Career Incumbent	CA	ES	....	....	....
Washington, DC	Malaria Coordinator...	David Walton	NA	ES	....	....	....
Washington, DC	Deputy Assistant Administrator........................	Nidhi Bouri	XS	AD	....	....	....
Washington, DC	Director...	Nicole Pasteur	XS	AD	....	....	....
Washington, DC	Chief of Staff...	Ashley Marie Boccuzzi.........	XS	AD	....	....	....
Washington, DC	Special Assistant...	Chelsea Chatterton	XS	AD	....	....	....
	BUREAU FOR AFRICA						
Washington, DC	Assistant Administrator for Africa....................	Monde Muyangwa	PAS	EX	IV	....	....
Washington, DC	Deputy Assistant Administrator........................	Career Incumbent	CA	ES	....	....	....
Washington, DC	Deputy Assistant Administrator........................	Tyler Beckelman	XS	AD	....	....	....
Washington, DC	Senior Advisor..	Mohyeldin Omer...................	XS	AD	....	....	....
Washington, DC	Coordinator..	British Robinson...................	XS	AD	....	....	....
Washington, DC	Special Advisor..	Patrick Meyers	XS	AD	....	....	....
	BUREAU FOR EUROPE AND EURASIA						
Washington, DC	Assistant Administrator for Europe and Eurasia.	Erin McKee..........................	PAS	EX	IV	....	....
Washington, DC	Deputy Assistant Administrator........................	Career Incumbent	CA	ES	....	....	....
Washington, DC	Deputy Assistant Administrator........................	Mark Simakovsky	XS	AD	....	....	....
Washington, DC	Senior Advisor..	Alexandre Tiersky...............	XS	AD	....	....	....
Washington, DC	Chief of Staff...	Leah Nodvin	XS	AD	....	....	....
	BUREAU FOR LATIN AMERICA AND THE CARIBBEAN						
Washington, DC	Deputy Assistant Administrator........................	Career Incumbent	CA	ES	....	....	....
Washington, DC	Deputy Assistant Administrator........................	Mileydi Guilarte	XS	AD	....	....	....
Washington, DC	Senior Advisor..	Clay Boggs	XS	AD	....	....	....
Washington, DC	Senior Advisor..	Michael Camilleri.................	XS	AD	....	....	....
Washington, DC	Special Assistant to Assistant Administrator....	Pablo Iraheta	XS	AD	....	....	....
	BUREAU FOR MANAGEMENT						
Washington, DC	Assistant Administrator for Management.........	Colleen Roberson Allen........	PA	EX	IV	....	....
Washington, DC	Deputy Assistant Administrator........................	Career Incumbent	CA	ES	....	....	....
Washington, DC	Deputy Assistant Administrator........................	Samir Goswami	XS	AD	....	....	....
Washington, DC	Deputy Chief Information Officer	Career Incumbent	CA	ES	....	....	....
	OFFICE OF HUMAN CAPITAL AND TALENT MANAGEMENT						
Washington, DC	Assistant to the Administrator..........................	Adetola Abiade	XS	AD	....	....	....
	BUREAU FOR MIDDLE EAST						
Washington, DC	Assistant Administrator for Middle East	Vacant	....	EX	....	....	....
Washington, DC	Deputy Assistant Administrator........................	Career Incumbent	CA	ES	....	....	....
Washington, DC	Deputy Assistant Administrator........................	John Walsh	XS	AD	....	....	....
	OFFICE OF THE EXECUTIVE SECRETARIAT						
Washington, DC	Executive Secretary..	Laila Elgohary	NA	ES	....	....	....
	BUREAU FOR HUMANITARIAN ASSISTANCE						
Washington, DC	Deputy Assistant Administrator........................	Marcia Wong........................	XS	AD	....	....	....
Washington, DC	Special Assistant...	Layla Siddig........................	XS	AD	....	....	....
	BUREAU FOR RESILIENCE, ENVIRONMENT, AND FOOD SECURITY						
Washington, DC	Deputy Assistant Administrator........................	Ann Vaughan	XS	AD	....	....	....
Washington, DC	Special Assistant...	Aaminah Tabassum.............	XS	AD	....	....	....
	BUREAU FOR CONFLICT PREVENTION AND STABILIZATION						
Washington, DC	Director, Civilian-Military Cooperation	Career Incumbent	CA	ES	....	....	....
Washington, DC	Director for the Office of Transition Initiatives.	Brittany Brown	XS	AD	....	....	....

UNITED STATES AGENCY FOR INTERNATIONAL DEVELOPMENT—Continued

Location	Position Title	Name of Incumbent	Type of Appt.	Pay Plan	Level, Grade, or Pay	Tenure	Expires
	BUREAU FOR INCLUSIVE GROWTH, PARTNERSHIPS, AND INNOVATION						
Washington, DC	Senior LGBTI Coordinator..........................	Jay Gilliam	XS	AD	....	....	....
Washington, DC	Deputy Assistant Administrator........................	Bama Athreya	XS	AD	....	....	....
	BUREAU FOR DEVELOPMENT, DEMOCRACY AND INNOVATION						
Washington, DC	Director of the Innovation, Technology and Research Hub.	Mohamed W Abdel-Kader....	XS	AD	....	....	....
	BUREAU FOR RESILIENCE, ENVIRONMENT, AND FOOD SECURITY						
Washington, DC	Senior Climate Finance Advisor........................	Jacqueline Musiitwa	XS	AD	....	....	....
Washington, DC	Senior Advisor..	Avinash Kaza......................	XS	AD	....	....	....
Washington, DC	Senior Advisor..	Aria Grabowski	XS	AD	....	....	....
Washington, DC	Chief of Staff..	Isabella Blecha	XS	AD	....	....	....
Washington, DC	Senior Advisor for Faith Engagement...............	Peter Mandaville..................	XS	AD	....	....	....
	OFFICE OF THE CHIEF ECONOMIST						
Washington, DC	Deputy Chief Economist	Career Incumbent	CA	ES	....	....	....
Washington, DC	Macroeconomist	Zulima Lealcalderon	XS	AD	....	....	....
	OFFICE OF POLICY						
Washington, DC	Deputy Assistant Administrator........................	Career Incumbent	CA	ES	....	....	....
Washington, DC	Senior Policy Advisor..........................	Daniel K Balke....................	XS	AD	....	....	....
Washington, DC	Senior Policy Advisor..........................	Francisco A Bencosme	XS	AD	....	....	....
Washington, DC	Senior Policy Advisor..........................	Genevieve Maricle...............	XS	AD	....	....	....
Washington, DC	Policy Advisor..........................	Holly Stevens......................	XS	AD	....	....	....
	BUREAU FOR DEMOCRACY, HUMAN RIGHTS, AND GOVERNANCE						
Washington, DC	Deputy Assistant Administrator........................	Career Incumbent	CA	ES	....	....	....
Washington, DC	Director..........................	Rosarie Tucci	XS	AD	....	....	....
Washington, DC	Assistant to the Administrator..........................	Shannon Green....................	XS	AD	....	....	....
Washington, DC	Deputy Assistant Administrator........................	Lesley Warner......................	XS	AD	....	....	....
Washington, DC	Senior Advisor..........................	Vera Zakem..........................	XS	AD	....	....	....
Washington, DC	Senior Advisor..........................	Sophia Lajaunie	XS	AD	....	....	....
Washington, DC	Special Assistant and Advisor	Filip Jotevski	XS	AD	....	....	....
	BUREAU FOR PLANNING, LEARNING, AND RESOURCE MANAGEMENT						
Washington, DC	Deputy Assistant Administrator........................	Career Incumbent	CA	ES	....	....	....
Washington, DC	Assistant to the Administrator..........................	Michele Sumilas..................	XS	AD	....	....	....
Washington, DC	Special Advisor..........................	Vacant	....	AD	....	....	....
Washington, DC	Advisor..........................	Maiesha Hossain	XS	AD	....	....	....
Washington, DC	Advisor for Policy and Global Engagement.......	Areeb Akbari......................	XS	AD	....	....	....
Washington, DC	Senior Advisor..........................	Naseam Alavi	XS	AD	....	....	....
	BUREAU FOR RESILIENCE, ENVIRONMENT, AND FOOD SECURITY						
Washington, DC	Deputy Assistant Administrator........................	Career Incumbent	CA	ES	....	....	....
Washington, DC	Assistant to the Administrator..........................	Dina Esposito	XS	AD	....	....	....
Washington, DC	Senior Advisor..........................	Kristen Joan Sarri	XS	AD	....	....	....

UNITED STATES AGENCY FOR INTERNATIONAL DEVELOPMENT OFFICE OF THE INSPECTOR GENERAL

Location	Position Title	Name of Incumbent	Type of Appt.	Pay Plan	Level, Grade, or Pay	Tenure	Expires
Washington, DC	Inspector General	Paul Kenneth Martin...........	PAS	OT	....	....	....

UNITED STATES COMMISSION ON CIVIL RIGHTS

Location	Position Title	Name of Incumbent	Type of Appt.	Pay Plan	Level, Grade, or Pay	Tenure	Expires
	COMMISSIONERS						
San Antonio, TX	Commissioner..	Rochelle Garza......................	PA	EX	IV	....	....
Los Angeles, CA	Vice-Chair..	Vacant	....	EX	....	....	....
San Francisco, CA...	Commissioner..	Mondaire Jones	XS	EX	IV	....	12/15/28

UNITED STATES COMMISSION ON CIVIL RIGHTS—Continued

Location	Position Title	Name of Incumbent	Type of Appt.	Pay Plan	Level, Grade, or Pay	Tenure	Expires
Las Vegas, NV	Commissioner	Glenn Magpantay	XS	EX	IV		12/12/28
Concord, MA	Vice Chairman	Vacant		EX			
San Diego, CA	Commissioner	Gail Heriot	XS	EX	IV		07/18/08
Cleveland, OH	Commissioner	Peter N Kirsanow	XS	EX	IV		12/16/19
New York, NY	Commissioner	Victoria Nourse	PA	EX	IV		
Washington, DC	Special Assistant	John Kinney Mashburn	SC	GS	14		
Washington, DC	Special Assistant to the Commissioner	Stephanie Mariette Wong	SC	GS	12		
Washington, DC	Vice Chairman	Vacant		EX			
Washington, DC	Commissioner	Stephen L Gilchrist	PA	EX	IV		
Fayetteville, NC	Commissioner (Vicechair)	J Christian Adams	PA	EX	IV		12/05/25
Washington, DC	Special Assistant	Nathalie Demirdjian-Rivest.	SC	GS	13		
Washington, DC	Special Assistant to the Commissioner	Irena Vidulovic	SC	GS	14		
Washington, DC	Special Assistant to the Commissioner	Alexis Fragosa	SC	GS	13		
Washington, DC	Special Assistant to the Commissioner	Carissa Beth Mulder	SC	GS	14		
Washington, DC	Special Assistant to the Commissioner	Yvesner Zamar	SC	GS	14		
	STAFF MEMBERS						
Washington, DC	Associate Deputy Staff Director	Vacant		ES			
Washington, DC	Assistant Staff Director for Civil Rights Evaluation.	Vacant		ES			
Washington, DC	Acting Staff Director	Vacant		ES			
Washington, DC	General Counsel	Vacant		ES			
Washington, DC	Assistant Staff Director for Congressional Affairs.	Vacant		ES			
Washington, DC	Staff Director	Mauro Albert Morales	NA	ES			
Washington, DC	Principal Advisor to the Commission	Vacant		ES			
Washington, DC	Special Assistance to the Commissioner	Thomas Simuel	SC	GS	14		
Washington, DC	Special Assistant to the Commissioner	Vacant		GS			

UNITED STATES COMMISSION FOR THE PRESERVATION OF AMERICA'S HERITAGE ABROAD

Location	Position Title	Name of Incumbent	Type of Appt.	Pay Plan	Level, Grade, or Pay	Tenure	Expires
Washington, DC	Chair	Star Jones	PA	WC		3	02/27/25
Washington, DC	Member	Nancy Berman	PA	WC		3	06/24/25
Washington, DC	Member	Herbert Block	PA	WC		3	07/13/25
Washington, DC	Member	Abba Cohen	PA	WC		3	06/24/25
Washington, DC	Member	Joseph Douek	PA	WC		3	08/09/25
Washington, DC	Member	William C Inboden	PA	WC		3	07/13/26
Washington, DC	Member	Emil Fish	PA	WC		3	06/24/10
Washington, DC	Member	Jonathan Greenwald	PA	WC		3	02/27/25
Washington, DC	Member	Martin B Gold	PA	WC		3	07/13/08
Washington, DC	Member	John Cordisco	PA				02/27/25
Washington, DC	Member	Nancy K Kaufman	PA	WC		3	02/27/25
Washington, DC	Member	Elizabeth Naftali	PA	WC		3	07/13/25
Washington, DC	Member	Michael Lozman	PA	WC		3	06/24/25
Washington, DC	Member	Michael Marquardt	PA	WC		3	02/27/25
Washington, DC	Member	Harley Lippman	PA	WC		3	06/24/25
Washington, DC	Member	Maureen Pikarski	PA	WC		3	02/27/25
Washington, DC	Member	Yair Robinson	PA	WC		3	02/27/25
Washington, DC	Member	Hershel Wein	PA	WC		3	08/17/25
Washington, DC	Member	Lesley Weiss	PA	WC		3	08/09/23
Washington, DC	Member	Vacant		WC		3	
Washington, DC	Member	Roselyne Swig	PA	WC		3	08/02/23

UNITED STATES ELECTION ASSISTANCE COMMISSION

Location	Position Title	Name of Incumbent	Type of Appt.	Pay Plan	Level, Grade, or Pay	Tenure	Expires
Silver Spring, MD	Member	Benjamin W Hovland	PAS	EX	IV	4	
Williamsburg, VA	Member	Christy A McCormick	PAS	EX	IV	4	
Jacksonville, FL	Member	Donald L Palmer	PAS	EX	IV	4	
Silver Spring, MD	Member	Thomas Hicks	PAS	EX	IV	4	
Washington, DC	Confidential Assistant	Heather Ford	PAS	EX	IV		
Washington, DC	Confidential Assistant	Kristen Mei Yin Lee	SC	OT			

UNITED STATES ELECTION ASSISTANCE COMMISSION—Continued

Location	Position Title	Name of Incumbent	Type of Appt.	Pay Plan	Level, Grade, or Pay	Tenure	Expires
Silver Spring, MD ...	Executive Director	Brianna Schletz	XS	AD	....	4	....
Silver Spring, MD ...	General Counsel	Camden Kelliher	XS	AD	....	4	12/20/24

UNITED STATES HOLOCAUST MEMORIAL MUSEUM

Location	Position Title	Name of Incumbent	Type of Appt.	Pay Plan	Level, Grade, or Pay	Tenure	Expires
Washington, DC	Council Chair	Stuart E Eizenstat	PA	WC	....	....	01/15/27
Washington, DC	Council Vice Chair	Allan M Holt	PA	WC	....	....	01/15/27
Washington, DC	Council Chair Emeritus	Tom A Bernstein	PA	WC	....	....	01/15/27
Washington, DC	Council Chair Emeritus	Howard M Lorber	PA	WC	....	....	01/15/25
Washington, DC	Council Vice Chair Emeritus	Joshua B Bolten	PA	WC	....	....	01/15/24
Washington, DC	Council Member	Kevin Abel	PA	WC	....	....	01/15/28
Washington, DC	Council Member	Michael S Beals	PA	WC	....	....	01/15/28
Washington, DC	Council Member	David Cicilline	PA	WC	....	....	01/15/29
Washington, DC	Council Member	Adam S Boehler	PA	WC	....	....	01/15/25
Washington, DC	Council Member	Susan Lowenberg	PA	WC	....	....	01/15/29
Washington, DC	Council Member	Theodore E Deutch	PA	WC	....	....	01/15/28
Washington, DC	Council Member	Kimberly M Emerson	PA	WC	....	....	01/15/28
Washington, DC	Council Member	Paul Fine	PA	WC	....	....	01/15/29
Washington, DC	Council Member	Abraham H Foxman	PA	WC	....	....	01/15/27
Washington, DC	Council Member	Meryl Frank	PA	WC	....	....	01/15/27
Washington, DC	Council Member	Andrew H Giuliani	PA	WC	....	....	01/15/26
Washington, DC	Council Member	Michael S Glassner	PA	WC	....	....	01/15/26
Washington, DC	Council Member	Judith Gold	PA	WC	....	....	01/15/27
Washington, DC	Council Member	Mark Goldfeder	PA	WC	....	....	01/15/25
Washington, DC	Council Member	Judith Schocken	PA	WC	....	....	01/15/29
Washington, DC	Council Member	Richard A Grenell	PA	WC	....	....	01/15/25
Washington, DC	Council Member	Alexander P Heckler	PA	WC	....	....	01/15/28
Washington, DC	Council Member	Danielle B Hertz	PA	WC	....	....	01/15/28
Washington, DC	Council Member	Daniel Huff	PA	WC	....	....	01/15/26
Washington, DC	Council Member	Marsha Z Laufer	PA	WC	....	....	01/15/28
Washington, DC	Council Member	Sam Lauter	PA	WC	....	....	01/15/27
Washington, DC	Council Member	Jonathan S Lavine	PA	WC	....	....	01/15/28
Washington, DC	Council Member	Susan G Levine	PA	WC	....	....	01/15/29
Washington, DC	Council Member	Alan D Listhaus	PA	WC	....	....	01/15/25
Washington, DC	Council Member	Nicholas F Luna	PA	WC	....	....	01/15/26
Washington, DC	Council Member	Marsha Borin	PA	WC	....	....	01/15/29
Washington, DC	Council Member	Sigal P Mandelker	PA	WC	....	....	01/15/25
Washington, DC	Council Member	David M Marchick	PA	WC	....	....	01/15/26
Washington, DC	Council Member	Cynthia Simon Skjodt	PA	WC	....	....	01/15/29
Washington, DC	Council Member	John T McNabb, II	PA	WC	....	....	01/15/25
Washington, DC	Council Member	Eli H Miller	PA	WC	....	....	01/15/25
Washington, DC	Council Member	Jeffrey Miller	PA	WC	....	....	01/15/26
Washington, DC	Council Member	Max L Miller	PA	WC	....	....	01/15/26
Washington, DC	Council Member	Martin Oliner	PA	WC	....	....	01/15/26
Washington, DC	Council Member	Jeffrey Peck	PA	WC	....	....	01/15/27
Washington, DC	Council Member	Leah Pisar	PA	WC	....	....	01/15/27
Washington, DC	Council Member	Jimmy Resnick	PA	WC	....	....	01/15/26
Washington, DC	Council Member	Curtis D Robinson	PA	WC	....	....	01/15/25
Washington, DC	Council Member	Irvin N Shapell	PA	WC	....	....	01/15/29
Washington, DC	Council Member	Mark A Siegel	PA	WC	....	....	01/15/27
Washington, DC	Council Member	Harry E Sloan	PA	WC	....	....	01/15/28
Washington, DC	Council Member	Jared Smith	PA	WC	....	....	01/15/25
Washington, DC	Council Member	Alan D Solomont	PA	WC	....	....	01/15/28
Washington, DC	Council Member	Susan K Stern	PA	WC	....	....	01/15/27
Washington, DC	Council Member	William H Stern	PA	WC	....	....	01/15/25
Washington, DC	Council Member	Howard D Unger	PA	WC	....	....	01/15/26
Washington, DC	Council Member	Mitchell Webber	PA	WC	....	....	01/15/26
Washington, DC	Council Member	Samantha Vinograd	PA	WC	....	....	01/15/29
Washington, DC	Council Member	Mark Wilf	PA	WC	....	....	01/15/29
Washington, DC	Council Member	Gary P Zola	PA	WC	....	....	01/15/28

UNITED STATES INSTITUTE OF PEACE

Location	Position Title	Name of Incumbent	Type of Appt.	Pay Plan	Level, Grade, or Pay	Tenure	Expires
	BOARD OF DIRECTORS						
Washington, DC	Chair, Board of Directors	Judy Ansley	PAS	PD	....	4	09/19/15
Washington, DC	Vice Chair, Board of Directors	Nancy M Zirkin	PAS	PD	....	4	01/19/11
Washington, DC	Member, Board of Directors	Jonathan W Burks	PAS	PD	....	4	08/08/26
Washington, DC	Member, Board of Directors	Joseph L Falk	PAS	PD	....	4	02/02/27
Washington, DC	Member, Board of Directors	Edward M Gabriel...............	PAS	PD	....	4	08/08/26
Washington, DC	Member, Board of Directors	Kerry Kennedy	PAS	PD	....	4	01/19/11
Washington, DC	Member, Board of Directors	Michael Singh......................	PAS	PD	....	4	08/08/26
Washington, DC	Member, Board of Directors	John Sullivan.......................	PAS	PD	....	4	05/05/28
Washington, DC	Member, Board of Directors	Mary Swig............................	PAS	PD	....	4	08/08/26
Washington, DC	Member, Board of Directors	Kathryn L Wheelbarger.......	PAS	PD	....	4	08/08/26
Washington, DC	Member, Board of Directors	Roger Zakheim	PAS	PD	....	4	02/02/27
Washington, DC	Member, Board of Directors	Vacant	....	PD	....	4	....

UNITED STATES INTERNATIONAL DEVELOPMENT FINANCE CORPORATION

Location	Position Title	Name of Incumbent	Type of Appt.	Pay Plan	Level, Grade, or Pay	Tenure	Expires
	OFFICE OF THE CHIEF EXECUTIVE						
Washington, DC	Board Member	Deven Jawahar Parekh........	PAS	EX	IV	....	12/21/23
Washington, DC	Board Member	Vacant	....	EX	....	....	....
Washington, DC	Board Member	Irving Widmer Bailey	PAS	EX	IV	....	12/21/23
Washington, DC	Board Member	Christopher P Vincze	PAS	EX	IV	....	12/17/19
Washington, DC	Chief of Staff..	Jane Rhee	XS	OT		....	....
Washington, DC	Vice President, External Affairs	Vacant	....	OT		....	....
Washington, DC	Senior Advisor	Vacant	....	GS		....	....
Washington, DC	Vice President and General Counsel.................	Sarah Elizabeth Fandell......	XS	OT		....	....
Washington, DC	Special Assistant.....................................	Alanna Paul.........................	SC	GS	9	....	....
Washington, DC	Advisor...	Abigail Wade	SC	GS	11	....	....
Washington, DC	Chief Operating Officer	Agnes Dasewicz...................	XS	OT		....	....
Washington, DC	Strategy Associate	Omar Ben Halim..................	XS	OT		....	....
Washington, DC	Senior Vice President for Administration.........	Vacant	....	OT		....	....
Washington, DC	Senior Advisor	Juan Sebastian Gonzalez.....	XS	OT		....	....
Washington, DC	Director, Climate Diversification	Ashley Thomas	XS	OT		....	....
Washington, DC	Program Manager	Neonu Jewell	XS	OT		....	....
Washington, DC	Strategy Associate	Patrick Deem	XS	OT		....	....
Washington, DC	Strategy Associate	Tara Boggaram....................	XS	OT		....	....
Washington, DC	Senior Advisor	Vanessa Holcomb Mann.......	XS	OT		....	....
Washington, DC	Senior Advisor	Lauren A Vargas	SC	GS	15	....	....
Washington, DC	Deputy Director, Diversity, Equity, Inclusion, and Accessibility.	Karmen Smith	XS	OT		....	....
Washington, DC	Deputy Chief of Staff for Strategy	Alexandra Kahan	XS	OT		....	....
Washington, DC	Chief Executive Officer	Scott Andrew Nathan	PAS	EX	II	....	....
Washington, DC	Advisor-Speechwriter	Diego Garcia........................	SC	GS	13	....	....
Washington, DC	Deputy Chief Executive Officer.......................	Nisha Desai Biswal.............	PAS	EX	III	....	....
Washington, DC	Senior Advisor	Michelle Czarniak	SC	GS	15	....	....
Washington, DC	Senior Advisor	Vacant	....	OT		....	....
Washington, DC	Senior Advisor	Richard Patrick Granfield ...	XS	OT		....	....
Washington, DC	Senior Advisor	Caitlin B Klevorick	XS	OT		....	....
Washington, DC	Senior Advisor	Joshua Kram	XS	OT		....	....
Washington, DC	Vice President, Office of Development Policy....	Elizabeth Boggs Davidsen ...	XS	OT		....	....
Washington, DC	Managing Director, Portfolio Strategy	Katherine Collins	XS	OT		....	....
Washington, DC	Senior Advisor for Co-Financing Partnerships..	Claire Foster Avett..............	XS	OT		....	....
Washington, DC	Chief Climate Officer	Jacob Caplan Levine............	XS	OT		....	....
Washington, DC	Deputy Chief, Climate Officer	Aparna Shrivastava	XS	OT		....	....
Washington, DC	Special Assistant.....................................	Jack Steel............................	SC	GS	9	....	....
Washington, DC	Senior Gender Policy Advisor	Hama Makino.......................	XS	OT		....	....
Washington, DC	Special Assistant.....................................	Merone Kahassai..................	SC	GS	12	....	....
Washington, DC	Advisor...	Philip Rounds	XS	OT		....	....
Washington, DC	Advisor...	Zhanrui Kuang.....................	XS	OT		....	....
	OFFICE OF FOREIGN POLICY						
Washington, DC	Vice President, Office of Foreign Policy	Vacant	....	OT	....	....	....

UNITED STATES INTERNATIONAL TRADE COMMISSION

Location	Position Title	Name of Incumbent	Type of Appt.	Pay Plan	Level, Grade, or Pay	Tenure	Expires
	OFFICE OF THE CHAIRMAN						
Washington, DC	Chairman	Amy A Karpel	PAS	EX	III		06/16/26
Washington, DC	Chief of Staff	Vacant		ES			
Washington, DC	Confidential Assistant	Gwendolyn Diggs	SC	GS	13		
Washington, DC	Confidential Assistant	Sally E Knight	SC	GS	13		
Washington, DC	Staff Assistant (Legal)	James H Ahrens	SC	GS	15		
Washington, DC	Staff Assistant	Juliana M Cofrancesco	SC	GS	15		
	OFFICE OF THE VICE CHAIRMAN						
Washington, DC	Vice Chairman	Vacant		EX			
	OFFICE OF COMMISSIONER JOHANSON						
Washington, DC	Commissioner	David Stanley Johanson	PAS	EX	IV	7	12/16/18
Washington, DC	Staff Assistant (Legal)	Michael Joseph Robbins	SC	GS	14		
Washington, DC	Staff Assistant (Legal)	Mark B Rees	SC	GS	15		
Washington, DC	Confidential Assistant	Anthony Courtney	SC	GS	12		
	OFFICE OF COMMISSIONER SCHMIDTLEIN						
Washington, DC	Commissioner	Rhonda Kay Schmidtlein	PAS	EX	IV	7	12/16/21
Washington, DC	Staff Assistant (Confidential Legal)	Elizabeth Argenti	SC	GS	15		
Washington, DC	Staff Assistant (Confidential) Legal	Michael J Leib	SC	GS	15		
Washington, DC	Staff Assistant (Legal)	Mark Beatty	SC	GS	15		
Washington, DC	Staff Assistant (Legal)	Richard Pancake	SC	GS	15		
Washington, DC	Confidential Assistant	Cordelia Odessa Stroman	SC	GS	13		
	OFFICE OF COMMISSIONER KEARNS						
Washington, DC	Commissioner	Jason E Kearns	PAS	EX	IV	7	12/16/24
Washington, DC	Staff Assistant (Legal)	Stuart M Weiser	SC	GS	15		
Washington, DC	Staff Assistant (Legal)	Lane Hurewitz	SC	GS	15		
Washington, DC	Staff Assistant (Economist)	Vilas Pathikonda	SC	GS	15		
Washington, DC	Confidential Assistant	Samira I Howard	SC	GS	11		
	OFFICE OF COMMISSIONER						
Washington, DC	Commissioner	Vacant		EX		7	
Washington, DC	Commissioner	Vacant		EX		7	

UNITED STATES PATENT AND TRADEMARK OFFICE

Location	Position Title	Name of Incumbent	Type of Appt.	Pay Plan	Level, Grade, or Pay	Tenure	Expires
Alexandria, VA	Deputy Under Secretary of Commerce for Intellectual Property and Director of U.S. Patent and Trademark Office.	Katherine Vidal	PAS	EX	III		
Alexandria, VA	Deputy Under Secretary for Intellectual Property and Deputy Director of U.S. Patent and Trademark Office.	Derrick Brent	XS	AD			
Alexandria, VA	Chief of Staff	Shirin Bidel-Niyat	NA	ES			
Alexandria, VA	Senior Advisor	Charesse Evans	SC	GS	15		
Alexandria, VA	Chief Communications Officer	John Fleming	SC	GS	15		
Alexandria, VA	Deputy Chief Communications Officer	Troy Blackwell Jr	SC	GS	14		
Alexandria, VA	Senior Legislative Advisor	Ellen McLaren	NA	ES			
Alexandria, VA	Senior Advisor	Catharine Young	SC	GS	15		
Alexandria, VA	Policy Advisor	Claudia Murguia	SC	GS	13		
Alexandria, VA	Chief Information Officer	Career Incumbent	CA	ES			
Alexandria, VA	General Counsel	Career Incumbent	CA	ES			
Alexandria, VA	Chief Administrative Officer	Career Incumbent	CA	ES			
Alexandria, VA	Chief Policy Officer and Director for International Affairs.	Career Incumbent	CA	ES			

UNITED STATES POSTAL SERVICE

Location	Position Title	Name of Incumbent	Type of Appt.	Pay Plan	Level, Grade, or Pay	Tenure	Expires
Washington, DC	Postmaster General, Chief Executive Officer	Louis Dejoy	XS	OT			
Washington, DC	Deputy Postmaster General	Douglas A Tulino	XS	OT			
Washington, DC	Governor (Chairman, Board of Governors)	Roman Martinez IV	PAS	OT			12/08/24

UNITED STATES POSTAL SERVICE—Continued

Location	Position Title	Name of Incumbent	Type of Appt.	Pay Plan	Level, Grade, or Pay	Tenure	Expires
Washington, DC	Governor (Vice Chairman, Board of Governors).	Amber F McReynolds...........	PAS	OT	....	....	12/08/26
Washington, DC	Governor...	Robert M Duncan.................	PAS	OT	....	....	12/08/25
Washington, DC	Governor...	Daniel M Tangherlini...........	PAS	OT	....	....	12/08/27
Washington, DC	Governor...	Derek Kan............................	PAS	OT	....	....	12/08/28
Washington, DC	Governor...	Ronald A Stroman................	PAS	OT	....	....	12/08/28
Washington, DC	Governor...	Vacant	....	OT	....	....	12/08/29
Washington, DC	Governor...	Vacant	....	OT	....	....	12/08/29
Washington, DC	Governor...	Anton G Hajjar....................	PAS	OT	....	....	12/08/23
Washington, DC	Secretary of the Board of Governors.................	Michael J Elston	XS	OT	....	....	....
Washington, DC	Chief Retail and Delivery Officer and Executive Vice President.	Joshua D Colin	XS	OT	....	....	....
Washington, DC	Chief Processing and Distribution Officer and Executive Vice President.	Isaac S Cronkhite.................	XS	OT	....	....	....
Washington, DC	Chief Logistics Officer and Executive Vice President.	Kelly R Abney......................	XS	OT	....	....	....
Washington, DC	Chief Commerce and Business Solutions Officer and Executive Vice President.	Jacqueline Krage Strako	XS	OT	....	....	....
Washington, DC	Chief Technology Officer and Executive Vice President.	Scott R Bombaugh	XS	OT	....	....	....
Washington, DC	Chief Information Officer and Executive Vice President.	Pritha N Mehra....................	XS	OT	....	....	....
Washington, DC	Chief Customer and Marketing Officer and Executive Vice President.	Steven W Monteith	XS	OT	....	....	....
Washington, DC	Chief Financial Officer and Executive Vice President.	Joseph Corbett......................	XS	OT	....	....	....
Washington, DC	General Counsel and Executive Vice President.	Thomas J Marshall	XS	OT	....	....	....
Washington, DC	Senior Vice President, Finance and Strategy....	Luke T Grossmann................	XS	OT	....	....	....
Washington, DC	Chief Postal Inspector	Gary R Barksdale.................	XS	OT	....	....	....
Washington, DC	Vice President, Corporate Affairs.....................	Judith A De Torok	XS	OT	....	....	....
Washington, DC	Vice President, Corporate Communications	Jeffrey A Adams	XS	OT	....	....	....
Washington, DC	Senior Vice President, Facilities and Fleet Management.	Ronnie J Jarriel...................	XS	OT	....	....	....
Washington, DC	Vice President, Government Relations and Public Policy.	Peter R Pastre	XS	OT	....	....	....
Florence, WI	Vice President, Human Resources.....................	Simon M Storey....................	XS	OT	....	....	....
Dallas, WI................	Vice President, Labor Relations	Thomas J Blum	XS	OT	....	....	....
Washington, DC	Vice President, Organization Development.......	Jennifer D Utterback..........	XS	OT	....	....	....
Washington, DC	Vice President, Customer Experience	Marc D McCrery..................	XS	OT	....	....	....
Washington, DC	Vice President, International, and Managing Director.	Robert H Raines..................	XS	OT	....	....	....
Washington, DC	Vice President, Marketing	Sheila B Holman.................	XS	OT	....	....	....
Washington, DC	Vice President, Product Solutions	Thomas J Foti......................	XS	OT	....	....	....
Washington, DC	Vice President, Sales	Shavon Keys	XS	OT	....	....	....
Washington, DC	Vice President, Sales Intelligence and Support.	Shibani S Gambhir	XS	OT	....	....	....
Washington, DC	Vice President, Controller.................................	Cara M Greene....................	XS	OT	....	....	....
Washington, DC	Vice President, Pricing and Costing..................	Sharon D Owens	XS	OT	....	....	....
Washington, DC	Vice President, Supply Management	Mark A Guilfoil	XS	OT	....	....	....
Falls Church, VA	Vice President, Chief Data and Analytics Officer.	Stephen M Dearing.............	XS	OT	....	....	....
Washington, DC	Vice President, Chief Information Security Officer.	Heather L Dyer	XS	OT	....	....	....
Washington, DC	Vice President, Network and Compute Technology.	William E Koetz	XS	OT	....	....	....
Washington, DC	Vice President, Technology Applications...........	Angela D Lawson	XS	OT	....	....	....
Washington, DC	Vice President, Logistics	Robert Cintron.....................	XS	OT	....	....	....
Washington, DC	Vice President, Transportation Strategy	Peter Routsolias	XS	OT	....	....	....
Washington, DC	Vice President, Processing and Maintenance Operations.	Dane A Coleman	XS	OT	....	....	....
Cincinnati, OH	Vice President, Regional Processing Operations - Eastern.	Todd S Hawkins	XS	OT	....	....	....
Phoenix, OR............	Vice President, Regional Processing Operations - Western.	John J Diperi......................	XS	OT	....	....	....
Washington, DC	Vice President, Delivery Operations	Angela H Curtis	XS	OT	....	....	....
Washington, DC	Vice President, Retail and Post Office Operations.	Elvin Mercado	XS	OT	....	....	....
Washington, DC	Vice President, Area Retail and Delivery Operations - Atlantic.	Scott P Raymond.................	XS	OT	....	....	....
Plano, TX	Vice President, Area Retail and Delivery Operations - Southern.	Linda K Crawford	XS	OT	....	....	....

UNITED STATES POSTAL SERVICE—Continued

Location	Position Title	Name of Incumbent	Type of Appt.	Pay Plan	Level, Grade, or Pay	Tenure	Expires
Carol Stream, IL.....	Vice President, Area Retail and Delivery Operations - Central.	Eric E Henry	XS	OT	....	....	....
San Diego, TX..........	Vice President, Area Retail and Delivery Operations - Westpac.	Eduardo H Ruiz	XS	OT	....	....	....
Merrifield, VA..........	Vice President, Engineering Systems	Linda M Malone	XS	OT	....	....	....
Washington, DC	Vice President, Innovative Business Technology.	Gary C Reblin......................	XS	OT	....	....	....
Washington, DC	Vice President, Plant and Process Modernization.	John M Dunlop.....................	XS	OT	....	....	....
Washington, DC	Vice President, Facilities....................................	Benjamin P Kuo	XS	OT	....	....	....
Arlington, WI...........	Judicial Officer...	Alan R Caramella	XS	OT	....	....	....

UTAH RECLAMATION MITIGATION AND CONSERVATION COMMISSION

Location	Position Title	Name of Incumbent	Type of Appt.	Pay Plan	Level, Grade, or Pay	Tenure	Expires
	COMMISSIONERS						
Salt Lake City, UT ..	Commission Chair	Brad Barber..........................	PA	PD	....	4	07/10/14
Salt Lake City, UT ..	Commissioner...	Robert Morgan.....................	PA	PD	....	4	07/10/18
Salt Lake City, UT ..	Commissioner...	Gene Shawcroft	PA	PD	....	4	11/20/20
Salt Lake City, UT ..	Commissioner...	Justin Shirley	PA	PD	....	4	11/06/25

WOODROW WILSON INTERNATIONAL CENTER FOR SCHOLARS

Location	Position Title	Name of Incumbent	Type of Appt.	Pay Plan	Level, Grade, or Pay	Tenure	Expires
	BOARD OF TRUSTEES						
Washington, DC	Chair..	Joseph Asher	PA	WC	....	....	....
Washington, DC	Vice Chair..	Leah Daughtry	PA	WC	....	....	....
Washington, DC	Trustee...	Nicholas Adams....................	PA	WC	....	....	....
Washington, DC	Trustee...	Bill Haslam..........................	PA	WC	....	....	....
Washington, DC	Trustee...	Brian Hook	PA	WC	....	....	....
Washington, DC	Trustee...	Elizabeth Hubbard...............	PA	WC	....	....	....
Washington, DC	Trustee...	Andrew Kerwin Maloney.....	PA	WC	....	....	....
Washington, DC	Trustee...	Timothy Pataki.....................	PA	WC	....	....	....
Washington, DC	Trustee...	Alan Rechtschaffen	PA	WC	....	....	....
Washington, DC	Trustee...	Enoh Ebong	PA	WC	....	....	....

WORLD BANK

Location	Position Title	Name of Incumbent	Type of Appt.	Pay Plan	Level, Grade, or Pay	Tenure	Expires
Washington, DC	United States Alternate Governor	Jose W. Fernandez................	PAS	EX	....	....	07/9/26
Washington, DC	United States Alternate Executive Director......	Felice Gorordo......................	PAS	EX	....	....	09/5/25
	INTERNATIONAL CENTRE FOR SETTLEMENT OF INVESTMENT DISPUTES						
Washington, DC	Arbitrator	Rosemary Barkett	PA	OT	....	....	....
Washington, DC	Arbitrator	Sean Murphy	PA	OT	....	....	....
Washington, DC	Conciliator...	Kathleen Claussen	PA	OT	....	....	....
Washington, DC	Conciliator...	Anna Spain Bradley.............	PA	OT	....	....	....
Washington, DC	Conciliator...	John Woods Jr	PA	OT	....	....	....
Washington, DC	Arbitrator	David Huebner	PA	OT	....	....	....
Washington, DC	Conciliator...	Melida Hodgson...................	PA	OT	....	....	....
Washington, DC	Arbitrator	Paolo Di Rosa	PA	OT	....	....	....

APPENDICES

APPENDIX NO. 1

SUMMARY OF POSITIONS SUBJECT TO NONCOMPETITIVE APPOINTMENT

PAS = Positions Subject to Presidential Appointment with Senate Confirmation
PA = Positions Subject to Presidential Appointment without Senate Confirmation
GEN = Positions Designated as Senior Executive Service "General"
NA = Senior Executive Service General Positions Filled by Noncareer Appointment
TA = Senior Executive Service Positions Filled by Limited Emergency or Limited Term Appointment
SC = Positions Filled by Schedule C Excepted Appointment
XS = Positions Subject to Statutory Excepted Appointment

Agency or Department	PAS	PA	GEN	NA	TA	SC	XS
ADMINISTRATIVE CONFERENCE OF THE UNITED STATES	1	0	0	0	0	1	0
ADVISORY COUNCIL ON HISTORIC PRESERVATION	1	10	0	0	0	0	0
AFRICAN DEVELOPMENT FOUNDATION	4	0	0	0	0	0	0
AFRICAN DEVELOPMENT BANK	1	0	0	0	0	0	0
AMERICAN BATTLE MONUMENTS COMMISSION	1	12	0	0	0	0	0
AMTRAK	6	0	0	0	0	0	0
APPALACHIAN REGIONAL COMMISSION	1	0	0	0	0	1	0
ARCHITECT OF THE CAPITOL	1	0	0	0	0	0	0
ARCTIC RESEARCH COMMISSION	0	7	1	0	0	0	0
ARMED FORCES RETIREMENT HOME	0	1	0	0	0	0	0
ASIAN DEVELOPMENT BANK	1	0	0	0	0	0	0
BARRY GOLDWATER SCHOLARSHIP AND EXCELLENCE IN EDUCATION FOUNDATION	7	0	0	1	0	0	0
CENTRAL INTELLIGENCE AGENCY	3	1	0	0	0	0	0
CHEMICAL SAFETY AND HAZARD INVESTIGATION BOARD	3	0	1	0	0	0	0
CIVIL RIGHTS COLD CASE RECORDS REVIEW BOARD	4	0	0	0	0	0	0
COMMISSION OF FINE ARTS	0	7	1	0	0	0	0
COMMODITY FUTURES TRADING COMMISSION	5	0	0	0	0	8	0
CONSUMER FINANCIAL PROTECTION BUREAU	1	0	0	0	0	8	0
CONSUMER PRODUCT SAFETY COMMISSION	5	0	5	3	0	13	0
CORPORATION FOR NATIONAL AND COMMUNITY SERVICE	8	0	0	0	0	0	14
CORPORATION FOR PUBLIC BROADCASTING	8	0	0	0	0	0	0
COURT SERVICES AND OFFENDER SUPERVISION AGENCY FOR THE DISTRICT OF COLUMBIA	1	0	1	0	0	0	0
DEFENSE NUCLEAR FACILITIES SAFETY BOARD	2	0	2	0	0	0	0
DELTA REGIONAL AUTHORITY	1	0	0	0	0	1	0
DEPARTMENT OF AGRICULTURE	12	8	126	41	1	190	0
DEPARTMENT OF COMMERCE	17	1	79	46	2	131	1
DEPARTMENT OF COMMERCE OFFICE OF THE INSPECTOR GENERAL	0	0	0	0	0	0	0
DEPARTMENT OF DEFENSE OFFICE OF THE SECRETARY OF DEFENSE	34	1	220	65	6	84	0
DEPARTMENT OF DEFENSE OFFICE OF THE INSPECTOR GENERAL	1	0	0	0	0	0	0
DEPARTMENT OF EDUCATION	11	1	41	21	0	111	1
DEPARTMENT OF EDUCATION OFFICE OF THE INSPECTOR GENERAL	1	0	0	0	0	0	0
DEPARTMENT OF ENERGY	13	0	76	85	6	77	1

Agency or Department	PAS	PA	GEN	NA	TA	SC	XS
DEPARTMENT OF ENERGY OFFICE OF THE INSPECTOR GENERAL	1	0	0	0	0	0	0
DEPARTMENT OF HEALTH AND HUMAN SERVICES	14	3	237	78	11	94	0
DEPARTMENT OF HEALTH AND HUMAN SERVICES OFFICE OF THE INSPECTOR GENERAL	1	0	0	0	0	0	0
DEPARTMENT OF HOMELAND SECURITY	10	11	101	63	7	97	154
DEPARTMENT OF HOMELAND SECURITY OFFICE OF THE INSPECTOR GENERAL	1	0	0	0	0	0	0
DEPARTMENT OF HOUSING AND URBAN DEVELOPMENT	6	1	39	23	5	59	0
DEPARTMENT OF HOUSING AND URBAN DEVELOPMENT OFFICE OF THE INSPECTOR GENERAL	1	0	0	0	0	0	0
DEPARTMENT OF JUSTICE	157	5	106	56	2	66	0
DEPARTMENT OF JUSTICE OFFICE OF THE INSPECTOR GENERAL	1	0	0	0	0	0	0
DEPARTMENT OF LABOR	11	3	41	23	1	73	0
DEPARTMENT OF LABOR OFFICE OF INSPECTOR GENERAL	1	0	0	0	0	0	0
DEPARTMENT OF STATE	201	6	147	40	2	116	12
DEPARTMENT OF STATE OFFICE OF THE INSPECTOR GENERAL	1	0	0	0	0	0	0
DEPARTMENT OF THE AIR FORCE	7	0	11	2	0	6	0
DEPARTMENT OF THE ARMY	8	0	29	9	6	6	4
DEPARTMENT OF THE INTERIOR	10	0	78	39	0	45	3
DEPARTMENT OF THE INTERIOR OFFICE OF THE INSPECTOR GENERAL	1	0	0	0	0	0	0
DEPARTMENT OF THE NAVY	7	0	14	3	0	7	1
DEPARTMENT OF THE TREASURY	15	5	125	28	2	66	2
DEPARTMENT OF THE TREASURY OFFICE OF THE INSPECTOR GENERAL	1	0	2	0	1	0	0
DEPARTMENT OF THE TREASURY TAX ADMINISTRATION OFFICE OF THE INSPECTOR GENERAL	1	0	2	0	1	0	0
DEPARTMENT OF TRANSPORTATION	9	3	150	40	1	52	3
DEPARTMENT OF TRANSPORTATION OFFICE OF THE INSPECTOR GENERAL	1	0	0	0	0	0	0
DEPARTMENT OF VETERANS AFFAIRS	8	2	336	16	4	8	157
DEPARTMENT OF VETERANS AFFAIRS OFFICE OF THE INSPECTOR GENERAL	1	0	0	0	0	0	0
ENVIRONMENTAL PROTECTION AGENCY	9	0	89	35	0	64	0
ENVIRONMENTAL PROTECTION AGENCY OFFICE OF THE INSPECTOR GENERAL	1	0	0	0	0	0	0
EQUAL EMPLOYMENT OPPORTUNITY COMMISSION	6	0	14	2	0	1	0
EXECUTIVE OFFICE OF THE PRESIDENT	12	212	7	26	0	53	61
EXPORT-IMPORT BANK	3	0	0	0	0	15	0
EXPORT-IMPORT BANK OFFICE OF THE INSPECTOR GENERAL	1	0	0	0	0	0	0
FARM CREDIT ADMINISTRATION	3	0	0	0	0	3	0
FEDERAL AGRICULTURAL MORTGAGE CORPORATION	4	0	0	0	0	0	0
FEDERAL COMMUNICATIONS COMMISSION	6	0	41	4	0	2	
FEDERAL DEPOSIT INSURANCE CORPORATION	4	0	0	0	0	0	0
FEDERAL ELECTION COMMISSION	6	0	0	0	0	0	22
FEDERAL ELECTION COMMISSION OFFICE OF THE INSPECTOR GENERAL	0	0	0	0	0	0	1
FEDERAL ENERGY REGULATORY COMMISSION	5	0	42	0	0	3	0
FEDERAL HOUSING FINANCE AGENCY	2	0	0	0	0	0	0
FEDERAL LABOR RELATIONS AUTHORITY	2	11	0	0	0	0	2
FEDERAL MARITIME COMMISSION	5	0	2	0	0	3	0
FEDERAL MEDIATION AND CONCILIATION SERVICE	0	0	1	0	0	1	1
FEDERAL MINE SAFETY AND HEALTH REVIEW COMMISSION	4	0	2	0	0	1	0

Agency or Department	PAS	PA	GEN	NA	TA	SC	XS
FEDERAL PERMITTING IMPROVEMENT STEERING COUNCIL	0	1	0	0	0	4	0
FEDERAL RESERVE SYSTEM	10	0	0	0	0	0	0
FEDERAL RETIREMENT THRIFT INVESTMENT BOARD	4	0	4	9	0	0	1
FEDERAL TRADE COMMISSION	5	0	30	9	0	5	0
GENERAL SERVICES ADMINISTRATION	1	0	16	14	1	18	0
GENERAL SERVICES ADMINISTRATION OFFICE OF THE INSPECTOR GENERAL	0	0	0	0	0	0	0
GOVERNMENT ACCOUNTABILITY OFFICE	1	0	0	0	0	0	0
GOVERNMENT PUBLISHING OFFICE	1	0	0	0	0	0	2
GREAT LAKES FISHERY COMMISSION	0	5	0	0	0	0	0
GULF COAST ECOSYSTEM RESTORATION COUNCIL	0	0	1	0	0	0	0
HARRY S TRUMAN SCHOLARSHIP FOUNDATION	4	0	1	0	0	0	0
INSTITUTE OF MUSEUM AND LIBRARY SERVICES	0	20	1	0	0	0	0
INTER-AMERICAN DEVELOPMENT BANK	1	0	0	0	0	0	0
INTER-AMERICAN FOUNDATION	4	0	0	0	0	0	0
INTERAGENCY COUNCIL ON THE HOMELESS	0	0	0	0	0	0	1
INTERNATIONAL BOUNDARY AND WATER COMMISSION	0	1	0	0	0	0	0
INTERNATIONAL JOINT COMMISSION	3	0	0	0	0	0	0
INTERSTATE COMMISSION ON THE POTOMAC RIVER BASIN	0	3	0	0	0	0	0
JAMES MADISON MEMORIAL FELLOWSHIP FOUNDATION	3	4	0	0	0	0	1
JAPAN-UNITED STATES FRIENDSHIP COMMISSION	0	0	1	0	0	0	0
LIBRARY OF CONGRESS	1	10	0	0	0	0	6
MARINE MAMMAL COMMISSION	3	0	0	0	0	0	0
MEDICAID AND CHIP PAYMENT AND ACCESS COMMISSION	0	0	0	0	0	0	20
MEDICARE PAYMENT ADVISORY COMMISSION	0	0	0	0	0	0	3
MERIT SYSTEMS PROTECTION BOARD	1	0	1	0	0	1	0
MILLENNIUM CHALLENGE CORPORATION	2	1	0	0	0	0	11
MORRIS K UDALL AND STUART L UDALL FOUNDATION	9	0	0	0	0	0	0
NATIONAL AERONAUTICS AND SPACE ADMINISTRATION	3	0	27	6	1	16	0
NATIONAL AERONAUTICS AND SPACE ADMINISTRATION OFFICE OF THE INSPECTOR GENERAL	0	0	0	0	0	0	0
NATIONAL ARCHIVES AND RECORDS ADMINISTRATION	1	0	0	0	0	0	13
NATIONAL CAPITAL PLANNING COMMISSION	0	3	0	0	0	0	0
NATIONAL COUNCIL ON DISABILITY	0	5	0	0	0	0	0
NATIONAL CREDIT UNION ADMINISTRATION	3	0	0	0	0	9	0
NATIONAL ENDOWMENT FOR THE ARTS	19	0	0	2	0	11	0
NATIONAL ENDOWMENT FOR THE HUMANITIES	25	0	4	2	0	5	0
NATIONAL ENDOWMENT FOR THE HUMANITIES OFFICE OF THE INSPECTOR GENERAL	0	0	1	0	0	0	0
NATIONAL INSTITUTE OF BUILDING SCIENCES	5	0	0	0	0	0	0
NATIONAL LABOR RELATIONS BOARD	5	0	12	4	0	3	0
NATIONAL MEDIATION BOARD	3	0	1	0	0	3	0
NATIONAL SCIENCE FOUNDATION	1	16	57	0	3	0	0
NATIONAL TRANSPORTATION SAFETY BOARD	5	0	2	1	0	10	0
NORTHERN BORDER REGIONAL COMMISSION	1	1	0	0	0	0	0
NATIONAL WOMEN'S BUSINESS COUNCIL	0	1	0	0	0	0	0
NUCLEAR REGULATORY COMMISSION	4	0	39	0	0	0	58
NUCLEAR REGULATORY COMMISSION OFFICE OF THE INSPECTOR GENERAL	1	0	0	0	0	0	0
NUCLEAR WASTE TECHNICAL REVIEW BOARD	0	8	1	0	0	0	0
OCCUPATIONAL SAFETY AND HEALTH REVIEW COMMISSION	1	0	1	1	1	1	0
OFFICE OF GOVERNMENT ETHICS	0	0	1	0	0	0	0
OFFICE OF PERSONNEL MANAGEMENT	1	0	12	13	2	19	0

Agency or Department	PAS	PA	GEN	NA	TA	SC	XS
OFFICE OF PERSONNEL MANAGEMENT OFFICE OF THE INSPECTOR GENERAL	1	0	0	0	0	0	0
OFFICE OF SPECIAL COUNSEL	1	0	4	0	0	3	0
OFFICE OF THE DIRECTOR FOR NATIONAL INTELLIGENCE	4	0	0	0	0	0	0
PEACE CORPS	2	0	0	0	0	0	31
PENSION BENEFIT GUARANTY CORPORATION	0	3	0	0	0	0	0
POSTAL REGULATORY COMMISSION	5	0	0	0	0	0	18
PRESIDENT'S COMMITTEE ON THE ARTS AND HUMANITIES	0	23	0	0	0	1	0
PRIVACY AND CIVIL LIBERTIES OVERSIGHT BOARD	3	0	0	0	0	0	0
PUBLIC BUILDINGS REFORM BOARD	0	6	0	0	0	0	0
RAILROAD RETIREMENT BOARD	3	0	0	0	0	0	0
RAILROAD RETIREMENT BOARD OFFICE OF THE INSPECTOR GENERAL	0	0	0	0	0	0	0
SECURITIES AND EXCHANGE COMMISSION	5	0	0	0	0	12	0
SECURITIES INVESTOR PROTECTION CORPORATION	5	0	0	0	0	0	0
SELECTIVE SERVICE SYSTEM	0	0	0	1	0	1	0
SMALL BUSINESS ADMINISTRATION	2	0	18	13	0	41	0
SMALL BUSINESS ADMINISTRATION OFFICE OF THE INSPECTOR GENERAL	1	0	0	0	0	0	0
SOCIAL SECURITY ADMINISTRATION	5	0	89	7	2	6	0
SOCIAL SECURITY ADMINISTRATION OFFICE OF THE INSPECTOR GENERAL	0	0	0	0	0	0	0
SOUTHWEST BORDER REGIONAL COMMISSION	2	0	0	0	0	0	0
SURFACE TRANSPORTATION BOARD	4	0	0	0	0	0	0
TENNESSEE VALLEY AUTHORITY	8	0	0	0	0	0	0
TENNESSEE VALLEY AUTHORITY OFFICE OF THE INSPECTOR GENERAL	1	0	0	0	0	0	0
TRADE AND DEVELOPMENT AGENCY	1	0	0	1	0	3	0
U.S. ABILITYONE COMMISSION	0	4	0	0	0	0	0
U.S. ACCESS BOARD	0	13	0	0	0	0	1
U.S. ADVISORY COMMISSION ON PUBLIC DIPLOMACY	2	0	0	0	0	0	0
U.S. AGENCY FOR GLOBAL MEDIA	7	0	2	1	1	4	0
UNITED STATES—CHINA ECONOMIC AND SECURITY REVIEW COMMISSION	0	0	0	0	0	0	7
UNITED STATES AGENCY FOR INTERNATIONAL DEVELOPMENT	6	1	18	4	1	0	98
UNITED STATES AGENCY FOR INTERNATIONAL DEVELOPMENT OFFICE OF THE INSPECTOR GENERAL	1	0	0	0	0	0	0
UNITED STATES COMMISSION FOR THE PRESERVATION OF AMERICA'S HERITAGE ABROAD	0	20	0	0	0	0	0
UNITED STATES COMMISSION ON CIVIL RIGHTS	0	4	0	1	0	8	4
UNITED STATES ELECTION ASSISTANCE COMMISSION	5	0	0	0	0	2	1
UNITED STATES HOLOCAUST MEMORIAL MUSEUM	0	55	0	0	0	0	0
UNITED STATES INSTITUTE OF PEACE	11	0	0	0	0	0	0
UNITED STATES INTERNATIONAL DEVELOPMENT FINANCE CORPORATION	5	0	0	0	0	7	23
UNITED STATES INTERNATIONAL TRADE COMMISSION	4	0	0	0	0	16	0
UNITED STATES PATENT AND TRADEMARK OFFICE	1	0	4	2	0	5	1
UNITED STATES POSTAL SERVICE	7	0	0	0	0	0	49
UTAH RECLAMATION MITIGATION AND CONSERVATION COMMISSION	0	4	0	0	0	0	0
WOODROW WILSON INTERNATIONAL CENTER FOR SCHOLARS	0	10	0	0	0	0	0
WORLD BANK	2	8	0	0	0	0	0
TOTAL (7148)	936	540	2371	776	54	1676	795

APPENDIX NO. 2

SENIOR EXECUTIVE SERVICE

The Senior Executive Service (SES) is a personnel system covering top level policy, supervisory, and managerial positions in most Federal agencies. Positions in Government corporations, the FBI and Drug Enforcement Administration, certain intelligence agencies, certain financial regulatory agencies, and the Foreign Service are exempt from the SES.

The SES includes most Civil Service positions above grade 15 of the General Schedule. An agency may establish an SES position only within an allocation approved by the U.S. Office of Personnel Management (OPM). Currently, there are 8,845 SES positions allocated by OPM to agencies.

Types of SES Positions

There are two types of SES positions: Career Reserved and General. About half of the SES positions are designated in each category. Once a position is designated by an agency, the designation may not be changed without prior OPM approval.

SES positions are designated Career Reserved when the need to ensure impartiality, or the public's confidence in the impartiality of the Government, requires that they be filled only by career employees (e.g., law enforcement and audit positions).

The remaining SES positions are designated General. A General position may be filled by a career appointee, a noncareer appointee, or, if the position meets the criteria described below, by a limited term or limited emergency appointee. Because of the limitations on the number of limited appointees, most General positions are filled by career appointees.

A given General position may be filled at one time by a career appointee and at another time by a noncareer or limited appointee, or vice versa. Because of the limitations on the number of noncareer and limited appointees, as discussed below, most General positions are filled by career appointees. This publication lists only General positions since Career Reserved positions must be filled by a career appointee.

Appointments to SES Positions

The legislation establishing the SES provides three methods of appointment. Veterans' preference is not applicable in the SES.

(1) Career appointment: Career appointments are made through a Governmentwide or an "all sources" merit staffing (competitive) process, including recruitment through a published announcement, rating and ranking of eligible candidates, approval by the agency of the professional qualifications of the selected candidate, and a further review and approval of the executive/managerial qualifications of the proposed selectee by an OPM-administered SES Qualifications Review Board.

A career appointee serves a 1-year probationary period. Upon completion, the appointee acquires tenure rights and may be removed from the SES only for cause or for poor performance. (A performance appraisal for a career appointee may not be made, however, within 120 days after the beginning of a new Presidential Administration, i.e., one where the President changes.)

When a career appointee is reassigned within an agency, he or she must be given at least a 15-day advance written notice. If the reassignment is to another commuting area, the notice period is 60 days; the agency first must consult with the individual as to the reasons and the individual's preferences.

A career appointee may not be involuntarily reassigned within 120 days after the appointment of a new agency head, or during the same period after the appointment of a noncareer supervisor who has the authority to make an initial appraisal of the career appointee's performance. A career appointee may not be involuntarily transferred to another agency.

Like all career Federal employees, a career SES appointee is entitled to protection against retaliatory or politically motivated personnel actions and may lodge a complaint with the Office of the Special Counsel if a prohibited personnel practice has occurred.

(2) Noncareer appointment: By law, no more than 10 percent of total SES positions Government-wide may be filled by noncareer appointees. The proportion of noncareer appointees may, however,

vary from agency to agency, generally up to a limit of 25 percent of the agency's number of SES positions. OPM approves each use of a noncareer authority by an agency, and the authority reverts to OPM when the noncareer appointee leaves the position.

Noncareer appointees may be appointed to any SES General position. There is no requirement for competitive staffing, but the agency head must certify that the appointee meets the qualifications requirements for the position.

Any noncareer appointee may be removed by the appointing authority (e.g., for loss of confidence or change in policy). There is no appeal right.

(3) Limited appointment: Limited appointments are used in situations where the position is not continuing (e.g., to head a special project), or where the position is established to meet a bona fide, unanticipated, urgent need. Limited term appointments may not exceed 3 years; limited emergency appointments, 18 months.

By law, limited appointments Governmentwide may not exceed 5 percent of total SES positions. The appointments may be made only to General positions. Generally, OPM allocates limited appointment authorities on a case-by-case basis. However, each agency has a small pool of limited authorities equal to 3 percent of their total SES position allocation from OPM. Such pool authorities may be used only for appointment of career or career-type Federal civil service employees. Selection procedures and qualification requirements are determined by the agency, and the incumbent serves at the pleasure of the appointing authority.

By law, the appointment to or removal from any SES position in an independent regulatory commission shall not be subject, directly or indirectly, to review or approval by an officer or entity within the Executive Office of the President.

APPENDIX NO. 3

SCHEDULE C POSITIONS

————

Schedule C positions are excepted from the competitive service because of their confidential or policy-determining character. Most such positions are at grade 15 of the General Schedule or lower. Schedule C positions above the GS-15 level are either in the Senior Level (SL) personnel system or are specifically authorized in law.

The decision concerning whether to place a position in Schedule C is made by the Director, U.S. Office of Personnel Management, upon agency request. Such requests are considered on a case-by-case basis. In addition to consideration of the justification submitted by the agency, OPM may conduct an independent review and analysis. In addition to the Schedule C positions authorized by the OPM Director, a limited number of positions may be placed under Schedule C by Executive Order of the President or by legislation.

Requests for Schedule C exception are appropriate when:

(1) The position involves making or approving substantive policy recommendations; or

(2) The work of the position can be performed successfully only by someone with a thorough knowledge of and sympathy with the goals, priorities, and preferences of an official who has a confidential or policy determining relationship with the President or the agency head. There are special requirements for the types of superiors who are eligible for Schedule C secretaries.

The immediate supervisor of a Schedule C position must be a Presidential appointee, a Senior Executive Service appointee (career or noncareer) occupying a General position, or a Schedule C appointee. The immediate supervisor may not occupy a position in the competitive service or a Career Reserved position in the Senior Executive Service.

The only time when OPM approval is not required for a Schedule C position is when a position is filled by a temporary Schedule C appointment during a Presidential transition, a change of agency head, or establishment of a new agency. Temporary Schedule C positions may be established for 120 days, with one extension of 120 days, under conditions prescribed by OPM. There is a limit on the number of such positions that can be established by an agency. New appointments may be made only during the 1-year period beginning on the date of the agency head's appointment, a new Administration or establishment of a new agency.

By law, the agency head must certify to OPM that both Schedule C and temporary Schedule C positions are not being requested for the sole purpose of detailing the incumbent to the White House.

Agencies may fill Schedule C positions noncompetitively. Because of the confidential or policy-determining nature of Schedule C positions, the incumbents serve at the pleasure of the appointing authority (usually the agency head) and may be removed at any time. They are not covered under conduct-based or performance-removal procedures that apply to certain other excepted Service appointees.

Schedule C positions authorized by OPM are automatically revoked when the incumbent leaves the position (i.e., there is no such thing as a "vacant" Schedule C position).

APPENDIX NO. 4

FEDERAL SALARY SCHEDULES FOR 2024

———

The information in the body of this report reflects grades or salaries in effect on the first pay period on or after January 1, 2024.

EXECUTIVE SCHEDULE (EX)

Level I	$246,400
Level II	$221,900
Level III	$204,000
Level IV	$191,900
Level V	$180,000

SENIOR EXECUTIVE SERVICE SCHEDULE (ES)

Pay ranges for the Senior Executive Service (SES) are established by law. The minimum is 120 percent of the rate of basic pay for GS–15, step 1. For agencies without a certified SES performance appraisal system, SES members' pay may not exceed the rate payable for level III of the Executive Schedule. For agencies with a certified SES performance appraisal system, SES members' pay may not exceed the rate payable for level II of the Executive Schedule. SES members are not entitled to locality-based comparability payments.**

Structure of the SES Pay System	Minimum	Maximum
Agencies with a Certified SES Performance Appraisal System	$147,649	$221,900
Agencies without a Certified SES Performance Appraisal System	$147,649	$204,000

SENIOR LEVEL (SL)

Pay for SL positions ranges from 120 percent of the rate of basic pay for GS–15, step 1 to the rate payable for level III of the Executive Schedule. For agencies without a certified SL performance appraisal system, SL members' pay may not exceed the rate payable for level III of the Executive Schedule. For agencies with a certified SL performance appraisal system, SL members' pay may not exceed the rate payable for level II of the Executive Schedule. SL members are not entitled to locality-based comparability payments. **

Structure of the SL Pay System	Minimum	Maximum
Agencies with a Certified SES Performance Appraisal System	$147,649	$221,900
Agencies without a Certified SES Performance Appraisal System	$147,649	$204,000

**Certain SES and SL employees in Non-Foreign Areas receive locality pay under provisions of the Non-Foreign Area Retirement Equity Assurance (AREA) Act (as contained in the National Defense Authorization Act for Fiscal Year 2010 (Pub. L. 111–84, October 28, 2009).

GENERAL SCHEDULE (GS)

Initial appointments to positions under the General Schedule are normally made at the minimum rate of the grade, although under certain circumstances, individuals with superior qualifications or fulfilling a special agency need may be paid at a rate above the minimum rate.

Step increases are granted to GS employees at the end of 52 weeks of service in steps 1, 2, and 3 of each grade; at the end of 104 weeks of service in steps 4, 5, and 6; and at the end of 156 weeks of service in steps 7, 8, and 9. An employee's work must be determined to be of an acceptable level of competence before granting a step increase. In addition to the periodic step increase, an employee whose work is outstanding may be advanced to the next higher step rate no more than once every 52 weeks. In addition to the 2024 basic pay rates listed below, GS employees are entitled to locality-based comparability payments for their respective locality pay area. The employee's locality rate of pay may not exceed the rate payable for level IV of the Executive Schedule. Certain GS employees may receive higher special rates instead of locality rates established to address significant recruitment or retention problems.

GENERAL SCHEDULE

Grade	2024 Annual Rates and Steps									
	1	2	3	4	5	6	7	8	9	10
GS–1	$21,986	$22,724	$23,454	$24,183	$24,912	$25,339	$26,063	$26,792	$26,821	$27,502
GS–2	24,722	25,310	26,129	26,821	27,124	27,922	28,720	29,518	30,316	31,114
GS–3	26,975	27,874	28,773	29,672	30,571	31,470	32,369	33,268	34,167	35,066
GS–4	30,280	31,289	32,298	33,307	34,316	35,325	36,334	37,343	38,352	39,361
GS–5	33,878	35,007	36,136	37,265	38,394	39,523	40,652	41,781	42,910	44,039
GS–6	37,765	39,024	40,283	41,542	42,801	44,060	45,319	46,578	47,837	49,096
GS–7	41,966	43,365	44,764	46,163	47,562	48,961	50,360	51,759	53,158	54,557
GS–8	46,475	48,024	49,573	51,122	52,671	54,220	55,769	57,318	58,867	60,416
GS–9	51,332	53,043	54,754	56,465	58,176	59,887	61,598	63,309	65,020	66,731
GS–10	56,528	58,412	60,296	62,180	64,064	65,948	67,832	69,716	71,600	73,484
GS–11	62,107	64,177	66,247	68,317	70,387	72,457	74,527	76,597	78,667	80,737
GS–12	74,441	76,922	79,403	81,884	84,365	86,846	89,327	91,808	94,289	96,770
GS–13	88,520	91,471	94,422	97,373	100,324	103,275	106,226	109,177	112,128	115,079
GS–14	104,604	108,091	111,578	115,065	118,552	122,039	125,526	129,013	132,500	135,987
GS–15	123,041	127,142	131,243	135,344	139,445	143,546	147,647	151,748	155,849	159,950

2024 LOCALITY PAY AREAS* AND RATES

ALASKA	31.96%
ALBANY–SCHENECTADY, NY–MA	20.25%
ALBUQUERQUE–SANTA FE–LAS VEGAS, NM	18.05%
ATLANTA—ATHENS–CLARKE COUNTY—SANDY SPRINGS, GA–AL	23.45%
AUSTIN–ROUND ROCK–GEORGETOWN, TX	19.99%
BIRMINGHAM–HOOVER–TALLADEGA, AL	17.91%
BOSTON–WORCESTER–PROVIDENCE, MA–RI–NH–CT–ME–VT	31.97%
BUFFALO–CHEEKTOWAGA–OLEAN, NY	21.99%
BURLINGTON–SOUTH BURLINGTON–BARRE, VT	18.97%
CHARLOTTE–CONCORD, NC–SC	19.26%
CHICAGO–NAPERVILLE, IL–IN–WI	30.41%
CINCINNATI–WILMINGTON–MAYSVILLE, OH–KY–IN	21.69%
CLEVELAND–AKRON–CANTON, OH–PA	22.01%
COLORADO SPRINGS, CO	19.73%
COLUMBUS–MARION–ZANESVILLE, OH	21.80%
CORPUS CHRISTI–KINGSVILLE–ALICE, TX	17.40%
DALLAS–FORT WORTH, TX–OK	26.91%
DAVENPORT–MOLINE, IA–IL	18.66%
DAYTON–SPRINGFIELD–KETTERING, OH	21.14%
DENVER–AURORA, CO	29.88%
DES MOINES–AMES–WEST DES MOINES, IA	17.68%
DETROIT–WARREN–ANN ARBOR, MI	28.82%
FRESNO–MADERA–HANFORD, CA	17.15%
HARRISBURG–LEBANON, PA	19.10%
HARTFORD–EAST HARTFORD, CT–MA	31.62%
HAWAII	21.79%
HOUSTON–THE WOODLANDS, TX	34.72%
HUNTSVILLE–DECATUR, AL–TN	21.48%
INDIANAPOLIS–CARMEL–MUNCIE, IN	17.89%
KANSAS CITY–OVERLAND PARK–KANSAS CITY, MO–KS	18.65%
LAREDO, TX	21.33%
LAS VEGAS–HENDERSON, NV–AZ	19.23%
LOS ANGELES–LONG BEACH, CA	35.84%
MIAMI–PORT ST. LUCIE–FORT LAUDERDALE, FL	24.42%
MILWAUKEE–RACINE–WAUKESHA, WI	22.15%
MINNEAPOLIS–ST. PAUL, MN–WI	27.15%
NEW YORK–NEWARK, NY–NJ–CT–PA	37.24%
OMAHA–COUNCIL BLUFFS–FREMONT, NE–IA	17.94%
PALM BAY–MELBOURNE–TITUSVILLE, FL	17.60%
PHILADELPHIA–READING–CAMDEN, PA–NJ–DE–MD	28.55%
PHOENIX–MESA, AZ	22.02%
PITTSBURGH–NEW CASTLE–WEIRTON, PA–OH–WV	20.78%
PORTLAND–VANCOUVER–SALEM, OR–WA	25.66%
RALEIGH–DURHAM–CARY, NC	21.90%
RENO–FERNLEY, NV	17.11%
RICHMOND, VA	21.91%
ROCHESTER–BATAVIA–SENECA FALLS, NY	17.35%
SACRAMENTO–ROSEVILLE, CA–NV	29.16%
SAN ANTONIO–NEW BRAUNFELS–PEARSALL, TX	18.49%
SAN DIEGO–CHULA VISTA–CARLSBAD, CA	33.05%
SAN JOSE–SAN FRANCISCO–OAKLAND, CA	45.41%

SEATTLE–TACOMA, WA	30.81%
SPOKANE–SPOKANE VALLEY–COEUR D'ALENE, WA–ID	17.18%
ST. LOUIS–ST. CHARLES–FARMINGTON, MO–IL	19.63%
TUCSON–NOGALES, AZ	18.92%
VIRGINIA BEACH–NORFOLK, VA–NC	18.46%
WASHINGTON–BALTIMORE–ARLINGTON, DC–MD–VA–WV–PA	33.26%
REST OF U.S.	16.82%

* Locality Pay Areas are defined in 5 CFR 531.603

WASHINGTON–BALTIMORE–NORTHERN VIRGINIA, DC–MD–VA–WV–PA
LOCALITY PAY SCHEDULE

The following salary tables reflect the locality pay rates for the Washington–Baltimore–Northern Virginia, DC–MD–VA–WV–PA locality pay area in 2024. The tables incorporate a locality payment of 33.26 percent.

Grade	Step 1	Step 2	Step 3	Step 4	Step 5	Step 6	Step 7	Step 8	Step 9	Step 10
1	$29,299	$30,282	$31,255	$32,226	$33,198	$33,767	$34,732	$35,703	$35,742	$36,649
2	32,945	33,728	34,820	35,742	36,145	37,209	38,272	39,336	40,399	41,463
3	35,947	37,145	38,343	39,541	40,739	41,937	43,135	44,333	45,531	46,729
4	40,351	41,696	43,040	44,385	45,730	47,074	48,419	49,763	51,108	52,452
5	45,146	46,650	48,155	49,659	51,164	52,668	54,173	55,677	57,182	58,686
6	50,326	52,003	53,681	55,359	57,037	58,714	60,392	62,070	63,748	65,425
7	55,924	57,788	59,653	61,517	63,381	65,245	67,110	68,974	70,838	72,703
8	61,933	63,997	66,061	68,125	70,189	72,254	74,318	76,382	78,446	80,510
9	68,405	70,685	72,965	75,245	77,525	79,805	82,085	84,366	86,646	88,926
10	75,329	77,840	80,350	82,861	85,372	87,882	90,393	92,904	95,414	97,925
11	82,764	85,522	88,281	91,039	93,798	96,556	99,315	102,073	104,832	107,590
12	99,200	102,506	105,812	109,119	112,425	115,731	119,037	122,343	125,650	128,956
13	117,962	121,894	125,827	129,759	133,692	137,624	141,557	145,489	149,422	153,354
14	139,395	144,042	148,689	153,336	157,982	162,629	167,276	171,923	176,570	181,216
15	163,964	169,429	174,894	180,359	185,824	191,289	191,900*	191,900*	191,900*	191,900*

* Rate limited to the rate for level IV of the Executive Schedule (5 U.S.C. 5304 (g)(1)).

SPECIAL LAW ENFORCEMENT OFFICER (LEO) PAY SCHEDULES

Law enforcement officers at grades GS–3 through GS–10 are entitled to special base rates that are higher than General Schedule base rates. Such LEOs receive the locality payments applicable in their locality pay area on top of these special base rates. The locality pay area definitions and pay percentages are the same as those used for regular General Schedule employees.

SPECIAL SALARY RATES FOR LEOS

Grade	Step 1	Step 2	Step 3	Step 4	Step 5	Step 6	Step 7	Step 8	Step 9	Step 10	Within Grade Amounts
3	$32,369	$33,268	$34,167	$35,066	$35,965	$36,864	$37,763	$38,662	$39,561	$40,460	$899
4	36,334	37,343	38,352	39,361	40,370	41,379	42,388	43,397	44,406	45,415	1,009
5	41,781	42,910	44,039	45,168	46,297	47,426	48,555	49,684	50,813	51,942	1,129
6	44,060	45,319	46,578	47,837	49,096	50,355	51,614	52,873	54,132	55,391	1,259
7	47,562	48,961	50,360	51,759	53,158	54,557	55,956	57,355	58,754	60,153	1,399
8	49,573	51,122	52,671	54,220	55,769	57,318	58,867	60,416	61,965	63,514	1,549
9	53,043	54,754	56,465	58,176	59,887	61,598	63,309	65,020	66,731	68,442	1,711
10	58,412	60,296	62,180	64,064	65,948	67,832	69,716	71,600	73,484	75,368	1,884

NOTE: These special base rates for law enforcement officers (as defined in 5 U.S.C. 5541(3) and 5 CFR 550.103) are authorized by section 403 of the Federal Employees Pay Comparability Act of 1990, as amended. By law, these rates must be the basis for computing locality payments. (5 CFR part 531, subpart F.)

THE FOREIGN SERVICE SCHEDULE

Class	Step 1	Step 2	Step 3	Step 4	Step 5	Step 6	Step 7	Step 8	Step 9	Step 10	Step 11	Step 12	Step 13	Step 14
1	123,041	126,732	130,534	134,450	138,484	142,638	146,917	151,325	155,865	159,950	159,950	159,950	159,950	159,950
2	99,700	102,691	105,772	108,945	112,213	115,580	119,047	122,618	126,297	130,086	133,988	138,008	142,148	146,413
3	80,787	83,211	85,707	88,278	90,926	93,654	96,464	99,358	102,339	105,409	108,571	111,828	115,183	118,638
4	65,461	67,425	69,448	71,531	73,677	75,887	78,164	80,509	82,924	85,412	87,974	90,613	93,332	96,132
5	53,043	54,634	56,273	57,962	59,700	61,491	63,336	65,236	67,193	69,209	71,285	73,424	75,627	77,895
6	47,419	48,842	50,307	51,816	53,371	54,972	56,621	58,319	60,069	61,871	63,727	65,639	67,608	69,636
7	42,391	43,663	44,973	46,322	47,711	49,143	50,617	52,136	53,700	55,311	56,970	58,679	60,439	62,253
8	37,896	39,033	40,204	41,410	42,652	43,932	45,250	46,607	48,006	49,446	50,929	52,457	54,031	55,652
9	33,878	34,894	35,941	37,019	38,130	39,274	40,452	41,666	42,916	44,203	45,529	46,895	48,302	49,751

SENIOR FOREIGN SERVICE SCHEDULE

The Senior Foreign Service (SFS) pay system is an open-range, performance-based pay system that is linked to the SES pay system. SFS members, like SES members, are not entitled to automatic across-the-board increases and locality-based comparability payments. Instead, pay adjustments are based on a member's individual performance and/or contribution to the agency's performance.

The Executive order prescribes three SFS salary classes that are linked to the SES as follows:

(1) Career Minister (CM). with a range from 94 percent of the rate payable to level III of the Executive Schedule to 100 percent of the rate payable to level III of the Executive Schedule (Note: Career Ambassador (CA) SFS members are also paid within the CM rate range);

(2) Minister-Counselor (MC) with a range from 90 percent of the rate payable to level III of the Executive Schedule to 100 percent of the rate payable to level III of the Executive Schedule; and

(3) Counselor (OC), with a range from 120 percent of the rate payable to GS–15, step 1 to 100 percent of the rate payable to level III of the Executive Schedule.

The 2024 pay ranges for the SFS classes are:

SFS Class	Minimum	Maximum
OC	$135,468	$191,046
MC	$135,468	$200,411
CM, CA	$135,468	$203,700

DEPARTMENT OF VETERANS AFFAIRS, VETERANS HEALTH ADMINISTRATION FEDERAL SALARY SCHEDULES EFFECTIVE ON THE FIRST DAY OF THE FIRST APPLICABLE PAY PERIOD BEGINNING ON OR AFTER JANUARY 1, 2024

SCHEDULE FOR THE OFFICE OF THE UNDER SECRETARY FOR HEALTH (38 U.S.C. 7306) AND DIRECTORS OF MEDICAL CENTERS AND VETERANS INTEGRATED SERVICE NETWORKS (38 U.S.C. 7401(4))*

	Minimum	Maximum
Assistant Under Secretaries for Health	$147,649	$221,900**
(Only applies to incumbents who are not physicians or dentists)		
Service Directors (non Physicians)	$147,649	$221,900
Physician and Dentist Base and Longevity Schedule*		
Physician Grade	$121,020	$177,496
Dentist Grade	121,020	177,496
Chiropractor, and Optometrist Schedule		
Chief Grade	$123,041	$159,950
Senior Grade	104,604	135,987
Intermediate Grade	88,520	115,079
Full Grade	74,441	96,770
Associate Grade	62,107	80,737

*Rate limited to level IV of the Executive Schedule

Expanded-Function Dental Auxiliary Schedule ***		
Director Grade	$123,041	$159,950
Assistant Director Grade	104,604	135,987
Chief Grade	88,520	115,079
Senior Grade	74,441	96,770
Intermediate Grade	62,107	80,737
Full Grade	51,332	66,731
Associate Grade	44,173	57,421
Junior Grade	37,765	49,096

*Pursuant to 38 U.S.C. 7404(a)(2)(A) and (e), this schedule does not apply to the Director of Nursing Service or any incumbents who are physicians, podiatrists, or dentists. Pursuant to 38 U.S.C. 7404(a)(2)(B), this schedule also does not apply to the basic pay of any incumbents who are registered nurses or physician assistants if that basic pay is determined by the Secretary under subchapter IV of chapter 74 of title 38, United States Code.

** Pursuant to 38 U.S.C. 7404(a)(3)(B), for positions that are covered by a certified performance appraisal system, the maximum rate of basic pay may not exceed the rate of basic pay payable for level II of the Executive Schedule. For positions that are not covered by a certified performance appraisal system, the maximum rate of basic pay may not exceed the rate of basic pay payable for level III of the Executive Schedule.

*** Pursuant to 38 U.S.C. 7431, Veterans Health Administration physicians, podiatrists, and dentists paid under the Physician, Podiatrist, and Dentist Base and Longevity Pay schedule may also be paid market pay and performance pay.

**** Pursuant to section 301(a) of Public Law 102–40, these positions are paid according to the Nurse Schedule in 38 U.S.C. 4107(b), as in effect on August 14, 1990, with subsequent adjustments.

Made in United States
Cleveland, OH
07 April 2025

15892052R00127

2025-2026 Edition

Digital SAT
Hard Verbal Modules

PREPVANTAGE

ISBN-13: 9798305576863

Visit us at **PrepVantageTutoring.com**

Digital SAT Reading: Literature and History
Copyright © 2025 PrepVantage Publishing

ISBN-13: 9798305576863

Table of Contents

CONTINUES ON THE NEXT PAGE

Test 6

Scan here for
online questions!

_____

Want even more practice?

We are partnered with EdisonOS, and some of our questions are
published on the EdisonOS digital platform.

- If you'd like to explore more digital tests, please visit the website at
  the following link: https://www.edisonos.com/sat-practice-tests.

Learn more about our strategies and question research!

Visit the background pages prepvantagetutoring.com/digitalreading
and prepvantagetutoring.com/digitalwriting for more information

_____

Reading and Writing

27 QUESTIONS

The questions in this section address a number of important reading and writing skills. Each question includes one or more passages, which may include a table or graph. Read each passage and question carefully, and then choose the best answer to the question based on the passage(s).

All questions in this section are multiple-choice with four answer choices. Each question has a single best answer.

1

By no means simply _____ to the animals that encounter them, snow deposits can in fact be used strategically by birds and mammals, from moose (which, when grazing, stand on snow banks to reach high-up branches) to the various woodland birds that dig into iced-over snow to create insulated shelters.

Which choice completes the text with the most logical and precise word or phrase?

A) suspicions

B) inventions

C) privileges

D) obstacles

2

Biographical films, or "biopics," about famous musicians have proliferated over the past fifteen years. Such recent biopics can be understood as continuing an earlier approach: among the important _____ here is *The Coal Miner's Daughter*, a film about country musician Loretta Lynn that appeared to critical acclaim in 1980.

Which choice completes the text with the most logical word or phrase?

A) incentives

B) outliers

C) relics

D) precedents

CONTINUE

3

Gretchen McCulloch's research on word usage over time cites women as _____ of transformations in written English even during the Renaissance, when the production of published drama and poetry was dominated by men. Women's interactions, argues McCulloch, are premised on large networks of contacts, and women have expedited new word usage—along with the abandonment of older usages like "doth" for "do"—through informal letter writing.

Which choice completes the text with the most logical and precise word or phrase?

A) opponents

B) investigators

C) facilitators

D) delegates

4

On Earth, geological disruptions like earthquakes and landslides can create jagged terrain. On Jupiter's moon Europa, seemingly _____ disruptions may have the opposite effect; indeed, scientists affiliated with NASA's Europa Clipper mission posit that "moonquakes" and landslides redistribute loose rocks and ice on Europa to smooth out this moon's frigid surface.

Which choice completes the text with the most logical and precise word or phrase?

A) dormant

B) imprecise

C) similar

D) eccentric

5

This text is adapted from William Wordsworth's poem "Lines Composed upon Westminster Bridge, September 3, 1802." Westminster Bridge itself is located in London and crosses the Thames, a river that runs through the center of the city.

Earth has not anything to show more fair:
Dull would he be of soul who could pass by
A sight so touching in its majesty:
This city now doth, like a garment, wear
The beauty of the morning; silent, bare,
Ships, towers, domes, theaters, and temples lie
Open unto the fields, and to the sky;
All bright and glittering in the smokeless air.

Which choice best states the main purpose of the text?

A) To depict a scene that makes a favorable impression on the speaker

B) To specify the causes of the speaker's sense of confusion

C) To investigate the social and moral virtues that the speaker associates with the city

D) To evoke a moment of crisis from the speaker's first arrival in the city

CONTINUE ▶

Plasmas frequently take the form of superheated gases with destabilized atomic structures: think of the hyper-energized matter that constitutes the powerful stars. <u>Yet lower-energy plasmas are now available in handheld devices.</u> One of these, a hand-cranked tool shaped like a snail shell, was developed by David Go of the University of Notre Dame and a team of collaborators; the potential utility of this device lies not in colossal energy production but in integration with the subtle moving parts of machinery for improved efficiency, according to a press release from the National Science Foundation.

Which choice best describes the purpose of the underlined portion in the text as a whole?

A) It juxtaposes two devices that were designed to utilize plasma-based energy, suggesting that only one of the devices operated as hoped.

B) It surveys the uses of a recent invention that utilizes low-energy plasma, hinting nonetheless at the limitations that users of this device have cited.

C) It explains why low-energy plasmas are safer for human use than higher-energy plasmas, citing one project that featured a low-energy plasma.

D) It draws a distinction between different types of plasma, presenting one type as useful in the creation of the tool discussed later in the passage.

India's largest stock exchange began, so the story goes, with a few men congregating under a banyan tree around 1875. Entrepreneur and financier Premchand Roychand took this tree in the city then known as Bombay (and known today as Mumbai) as a gathering place for his business associates, who joined him in creating the Bombay Stock Exchange (BSE). Yet while the ever-expanding BSE became central to India's finance industry, official recognition did not follow immediately, or even soon. India's government only formally recognized the BSE as the country's first stock exchange in 1957.

Which choice best describes the main purpose of the text as a whole?

A) To explain the reasoning behind India's decision to delay formal recognition of the BSE

B) To compare the principles that led to the creation of the BSE with the ideals that the BSE came to embody as it gained prominence

C) To enumerate a few of the historical and economic factors that led to the rapid growth of the BSE

D) To discuss how the BSE evolved from a local and personal endeavor into a nationally significant organization

8

CONTINUE ▶

8

The following text is from Charles W. Chesnutt's 1900 novel *The House Behind the Cedars*. George Tryon has recently returned home to stay with Mrs. Tryon, his mother.

"What is the matter, George, dear?" [Mrs. Tryon] would ask, stroking his hot brow with her small, cool hand as he sat moodily nursing his grief. "Tell your mother, George. Who else could comfort you so well as she?"

"Oh, it's nothing, mother—nothing at all," he would reply, with a forced attempt at lightness. "It's only your fond imagination, you best of mothers."

It was Mrs. Tryon's turn to sigh and shed a clandestine tear. Until her son had gone away on this trip to South Carolina, he had kept no secrets from her: his heart had been an open book, of which she knew every page.

Which choice best states the main idea of the text?

A) George's mother does not believe that George truly has respect for her.

B) George has led his mother to dwell on an unpleasant moment from her distant past.

C) George's unwillingness to confide in his mother brings sadness to Mrs. Tryon.

D) George expresses affection in a manner that his mother does not find sincere.

9

Sweeping visions of the pulsating stars and swirling galaxies have guided visionary composers, as has the history of astronomy itself, inspiring music that commemorates breakthroughs in astrophysics and space exploration. For Hungarian composer Peter Eötvös, the spaceflight adventures of astronauts and the universe's origins in the Big Bang motivated the instrumental music of Cosmos. Other composers such as Henryk Gorecki, who honored astronomer Nicholas Copernicus, and Philip Glass, who crafted operas devoted to Kepler and Galileo, have offered tribute to scientists and mathematicians who laid the foundations of modern astronomy.

Which choice best describes the main idea of the text?

A) Music based on topics in astronomy varies considerably, with composers increasingly drawn to opera as a preferred mode.

B) Instrumental music has enabled composers to represent astronomy-based topics that opera proved unable to depict.

C) Composers have been inspired both by specific astronomers and by phenomena from astronomy as a broad field of investigation.

D) New approaches to astronomy-based topics have resulted from dialogues involving diverse composers.

10

This text is adapted from Lucy Maud Montgomery's 1919 novel *The Rainbow Valley*.

[Little Jem] had a standing feud with [his mother] because she would not give up calling him Little Jem. It was outrageous, thought thirteen-year-old Jem. Mother had more sense.

"I'm not little any more, Mother," he had cried indignantly, on his eighth birthday. "I'm awful big."

Mother had sighed and laughed and sighed again; and she never called him Little Jem again—in his hearing at least.

He was and always had been a sturdy, reliable little chap. He never broke a promise.

Which choice best states the main purpose of the text?

A) To illustrate Jem's traits by noting both a specific issue that offends him and more general attributes

B) To critique Jem's immaturity and impulsivity through juxtaposition with his mother's more thoughtful approach

C) To demonstrate how Jem's conflict with his mother led him to value honesty in other contexts

D) To reveal how Jem's ideas changed by contrasting different stages of his relationship with his mother

11

The Land of Little Rain is a 1903 book by Mary Hunter Austin. In this collection of short narratives, Austin herself describes the plantlife of the American Southwest but acknowledges that precise observation can be difficult: _____

Which choice from *The Land of Little Rain* most effectively illustrates the claim?

A) "For all the toll the desert takes of a man it gives compensations, deep breaths, deep sleep, and the communion of the stars."

B) "We have fallen on a very careless usage, speaking of wild creatures as if they were bound by some such limitation as hampers clockwork."

C) "[My neighbor's] field is not greatly esteemed of the town, not being put to the plough nor affording firewood, but breeding all manner of wild seeds that go down in the irrigating ditches to come up as weeds in the gardens and grass plots."

D) "It is not easy always to be attentive to the maturing of wild fruit. Plants are so unobtrusive in their material processes, and always at the significant moment some other bloom has reached its perfect hour."

12

Decision Making Times for Four Students

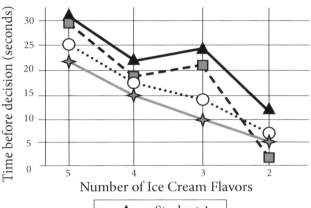

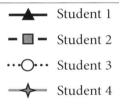

To test whether having more choices results in slower decision making, a student conducted an experiment with four of her classmates as participants. She presented them with different flavors of ice cream in sets of five, four, three, and two; for each set, she recorded how long it took each student to name a favorite flavor from among those in the set. The student had predicted that decision making time would progressively decrease as the number of flavors decreased. This prediction is most aligned with the results from _____

Which choice best uses information from the graph to complete the statement?

A) student 1 and student 3.

B) student 2 and student 3.

C) student 2 and student 4.

D) student 3 and student 4.

13

Lifespans of Various Fish Species

Fish Species	Maximum Lifespan (years)	Lifespans for Related Species (years)
Rougheye Rockfish	205	2-100
Shortraker Rockfish	157	2-100
Lake Sturgeon	152	50-60
Orange Roughy	149	95-110

For a marine biology seminar, a student has been collecting statistics on fish that have exceptionally long lifespans. Initially, the student had hypothesized that fish species with extremely long lifespans lived much longer than related species, but this hypothesis would be most strongly challenged by statistics for the _____

Which choice most effectively completes the text with information from the table?

A) rougheye rockfish and its related species.

B) shortraker rockfish and its related species.

C) lake sturgeon and its related species.

D) orange roughy and its related species.

CONTINUE

14

Even an activity as straightforward as sorting Halloween candy can foster important mathematical skills in children, note professors Sheri-Lynn Swarchuk, Erin A. Maloney, and Heather P. Douglas. In an article published during the 2021 Halloween season, the co-authors encouraged parents and caretakers to actively challenge children to think of Halloween candy in terms of fractions and counted sequences, ideally through cooperative activities involving statistics for the collected candy. Given this emphasis, the authors might not attribute the same benefits to _____

Which choice most logically completes the text?

A) mathematical tasks that involve candy but lack an interactive or participatory element.

B) Halloween-based mathematical activities that require multiple age groups to collaborate.

C) structured activities that require children to analyze a small number of everyday objects.

D) Halloween activities that suggest multiple methods for completing a single task.

15

White-Out, which was first branded as Liquid _____ was invented by Bette Nelson Graham, whose experience as an office worker in the 1950s alerted her to the time consumed in correcting typewritten documents. With her invention, an error could be "whited out" and typed over.

Which choice completes the text so that it conforms to the conventions of Standard English?

A) Paper,

B) Paper;

C) Paper

D) Paper—

16

Gary Paulsen's most famous novels center on young men who must survive in the American wilderness, much as Paulsen himself once did. *Dogsong* (1985) and *Hatchet* (1986) are tales of endurance, and the heroes of these stories exhibit some of the same survival skills that Paulsen _____ fishing, hunting, building shelters, and driving teams of sled dogs across the frozen expanses of northern Canada.

Which choice completes the text so that it conforms to the conventions of Standard English?

A) mastered

B) mastered,

C) mastered:

D) mastered;

CONTINUE ➜

17

During times of scarcity, new recipes can emerge. Water _____ became popular during the Great Depression; the recipe calls for a pie crust and a filling made of sugar, butter, and water. Normally, eggs would have been used in a custard-like filling of this sort, but they were hard to find during the Depression.

Which choice completes the text so that it conforms to the conventions of Standard English?

A) pie, a simple dessert,

B) pie, a simple dessert

C) pie a simple dessert

D) pie a simple dessert,

18

Having emerged as a flourishing hub of culture and commerce by the early 800s CE, _____ —from the overland traders who arrived along the Silk Road to those who arrived by sea, bearing luxury goods from ancient Persia.

Which choice completes the text so that it conforms to the conventions of Standard English?

A) merchants from different cultures were drawn to the Korean city of Gyeongju

B) different cultures' merchants were drawn to Geyongju, a Korean city

C) the Korean city of Gyeongju drew merchants from very distant cultures

D) different cultures, through their merchants, were drawn to the Korean city of Gyeongju

19

Unlike botanists, who use their expertise in the zoology of plants mostly for research purposes, horticulturists take a direct hand in fostering plant populations. Horticulturists' contributions to plant management include cross-breeding _____ overseeing flower gardens to keep ornamental plants healthy; and maintaining food-producing gardens and orchards.

Which choice completes the text so that it conforms to the conventions of Standard English?

A) plants from shrubs to apple trees; to create durable breeds;

B) plants; from shrubs to apple trees, to create durable breeds,

C) plants, from shrubs to apple trees, to create durable breeds,

D) plants, from shrubs to apple trees, to create durable breeds;

20

Perhaps the most unusual distinction that Toronto has earned is its status as "The Raccoon Capital of the World." Indeed, the city's raccoons have been widespread recently, with the count estimated at 100,000 in 2017 and then at 200,000 in _____ instead of directly reducing the raccoon count, Toronto now promotes measures—warning visitors against feeding raccoons, for example— to discourage the raccoons from becoming bothersome.

Which choice completes the text so that it conforms to the conventions of Standard English?

A) 2022, now:

B) 2022, now

C) 2022. Now,

D) 2022, now,

21

How a jury is selected can vary considerably even in countries with largely comparable legal and political systems. To screen potential jury members, a judge in the United States will ask about several factors, including past involvement in lawsuits or employment in the legal system; _____ a judge in Australia will typically request little more than name and age.

Which choice completes the text so that it conforms to the conventions of Standard English?

A) furthermore,

B) by contrast,

C) more precisely,

D) to this end,

22

Director Sergio Leone, who is best known for his action and adventure sagas set in the American West, filmed large portions of his 1964 breakthrough Western *A Fistful of Dollars* at a public park in Spain. _____ he altered his approach to prioritize filming in the actual landscapes he depicted, staging important scenes in *Once Upon a Time in the West* (1968) in the deserts of Arizona.

Which choice completes the text with the most logical and precise word or phrase?

A) Consequently,

B) Concurrently,

C) Recently,

D) Subsequently,

23

While researching a topic, a student has taken the following notes:

- Dendrochronologists are scientists who study the growth patterns of trees.

- Projects that involve conserving tree populations and maintaining national parks often utilize the services of dendrochronologists.

- In 2023, observers at Dinosaur National Monument, a nature preserve in Utah, noticed groups of ponderosa pines growing in unexpected locations.

- United States Geological Survey dendrochronologist Becky Brice examined the trees.

- Brice drilled small samples from the pine trees' trunks to evaluate how the tree population initially dispersed and then adapted to different locations.

The student wants to emphasize Brice's contribution to a specific project. Which choice most effectively uses relevant information from the notes to accomplish this goal?

A) Brice and other dendrochronologists study how trees grow by evaluating evidence such as small samples from the trunks of trees.

B) Dendrochronologists such as Brice participate in projects that center on the tree populations found in national parks.

C) After an unusual dispersal pattern was observed among the ponderosa pines at Dinosaur National Monument in 2023, Brice traveled to this nature preserve.

D) In a study of ponderosa pines at Dinosaur National Monument, Brice used small samples from tree trunks to analyze growth and dispersion patterns.

CONTINUE

24

While researching a topic, a student has taken the following notes:

- "Land Art" involves large-scale works that are situated outdoors.

- These works are responsive to environmental changes and are sometimes made of natural materials such as rocks and plants.

- Robert Smithson's *Spiral Jetty* (1970) is in Utah.

- Smithson's jetty consists of rocks that spiral out into a lake to form a walkable surface.

- Nancy Holt's *Sun Tunnels* (1973-1976) is in Utah.

- Holt's tunnels are four concrete cylinders that are carefully aligned with the movements of the sun.

The student wants to specify a contrast between *Spiral Jetty* and *Sun Tunnels*. Which choice most effectively uses relevant information from the notes to accomplish this goal?

A) Situated in Utah, *Spiral Jetty* (1970) is made of stones that form a surface, and *Sun Tunnels*, which was composed a few years later, is also situated outdoors.

B) Land Art consists of substantial outdoor artworks; two outdoor works, *Sun Tunnels* and *Spiral Jetty*, occupy natural surroundings in Utah.

C) While works of Land Art can feature plants, Nancy Holt's *Sun Tunnels* is made up of concrete cylinders instead.

D) Smithson's *Spiral Jetty* is made of rocks, but Holt's *Sun Tunnels*, which is in Utah as well, consists of concrete cylinders.

25

While researching a topic, a student has taken the following notes:

- Individual dog breeds are known for specific personality traits that make them desirable to owners.

- Crossbreeding can produce a new breed that captures desirable traits from both of its parent breeds.

- Beagles are popular for their high intelligence and sociable temperament.

- Cavalier King Charles spaniels are popular for their protective nature and loyalty to their owners.

- "Beagliers," which represent a beagle-Cavalier King Charles Spaniel hybrid, are popular for their high intelligence and strong emotional connection to their owners.

The student wants to emphasize a specific similarity between beagles and "beagliers." Which choice most effectively uses relevant information from the notes to accomplish this goal?

A) Beagliers, which combine traits of the beagle and the Cavalier King Charles Spaniel, have proven popular because these crossbred dogs form strong emotional bonds with their owners.

B) Beagles are popular for their sociable temperaments; Cavalier King Charles Spaniels, which have been crossbred with beagles, are popular for their protective nature.

C) Representing a hybrid of beagles and Cavalier King Charles Spaniels, beagliers are popular for the high intelligence attributed to beagles.

D) Crossbreeding beagles and Cavalier King Charles Spaniels has produced a new breed with desirable traits: the beaglier.

CONTINUE

26

While researching a topic, a student has taken the following notes:

- Mónica Carvalho and Carlos Jaramillo researched how the Chicxulub Impact affected plants.

- The Chicxulub Impact, a meteor strike that took place 66 million years ago, arguably led to the mass extinction of the dinosaurs.

- A team including Carvalho and Jaramillo investigated fossilized plants in Central and South America.

- Jaramillo, a paleontologist, examined traces of prehistoric pollen from 39 sites.

- The investigation revealed that the Chicxulub Impact led to mass extinctions among large coniferous trees.

- Smaller trees and ferns replaced these coniferous trees to form rainforests.

The student wants to explain the study's findings to an audience familiar with the Chicxulub Impact. Which choice most effectively uses relevant information from the notes to accomplish this goal?

A) An asteroid strike that occurred 66 million years ago, the Chicxulub Impact was investigated by researchers.

B) The Chicxulub Impact, an asteroid strike that presumably led to a dinosaur extinction 66 million years ago, also led to a widespread plant extinction, according to Carvalho and Jaramillo.

C) By focusing on clues such as pollen traces, Jaramillo and other researchers investigated the fossil record to trace how the Chicxulub Impact affected plantlife in Central and South America.

D) Carvalho and Jaramillo,determined that the Chicxulub Impact eliminated coniferous trees in Central and South America and that these trees were replaced by other plants.

27

While researching a topic, a student has taken the following notes:

- Nara is a significant cultural center in Japan.

- Tourists interested in traditional Japanese architecture have often been drawn to the monumental Shinto shrines in Nara.

- Nara is famous for the friendly "sacred deer" that roam some of its sites.

- Visitors are encouraged to interact with the deer and can purchase small biscuits known as shika senbei to feed to these animals.

- The deer appear to respond well to human visitors and have been recorded "bowing" to visitors in photos and video footage.

The student wants to describe the sacred deer for an audience unfamiliar with Nara. Which choice most effectively uses relevant information from the notes to accomplish this goal?

A) The "sacred deer" that roam through Nara are notable for a few different reasons: these friendly animals have been recorded "bowing" to visitors and are tame enough to accept food from tourists as well.

B) Nara's "sacred deer" are famous, and Nara visitors are in fact encouraged to buy small biscuits known as shika senbei, which can then be used to feed the deer.

C) Nara, a Japanese cultural center notable for its Shinto shrines, is home to a population of "sacred deer" that wander freely and even appear to "bow" to tourists.

D) In video footage and in photographic evidence, Nara's friendly "sacred deer" have been documented "bowing" to human visitors.

STOP
If you finish these exercises, you may check your work on this section only.
Do not turn to any other section in the book.

No Test Content on This Page

Reading and Writing

27 QUESTIONS

The questions in this section address a number of important reading and writing skills. Each question includes one or more passages, which may include a table or graph. Read each passage and question carefully, and then choose the best answer to the question based on the passage(s).

All questions in this section are multiple-choice with four answer choices. Each question has a single best answer.

1

Korea's Choson Dynasty ruled from 1392 to 1910 CE, often _____ power by adhering to a strategy of non-engagement with the rest of the world. Even as Choson Korea remained isolated and fairly steady, nearby powers such as Ming Dynasty China pursued global trade with uneven results.

Which choice completes the text with the most logical and precise word or phrase?

A) refusing

B) proclaiming

C) maintaining

D) relaxing

2

In 2004, *New York Times* columnist William Safire published the opinion essay "Abolish the Penny," arguing that pennies had become increasingly inefficient in everyday transactions. Safire's article appears remarkably _____ in retrospect: in the years since, the rise of digital payments has reduced pennies to frequent irrelevance.

Which choice completes the text with the most logical and precise word or phrase?

A) erudite

B) bombastic

C) prescient

D) reclusive

3

Several insights about the _____ of bacteria—which can transmit genetic material to one another and are themselves vulnerable to DNA-attacking viruses known as bacteriophages—can be traced to the work of cell biologist and geneticist Esther Lederberg, who in 1951 became the first scientist to detect the lambda bacteriophage.

Which choice completes the text with the most logical and precise word or phrase?

A) corroborations

B) magnitude

C) transactions

D) dynamics

4

Discounts often prompt shoppers to make purchases that they do not need, value, or even want in retrospect. According to a 2023 Ipsos poll, 42 percent of American shoppers regret buying at least one item on discount—with almost two thirds of these regretful shoppers deeming the item _____ and its presence an unimportant addition to their lives, if not simply a nuisance.

Which choice completes the text with the most logical and precise word or phrase?

A) tenacious

B) derogatory

C) idiosyncratic

D) superfluous

5

Text 1
Narwhals, carnivorous whales that inhabit the waters surrounding the North Pole, do not in fact possess teeth for chewing; instead, narwhals swallow fish and other prey whole. Still, a narwhal is classified as a toothed whale because male and, in rare cases, female narwhals grow a single elongated tooth. Analyzing this tooth (which resembles a spear-like horn), professor of aquatic sciences Kristin Laidre posits that, <u>because only male narwhals regularly grow this "horn," it is used in rivalries pitting males against males, not for catching food.</u>

Text 2
For Megan Montemurno of the Ocean Conservancy, there are multiple plausible purposes for the long, thin "horn" characteristic of male narwhals. She notes that narwhals do not actually use the horn to spear food (despite its appearance) but may use it to tap and stun prey, that narwhals could use the horn to break through layers of ice, and that the horn houses abundant nerve endings and, thus, may help a narwhal to better assess and navigate its surroundings.

Based on the texts, how would Megan Montemurno (Text 2) respond to the underlined claim in Text 1?

A) By highlighting the ways in which female narwhals also use their horns for purposes such as navigation and competition

B) By conceding that a narwhal's horn is of limited use in hunting due to the extraordinary sensitivity of the horn itself

C) By emphasizing that the horn may in fact be used in hunting but could prove useful in the absence of prey as well

D) By suggesting that additional observations of narwhals are needed to confirm the idea that male narwhals exhibit competitive behavior

CONTINUE ▶

6

This text is adapted from Gottfried Keller's 1862 novel *The Banner of the Upright Seven*.

Kaspar Hediger, master tailor of Zurich, had reached the age at which an industrious craftsman begins to allow himself a brief hour of rest after dinner. So it happened that one beautiful March day he was sitting not in his manual but in his mental workshop, a small, separate room which for years he had reserved for himself. He was glad that the weather was warm enough for him to occupy it again.

Which choice best states the main idea of the passage?

A) Kaspar has earned respect as a result of his recent intellectual pursuits.

B) Kaspar is a dedicated worker who nonetheless values repose and reflection.

C) Kaspar's professional and intellectual efforts both flourish when the weather grows warmer.

D) Kaspar's reputation for hard work could be undermined by his new habits.

7

This text is adapted from Emma Lazarus's 1883 poem "In Exile." The speaker is describing a group of Russian men who have relocated to the United States and work as farm laborers in Texas.

Hark! through the quiet evening air, their song
Floats forth with wild sweet rhythm and glad
    refrain.
They sing the conquest of the spirit strong,
The soul that wrests the victory from pain;
The noble joys of manhood that belong
To comrades and to brothers. In their strain
Rustle of palms and Eastern streams one hears,
And the broad prairie melts in mist of tears.

Which choice best states the main idea of the text?

A) The singing of the men combines tones of sorrow and triumph in a manner that is quite moving.

B) The speaker appreciates the men's song even though it is unlikely that other people will find the song equally affecting.

C) The men's song indicates that they are eager to forget their past and build a new life through hard work.

D) The speaker feels sadness for the men because they do not understand the extent of their misfortunes.

CONTINUE

Sharp deviations from expected product shapes have conflicting effects: while manufacturing a household staple such as soap in a nonstandard form—a cone, perhaps—can captivate customers, those same customers may ultimately find the unconventionally shaped product inefficient for use or unnerving due to its associations with other products. Some currently available conical soaps, for instance, are readily confused with conical candles. For the boutique soap company Nectarlife, the solution is to embrace these potentially paradoxical product features, and Nectarlife's own conical soaps are novelty items that are not intended for offhand everyday use and that are shaped, in a further twist, like ice cream cones.

Which choice most effectively states the main idea of the text?

A) Customers can be led to adopt nonstandard product shapes if these shapes appear primarily in boutique products.

B) Nectarlife's approach to soap production resolves two problems associated with nonstandard product shapes.

C) Nectarlife's product design strategy changed dramatically as a result of concerns about the classification of products such as conical soap.

D) Problems with marketing and distributing conical soap exemplify the likely liabilities of nonstandard product shapes.

9

Pierre: or the Ambiguities is an 1852 novel by Herman Melville. In the novel, Pierre is notable for his emotional and impulsive personality but displays dramatic changes of mood as well: _____

Which quotation from *Pierre: or the Ambiguities* most effectively illustrates the claim?

A) "Pierre, gladly plunging into this welcome current of talk, was enabled to attend his mother home without furnishing further cause for her concern or wonderment. But not by any means so readily could he allay his own concern and wonderment."

B) "Not into young Pierre, did there then steal that thought of utmost sadness; pondering on the inevitable evanescence of all earthly loveliness; which makes the sweetest things of life only food for ever-devouring and omnivorous melancholy. Pierre's thought was different from this, and yet somehow akin to it."

C) "It was long after midnight when Pierre returned to the house. He had rushed forth in that complete abandonment of soul, which, in so ardent a temperament, attends the first stages of any sudden and tremendous affliction; but now he returned in pallid composure."

D) "Deep, deep, and still deep and deeper must we go, if we would find out the heart of a man; descending into which is as descending a spiral stair in a shaft, without any end, and where that endlessness is only concealed by the spiralness of the stair, and the blackness of the shaft."

10

Document	Letters in Document	Letters per Minute, by Hand	Letters per Minute, Typed
1	2037	50	211
2	2201	41	219
3	2033	51	212
4	2120	43	223
5	2294	37	209

For adults writing in English, average writing speeds vary depending on a few different factors, particularly whether the writer is writing by hand or is typing, though the nature of the assigned writing task can account for differences as well. To determine whether differences in average word length impact typing speed, a student wrote and then typed five documents with the same base word count: 500 words. The results were mixed, and the best evidence that average word length can meaningfully impact writing speed is offered by comparing _____.

Which choice presents information from the table that logically completes the statement?

A) handwritten letters per minute for Document 1 and handwritten letters per minute for Document 3.

B) typed letters per minute for Document 2 and handwritten letters per minute for Document 4.

C) handwritten letters per minute for Document 1 and handwritten letters per minute for Document 5.

D) handwritten letters per minute for Document 3 and typed letters per minute for Document 3.

11

On the basis of research in social psychology, singing in group formats increases individual well-being and simultaneously creates a sense of belonging. These benefits were pinpointed by Robin Dunbar in a 2015 study, which found that singing in a large group, as a cooperative task without competitive pressures, creates a powerful bonding mechanism—making singers who are mostly perfect strangers comfortable with one another, as though, in Dunbar's words, "they'd known each other since primary school." Corroborating research by Daisy Fancourt emphasizes that group singing promotes well-being because it offers an escape from everyday pressures.

Which finding, if true, would most directly challenge the claims of Fancourt, Dunbar, and the other researchers?

A) The majority of the singers who have participated in recent studies of group singing did not know one another from any previous activities.

B) Another study asked participants whether group singing made them feel acceptance, antagonism, or indifference towards their fellow singers and found participants split evenly among the three possible responses.

C) In a further study, participants were provided with "before" and "after" questionnaires and mostly reported feelings of anxiety before a group singing event and feelings of enthusiasm after a group singing event.

D) Additional research has proven that group singing results in the release of endorphins, which are hormones that normally relieve pain but can also lead to short-term sensations of happiness.

12

Paleontologists have uncovered fossilized dinosaur eggs with increasing frequency over the past four decades, although some fossils of this nature were first unearthed in the 1920s. With increasing frequency has emerged an increased understanding of how dinosaurs distributed and safeguarded their eggs before these eggs hatched. Drawing on fossil evidence, one paleontologist has claimed that otherwise dissimilar dinosaurs nonetheless adopted comparable "caregiver" attitudes towards eggs and hatchlings.

Which of the following findings, if true, would most effectively support the paleontologist's claim?

A) Fossilized eggs attributed to the oviraptor, a birdlike dinosaur that died out 66 million years ago, have been found in communal nests that recall those of the triceratops, a larger dinosaur that emerged 65 million years ago and walked on four legs.

B) Two distinct oviraptor breeds, the standard oviraptor and the giant oviraptor, were known to lay eggs and build nesting structures, and paleontologist Darla K. Zelenitsky has noted that more of the standard oviraptor's smaller eggs have been unearthed through fossil-hunting expeditions.

C) The oviraptor was once assumed to be an "egg thief" that raided the nests of a triceratops ancestor, the protoceratops, but this view has been abandoned as a result of genetic evidence that oviraptors laid several of the eggs now known in well-preserved fossils.

D) Oviraptor fossil discoveries indicate several commonalities between oviraptors and birds, some of them linked to the positioning of embryos and then hatchlings within their eggs, despite the strong likelihood that oviraptors were primarily ground-dwelling.

13

In 2012, Jessica de Bloom, Sabine Guerts, and Michael Kompier published a study quantifying the levels of relaxation present over the course of a typical vacation. According to the study's computations, which were revisited and reaffirmed by de Bloom early in 2024, the relaxation that a vacationer experiences peaks on the eighth day of a given vacation. The research, however, was not meant to guide potential vacationers but was intended as an interpretive study of trends gleaned from a dataset, making it unlikely that _____

Which choice most logically completes the text?

A) the initial research by de Bloom and colleagues resembled later research projects on vacation time and relaxation.

B) vacationers themselves would find the conclusions reached by de Bloom and colleagues readily understandable.

C) de Bloom and colleagues directly recommended ideal vacation durations to the vacationers observed in the study.

D) the 2012 study sampled a sufficient number of vacationers to preclude a follow-up study on the experience of relaxation.

14

Squirrels possess a few different strategies that are useful for dealing with high temperatures, a process known as thermoregulation. One is linked to the distinctive feature of many squirrel species: a squirrel's large, bushy tail can in fact be used as a sunshade. Another—a posture known as a sploot—is used across species. Here, a squirrel (or a dog, or a cat) stretches out flat along the ground, so that heat can rise more easily from the expanded surface area of the animal's body. Though effective in thermoregulation, a sploot is _____

Which choice most logically completes the text?

A) typically less helpful to a squirrel than the use of its bushy tail as a sunshade.

B) more of an asset to dogs and cats than it is to squirrels.

C) best suited to temperatures that are not higher than average.

D) not dependent on any distinctive feature of a squirrel's body.

Until the Second Vatican Council (1962-1965) revised the Catholic Church's protocols for conducting church services, masses presided over by Catholic priests featured extended prayers delivered in Latin. The replacement of these prayers with mostly identical prayers delivered in the congregation's daily language of choice, or vernacular, was soon followed by a change in the education of Catholic priests, as the Roman universities that traditionally educated priests discontinued rigorous Latin courses starting in 1967. This further decision effectually ensured that _____

Which choice most logically completes the text?

A) the vernacular versions of the Latin prayers would over time be replaced by vernacular prayers that would not have any clear equivalents from the pre-Vatican Latin mass.

B) prayers from the Latin mass would increasingly be used to teach priests Latin even as fewer priests overall achieved proficiency in Latin itself.

C) further changes to the vernacular mass would most likely result from deviations from the Latin mass promoted by priests who had themselves achieved some proficiency in Latin.

D) the Latin mass would be difficult or even impossible to reinstitute at a later date due to a likely shortage of priests with a strong command of the language.

CONTINUE

16

Biology and chemistry intersect in Valeria Molinaro's inquiries, and one of this theoretical chemist's most recent _____ freezing point from a surprising perspective. Water in its pure form actually freezes at −50 degrees Fahrenheit; Molinaro is looking into the possibility that impurities, particularly protein figments, help water crystallize at its "classic" 32 degrees Fahrenheit freezing point.

Which choice completes the text so that it conforms to the conventions of Standard English?

A) projects' delves into water's

B) projects delves into water's

C) projects delves into waters'

D) projects' delves into waters'

17

Known today as the "father of robotics," Islamic inventor Al-Jazari devised automatons that were notable more for their ingenuity of design than for their practical uses. His purported inventions—several of them traceable to the early 1200s—include an _____ and capable of generating music when wound up and then set in motion.

Which choice completes the text so that it conforms to the conventions of Standard English?

A) orchestra, composed of four miniature figures in a small boat

B) orchestra, composed of four miniature figures in a small boat,

C) orchestra composed of four miniature figures in a small boat,

D) orchestra composed of four miniature figures in a small boat

18

Kindergarten, though meant to ease the transition preschool and first grade, can itself involve difficult transitions for students. Gathered from a large Ohio school district and recorded as part of an Ohio State University study, _____ roughly 70 percent of the children studied had trouble transitioning into a kindergarten classroom, with detrimental impacts on later academic success.

Which choice completes the text so that it conforms to the conventions of Standard English?

A) helping kindergarteners adapt is important, as indicated by statistics on 624 children:

B) the importance of helping kindergarteners adapt is indicated by statistics on 624 children:

C) statistics on 624 children indicate the importance of helping kindergarteners adapt:

D) 624 children statistically indicate the importance of helping kindergarteners adapt:

CONTINUE

19

The psychological importance of a "goodbye" that is well understood was publicized by B. Schwörer and others in a 2020 scholarly _____ claiming that a decisive goodbye can facilitate "an easy transition into the next life phase," in part because saying "goodbye" in this manner provides a basis for continuing a valued connection in a new form.

Which choice completes the text so that it conforms to the conventions of Standard English?

A) article and

B) article; and

C) article:

D) article

20

Compared to those constructed in the Holy Roman Empire, _____ were relatively compact. While the Byzantine structures of northern Italy were laid out on square foundations, Holy Roman Empire churches had more elongated rectangular foundations.

Which choice completes the text so that it conforms to the conventions of Standard English?

A) Byzantine architects who constructed churches in the Middle Ages

B) the Byzantine architects of the Middle Ages constructed churches that

C) the Middle Ages' Byzantine architects constructed churches that

D) the churches constructed by Byzantine architects in the Middle Ages

21

The famously erudite British novelists of the Victorian era were alert to the pitfalls of a scholarly yet detached mentality; among their characters, Edward Casaubon, whose excessive learning and problematic marriage lend both complexity and sadness to George Eliot's *Middlemarch*, and Jude Fawley, whose idealistic pursuit of knowledge leads to disaster in Thomas Hardy's *Jude the Obscure*, _____ the self-destructive nature of scholarly self-absorption.

Which choice completes the text so that it conforms to the conventions of Standard English?

A) symbolize

B) is symbolizing

C) has symbolized

D) symbolizes

22

How old is Earth's moon, exactly? While the longstanding figure for the moon's age was, by past approximations, 4.42 billion years, new research from Northwestern University has yielded a new figure, 4.46 billion _____ determined through atom-level analysis of the zircon crystals in a sample of lunar dust.

Which choice completes the text so that it conforms to the conventions of Standard English?

A) years, was

B) years was

C) years,

D) years

23

Much evolution has been classified as divergent: branching off from a species known as a common ancestor, organisms progressively develop specialized traits. However, the converse, "convergent evolution," has also been observed. _____ the pitcher plant and the venus flytrap hail from different evolutionary lineages, but both evolved to trap and consume insects.

Which choice completes the text with the most logical transition?

A) In retrospect,

B) As noted,

C) Nevertheless,

D) For example,

24

Questionnaires primarily serve to glean raw data from the focus groups and sample populations targeted in research projects; however, as the Pew Research Center notes, questionnaire design itself requires exceptional rigor. _____ researchers run preliminary focus groups to determine that questionnaires are sufficiently straightforward and then send fine-tuned questionnaires to the actual survey participants.

Which choice completes the text with the most logical transition?

A) Meanwhile,

B) By contrast,

C) Afterwards,

D) To this end,

25

Ancient Roman theaters were devised by architects who both revered ancient Greek models and adapted them to mass audiences. _____ edifices such as the Theater of Pompey, a Roman entertainment venue that could accommodate up to 20,000 spectators, paid tribute to the open-form theaters of the Greek city states and their Hellenistic successors.

Which choice completes the text with the most logical transition?

A) More broadly,

B) That said,

C) In this spirit,

D) In comparison,

While researching a topic, a student has taken the following notes:

- Cactus pears are produced by the various cactus species in the Opuntia genus.

- These oblong pink fruits are edible and taste somewhat like melons.

- Cactus pears can survive drought conditions and require little water to sprout.

- Tiffany Kozsan of the University of Nevada speculates that cactus pears could become an alternative to mass-produced crops like corn and soybeans.

- Kozsan notes that this situation could emerge as "long-term drought events [increase] in duration and intensity."

The student wants to explain one of Kozsan's hypotheses to an audience unfamiliar with cactus pears. Which choice most effectively uses relevant information from the notes to accomplish this goal?

A) Oblong and pink, cactus pears taste somewhat like melons and can survive drought conditions.

B) The oblong pink fruits of Opuntia genus cactus species are known as cactus pears, and Tiffany Kozsan of the University of Nevada has speculated about these fruits.

C) Kozsan speculates that the cactus pear will become a viable alternative to mass produced crops in the event of intense "long-term drought events."

D) For Kozsan, one potential alternative to mass-produced crops like corn is the cactus pear, an pink oblong fruit produced by cactus plants of the Opuntia genus.

While researching a topic, a student has taken the following notes:

- Sheets of paper are often recyclable, even if they are only a few inches wide and a few inches long.

- Paper that has been put through shredding machines, such as those common in office buildings, cannot be recycled.

- The shredding process weakens paper fibers.

- Because its fibers are weak, shredded paper cannot be used in products made from recycled paper.

- The New Jersey Department of Environmental Protection notes that shredded paper can "contaminate" a batch of recyclable paper.

The student wants to make and support a generalization about the types of paper that can be recycled. Which choice most effectively uses relevant information from the notes to accomplish this goal?

A) Whether paper has been shredded determines whether it can be recycled: small pieces of paper that have not been shredded are recyclable, but shredded paper cannot be recycled because its fibers have been weakened.

B) The shredding machines used in office buildings both shred paper and weaken the paper's fibers, and it is impossible to create new paper products from paper that has been shredded in this manner.

C) Shredded paper has the potential to contaminate otherwise recyclable paper if it is present in a batch of paper that, for the most part, has not been shredded.

D) Shredded paper can undermine the recycling process, as noted by the New Jersey Department of Environmental Protection.

STOP
If you finish these exercises, you may check your work on this section only.
Do not turn to any other section in the book.

No Test Content on This Page

Test 1 Modules
— Pages 6-28 —

<table>
<tr><td colspan="6" align="center">Pages 6-16
Module 1: Baseline</td></tr>
<tr><td>1</td><td>D</td><td>10</td><td>A</td><td>19</td><td>D</td></tr>
<tr><td>2</td><td>D</td><td>11</td><td>D</td><td>20</td><td>C</td></tr>
<tr><td>3</td><td>C</td><td>12</td><td>D</td><td>21</td><td>B</td></tr>
<tr><td>4</td><td>C</td><td>13</td><td>D</td><td>22</td><td>D</td></tr>
<tr><td>5</td><td>A</td><td>14</td><td>A</td><td>23</td><td>D</td></tr>
<tr><td>6</td><td>D</td><td>15</td><td>A</td><td>24</td><td>D</td></tr>
<tr><td>7</td><td>D</td><td>16</td><td>C</td><td>25</td><td>C</td></tr>
<tr><td>8</td><td>C</td><td>17</td><td>A</td><td>26</td><td>D</td></tr>
<tr><td>9</td><td>C</td><td>18</td><td>C</td><td>27</td><td>C</td></tr>
</table>

<table>
<tr><td colspan="6" align="center">Pages 18-28
Module 2: Hard</td></tr>
<tr><td>1</td><td>C</td><td>10</td><td>C</td><td>19</td><td>D</td></tr>
<tr><td>2</td><td>C</td><td>11</td><td>B</td><td>20</td><td>D</td></tr>
<tr><td>3</td><td>D</td><td>12</td><td>A</td><td>21</td><td>A</td></tr>
<tr><td>4</td><td>D</td><td>13</td><td>C</td><td>22</td><td>C</td></tr>
<tr><td>5</td><td>C</td><td>14</td><td>D</td><td>23</td><td>D</td></tr>
<tr><td>6</td><td>B</td><td>15</td><td>D</td><td>24</td><td>D</td></tr>
<tr><td>7</td><td>A</td><td>16</td><td>B</td><td>25</td><td>C</td></tr>
<tr><td>8</td><td>B</td><td>17</td><td>D</td><td>26</td><td>D</td></tr>
<tr><td>9</td><td>C</td><td>18</td><td>C</td><td>27</td><td>A</td></tr>
</table>

Want to learn more?
Visit prepvantagetutoring.com for Digital SAT updates and for the research sources for our passages

Module 1: Baseline
— Pages 6-16 —

Question 1: Choice D
Word in Context
Difficulty - **Easy** | Topic - **Science**

Choice D is the best answer because the "By no means . . . in fact" construction sets up an opposing relationship. Using snow deposits strategically is a benefit to the animal, so the underlined word must mean a hindrance to the animal.

Choice A is incorrect because, while "suspicions" is a negative word, suspicions are thoughts, not objects. Choice B is incorrect because snow deposits are naturally occurring structures; they were not invented by animals. Choice C is incorrect because "privileges" is positive, whereas the "By no means . . in fact" construction makes the underlined word negative.

Question 2: Choice D
Word in Context
Difficulty - **Medium** | Topic - **Humanities**

Choice D is the best answer because the passage describes the film *The Coal Miner's Daughter* as an early example of a trend (films portraying the lives of famous musicians) that continued to expand and grow in subsequent years. Choose D to best capture the sense of *The Coal Miner's Daughter* being a precursor to other similar films.

Choice A is incorrect because it positions *The Coal Miner's Daughter* as a reward for other films, rather than an early example of a trend in filmmaking. Choice B is incorrect because it implies that *The Coal Miner's Daughter* is different or exceptional, rather than an example of a trend. Choice C is incorrect because it implies that *The Coal Miner's Daughter* is left over or lingering from a previous trend or model, rather than an example marking the start of a pattern that would develop over time.

Question 3: Choice C
Word in Context
Difficulty - **Medium** | Topic - **Social Studies**

Choice C is the best answer because "women have expedited new word usage [and] the abandonment of older usages," so women have facilitated "transformations in written English." Choice A is incorrect because women were catalysts of, not antagonists of, "transformations in written English." Choice B is incorrect because women caused verbal changes by writing letters; they did not research those changes. Choice D is incorrect because women were not representing anyone other than themselves.

Question 4: Choice C
Word in Context
Difficulty - **Medium** | Topic - **Science**

Choice C is the best answer because the context clue "seemingly" indicates a tension between the disruptions being alike and the fact that they "have the opposite effect." For example, "'moonquakes' and landslides" are akin to "earthquakes and landslides," but the former can "smooth out this moon's frigid surface" while the latter "can create jagged terrain." Thus, the underlined word must indicate that the disruptions are alike.

Choice A is incorrect because, though some geological processes may appear dormant, quakes and landslides are, by nature, active. Choice B is incorrect because, if the disruptions were "seemingly" imprecise, the rest of the passage would have to show that they were, in fact, precise, which it does not. Choice D is incorrect because, though "moonquakes" might seem odd, Choice D fails to draw a parallel between "moonquakes" and earthquakes.

Question 5: Choice A
Text Structure and Purpose
Difficulty - **Easy** | Topic - **Literature**

Choice A is the best answer because the narrator keeps emphasizing how beautiful the city is (e.g., it is "fair" and full of "beauty."). Moreover, the narrator finds this beauty "touching in its majesty," so the view makes a favorable impression on the narrator.

Choice B is incorrect because, while the passage gives reasons for the speaker's intense emotional state, the speaker is awestruck, not confused. Choice C is incorrect because, though the passage describes the city, it states physical attributes, not a broader set of social and moral virtues. Choice D is incorrect because the speaker feels positively, not negatively, when regarding the city. In a different context, "silent [and] bare" could be negative, but they are not negative here and instead contribute to the speaker's sense of awe.

Question 6: Choice D
Text Structure and Purpose
Difficulty - **Medium** | Topic - **Science**

Choice D is the best answer because the passage begins by mentioning one form of plasma (superheated gases) and then the underlined sentence introduces a different type (a lower energy form). This second type of plasma is discussed in more detail in the remainder of the passage.

Choice A is incorrect because the preceding sentence mentions a different form of plasma (superheated gases), NOT a different type of device. Choice B is incorrect because the sentence begins to introduce a device, but does not elaborate on its advantages or limitations. Choice C is incorrect because the sentence initially only mentions that lower energy plasma exists alongside superheated gas forms.

Question 7: Choice D
Text Structure and Purpose
Difficulty - **Hard** | Topic - **History**

Choice D is the best answer because the passage provides a history of the founding and growth of the BSE. Moreover, the origins of the BSE were local and personal (Roychand and a small group of other businesspeople gathering beneath a tree), whereas the current BSE is "central to India's finance industry."

Choice A is incorrect because, while the passage mentions India's delay in formally recognizing the BSE, it does not give India's reasoning for the delay. Choice B is incorrect because, while the passage contrasts the original BSE with the BSE as it gained prominence, it does not compare the BSE's original ideals to its later ideals. Choice C is incorrect because, while the rapid growth of the BSE is mentioned, the reasons for that growth are not.

Question 8: Choice C
Central Ideas and Details
Difficulty - **Medium** | Topic - **Literature**

Choice C is the best answer because George's insistence that his sorrow is "nothing at all" represents a change in his previously open relationship with his mother. Mrs. Tryon is herself moved to sorrow because George's trip to South Carolina represents a change from the earlier time, when he "kept no secrets from her," to the apparent new period of sadness and less open communication.

Choice A is incorrect because Mrs. Tryon feels sad but not that George, despite his apparent unwillingness to talk to her about his sorrows, is in fact disrespectful of her; she simply acknowledges that George is uncommunicative. Choice

B is incorrect because an unpleasant yet vague portion of George's past, not a portion of Mrs. Tryon's past, is central to the passage. Choice D is incorrect because George's mother is upset by her son's apparent unwillingness to communicate but does not question his affection itself and in fact tries to show him kindness.

Question 9: Choice C
Central Ideas and Details
Difficulty - **Medium** | Topic - **Humanities**

Choice C is the best answer because the passage is primarily about how astronomy and astronomers "have guided visionary composers" and "inspir[ed works of] music."

Choice A is incorrect because, while the passage mentions various musical works and the genre of opera, it is not about the diversity of music or anyone's preference for opera. Choice B is incorrect because, while the passage mentions opera and instrumental music, it does not say that opera was unable to depict certain topics. Choice D is incorrect because, while the passage mentions composers, it does not mention dialogues between composers.

Question 10: Choice A
Text Structure and Purpose
Difficulty - **Medium** | Topic - **Literature**

Choice A is the best answer because most of the passage is about Jem's resentment at being called "Little Jem," and the end of the passage describes his general traits ("He was . . . a promise.").

Choice B is incorrect because, while the passage contrasts Jem with his mother, it does not paint Jem in a negative light. Choice C is incorrect because, while the passage mentions Jem's conflict with his mother and his honesty, it does not imply a causal link between those two things. Choice D is incorrect because, while the focus of the passage shifts, Jem's ideas do not change over the course of the passage.

Question 11: Choice D
Textual Command of Evidence
Difficulty - **Medium** | Topic - **Literature**

Choice D is the best answer because "It is not easy always to be attentive to the maturing of wild fruit" supports the claim that "precise observation [of plantlife] can be difficult." Moreover, choice D describes how it is difficult to catch the precise moment of a bloom or other maturation process because one may be observing a different plant at that moment.

Choice A is incorrect because, while it references people, it does so purely with regard to what the desert gives and "takes of a man" rather than with regard to human observation. Choice B is incorrect because, though it references a "limitation," the limitation is stated to be incorrect rather than actual, and it does not have to do with human observation. Choice C is incorrect because, while it provides the narrator's observations of plantlife, it does not describe a difficulty with precise observation.

Question 12: Choice D
Quantitative Command of Evidence
Difficulty - **Medium** | Topic - **Social Studies**

Choice D is the best answer because the decision making times of student 3 and student 4 decreased each time the number of flavors decreased.

Choice A is incorrect because student 1 took longer to decide among three flavors than among four flavors. Choice B is incorrect because student 2 took longer to decide among three flavors than among four flavors, so that student's decision making times did not "progressively decrease as the number of flavors decreased." Choice C is incorrect because student 2 took longer to decide among three flavors than among four flavors.

Question 13: Choice D
Quantitative Command of Evidence
Difficulty - **Medium** | Topic - **Science**

Choice D is the best answer because the claim that "fish species with extremely long lifespans lived much longer than related species" would be challenged by evidence showing that a fish species and its related species have fairly similar lifespan. The orange roughy lives for 149 years while its related species can live for 95-110 years, and this evidence presents a relatively small difference in lifespans.

Choice A is incorrect because the rougheye rockfish lives significantly longer than its related species; some of these live for only 2 years while the rougheye rockfish lives for 205 years. Choice B is incorrect because the shortraker rockfish lives significantly longer than its related species; some of these live for only 2 years while the shortraker rockfish lives for 157 years. Choice C is incorrect because the difference between the lifespans for the lake sturgeon and related species is larger than the difference for the orange roughy and related species. Though species related to the lake sturgeon have relatively long lifespans, at minimum and maximum, there is still a difference of almost 100 years between the maximum for a lake sturgeon and the maximum for its related species.

Question 14: Choice A
Inferences
Difficulty - **Hard** | Topic - **Science**

Choice A is the best answer because the research described in the text emphasizes activities in which "parents and caretakers to actively challenge children" and "cooperative activities." This emphasis makes it likely that the research authors, who "encouraged" activities of precisely this sort, might not find less interactive and involved activities equally useful.

Choice B is incorrect because the researchers do find activities that bring together multiple age groups (children long with parents or caretakers) extremely helpful; this choice is directly contradicted by the text. Choice C is incorrect because it is unclear whether the researchers would want a small or a large number of pieces of candy for the activities mentioned in the text. While this fact is not clarified, the researchers would most likely endorse structured and analytical activities, on the basis of the text. Choice D is incorrect because the text does not directly raise the issue of whether multiple methods or a single method would be preferable. It is in fact possible that the researchers, who promote multiple mathematical activities, would be willing to endorse multiple methods for learning about math using Halloween candy.

Question 15: Choice A
Boundaries
Difficulty - **Easy** | Topic - **History**

Choice A is the best answer because the nonessential clause ("which was . . . Paper") is set off by commas from the noun that it describes ("White-Out"). The nonessential clause should be integrated into the rest of the sentence in this manner, since other options create incomplete independent clauses and faulty nonessential phrases.

Choice B is incorrect because it produces an incomplete independent clause ("White-Out . . . Paper"). Choice C is incorrect because it treats "White-Out . . . Graham" as a nonessential clause, which it is not. Choice D is incorrect because it mixes punctuation marks in setting off the nonessential clause ("which was . . . Paper"). All of these false answers result in errors in independent clauses and nonessential phrases.

Question 16: Choice C
Boundaries
Difficulty - **Medium** | Topic - **Humanities**

Choice C is the best answer because the sentence ("Dogsong . . . Canada") consists of an independent clause ("Dogsong . . . mastered") followed by detail about that clause ("fishing . . . Canada"), so the independent clause should end with a colon.

Choice A is incorrect because it fuses the explanatory list with the independent clause. Choice B is incorrect because it treats the independent clause as part of the list. Choice D is incorrect because it treats the explanatory list as a second independent clause.

Question 17: Choice A
Boundaries
Difficulty - **Easy** | Topic - **History**

Choice A is the best answer because it correctly sets off the appositive with commas. The appositive ("a simple dessert") should be set off from the rest of the independent clause ("Water . . . Depression") in this manner, since other options result in changes in meaning.

Choice B is incorrect because the lack of a comma after the appositive excludes "water pie" from the independent clause. Choice C is incorrect because the lack of commas makes the appositive part of the name of the dessert. Choice D is incorrect because the lack of a comma before the appositive leaves the independent clause without a subject. All of these false answers result in errors in the coordination of phrases and independent clauses.

Question 18: Choice C
Form, Structure, and Sense
Difficulty - **Medium** | Topic - **History**

Choice C is the best answer because the dependent content that begins the sentence indicates a "flourishing hub of culture and commerce," and a cosmopolitan "Korean city" could naturally be described as such a "hub" of activity. This choice properly places a reference to "the Korean city of Gyeongju" directly after the dependent content to avoid a modifier error.

Choice A is incorrect because this positioning would indicate that "merchants" themselves, not the city visited by the merchants, would be a place or a "hub" of commerce. Choice B is incorrect because "merchants" are wrongly being described as a "hub" or a place, since the possessive "different cultures'" must be factored out. Choice D is incorrect because

"different cultures" gravitated to the commercial hub in Korea but were not themselves the "hub" designated by the modifier phase. All of these choices introduce illogical references and modifier errors.

Question 19: Choice D
Boundaries
Difficulty - **Hard** | Topic - **Social Studies**

Choice D is the best answer because semicolons are used to separate items in a list when any of the items contains one or more commas. The first item in the list is "cross-breeding plants, from shrubs to apple trees, to create durable breeds." Thus, that item should be followed by a semicolon.

Choice A is incorrect because the first item in the list is "cross-breeding plants, from shrubs to apple trees, to create durable breeds." Thus, that text should not contain a semicolon.
Choice B is incorrect because an item in a list should not contain a semicolon. Choice C is incorrect because the first item in the list ("cross-breeding plants, from shrubs to apple trees, to create durable breeds") should be followed by a semicolon, not a comma.

Question 20: Choice C
Boundaries
Difficulty - **Medium** | Topic - **Science**

Choice C is the best answer because the period is properly used to coordinate two independent clauses, "the city's . . . recently" and "Toronto's . . . bothersome." In this instance, portions of the text that should be treated as dependent clauses ("with . . . 2022," "Now," "instead . . . count") are properly set off from the independent clauses with commas.

Choice A is incorrect because the word "now" should describe a further situation presented in a new clause construction ("Toronto's . . . bothersome"). Instead, this version illogically groups "now" with earlier content to suggest that 2022, a year that has already passed, is happening "now." Choice B is incorrect because it creates a comma splice by placing a long dependent clause ("now . . . count") between two independent clauses joined with only a comma. Choice D is incorrect because it creates a comma splice by avoiding a period, a semicolon, or a coordinating conjunction; the dependent clauses are properly configured but the independent clauses cannot be joined with only a comma.

Question 21: Choice B
Transitions
Difficulty - **Medium** | Topic - **Social Studies**

Choice B is the best answer because "by contrast" indicates that the jury selection process of the United States differs from that of Australia, which supports the "vary considerably" claim in the passage. This transition properly signals an opposing relationship.

Choice A is incorrect because "furthermore" introduces an extension relationship and wrongly indicates that the jury selection process of Australia follows from the jury selection process of the United States. Choice C is incorrect because "more precisely" introduces a support relationship and wrongly indicates that the jury selection process of Australia is a more specific version of the jury selection process of the United States. Choice D is incorrect because "to this end" introduces a goal and method relationship and wrongly indicates that the jury selection process of Australia is a means of achieving the jury selection process of the United States.

Question 22: Choice D
Transitions
Difficulty - **Medium** | Topic - **Humanities**

Choice D is the best answer because "subsequently" indicates that Leone's 1968 movie was filmed after his 1964 movie was filmed. This transition properly signals a temporal relationship.

Choice A is incorrect because "consequently" introduces a cause and effect relationship, which wrongly indicates that Leone's 1968 movie was filmed because his 1964 movie was filmed. Choice B is incorrect because, while "concurrently" introduces a temporal relationship, it wrongly indicates that Leone's 1968 movie was filmed while his 1964 movie was being filmed. Choice C is incorrect because, while "recently" introduces a temporal relationship, it draws a connection between 1968 and now rather than drawing a connection between 1968 and 1964.

Question 23: Choice D
Rhetorical Synthesis
Difficulty - **Medium** | Topic - **Science**

Choice D is the best answer because it states what Brice did in the study, with particular emphasis on how she used "small samples" to analyze the growth and dispersion of trees. This choice is consistent with the student's goal of "emphasiz[ing] Brice's contribution to a specific project."

Choice A is incorrect because it explains what dendro-chronologists do in general rather than focusing on Brice and on one study. Choice B is incorrect because it does not state how Brice contributed to a project or note specific activities within that project; instead, this choice simply indicates the sort of project that Brice could be involved in. Choice C is incorrect because it mentions the Dinosaur

National Monument project without clarifying how Brice was involved in a specific aspect of the project. At most, this choice indicates her involvement in a very general manner.

Question 24: Choice D
Rhetorical Synthesis
Difficulty - **Hard** | Topic - **Humanities**

Choice D is the best answer because it states that Spiral Jetty is made of rocks while Sun Tunnels is made of concrete. This choice is consistent with the student's goal of "specify[ing] a contrast between Spiral Jetty and Sun Tunnels."

Choice A is incorrect because, though it is about Spiral Jetty and Sun Tunnels, it does not state a difference between the two works. Choice B is incorrect because, though it mentions Spiral Jetty and Sun Tunnels, it does not contrast the two works. Choice C is incorrect because, though it mentions Sun Tunnels, it does not say anything about Spiral Jetty.

Question 25: Choice C
Rhetorical Synthesis
Difficulty - **Medium** | Topic - **Science**

Choice C is the best answer because it explains that both beagles and beagliers are intelligent. This choice is consistent with the student's goal of "emphasiz[ing] a specific similarity between beagles and 'beagliers.'"

Choice A is incorrect because, though it states that beagliers have some beagle traits, it does not specify what those traits are. Choice B is incorrect because it is only about beagles and Cavalier King Charles Spaniels, not beagliers. Choice D is incorrect because it is about the genetic heritage of beagliers, not any specific similarity between beagles and beagliers.

Question 26: Choice D
Rhetorical Synthesis
Difficulty - **Hard** | Topic - **Science**

Choice D is the best answer because it mentions the Chicxulub Impact without explaining what it is and states the study's findings. This choice is consistent with the student's goal of "explain[ing] the study's findings to an audience familiar with the Chicxulub Impact."

Choice A is incorrect because it explains what the Chicxulub Impact is and fails to state the study's findings. Choice B is incorrect because, while it does state the study's findings, it explains what the Chicxulub Impact is, which is not appropriate for "an audience familiar with the Chicxulub Impact." Choice C is incorrect because it does not state the study's findings but rather only states the topic of the study.

Question 27: Choice C
Rhetorical Synthesis
Difficulty - **Medium** | Topic - **Social Studies**

Choice C is the best answer because it explains what Nara is and introduces sacred deer in the context of Nara. This is consistent with the student's goal of "describ[ing] the sacred deer for an audience unfamiliar with Nara."

Choice A is incorrect because, though it mentions sacred deer, it does not explain what Nara is, which does not match the student's goal of writing "for an audience unfamiliar with Nara." Choice B is incorrect because, though it mentions sacred deer, it does not explain what Nara is, and it focuses on details that are too specific for an introduction. Choice D is incorrect because, though it mentions sacred deer, it does not explain what Nara is.

Module 2: Hard
— Pages 18-28 —

Question 1: Choice C
Word in Context
Difficulty - **Easy** | Topic - **History**

Choice C is the best answer because the text is about the success of the Choson Dynasty over many centuries. "Maintaining" appropriately indicates that the dynasty stayed in power for a long time.

Choice A is incorrect because "refusing" would wrongly indicate that the Choson Dynasty chose not to stay in power. Choice B is incorrect because "proclaiming" would wrongly indicate that the Choson Dynasty used a strategy of non-engagement to state that it was in power. Choice D is incorrect because "relaxing" would wrongly indicate that the Choson Dynasty loosened its grip on power.

Question 2: Choice C
Word in Context
Difficulty - **Hard** | Topic - **Social Studies**

Choice C is the best answer because pennies have been "reduced . . . to frequent irrelevance," which matches Safire's argument "that pennies had become increasingly inefficient in everyday transactions." Thus, Safire's 2004 essay predated what happened "in the years since," which makes the essay appear prescient.

Choice A is incorrect because, while someone who seems to have predicted a trend might be well educated, nothing about Safire's education is mentioned. Choice B is incorrect because, though Safire might seem overly-opinionated, the passage does not fault him for it. Choice D is incorrect because an article cannot be reclusive (only a person can be reclusive).

Question 3: Choice D
Word in Context
Difficulty - **Hard** | Topic - **Science**

Choice D is the best answer because Esther Lederberg researched the traits of bacteria. The information between the dashes describes genetic transfer and infection, both of which are processes, so "dynamics" fits.

Choice A is incorrect because, while scientific evidence is often corroborated, nothing is being verified or backed up, so "corroborations" does not fit. Choice B is incorrect because "magnitude" refers to size. While bacteria are known for being small, the size of the bacteria is not mentioned in the passage. Choice C is incorrect because, while genetic transfer and infection are processes, they are not transactions, as nothing is being paid or bartered.

Question 4: Choice D
Word in Context
Difficulty - **Hard** | Topic - **Social Studies**

Choice D is the best answer because the purchases are items that the shoppers "do not need, value, or even want." Thus, the underlined word must reflect that definition. "Superfluous" appropriately indicates that the discounted items purchased were of no use or value to the shoppers.

Choice A is incorrect because only a person, not a thing, can be tenacious. Choice B is incorrect because, though "derogatory" is appropriately negative, the items were not insulting but rather unnecessary. Choice C is incorrect because, though impulse buys often reflect the idiosyncrasies of the shopper, the passage is making the point that the items were ultimately unwanted.

Question 5: Choice C
Cross-Text Connections
Difficulty - **Hard** | Topic - **Science**

Choice C is the best answer because, while Montemurno agrees "that narwhals do not actually use the horn to spear food," she argues that they might "use it to tap and stun prey." Therefore, she would disagree with the "not for catching food" part of the underlined claim. Moreover, she argues that the horn has non-food purposes too ("narwhals could use the horn to break through layers of ice, and . . . navigate [their] surroundings").

Choice A is incorrect because, though Montemurno lists uses of the horn that do not seem sex-specific, she agrees that the horn is "characteristic of male narwhals." Choice B is incorrect because, though Montemurno agrees "that narwhals do not actually use the horn to spear food," she argues that they might "use it to tap and stun prey." Moreover, her comment about the horn's "abundant nerve endings" is support for her claim that the horn is useful. Choice D is incorrect because, though Montemurno does not claim that male narwhals exhibit competitive behavior, she does not suggest that additional observations are needed to confirm that behavior.

Question 6: Choice B
Central Ideas and Details
Difficulty - **Medium** | Topic - **Literature**

Choice B is the best answer because the passage refers to the "master tailor" Kaspar as an "industrious craftsman" who, when he is not working, gravitates to "rest" and places importance on a room known as his "mental workshop." This combination of hard work with specific mental and restful activities is central to Kaspar's character as depicted in the text.

Choice A is incorrect because Kaspar's intellectual pursuits, though valued by Kaspar himself, are not described in the context of how other people see Kaspar. It is unclear how the other people in Zurich regard Kaspar's "mental workshop." Choice C is incorrect because the passage never indicates whether Kaspar's professional pursuits flourish with warm weather, even though Kaspar's intellectual pursuits in the "mental workshop" are indeed linked to warm weather. Choice D is incorrect because the text characterizes Kaspar's "rest" and "metal workshop" as features that are allowed and that coexist with his industrious habits, not as potential weaknesses that would be described with a strong negative tone.

Question 7: Choice A
Central Ideas and Details
Difficulty - **Medium** | Topic - **Literature**

Choice A is the best answer because the passage references both positive ("glad refrain," "victory," and "noble joys") and negative ("pain" and "tears") elements of the music. Moreover, the text uses vivid language to show that the singing is quite moving.

Choice B is incorrect because, while the speaker is moved by the men's song, the passage does not reference how other people will feel about the song. Choice C is incorrect because, though the introduction implies that the men want to build a new life through hard work, the song is not about that. Choice D is incorrect because, though the text lists sad ("pain" and "tears") elements of the music, it does not say that the men do not understand the extent of their misfortunes.

Question 8: Choice B
Central Ideas and Details
Difficulty - **Hard** | Topic - **Social Studies**

Choice B is the best answer because the text indicates that products such as conical soap can confuse consumers and may not have a perceived immediate use. Then, the text presents the example of one company, Nectarlife, that has addressed these problems by successfully marketing conical soap in the form of a novelty product shaped like an ice cream cone.

Choice A is incorrect because, though Nectarlife is using nonstandard product shapes for its boutique products, the text does not say that the success of such products depends on boutiques being their primary retailers. Choice C is incorrect because, while the text describes two phenomena associated with nonstandard product shapes, the text does not chart a dramatic change in Nectarlife's approach over time. Instead, the analysis mostly centers on how the company addressed perceived problems with products such as conical soap through a single project. Choice D is incorrect because, while the text describes problems with marketing nonstandard product shapes, it does not discuss distributing them.

Question 9: Choice C
Textual Command of Evidence
Difficulty - **Hard** | Topic - **Literature**

Choice C is the best answer because it shows Pierre's emotional and impulsive personality ("He had rushed forth in that complete abandonment of soul, which, in so ardent a temperament, attends the first stages of any sudden and tremendous affliction") as well as his dramatic change of mood from a state of frenzy to "pallid composure."

Choice A is incorrect because, while "gladly plunging" hints at an impulsive personality, choice A does not show a change of mood. Choice B is incorrect because, while emotions are mentioned, "omnivorous melancholy" is neither impulsive nor capricious. Choice D is incorrect because it is about human psychology in general, not about Pierre's psychology in particular.

Question 10: Choice C
Quantitative Command of Evidence
Difficulty - **Hard** | Topic - **Social Studies**

Choice C is the best answer because it compares the same type of writing (handwritten letters) for two documents with notably different average word length (based on having notably different letter counts and the same word count) and because the two data points cited show notably different writing speeds. This supports the claim that "average word length can meaningfully impact writing speed."

Choice A is incorrect because, though it compares the same type of writing, Documents 1 and 3 have almost the same average word length (based on having approximately the same letter counts and the same word count), so they cannot support a claim about the effect of word length. Choice B is incorrect because, though the numbers cited are different speeds, they are not the same type of writing, so average word length is not the only variable between them. Choice D is incorrect because, though the speeds cited are different, they differ only in the type of writing, not word length, so they show the effect of handwriting vs. typing, not of word length.

Question 11: Choice B
Textual Command of Evidence
Difficulty - **Hard** | Topic - **Social Studies**

Choice B is the best answer because "acceptance, antagonism, [and] indifference" are positive, negative, and neutral, respectively. Having "participants split evenly among the three possible responses" would indicate that group singing is just as likely to produce negative feelings as positive feelings "towards . . . fellow singers." This undermines the claim that group singing makes "singers who are mostly perfect strangers comfortable with one another."

Choice A is incorrect because having the singers "not know one another from any previous activities" would strengthen the claim that group singing makes "singers who are mostly perfect strangers comfortable with one another." Choice C is incorrect because "feelings of anxiety before a group singing event and feelings of enthusiasm after a group singing event" indicates that group singing changed the participants'

feelings for the better, so it "promotes well-being." Choice D is incorrect because having "group singing result[] in the release of endorphins" would support the claim that it "promotes well-being."

Question 12: Choice A
Textual Command of Evidence
Difficulty - **Hard** | Topic - **Science**

Choice A is the best answer because the claim "that dinosaurs at otherwise dissimilar evolutionary stages nonetheless adopted comparable 'caregiver' attitudes towards eggs and hatchlings" can best be supported by evidence of similar caretaking among dinosaurs that evolved at very different times. Choice A does that because oviraptor died out before triceratops emerged, yet the two species had similar nesting patterns.

Choice B is incorrect because, though it compares the nesting habits of two types of dinosaurs, there is nothing to suggest that the standard oviraptor and the giant oviraptor evolved at very different times. Choice C is incorrect because, though it mentions two types of dinosaurs and their eggs, protoceratops and oviraptor were contemporaries. Choice D is incorrect because, though it mentions similarities between the eggs of animals that lived during different times, it does not compare two types of dinosaurs.

Question 13: Choice C
Inferences
Difficulty - **Hard** | Topic - **Social Studies**

Choice C is the best answer because the project "quantifying the levels" of relaxation was "not meant to guide potential vacationers." With these conditions, de Bloom and colleagues most likely avoided making direct recommendations in order to focus on conclusions drawn from "a dataset" instead.

Choice A is incorrect because the passage does not directly mention any later research; the reference to de Bloom's multiple considerations of the same data (in 2012 and in 2024) should not be misread as indicating multiple studies. Choice B is incorrect because the passage does not directly indicate whether the conclusions are understandable to vacationers themselves. Instead, the passage emphasizes that the study is not intended primarily for practical use and is instead "an interpretive study of trends." Choice D is incorrect because the passage does not evaluate the need for a follow-up study and instead, at most, notes that de Bloom returned to previously-assessed data from an existing study.

Question 14: Choice D
Inferences
Difficulty - **Hard** | Topic - **Science**

Choice D is the best answer because the passage indicates that a dog or a cat can perform a sploot in much the same way that a squirrel can. Performing a sploot is a tendency observed across species, and a sploot (unlike the use of a tail as a sunshade) does not rely on a specific anatomical trait of a squirrel.

Choice A is incorrect because the passage mentions two approaches to thermoregulation (the sunshade usage and the sploot) without directly indicating which of these two different methods is more effective. Choice B is incorrect because the passage notes that multiple animals use sploots but does not evaluate this topic in terms of which animals find sploots useful; at most, the passage indicates that a sploot is only one method available to squirrels. Choice C is incorrect because the passage indicates that sploots are useful but does not specify the temperatures (high, low, or average) that are most suited to sploot usage.

Question 15: Choice D
Inferences
Difficulty - **Hard** | Topic - **History**

Choice D is the best answer because the text is about the replacement of Latin masses with vernacular masses. The associated discontinuation of rigorous Latin courses for priests would result in a shortage of priests who were able to conduct masses in Latin.

Choice A is incorrect because, while it is about the replacement of mass material, the passage does not suggest that the content of the masses has changed (rather, only the languages in which the masses are delivered have changed). Choice B is incorrect because, though fewer priests overall achieved proficiency in Latin, the Catholic church decided not to teach priests Latin at all (not merely to stop teaching Latin via coursework). Choice C is incorrect because, while it is possible that further changes would occur, the text does not mention what priests who had achieved proficiency in Latin were promoting.

Question 16: Choice B
Form, Structure, and Sense
Difficulty - **Hard** | Topic - **Science**

Choice B is the best answer because the plural noun "projects" is necessary because the sentence is about "one of" multiple projects. The singular possessive "water's" properly indicates that the freezing point is of water in general, not of certain bodies of water.

Choice A is incorrect because the plural possessive "projects'" lacks a noun, thereby leaving the verb "delves" without an object. Choice C is incorrect because the plural possessive "waters'" would indicate that the freezing point is of bodies of water. Choice D is incorrect because the plural possessive "projects'" lacks a noun and because the plural possessive "waters'" would indicate that the freezing point is of bodies of water.

Question 17: Choice D
Boundaries
Difficulty - **Hard** | Topic - **Humanities**

Choice D is the best answer because the list of the orchestra's traits ("composed of four miniature figures in a small boat" and "capable of generating music when wound up and then set in motion") is essential and is only two items long, so those two items should not be separated by any commas.

Choice A is incorrect because it treats "composed of . . . in motion" as nonessential. Choice B is incorrect because it treats "composed of . . . small boat" as nonessential. Choice C is incorrect because the list of the orchestra's traits is only two items long, so those two items should not be separated with a comma.

Question 18: Choice C
Form, Structure, and Sense
Difficulty - **Hard** | Topic - **Social Studies**

Choice C is the best answer because the introductory clause ("Gathered . . . University study") must modify the first noun after the comma. Statistics were gathered and recorded.

Choice A is incorrect because "helping kindergarteners adapt" is not something that can be gathered and recorded. Choice B is incorrect because "the importance of helping kindergarteners adapt" is not something that can be gathered and recorded. Choice D is incorrect because 624 children were not gathered and recorded by the study (rather, statistics about the children were gathered and recorded by the study).

Question 19: Choice D
Boundaries
Difficulty - **Medium** | Topic - **Social Studies**

Choice D is the best answer because it correctly includes the modifier ("claiming that . . . new form") in the independent clause ("The psychological . . . new form") so that it modifies "article." The modifier should be included in the independent clause in this manner, since other options result in alterations in meaning.

Choice A is incorrect because "and" makes the modifier part of a second clause, thereby indicating that the claim about goodbyes was not made in the article. Choice B is incorrect because a semicolon cannot join an independent clause with a dependent clause. Choice C is incorrect because the colon makes the modifier part of a second clause. "Claiming" in that clause would then be a gerund (noun), which would lack a verb. All of these false answers result in errors in the coordination of independent and dependent clauses.

Question 20: Choice D
Form, Structure, and Sense
Difficulty - **Medium** | Topic - **Humanities**

Choice D is the best answer because the dependent content that begins the sentence should refer to something that was "constructed in the Holy Roman Empire." The noun "churches" would be appropriate for buildings that could be "constructed," and placing this noun directly after the dependent content that begins the sentence would avoid a modifier error.

Choice A is incorrect because it indicates that architects themselves would be "constructed," not that the churches would be constructed by architects. This choice also indicates, towards the end of the sentence, that the architects (not the churches) were "relatively compact." Choice B is incorrect because it indicates that Byzantine architects were constructed, not that Byzantine architects constructed churches. Choice C is incorrect because it indicates that architects from an era were themselves constructed in the manner of buildings. All of these choices result in illogical descriptions and modifier errors.

Question 21: Choice A
Form, Structure, and Sense
Difficulty - **Hard** | Topic - **Humanities**

Choice A is the best answer because "Edward Casaubon . . . and Jude Fawley" is the plural subject of the underlined plural verb "symbolize." The subject may be hard to locate due to the interrupter phrase ("whose excessive . . . *Middlemarch*") separating Edward Casaubon from Jude Fawley.

Choice B is incorrect because the singular verb "is symbolizing" does not agree with the plural subject. Choice C is incorrect because the singular verb "has symbolized" does not agree with the plural subject. Choice D is incorrect because the singular verb "symbolizes" does not agree with the plural subject.

Question 22: Choice C
Boundaries
Difficulty - **Hard** | Topic - **Science**

Choice C is the best answer because it positions the nonessential phrase ("4.46 billion years") between two commas. This phrase should be set off with commas because it is an appositive phrase.

Choice A is incorrect because it treats the appositive phrase as the subject of an independent clause ("a new figure . . . lunar dust"). Choice B is incorrect because it joins two independent clauses ("new research . . . new figure" and "4.46 billion . . . lunar dust) with a comma. Choice D is incorrect because it treats "4.46 billion . . . lunar dust" as the appositive phrase.

Question 23: Choice D
Transitions
Difficulty - **Medium** | Topic - **Science**

Choice D is the best answer because "for example" signals that the shared trait (trapping and consuming insects) between the pitcher plant and the Venus flytrap is an example of convergent evolution. This transition properly signals a support relationship.

Choice A is incorrect because "in retrospect" introduces a correction relationship, which wrongly indicates that it was previously believed that the similarity between the pitcher plant and the Venus flytrap did not result from convergent evolution. Choice B is incorrect because "as noted" introduces a reiteration relationship, which wrongly indicates that it was previously stated in the text that the pitcher plant and the Venus flytrap share a trait because of convergent evolution. Choice C is incorrect because "nevertheless" introduces an opposing relationship, which wrongly indicates that the pitcher plant and the Venus flytrap share a trait despite convergent evolution.

Question 24: Choice D
Transitions
Difficulty - **Hard** | Topic - **Social Studies**

Choice D is the best answer because "to this end" signals that "researchers run preliminary focus groups to determine that questionnaires are sufficiently straightforward" in an effort to ensure "exceptional rigor" in questionnaire design. This transition properly signals a goal relationship.

Choice A is incorrect because "meanwhile" introduces an alternative relationship, which wrongly indicates that the fact that "researchers run preliminary focus groups to determine that questionnaires are sufficiently straightforward" undermines the supposed "exceptional rigor" of their questionnaire design. Choice B is incorrect because "by contrast" introduces an opposing relationship, which wrongly indicates that running "preliminary focus groups to determine that questionnaires are sufficiently straightforward" is inconsistent with "exceptional rigor" in questionnaire design. Choice C is incorrect because "afterwards" introduces a chronological relationship, which wrongly indicates that "researchers run preliminary focus groups to determine that questionnaires are sufficiently straightforward" after "questionnaire design . . . requires exceptional rigor."

Question 25: Choice C
Transitions
Difficulty - **Hard** | Topic - **Humanities**

Choice C is the best answer because "in this spirit" signals that the design of the Roman theaters was inspired by ancient Greek models and the desire to adapt those models to large audiences. This transition properly signals a cause and effect relationship.

Choice A is incorrect because "more broadly" introduces a generalization relationship, which wrongly indicates that the design of the Roman theaters was a generalization of the ancient Greek models that inspired it. Choice B is incorrect because "that said" introduces a caveat relationship, which wrongly indicates that the design of the Roman theaters was an exception to ancient Greek models. Choice D is incorrect because "in comparison" introduces a contrasting relationship, which wrongly indicates that Roman theaters were very different from the ancient Greek models that inspired them.

Question 26: Choice D
Rhetorical Synthesis
Difficulty - **Hard** | Topic - **Science**

Choice D is the best answer because it explains "one potential alternative" according to Kozsan, and it states what a cactus pear is. This choice is consistent with the student's goal of "explain[ing] one of Kozsan's hypotheses to an audience unfamiliar with cactus pears."

Choice A is incorrect because, though it explains what a cactus pear is, it does not explain one of Kozsan's hypotheses. Choice B is incorrect because, though it mentions Kozsan and explains what a cactus pear is, it does not explain one of Kozsan's hypotheses. Choice C is incorrect because, though it explains one of Kozsan's hypotheses, it does not explain what a cactus pear is, so it is not written for "an audience unfamiliar with cactus pears."

Question 27: Choice A
Rhetorical Synthesis
Difficulty - **Hard** | Topic - **Science**

Choice A is the best answer because it states that the recyclability of paper depends upon whether it has been shredded. This is consistent with the student's goal of "mak[ing] . . . a generalization about the types of paper that can be recycled." Moreover, Choice A states that "small pieces of paper that have not been shredded are recyclable, but shredded paper cannot be recycled because its fibers have been weakened," which is consistent with the student's goal of "support[ing] a generalization about the types of paper that can be recycled."

Choice B is incorrect because, though it states a problem with shredded paper, it does not make a generalization about the types of paper that can be recycled. Choice C is incorrect because, though it references "recyclable paper," it does not make a generalization about the types of paper that can be recycled. Choice D is incorrect because it focuses on cardboard, not paper.

Reading and Writing

27 QUESTIONS

The questions in this section address a number of important reading and writing skills. Each question includes one or more passages, which may include a table or graph. Read each passage and question carefully, and then choose the best answer to the question based on the passage(s).

All questions in this section are multiple-choice with four answer choices. Each question has a single best answer.

1

Ethnographers are sociologists who investigate community-level interactions and values, while botanists are scientists who study plants. Naturally, experts in ethnobotany borrow from both ethnography and botany. This _____ field addresses how different plants are significant within particular historical communities and social structures.

Which choice completes the text with the most logical and precise word or phrase?

A) hybrid

B) corrected

C) unknown

D) unintended

2

Desks that enable both standing and sitting postures are not _____ in Japan, according to Jiameng Ma and her fellow physical education researchers at Sendai University. Nonetheless, Ma and colleagues have found that the relatively few Japanese office workers who use hybrid stand-sit desks report improved performance and wellbeing—promising results, particularly if the desks become more popular.

Which choice completes the text with the most logical and precise word or phrase?

A) viable

B) understood

C) widespread

D) beneficial

CONTINUE

3

It seems like a situation pulled directly from a science fiction novel: a mysterious planet, known only as "Planet X" or "Planet 9" and presumed to be 10 times as large as Earth, might be orbiting beyond Pluto in the far reaches of the Solar System. However, NASA scientists find this _____ plausible. Gravitational measurements indicate that this mysterious planet may, in fact, exist.

Which choice completes the text with the most logical and precise word or phrase?

A) conflict

B) disaster

C) scenario

D) experiment

4

While historians regard James Madison's US presidential administration (1809-1817) as mostly competent, Madison's accomplishments as president were, by some assessments, _____ by his resounding achievements from decades earlier, particularly his profound contributions to the nation's founding documents—contributions that earned him the title "Father of the Constitution."

Which choice completes the text with the most logical and precise word or phrase?

A) undermined

B) overshadowed

C) anticipated

D) justified

5

Urban beekeeping seems to offer a ready means of supplementing the number of pollinating insects in major cities, yet conservation scientist Sheila Colla warns that well-meaning urban beekeeping projects could _____ lead to biodiversity loss. As she sees it, the robust honeybees brought in by urban beekeepers could crowd out other bee species in competition for limited resources.

Which choice completes the text with the most logical and precise word or phrase?

A) helpfully

B) sparingly

C) inadvertently

D) carefully

6

This text is adapted from Stendhal's 1830 novel *The Red and the Black*. Julien Sorel, a young man from a countryside town in France, has recently begun a job tutoring children in a wealthy household.

> The children adored Julien, but he did not <u>like</u> them in the least. His thoughts were elsewhere. But nothing which the "little brats" ever did made him lose his patience. Cold, just, and impassive, and nonetheless liked, inasmuch his arrival had more or less driven ennui out of the house, he was a good tutor.

As used in the text, what does the word "like" most nearly mean?

A) Provide assistance to

B) Enjoy

C) Understand

D) Become aware of

CONTINUE ➡

7

To create the monochromatic artworks in her 1998 *Tension* series, Jungsook Ahn constructed specialized rectangular frames. She then stretched a painting canvas over each one, using the natural tension between the canvas surface and specially-placed underlying supports to create one or two sharp curves in the picture plane. Ahn's works call to mind the similarly monochromatic paintings of Italian artist Lucio Fontana, but with a difference: Fontana cut directly into his canvases to create lines, while Ahn uses a taut surface to hint at lines of force.

Which choice best states the main idea of the text?

A) By embracing tension rather than cutting into her canvases, Ahn created painting-like works that are more appealing than Fontana's otherwise similar creations.

B) Ahn created the *Tension* series without slicing into her canvases, in contrast to Fontana in his monochrome paintings.

C) Ahn's use of rectangular frames in the *Tension* series enabled a surprising range of expression within a simple format.

D) The *Tension* series represents one of the high points of Ahn's career.

8

This text is adapted from Mary Shelley's 1832 short story "The Dream." The story is set during the Renaissance and here depicts Constance, a member of an affluent French family.

Constance had left the castle to wander in the neighbouring grounds. Lofty and extensive as were the apartments of her abode, she felt pent up within their walls, beneath their fretted roofs. The spreading uplands and the antique wood, associated to her with every dear recollection of her past life, enticed her to spend hours and days beneath their leafy coverts. The motion and change eternally working, as the wind stirred among the boughs, or the journeying sun rained its beams through them, soothed and called her out of that dull sorrow which clutched her heart with so unrelenting a pang beneath her castle roof.

Which choice best states the main idea of the passage?

A) Constance remains isolated despite her eagerness to communicate with people who live beyond the castle grounds.

B) Constance's sense of guilt is alleviated whenever she is near the castle.

C) Constance feels intense sadness but finds some solace in the presence of nature.

D) Constance's daily routine has erased memories of the happier times in her life.

CONTINUE

9

Developmental psychologist Sarah Kollat has investigated the benefits of fear-inducing experiences—benefits that turn out to be considerable and even inspiring, in her telling. Although her ideas do not necessarily extend to all fear-inducing experiences, her work locates beneficial links between a "controlled fear experience" such as watching a scary movie and outcomes such as better regulation of anxiety, heightened situational awareness, and social bonding. The last benefit can also emerge from work that involves an element of fear or at least suspense, as Kollat, a volunteer firefighter, further explains.

Which choice best states the main idea of the text?

A) Kollat's research indicates that some forms of fear can be assets.

B) Although Kollat's work relies heavily on hypothetical scenarios, her insights have been applied by other researchers.

C) By researching various activities, Kollat has drawn a distinction between "controlled" fear and other forms of fear.

D) Kollat's work as a volunteer firefighter inspired her research on fear responses.

10

"Dr. Heidegger's Experiment" is an 1837 short story by Nathaniel Hawthorne. In the text, Hawthorne's narrator describes Dr. Heidegger as an unusual man who, somewhat unfortunately, has inspired a large number of rumors: _____

Which choice most effectively uses evidence from "Dr. Heidegger's Experiment" to illustrate the claim?

A) "If all stories were true, Dr. Heidegger's study must have been a very curious place. It was a dim, old-fashioned chamber festooned with cobwebs and besprinkled with antique dust."

B) "Now, Dr. Heidegger was a very strange old gentleman whose eccentricity had become the nucleus for a thousand fantastic stories. Some of these fables—to my shame be it spoken—might possibly be traced back to mine own veracious self."

C) "But without waiting for a reply Dr. Heidegger hobbled across the chamber and returned with the same ponderous folio bound in black leather which common report affirmed to be a book of magic."

D) "[Dr. Heidegger's] guests shivered again. A strange dullness—whether of the body or spirit they could not tell—was creeping gradually over them all."

CONTINUE ➤

11

Speed of an Aircraft at Different "Mach" Ratings

Number	Miles per Hour	Aircraft capable of the given Mach
Mach 1	770	Supersonic experimental aircraft, passenger jumbo jets
Mach 2	1540	US Air Force fighter planes
Mach 3	2310	US Air Force stealth and reconnaissance aircraft
Mach 4	3080	Experimental hypersonic rocket planes, US Space Shuttle

Typically used to explain aircraft speeds, Mach numbers indicate how fast an aircraft is moving in comparison to the speed of sound, which is 770 miles per hour in Earth's atmosphere. Aircraft that are capable of speeds that are three times the speed of sound or even faster include _____

Which choice uses relevant and accurate information from the table to complete the statement?

A) US space shuttles and US Air Force stealth aircraft.

B) US Air Force reconnaissance aircraft and supersonic experimental aircraft.

C) experimental hypersonic rocket planes and US Air Force fighter planes.

D) US Air Force fighter planes and US Air Force stealth aircraft.

12

Figurative language often accentuates the seriousness of a moment, but devices such as metaphors, similes, and personification can be used for comedic effect as well. To achieve such an effect, writers and comedians deploy incongruous tones and surprising pairings of ideas. For instance, on the television comedy *Seinfeld*, one character famously begins a story by describing a turbulent sea and then comparing it to an angry old man in a small restaurant—not to something grandiose or dignified. The humor here involves _____

Which choice most logically completes the text?

A) a logical inconsistency between the events described in the story and the character's actual circumstances.

B) a comparison between elements that would normally be depicted as incompatible.

C) an analogy that is meant to be insightful but is ultimately incomprehensible.

D) an elevated style of description that does not fit the character's apparent personality.

CONTINUE

13

Traces of a 500 year-old wooden ship were first discovered off the coast of Kenya in 2013. At the time, researchers suspected that this large galleon played a role in Portuguese exploration and commerce; more precise information could be hard to obtain, since the ship's hull had been integrated into a coral reef and thus anchored to the ocean's floor. Yet in 2024, scholars from the University of Coimbra determined that the ship could be the São Jorge, a vessel that was part of famed explorer Vasco da Gama's fleet, arriving at this conjecture by _____

Which choice most logically completes the text?

A) investigating how the ship eventually resurfaced from the bottom of the ocean.

B) exploring the several other large ships that sank near the ship discovered in 2013.

C) examining small samples of the hull rather than returning the ship to the ocean's surface.

D) gathering new evidence demonstrating that the São Jorge sank far from the coast of Kenya.

14

Although rubber is typically white when manufactured in its basic form, rubber tires have historically been black because carbon black, a hardening agent, is necessary in manufacturing durable _____ white tires display dirt more easily than black tires do and are thus aesthetically unappealing.

Which choice completes the text so that it conforms to the conventions of Standard English?

A) tires, in addition

B) tires in addition,

C) tires; in addition,

D) tires, in addition,

15

Even as consumer technologies become outmoded, those same technologies could provide artists with raw materials for exciting new compositions. Take DVDs: though no longer particularly popular for storing and viewing _____ were used to create a massive sculpture of a fish at the 2011 Glastonbury Festival—and might find future aesthetic uses.

Which choice completes the text so that it conforms to the conventions of Standard English?

A) videos, DVDs;

B) videos; DVDs

C) videos, DVDs

D) videos DVDs

CONTINUE

16

Artists have created striking new versions of the American flag to deliver historical commentary. For instance, _____ classic red, white, and blue were swapped out for red, green, and black—the colors of the pan-African Flag—by African American conceptual artist David Hammons, whose flag encourages viewers to contemplate the intersections of African and American politics.

Which choice completes the text so that it conforms to the conventions of Standard English?

A) it's

B) its

C) they're

D) their

17

At a 2021 symposium on free public transportation convened by the Boston Greater Debate Series, participating speakers weighed whether eliminating public transit fares helps bus _____ train or streetcar conductors to operate more efficiently. Eliminating free public transit itself was not debated as intensely: after all, over 100 cities in the US have partially fare-free systems.

Which choice completes the text so that it conforms to the conventions of Standard English?

A) drivers and

B) drivers, and

C) drivers

D) drivers,

18

Laboratory studies involving animal subjects can be hampered if a test population—for instance, two hundred mice assigned to navigate different mazes— _____ test subjects with different genetic traits that skew results. In this case, some mice may be predisposed to navigate more easily based on an undetected genetic aptitude.

Which choice completes the text so that it conforms to the conventions of Standard English?

A) include

B) are including

C) includes

D) have included

19

Noting that the powers of artificial intelligence technologies have been historically overestimated, researcher Danielle Williams has documented the debut of the _____ that appeared in 1958. This device, it was assumed, was meant to lead to a new era of sentient technology, yet even today's "smart machines" remain error-prone.

Which choice completes the text so that it conforms to the conventions of Standard English?

A) Perceptron, a machine,

B) Perceptron, a machine

C) Perceptron a machine,

D) Perceptron a machine

20

By venturing to the mountains of rural Taiwan and deploying drones to survey rock formations, researchers from Pennsylvania State University _____ how rivers have moved boulders and discerned a precise sequence of geologic events: strong rivers typically moved boulders down mountains first and then began to erode the mountains themselves.

Which choice completes the text so that it conforms to the conventions of Standard English?

A) examined

B) examining

C) to examine

D) having examined

21

Televised in Afghanistan, the children's program *Baghch-e-Simsim*, or *Sesame Garden*, translates the format of its United States counterpart *Sesame Street*—short educational segments featuring lively puppets—into a new cultural context. _____ it uses its puppet characters, such as the brother-sister duo of Zeerak and Zari, to channel the same themes of friendship and inclusivity that have endeared *Sesame Street* to generations of viewers.

Which choice completes the text with the most logical transition?

A) Moreover,

B) Alternatively,

C) More broadly,

D) As noted,

22

Research from social psychologists Shigehiro Oishi and Selin Kesebir posits a correlation between the size of friend groups and socioeconomic conditions, with larger, looser friend groups forming in times of high prosperity and social mobility. _____ economic downturns cause the formation of smaller, more collaborative, more interdependent friend groups.

Which choice completes the text with the most logical transition?

A) Regardless,

B) Next,

C) Conversely,

D) In other words,

23

In 2005, instructor Miranda Hamilton published an article praising the capabilities of interactive, computer-connected whiteboards. These classroom technologies appeared to hold remarkable promise in keeping students engaged—at the time. Today, _____ such interactive whiteboards are a rarity in physical classrooms and are often neglected even when present.

Which choice completes the text with the most logical transition?

A) in addition,

B) as noted,

C) furthermore,

D) though,

CONTINUE

24

While researching a topic, a student has taken the following notes:

- Supermassive black holes can be billions of times more massive than the Sun.

- A black hole of this sort is at the center of the galaxy that contains Earth and the Sun.

- Earth's galaxy is referred to as the Milky Way or as Sagittarius A.

- A black hole of this sort is also at the center of Galaxy NGC 2217.

- This galaxy forms one of the points in the Canis Major (or Larger Dog) constellation.

The student wants to specify the location of a supermassive black hole in a single galaxy. Which choice most effectively uses relevant information from the notes to accomplish this goal?

A) In Galaxy NGC 2217, a black hole occupies the galaxy's center.

B) Galaxy NGC 2217 and Sagittarius A both contain black holes.

C) A supermassive black hole is present in Earth's galaxy, which is known as the Milky Way.

D) Billions of times more massive than the Sun, supermassive black holes are present in galaxies such as the Milky Way and Galaxy NGC 2217.

25

While researching a topic, a student has taken the following notes:

- An archipelago is typically a group consisting of several islands.

- The term "vertical archipelago" was coined by anthropologist John Victor Murra.

- Murra applied this term to the ancient Incas, who inhabited the Andes mountains.

- Inca communities formed at different elevations, from sea-level to mountaintop.

- Each community in the vertical archipelago distributed the resources unique to its elevation to communities at other elevations.

The student wants to emphasize the origins of the term "vertical archipelago." Which choice most effectively uses relevant information from the notes to accomplish this goal?

A) For the Incas, resource distribution involved communities at different elevations.

B) John Victor Murra, an anthropologist, coined the term "vertical archipelago" and used it to describe Inca communities.

C) Ancient Inca communities have been described using the term "vertical archipelago," which is applied to connected communities at different elevations.

D) An archipelago is typically a group of islands, but a vertical archipelago involves land-based communities.

26

While researching a topic, a student has taken the following notes:

- Mensa is a society that seeks out intellectually gifted members.
- It was founded in 1946 in England and is active in the US today.
- The word "mensa" is Latin for "table."
- For Mensa, the image of a table symbolizes the inclusive nature of the organization as a whole.
- The main requirement for joining Mensa is high performance on an intelligence quotient (IQ) test.
- The Stanford-Binet and the Cattell are two IQ tests accepted by Mensa.

The student wants to explain how a person can become a member of Mensa. Which choice most effectively uses relevant information from the notes to accomplish this goal?

A) High performance on an IQ test such as the Cattell is the central requirement for Mensa membership.

B) Founded in 1946, Mensa is an inclusive organization with one main membership requirement.

C) Mensa's name means "table" in Latin and is meant to convey the inclusive nature of Mensa itself.

D) One of the IQ tests that Mensa considers is the Stanford-Binet test.

27

While researching a topic, a student has taken the following notes:

- Engineering researchers Jochen Mueller and Lorna Gibson recently investigated how birds' feathers retain water during flight.
- The researchers studied the African sandgrouse, which retains up to 15% of its body weight in water using a network of belly feathers.
- Mueller and Gibson inspected sandgrouse feathers using high-precision microscopes.
- The researchers traced water retention to the arrangement of barbs (strands which branch off the main branch of a feather) and barbules (strands which branch off the barbs) in sandgrouse feathers.
- Barbules in particular were instrumental in retaining water droplets.

The student wants to specify how the African sandgrouse retains water. Which choice most effectively uses relevant information from the notes to accomplish this goal?

A) To determine how the African sandgrouse retains water, Mueller and Gibson used high-precision microscopes to inspect this bird's distinctive belly feathers.

B) Focusing on the African sandgrouse, which can retain up to 15% of its body weight in water, Mueller and Gibson investigated the barbs and barbules of African sandgrouse feathers.

C) The arrangement of barbs and barbules on a sandgrouse's belly feathers allows the sandgrouse to retain water, with the barbules proving especially instrumental.

D) The African sandgrouse has a distinctive arrangement of barbs, or strands branching from the main branch of a feather, and barbules, or strands branching from the barbs, on its belly feathers.

STOP
If you finish these exercises, you may check your work on this section only.
Do not turn to any other section in the book.

Reading and Writing

27 QUESTIONS

DIRECTIONS

The questions in this section address a number of important reading and writing skills. Each question includes one or more passages, which may include a table or graph. Read each passage and question carefully, and then choose the best answer to the question based on the passage(s).

All questions in this section are multiple-choice with four answer choices. Each question has a single best answer.

1

Skepticism of popular and dramatic accounts of scientific discoveries is often warranted, yet the prevalence of accounts linking scientific breakthroughs to dreaming indicates that sleep may be useful to scientists who are _____ complex constructs. Apparently, a dream helped Russian chemist Dmitri Mendeleev (1834-1907) to clarify his ideas about the final design of the Periodic Table.

Which choice completes the text with the most logical and precise word or phrase?

A) rehearsing

B) juxtaposing

C) pondering

D) inciting

2

In earlier centuries, when professional authors were relatively scarce, librarians could easily create _____ lists of available books; arduous readers could probably work their way through all of the cataloged titles, much as British poet Samuel Taylor Coleridge (1772-1834), who read through the entire book list of a local library, once did.

Which choice completes the text with the most logical and precise word or phrase?

A) pretentious

B) exhaustive

C) credulous

D) ameliorated

CONTINUE ▶

3

Scholars who understand the 1890 Sherman Antitrust Act as the sole defining achievement of Ohio Senator John Sherman's illustrious career risk _____ Sherman's other contributions to political reform. He was, after all, a vocal and influential proponent of the abolition of slavery before he turned his attention, with the Antitrust Act, to corporate governance.

Which choice completes the text with the most logical and precise word or phrase?

A) overriding

B) discounting

C) underscoring

D) extolling

4

Fashion designer Kofi Ansah pursued a variety of measures that _____ the clothing and accessories industry in his home country, Ghana, in the early 1990s: his promotion of Ghanaian traditional fabrics in mass-produced and high-quality garments was complemented by his sponsorship of popular fashion-related events, sometimes with the help of Ghana's government ministers.

Which choice completes the text with the most logical word or phrase?

A) galvanized

B) resurrected

C) released

D) authorized

CONTINUE ➡

5

This text is adapted from Natsume Soseki's novel *The Master*, in a 1919 translation by Yasutaro Moro. Here, the narrator has just received a letter from a close friend.

I am quick-tempered and would refuse to read such a long, unintelligible letter for five yen [coins], but I read this seriously from the first to the last. <u>It is a fact that I read it through.</u> My efforts were mostly spent in untangling letters and sentences; so I started reading it over again. The room had become a little dark, and this rendered it harder to read it; so finally I stepped out to the porch where I sat down and went over it carefully.

Which choice best states the function of the underlined portion in the text as a whole?

A) It defines the setting that the narrator describes in greater detail later on in the text.

B) It communicates the narrator's fulfillment and relief upon finishing a challenging task.

C) It qualifies the narrator's earlier remarks on the letter by alluding to the letter's admirable qualities.

D) It emphasizes the narrator's ultimate response to difficulties mentioned elsewhere in the text.

6

Art and literature critics often call an era in which a particular form of expression was brilliantly reinvented a "renaissance," appropriating the term applied to the creatively fertile revival of classical forms that took place in Europe centuries ago. So-called renaissances are not confined to media such as sculpture: <u>in animation, Walt Disney Studios experienced a "renaissance" of its own.</u> After producing masterpieces from the 1930s to the 1960s, the Disney animation division fell into critical and financial decline—only for beloved feature films such as *The Little Mermaid* to usher in the Disney Renaissance of the 1980s and 1990s.

Which choice best explains the function of the underlined portion in the text as a whole?

A) It demonstrates that the concept of a renaissance is not normally applied to animation.

B) It signals that earlier definitions of a concept are outdated and proposes a new definition.

C) It notes an unusual trend that appears to weaken an argument introduced earlier in the text.

D) It returns to a concept mentioned earlier while raising a new and relevant context.

This text is adapted from Frances E.W. Harper's 1896 poem "Songs for the People."

> Let me make the songs for the weary,
> Amid life's fever and fret,
> Till hearts shall relax their tension,
> And careworn brows forget.
>
> Let me sing for little children,
> Before their footsteps stray,
> Sweet anthems of love and duty,
> To float over life's highway.

Which choice best states the main purpose of the text as a whole?

A) To present various artistic principles and show how they originated from the speaker's experiences

B) To define specific audiences and explain how they will benefit from the speaker's compositions

C) To depict contrasting groups and illustrate how they can empathize with one another through the speaker's influence

D) To provide moral instruction and suggest that the principles set forward have guided the speaker's interactions with other people

This text is adapted from Vachel Lindsay's 1916 poem "The Moon Is a Mirror." Here, the speaker encounters a wanderer who earns money by sharpening household implements.

> The old man had his box and wheel
> For grinding knives and shears.
> No doubt his bell in village streets
> Was joy to children's ears.
> And I bethought me of my youth
> When such men came around,
> And times I asked them in, quite sure
> The scissors should be ground.
> The old man turned and spoke to me,
> His face at last in view.
> And then I thought those curious eyes
> Were eyes that once I knew.

Which choice best describes the structure of the text as a whole?

A) The speaker reflects on the significance of the old man's work, then the old man confronts the speaker and provides a new interpretation.

B) The old man draws the attention of the speaker, then the speaker contemplates a contrast between the past and the present.

C) The speaker observes the old man and contemplates the past, then the old man interacts with the speaker.

D) The old man evokes the speaker's pleasant childhood, then the speaker recalls the struggles of adulthood.

Text 1
The first silver dollars minted by the US were created in response to the 1859 discovery of the Comstock Lode, a Nevada-based vein of precious metals that almost instantaneously increased the country's available silver supply. Subsequently, legislation designed to make the value of US currency dependent on the silver supply moved through Congress and led, in 1878, to the debut of the first Morgan Silver Dollar, a coin named after its principal designer, George T. Morgan, but contingent upon a lucky find and political forces.

Text 2
When, following the demise of the Morgan Silver Dollar in the 1920s, US silver dollars were reintroduced later in the century, the intention was not to respond to changing financial and political realities through a new form of coinage. Rather, the 1971 silver dollar served commemorative purposes, with engravings that celebrated Dwight Eisenhower—a heroic World War II general and popular president—and the Space Race, particularly the Apollo 11 Moon Landing.

Which choice best describes the relationship between Text 1 and Text 2?

A) Text 1 claims that the Morgan Silver Dollar was historically influential despite its origins in a chance discovery, while Text 2 suggests that later silver dollars mostly celebrate historical accomplishments.

B) Text 1 demonstrates the manner in which the creation of the Morgan Silver Dollar impacted US legislation, while Text 2 asserts that later silver dollar coinage did not have a similarly significant impact on US finances and policy.

C) Text 1 illustrates how a discovery and subsequent legislation led to the production of the Morgan Silver Dollar, while Text 2 argues that a different silver dollar was commemorative in intent.

D) Text 1 indicates that creation of the Morgan Silver Dollar was initially met with resistance, while Text 2 suggests that silver dollars became popular mostly as historical curiosities.

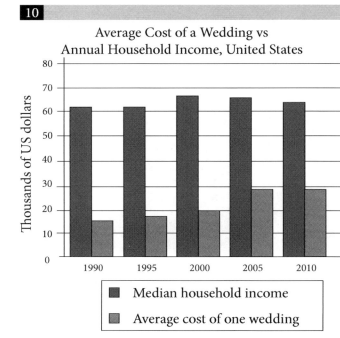

Average Cost of a Wedding vs Annual Household Income, United States

Median household income

Average cost of one wedding

While the percentage of household income allotted to some expenditures typically grows over time, others remain stable as a percentage of median US household income (a widely-accepted measure of the income of a "typical" US household). One economist cites wedding expenses as representative of such stability, with the share of income that a typical household would allot to wedding expenses presumably unchanged from 1990 onwards. However, this economist's claim would be challenged by a comparison of _____

Which choice effectively uses relevant information from the chart to complete the statement?

A) the cost of one wedding as a portion of median household income in 1990 and then in 2000.

B) the cost of one wedding as a portion of median household income in 2000 and then in 2010.

C) median household income between 1990 and 2010 and the cost of one wedding in 2000.

D) median household income between 1990 and 2010 and the cost of one wedding in 2010.

CONTINUE

11

The Uncalled is an 1898 novel by Paul Laurence Dunbar. In the novel, Dunbar's narrator describes how Hester Prime, a forty year-old woman, lives according to a firm moral code: _____

Which quotation from *The Uncalled* most effectively illustrates the claim?

A) "Looking down upon its meaner neighbours in much the same way that its mistress looked upon the denizens of the street, stood Miss Prime's cottage. It was not on the mean street—it would have disdained to be—but sat exactly facing it in prim watchfulness over the unsavoury thoroughfare which ran at right angles."

B) "In summer [Hester's] front yard was filled with flowers, hollyhocks, bachelor's-buttons, sweet-william, and a dozen other varieties of blooms. But they were planted with such exactness and straightness that the poor flowers looked cramped and artificial and stiff as a party of angular ladies dressed in bombazine. Here was no riot nor abandon in growth. Everything had its place, and stayed therein or was plucked up."

C) "In the world about her [Hester] saw so much of froth and frivolity that she tried to balance matters by being especially staid and stern herself. She did not consider that in the seesaw of life it takes more than one person to toss up the weight of the world's wickedness."

D) "Miss Prime's idea of floors was that they were to be walked on, scrubbed, measured, and carpeted; she did not remember in all the extent of her experience to have seen one used as a reading-desk before."

12

Flight Statistics for Various North American Birds

Bird	Wing beats per second	Maximum flight speed (miles per hour)	Average body mass, adult female (grams)
Ruby-throated hummingbird	70	45	4.1
Scarlet tanager	2.7	25	37
American robin	2.3	36	85

Birds with smaller body masses are famous for achieving higher flight speeds by beating their wings rapidly, much as some insects stay aloft through high-frequency wing movements. Nonetheless, a higher number of wing beats per second does not directly correlate with a higher maximum flight speed among birds, since _____

Which choice most effectively completes the statement with accurate information from the table?

A) the American robin normally beats its wings slightly less often than a scarlet tanager does but can achieve a flight speed over 10 miles per hour higher.

B) wing beats per second is significantly higher for a ruby-throated hummingbird than for a scarlet tanager.

C) the scarlet tanager exhibits only a slightly higher number of wing beats per second than the American robin, a bird with significantly higher average body mass.

D) the ruby-throated hummingbird beats its wings significantly more often than either the scarlet tanager or the American robin, two birds with nearly-identical wing speeds and maximum flight speeds but significantly different body masses.

CONTINUE

13

"The River" is an 1827 poem by Ralph Waldo Emerson. In this poem, the speaker observes a natural landscape that, though familiar and understandable, is disheartening for the speaker to contemplate: _____

Which choice best uses evidence from "The River" to illustrate the claim?

A) "Look, here [the river] is, unaltered, save that now / He hath broke his banks and flooded all the vales / With his redundant waves. / Here is the rock where, yet a simple child, / I caught with bended pin my earliest fish."

B) "I am not the same, / But wiser than I was, and wise enough / Not to regret the changes, though they cost / Me many a sigh."

C) "Oh, call not Nature dumb; / These trees and stones are audible to me, / These idle flowers, that tremble in the wind, / I understand their faery syllables, / And all their sad significance."

D) "The wind, / That rustles down the well-known forest road— / It hath a sound more eloquent than speech."

14

Ultraviolet light, which is invisible to humans, is readily detected by reindeer and plays a significant role in the foraging habits of arctic reindeer herds. Dependent on the *Cladonia rangiferina* lichen more popularly known as "reindeer moss" for subsistence, reindeer must discriminate this whitish lichen from the winter snows of their habitat. Reindeer moss, according to researchers from Dartmouth University and the University of St. Andrews, does not reflect ultraviolet light; these specialists further claim that reindeer's ultraviolet vision evolved as a mechanism for spotting this dietary staple.

Which finding, if true, would most directly support the researchers' claim about reindeer?

A) Using visual means to locate food from a distance allows arctic reindeer to conserve energy while foraging, thus increasing their survival prospects even when access to *Cladonia rangiferina* is limited.

B) Ultraviolet light has been presented in visual simulations during studies of how reindeer perceive their surroundings, and light of this sort might appear to be of an intense purple or indigo color if human eyes could see it directly.

C) Of the over 1,500 lichen species that arctic reindeer can encounter, several species have a whitish color that makes it difficult to tell them apart from snow.

D) Reindeer discern *Cladonia rangiferina* as a non-reflecting blank spot in the middle of an expanse of ultraviolet light reflected from snow, but reindeer must approach the lichen to ensure that it is *Cladonia rangiferina* and not another species.

CONTINUE

15

For individuals with multiple types of debt, two widely-touted payment strategies are possible: the "debt avalanche" method and the "debt snowball" method. The debt avalanche method is to some extent the more logical of the two: because people who owe money must often pay additional sums (or interest) on the money owed, rapidly paying off extremely high-interest debts in a single "avalanche" can be financially beneficial. The debt snowball method, though, involves paying off small debts first (and regardless of interest rate) to build the confidence to progressively pay off larger debts. This "snowball" approach can be quite popular, indicating that people who owe money _____

Which choice most logically completes the text?

A) normally turn to the snowball method after attempting to pay off debts using the avalanche method.

B) combine aspects of the snowball and avalanche methods in an approach that borrows primarily from the snowball method.

C) to some extent disregard factors such as high interest rates when paying off debts.

D) are rather likely to accumulate further debts while using the avalanche method.

16

Lighthearted entertainments that combined song and dance with elaborate costumes and somewhat simplistic narratives, court masques rose to popularity in Renaissance England, as prominent poets such as Ben Jonson and John Milton scripted and designed court masques of their own. To some scholars, Milton's participation in the court masque genre was unusual: both at the time of his most famous court masque—*Comus* (1637)—and after, Milton gravitated to modes of narrative and symbolic poetry notable for its intricate storytelling. Apparently, Milton _____

Which choice most logically completes the text?

A) crafted court masques that were more elaborate than those of earlier authors.

B) prioritized narrative complexity while minimizing the use of song and dance when composing his court masques.

C) regarded his work on masques such as *Comus* as a diversion from the creation of serious poetry.

D) decided to work within the court masque genre despite its presumed narrative simplicity.

CONTINUE

17

According to collaborating scientists Konstantin Batygin and Alessandro Morbidelli, the planets in our solar system could have _____ an inner ring, where smaller rocky planets cohered, and an outer ring, where the gas giants took shape. Systems dominated by large rocky planets, as Batygin and Morbidelli acknowledge, could have formed differently.

Which choice completes the text so that it conforms to the conventions of Standard English?

A) formed: in two "rings" of material

B) formed in; two "rings" of material,

C) formed in two "rings" of material:

D) formed, in two "rings" of material;

18

In the early decades of the 21st century, deep sea explorers such as Lucy Woodall—whose team, around 2020, examined undersea mountains in the Indian Ocean—built upon the ventures of deep sea pioneers William Beebe and Otis Barton, who, with a pressurized capsule known as the "bathysphere," _____ a depth of 3000 feet below the surface in 1930.

Which choice completes the text so that it conforms to the conventions of Standard English?

A) have reached

B) had reached

C) reach

D) were reaching

19

For some large waterbird species (the flamingo, for example), adult males and adult females are virtually identical in coloration. Male and female spoonbills, though, exhibit slight differences in _____ the male of this species is notable for the dark markings near its eyes and the vivid pink feathers near its wings, while the female lacks the dark markings and has more mute pink features.

Which choice completes the text so that it conforms to the conventions of Standard English?

A) adulthood:

B) adulthood: as

C) adulthood,

D) adulthood. As

20

At the core of Book 1 of Edmund Spenser's *The Faerie Queene*, a sweeping epic poem from the English Renaissance, _____ the various influences that Spenser absorbed during his time at the University of Cambridge, where, between 1569 and 1573, he steeped himself in the Greek and Latin classics and in more recent poetic forms from France and Italy.

Which choice completes the text so that it conforms to the conventions of Standard English?

A) are

B) was

C) is

D) has been

21

Professor Rachel J.C. Fu specializes in the tourism and hospitality industries, areas of the world economy that, in the years ahead, could be stimulated by events such as Formula 1 motor races, which Fu (herself a Formula 1 enthusiast) links to such _____ "expanded broadcasting rights, sponsorship deals, and a growing global fan base."

Which choice completes the text so that it conforms to the conventions of Standard English?

A) assets as

B) assets, as

C) assets as:

D) assets as,

22

Dialogue between individuals who are dreaming and awake seems like an unlikely prospect, but Northwestern University researcher Karen Konkoly and an experiment _____ achieved exactly this type of connection in 2021. Mazurek entered a state of rapid eye movement (REM) sleep; according to readings of his brain activity during REM dreaming, he could solve simple math problems posed by Konkoly.

Which choice completes the text so that it conforms to the conventions of Standard English?

A) participant, Christopher Mazurek

B) participant, Christopher Mazurek,

C) participant Christopher Mazurek

D) participant Christopher Mazurek,

23

"It is surprising how much we have in common with zebrafish," notes scientist Diana W. Bianchi, whose specialty in human genetics and development from early childhood forward has been illuminated in new ways by the recently-discovered fact that, like humans, zebrafish possess lymphatic _____ connecting their brains to their circulatory systems.

Which choice completes the text so that it conforms to the conventions of Standard English?

A) vessels: which

B) vessels:

C) vessels

D) vessels, which

24

Political polarization, in which opposed liberal and conservative parties embrace starkly incompatible positions, has followed differing trends in neighboring countries over the past 40 years. According to research from Brown University economist Jesse Shapiro, polarization has increased in New Zealand and decreased in nearby Australia; _____ polarization has fallen in Germany and risen in Switzerland, which borders Germany.

Which choice completes the text with the most logical transition?

A) conversely,

B) nonetheless,

C) likewise,

D) thus,

25

African American engineer and astronaut Mae Jamison has been cited as a direct inspiration by scientists and educators who, though earthbound, share Jamison's passion for investigating the cosmos—for instance, Susan Mbara of Kenya. As the organizer of the telescope-based Star Safari education programs, Mbara is not herself an astronaut; she hopes, _____ that Jamison's example will inspire African girls to become astronauts one day.

Which choice completes the text with the most logical transition?

A) conversely,

B) though,

C) by this logic,

D) furthermore,

26

Special effects expert John Dykstra worked at the University of California Environmental Simulation laboratory and then contributed to the *Star Wars* series; here, by moving a movie camera in front of a stationary object (often a model of a spaceship), he conjured the impression that the object itself was moving. Under Dykstra's manipulations, _____ the spaceships of *Star Wars* never actually moved— but the illusion of movement remains breathtaking.

Which choice completes the text with the most logical transition?

A) for example,

B) in addition,

C) in other words,

D) to some extent,

27

While researching a topic, a student has taken the following notes:

- Sea angels and sea butterflies are marine snails that move by flapping two wing-like appendages.

- These organisms possess shells made of aragonite, which dissolves more readily than the calcite that land-dwelling snails use to create their shells.

- A research team led by Katja Peijnenburg performed genetic analysis to better understand the evolution of sea angels and sea butterflies.

- The research team determined that sea angels and sea butterflies "are much older than previously thought and must have survived previous episodes of widespread ocean acidification," according to a report by Peijnenburg.

- Two of the "previous episodes" cited by Peijnenburg took place 66 million years ago and 56 million years ago.

The student wants to summarize the aim and findings of Peijnenburg's research. Which choice most effectively uses relevant information from the notes to accomplish this goal?

A) Peijnenburg and colleagues determined that sea angels and sea butterflies were resilient enough to survive in periods of ocean acidification.

B) Peijnenburg's research resulted in an evaluation of these organisms' survival aptitudes: in Peijnenburg's words, sea angels and sea butterflies "are much older than previously thought."

C) Charting the evolution of sea angels and sea butterflies, Peijnenburg and colleagues concluded that these organisms successfully survived two periods of ocean acidification.

D) Peijnenburg and colleagues set out to perform genetic analysis of sea angels and sea butterflies, organisms that experienced ocean acidification.

STOP
If you finish these exercises, you may check your work on this section only.
Do not turn to any other section in the book.

No Test Content on This Page

Answer Key
Test 2 Modules
— Pages 42-62 —

Pages 42-51						
Module 1: Baseline						
1	A	10	B	19	B
2	C	11	A	20	A
3	C	12	B	21	A
4	B	13	C	22	C
5	C	14	C	23	D
6	B	15	C	24	A
7	B	16	B	25	B
8	C	17	A	26	A
9	A	18	C	27	C

Pages 52-62						
Module 2: Hard						
1	C	10	B	19	A
2	B	11	C	20	A
3	B	12	A	21	A
4	A	13	C	22	B
5	D	14	D	23	C
6	D	15	C	24	C
7	B	16	D	25	B
8	C	17	C	26	C
9	C	18	B	27	C

Want to learn more?
Visit prepvantagetutoring.com for Digital SAT updates and for the research sources for our passages

Module 1: Baseline
— Pages 42-51 —

Question 1: Choice A
Word in Context
Difficulty - **Easy** | Topic - **Social Studies**

Choice A is the best answer because "experts in ethnobotany borrow from both ethnography and botany," so they combine the fields of ethnography and botany. Thus, the field of ethnobotany is a mixture of two fields. "Hybrid" appropriately fits the context of academic disciplines.

Choice B is incorrect because, though scientists often correct prior misunderstandings, the field of ethnobotany is not being corrected. Choice C is incorrect because, though ethnobotany may not be well known, the passage is not discussing the obscurity of ethnobotany. Choice D is incorrect because, though academic disciplines sometimes come together unexpectedly, there is nothing in the text to suggest that ethnobotany resulted from an unintended blending of fields.

Question 2: Choice C
Word in Context
Difficulty - **Medium** | Topic - **Social Studies**

Choice C is the best answer because "relatively few Japanese office workers . . . use hybrid stand-sit desks," and the desks are not yet popular. Thus, the correct answer, along with the word "not" before it, should indicate that such desks are not used by many people.

Choice A is incorrect because "not viable" would mean that such desks could not be used in Japan, which is false because few, not zero, people in Japan use them. Choice B is incorrect because, while few people use them, there is nothing to indicate that people don't understand how to use them. Choice D is incorrect because those who use stand-sit desks "report improved performance and wellbeing."

Question 3: Choice C
Word in Context
Difficulty - **Easy** | Topic - **Science**

Choice C is the best answer because the text is about "a situation" that seems like science fiction but is actually plausible. Thus, the underlined word must mean "situation." "Scenario" fits this meaning and appropriately indicates that "Planet X" or "Planet 9" might actually exist.

Choice A is incorrect because, though something that seems like science fiction might seem to conflict with reality, the passage says that "this mysterious planet may, in fact, exist." Moreover, it is a planet, not a conflict, that seems plausible. Choice B is incorrect because the text does not mention a disaster. Choice D is incorrect because, though science often involves experiments, the text does not mention an experiment.

Question 4: Choice B
Word in Context
Difficulty - **Medium** | Topic - **History**

Choice B is the best answer because the text indicates that "Madison's accomplishments as president were" not as acclaimed as "his resounding achievements from decades earlier" were. Thus, the underlined word must approximate the meaning of "outdone." "Overshadowed" fulfills this requirement because it indicates that Madison's earlier achievements were more well regarded than his accomplishments as president were.

Choice A is incorrect because, while "undermined" is negative, it would indicate that Madison's earlier achievements stymied his accomplishments as president, which was not the case. Choice C is incorrect because, while Madison's earlier achievements predated his accomplishments as president, that is not the point that the author is making. The introductory clause ("While historians . . . competent") makes it clear that the passage is about how Madison is perceived by historians. Choice D is incorrect because, while Madison's actions as president may have been justified, the underlined word needs to be negative in order to contrast with the introductory clause.

Question 5: Choice C
Word in Context
Difficulty - **Medium** | Topic - **Science**

Choice C is the best answer because the "urban beekeeping projects" are "well-meaning," so they do not aim to create "biodiversity loss." "Inadvertently" correctly indicates that the biodiversity loss is unintentional.

Choice A is incorrect because, while urban beekeepers are well-meaning, biodiversity loss is negative ("honeybees brought in by urban beekeepers could crowd out other bee species"), not helpful. Choice B is incorrect because the problem is substantial and widespread, not small or infrequent. Choice D is incorrect because, while beekeepers must be careful, the biodiversity loss is unintentional, so urban beekeepers are not taking care to cause it.

Question 6: Choice B
Word in Context
Difficulty - **Medium** | Topic - **Literature**

Choice B is the best answer because the context clue that "the children adored Julien" means that the underlined word must mean something akin to "adore." "Enjoy" fulfills this meaning and appropriately describes the fact that he did not delight in the children's company.

Choice A is incorrect because, though his thoughts were elsewhere, "he was a good tutor," so he did provide them with assistance. Choice C is incorrect because, while he might not have understood the children's behavior, not understanding the children does not contrast with "the children adored Julien." Choice D is incorrect because, though his thoughts were elsewhere, he could not have been unaware of the children given that he was tutoring them.

Question 7: Choice B
Central Ideas and Details
Difficulty - **Medium** | Topic - **Humanities**

Choice B is the best answer because the passage is about how Jungsook Ahn "create[d] the monochromatic artworks in her 1998 Tension series." Specifically, it contrasts Ahn's and Fontana's methods of creating lines with regard to whether they cut their canvases.

Choice A is incorrect because, though Ahn used tension rather than cutting into her canvases, the text does not say which method is more appealing. Choice C is incorrect because, though Ahn did use rectangular frames, the text does not say that the frames enabled a surprising range of expression. Choice D is incorrect because, though the text is about Ahn's Tension series, it does not say that the series represents one of the high points of her career.

Question 8: Choice C
Central Ideas and Details
Difficulty - **Hard** | Topic - **Literature**

Choice C is the best answer because Constance feels "pent up" near the castle but experiences different emotions in "the antique wood," which helps to alleviate the "sorrow" that is such a strong emotion for her in other contexts. Constance's experience thus combines a strong negative tone of sadness

with the positive tone that characterizes her encounters with nature in the woods.

Choice A is incorrect because the passage emphasizes Constance's experiences entirely and does not in fact specify any other characters, though other characters may in fact inhabit the castle. Choice B is incorrect because it wrongly cites "guilt" as Constance's negative emotion; despite Constance's sadness, it is not clear that Constance has done anything wrong. Moreover, Constance's negative feelings are increased, not lessened, when she is near the castle. Choice D is incorrect because Constance experiences the "dear recollection of her past life" when she is in the woods; her pleasant memories have not been erased but are probably less pronounced when she is near the castle.

Question 9: Choice A
Central Ideas and Details
Difficulty - **Medium** | Topic - **Social Studies**

Choice A is the best answer because Kollat's research is about "the benefits of fear-inducing experiences." Moreover, these benefits "turn out to be considerable and even inspiring."

Choice B is incorrect because, though the text mentions various scenarios, it does not mention other researchers. Choice C is incorrect because, though Kollat has researched "controlled fear experience[s]," the passage is not primarily about the distinction between "controlled" fear and other forms of fear. Choice D is incorrect because, though the text notes Kollat's work as a volunteer firefighter, it does not say that her volunteer work inspired her research on fear responses.

Question 10: Choice B
Textual Command of Evidence
Difficulty - **Medium** | Topic - **Literature**

Choice B is the best answer because "Dr. Heidegger was a very strange old gentleman " illustrates the claim that "Dr. Heidegger [w]as an unusual man." Moreover, "whose eccentricity had become the nucleus for a thousand fantastic stories" illustrates the claim that "Dr. Heidegger has inspired a large number of rumors." Lastly, "to my shame be it spoken" supports the notion that the rumors were "somewhat unfortunate[]."

Choice A is incorrect because, while it references stories about Dr. Heidegger and his "very curious" study, it does not portray him as an unusual man but rather portrays his study as an unusual place. Moreover, it does not portray the stories as somewhat unfortunate. Choice C is incorrect because, though it references Dr. Heidegger, it does not reference any rumors about him. Choice D is incorrect because, though it references odd events, it does not reference rumors.

Question 11: Choice A
Quantitative Command of Evidence
Difficulty - **Medium** | Topic - **Science**

Choice A is the best answer because "three times the speed of sound or even faster" includes speeds greater than or equal to 2310 miles per hour. This corresponds to the bottom two rows of the table, so the correct answer must include aircraft only from one or both of those rows. US space shuttles and US Air Force stealth aircraft are from the bottom two rows.

Choice B is incorrect because, though US Air Force reconnaissance aircraft are from one of the bottom two rows of the table, supersonic experimental aircraft are not. Choice C is incorrect because, though experimental hypersonic rocket planes are from one of the bottom two rows of the table, US Air Force fighter planes are not. Choice D is incorrect because, though US Air Force stealth aircraft are from one of the bottom two rows of the table, US Air Force fighter planes are not.

Question 12: Choice B
Inferences
Difficulty - **Medium** | Topic - **Humanities**

Choice B is the best answer because the passage is about how comedy uses figurative language for comedic effect by using it in novel ways, such as "incongruous tones and surprising pairings." Choice B is consistent with this idea, since "elements that would normally be depicted as incompatible" are "incongruous," and because a grandiose description of the sea would normally be depicted as incompatible with "an angry old man in a small restaurant."

Choice A is incorrect because, while it is about a discrepancy, it is about "a logical inconsistency" rather than an inconsistency of tone or topics. Choice C is incorrect because, though the *Seinfeld* example uses an analogy, it is not incomprehensible. Choice D is incorrect because, though the *Seinfeld* example uses an elevated style of description that does not fit the topic of "an angry old man in a small restaurant," it is not the old man's personality that causes the discrepancy.

Question 13: Choice C
Inferences
Difficulty - **Medium** | Topic - **Social Studies**

Choice C is the best answer because the passage states that "the ship's hull had been integrated into a coral reef and thus anchored to the ocean's floor." Therefore, any efforts to examine the ship would have to be done either underwater or by extracting samples.

Choice A is incorrect because, though the ship was anchored underwater, there is nothing to suggest that it broke free of the coral reef. Choice B is incorrect because, though the ship was discovered in 2013, the passage is not about other ships. Choice D is incorrect because, though the ship was "discovered off the coast of Kenya," there is nothing to suggest that it sank further away and then drifted toward Kenya.

Question 14: Choice C
Boundaries
Difficulty - **Medium** | Topic - **Science**

Choice C is the best answer because it joins two independent clauses with a semicolon. The first independent clause ("rubber tires ... durable tires") and the second independent clause ("in addition . . . unappealing") should be joined in this manner, since other options produce run-on sentences and comma splices.

Choice A is incorrect because it lacks a comma after the introductory phrase "in addition" and because it uses a comma to join two independent clauses. Choice B is incorrect because it incorrectly treats "in addition" as part of the first independent clause and because it uses a comma to join two independent clauses. Choice D is incorrect because a comma cannot be used to join two independent clauses. All of these false answers result in errors in the coordination of independent clauses.

Question 15: Choice C
Boundaries
Difficulty - **Medium** | Topic - **Humanities**

Choice C is the best answer because it correctly separates the dependent clause ("though no . . . videos") and the independent clause ("DVDs were ... Festival") with a comma. The clauses should be joined in this manner, since other options result in incomplete and expanded independent clauses.

Choice A is incorrect because it excluded "DVDs" from the independent clause, thereby leaving the verb "were used" without a subject. Choice B is incorrect because a semicolon cannot join an independent clause with a dependent clause. Choice D is incorrect because it fuses an independent clause with a dependent clause without any punctuation between them. All of these false answers result in errors in the coordination of independent and dependent clauses.

Question 16: Choice B
Form, Structure, and Sense
Difficulty - **Medium** | Topic - **Humanities**

Choice B is the best answer because the singular pronoun "its" agrees with the singular antecedent "flag" to effectively indicate that the flag is red, white, and blue. "Its" is a possessive pronoun, so it indicates that the "classic red, white, and blue" colors belong to the flag.

Choice A is incorrect because the singular contraction "it's" is a subject-verb contraction, so it would leave the verb "were" without a subject. Even though "it's" is singular, the underlined word must be a possessive adjective rather than a subject-verb contraction. Choice C is incorrect because "they're" is a subject-verb contraction, so it would leave the verb "were" without a subject. Moreover, the plural contraction "they're" does not agree with the singular antecedent "flag." Choice D is incorrect because the plural pronoun "their" does not agree with the singular antecedent "flag."

Question 17: Choice A
Boundaries
Difficulty - **Hard** | Topic - **Social Studies**

Choice A is the best answer because the "and" connects two directly paired noun phrases, "bus drivers" and "train or streetcar conductors." The connected elements should not be split with a comma but require the "and" for proper coordination of two parallel nouns.

Choice B is incorrect because it splits two items connected by "and" with a single comma and thus disrupts the convention ("drivers and conductors") required by the sentence. Choice C is incorrect because it avoids a conjunction entirely and thus runs together two nouns that indicate separate groups. Choice D is incorrect because it introduces a comma and thus wrongly treats "train or streetcar conductors . . . " as a dependent phrase; instead, the description of the "conductors" should be paired with the reference to "bus drivers" in the main independent clause.

Question 18: Choice C
Form, Structure, and Sense
Difficulty - **Medium** | Topic - **Science**

Choice C is the best answer because "test population" is the singular subject of the underlined singular verb "includes." The subject may be hard to locate due to the long intervening clause.

Choice A is incorrect because the plural verb "include" does not agree with the singular subject. Choice B is incorrect because the plural verb "are including" does not agree with the singular subject. Choice D is incorrect because the plural verb "have included" does not agree with the singular subject.

Question 19: Choice B
Boundaries
Difficulty - **Easy** | Topic - **History**

Choice B is the best answer because it correctly connects an independent clause and an appositive with a comma. The independent clause ("researcher . . . Perceptron") and the appositive ("a machine . . . in 1958") should be joined in this manner, since other options result in run-on sentences and alterations in meaning.

Choice A is incorrect because it treats "a machine" as the complete appositive. Choice C is incorrect because it treats "that appeared in 1958" as the complete appositive. Choice D is incorrect because it fuses an independent clause and an appositive with no punctuation. All of these false answers result in errors in the coordination of dependent and independent clauses.

Question 20: Choice A
Form, Structure, and Sense
Difficulty - **Easy** | Topic - **Science**

Choice A is the best answer because the sentence requires the finite verb form "examined" to create an independent clause with a parallel list. The verb form should take the subject "researchers." The independent clause's other verb ("discerned") in the list of things that the researchers did is a past tense verb, so the underlined verb should match that tense.

Choice B is incorrect because the nonfinite verb form "examining" is the present participle, which leaves the sentence without an independent clause. Choice C is incorrect because the nonfinite verb form "to examine" is the infinitive form, which does not create an independent clause. Choice D is incorrect because the nonfinite verb form "having examined" is the perfect participle, which does not create an independent clause.

Question 21: Choice A
Transitions
Difficulty - **Hard** | Topic - **Humanities**

Choice A is the best answer because "moreover" indicates that the thematic similarities between Baghch-e-Simsim and Sesame Street are consistent with the similarities between the formats of Baghch-e-Simsim and Sesame Street. This transition properly signals an extension relationship.

Choice B is incorrect because "alternatively" introduces an opposing relationship and wrongly indicates that the thematic similarities between Baghch-e-Simsim and Sesame Street are inconsistent with the similarities between the formats of Baghch-e-Simsim and Sesame Street. Choice C is incorrect because "more broadly" introduces a generalization relationship and wrongly indicates that the similarities between the formats of Baghch-e-Simsim and Sesame Street are a subset of the thematic similarities between Baghch-e-Simsim and Sesame Street. Choice D is incorrect because "as noted" introduces a reiteration relationship and wrongly indicates that the thematic similarities between Baghch-e-Simsim and Sesame Street are the same as the similarities between the formats of Baghch-e-Simsim and Sesame Street.

Question 22: Choice C
Transitions
Difficulty - **Medium** | Topic - **Social Studies**

Choice C is the best answer because "conversely" indicates that "smaller, more collaborative, more interdependent friend groups" are the opposite of "larger, looser friend groups" and that "high prosperity" is the opposite of "economic downturns." This transition properly signals a contrasting relationship.

Choice A is incorrect because, while "regardless" introduces a contrasting relationship, it wrongly indicates that the correlation between economic downturns and more closely knit friend groups occurs despite the correlation between prosperity and looser friend groups. Choice B is incorrect because "next" introduces a temporal relationship and wrongly indicates that economic downturns follow times of prosperity. Choice D is incorrect because "in other words" introduces a reiteration relationship and wrongly indicates that economic downturns and more closely knit friend groups are the same as prosperity and looser friend groups.

Question 23: Choice D
Transitions
Difficulty - **Medium** | Topic - **Social Studies**

Choice D is the best answer because "though" indicates that the scarcity and neglect of interactive whiteboards today lies in contrast with Hamilton's 2005 expectations. This transition properly signals an opposing relationship.

Choice A is incorrect because "in addition" introduces an extension relationship and wrongly indicates that the scarcity and neglect of interactive whiteboards today is a second support point for Hamilton's 2005 expectations. Choice B is incorrect because "as noted" introduces a reiteration relationship and wrongly indicates that the scarcity and neglect of interactive whiteboards today is the same thing as Hamilton's 2005 expectations. Choice C is incorrect because

"furthermore" introduces an extension relationship and wrongly indicates that the scarcity and neglect of interactive whiteboards today is a logical extension of the fact that interactive whiteboards in 2005 "appeared to hold remarkable promise in keeping students engaged."

Question 24: Choice A
Rhetorical Synthesis
Difficulty - **Medium** | Topic - **Science**

Choice A is the best answer because it states that a black hole resides in the center of Galaxy NGC 2217. Furthermore, the student's notes specify that the black hole in Galaxy NGC 2217 is "of this sort," which means that it is a supermassive black hole. This choice is consistent with the student's goal of "specify[ing] the location of a supermassive black hole in a single galaxy."

Choice B is incorrect because, though it mentions black holes in galaxies, it does not specify the location of a black hole within a galaxy. Choice C is incorrect because, though it mentions a supermassive black hole in a particular galaxy, it does not specify the location of the black hole within the galaxy. Choice D is incorrect because, though it mentions supermassive black holes in galaxies, it does not specify the location of any black hole within a galaxy.

Question 25: Choice B
Rhetorical Synthesis
Difficulty - **Medium** | Topic - **Social Studies**

Choice B is the best answer because it states who "coined the term 'vertical archipelago,'" and what it was used to describe. This choice is consistent with the student's goal of "explain[ing] the origins of the term 'vertical archipelago.'"

Choice A is incorrect because, though the term "vertical archipelago" was used to describe Inca communities, Choice A is not about the term "vertical archipelago." Choice C is incorrect because, though it is about a use of the term "vertical archipelago," it does not specify the origins of the term. Choice D is incorrect because, though it describes what a vertical archipelago is, it does not state the origins of the term "vertical archipelago."

Question 26: Choice A
Rhetorical Synthesis
Difficulty - **Medium** | Topic - **History**

Choice A is the best answer because it states that a high IQ score is the main requirement to become a member of Mensa. This choice is consistent with the student's goal of "explain[ing] how a person can become a member of Mensa."

Choice B is incorrect because, though it mentions one main membership requirement, it does not say what that requirement is. Choice C is incorrect because, though it discusses Mensa, it does not state a requirement for membership. Choice D is incorrect because, though it names an IQ test used by Mensa, it does not specify that a high score is required for membership.

Question 27: Choice C
Rhetorical Synthesis
Difficulty - **Hard** | Topic - **Science**

Choice C is the best answer because it explains that a sandgrouse retains water by using the barbs and barbules on its belly feathers. This choice is consistent with the student's goal of "specify[ing] how the African sandgrouse retains water."

Choice A is incorrect because, though it alludes to the African sandgrouse retaining water, it does not specify how the bird does that. Choice B is incorrect because, though it mentions the barbs and barbules of African sandgrouse feathers, it does not explain how they are used to retain water. Choice D is incorrect because, though it is about the African sandgrouse's feathers, it does not say that they are used to retain water.

Module 2: Hard
— Pages 52-62 —

Question 1: Choice C
Word in Context
Difficulty - **Hard** | Topic - **Science**

Choice C is the best answer because the passage is about how dreaming helps to clarify the thoughts of scientists who are thinking about complex constructs. Thus, the underlined word must mean "thinking about." "Pondering" satisfies that requirement and is appropriate in the context of complex ideas.

Choice A is incorrect because, while repetition is important in scientific thought, "rehearsing" would wrongly indicate that scientists were practicing ideas. Choice B is incorrect because, while scientific ideas are often compared to each other, the scientists in the passage are mulling over ideas rather than comparing them. Choice D is incorrect because one can only incite actions, not thoughts.

Question 2: Choice B
Word in Context
Difficulty - **Hard** | Topic - **History**

Choice B is the best answer because only "arduous readers could probably work their way through all of the cataloged titles." Therefore, the "lists of available books" were quite long. "Exhaustive" properly indicates that the book lists were extensive.

Choice A is incorrect because, while one might be pretentious about being an avid reader, the underlined word modifies "lists," not "readers." Choice C is incorrect because, while the library patrons may have trusted the librarians, the underlined word modifies "lists," not "readers." Choice D is incorrect because, though the lists may have ameliorated the need for reading material, the lists themselves were not ameliorated.

Question 3: Choice B
Word in Context
Difficulty - **Hard** | Topic - **History**

Choice B is the best answer because scholars who view the 1890 Sherman Antitrust Act as Sherman's "sole defining achievement" do so because they downplay or ignore "Sherman's other contributions." "Discounting" properly indicates that these scholars attribute less significance to Sherman's other contributions than they should.

Choice A is incorrect because, though the scholars might not realize how important Sherman's other contributions were, they are not vetoing them. Choice C is incorrect because, though the text is about the perceived relative importance of Sherman's achievements, the scholars are underestimating, not highlighting, the importance of Sherman's other achievements. Choice D is incorrect because, though the scholars likely extol the 1890 Sherman Antitrust Act, they do not view Sherman's other achievements as praiseworthy.

Question 4: Choice A
Word in Context
Difficulty - **Hard** | Topic - **Humanities**

Choice A is the best answer because Kofi Ansah's measures helped the clothing and accessories industry in Ghana to develop and expand. The information after the colon makes it clear that Ansah's work helped to publicize and popularize his home country's clothing and accessories.

Choice B is incorrect because there is nothing to indicate that the clothing and accessories industry in Ghana had once been larger than it was when Ansah began his work. Choice C is incorrect because an industry cannot be released. Choice D is incorrect because, while the passage mentions Ghana's government, Ansah was not part of the government, so he had no authority to authorize anything.

Question 5: Choice D
Text Structure and Purpose
Difficulty - **Medium** | Topic - **Literature**

Choice D is the best answer because the underlined sentence does not provide any new information. Rather, it emphasizes the fact that the narrator read the letter, which is elsewhere described negatively as "unintelligible" and as requiring "untangling."

Choice A is incorrect because, while the setting is described later in the passage, the setting is not mentioned in the underlined sentence. Choice B is incorrect because, while the narrator might feel fulfillment and relief upon finishing the letter, the narrator's feelings are not mentioned in the underlined sentence. Choice C is incorrect because, while it qualifies the narrator's earlier remarks about not typically reading such a letter, the letter's admirable qualities are not mentioned in the underlined sentence.

Question 6: Choice D
Text Structure and Purpose
Difficulty - **Medium** | Topic - **History**

Choice D is the best answer because the underlined portion supports the claim that "so-called renaissances are not confined to media such as sculpture." By showing that Walt Disney studios experienced a "renaissance," the underlined portion applies the concept of a renaissance to a new context (animation).

Choice A is incorrect because, though the concept of a renaissance is not normally applied to animation, the underlined portion provides an example of when "renaissance" is applied to animation. Choice B is incorrect because, though it applies the concept of a renaissance to a

new context, it does not propose a new definition. Choice C is incorrect because, though it provides an unusual application of the concept of a renaissance, it does not weaken an argument introduced earlier in the text.

Question 7: Choice B
Text Structure and Purpose
Difficulty - **Hard** | Topic - **Literature**

Choice B is the best answer because the speaker lists different groups of people ("the weary" and "little children") and describes how they will feel soothed by the author's songs. For example, the weary's "hearts shall relax" upon hearing the speaker sing.

Choice A is incorrect because, while the poem is about the speaker's future experiences, it does not mention artistic principles. Choice C is incorrect because, while the poem mentions contrasting groups, it does not discuss those groups empathizing with one another. Choice D is incorrect because, while the poem is about the speaker's future interactions with other people, the poem does not provide moral instruction.

Question 8: Choice C
Text Structure and Purpose
Difficulty - **Hard** | Topic - **Literature**

Choice C is the best answer because the text opens with the speaker looking at the old man, which triggers memories of hiring someone to sharpen household implements in the past. After that, the old man talks with the speaker. Thus, all parts of choice C are correct and in the right order.

Choice A is incorrect because, while the old man talks to the speaker, he does not provide a new interpretation of anything. Choice B is incorrect because, though the old man draws the attention of the speaker, who then describes the past, the speaker does not contemplate a contrast between the past and the present. Choice D is incorrect because, though the speaker recalls the past, the speaker does not recount the struggles of adulthood.

Question 9: Choice C
Cross-Text Connections
Difficulty - **Hard** | Topic - **History**

Choice C is the best answer because Text 1 discusses how the "discovery of the Comstock Lode" led to "legislation designed to make the value of US currency dependent on the silver supply," which in turn "led . . . to the debut of the first Morgan Silver Dollar" in 1878. Moreover, Text 2 states that "the 1971 silver dollar served commemorative purposes."

Choice A is incorrect because, though Text 2 suggests that later silver dollars have mostly served to celebrate historical "achievements," and Text 1 states that the "Morgan Silver Dollar [was] named after its principal designer," it does not say that the coin was meant to commemorate him, nor does it suggest that the coin was historically influential. Choice B is incorrect because, while Text 2 asserts that "the intention [of later silver dollars] was not to respond to changing financial and political realities," Text 1 states that the Morgan Silver Dollar resulted from US legislation, not that it influenced legislation. Choice D is incorrect because, though Text 2 connects silver dollars to historical facts and people, Text 1 states that silver dollar legislation "moved through Congress," which suggests that it was not met with resistance.

Question 10: Choice B
Quantitative Command of Evidence
Difficulty - **Hard** | Topic - **Social Studies**

Choice B is the best answer because the claim that "the share of income that a typical household would allot to wedding expenses [has been] presumably unchanged from 1990 onwards" is undermined by a pair of years in which the respective shares of income that a typical household allotted to wedding expenses were quite different. The share of income that a typical household allotted to wedding expenses in 2000 was roughly 30%, versus 45% in 2010.

Choice A is incorrect because, though it cites two years in which the respective shares of income that a typical household allotted to wedding expenses were different, those shares were barely different in 1990 and 2000 (roughly 25% vs. 30%). Choice C is incorrect because, though it refers to median household incomes in multiple years, the share of income that a typical household allotted to wedding expenses cannot be calculated from medium incomes and wedding costs from different years (1990 and 2010 vs. 2000). Choice D is incorrect because, though the share of income that a typical household allotted to wedding expenses differed quite a bit between 1990 and 2010, choice D refers to the average cost of weddings in only one of those two years.

Question 11: Choice C
Textual Command of Evidence
Difficulty - **Hard** | Topic - **Literature**

Choice C is the best answer because Hester's attempt to live her life in a way that "balance[s] matters by being especially staid and stern herself" supports the claim that "Hester . . . lives according to a firm moral code." Moreover, since she is living in a way opposite of how those around her live ("froth and frivolity"), she must be living according to her own principles rather than according to external norms.

Choice A is incorrect because, though it contrasts Hester's house with other homes and states that she looks down upon her neighbors, it is not about how Hester lives her life. Choice B is incorrect because, though it is about one of Hester's traits (precision), it is not about her ethics. Choice D is incorrect because, though it implies one of Hester's traits (close-mindedness), it is not about her moral code.

Question 12: Choice A
Quantitative Command of Evidence
Difficulty - **Hard** | Topic - **Science**

Choice A is the best answer because the claim is that the number of wing beats per second does not directly correlate with flight speed among birds. Choice A supports that claim by providing an example of a bird (the American robin) that has both a lower number of wing beats per second and a higher maximum flight speed than a different bird (the scarlet tanager) does.

Choice B is incorrect because, though it is true that wing beats per second is significantly higher for a ruby-throated hummingbird than for a scarlet tanager, it is also true that flight speed is significantly higher for a ruby-throated hummingbird than for a scarlet tanager. Choice C is incorrect because, though it is true that the American robin has a significantly higher average body mass, the claim being supported by the underlined text is not about body mass. Choice D is incorrect because, though it is true that the scarlet tanager and the American robin have nearly-identical wing speeds, they do not have nearly-identical maximum flight speeds.

Question 13: Choice C
Textual Command of Evidence
Difficulty - **Hard** | Topic - **Literature**

Choice C is the best answer because the speaker's remarks that the "trees and stones are audible to me" and "I understand their faery syllables" support the notion that the natural landscape is familiar and understandable. "And all their sad significance" supports the notion that the natural landscape is disheartening to contemplate.

Choice A is incorrect because, though it portrays nature as familiar to the speaker, it does not show that it is disheartening to contemplate. Choice B is incorrect because, while it references negative experiences, it is not about nature. Choice D is incorrect because, though it portrays nature as familiar and understandable to the speaker, it does not show that it is disheartening to contemplate.

Question 14: Choice D
Textual Command of Evidence
Difficulty - **Hard** | Topic - **Science**

Choice D is the best answer because the claim is that reindeer's ultraviolet vision evolved as a mechanism for differentiating reindeer moss, which does not reflect ultraviolet light, from snow, which does reflect ultraviolet light. Choice D supports this claim by showing how reindeer perceive this difference.

Choice A is incorrect because, though it is about a visual means of foraging, the claim is not about long-distance vision. Choice B is incorrect because, though it is about ultraviolet light, it is not about reindeer moss or foraging. Choice C is incorrect because, though it is about the appearance of lichen versus snow, it merely restates the problem of similar appearance rather than supporting the claim that ultraviolet light solves that problem.

Question 15: Choice C
Inferences
Difficulty - **Hard** | Topic - **Social Studies**

Choice C is the best answer because the avalanche method takes into account high interest rates when prioritizing debts to pay off, whereas the snowball method pays off debts in the reverse order. Therefore, the snowball method does not take into account high interest rates. The popularity of the snowball method, then, shows that its adherents disregard factors such as high interest rates when paying off debts.

Choice A is incorrect because, while a popular method might replace a different method, the popularity of the snowball method does not show that its adherents previously used the avalanche method. Choice B is incorrect because the popularity of the snowball method does not show that its adherents also use elements of the avalanche method. Choice D is incorrect because, while a popular method might be better than a different method, the popularity of the snowball method merely shows that it has many adherents; it does not show that people are likely to accumulate further debts while using the avalanche method.

Question 16: Choice D
Inferences
Difficulty - **Hard** | Topic - **Humanities**

Choice D is the best answer because the court masque genre was atypical for Milton. "Milton gravitated to modes of narrative and symbolic poetry notable for its intricate storytelling," yet court masques were "lighthearted entertainments . . . with . . . simplistic narratives." Thus, Milton decided to write court masques despite the narrative simplicity of the genre.

Choice A is incorrect because, though Milton generally worked in more complex genres, the text suggests that his court masques were atypically lighthearted for him, not that his masques were atypically elaborate for the genre. Choice B is incorrect because, though Milton's other work had more narrative complexity, the text does not suggest that he prioritized narrative complexity or minimized the use of song and dance in his masques. Choice C is incorrect because, though Milton generally wrote more serious work, the text does not suggest that he regarded his masques as a diversion from more serious work.

Question 17: Choice C
Boundaries
Difficulty - **Medium** | Topic - **Science**

Choice C is the best answer because the sentence designates two rings of material in an independent clause before indicating what the two rings are by listing out an "inner ring" and an "outer ring" as two items. This structure of an independent clause indicating further explanatory content and followed by a list would be properly punctuated by a colon.

Choice A is incorrect because it uses a colon to incorrectly break the connected phrase "formed in" and treats the word "rings" as part of a list, not as an item followed by further explanatory content. Choice B is incorrect because it places content that is not an independent clause after a semicolon and further uses the one semicolon to break the integrated phrase "in two." Choice D is incorrect because it uses a comma to incorrectly break the connected phrase "formed in" and uses a semicolon, not a colon, to introduce a list.

Question 18: Choice B
Form, Structure, and Sense
Difficulty - **Hard** | Topic - **Science**

Choice B is the best answer because the context clues "built upon" and "in 1930" indicate that a past perfect tense verb is necessary. The verb "had reached" appropriately fits the context of describing what William Beebe and Otis Barton had done before Lucy Woodall's 2020 expedition occurred.

Choice A is incorrect because the verb "have reached" is present perfect tense, which would fail to indicate that William Beebe and Otis Barton went on their expedition before Lucy Woodall went on hers. Choice C is incorrect because the verb "reach" is present tense, which is a mismatch for describing something that happened in 1930. Choice D is incorrect because the verb "were reaching" is past continuous tense, which would indicate that William Beebe and Otis Barton were on their expedition while Lucy Woodall was on hers.

Question 19: Choice A
Boundaries
Difficulty - **Hard** | Topic - **Science**

Choice A is the best answer because the colon properly coordinates an explanation that is structured as a full independent clause. While the independent clause before the colon notes "slight differences" in bird coloration, the content immediately after the colon explains the exact differences in an independent clause description ("the male . . . wings") of the male spoonbill.

Choice B is incorrect because the word "as" after the colon creates two dependent clauses with the phrases "as the male" and "while the female," but a colon should only be followed by discrete items or by an independent clause construction. Choice C is incorrect because the comma creates a comma splice that wrongly coordinates the independent clauses "Male . . . adulthood" and "the male . . . wings." Choice D is incorrect because the period should coordinate full independent clause constructions, yet the presence of the word "As" creates a sentence fragment after a period.

Question 20: Choice A
Form, Structure, and Sense
Difficulty - **Hard** | Topic - **History**

Choice A is the best answer because "the various influences that Spenser absorbed during his time at the University of Cambridge" is the plural subject of the underlined plural verb "are." The subject may be hard to locate due to the inverted subject-verb pair.

Choice B is incorrect because the singular verb "was" does not agree with the plural subject. Choice C is incorrect because the singular verb "is" does not agree with the plural subject. Choice D is incorrect because the singular verb "has been" does not agree with the plural subject.

Question 21: Choice A
Boundaries
Difficulty - **Hard** | Topic - **Social Studies**

Choice A is the best answer because the phrase "such assets as expanded broadcasting rights" should be treated as connected phrasing within a dependent clause, despite the presence of a quotation mark. This choice avoids the presence of single commas that would disrupt connected phrases such as "such assets as" and "as expanded broadcasting rights, and commas should not be used to set off quotations that are integrated with other sentence elements.

Choice B is incorrect because it uses a single comma to break the integrated phrase "assets as." Choice C is incorrect

because it creates a fragmentary phrase before the quotation with "which Fu . . . links to such assets as." Instead, a colon should follow a fully articulated independent clause rather than a clause that trails off with a transition such as "as." Choice D is incorrect because it breaks the integrated phrase "such assets as expanded broadcasting rights" with a single comma, yet commas should be used to set dependent content off from independent clause quotations. The sentence does not in fact follow this structure and integrates the quotation with parts of a dependent clause.

Question 22: Choice B
Boundaries
Difficulty - **Hard** | Topic - **Social Studies**

Choice B is the best answer because it places the appositive ("Christopher Mazurek") between commas. An appositive is nonessential text, so it should be separated from the rest of the sentence by commas.

Choice A is incorrect because it treats "Karen Konkoly and an experiment participant" as a modifying phrase for "Christopher Mazurek." Choice C is incorrect because it treats "Christopher Mazurek" as essential text. Choice D is incorrect because it places Karen Konkoly and Christopher Mazurek outside of the independent clause, thereby leaving the verb "achieved" without a subject.

Question 23: Choice C
Boundaries
Difficulty - **Hard** | Topic - **Science**

Choice C is the best answer because the essential phrase ("connecting their . . . circulatory systems") is not set off by a punctuation mark. This phrase should be incorporated into the rest of the sentence in this manner, since other options result in errors in the coordination of independent clauses and essential phrases.

Choice A is incorrect because the colon omits the essential phrase from the independent clause and because a colon should not immediately precede the word "which" unless the word after "which" is a noun. Choice B is incorrect because the colon omits the essential phrase from the independent clause. Choice D is incorrect because "which" would require the finite verb "connect" instead of the nonfinite verb form "connecting." All of these false answers result in errors in essential phrases and verb forms..

Question 24: Choice C
Transitions
Difficulty - **Hard** | Topic - **Social Studies**

Choice C is the best answer because "likewise" indicates that the opposite polarization trends in Switzerland and Germany mirror the opposite polarization trends in New Zealand and Australia. This transition properly signals a similarity relationship.

Choice A is incorrect because "conversely" introduces an opposing relationship and wrongly indicates that the polarization trends in Switzerland and Germany are the opposite of the polarization trends in New Zealand and Australia. Choice B is incorrect because "nonetheless" introduces an opposing relationship and wrongly indicates that the polarization trends in Switzerland and Germany exist in spite of the polarization trends in New Zealand and Australia. Choice D is incorrect because "thus" introduces a causal relationship and wrongly indicates that the polarization trends in Switzerland and Germany have resulted from the polarization trends in New Zealand and Australia.

Question 25: Choice B
Transitions
Difficulty - **Hard** | Topic - **History**

Choice B is the best answer because "though" signals that, despite the fact that Mbara is not herself an astronaut, she hopes that Jamison's example will inspire African girls to become astronauts. This transition properly signals a contrasting relationship.

Choice A is incorrect because, while "conversely" introduces an opposing relationship, it wrongly indicates that Mbara's hope is an alternative to her not being an astronaut. Choice C is incorrect because "by this logic" introduces a parallel relationship, which wrongly indicates that Mbara's hope is analogous to her not being an astronaut. Choice D is incorrect because "furthermore" introduces an extension relationship, which wrongly indicates that Mbara's hope is an extension of the fact that Mbara is not an astronaut.

Question 26: Choice C
Transitions
Difficulty - **Hard** | Topic - **Humanities**

Choice C is the best answer because the text indicates that Dykstra "by moving a movie camera" created "the impression" that an object such as a model spaceship was moving. The text later presents the identical idea that "the spaceships of Star Wars never actually moved" and thus restates content from earlier.

Choice A is incorrect because the text restates an idea for emphasis rather than moving on to new information that provides an example illustrating an idea mentioned earlier. Choice B is incorrect because the text does not present new information; instead, the same idea is articulated in a slightly different manner. Choice D is incorrect because "to some extent" would indicate that there were possible exceptions or that Dykstra's methods did not extend to all cases. The text instead returns to an idea about Dykstra's methods without noting special cases.

Question 27: Choice C
Rhetorical Synthesis
Difficulty - **Hard** | Topic - **Science**

Choice C is the best answer because it mentions what the study was "meant to" do and then moves on to note what the researchers "concluded" as a result of their work. This content effectively fits the student's goal of noting the "aim and findings" of a specific research project on sea angels and sea butterflies.

Choice A is incorrect because it only notes the findings of Peijnenburg and colleagues' study without clearly indicating the aim of the study. Instead, this choice brings in a fact about sea angels and sea butterflies that is unrelated to the direct emphasis of Peijnenburg and colleagues' research. Choice B is incorrect because it only notes the results of Peijnenburg and colleagues' research without clearly indicating the aim of the research. Choice D is incorrect because it notes the aim of the research without directly indicating the outcomes of the research project. At most, this choice raises the topic of ocean acidification without clearly indicating how Peijnenburg and colleagues evaluated the way in which sea angels and sea butterflies responded to ocean acidification.

Reading and Writing

27 QUESTIONS

1

Benjamin Graham's classic 1949 investing guidebook *The Intelligent Investor* has frequently been _____ with new material that "updates" Graham's principles to account for new historical contingencies: a 2006 edition, for example, reproduced Graham's original chapters and appended more recent commentary on investing in 21st-century technology stocks.

Which choice completes the text with the most logical and precise word or phrase?

A) confounded

B) abridged

C) reissued

D) epitomized

2

Whales have asymmetrical skulls, and marine bioscientist Ellen Coombs and colleagues have correlated such asymmetry with the diet and size of specific whale species. Medium-sized whales that hunt large prey exhibit stark asymmetry; larger whales that _____ numerous small organisms have mostly symmetrical skulls.

Which choice completes the text with the most logical and precise word or phrase?

A) feed on

B) turn from

C) spread out

D) continue with

3

Visual art on the Southeast Asian island of Bali changed as Balinese painters _____ influences from beyond their home territory. In the 1800s, notes journalist Baladika Badra Anggakara, contact with Europeans caused Balinese artists to modify their longstanding emphasis on monumental religious compositions and begin depicting everyday scenes that reflected European conventions of painting.

Which choice completes the text with the most logical and precise word or phrase?

A) pioneered

B) refuted

C) assimilated

D) repulsed

4

The following text is from Ann S. Stephens's 1866 novel *The Gold Brick*. In this excerpt, the action takes place on a ship recently under the charge of Captain Mason.

Thrasher, who was the commander now, sat in his cabin at breakfast. He held in one hand a cup of coffee which seemed to have excited his disfavor, for setting it on the table and dashing the spoon so angrily into the coffee that it <u>scattered</u> the drops all around, he called out, "Come here, you brat."

Paul, the little boy whom Captain Mason had saved, came reluctantly forward, his black eyes heavy with fear.

As used in the text, what does the word "scattered" most nearly mean?

A) Dispersed

B) Separated

C) Banished

D) Interspersed

5

This text is adapted from Edna Ferber's 1915 short story "An Etude for Emma."

In her sunny little private office on the twelfth floor of the great loft-building that housed the T. A. Buck Company, Emma McChesney Buck sat listening to the street-sounds that were wafted to her, mellowed by height and distance. <u>The noises, taken separately, were the nerve-racking sounds common to a busy down-town New York cross-street.</u> By the time they reached the little office on the twelfth floor, they were softened, mellowed, debrutalized, welded into a weird choirlike chant first high, then low, rising, swelling, dying away, rising again to a dull roar, with now and then vast undertones like the rumbling of a cathedral pipe-organ.

Which choice best describes the function of the underlined sentence in the text as a whole?

A) It pinpoints a few aspects of a scene which disturbs Emma despite her air of detachment.

B) It conveys a response that forms a sharp contrast with Emma's own impressions.

C) It illustrates Emma's method for coping with the disturbances common in New York.

D) It highlights the exceptional nature of the sounds that Emma discerns from her office.

CONTINUE

6

When scientists Can Kabadayi and Mathias Osvarth set out to study ravens, their goal was not to prove that ravens are intelligent—<u>a well-accepted fact among zoologists</u>—but to assess exactly how far raven intelligence could extend. Various trials by Kabadayi and Osvarth tested whether ravens exhibited high level cognitive abilities mostly associated with humans: tool usage, ability to plan ahead, and willingness to pass up a smaller immediate reward in favor of a larger eventual reward—a phenomenon known as "delayed gratification." The ravens exhibited them all.

Which choice best describes the purpose of the underlined portion in the text as a whole?

A) It calls attention to a factor that was not the exact motivation for Kabadayi and Osvarth's investigation.

B) It paraphrases a longstanding idea that Kabadayi and Osvarth's experiments were designed to overturn.

C) It summarizes the conclusions that were reached in the course of Kabadayi and Osvarth's research on ravens.

D) It alludes to the analogies between humans and ravens that Kabadayi and Osvarth developed in the course of their project.

7

Reflecting on the skills fostered by skateboarding—both as a competitive sport and a shared culture—researcher Zoë B. Corwin and colleagues have located benefits that vary in scope. For some skateboarders, joining a local skateboarding community provides a long-term confidence boost. Others develop situational awareness simply by following safety procedures during complex stunts or determining whether a neighborhood is skateboarder-friendly. But Corwin and colleagues, in the report "Beyond the Board," acknowledge that much work lies ahead, since society still "struggles to articulate the clear connections between the skills demonstrated in skate contexts and other contexts."

Which choice best describes the purpose of the text?

A) To indicate that Corwin and colleagues' various insights might nonetheless represent preliminary stages of a larger inquiry

B) To illustrate a few of the reasons that Corwin and colleagues decided not to issue a definitive "Beyond the Board" report

C) To argue that Corwin and colleagues were justifiably cautious in presenting ideas about the benefits of skateboarding culture

D) To validate a few of the conclusions drawn by Corwin and colleagues by presenting a set of anecdotes

CONTINUE

8

Text 1

Powering an entire car with an external form of energy like incoming solar rays or radio waves is not yet possible, but the MilliMobile, a thumbprint-sized robot developed by researchers at the University of Washington, points the way to such futuristic vehicles. Each MilliMobile robot moves along on wheels and can carry equipment much like a lunar rover does. Individual robots can even be programmed to gravitate toward the same light sources that power MilliMobile engines, massing to move unexpectedly large obstacles.

Text 2

Despite innovations in powering small robots with renewable energy, the real potential of such robots resides in aggregates—in the ability of robot clusters to complete construction or surveying tasks. Aggregates of this sort could also address one of the inherent disadvantages of larger single robots, which must be engineered for flexibility component by component and break easily. If one small robot slips out of place and breaks, dozens will be waiting to replace it.

Based on the texts, the author of Text 1 and the author of Text 2 would most likely agree with which statement?

A) Several small robots could be programmed to cooperate on tasks that a single small robot might not be able to fulfill on its own. X

B) Current small robot designs were often intended as miniaturized versions of designs for larger robots, including robots that move like wheel-based rovers.

C) The use of renewable energy in aggregating small robots directly would directly remove some of the liabilities associated with larger robots.

D) The physical tasks that small robots could perform are most efficiently completed at present by vehicles and devices that require constant human supervision.

5

This text is adapted from Madeline Leslie's 1870 short novel *Ida's New Shoes.*

> Ida Kent was a very handsome child. Her face was round and fair, her eyes deep-blue, her mouth small and rosy, and her hair rippled and curled all over her head. This was a great affliction to Ida; for, as it hung in ringlets over her neck, it took a long time in the morning to comb out the snarls.
>
> Mrs. Kent, too, used to dread the job and was always happy when it was completed without arousing Ida's temper.

Which choice best states the main idea of the text?

A) Ida's irrationality forms a contrast with Mrs. Kent's maturity.

B) Ida and Mrs. Kent solve a problem by following an unusual approach.

C) Mrs. Kent's treats Ida unfairly.

D) Ida and Mrs. Kent find a particular routine extremely unpleasant.

CONTINUE ▶

10

Library Items for Four Months in 2022
Number of Times Checked Out

Item	February	March	April	May
Manuscript from 1613	3	12	10	12
Manuscript from 1627	12	13	14	9
Book from 1614	3	23	4	7
Book from 1639	7	9	9	12

A research librarian at a major university is reviewing the records for items in a collection of rare books and manuscripts from the 1600s; these items are checked out for one-day use within the library. When a book or manuscript is checked out much more often than it is on average, it is most likely the subject of a small group seminar in one of the university's humanities departments. In 2022, there was most likely a small group seminar that included the _____

Which choice uses accurate information from the table to complete the statement?

A) 1613 manuscript and took place in February.

B) 1627 manuscript and took place in April.

C) 1614 book and took place in March.

D) 1639 book and took place in May.

11

Presidential elections have sometimes hinged on financial considerations, with candidates publicizing their successes in the realms of business and finance in order to garner votes. However, one political historian claims that early presidential elections do not fit this trend and that one of the most celebrated US presidents, Thomas Jefferson, was in fact simultaneously regarded as a financial "failure" and a political success.

Which of the following pieces of information, if true, would best support the historian's claim?

A) Jefferson had significant holdings of land in Virginia, though, as a member of the state's cash-crop economy, he did not attain the same level of wealth as George Mason, who attended the United States Constitution Convention but never served as president.

B) Despite Jefferson's ownership of vast tracts of land, Jefferson as president promoted policies meant to favor the well-being of small farmers, arguably to the detriment of large landholders.

C) Jefferson's limited political success in areas dominated by large cities and maritime trade, particularly New England, was explained in part by divergences in the industries favored by early Northern, Southern, and Midwestern states.

D) For much of his adult life, Thomas Jefferson was troubled by debts that, at their height, reached two million dollars (adjusted to today's currency) and that were known at least in passing to many of the electors who supported Jefferson's election in 1800.

12

World Population by Age Group

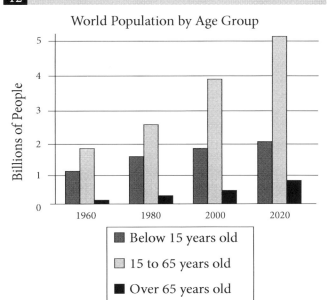

According to some social scientists who study demographic changes, the global population has "grown older" over the past century, as age groups composed of older people have experienced higher growth rates than younger groups. Evidence compiled by the nonprofit OurWorldInData suggests the validity of this idea, since _____

Which choice completes the text with relevant and accurate information from the graph?

A) people over 65 represented a small fraction of the world's population in 1960, and the number of people over 65 would remain constant over the subsequent 60 years.

B) there were roughly 2 billion people under 15 in 2020, while more than twice as many people were between 15 and 65 during the same year.

C) the number of people below age 15 changed relatively little between 2000 and 2020, while the number of people between 15 and 65 grew by one billion people over the same period.

D) the number of people older than 65 and the number of people below age 15 grew at comparable rates between 1980 and 2020, even though the number of people below age 15 was significantly higher throughout this period.

12

The Group: A Farce is a 1775 satirical play by Mercy Otis Warren. In this text, Monsieur François has arrived in Massachusetts; he expresses his desire to be honored and remembered, as is made apparent when _____

Which quotation from *The Group* best illustrates the claim?

A) he explains to another character that "the impressions of my early youth, / Infix'd by precepts of my pious sire, / Are stings and scorpions in my goaded breast."

B) after relocating to Boston he signals his unwillingness to "[erase] the sacred bonds, / And help to clank the tyrant's iron chains / O'er these blest shores."

C) he speculates that "If e'er oppression reach'd the western world" he would "Resist [oppression's] force, and break the servile yoke."

D) he acknowledges to another character the "itch I feel for titl'd place, / Some honorary post, some small distinction, / To save my name from dark oblivion's jaws."

CONTINUE ➡

14

Part dark comedy, part character study, the 2013 film *Inside Llewyn Davis* depicts a 1960s folk and blues musician who bears passing resemblances to one of the legendary singers and songwriters of the time: Bob Dylan. Directors Joel and Ethan Coen, however, are careful to differentiate the fictional Llewyn Davis from the real-life Dylan. When, at the end of the film, Davis overhears Dylan himself playing the Bob Dylan classic "Farewell," the Coens use this sequence to emphasize the _____

Which choice most logically completes the text?

A) ascendancy of Dylan's music at the expense of Davis's own singing and songwriting.

B) possibility that Dylan himself was inspired by Davis's music.

C) identity of Davis as a discrete character, not a depiction of Bob Dylan.

D) simultaneously comedic and serious tone applied to Davis and Dylan throughout the film.

15

According to planetary scientist Eryn Cangi, the planet Venus once held abundant stores of water. Venus is close enough to the Sun to be bombarded with intense sunlight, which changed large amounts of water vapor into water's constituent elements, hydrogen and oxygen, millions of years ago. These elements exist as gases in their natural state, and much of the lightweight hydrogen produced by this reaction escaped Venus's gravity and drifted into space. Today, it is likely that _____

Which choice most logically completes the text?

A) some hydrogen gas has been drawn back into Venus's atmosphere by Venus's gravity.

B) water still exists on Venus in substantial amounts, though it is likely that this water exists in the form of clouds and vapors.

C) there is still oxygen on Venus, provided that oxygen gas is not light enough to escape Venus's gravity.

D) Venus is no longer being bombarded with intense sunlight that could break water into hydrogen and oxygen.

16

Even today, galaxies are grouped in categories _____ Edwin Hubble around 1923. Spiral galaxies, like the one that contains Earth, form one of Hubble's major categories. Elliptical galaxies—older, dimmer, and more abundant than spiral galaxies—constitute another.

Which choice completes the text so that it conforms to the conventions of Standard English?

A) developed, by revered astronomer

B) developed, by revered astronomer,

C) developed by revered astronomer,

D) developed by revered astronomer

17

As conceived by Joseph Woodland and Bernard Silver in the late 1940s, the very first barcodes were not, in fact, patterned with actual bars. Had the original design been put in successful circulation, each of today's barcodes _____ of a circular bull's eye pattern instead of the now-iconic vertical stripes.

Which choice completes the text so that it conforms to the conventions of Standard English?

A) were consisting

B) have consisted

C) consist

D) would consist

18

If you've ever envisioned _____ in an interior design career, or simply want to try different design options for your living space, user-friendly digital tools are right within your reach. Interior design platforms such as SketchUp and Roomstyler 3D are but a few of many that enable you to create digital models of colorful, easily navigated interior spaces.

Which choice completes the text so that it conforms to the conventions of Standard English?

A) yourself

B) themselves

C) you

D) them

19

Today, the various Inuit peoples whose distant ancestors _____ communities in the northernmost reaches of Canada refer to their home territory as "Nunangat," though this territory should not be understood solely in terms of landmass. Nunangat, as defined by its current Inuit inhabitants, encompasses interconnected islands, peninsulas, waters, and ice floes that border the Arctic Circle.

Which choice completes the text so that it conforms to the conventions of Standard English?

A) will form

B) formed

C) form

D) are forming

20

Reviewers often explain a newly-published _____ by noting comparisons with the works of older, more established writers. When Kali Fajardo-Anstine released her debut collection of short stories, *Sabrina and Corina*, in 2020, some critics drew analogies between Fajardo-Anstine narratives and those of celebrated Canadian writer Alice Munro.

Which choice completes the text so that it conforms to the conventions of Standard English?

A) author's short story's

B) authors short stories'

C) author's short stories

D) authors short stories

21

Materials scientist Michel Barsoum employs electron microscopes and other fine-tuned devices to investigate structures made of bricks, stucco, and ceramics. _____ this expertise, he has turned his attention to the question of how the Great Pyramids were constructed.

Which choice completes the text so that it conforms to the conventions of Standard English?

A) Utilized

B) Utilize

C) Utilizing

D) Utilizes

22

The first time I visited Australia, I was surprised to encounter beach and hiking trail signs warning me to be "casso-wary"— _____ to be cautious of the large flightless birds known as cassowaries, which are best kept at a distance because they act aggressively towards humans when approached or provoked.

Which choice completes the text with the most logical transition?

A) that is,

B) for example,

C) furthermore,

D) granted,

23

Waiting in a longer line, as three Georgetown University professors claim, often prompts shoppers to buy more goods. In the paper "Making the Wait Worthwhile," Sezer Ülkü, Chris Hydock, and John Cui note that shoppers want to feel that their time has been well spent. _____ a shopper faced with a long line will pick up additional products, generating a sensation of purposeful activity during a long wait.

Which choice completes the text with the most logical transition?

A) Granted,

B) Nevertheless,

C) For this reason,

D) More broadly,

Colombo, the largest city in Sri Lanka, boasts both traditional art galleries and a vibrant open-air art scene—the latter exemplified by the Nelum Pokuna Art Street. _____ pedestrians can amble past rows of vivid paintings before returning to more "mainstream" attractions, like the nearby National Museum of Columbo.

Which choice completes the text with the most logical transition?

A) That said,

B) Regardless,

C) Surprisingly,

D) Here,

25

If you have ever watched a famous actor become so immersed in a role as to become virtually unrecognizable, then you have witnessed a feat of "method acting." This level of self-effacement is prized by actors who seek to portray their characters with maximum intensity; _____ there are popular alternatives to method acting. So-called "character actors," for instance, retain key aspects of their off-screen personas in role after role.

Which choice completes the text with the most logical transition?

A) still,

B) indeed,

C) consequently,

D) finally,

26

While researching a topic, a student has taken the following notes:

- Ammonia (NH_3) consists of one nitrogen atom and three hydrogen atoms.

- Molecules of ammonia are typically produced through reactions between nitrogen gas (N_2) and hydrogen gas (H_2).

- These reactions require high temperatures, high temperatures, and metal compounds that serve as catalysts.

- The Haber-Bosch process is the name for this method of ammonia formation.

- Scientists at the University of California recently developed an alternative method that could produce ammonia at room temperature.

The student wants to emphasize a difference between the Haber-Bosch process and the method developed at the University of California. Which choice most effectively uses relevant information from the notes to accomplish this goal?

A) University of California researchers have developed a way to create ammonia at relatively low temperatures and without metal catalysts.

B) The Haber-Bosch process requires high temperatures, yet another method, developed at the University of California, creates ammonia at room temperature.

C) Hydrogen gas and nitrogen gas react to produce ammonia, and two methods for creating ammonia, one called the Haber-Bosch process and the other recently developed at the University of California, are now known.

D) Ammonia can be developed under high temperature and high pressure or using an alternative method.

27

While researching a topic, a student has taken the following notes:

- The Renaissance lasted from approximately the fourteenth to the seventeenth century in Europe and witnessed a general tendency towards economic growth and stability.

- Financial panics and banking catastrophes still occurred during the Renaissance.

- Between 1499 and 1500, the Italian city-state of Venice saw its banking system collapse.

- Venice's four privately-held banks were known as the "four pillars" of its finances.

- Three of these four banks failed by 1500.

The student wants to provide a summary of Venice's banking crisis. Which choice most effectively uses relevant information from the notes to accomplish this goal?

A) The Venetian banking system collapsed between 1499 and 1500; during this time, Venice was home to four important private banks, three of which would quickly fail.

B) The Renaissance witnessed financial panics and crises despite robust economic growth; one such panic occurred in Venice.

C) Venice during the late 1400s was the site of four privately-held banks known as the "four pillars" of the city-state's.

D) Venice experienced a financial crisis in the fifteenth century; the Renaissance lasted from the fourteenth to the seventeenth century.

STOP
If you finish these exercises, you may check your work on this section only.
Do not turn to any other section in the book.

No Test Content on This Page

Reading and Writing

27 QUESTIONS

DIRECTIONS

The questions in this section address a number of important reading and writing skills. Each question includes one or more passages, which may include a table or graph. Read each passage and question carefully, and then choose the best answer to the question based on the passage(s).

All questions in this section are multiple-choice with four answer choices. Each question has a single best answer.

1

For civil rights leader A. Philip Randolph, the 1963 March on Washington was a triumphant moment. It was a point of _____ in the long career of Randolph himself (then 74) and a "passing of the torch" to a new generation of African American leaders.

Which choice completes the text with the most logical and precise word or phrase?

A) relief

B) culmination

C) origin

D) negation

2

When Yan Martel's *Life of Pi* appeared in 2001, this bestselling novel called attention to the city of Pondicherry in southeast India, depicting the workings of the Pondicherry Zoo in painstaking detail. Yet readers who expected to find an actual zoo in Pondicherry discovered that this attraction was a meticulous _____, not a real place.

Which choice completes the text with the most logical and precise word or phrase?

A) concession

B) superfluity

C) geniality

D) fabrication

3

To classify different types of studies, demographers have _____ two terms from geography: latitude, which indicates horizontal positioning, and longitude, which indicates vertical positioning. A "longitudinal study" assesses the same population over different time periods, while a "latitudinal study" assesses several populations across one time period.

Which choice completes the text with the most logical and precise word or phrase?

A) amalgamated

B) recanted

C) redressed

D) appropriated

4

When Henry Luce launched *Sports Illustrated* magazine in 1954, he did so not out of any personal devotion to sports himself. The magazine was a _____ venture, meant as a new iteration of the fusion of photography and journalism that Luce, already, had used to turn handsome profits from three of his three previous magazines: *Time*, *Life*, and *Fortune*.

Which choice completes the text with the most logical and precise word or phrase?

A) regulatory

B) benevolent

C) tangential

D) commercial

5

In chess, the idea that players "peak" at remarkably young ages is at once prevalent and, ultimately, rather suspect: research indicates that chess players often deliver their most remarkable performances around age 35. Accounts of young players who achieve remarkable feats nonetheless have a remarkable hold on the imaginations of both the public and fellow chess players. One such chess prodigy, Judit Polgár, achieved the coveted position of grandmaster when she was only fifteen, but her rise to prowess should not be taken as representative of how top-level chess masters operate.

Which choice best describes the overall structure of the text?

A) It introduces a questionable belief, notes how a specific fact contradicts the belief, and demonstrates how further information has led to a faulty conclusion.

B) It lays out the premises behind a debate, emphasizes that one perspective in the debate is growing in popularity, and argues that this perspective has been misconstrued.

C) It presents evidence that is accepted as authoritative, suggests that the interpretation of the evidence is flawed, and proposes a superior method for gathering reliable information.

D) It catalogs the traits of a specific type of individual, pinpoints the traits that have not remained constant over time, and corrects a widespread misinterpretation.

CONTINUE

6

This text is adapted from William Cullen Bryant's 1825 poem "Lines on Revisiting the Country."

> Here, I have escaped the city's stifling heat,
> Its horrid sounds, and its polluted air;
> And, where the season's milder fervours beat,
> And gales, that sweep the forest borders, bear
> The song of bird, and sound of running stream,
> I have come awhile to wander and to dream.

Which choice best states the main purpose of the text?

A) It describes mostly dissimilar settings that nonetheless both distract the speaker from earlier problems.

B) It records the feelings of relief that the speaker experiences after leaving a city.

C) It outlines the speaker's motives for abandoning a lifestyle that was once appealing.

D) It demonstrates how the speaker's enjoyment of nature has gradually increased.

7

Heads of state and sharp differences in national customs shaped the eventual adoption of forks across Europe, if centuries-old narratives are to be believed. By some accounts, Henry III of France (1551-1589) promoted the fork within his royal court, though nations such as England, where even the nobility preferred to eat by hand, resisted the fork. Descriptions of how the fork changed function, though, indicate that Henry's forks were not the absolute first ones; indeed, two-pronged forks were used at least since the early Middle Ages to hold food in place for cutting and evolved into utensils for bringing food directly to the mouth.

According to the text, what is true about the forks that appeared before the reign of Henry III?

A) They were designed to be larger and sturdier than the forks that Henry later popularized.

B) They were readily embraced by the French nobility but were initially rejected by the English nobility.

C) They were used to keep food from moving around while it was being prepared.

D) They increased in popularity because they were perceived as more efficient than otherwise comparable utensils.

90

CONTINUE

8

This text is adapted from Fyodor Dostoevsky's 1872 novel *The Possessed*, in a 1912 translation by Constance Garnett. The speaker here is a resident of a town in Russia.

A crowd of people, the hands from Shpigulin's factory, seventy or more in number, had been marching through the town, and had been an object of curiosity to many spectators. They walked intentionally in good order and almost in silence. Afterwards it was asserted that these seventy had been elected out of the whole number of factory hands, amounting to about nine hundred, to go to the governor and to try and get from him, in the absence of their employer, a just settlement of their grievances against the manager, who, in closing the factory and dismissing the workmen, had cheated them all in an impudent way—a fact which has since been proved conclusively.

Which choice best states the main idea of the text?

A) The community is temporarily puzzled by the conduct of the factory hands, and the speaker feels compelled to explain the situation in order to avoid a misunderstanding.

B) The factory hands have decided to calmly address a problem that involves their manager, and the speaker finds the discontent of the factory hands to be justified.

C) The factory hands have earned the sympathy of the community through their action, and the speaker anticipates heightened conflict despite the good conduct of the factory hands.

D) The community supports the strategy adopted by the factory hands, and the speaker speculates that the governor will be receptive to their proposal.

9

Helium-3 has recently gained attention as much for its vast commercial promise as for its connections, at least in speculation, to the subtleties of how Earth was formed. This gas isotope is exceedingly rare on Earth, more abundant on the Moon, and potentially invaluable in the creation of everything from fusion energy reactors to advanced digital imaging systems. But helium-3 was assumed not to occur naturally on Earth or the Moon—at least until a 2022 study noted the helium-3 leaking from Earth's surface, in a possible sign that Earth was formed from a solar nebula once rich in this substance.

Which choice best states the main idea of the text?

A) New technological uses for helium-3 have been suggested by research that originally aimed to explain Earth's formation by mapping the distribution of helium-3 on Earth and the Moon.

B) Due to the scarcity of helium-3 on Earth's surface, research on this substance is gradually shifting from practical applications to theoretical questions involving Earth's formation.

C) With growing interest in the commercial uses of helium-3, earlier attempts to harvest this substance on earth have been abandoned even as theoretical research on helium-3 has intensified.

D) Research on helium-3, a substance that could power useful technologies, has complicated the view that helium-3 has no natural sources on Earth itself.

10

As You Like It is a 1603 play by William Shakespeare. In the play, a nobleman named Orlando and his elderly servant Adam journey through a wild landscape. Though Adam finds the journey difficult, Orlando is eager to offer reassurance, as indicated when _____

Which choice most effectively uses a quotation from *As You Like It* to illustrate the claim?

A) Adam asks Orlando to "Let me be your servant. / Though I look old, yet I am strong and lusty,"

B) Orlando tells Adam, just before setting off, that "Thou art not for the fashion of these times, / Where none will sweat but for promotion."

C) Adam claims that he "can go no further" and is overheard by Orlando, who asks aloud if Adam has "No greater heart in thee."

D) Orlando asserts that he will find "shelter and [Adam] shalt not die for lack of a dinner if there live anything in this desert."

11

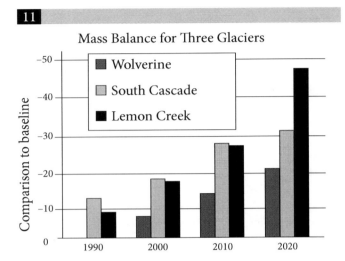

Mass Balance for Three Glaciers

Climate scientists use a metric known as mass balance to determine how much a glacier is diminishing in size: this balance is computed as a negative number that shows the cumulative change from a starting point—in one recent study, the mass of three glaciers in 1980. Much of the loss of glacier mass since 1990 has been attributed to a steady increase in global temperatures, but mass loss has not proceeded steadily in the case of individual glaciers, as indicated by the fact that _____

Which choice effectively uses relevant information from the chart to complete the statement?

A) Wolverine exhibited a consistent mass balance change of roughly –7.0 every ten years between 1990 and 2020.

B) the mass balance change for Lemon Creek was higher than the mass balance change for South Cascade over every ten year interval studied since 1980.

C) South Cascade consistently exhibited mass balance loss but with a sharp loss between 2000 and 2010 and a much smaller loss between 2010 and 2020.

D) Wolverine and South Cascade had approximately the same mass balance change of –27.0 in 2010.

CONTINUE

12

A visual tool first developed by the Toyota Company in the 1940s, a kanban board enables workers to chart the progress of individual projects by relying on a series of cards that break workflow down into various stages and objectives. (In Japanese, "kanban" means "visible card.") The main virtue of a kanban board, according to some managers, is that it streamlines duties by steering workers away from unnecessary projects and prevents work teams from becoming over-extended.

Which of the following pieces of information, if true, would best support the position of the managers as described in the text?

A) The kanban mentality shares an emphasis on continuous improvement over time with Lean Management, a workplace philosophy popular in both the United States and Japan.

B) Among other benefits arising from its visual format, a kanban board can reduce points of uncertainty or confusion surrounding project due dates.

C) The first card on a typical kanban board prompts employees to visualize their given project, while the second prompts employees to take on a moderate amount of work and achieve a few aims at a time.

D) Some of the intermediate cards on a traditional kanban board are meant to facilitate communication once a project is underway, though the expected final card, which cites improvement as an end goal, can signal the starting point for a new project.

13

Honeybee Colony Population Losses
Winter of 2020-2021

State	Percent Loss
Minnesota	31.6
Wisconsin	23.1
Michigan	50.9
Iowa	58.4
Illinois	47.0
Indiana	28.4
Missouri	34.2
All 50 States	43.5

Even in the absence of unexpected environmental stresses, honeybee colonies across the US typically experience seasonal population losses due to cold weather. These population losses can vary considerably from state to state; two states whose percentages for honeybee survival were significantly higher than the national aggregate in the winter of 2020-2021 were _____

Which choice most effectively uses data from the table to complete the statement?

A) Indiana and Wisconsin.

B) Minnesota and Illinois.

C) Iowa and Illinois.

D) Iowa and Michigan.

93

CONTINUE

14

Launched in 2021, the Dark Energy Spectroscopic Instrument (DESI) Survey seeks to map the wide-scale effect of dark energy, an invisible force that is conjectured to counteract gravity and cause the universe's expansion. At the core of this endeavor is an apparatus that consists of 5000 automated eyes that can collectively survey hundreds of thousands of galaxies every day, collecting data and measurements that can then be synthesized into visual charts of the universe. Researchers have hailed the DESI initiative as a success so far, even though _____

Which choice most logically completes the text?

A) the DESI apparatus can record the effects of gravity on the expansion of the universe with greater accuracy than it can presently record the reciprocal effects of dark matter.

B) the galaxy dataset that the DESI apparatus is meant to survey is likely to become increasingly difficult to monitor in the project's later stages.

C) the eyes in the DESI apparatus primarily record minute images that must then be analyzed to create a composite model of the effects of gravity on the universe's expansion.

D) none of the eyes used in the DESI apparatus have successfully provided a photographic image of dark energy itself.

15

The first Black person to become a US Senator, Hiram Revels of Mississippi, was a remarkable man: serving as Methodist-Episcopal church leader, leading a Union regiment in the Civil War, and vocally denouncing racial prejudice _____ some of the accomplishments that he is best remembered for. Unfortunately, his term in the Senate lasted only a single year, ending in 1870.

Which choice completes the text so that it conforms to the conventions of Standard English?

A) was

B) is

C) are

D) has been

16

A relatively easy factor to adjust in experiments that require participants to respond to an image and perform a task (for instance, naming incongruous elements or quickly associating an image with a past memory), _____

Which choice completes the text so that it conforms to the conventions of Standard English?

A) image resolution can be calibrated by researchers to prevent participants from being distracted by blurry or indistinct features.

B) researchers can calibrate image resolution to prevent participants from being distracted by blurry or indistinct features.

C) participants would not be distracted by blurry or indistinct features in an image that, in terms of resolution, has been calibrated by researchers.

D) participants' distraction by blurry or indistinct features can be prevented by researchers' calibration of image resolution.

17

Airline travelers often regard voluntary questionnaires as trivial, but designing a questionnaire to resemble an official boarding document—essentially, a document that is not voluntary—can increase participation _____ the questionnaire during a high-stress interval immediately before takeoff can lead passengers, particularly those afraid of leaving actual requirements unfulfilled, to complete the document.

Which choice completes the text so that it conforms to the conventions of Standard English?

A) rates, furthermore distributing

B) rates, furthermore, distributing

C) rates. Furthermore, distributing

D) rates, furthermore. Distributing

Jawless fish that inhabit the Atlantic Ocean, sea lampreys possess astonishingly adaptable immune systems. Biologists recently put the roughly 100 trillion disease-fighting protein receptors found in sea lampreys to the test, exposing the animals to a _____ never encountered by these sea creatures in the wild. For the lampreys, it took only four weeks to develop the right receptor combination to neutralize the anthrax threat.

Which choice completes the text so that it conforms to the conventions of Standard English?

A) pathogen—anthrax—

B) pathogen anthrax,

C) pathogen, anthrax—

D) pathogen—anthrax

CONTINUE

19

Fish that inhabit the ocean surrounding Antarctica _____ with freezing water using specialized "antifreeze" proteins, some of which stifle the growth of ice crystals in the blood of these well-adapted species. Thanks to this antifreeze mechanism, these fish can survive at consistent subzero water temperatures.

Which choice completes the text so that it conforms to the conventions of Standard English?

A) to cope

B) having coped

C) cope

D) coping

20

The architectural marvel Nan Madol served as a ceremonial and administrative center in Micronesia between 1200 and 1500 CE. Technically a network of 100 island-like structures, Nan Madol consists of heavy basalt slabs positioned atop coral _____ art historians note, were exceptionally difficult to quarry, transport, and lift into place.

Which choice completes the text so that it conforms to the conventions of Standard English?

A) foundations and these slabs,

B) foundations, and these slabs

C) foundations and, these slabs

D) foundations, and these slabs,

21

Works of modernist sculpture often entered into a tension between accurate representation of anatomy and pure abstraction. This is the principle that Henri Matisse's and later Henry Moore's sculptures were premised _____ carefully studied the human figure but then created totemic, blocklike figure sculptures on the basis of such study.

Which choice completes the text so that it conforms to the conventions of Standard English?

A) on and both modernists

B) on. Both modernists

C) on; and both modernists

D) on both modernists

22

While monitoring migratory mule deer in the Wyoming desert, researchers from the United States Geological Survey observed that deer will reach key sites at the same time regardless of whether the deer start early, late, or at the expected time in the migration season, with late-starting deer speeding up their pace and early-starting deer slowing theirs. _____ start time does not meaningfully determine a mule deer's date of arrival.

Which choice completes the text with the most logical transition?

A) Furthermore,

B) Meanwhile,

C) In contrast,

D) In short,

CONTINUE

23

Australia's first radio station broadcast, which took place late in November of 1923, brought a performance by the St. Andrews Choir to households around the country, though the broadcast itself was more than a serene moment of artistic appreciation. _____ two radio stations then known as 2SB and 2FC had been competing to secure a historic first. The 1923 broadcast was 2SB's victory.

Which choice completes the text with the most logical transition?

A) Moreover,

B) Regardless,

C) After all,

D) In comparison,

24

Frilled sharks dwell in the deep reaches of the sea, feeding primarily on the various squids that inhabit these areas, where light seldom reaches. For their part, fieldwork expeditions seldom reach this far below the surface, so much knowledge of the squid species in these deep-sea regions has been gleaned secondhand, from squid specimens that float to lower depths. _____ knowledge of the frilled shark relies little on direct observation.

Which choice completes the text with the most logical transition?

A) Secondly,

B) Likewise,

C) Instead,

D) Alternatively,

25

While researching a topic, a student has taken the following notes:

- Red sprites are electrical discharges from storm clouds and resemble long downward-hanging bulbs and strands.

- Blue jets are electrical discharges from storm clouds and resemble long thin columns.

- Both red sprites and blue jets typically burst upward from a lower to a higher altitude.

- These two forms of electrical discharge only appear during intense thunderstorms.

- The same thunderstorms often produce lightning, which bursts downward from a higher to a lower altitude

The student wants to describe the conditions that result in the three types of electrical discharge. Which choice most effectively uses relevant information from the notes to accomplish this goal?

A) Blue jets resemble long thin columns, while red sprites resemble downward-hanging bulbs and strands; both of these forms of electrical discharge, however, move from lower to higher altitudes.

B) Unlike lightning, which moves from higher to lower altitudes, red sprites and blue jets both move from lower to higher altitudes.

C) Red sprites originate from storm clouds and appear to hang downward; lightning, which also originates during thunderstorms, moves downward after it is produced.

D) Lightning, red sprites, and blue jets are all produced by intense activity during thunderstorms, and red sprites and blue jets both originate from storm clouds.

26

While researching a topic, a student has taken the following notes:

- Chinua Achebe's novel *Things Fall Apart* depicts the contact between Igobo villagers in Nigeria and English colonizers towards the end of the 1800s.

- Chimamanda Adichie's short story "The Headstrong Historian" addresses the same cultural context with a different narrative.

- Achebe's protagonist is a man named Okonkwo.

- Adichie's text gives the name Okonkwo to a minor character who is mentioned in passing.

- One significant character in Achebe's novel is Obierika, a close friend of Achebe's protagonist.

- Adichie's text gives the name Obierika to the husband of Adichie's female protagonist.

The student wants to note a contrast between Achebe's novel and Adichie's story. Which choice most effectively uses relevant information from the notes to accomplish this goal?

A) In "The Headstrong Historian," one of the minor characters is Okonkwo; in *Things Fall Apart*, which in some ways resembles "The Headstrong Historian," a character named Obierika is the husband of the protagonist.

B) Achebe's *Things Fall Apart* features a male protagonist named Okonkwo; for its part, Adichie's "The Headstrong Historian" assigns the names Obierika and Okonkwo to minor characters who are only briefly mentioned.

C) Even though both *Things Fall Apart* and "The Headstrong Historian" depict Igbo villages during the 1800s, Adichie's protagonist is female while Achebe's is male.

D) Like *Things Fall Apart*, "The Headstrong Historian" depicts Igbo villagers, and characters named Obierika and Okonkwo appear in Adichie's text.

27

While researching a topic, a student has taken the following notes:

- Mammal lungs typically follow an inhalation and exhalation pattern known as "tidal" airflow.

- Oxygen enters a mammal lung and disperses to a large number of tiny air sacs, where it is converted into carbon dioxide before it is expelled.

- Bird lungs follow an inhalation and exhalation pattern of "unidirectional" airflow.

- Oxygen enters a bird lung and moves toward a group of air sacs at the back of the lung, displacing the air already in these sacs towards the front of the lung so that this displaced air can then be expelled as carbon dioxide.

- Some lizards have "hybrid" lungs that combine tidal and unidirectional airflow.

The student wants to specify a similarity between tidal and unidirectional airflow. Which choice most effectively uses relevant information from the notes to accomplish this goal?

A) Mammals primarily rely on tidal airflow to convert oxygen into carbon dioxide, yet some bird species rely on a combination of tidal airflow and unidirectional airflow.

B) Lizards with "hybrid" lungs utilize unidirectional airflow in a manner that recalls the inhalation and exhalation of birds, which have two groups of air sacs in their own lungs.

C) Both mammals and some reptiles rely on tidal airflow during inhalation and exhalation, and this form of breathing involves the movement of air between groups of air sacs at the front and the back of the lung.

D) Tidal airflow involves air sacs that receive oxygen, and unidirectional airflow also involves air sacs, though here different groups of sacs are positioned towards the front and the back of the lung.

STOP
If you finish these exercises, you may check your work on this section only.
Do not turn to any other section in the book.

No Test Content on This Page

Test 3 Modules
— Pages 76-98 —

Pages 76-86 Module 1: Baseline					
1	C	10	C	19	B
2	A	11	D	20	C
3	C	12	D	21	C
4	A	13	C	22	A
5	B	14	C	23	C
6	A	15	C	24	D
7	A	16	D	25	A
8	A	17	D	26	B
9	D	18	A	27	A

Pages 88-98 Module 2: Hard					
1	B	10	D	19	C
2	D	11	C	20	D
3	D	12	C	21	B
4	D	13	A	22	D
5	A	14	D	23	C
6	B	15	C	24	B
7	C	16	A	25	D
8	B	17	C	26	C
9	D	18	A	27	D

Want to learn more?
Visit prepvantagetutoring.com for Digital SAT updates
and for the research sources for our passages

Module 1: Baseline
— Pages 76-86 —

Question 1: Choice C
Word in Context
Difficulty - **Easy** | Topic - **Social Studies**

Choice C is the best answer because the sentence indicates that new material has been added to the original edition to update it. Therefore, the underlined word must indicate that a new version of the book has been published.

Choice A is incorrect because, while new material could obfuscate the original aim of a book, there is nothing to indicate that here. In the passage, updating the book is presented as positive. Choice B is incorrect because, while "abridged" is a word that is often used for new editions of books, it means shortened, whereas the sentence describes material being added. Choice D is incorrect because, while educational books typically contain examples, the added material is not the epitome of the original edition.

Question 2: Choice A
Word in Context
Difficulty - **Easy** | Topic - **Science**

Choice A is the best answer because the text compares the "stark asymmetry" of the skulls of "medium-sized whales that hunt large prey" with the "mostly symmetrical skulls" of "larger whales that [hunt] numerous small organisms." Therefore, the underlined phrase must mean "eat" or "hunt." "Feed on" properly indicates that larger whales eat numerous small organisms.

Choice B is incorrect because, though the text makes a comparison, it compares what medium and large whales eat; it does not contrast hunting with avoiding. Choice C is incorrect because, though schools of fish may spread out when being hunted, the text is discussing what whales eat. Choice D is incorrect because the text does not mention anything about medium whales stopping or continuing an action, so it would not be logical to talk about large whales continuing with anything.

Question 3: Choice C
Word in Context
Difficulty - **Medium** | Topic - **Humanities**

Choice C is the best answer because the Balinese artists adopted "European conventions of painting." Therefore, Balinese painters incorporated "influences from beyond their home territory," so the underlined word must mean something akin to "incorporated." "Assimilated" fits this definition and is appropriate for indicating the adoption of artistic influences.

Choice A is incorrect because, though the passage describes a novel addition to Balinese art, Balinese painters could not have invented "influences from beyond their home territory." Moreover, the passage states that those influences came from Europe. Choice B is incorrect because, though the passage describes a difference between traditional Balinese art and European art, Balinese painters began to use European conventions rather than eschewing them. Choice D is incorrect because the passage describes a positive and willing combination of artistic traditions rather than a negative reaction to foreign traditions.

Question 4: Choice A
Word in Context
Difficulty - **Medium** | Topic - **Literature**

Choice A is the best answer because the passage describes Captain Mason aggressively stirring his coffee and spilling it as a result of this action. Choose A to convey the sense of the coffee droplets being jolted out of the cup, and spread around the surrounding area.

Choice B is incorrect because it implies one portion being segregated from others, and does not convey the implication of the coffee droplets being spread around at random. Choice C is incorrect because it implies someone being intentionally sent away as a form of punishment, whereas the coffee droplets escape the cup due to the laws of physics. Choice D is incorrect because it implies something being located at intervals with something else, whereas the coffee drops are randomly sent flying to new locations outside of the cup.

Question 5: Choice B
Text Structure and Purpose
Difficulty - **Hard** | Topic - **Literature**

Choice B is the best answer because the underlined sentence is negative (e.g., "nerve-racking"), while the rest of the passage is pleasant. The rest of the passage describes the sounds as they are when they reach Emma, so the underlined sentence serves as a foil for that.

Choice A is incorrect because, while the underlined sentence is negative, there is nothing to suggest that Emma is disturbed by the sounds. In fact, the sounds in her office are described in positive terms. Choice C is incorrect because, while someone might try to view noise as pleasant to cope with it, there is nothing to suggest that Emma is initially disturbed by the sounds. Choice D is incorrect because, while the passage describes the sounds that Emma discerns from her office, the underlined sentence states that the sounds are "common," so they are not exceptional.

Question 6: Choice A
Text Structure and Purpose
Difficulty - **Medium** | Topic - **Science**

Choice A is the best answer because the underlined text supports the text immediately before it in explaining why Kabadayi and Osvarth did not set out to prove that ravens are intelligent. The scientists would have no need to prove something that is already "a well-accepted fact among zoologists."

Choice B is incorrect because, while the underlined text references a longstanding idea, Kabadayi and Osvarth's experiments were not designed to overturn that idea. Choice C is incorrect because, though ravens are intelligent, that fact was not discovered by Kabadayi and Osvarth. Choice D is incorrect because, though Kabadayi and Osvarth drew analogies between humans and ravens for their study, the underlined text is not about the study but rather a pre-existing notion.

Question 7: Choice A
Text Structure and Purpose
Difficulty - **Medium** | Topic - **Social Studies**

Choice A is the best answer because most of the passage is about "the skills fostered by skateboarding," but the end of the text "acknowledge[s] that much work lies ahead" with regard to societal acceptance and understanding of the transferability of those skills. Thus, Corwin and colleagues' insights represent the preliminary stage of a larger inquiry.

Choice B is incorrect because, though there is an area that warrants further work, Corwin and colleagues did issue a "Beyond the Board" report. Moreover, identifying an area that warrants further work does not make a report inconclusive. Choice C is incorrect because, though the report "acknowledge[s] that much work lies ahead," Corwin and colleagues were not unsure about the benefits of skateboarding. Choice D is incorrect because, though the text presents concrete examples of the benefits of skateboarding, those examples are not in the narrative form of anecdotes.

Question 8: Choice A
Cross-Text Connections
Difficulty - **Hard** | Topic - **Science**

Choice A is the best answer because Text 1 mentions that small robots could move "unexpectedly large obstacles" while Text 2 approvingly addresses the potential for several small robots to replace "larger single robots" in completing physical tasks. Both texts indicate that aggregates of small robots are potentially useful in physical tasks that are logically premised on a large scale. Moreover, if a single small robot could perform the sort of tasks mentioned in Text 1 and Text 2, it would be illogical for the authors to promote robot aggregates as necessary.

Choice B is incorrect because Text 1 presents a comparison between small robots and the rover-like vehicles that they resemble but does not clearly indicate that the rover designs inspired the robot designs. Moreover, Text 2 indicates that small robots are different from and preferable to larger robots and devices in design. Choice C is incorrect because Text 2 does not discuss the use of renewable energy as an overwhelming asset. According to Text 2, the aggregating and cooperative abilities of small robots, not the use of renewable energy, would remove liabilities associated with larger robots. Choice D is incorrect because neither text directly analyzes human supervision at length. Instead, Text 1 emphasizes the benefits of small robots and Text 2 is concerned with a comparison between larger and smaller robots.

Question 9: Choice B
Central Ideas and Details
Difficulty - **Easy** | Topic - **Literature**

Choice B is the best answer because the passage focuses on the unpleasantness of combing Ida's hair. The task "was a great affliction to Ida," and "Mrs. Kent, too, used to dread the job." Moreover, the passage states the reason for the unpleasantness: Ida's hair is difficult to comb.

Choice A is incorrect because, though Ida has a temper, her dislike of combing her hair is not portrayed as irrational. Choice B is incorrect because, while Ida and Mrs. Kent both address the problem of Ida's unruly hair, they do not do so by following an unusual approach. Choice C is incorrect because, though "Mrs. Kent . . . used to dread the job" of combing Ida's hair, there is nothing to indicate that she treated Ida unfairly despite her dislike of combing Ida's hair.

Question 10: Choice C
Quantitative Command of Evidence
Difficulty - **Medium** | Topic - **Social Studies**

Choice C is the best answer because the 1614 illustrated book was checked out substantially more times in March than in any other month in the table. According to the text, "when a book or manuscript is checked out much more often than it is on average, it is most likely the subject of a small group seminar." Thus, there was most likely a small group seminar that included the 1614 illustrated book in March.

Choice A is incorrect because, though February was an anomalous month for the 1613 manuscript, the checkouts were abnormally low, not abnormally high. Choice B is incorrect because, though April had the most checkouts for the 1627 manuscript, 14 is barely above the 1627 manuscript's average monthly checkouts. Choice D is incorrect because, though May had the most checkouts for the 1639 illustrated book, 19 is not as far above the 1639 illustrated book's average monthly checkouts as 23 is above the 1614 illustrated book's average monthly checkouts, so it is not the best example of being "checked out much more often than it is on average."

Question 11: Choice D
Textual Command of Evidence
Difficulty - **Medium** | Topic - **History**

Choice D is the best answer because it states that Jefferson was in substantial debt and that his debt was known to people who supported him politically. This supports both the broader claim that financial success was not tied to political success in early presidential elections and the narrower claim that "Thomas Jefferson, was in fact simultaneously regarded as a financial "failure" and a political success."

Choice A is incorrect because, though it points out that Jefferson was less wealthy than Mason was, it does not suggest that Jefferson was politically successful. Choice B is incorrect because, though it is about Jefferson as president, it does not suggest that Jefferson was "regarded as a financial failure." Choice C is incorrect because, though it is about Jefferson's political success, it states that his political success was limited, which opposes the historian's claim that "Thomas Jefferson, was . . . regarded as . . . a political success."

Question 12: Choice C
Quantitative Command of Evidence
Difficulty - **Hard** | Topic - **Social Studies**

Choice C is the best answer because the number of people below age 15 (the left bar in each set of three bars) did not change substantially between 2000 and 2020, whereas the number of people between 15 and 65 (the middle bar in each set of three bars) grew from less than four billion people to more than five billion people over the same period.

Choice A is incorrect because, though people over 65 represented a small fraction of the world's population in 1960, and the number of people over 65 increased substantially over the subsequent 60 years. Moreover, if the number of people over 65 had remained constant, that would have undermined rather than "suggest[ed] the validity of" the claim. Choice B is incorrect because, though it states true information, that information does not "suggest[] the validity of" the claim since the claim is about population changes over time, not population demographics in a single year. Choice D is incorrect because, though it states true information, that information undermines rather than "suggests the validity of" the claim since it shows a younger demographic growing as much as the older demographic did.

Question 13: Choice D
Textual Command of Evidence
Difficulty - **Medium** | Topic - **Literature**

Choice D is the best answer because the underlined text must support the claim that Monsieur François "expresses his desire to be honored and remembered." The "itch" that he feels is his desire, and the "honorary post, some small distinction" is the honor. That honor will help him to be remembered (i.e., it will "save [his] name from dark oblivion's jaws").

Choice A is incorrect because, though it is about the correct character, it is about his past, not his legacy. Choice B is incorrect because, though it references significant events, those events are of the past, not of the future. Choice C is incorrect because, though resisting oppression might grant Monsieur François a legacy, the legacy itself is not referenced in Choice C.

Question 14: Choice C
Inferences
Difficulty - **Medium** | Topic - **Humanities**

Choice C is the best answer because emphasizing the "identity of Davis as a discrete character, not a depiction of Bob Dylan" supports the claim that the directors were "careful to differentiate the fictional Llewyn Davis from the real-life Dylan."

Choice A is incorrect because, though Dylan was a very influential songwriter, there is nothing in the passage about anything being at the expense of Davis's singing and songwriting. Choice B is incorrect because, though Davis resembles Dylan, Davis's musical influences are not discussed. Choice D is incorrect because, though the film is "part dark comedy," Dylan does not appear "throughout the film."

Question 15: Choice C
Inferences
Difficulty - **Hard** | Topic - **Science**

Choice C is the best answer because the passage indicates that chemical reactions on Venus broke water into gaseous hydrogen and gaseous oxygen, with hydrogen escaping Venus's gravity. It is plausible that some of the resulting oxygen remained on Venus under the condition that oxygen, unlike hydrogen, is too heavy to escape Venus's gravitational pull.

Choice A is incorrect because the passage explains that hydrogen could escape Venus's gravity and does not specify any changes on Venus that would increase its gravitational pull and bring back the escaped hydrogen. Choice B is incorrect because the passage indicates that Venus "once held" water but that it no longer does, since sunlight broke this water into hydrogen and oxygen. Choice D is incorrect because it is unclear whether Venus is still being bombarded with sunlight; it is possible that the sunlight that bombards Venus is still strong even though the reactions that turned water into hydrogen and oxygen mostly took place in the distant past.

Question 16: Choice D
Boundaries
Difficulty - **Medium** | Topic - **Science**

Choice D is the best answer because the essential phrase ("developed by revered astronomer") is not set off with commas or interrupted by one or more commas. This phrase should be incorporated into the rest of the sentence in this manner, since other options treat an essential phrase as nonessential.

Choice A is incorrect because it treats "galaxies are . . . developed" as nonessential, thereby producing an incomplete independent clause. Choice B is incorrect because it treats "by revered astronomer" as nonessential, thereby producing an incomplete independent clause. Choice C is incorrect because it treats "galaxies are . . . revered astronomer" as nonessential, thereby producing an incomplete independent clause. All of these false answers result in incomplete independent clauses.

Question 17: Choice D
Form, Structure, and Sense
Difficulty - **Medium** | Topic - **History**

Choice D is the best answer because the sentence requires the conditional verb form "would consist" to align with the hypothetical scenario "had the original design been put in successful circulation." The sentence describes a scenario that did not in fact happen, so the traits of the barcodes in that scenario require the conditional verb form.

Choice A is incorrect because "were consisting" is in the past continuous tense, which does not align with a scenario that did not take place in the past. Choice B is incorrect because "have consisted" is in the present perfect tense, which does not align with a hypothetical scenario. Choice C is incorrect because "consist" is in the present tense, which is not used to describe a hypothetical scenario.

Question 18: Choice A
Form, Structure, and Sense
Difficulty - **Easy** | Topic - **Humanities**

Choice A is the best answer because the singular pronoun "yourself" agrees with the singular antecedent "you" to effectively indicate that the reader is imagining himself or herself "in an interior design career." "Yourself" is a reflexive pronoun, so it indicates that the doer of the action is also the recipient of the action (the person is the thinker and the one being thought about).

Choice B is incorrect because, though the plural pronoun "themselves" is reflexive, it does not agree with the singular antecedent "you." Choice C is incorrect because, though the singular pronoun "you" agrees with the singular antecedent "you," it is not reflexive. Choice D is incorrect because the plural pronoun "them" does not agree with the singular antecedent "you," so it would indicate that the reader is envisioning other people "in an interior design career." This also creates a plural-singular mismatch between the plural "them" and the singular "an interior design career."

Question 19: Choice B
Form, Structure, and Sense
Difficulty - **Medium** | Topic - **History**

Choice B is the best answer because the context clue "distant ancestors" indicates that a past tense verb is necessary. The verb "formed" appropriately fits the context of describing the establishment of communities.

Choice A is incorrect because the verb "will form" is future tense, which would indicate that past occurrences have not yet happened. Choice C is incorrect because the verb "form" is present tense, which is a mismatch for a description of past occurrences. Choice D is incorrect because the verb "are forming" is present continuous tense, which would indicate that distant ancestors are currently forming communities.

Question 20: Choice C
Form, Structure, and Sense
Difficulty - **Medium** | Topic - **Humanities**

Choice C is the best answer because the singular possessive "author's" properly indicates that the short stories were written by their author. The plural noun "short stories" is necessary because "short stories" are being compared to "the works of older, more established writers."

Choice A is incorrect because the singular possessives "author's" and "story's" are both adjectives, thereby leaving "explain" without an indirect object. Choice B is incorrect because the plural possessive "stories'" is an adjective that does not modify a noun. Choice D is incorrect because the plural noun "authors" does not match the singular article "a."

Question 21: Choice C
Form, Structure, and Sense
Difficulty - **Easy** | Topic - **Social Studies**

Choice C is the best answer because the sentence requires the nonfinite verb form "utilizing" to create a dependent clause. The verb form should be the present participle ("-ing" form) in order to create an introductory clause that describes how Barsoum uses his technical skills in his work.

Choice A is incorrect because the finite verb form "utilized" is the simple past tense, so it is not appropriate for describing work that is currently being done. Choice B is incorrect because the finite verb form "utilize" is the simple present tense and does not match the third-person singular subject (Barsoum). Choice D is incorrect because the finite verb form "utilizes" is the simple present tense, so it treats the introductory clause as an independent clause.

Question 22: Choice A
Transitions
Difficulty - **Medium** | Topic - **Social Studies**

Choice A is the best answer because "that is" indicates that "cautious of . . . cassowaries" defines what "casso-wary" means. This transition properly signals a clarification or definition relationship.

Choice B is incorrect because "for example" introduces a support relationship and wrongly indicates that being "cautious of the large flightless birds known as cassowaries" is an example of what "casso-wary" means rather than a complete

definition of it. Choice C is incorrect because "furthermore" introduces an extension relationship and wrongly indicates that being "cautious of the large flightless birds known as cassowaries" is something different from being "casso-wary." Choice D is incorrect because "granted" introduces a caveat relationship and wrongly indicates that being "cautious of the large flightless birds known as cassowaries" is incongruous with being "casso-wary."

Question 23: Choice C
Transitions
Difficulty - **Medium** | Topic - **Social Studies**

Choice C is the best answer because "for this reason" indicates that the shoppers' desire "to feel that their time has been well spent" is the reason that they pick up additional items while waiting in line. This transition properly signals a cause and effect relationship.

Choice A is incorrect because "granted" introduces a contrast relationship, which wrongly indicates the shoppers' desire "to feel that their time has been well spent" lies in opposition to their tendency to pick up additional items while waiting in line. Choice B is incorrect because "nevertheless" introduces a contrast relationship, which wrongly indicates the shoppers' tendency to pick up additional items while waiting in line occurs despite their desire "to feel that their time has been well spent." Choice D is incorrect because "more broadly" introduces a generalization relationship, which wrongly indicates that the shoppers' desire "to feel that their time has been well spent" is a more specific version of their tendency to pick up additional items while waiting in line.

Question 24: Choice D
Transitions
Difficulty - **Medium** | Topic - **Humanities**

Choice D is the best answer because "here" indicates that "pedestrians can amble past rows of vivid paintings" at "the Nelum Pokuna Art Street." This transition properly signals a location relationship.

Choice A is incorrect because "that said" introduces an opposing relationship and wrongly indicates that the opportunity to "amble past rows of vivid paintings" exists despite "the Nelum Pokuna Art Street." Choice B is incorrect because "regardless" introduces an opposing relationship and wrongly indicates that "pedestrians can amble past rows of vivid paintings" despite the existence of "the Nelum Pokuna Art Street." Choice C is incorrect because "surprisingly" introduces an incongruous relationship and wrongly indicates that the opportunity to "amble past rows of vivid paintings" is surprising in light of the existence of "the Nelum Pokuna Art Street."

Question 25: Choice A
Transitions
Difficulty - **Medium** | Topic - **Humanities**

Choice A is the best answer because "still" indicates that "there are popular alternatives to method acting" despite the fact that "'method acting' . . . is prized by actors." This transition properly signals an opposing relationship.

Choice B is incorrect because "indeed" introduces an additive relationship and wrongly indicates that the existence of "popular alternatives to method acting" is an extension of the fact that "'method acting' . . . is prized by actors." Choice C is incorrect because "consequently" introduces a causal relationship and wrongly indicates that the existence of "popular alternatives to method acting" is a result of the fact that "'method acting' . . . is prized by actors." Choice D is incorrect because "finally" introduces a temporal relationship and wrongly indicates that "alternatives to method acting" became popular after method acting did.

Question 26: Choice B
Rhetorical Synthesis
Difficulty - **Medium** | Topic - **Science**

Choice B is the best answer because it contrasts the temperatures used in the Haber-Bosch process with those used in the method developed at the University of California. This choice is consistent with the student's goal of "emphasiz[ing] a difference between the Haber-Bosch process and the method developed at the University of California."

Choice A is incorrect because, though it discusses the method developed at the University of California, it does not mention the Haber-Bosch process. Choice C is incorrect because, though it discusses both methods, it does not state a difference between them. Choice D is incorrect because, though it alludes to two methods, it does not specify what either one is or how they differ from each other.

Question 27: Choice A
Rhetorical Synthesis
Difficulty - **Medium** | Topic - **History**

Choice A is the best answer because it focuses on the structure and collapse of the Venetian banking system. This choice is consistent with the student's goal of "provid[ing] a summary of Venice's banking crisis."

Choice B is incorrect because, though it mentions Venice's financial panic, it does not summarize Venice's banking crisis. Choice C is incorrect because, though it mentions Venetian banks, it does not mention a banking crisis. Choice D is incorrect because, though it mentions Venice's financial crisis, it does not provide a summary of it.

Module 2: Hard
— Pages 88-98 —

Question 1: Choice B
Word in Context
Difficulty - **Easy** | Topic - **History**

Choice B is the best answer because the text describes the March on Washington as "triumphant" for Randolph, who was older at the time and who would be giving leadership to a "new generation." The word "culmination" indicates both a high point and a point of conclusion and would thus be appropriate for the given context.

Choice A is incorrect because "relief" indicates the removal of a problem and suggests a negative tone that is not supported by the passage, which depicts the March on Washington as an inspiring moment. Choice C is incorrect because the March on Washington could be a point of "origin" for younger African American leaders but not for Randolph, who had already had a "long career." Choice D is incorrect because it suggests cancellation or conflict, introducing a negative tone into a text that depicts Randolph and the March on Washington positively.

Question 2: Choice D
Word in Context
Difficulty - **Hard** | Topic - **Humanities**

Choice D is the best answer because the underlined text must match "not a real place" in meaning. "Fabrication" correctly indicates that the details about the zoo were created by the author.

Choice A is incorrect because, though zoos often sell food, the zoo itself is not a concession stand. Choice B is incorrect because, though the zoo is an addition to reality, the passage does not suggest that the zoo is unnecessary to the novel.

Choice C is incorrect because, though visitors are often happy at zoos, a zoo is not friendliness itself.

Question 3: Choice D
Word in Context
Difficulty - **Hard** | Topic - **Social Studies**

Choice D is the best answer because the terms "latitude" and "longitude" come from geography but are now being used by demographers for a different purpose. "Appropriated" conveys that these terms have been taken from their original context.

Choice A is incorrect because, though the terms "latitude" and "longitude" have been incorporated into research studies, they haven't been mixed with each other. Choice B is incorrect because, though the text is about a change, the terms "latitude" and "longitude" have not been disavowed by demographers. Choice C is incorrect because, though it may seem wrong to apply geography terms to research studies, the text is not about remedying a situation or compensating anyone for a wrongful act.

Question 4: Choice D
Word in Context
Difficulty - **Hard** | Topic - **History**

Choice D is the best answer because Luce's aim was to generate "handsome profits" with his publications. Therefore, Sports Illustrated was a commercial venture. Moreover, "Luce launched Sports Illustrated . . . not out of any personal devotion to sports," so it is clear that his only motivation was profit.

Choice A is incorrect because magazines are not government publications, so they cannot serve a regulatory purpose. Choice B is incorrect because, though someone could donate their profits, Luce's aim was to generate "handsome profits" for himself, not for charity. Choice C is incorrect because, though sports might be tangential to the topics of his three previous magazines, there is nothing to indicate that Sports Illustrated was secondary to those publications.

Question 5: Choice A
Text Structure and Purpose
Difficulty - **Hard** | Topic - **History**

Choice A is the best answer because the passage begins by stating that "the idea that players 'peak' at remarkably young ages" is "rather suspect." It goes on to provide a research finding ("chess players often deliver their most remarkable performances around age 35") to support its stance and then notes that "accounts of young players who achieve remarkable feats" are responsible for the incorrect belief.

Choice B is incorrect because, though it presents two views, it does not state that one of them is growing in popularity. Choice C is incorrect because, though it points to flawed reasoning, it does not propose a new method for gathering reliable information. Choice D is incorrect because, though it corrects a widespread belief and mentions an individual (Judit Polgár), it does not catalogs her traits or pinpoint those that have changed over time.

Question 6: Choice B
Text Structure and Purpose
Difficulty - **Hard** | Topic - **Literature**

Choice B is the best answer because the speaker has "escaped" a city that is described using strong negative tones. The speaker is then in a new setting with much more appealing features, including opportunities "to wander and to dream" at ease. This movement from a negative to a positive emphasis in the poem supports the idea of "relief" as one of the speaker's central emotions.

Choice A is incorrect because the text never specifies that the city setting provides a distraction from earlier problems, even though the more natural setting seems to offer an escape. Instead, the city setting is itself the source of some of the speaker's negative emotions. Choice C is incorrect because the speaker notes possible reasons for abandoning an unappealing lifestyle and finds a more appealing alternative. The text does not explain why the speaker, most likely at some earlier stage, went to the city instead of to a more appealing setting. Choice D is incorrect because the speaker does not note a gradual increase in enjoyment of nature. Instead, the speaker feels a strong enjoyment upon leaving the city, but it is never argued that the speaker's enjoyment progressively increases during the speaker's time in natural surroundings.

Question 7: Choice C
Central Ideas and Details
Difficulty - **Hard** | Topic - **History**

Choice C is the best answer because "two-pronged forks were used at least since the early Middle Ages to hold food in place for cutting and evolved into utensils for bringing food directly to the mouth." Thus, the two-pronged forks were not used for eating but rather for food preparation.

Choice A is incorrect because, while food preparation forks are often large, their size is not mentioned in the passage. Choice B is incorrect because, though Henry III's forks were "initially rejected by the English nobility," the passage does not say the same of forks that predated Henry III. Choice D is incorrect because, while forks increased in popularity, the passage does not say that they were perceived as more efficient.

Question 8: Choice B
Textual Command of Evidence
Difficulty - **Hard** | Topic - **Literature**

Choice B is the best answer because the factory hands are calm (they "walked intentionally in good order and almost in silence") in attempting to get "a just settlement of their grievances against the manager." Moreover, the speaker finds the discontent of the factory hands to be justified because "the manager, . . . in closing the factory and dismissing the workmen, had cheated them all in an impudent way."

Choice A is incorrect because, though the community is temporarily puzzled by the conduct of the factory hands, the speaker is not explaining their conduct for the sake of avoiding a misunderstanding. Choice C is incorrect because, though the factory hands have earned the sympathy of the speaker, the narrator does not predict heightened conflict. Choice D is incorrect because, though the factory hands are going to the governor, the speaker does not predict whether the governor will be receptive to their proposal.

Question 9: Choice D
Central Ideas and Details
Difficulty - **Hard** | Topic - **Science**

Choice D is the best answer because the main point being made about helium is that it was previously believed to have no natural sources on Earth but is now known to be leaking from Earth's surface. Moreover, the passage notes that helium is "potentially invaluable in the creation of everything from fusion energy reactors to advanced digital imaging systems," which supports the notion that it "could power useful technologies."

Choice A is incorrect because, though new technological uses for helium-3 have been suggested, they were not suggested by research that originally aimed to explain Earth's formation. Furthermore, the study discussed in the passage did not involve the Moon. Choice B is incorrect because, though the passage describes questions involving Earth's formation and research about helium-3 on Earth's surface, that research is not shifting from practical applications to theoretical questions involving Earth's formation. Choice C is incorrect because, though there is growing interest in the commercial uses of helium-3, attempts to harvest it on earth have not been abandoned.

Question 10: Choice D
Textual Command of Evidence
Difficulty - **Hard** | Topic - **Literature**

Choice D is the best answer because Orlando's optimistic prediction that he and Adam will find shelter and food in the desert supports the claim that "Orlando is eager to offer reassurance" to Adam.

Choice A is incorrect because, though it is about reassurance, it is about Adam reassuring Orlando of Adam's abilities rather than Orlando reassuring Adam about their journey. Choice B is incorrect because, though it is about what Orlando tells Adam, it is not about Orlando reassuring Adam regarding their journey. Choice C is incorrect because, though it supports the notion that Adam finds the journey difficult, it does not provide an example of Orlando reassuring Adam.

Question 11: Choice C
Quantitative Command of Evidence
Difficulty - **Hard** | Topic - **Science**

Choice C is the best answer because the idea of uneven mass balance loss supports the required claim that "mass loss has not proceeded steadily." The chart indicates that South Cascade has consistently lost mass but not always at the same rate, with a roughly −10 change between 2000 and 2010 and a much smaller change between 2010 and 2020.

Choice A is incorrect because it in fact contradicts the claim about differences in rate by citing a glacier, Wolverine, that has exhibited a consistent rate of loss over the period mentioned. Choice B is incorrect because it notes that one rate was higher than another rate but does not indicate different increments for a single rate; the correct choice should much more directly indicate that "mass loss has not proceeded steadily" for at least one glacier. Choice D is incorrect because it indicates comparable changes for two glaciers but does not clearly indicate whether either glacier exhibited losses that proceeded at uneven rates.

Question 12: Choice C
Textual Command of Evidence
Difficulty - **Hard** | Topic - **Social Studies**

Choice C is the best answer because "prompt[ing] employees to visualize their given project" is a means of "steering workers away from unnecessary projects," and "tak[ing] on a moderate amount of work and achiev[ing] a few aims at a time" is a means of "prevent[ing] work teams from becoming over-extended."

Choice A is incorrect because, though the passage mentions a company that is popular in the United States, the managers' claim is not about parallels between the United States and Japan. Moreover, the managers' claim is not about continuous improvement over time. Choice B is incorrect because, though the text describes benefits of the kanban board, the managers' claim is not about project due dates. Choice D is incorrect because, though waiting to start a new project is consistent with "prevent[ing] work teams from becoming over-extended," the managers' claim is not about communication or improvement.

Question 13: Choice A
Quantitative Command of Evidence
Difficulty - **Medium** | Topic - **Science**

Choice A is the best answer because Indiana and Wisconsin's numbers are below the average in the table. The numbers in the table show honeybee population losses, so low numbers indicate high survival.

Choice B is incorrect because, though Minnesota had an above-average survival, Illinois did not. Choice C is incorrect because, though the numbers in the table for Iowa and Illinois are higher than the national average, those numbers show honeybee population losses, so high numbers indicate low survival. Choice D is incorrect because, though the numbers in the table for Iowa and Michigan are the highest in the table, those numbers show honeybee population losses, not survival.

Question 14: Choice D
Inferences
Difficulty - **Hard** | Topic - **Science**

Choice D is the best answer because "even though" sets up a negative statement that does not negate the success of the DESI initiative. Choice D shows a shortcoming of the DESI apparatus that does not hinder the success of its goal, which is to "map the wide-scale effect of dark energy." Moreover, dark energy is "an invisible force," so no apparatus would be able to provide a photographic image of dark energy itself.

Choice A is incorrect because, though it shows that the DESI apparatus is better at something other than recording the effects of dark matter, it does not provide any information about how good the DESI apparatus is at recording the effects of dark matter. Choice B is incorrect because, though it presents a problem, the claim is about "the DESI initiative . . . so far," so a future problem is not relevant to the claim. Choice C is incorrect because, though it points out that analyzing DESI data is laborious, it is about gravity data, while the claim is about dark matter data.

Question 15: Choice C
Form, Structure, and Sense
Difficulty - **Hard** | Topic - **History**

Choice C is the best answer because the plural verb "are" agrees with the plural subject "serving as . . . racial prejudice." The subject may be difficult to identify due to the fact that it is a list of gerunds ("-ing" words that function as nouns rather than verbs).

Choice A is incorrect because the singular verb "was" does not agree with the plural subject. Choice B is incorrect because the singular verb "is" does not agree with the plural subject. Choice D is incorrect because the singular verb "has been" does not agree with the plural subject.

Question 16: Choice A
Form, Structure, and Sense
Difficulty - **Hard** | Topic - **Science**

Choice A is the best answer because the modifier ("A relatively . . . past memory)") must modify the noun immediately after it. Image resolution is the "relatively easy factor to adjust," so "image resolution" must be the beginning of the correct answer.

Choice B is incorrect because it would make the modifier modify "researchers," which are not the "relatively easy factor to adjust." Choice C is incorrect because it would make the modifier modify "participants," which are not the "relatively easy factor to adjust." Choice D is incorrect because it would make the modifier modify "participants' distraction," which is not the "relatively easy factor to adjust."

Question 17: Choice C
Boundaries
Difficulty - **Hard** | Topic - **Social Studies**

Choice C is the best answer because it uses a period to structure the two independent clauses "Airline travelers . . . rates" and "distributing . . . document." This sentence structure properly configures the independent clauses, while the dependent transition "Furthermore" is properly placed at the beginning of the sentence after the period to indicate movement into a new independent clause that builds upon the previous independent clause.

Choice A is incorrect because it joins two independent clauses with only a comma and thus creates a comma splice, since "furthermore" is a dependent transition and cannot (like "and" or "but") connect independent clauses. Choice B is incorrect because it sets "furthermore" off with two commas as dependent content to create a comma splice. Choice D is incorrect because it positions the transition in the first independent clause to suggest that an earlier idea is being built upon, but no idea is present before the independent clause "Airline travelers . . . rates." Instead, the transition should instead indicate that the second independent clause ("distributing . . . document") builds upon the first.

Question 18: Choice A
Boundaries
Difficulty - **Hard** | Topic - **Science**

Choice A is the best answer because it uses two dashes to set off dependent content that further describes the "pathogen" mentioned earlier in the sentence. If this content is omitted, the phrasing that ends the sentence is both grammatically correct and understandable: "exposing the animals to a pathogen [. . .] never encountered by these sea creatures in the wild."

Choice B is incorrect because it awkwardly treats "anthrax" as part of the same dependent clause that contains "pathogen," no as part of a new dependent construction that describes the "pathogen" further. Choice C is incorrect because it combines a comma with a dash, yet two identical punctuation marks are needed to set off dependent content. Choice D is incorrect because the content at the end of the sentence ("never encountered . . . ") further describes the word "pathogen" as part of the same dependent clause. This choice wrongly creates the awkward phrase "anthrax never encountered" to indicate that "never encountered" defines what "anthrax" is generally; instead, the text describes a specific pathogen, notes its name in an appositive construction, and continues the description of the "pathogen" itself.

Question 19: Choice C
Form, Structure, and Sense
Difficulty - **Medium** | Topic - **Science**

Choice C is the best answer because the sentence requires the finite verb form "cope" to create an independent clause. The verb form should take the subject "fish." The other subject-finite verb pair in the sentence is located in a dependent clause, so it could not be the main subject-verb pair of the sentence.

Choice A is incorrect because the nonfinite verb form "to cope" is the infinitive form, which does not create an independent clause. Choice B is incorrect because the nonfinite verb form "having coped" is the perfect participle, which leaves the sentence without an independent clause. Choice D is incorrect because the nonfinite verb form "coping" is the present participle, which does not create an independent clause.

Question 20: Choice D
Boundaries
Difficulty - **Hard** | Topic - **History**

Choice D is the best answer because it properly punctuates the dependent clause "art historians note" with two commas; this clause can thus be set aside from the independent clause

"these slabs . . . place." Moreover, this choice properly places a comma and the word "and" between two independent clauses, "Nan . . . foundations" and "these slabs . . . place."

Choice A is incorrect because it omits the comma which is needed after "foundations" in order to properly connect two independent clauses, even though this choice properly punctuates the dependent clause. Choice B is incorrect because it omits the first comma necessary to set off "art historians note" as a dependent clause. Choice C is incorrect because it connects "these slabs" and "art historians note" in a single dependent clause. When this clause is omitted, the non-grammatical independent clause "Nan Madol consists . . . and were exceptionally difficult" results and wrongly attributes the plural verb "were" to the singular noun "Nan Madol."

Question 21: Choice B
Boundaries
Difficulty - **Hard** | Topic - **Humanities**

Choice B is the best answer because it uses a period to separate two independent clauses, "This is . . . premised on" and "Both . . . study."

Choice A is incorrect because it introduces the coordinating conjunction "and" without the comma that would be necessary to use "and" to join two independent clauses. Choice C is incorrect because it places a phrase introduced by "and" after a semicolon and thus does not properly punctuate or configure a second independent clause. Choice D is incorrect because it avoids any punctuation for the independent clause "both . . . study" and thus creates a fused run-on sentence.

Question 22: Choice D
Transitions
Difficulty - **Hard** | Topic - **Science**

Choice D is the best answer because the text indicates that mule deer "will reach key sites at the same time regardless" of start time, and the portion introduced by the transition rephrases this idea with the statement that "start time does not meaningfully determine a mule deer's date of arrival." The transition "in short" properly indicates that the text is returning to earlier content for a concise statement of a central point without introducing new material.

Choice A is incorrect because "Furthermore" indicates that new information is being presented to support a point, not that previous information is being rephrased for emphasis. Choice B is incorrect because "Meanwhile" indicates that two separate events are happening at the same time. Despite seeming to introduce a similarity, this transition creates a relationship based on simultaneous times and thus deviates from the passage's emphasis on returning to a point mentioned earlier for analysis. Choice C is incorrect because "In contrast" indicates a new and different point that opposes an earlier idea, but the content after the transition rephrases content from before the transition without deviating from previous ideas.

Question 23: Choice C
Transitions
Difficulty - **Hard** | Topic - **History**

Choice C is the best answer because "After all" indicates that the broadcast was "more than a serene moment of artistic appreciation" because of the fact that "the 1923 broadcast [served as] 2SB's victory." This transition properly signals a support relationship.

Choice A is incorrect because "moreover" introduces an extension relationship and wrongly indicates that "2SB's victory" is a different phenomenon than the broadcast being "more than a serene moment of artistic appreciation." Choice B is incorrect because "regardless" introduces an opposing relationship and wrongly indicates that "2SB's victory" occurred despite the broadcast being "more than a serene moment of artistic appreciation." Choice D is incorrect because "in comparison" introduces an opposing relationship and wrongly indicates that "2SB's victory" is a foil for the broadcast being "more than a serene moment of artistic appreciation."

Question 24: Choice B
Transitions
Difficulty - **Hard** | Topic - **Science**

Choice B is the best answer because "likewise" signals that the fact that "knowledge of the frilled shark relies little on direct observation" is similar to the fact that "much knowledge of the squid species in these deep-sea regions has been gleaned secondhand." This transition properly signals a similarity relationship.

Choice A is incorrect because "secondly" introduces an extension relationship, which wrongly indicates that the fact that "knowledge of the frilled shark relies little on direct observation" is the second in a list of statements meant to support the same point. Choice C is incorrect because "instead" introduces a contrast relationship, which wrongly indicates that the fact that "knowledge of the frilled shark relies little on direct observation" replaces the fact that "much knowledge of the squid species in these deep-sea regions has been gleaned secondhand." Choice D is incorrect because "alternatively" introduces an opposing relationship, which wrongly indicates that the fact that "knowledge of the frilled shark relies little on direct observation" is mutually exclusive with the fact that "much knowledge of the squid species in these deep-sea regions has been gleaned secondhand."

Question 25: Choice D
Rhetorical Synthesis
Difficulty - **Hard** | Topic - **Science**

Choice D is the best answer because it describes the storm conditions ("intense activity" and "storm clouds") that produce the three types of electrical discharge ("lightning, red sprites, and blue jets"). This is consistent with the student's goal of "describ[ing] the conditions that result in the three types of electrical discharge."

Choice A is incorrect because, though it mentions two types of electrical discharge, it does not mention the third one, and it does not describe the storm conditions that produce discharges. Choice B is incorrect because, though it mentions the three types of electrical discharge, it does not describe the storm conditions that produce them. Choice C is incorrect because, though it states how red sprites and lightning originate, it does not say how blue jets originate.

Question 26: Choice C
Rhetorical Synthesis
Difficulty - **Hard** | Topic - **Humanities**

Choice C is the best answer because it states that "Adichie's protagonist is female while Achebe's is male." This choice is consistent with the student's goal of "not[ing] a contrast between Achebe's novel and Adichie's story."

Choice A is incorrect because, though it gives two different character names, it portrays the works as somewhat similar ("Things Fall Apart . . . in some ways resembles 'The Headstrong Historian'") rather than different. Choice B is incorrect because, though it mentions both works, it does not contrast them. Choice D is incorrect because it portrays the works as similar (they both depict Igbo villagers) rather than different.

Question 27: Choice D
Rhetorical Synthesis
Difficulty - **Hard** | Topic - **Science**

Choice D is the best answer because it states that both tidal and unidirectional airflow involve air sacs. This choice is consistent with the student's goal of "specify[ing] a similarity between tidal and unidirectional airflow."

Choice A is incorrect because it contrasts the types of animals that use tidal and unidirectional airflow rather than providing a similarity between tidal and unidirectional airflow. Choice B is incorrect because, though it provides a similarity, it does not state a similarity between tidal and unidirectional airflow. Choice C is incorrect because it is only about tidal airflow, not unidirectional airflow.

Reading and Writing

27 QUESTIONS

DIRECTIONS

The questions in this section address a number of important reading and writing skills. Each question includes one or more passages, which may include a table or graph. Read each passage and question carefully, and then choose the best answer to the question based on the passage(s).

All questions in this section are multiple-choice with four answer choices. Each question has a single best answer.

1

For esteemed nineteenth century art critic John Ruskin, _____ sketching, even without the prospect of achieving excellence, could nonetheless be fulfilling—an idea evident from Ruskin's advocacy of drawing classes for factory workers, men who had little interest in becoming master draftsmen but came to appreciate natural beauty and well-formed proportions through art.

Which choice completes the text with the most logical and precise word or phrase?

A) triumphing in

B) venturing towards

C) turning against

D) participating in

2

Residents of Washington DC have not always _____ the right to cast votes for president. From 1801 to 1961, DC residents did not directly cast ballots in elections for the nation's highest office—until an act of Congress granted Washington DC a say in presidential elections.

Which choice completes the text with the most logical and precise word or phrase?

A) possessed

B) appreciated

C) understood

D) studied

CONTINUE

3

Rising global temperatures pose an obvious liability to snow-dependent sports like skiing and a less _____ but still considerable liability to sports like golf, a sport itself impeded by snow. Irregularities in rainfall can disrupt golf tournaments, and sea-level increases can undermine low-lying terrain of golf courses—and both problems have been subtly linked to worldwide temperature increases.

Which choice completes the text with the most logical and precise word or phrase?

A) nuanced

B) satisfying

C) meaningful

D) overt

4

This text is adapted from Charles Baudelaire's 1869 short character sketch "The Cake."

I was traveling. The landscape in the midst of which I was seated was of an irresistible grandeur and sublimity. Something no doubt at that moment passed from it into my soul. My thoughts fluttered with a lightness like that of the atmosphere.

As used in the text, what does the phrase "an irresistible" most nearly mean?

A) A glamorous

B) A powerful

C) A tempting

D) An upsetting

5

The following text is from Willa Cather's 1915 novel *The Song of the Lark*. This passage centers on the Kronborg family and their daily life in Colorado.

Anna, the elder daughter, was her mother's lieutenant. All the children knew that they must obey Anna, who was an obstinate contender for proprieties and not always fair minded. To see the young Kronborgs headed for Sunday School was like watching a military drill. Mrs. Kronborg let her children's minds alone. She did not pry into their thoughts or nag them. She respected them as individuals, and outside of the house they had a great deal of liberty. But their communal life was definitely ordered.

Which choice best describes the function of the underlined sentence in the text as a whole?

A) It summarizes the principles that guide Mrs. Kronborg's unusual parenting style.

B) It documents Anna's efforts in a manner that sets up a contrast between Anna and Mrs. Kronborg.

C) It paraphrases the younger Kronborg children's complaints about Mrs. Kronborg's habits.

D) It criticizes Anna for holding herself to an unrealistic set of standards.

CONTINUE

6

Two approaches to how ideas affect social networks, "top-down" and "bottom-up" diffusions of information, have been championed by social scientists. The "top-down" possibility arose in Malcolm Gladwell's 2000 book *The Tipping Point*, which pinpoints the single most prominent person in a network as central to diffusing new knowledge. The "bottom-up" possibility is at the core of 2021 published research by Gabriel Rossman and Jacob Fisher. Here, they posit that a small amount of publicity for a new idea can initiate interactions among less prominent people in the network, spreading information more readily than reliance on the most prominent person would.

Which choice best describes the function of the underlined sentence in the text as a whole?

A) It introduces a research project that did not embrace the "top-down" concept.

B) It contrasts the core principles of the "top-down" and "bottom-up" theories.

C) It demonstrates why Rossman and Fisher find the "bottom-up" model more realistic than the "top-down" model.

D) It suggests that Gladwell's "top-down" argument does not seem convincing to most social scientists.

7

This text is adapted from Arthur Conan Doyle's 1915 novel *The Valley of Fear*.

The house had been untenanted for some years and was threatening to moulder into a picturesque decay when the Douglases took possession of it. This family consisted of only two individuals—John Douglas and his wife. Douglas was a remarkable man, both in character and in person. In age he may have been about fifty, with a strong-jawed, rugged face, a grizzling moustache, peculiarly keen gray eyes, and a wiry, vigorous figure which had lost nothing of the strength and activity of youth.

Which choice best describes the function of the underlined sentence?

A) It leads into the subsequent descriptions by setting forth an approving stance.

B) It casts doubt upon an assessment of John Douglas from earlier in the passage.

C) It indicates a contrast between John Douglas and his wife.

D) It evokes additional features of a memorable setting.

CONTINUE

8

This text is adapted from Emile Zola's 1885 novel *Germinal*, which depicts the harsh working conditions in a French mining town. Catherine is a young woman who lives with her parents and several siblings. Here, her family is preparing for work.

Catherine, in front of the sideboard, was reflecting. There only remained the end of a loaf, cheese in fair abundance, but hardly a morsel of butter; and she had to provide bread and butter for four. At last she decided, cut the slices, took one and covered it with cheese, spread another with butter, and stuck them together; that was the "brick," the bread-and-butter sandwich taken to the [mining] pit every morning. The four bricks were soon on the table, in a row, cut with severe justice.

According to the text, what challenge does Catherine face?

A) Her family cannot afford to buy additional bread to make the "bricks."

B) One of the ingredients for making the "bricks" is in short supply.

C) Catherine does not know if her family will find the "bricks" appetizing.

D) Catherine finds making the "bricks" to be an unfulfilling task.

9

When Columbia University PhD student Boyaun Chen debuted Eva, a humanoid robot, around 2021, doubts arose about whether Eva could effectively replicate human emotions. That replication was Eva's entire purpose: Chen, a computer science specialist, equipped the robot's face with computerized "muscle" components that shift to various expressions, from joy to fear. Chen, alert to Eva's somewhat uncanny appearance, acknowledged that the Eva project was in its infancy and envisioned a possible future for expressive robots in medicine. This future may be arriving, as "emotional" medical robots are increasingly envisioned as sources of comfort for patients.

Which choice best states the main idea of the text?

A) The Eva project has raised skepticism while pointing to future applications.

B) The difficulties surrounding the Eva project led Chen to change her strategies.

C) Responses to the Eva project have shifted from hostility to enthusiasm in a short time.

D) The purpose of the Eva project changed from replicating human emotions to emphasizing the differences between humans and robots.

10

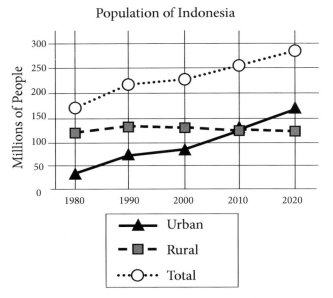

Population of Indonesia

Legend: Urban, Rural, Total

Over the past five decades, the nation of Indonesia has experienced urban population growth and pronounced population growth overall. Driven by the expansion of large cities such as Jakarta and Surabaya, Indonesia's urban population growth, as one demographer claims, has accounted for almost all of the total population growth in the country in the recent past.

Which choice uses relevant and accurate information from the graph to support the demographer's claim?

A) Between 2000 and 2020, Indonesia's rural population exhibited a very small decline that was more than offset by the roughly twofold increase in its urban population.

B) Population growth in Indonesia was slowest between 1990 and 2000, but the urban population nonetheless increased during this period.

C) In Indonesia, urban and rural population counts were almost identical in 2010 but diverged in other years between 1980 and 2020.

D) The urban population of Indonesia, for the period studied, was at its lowest in 1980 and increased over every subsequent ten-year interval.

11

Overtiredness should make sleep easier; ironically, the exact opposite may be true. Today, according to health and wellness experts like Vik Veer, overtiredness often results from a state of constant engagement with new information sources and different social obligations. This conundrum, notes Veer, is also age-dependent, since people in their 30s and 40s are often at particularly busy times in their professional lives and may continue thinking about high-pressure obligations even while attempting to fall asleep.

Which finding, if true, would best support Veer's claim about risks of overtiredness in specific age groups?

A) Across age groups, social media leads to simultaneous sleeplessness and overtiredness by presenting a constant source of new information.

B) People in their 30s often find that they experience fewer instances of overtiredness every month as they near their 40s.

C) Instead of easing the transition into sleep, time in bed prompts people in their 30s to analyze recent professional events and future obligations.

D) Sleep has traditionally been seen as a biological necessity, but wellness experts are redefining sound sleep as a psychological and professional source of fulfillment.

CONTINUE

12

"The Snowstorm" is an 1831 short story by Alexander Pushkin. In the text, a young woman named Masha is in a troubled state of mind, and other characters notice Masha's distress: _____

Which quotation from "The Snowstorm" best illustrates the claim?

A) "On the eve of the decisive day, [Masha] did not sleep all night; she was packing and tying up linen and dresses. She wrote, moreover, a long letter to a friend of hers, a sentimental young lady."

B) "Both her father and her mother remarked on her indisposition. Their tender anxiety and constant inquiries, 'What is the matter with you, Masha—are you ill?' cut her to the heart."

C) "The idea that [Masha] was passing the day for the last time in the midst of her family oppressed her. In her secret heart she took leave of everybody, of everything which surrounded her."

D) "Everything was ready. In half-an-hour Masha would leave for ever her parents' house, her own room, her peaceful life as a young girl."

13

Though consumers worldwide crave shoes that are at once comfortable and fashionable, the definition of comfort in footwear remains rather amorphous. When podiatry specialists Hylton Menz and Daniel R. Bonanno performed a comprehensive 2021 assessment of social science articles on comfortable footwear, the two researchers determined that "no studies specifically defined comfort, and a wide range of assessment scales were used." Comfort in footwear is a challenging concept to discuss precisely, yet _____

Which choice completes the text so that it conforms to the conventions of Standard English?

A) comfort continues to be valued by consumers in spite of this imprecision.

B) fashionable shoes are still less desirable than highly comfortable shoes.

C) inconsistencies surrounding the idea of comfort have been resolved by Menz and Bonanno's assessment.

D) Menz and Bonanno have provided a mostly compelling definition of comfort.

CONTINUE ➤

14

Depictions in film, theater, and television can signify changes in how individuals view civic responsibilities—for instance, serving on a jury. For screenwriter and scriptwriter Reginald Rose, author of the courtroom drama *12 Angry Men* (1954), jury service offered an expansive view of human nature and a forum for life-altering, fair-minded justice. More recent screenwriters, such as the creators of the sitcom *Jury Duty* (2023), have presented jury service as an ordeal to be avoided. If these differing depictions are indeed symptomatic of a real-life shift in perceptions, today's prospective jurors would be expected to _____

Which choice most logically completes the text?

A) understand serving on a jury as a process that is socially worthwhile yet personally burdensome.

B) regard jury service as somewhat burdensome and thus attempt to avoid serving on a jury.

C) serve on a jury primarily in order to gain a larger and more reasonable view of human nature.

D) change their views of jury service only if they are in fact called to serve on a jury.

15

Formerly known as Denimu, British artist Ian Barry crafts works that are informed by a quirky question: exactly how _____ Quite versatile, it turns out. Barry has fashioned everything from photorealistic images to artistic installations like *Secret Garden*, with its denim flowers, from the discarded jeans that are his material of choice.

Which choice completes the text so that it conforms to the conventions of Standard English?

A) versatile are old blue jeans, as an artistic medium?

B) versatile, as old blue jeans are an artistic medium?

C) versatile, as old blue jeans are an artistic medium.

D) versatile are old blue jeans, as an artistic medium.

16

Famous for developing next-generation aerospace technology, NASA also fosters the talents of aspiring engineers. Each year, _____ high school students to participate in its BIG (short for "Breakthrough, Innovative, and Game-Changing") Idea Challenge, a contest that revolves around unconventional tasks like designing inflatable vehicles for low-gravity environments.

Which choice completes the text so that it conforms to the conventions of Standard English?

A) some invite

B) you invite

C) they invite

D) it invites

17

Typically, "endangered languages" are spoken by only a few thousand or a few hundred _____ these languages are sometimes strongly related to languages that are by no means endangered. Both Xhosa, a language spoken by over 9 million people in South Africa, and Nluu, a language that faces possible extinction, are part of the Khoisan family of languages.

Which choice completes the text so that it conforms to the conventions of Standard English?

A) people but

B) people, but

C) people,

D) people

18

Legendary even now for unifying China during a period of intense factional conflict, the _____ founded the long-lived Song Dynasty in the middle of the tenth century CE. Yet wise governance is only part of Taizu's legend: his simple lifestyle, personal bravery, and canny negotiating abilities all form parts of his mythos.

Which choice completes the text so that it conforms to the conventions of Standard English?

A) emperor—known as Taizu

B) emperor known as—Taizu

C) emperor known as Taizu

D) emperor known—as Taizu—

CONTINUE

19

Celebrated entomologist Marla Spivak began her work on bee populations when, during her college years, she randomly picked up a book on bees. Intrigued, _____ taking the first step towards a career that would include research in colony collapse disorder, a condition that imperils bee population.

Which choice completes the text so that it conforms to the conventions of Standard English?

A) Spivak's beginning was in beekeeping work,

B) beekeeping was what Spivak began working in,

C) Spivak's work in beekeeping began,

D) Spivak began working in beekeeping,

20

Between 1996 and 2016, the Hubble Space Telescope photographed Nebula Hen3-1357, nicknamed the "Stingray Nebula," and in doing so revealed the disappearance of this nebula's defining _____ the two expanses of cosmic gas that had once formed the "wings" of the stingray shape and the aquatic green hue of the 1996 nebula, none of which were evident in the 2016 image.

Which choice completes the text so that it conforms to the conventions of Standard English?

A) features: of

B) features;

C) features of:

D) features:

21

When scientists discovered a human-produced breach of the ozone layer in 1985, governments worldwide reacted with alarm, concerned that pollution had contributed to the recently-noticed Ozone Hole and would further diminish the ozone layer, which absorbs harmful ultraviolet radiation before it reaches Earth. _____ the international Montreal Protocol—designed to safeguard Earth's ozone—came into being in 1987.

Which choice completes the text with the most logical transition?

A) However,

B) Before then,

C) As a result,

D) In summary,

22

Japanese has historically been considered a difficult language for speakers of English to learn, if not the single most difficult, according to a 2010 report from the US Foreign Services Institute. _____ English is itself a challenging language for speakers of Japanese to master; despite English's growth as a language of international commerce, only 2 to 8 percent of Japanese speakers are likely fluent in English.

Which choice completes the text with the most logical transition?

A) In other words,

B) Specifically,

C) Nonetheless,

D) Likewise,

23

Psychologist and novelist Hala Alyan's 2024 essay "The Power of Changing Your Mind" links its central topic not to moments of confusion or indecisiveness but to mental discipline. Changing to a new and preferable set of beliefs, for Alyan, is not natural: _____ it "resembles marathoning or playing an instrument" and requires purposeful focus.

Which choice completes the text with the most logical transition?

A) later,

B) in reality,

C) there,

D) secondly,

24

Josephine Jue honed her mathematical skills from a young age, by managing the bookkeeping and working the cash register in her parents' Houston grocery store. This talent with numbers was instrumental to her influential career at NASA. She was hired in 1963, ran calculations for manned spaceflight missions in the 1970s and 1980s, and, _____ headed NASA's Space Station Program Office in the years before her 1997 retirement.

Which choice completes the text with the most logical transition?

A) however,

B) as noted,

C) in summary,

D) finally,

25

While researching a topic, a student has taken the following notes:

- Agnes Martin was an American painter best known for her large abstract canvases.

- According to one art critic, Martin "often explained her work in terms of beauty, perception, [and] understanding."

- Martin once taught drawing and painting fundamentals in a night course for adults.

- As Martin herself explained, one student from the course was a "woman who painted her back yard, and she said it was the first time she had ever really looked at it."

- Martin's most famous abstract compositions incorporate soft colors, recalling foggy skies and peaceful sunsets.

The student wants to compare Martin's ideas to the ideas of Martin's painting student. Which choice most effectively uses relevant information from the notes to accomplish this goal?

A) Martin's principles of "beauty" and "understanding," as explained by one critic, guided some of Martin's abstract compositions.

B) Though Martin's better-known canvases are abstract, some of these compositions recall the varying colors of the sky.

C) Martin was a teacher of adults, one of whom decided to paint scenes of a backyard and found the experience illuminating.

D) One of Martin's painting students, like Martin herself, valued close perception as part of the artistic process.

26

While researching a topic, a student has taken the following notes:

- Cilia are cell structures that resemble hairs or threads.

- In humans and other mammals, olfactory cilia account for the sense of smell.

- These cilia can be found in the nasal cavity.

- The loss of the sense of smell can result from a genetic precondition.

- Researchers from the University of Michigan have used a targeted gene therapy to restore the sense of smell in mice.

- According to the researchers, a comparable therapy could be used to modify the olfactory cilia of humans.

The student wants to explain the University of Michigan study and its outcomes. Which choice most effectively uses relevant information from the notes to accomplish this goal?

A) Similar to hairs or threads in appearance, the olfactory cilia have been studied by a research team from the University of Michigan.

B) Like the olfactory cilia of humans, the olfactory cilia of mice are essential to the sense of smell.

C) Researchers investigating the olfactory cilia have arrived at a gene therapy method that could restore the sense of smell in human subjects.

D) A genetic precondition can impair the sense of smell in mammals; naturally, researchers interested in the olfactory cilia have gravitated to gene therapy.

27

While researching a topic, a student has taken the following notes:

- Jane Gregory is a researcher, professor, and published author from Australia.

- Her book *Sounds like Misophonia* was released in November of 2023.

- Misophonia is the condition of finding certain sounds unbearable.

- By some estimates, between 10% and 20% of all people in the world suffer from a version of misophonia.

- Gregory notes that strong negative reactions to the noises made by dogs or pigeons are symptoms of misophonia.

- Negative reactions to clashing or banging sounds can also indicate misophonia.

The student wants to introduce Gregory's book to an audience unfamiliar with misophonia. Which choice most effectively uses relevant information from the notes to accomplish this goal?

A) Jane Gregory has investigated misophonia, a condition that could affect as many as 10% to 20% of individuals worldwide, in a book-length release.

B) Misophonia, a condition in which specific sounds or noises are found unbearable by a hearer, is the topic of Jane Gregory's 2023 book *Sounds like Misophonia*.

C) Jane Gregory, the author of the book *Sounds like Misophonia*, has linked misophonia to noises made by animals such as dogs and pigeons, as well as to clashing and banging sounds.

D) In misophonia, certain sounds become unbearable to a hearer, and this condition has been investigated by Jane Gregory.

STOP
If you finish these exercises, you may check your work on this section only.
Do not turn to any other section in the book.

No Test Content on This Page

Reading and Writing

27 QUESTIONS

DIRECTIONS

The questions in this section address a number of important reading and writing skills. Each question includes one or more passages, which may include a table or graph. Read each passage and question carefully, and then choose the best answer to the question based on the passage(s).

All questions in this section are multiple-choice with four answer choices. Each question has a single best answer.

1

Folk art must fulfill a few different _____ to earn the "folk" designation: it must be produced by an artist with limited formal training and crafted in a "utilitarian" medium (carved wood, quilting, metalwork) rather than in a traditional "studio" medium (oil on canvas, carved marble). These standards seem lucid enough, though they are in fact open to dispute.

Which choice completes the text with the most logical and precise word or phrase?

A) criteria

B) quarrels

C) benefits

D) segments

2

After spending his early career investigating thoughts and feelings _____ humans—particularly the phenomenon of "learned helplessness," a conditioned acceptance of unpleasant situations—University of Pennsylvania professor Martin Seligman changed tactics, delving into questions of self-actualization and self-knowledge under an approach known as positive psychology.

Which choice completes the text with the most logical and precise word or phrase?

A) synchronized with

B) inimical to

C) prohibited by

D) ostracized from

CONTINUE

3

For his much-lauded musical *Hamilton*, playwright and composer Lin Manuel Miranda relied upon both readily-recognized facts and more _____ knowledge of the American Revolution. His play features well-known historical protagonists like George Washington alongside figures like Hercules Mulligan, an 18th-century spy whom few people beyond scholars of American history would know of offhand.

Which choice completes the text with the most logical and precise word or phrase?

A) fickle

B) genial

C) esoteric

D) worthwhile

4

Typically, students are taught to understand friction as involving physical, not chemical, interactions: the interaction of two surfaces can change the configuration but not the inherent properties of molecules. Yet in a 2013 paper, researchers from the University of Amsterdam assert that friction _____ the "forming and rupturing of microscopic chemical bonds."

Which choice completes the text with the most logical and precise word or phrase?

A) entails

B) sequesters

C) amalgamates

D) redresses

5

This text is adapted from Willa Cather's 1912 novel *Alexander's Bridge*, which centers on the character of Bartley Alexander, a renowned engineer.

After dinner Alexander took Wilson up to his study. It was a large room over the library, and looked out upon the black river and the row of white lights along the Cambridge Embankment. The room was not at all what one might expect of an engineer's study. Wilson felt at once the harmony of beautiful things that have lived long together without obtrusions of ugliness or change.

Which choice best describes the function of the underlined portion in the text as a whole?

A) It conveys the suddenness of Wilson's impressions while still suggesting the settled and longstanding quality of the arrangements in Alexander's room.

B) It communicates Wilson's puzzlement about the fine points of Alexander's personality while emphasizing Alexander's own sense of composure.

C) It qualifies a previous statement about Alexander's lifestyle while indicating Wilson's desire to emulate Alexander.

D) It offers a generality about Alexander's profession while specifying the features of Alexander's living space that Wilson most admires.

CONTINUE ➤

6

This text is adapted from Isabella Valancy Crawford's 1887 poem "The City Tree." Here, the tree of the title is personified and serves as the speaker of the poem.

I stand within the stony, arid town,
I gaze for ever on the narrow street;
I hear forever passing up and down,
The ceaseless tramp of feet.

I know no brotherhood with far-lock'd woods,
Where branches bourgeon from a kindred sap;
Where o'er moss'd roots, in cool, green solitudes,
Small silver brooklets lap.

No emerald vines creep wistfully to me,
And lay their tender fingers on my bark;
High may I toss my boughs, yet never see
Dawn's first most glorious spark.

Which choice best states the main purpose of the text?

A) To illustrate the monotony of the tree's existence by juxtaposing the tree's past and present states

B) To emphasize the fulfillment associated with nature by depicting the activities in a dreary and unappealing town

C) To demonstrate how human activity has changed a natural setting by focusing on the tree's unpleasant situation

D) To convey the tree's isolation from the natural landscape by presenting a series of vivid images

7

Text 1
Yeast, which consists of single-celled organisms, is perhaps best known for widespread use in cooking various pastries, yet a National Institutes of Health study has revealed a convergence of genetics, cell biology, and toxicology—all using yeast. Researchers infected one group of yeast cells with the toxin K28, then exposed these cells to a second, uninfected group. While the infected yeast cells, rather than dying off, began secreting K28 themselves, the uninfected yeast developed resistance to K28 through activation of the protein KTD1, which isolated and neutralized figments of K28.

Text 2
Though molecular chemists and cell biologists have been rigorously investigating toxin-producing yeast variants since at least the 1960s, breakthroughs in the study of these yeasts have occurred decades apart. After all, the first full examination of the genetic subtleties of K28, a toxin produced by some strains of yeast, appeared in 1990, and a scrupulous examination of how yeast counteracts K28 using the KTD1 protein appeared 30 years later.

Based on the texts, what would the author of Text 2 say about the research described in Text 1?

A) It properly explains how K28 functions in yeast while relying on a somewhat debatable understanding of how KTD1 functions.

B) It successfully overturns the current conception of yeast as a household substance with simple chemical and genetic properties.

C) It is open to criticism at present even though it suggests new possibilities for counteracting toxic substances.

D) It is extremely compelling despite some reliance on information dating from earlier decades.

CONTINUE

8

Almost across film genres, contemporary movie posters present overwhelming amounts of information about the films that they advertise: think, for example, of the dozens of characters crowded onto the posters for today's superhero movies. But for the most iconic movie posters, a principle of careful minimalism is often central. The poster for director Roman Polanski's film *Rosemary's Baby* (1968) presents only one of the film's actors, female lead Mia Farrow, and relies on mysterious touches (eerie green coloring, a small silhouette of a baby carriage) to command a viewer's fascination.

Which best states the main idea of the text?

A) Various movie posters today rely on a visually crowded format that more memorable posters, such as the poster for *Rosemary's Baby*, do not follow.

B) Stark film images like the one on the poster for *Rosemary's Baby* were created in response to a series of unappealing aesthetic choices.

C) Movie posters that feature too many characters alienate moviegoers.

D) Movies that become classics tend to be advertised with minimalistic posters.

9

Rodents such as mice and guinea pigs are common in scientific testing, yet the same cannot be said for the world's largest rodent: the 120-pound Capybara. Nonetheless, a project monitoring the therapeutic effects of hot spring bathing found a fitting test subject in these leisurely animals. Exploiting the fact that Capybaras are already water-loving and would gravitate to a "hot spring in the cold winter," researchers from Japan's Yamaguchi University investigated how hot springs facilitate skin health in Capybaras and perhaps in humans.

According to the text, why did the researchers choose to monitor Capybaras?

A) Capybaras and humans are both known to ensure skin health by adopting leisurely habits.

B) Capybaras already have a documented preference for soaking in hot water.

C) Capybaras benefit from the features of hot spring water that are known to aid humans.

D) Capybaras are slower-moving and thus easier to observe than mice and guinea pigs.

10

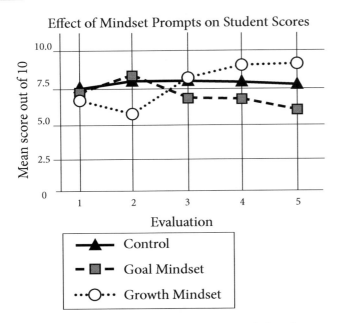

Effect of Mindset Prompts on Student Scores

Mean score out of 10

Evaluation

— ▲ — Control

- ■ - Goal Mindset

···O··· Growth Mindset

Psychologist Carol Dweck has promoted the idea of a "growth mindset"—that is, an approach that emphasizes incremental improvement over rigid benchmarks—in education. A teacher in a high school English course recently assessed Dweck's ideas with five consecutive vocabulary quiz evaluations. For the five evaluations, the teacher split her class into thirds: a group told to focus on improvement (growth mindset), a group told to get the highest possible score (goal mindset), and a group told nothing at all (control). The teacher found that <u>the growth mindset students, though possibly disoriented by their initial instructions, achieved the best results.</u>

Which choice most effectively uses data from the graph to support the underlined claim?

A) While the goal mindset students earned the best results on the second quiz, these students underperformed the growth mindset students and the control students on the remaining quizzes.

B) Despite earning relatively low scores on the second quiz, the growth mindset students outperformed both the goal mindset students and the control students on the remaining quizzes.

C) Comparison of the first quiz and the fifth quiz reveals that, between these two assessments, the growth mindset students improved by more than two points on average on the teacher's ten-point scale.

D) The growth mindset students improved most dramatically between the second and third of the five quizzes.

CONTINUE

11

Physical Properties of Saturn's Moons

Moon	Density (grams/cm³)	Orbital period (hours)	Distance from Saturn's center (km)
Rhea	1.23	108.43	527,070
Titan	1.88	382.80	1,221,870
Hyperion	0.54	510.72	1,500,880
Iapetus	1.08	1903.92	3,560,840

By some estimates, Saturn has as many as 140 moons or more, including some that have irregular oblong shapes, inconsistent densities, and erratic orbits. Saturn's largest moons—including Rhea, Titan, Hyperion, and Iapetus—exhibit behaviors and properties that correlate with their distance from Saturn, though such correlations do not exist for all such traits; in particular, _____

Which choice most effectively completes the statement with information from the table?

A) Rhea has a relatively low orbital period of 108.43 hours, which is roughly one fourth the orbital period of Titan and roughly one fifth the orbital period of Hyperion.

B) Hyperion, a moon with a density of 0.54 grams/cm³, is farther from Saturn than Rhea (1.23 grams/cm³) and closer to Saturn than Iapetus (1.08 grams/cm³).

C) Rhea has a density of 1.23 grams/cm³ and an orbital period of 108.34 hours, while Iapetus has a density of 1.08 grams/cm³ and an orbital period of 1903.92 hours.

D) Hyperion's distance from Saturn is almost 300,000 km greater than Titan's, but Hyperion's density is almost grams/cm³ 1.3 lower than Titan's.

12

On the basis of ongoing research from the consumer advocacy organization Which?, the number of oversized car models in the United Kingdom continues to grow; "oversized," here, indicates that a car is too long grille-to-trunk to fit in a standard parking space. Which? determined that the number of oversized car models by length grew from 129 models in 2019 to 161 models in 2023, yet one automotive journalist claims that a few luxury car brands are mostly responsible for the growing number of oversized cars and the problems associated with these vehicles.

Which finding about the 2023 statistics, if true, would most directly weaken the journalist's claim?

A) Of the 161 models classified as oversized by length, only 23, along with a few car models not classified as oversized by length, were also classified as oversized by width, as defined by the distance between the car's two front wheels.

B) The luxury cars in the dataset were seldom too wide to fit in standard parking spaces but, on average, exceeded the length of a typical parking space by over 6 inches.

C) More than half of the car models considered oversized by length were pickup trucks and utility vehicles marketed for their affordability, and these same models were the longest vehicles considered in the dataset.

D) A large number, but not a majority, of the car models considered in the 2019 dataset were discontinued or were subjected to significant design updates by 2023.

CONTINUE

13

Notes from Underground is an 1864 novel by Fyodor Dostoevsky. In the text, Dostoevsky's narrator and protagonist, the so-called "Underground Man" of the title, expresses high regard for his own abilities but admits that he is incapable of asserting himself: _____

Which quotation from *Notes from Underground* most effectively illustrates the claim?

A) "I have always considered myself cleverer than any of the people surrounding me, and sometimes, would you believe it, have been positively ashamed of it. At any rate, I have all my life, as it were, turned my eyes away and never could look people straight in the face."

B) "As though of design I used to get into trouble in cases when I was not to blame in any way. That was the nastiest part of it. At the same time I was genuinely touched and penitent, I used to shed tears and, of course, deceived myself."

C) "You know the direct, legitimate fruit of consciousness is inertia, that is, conscious sitting-with-the-hands-folded. I have referred to this already. I repeat, I repeat with emphasis: all 'direct' persons and men of action are active just because they are stupid and limited."

D) "Oh, if I had done nothing simply from laziness! Heavens, how I should have respected myself, then. I should have respected myself because I should at least have been capable of being lazy."

14

Native to Madagascar, the chameleons of the *Brookesia* genus stand out for their diminutive dimensions, in a paradoxical sense; these fingernail-sized creatures, which can hide behind small leaves and naturally blend in with Madagascar's plantlife, are adept at eluding fieldwork zoologists. Tinier and tinier *Brookesia* lizards have been discovered over the past several years, with the half-inch long *Brookesia micra* detected only in 2012 and the even smaller *Brookesia nana* detected in 2021. Given these trends, it is highly plausible that _____

Which choice most logically completes the text?

A) the chameleons of the *Brookesia* genus will grow larger over time as their current strategies of evasion prove increasingly unsuccessful in the wild.

B) the scientists who study the *Brookesia* genus will shift the focus of their inquiries to the mutually beneficial relationship between *Brookesia* chameleons and Madagascar's plantlife.

C) a *Brookesia* species smaller than *Brookesia nana* exists in the wild but has escaped the attention of scientists at least for the present.

D) the chameleons currently classified as *Brookesia micra* and *Brookesia nana* are in fact members of a single species despite behavioral differences.

Amish Dave and Daniel Margoliash, two biologists from the University of Chicago, have monitored the brainwaves of zebra finches to arrive at an intriguing possibility: animals might be capable of dreaming about their own signature activities. Particularly during the rapid eye movement (REM) sleep widely associated with dreaming, the finches observed by the researchers exhibited brain activity similar to the brain activity that they exhibited when singing—that is, during one of their signature activities. Still, the possibility that the finches were dreaming about singing would be called into question if _____

Which choice most logically completes the text?

A) the researchers identified a correlation between a different pattern of REM sleep brainwaves and those observed during a second signature activity of the zebra finches.

B) the zebra finches exhibited a higher intensity of brain activity during a second waking activity than they exhibited both during REM sleep and while singing.

C) the pattern of brainwaves observed for the zebra finches during REM sleep closely approximated a pattern observed when the finches were silently performing a particular activity.

D) none of the zebra finches began singing or engaged in other activities understood as the signature activities of their species immediately after emerging from REM sleep.

16

During the 1849 California Gold Rush, prospectors required cheap, sturdy, easily constructed new houses. The needs of these adventurers and wealth-seekers _____ companies around the globe to ship prefabricated, or largely pre-made, small houses to the state, including a few that reached California from as far away as France and China.

Which choice completes the text so that it conforms to the conventions of Standard English?

A) to be leading

B) leading

C) to lead

D) led

17

Arguably an unremarkable presidency otherwise, _____ This piece of legislation, which President Arthur signed into law in 1883, instituted a merit-based, not political loyalty- or party affiliation-based, protocol for appointments to US government posts.

Which choice completes the text so that it conforms to the conventions of Standard English?

A) Chester A. Arthur's administration (1881-1885) oversaw the passage of the Pendleton Civil Service Act.

B) the Pendleton Civil Service Act, as overseen by Chester A. Arthur's administration (1881-1885), was passed.

C) the passage of the Pendleton Civil Service Act was overseen by Chester A. Arthur's administration (1881-1885).

D) Chester A. Arthur oversaw the passage of the Pendleton Civil Service Act under his administration (1881-1885).

CONTINUE ▶

18

Despite the stark differences in size, geography, and population that separate of Vermont and Texas today, these states have a historical _____ each state at one point existed as an independent republic and rather quickly moved towards statehood, with Vermont (a republic starting in 1777) becoming a state in 1791 and Texas (a republic starting in 1836) itself becoming a state in 1846.

Which choice completes the text so that it conforms to the conventions of Standard English?

A) commonality:

B) commonality: with

C) commonality,

D) commonality, with

19

Widely depicted as pitting two esteemed 19th century painters against one another, the relationship between Edouard Manet and Edgar Degas was more complex than art critics who understand this relationship as a mere "rivalry" _____ . After all, the two began their careers as friends and exhibited stylistic affinities even after their relationship soured.

Which choice completes the text so that it conforms to the conventions of Standard English?

A) suggests

B) has suggested

C) suggest

D) is suggesting

20

With their furry faces and broad wings, _____ Nonetheless, just like we do, these airborne animals can form friend groups and gravitate repeatedly to specific friends in group settings, as Angelo Forli of the Yartsevs NeuroBat Lab has noticed.

Which choice completes the text so that it conforms to the conventions of Standard English?

A) there is a seeming difference between fruit bats and humans.

B) humans and fruit bats seem quite different.

C) fruit bats seem quite different from humans.

D) humans seemingly differ from fruit bats.

21

Peter Paul Rubens, a prolific Flemish Renaissance painter, did not create all elements of the paintings attributed to _____ they had reviewed a sketch of Rubens's intended composition, artists employed in Rubens's painting studio would render the image on a canvas that could stretch twenty feet wide, and Rubens himself would later provide the final embellishments.

Which choice completes the text so that it conforms to the conventions of Standard English?

A) him after

B) him:

C) him, after

D) him: after

22

The residents of Salvador de Bahia, a vibrant small city in Brazil, are notable as for their hybrid culture as for the guiding principle of their city life: axé. Translated as "energy," according to travel journalist Kate Schoenbach, _____ African, Portuguese, and South American traditions to make this city, in Schoenbach's analysis, Brazil's "capital of happiness."

Which choice completes the text so that it conforms to the conventions of Standard English?

A) axé enlivens a cultural fusion of

B) they fuse axé with a lively culture of

C) their lively culture fuses axé with

D) there is a lively cultural fusion of axé and

23

In a series of experiments designed by Alexandra Schnell and colleagues, octopuses, crabs, and other sea creatures were subjected to stimuli known to induce mild pain in mammals. Octopuses in particular exhibited sensitive responses and critical thinking: these intelligent cephalopods learned to quickly withdraw from harmful scenarios and, _____ to seek out ways to alleviate any harmful effects already incurred.

Which choice completes the text with the most logical transition?

A) before then,

B) regardless,

C) moreover,

D) for this reason,

24

Superconductors are substances that enable the flow of electricity with maximum efficiency and minimal resistance, but many of these materials (which include metal compounds such as copper oxide) only exhibit their superconducting properties at extremely low temperatures. _____ material scientists and engineers are searching for ways to create superconductors that are not so situation specific.

Which choice completes the text with the most logical transition?

A) By contrast,

B) In theory,

C) As noted,

D) Accordingly,

25

Vulnerable to environmental shocks, the world's various freshwater dolphins have been given renewed attention from conservationists since China's Yangtze River Dolphin was declared extinct. _____ different freshwater dolphin species inhabit rivers in India, Cambodia, and Brazil, and this geographic spread, combined with the diversity of the species themselves and of the human cultures that must coexist with them, can complicate conservation efforts.

Which choice completes the text with the most logical transition?

A) In other words,

B) Accordingly,

C) At present,

D) In retrospect,

CONTINUE

26

While researching a topic, a student has taken the following notes:

- The Underground City is a loosely connected network of passageways and public courts that run below street level in Montreal.

- Restaurants, clothing stores, bookstores, coffee shops, and cultural institutions are all accessible through the Underground City.

- The main building of the Montreal Museum of Contemporary Art (MAC) and the nearby Salle Wilfrid-Pelletier, a large theater, are both accessible through the Underground City.

- In 2023, the MAC closed its main building for renovations, which were estimated to be completed by 2026.

- The MAC moved its exhibitions to a temporary location accessible from the Underground City.

The student wants to make and support a generalization about the Montreal Underground City. Which choice most effectively uses relevant information from the notes to accomplish this goal?

A) The Salle Winfrid-Pelletier is an arts and culture institution that is accessible through the Montreal Underground City.

B) Several different types of venues and businesses can be accessed through the Montreal Underground City, though the Underground City itself is somewhat loosely organized.

C) After temporarily closing its main building in 2023, the Montreal Museum of Contemporary Art relocated its exhibitions to a new location that, like the Museum's previous location, could be accessed through the Underground City.

D) Montreal's Underground City is connected to both cultural institutions and various businesses, with bookstores, restaurants, and arts venues such as the Salle Wilfrid-Pelletier accessible through its routes.

27

While researching a topic, a student has taken the following notes:

- In 2024, researchers associated with the journal Lancet Planetary Health monitored the movements of venomous snake populations.

- The researchers considered 209 snake species and estimated the likely geographic range of each species by 2070.

- Many of the species native to tropical regions are projected to see contractions in range due to habitat loss.

- Species that could thrive in geographically diverse regions are projected to see expansions of range if global temperatures increase.

- Two viper species, the European horned viper and the African gaboon viper, could see their ranges double by 2070 due to temperature increases.

The student wants to explain why the geographic ranges for some snake species could change by 2070. Which choice most effectively uses relevant information from the notes to accomplish this goal?

A) It is possible that the African gaboon viper and the European horned viper will experience considerable increases in geographic range by 2070.

B) By 2070, global temperature increases might lead to considerable increases in the geographic range of two viper populations.

C) Of the 209 snake species considered in a 2024 Lancet Planetary Health study, the European horned viper could see its geographic range increase considerably by 2070.

D) By 2070, several snake species could see diminished geographic ranges as a result of temperature increases.

STOP
If you finish these exercises, you may check your work on this section only.
Do not turn to any other section in the book.

No Test Content on This Page

Test 4 Modules
— Pages 112-134 —

Pages 112-122					
Module 1: Baseline					
1	D	10	A	19	D
2	A	11	C	20	D
3	D	12	B	21	C
4	B	13	A	22	D
5	B	14	B	23	B
6	A	15	A	24	D
7	A	16	D	25	D
8	B	17	B	26	C
9	A	18	C	27	B

Pages 124-134					
Module 2: Hard					
1	A	10	B	19	C
2	B	11	B	20	C
3	C	12	C	21	D
4	A	13	A	22	A
5	A	14	C	23	C
6	D	15	C	24	D
7	D	16	D	25	C
8	A	17	A	26	D
9	B	18	A	27	B

Want to learn more?
Visit prepvantagetutoring.com for Digital SAT updates and for the research sources for our passages

Module 1: Baseline
— Pages 112-122 —

Question 1: Choice D
Word in Context
Difficulty - **Medium** | Topic - **Humanities**

Choice D is the best answer because the passage discusses the activity of drawing by people who are not pursuing artistic careers or technical mastery. Thus, the underlined phrase should indicate the doing of an action without implying a greater goal or achievement.

Choice A is incorrect because "triumphing in" indicates the achievement of technical mastery, whereas the passage is discussing art as a casual activity. Choice B is incorrect because "venturing towards" indicates a goal-oriented pursuit, whereas the passage is discussing art as a casual activity. Choice C is incorrect because "turning against" indicates the refusal to sketch, whereas the passage is discussing people who do draw.

Question 2: Choice A
Word in Context
Difficulty - **Easy** | Topic - **History**

Choice A is the best answer because the second sentence makes it clear that, "from 1801 to 1961, DC residents did not" have the right to vote for president. Thus, the underlined word must mean "had," as the first sentence is saying that Washington DC residents have not always had the right to vote for their president. In this context, "possessed" means "had," and it appropriately conveys that, in the past, Washington DC residents could not vote in presidential elections.

Choice B is incorrect because, though many people take for granted the right to vote, "appreciated" would wrongly indicate that Washington DC residents have always had the right to vote in presidential elections but simply did not value it. Choice C is incorrect because, though people can misunderstand how to vote, "understood" would wrongly indicate that Washington DC residents have always had the right to vote in presidential elections but simply did not comprehend how to vote. Choice D is incorrect because, though the passage's tone is academic, "studied" would wrongly put the focus on Washington DC residents' education rather than their legal rights.

Question 3: Choice D
Word in Context
Difficulty - **Medium** | Topic - **Social Studies**

Choice D is the best answer because the underlined word must mean "obvious" given that the "obvious liability to snow-dependent sports" is being contrasted with the "less [obvious] but still considerable liability to sports like golf." "Overt" satisfies this requirement and appropriately indicates that the risk to sports like golf is less immediately apparent than the risk to snow-dependent sports.

Choice A is incorrect because, though "nuanced" contrasts with "obvious," "less" already indicates the contrast, so the underlined word must mean "obvious" as opposed to the opposite of "obvious." Choice B is incorrect because a risk cannot be "satisfying." Choice C is incorrect because, though "less meaningful" would indicate a contrast in scale, it would mean that the "liability to sports like golf" was less impactful, which contradicts the point of the passage.

Question 4: Choice B
Word in Context
Difficulty - **Hard** | Topic - **Literature**

Choice B is the best answer because "grandeur and sublimity" are emotionally affecting traits. Moreover, "something no doubt at that moment passed from it into my soul," further emphasizes the fact that the landscape deeply affects the narrator.

Choice A is incorrect because, while the landscape may be beautiful, the passage's emphasis is on how the landscape struck the narrator emotionally, not on its physical appearance. Choice C is incorrect because, though the landscape affected the narrator's thoughts, the narrator does not mention being tempted to do something or to go somewhere. Choice D is incorrect because, though the second sentence taken out of context might sound ominous, the third sentence makes it clear that the effect is purely positive.

Question 5: Choice B
Text Structure and Purpose
Difficulty - **Medium** | Topic - **Literature**

Choice B is the best answer because the sentence provides a specific example of how Anna enforces order and discipline amongst her siblings, by comparing the children to soldiers engaging in a military drill.

Choice A is incorrect because the sentence provides an example as supporting evidence of a parenting style, not a summary of broad principles. Choice C is incorrect because the passage does not necessarily imply that the children are unhappy with the way they are raised. Choice D is incorrect because the sentence shows how Anna successfully achieves her goals of disciplining the younger children, and does not imply that her standards are unrealistic.

Question 6: Choice A
Text Structure and Purpose
Difficulty - **Medium** | Topic - **Social Studies**

Choice A is the best answer because it is the first time that the 2021 "bottom-up" study is mentioned. Moreover, it sets up the sentence after it, which describes the "bottom-up" research project's hypothesis.

Choice B is incorrect because, though it sets up a sentence that shows why the "bottom-up" theory is different from the "top-down" theory, the underlined text itself does not state the core principles of either theory. Choice C is incorrect because, though Rossman and Fisher do find the "bottom-up" model more realistic than the "top-down" model, the underlined text does not say why. Choice D is incorrect because, though Rossman and Fisher do not find the "top-down" argument convincing, the underlined text does not suggest anything about what most social scientists think.

Question 7: Choice A
Text Structure and Purpose
Difficulty - **Medium** | Topic - **Literature**

Choice A is the best answer because the underlined sentence is positive ("Douglas was a remarkable man") and because the "in person" part of it leads into the physical description of Douglas's person in the next sentence.

Choice B is incorrect because, though one might assume negative things about a man who moved into a decaying home, the passage does not present an assessment of John Douglas earlier in the passage. Choice C is incorrect because, though Douglas's wife does not look just like him, the text does not describe his wife. Choice D is incorrect because, though the underlined sentence describes features of John Douglas, it does not describe features of the setting.

Question 8: Choice B
Central Ideas and Details
Difficulty - **Medium** | Topic - **Literature**

Choice B is the best answer because the passage specifies that the "bricks" are sandwiches composed of bread and butter, and that there is "hardly a morsel of butter." Choose B to reflect that Catherine struggles to make sandwiches due to having only a limited amount of butter.

Choice A is incorrect because the passage mentions a somewhat limited amount of bread, but does not explicitly specify that the family is lacking the funds to buy more. Choice C is incorrect because the passage focuses on a description of Catherine assembling the sandwiches, and does not include any mention of concerns about whether or not the family will enjoy the sandwiches. Choice D is incorrect because the passage only describes Catherine's actions, not her emotions or internal state.

Question 9: Choice A
Central Ideas and Details
Difficulty - **Medium** | Topic - **Social Studies**

Choice A is the best answer because "doubts arose about whether Eva could effectively replicate human emotions," yet there is "a possible future for expressive robots in medicine." Thus, the Eva project raised skepticism about the robot's abilities while pointing to future applications in medical settings.

Choice B is incorrect because, though doubts about Eva arose, Chen did not change her strategies. Choice C is incorrect because, though the idea of medical robots has become more mainstream, doubts do not constitute hostility. Choice D is incorrect because, though the purpose of the Eva project is to replicate human emotions, that purpose has not changed.

Question 10: Choice A
Quantitative Command of Evidence
Difficulty - **Medium** | Topic - **Social Studies**

Choice A is the best answer because it indicates that Indonesia's population decreased slightly in rural areas and increased significantly in urban areas. This evidence effectively reflects valid information from the graph in "the recent past" and supports the claim that urban population growth has been significant; the "twofold" increase from roughly 75 million to roughly 150 million in urban population has more than offset a slight rural population decrease.

Choice B is incorrect because it does not clearly indicate that urban population growth has "accounted for almost all of the total population growth" in Indonesia; instead, this choice notes that urban population increased over one interval without specifying a comparison with rural population. Choice C is incorrect because it notes differences in urban and rural populations without specifying that urban population growth has been higher. Choice D is incorrect because it notes an increase in urban population without specifying rural population trends; comparison of this sort is needed to specify that urban population growth has "accounted for almost all of the total population growth" in recent years.

Question 11: Choice C
Textual Command of Evidence
Difficulty - **Medium** | Topic - **Social Studies**

Choice C is the best answer because Veer notes that the "conundrum" (or problem) of simultaneous overtiredness and deficient sleep is "age-dependent," with professionally active people in their 30s and 40s at risk. This choice notes that people "in their 30s" would be likely to remain active by analyzing professional events instead of falling asleep, and this evidence properly fits an aspect of Veer's idea.

Choice A is incorrect because it indicates results involving sleeplessness and overtiredness "Across age groups" instead of targeting the age groups (30s and 40s) central to Veer's claim. Choice B is incorrect because it indicates that the trend noted by Veer is valid for one group that Veer cites (30s) but could diminish at a point relevant to the other age group (40s); in fact, this evidence that overtiredness diminishes could contradict Veer's claim about severe overtiredness. Choice D is incorrect because it notes the topics of sleep and well-being without specifying an age group in order to fit Veer's exact claim.

Question 12: Choice B
Textual Command of Evidence
Difficulty - **Medium** | Topic - **Literature**

Choice B is the best answer because the claim that "Masha is in a troubled state of mind" is supported by the fact that her parents' concerns over her "indisposition . . . cut her to the heart." Moreover, the claim that "other characters notice Masha's distress" is supported by "Both her father and her mother remarked on her indisposition" and the fact that they kept asking, "What is the matter with you, Masha—are you ill?"

Choice A is incorrect because, though Masha "did not sleep all night," Choice A does not say anything about how others perceived her distress. Choice C is incorrect because, though

it describes Masha's distress and mentions her family, it does not say whether her family noticed her distress. Choice D is incorrect because, though it presents a tense situation, it does not say whether anyone noticed Masha's state of mind.

Question 13: Choice A
Inferences
Difficulty - **Medium** | Topic - **Social Studies**

Choice A is the best answer because the passage indicates that "consumers worldwide crave shoes that are at once comfortable and fashionable" even while describing the uncertainties surrounding the definition of "comfort." The research of Menz and Bonanno highlights this uncertainty, yet the text indicates that comfort is still seen as desirable and suggests that such an "amorphous" definition of comfort does not weaken consumer preferences.

Choice B is incorrect because the text mentions "comfortable and fashionable" footwear without providing an indication of whether fashion or comfort is preferred. The emphasis of the analysis is on comfort, but a more extensive comparison of fashion and comfort would be needed to support this choice. Choice C is incorrect because the researchers highlight inconsistencies and mostly note that such inconsistencies are ongoing, not resolved. Choice D is incorrect because the researchers do not in fact define comfort themselves; they note that other studies have failed to provide definitions, yet it is not clear that Menz and Bonanno have developed an effective definition of their own.

Question 14: Choice B
Inferences
Difficulty - **Medium** | Topic - **Humanities**

Choice B is the best answer because, if the films' depictions of jury duty "are indeed symptomatic of a real-life shift in perceptions, today's prospective jurors would be expected to" share the view presented in Jury Duty (2023), which is that "jury service as an ordeal to be avoided."

Choice A is incorrect because, though it is true that today's jurors would view jury duty as personally burdensome, they would not see it as being socially worthwhile. Choice C is incorrect because, though "an expansive view of human nature" is mentioned in the passage, that view is from the 1954 film, not the 2023 film. Choice D is incorrect because, though views of jury service have changed over the years, the text does not attribute that shift to being called to serve on a jury.

Question 15: Choice A
Boundaries
Difficulty - **Medium** | Topic - **Humanities**

Choice A is the best answer because the "quirky question" ("exactly how . . . medium?") ends with a question mark. Moreover, the inverted subject-verb order (the verb "are" precedes the subject "old blue jeans") is correct for a question, and the nonessential phrase ("as an artistic medium") is separated from the independent clause ("exactly how . . . jeans") by a comma. The independent clause and the nonessential phrase should be joined in this manner, since other options produce changes in meaning and incorrect punctuation.

Choice B is incorrect because the comma placement causes the question not to have an independent clause. Choice C is incorrect because the comma placement causes the question not to have an independent clause, and a question must end with a question mark. Choice D is incorrect because the sentence must end with a question mark since a question is being asked. All of these false answers result in errors in the coordination of phrases and independent clauses.

Question 16: Choice D
Form, Structure, and Sense
Difficulty - **Hard** | Topic - **Science**

Choice D is the best answer because the singular, impersonal pronoun "it" refers to the singular antecedent "NASA," which is a space program. Moreover, the singular verb "invites" is the correct verb form for the singular subject "it."

Choice A is incorrect because it uses a plural pronoun ("some") for a singular subject ("NASA"). Choice B is incorrect because it uses a personal pronoun ("you") for a subject ("NASA") that is not a person. Choice C is incorrect because it uses a plural pronoun ("they") for a singular subject ("NASA").

Question 17: Choice B
Boundaries
Difficulty - **Easy** | Topic - **Social Studies**

Choice B is the best answer because it uses a comma and a coordinating conjunction ("but") to join two independent clauses ("Typically . . . hundred people" and "these languages . . . endangered"). These independent clauses should be joined in this manner, since other options produce comma splices and run-on sentences.

Choice A is incorrect because two independent clauses joined with a coordinating conjunction also need a comma between them. Choice C is incorrect because the two independent

clauses are joined with only a comma. Choice D is incorrect because two independent clauses are joined without any separation. All of these false answers result in errors in the coordination of independent clauses.

Question 18: Choice C
Boundaries
Difficulty - **Easy** | Topic - **History**

Choice C is the best answer because "the emperor known as Taizu" is part of a single independent clause and thus should not be broken with punctuation. This choice properly avoids setting off content that is in fact essential and does not break any connected phrases with single units of punctuation.

Choice A is incorrect because it breaks the integrated phrase "emperor known" and wrongly uses a single dash to break the subject and verb combination "the emperor . . . founded." Choice B is incorrect because it breaks the connected phrase "known as Taizu" and wrongly places a single dash between subject and verb. Choice D is incorrect because it treats the phrase "as Taizu" as non-essential and would create the non-grammatical construction "the emperor known [. . .] founded" when the phrase is disregarded.

Question 19: Choice D
Form, Structure, and Sense
Difficulty - **Medium** | Topic - **Science**

Choice D is the best answer because the word that follows "Intrigued" should logically indicate a person who was intrigued in order to avoid a modifier error. In context, Spivak herself was interested in bees and would thus be "Intrigued" by a book on these insects.

Choice A is incorrect because it describes a "beginning" rather than a person as "Intrigued" and thus introduces a modifier error. The possessive "Spivak's" itself describes the noun "beginning" and must be factored out. Choice B is incorrect because it describes "beekeeping" as itself "Intrigued," yet a person should be intrigued by a pursuit such as beekeeping instead. Choice C is incorrect because it describes "work" as "Intrigued" rather than directly describing the person performing the work as "Intrigued." All of these choices result in modifier errors.

Question 20: Choice D
Boundaries
Difficulty - **Hard** | Topic - **Science**

Choice D is the best answer because the independent clause immediately before the colon indicates two "defining features" of a specific nebula, while the content that appears after the colon directly lists the two features. This use of two explanatory items, the "expanses" and "green hue," properly follows a standard sentence structure for explanatory content with a colon.

Choice A is incorrect because it places a prepositional phrase beginning with "of" directly after a colon, but a colon should only be followed by discrete listed items or with an independent clause. Choice B is incorrect because a semicolon should only introduce an independent clause, not a set of discrete items that specify "features" mentioned earlier. Choice C is incorrect because the placement of the colon after the word "of" disrupts the construction of the full independent clause that begins the sentence, since the "of" that ends the independent clause does not clearly connect to a noun that is part of the same clause.

Question 21: Choice C
Transitions
Difficulty - **Easy** | Topic - **Science**

Choice C is the best answer because "as a result" indicates that the Montreal Protocol was put in place because of the Ozone Hole and concerns that pollution "would further diminish the ozone layer." This transition properly signals a cause and effect relationship.

Choice A is incorrect because "however" introduces an opposing relationship and wrongly indicates that the Montreal Protocol was put in place despite concerns that pollution "would further diminish the ozone layer." Choice B is incorrect because "before then" introduces a reverse temporal relationship and wrongly indicates that the Montreal Protocol was put in place before the world was concerned about pollution. Choice D is incorrect because "in summary" introduces a reiteration relationship and wrongly indicates that the creation of the Montreal Protocol is the same thing as concerns about pollution.

Question 22: Choice D
Transitions
Difficulty - **Medium** | Topic - **History**

Choice D is the best answer because "likewise" indicates that the difficulty that speakers of English face when learning Japanese is akin to the difficulty that speakers of Japanese face when learning English. This transition properly signals a similar relationship.

Choice A is incorrect because "in other words" introduces a reiteration relationship and wrongly indicates that the difficulty that speakers of Japanese face when learning English is the same thing as the difficulty that speakers of English face when learning Japanese. Choice B is incorrect because "specifically" introduces a support relationship and wrongly indicates that the difficulty that speakers of Japanese

face when learning English is an example of the difficulty that speakers of English face when learning Japanese. Choice C is incorrect because "nonetheless" introduces an opposing relationship and wrongly indicates that the difficulty that speakers of Japanese face when learning English is an exception to the difficulty that speakers of English face when learning Japanese.

Question 23: Choice B
Transitions
Difficulty - **Medium** | Topic - **Social Studies**

Choice B is the best answer because "in reality" indicates that "changing to a new and preferable set of beliefs . . . is not natural." Rather, "it 'resembles marathoning or playing an instrument' and requires purposeful focus." This transition properly signals an opposing relationship.

Choice A is incorrect because "later" introduces a temporal relationship and wrongly indicates that changing one's mind becomes a purposeful act after it is an effortless, natural act. Choice C is incorrect because "there" introduces a subset relationship and wrongly indicates that changing one's mind is a purposeful act only in a certain location or set of circumstances. Choice D is incorrect because "secondly" introduces an extension relationship and wrongly indicates that the mental change being purposeful and labor-intensive is consistent with it being effortless and natural.

Question 24: Choice D
Transitions
Difficulty - **Medium** | Topic - **Science**

Choice D is the best answer because "finally" signals that Jue "headed NASA's Space Station Program Office" after she "ran calculations for manned spaceflight missions in the 1970s and 1980s." This transition properly signals a temporal relationship.

Choice A is incorrect because "however" introduces an opposing relationship, which wrongly indicates that Jue "headed NASA's Space Station Program Office" despite the fact that she "ran calculations for manned spaceflight missions in the 1970s and 1980s." Choice B is incorrect because "as noted" introduces a reiteration relationship, which wrongly indicates that Jue's position as the head of NASA's Space Station Program Office was the same as the position in which she "ran calculations for manned spaceflight missions in the 1970s and 1980s." Choice C is incorrect because "in summary" introduces an overall reiteration relationship, which wrongly indicates that Jue's running NASA's Space Station Program Office was the same as her being hired and her running "calculations for manned spaceflight missions in the 1970s and 1980s."

Question 25: Choice D
Rhetorical Synthesis
Difficulty - **Medium** | Topic - **Humanities**

Choice D is the best answer because it "compare[s] Martin's ideas to the ideas of the painting student" by noting that both of them "valued close perception as part of the artistic process." This information is consistent with the student's second and fourth notes.

Choice A is incorrect because it is only about Martin's principles, not her student's principles, so it fails to "compare" them. Likewise, Choice B is incorrect because it is only about Martin's work, not her student's work, so it fails to "compare" them. Choice C is incorrect because, while it is about both Martin and her student, it is not about "Martin's ideas" or "the ideas of the painting student."

Question 26: Choice C
Rhetorical Synthesis
Difficulty - **Medium** | Topic - **Science**

Choice C is the best answer because it explains that the research is about "investigating the olfactory cilia" and that the "[r]esearchers . . . have arrived at a treatment method that could restore the sense of smell in human subjects." These statements fulfill the student's goal of "explain[ing] the gene therapy study and its outcomes." Choice C is supported by the student's fifth and sixth notes.

Choice A is incorrect because it is about the study's subject, not its "outcomes." Choice B is incorrect because it is not about "the gene therapy study [or] its outcomes." Choice D is incorrect because it merely introduces gene therapy without stating the "outcomes" of the gene therapy study.

Question 27: Choice B
Rhetorical Synthesis
Difficulty - **Hard** | Topic - **Social Studies**

Choice B is the best answer because it explains what misophonia is, and it states both the title and the topic of Gregory's book. This choice is consistent with the student's goal of "introduc[ing] Gregory's book to an audience unfamiliar with misophonia."

Choice A is incorrect because, though it explains what misophonia is and states the topic of Gregory's research, it does not mention the book by name. Choice C is incorrect because, though it mentions the book by name, it does not explain what misophonia is for an audience unfamiliar with that topic. Choice D is incorrect because, though it explains what misophonia is, it does not mention Gregory's book.

Module 2: Hard
— Pages 124-134 —

Question 1: Choice A
Word in Context
Difficulty - **Medium** | Topic - **Humanities**

Choice A is the best answer because "it must be. . . carved marble" is a list of requirements for art to be considered folk art, and that list is referred to as "these standards." Thus, the underlined word must mean "requirements" or "standards." "Criteria" appropriately conveys that the list in the first sentence is a set of traits that art must have in order to be considered folk art.

Choice B is incorrect because, while the standards are "open to dispute," art itself cannot argue. Choice C is incorrect because, though the requirements might be seen as positive, they are not necessarily beneficial. Choice D is incorrect because, though traits are parts of the artwork, they are not physical subunits of the art.

Question 2: Choice B
Word in Context
Difficulty - **Hard** | Topic - **Social Studies**

Choice B is the best answer because the underlined word must align with an "acceptance of unpleasant situations" and must contrast with "positive psychology." Thus, the underlined word must have a negative meaning. "Inimical to" appropriately conveys that "learned helplessness" is negative.

Choice A is incorrect because, though people can be in tune with their feelings, they are not synchronized with them. Choice C is incorrect because, though people often try to block themselves from experiencing negative emotions, people cannot outlaw or prevent emotions. Choice D is incorrect because, though people often try to avoid negative emotions, people cannot be cast out or treated as pariahs by their own emotions.

Question 3: Choice C
Word in Context
Difficulty - **Hard** | Topic - **Humanities**

Choice C is the best answer because the underlined word is contrasted with "readily-recognized," so it must mean not well-known. Moreover, some of the characters are people "whom few people beyond scholars of American history would know of offhand." "Esoteric" appropriately conveys that the "knowledge of the American Revolution" is more obscure that the "readily-recognized facts" are.

Choice A is incorrect because, though people's understanding of history can change over time, information is not capricious. Choice B is incorrect because, though Lin Manuel Miranda is known for being friendly and outgoing, knowledge cannot be genial. Choice D is incorrect because, though acquiring knowledge is a worthwhile endeavor, "worthwhile" does not provide a contrast with "readily-recognized."

Question 4: Choice A
Word in Context
Difficulty - **Hard** | Topic - **Science**

Choice A is the best answer because, contrary to the usual concept of friction as purely physical, the description of friction in the 2013 paper describes it as involving chemical bonds. "Entails" appropriately conveys that friction involves chemical bonds.

Choice B is incorrect because, though friction occurs on surfaces, friction itself does not isolate anything. Choice C is incorrect because, though the paper discusses a set of bonds, friction does not gather the bonds together. Choice D is incorrect because, though the paper proposes a new concept of friction, it is not addressing or paying for a harmful act.

Question 5: Choice A
Text Structure and Purpose
Difficulty - **Hard** | Topic - **Literature**

Choice A is the best answer because "Wilson felt at once" shows the suddenness of Wilson's impressions, and "things that have lived long together without obtrusions of ugliness or change" shows that the items in Alexander's study had been in their current arrangement for a long time.

Choice B is incorrect because, though Wilson was surprised by Alexander's study, he was not confused about Alexander's personality. Moreover, the underlined text is about the appearance of the study, not Alexander's sense of composure. Choice C is incorrect because, though it relates to the prior sentence, it supports it rather than qualifying it. Moreover, it does not suggest that Wilson desires to emulate Alexander.

Choice D is incorrect because, though it specifies a feature of Alexander's study that Wilson likes, it does not offer a generality about Alexander's profession.

Question 6: Choice D
Text Structure and Purpose
Difficulty - **Hard** | Topic - **Literature**

Choice D is the best answer because the text places the tree in an urban setting (a "narrow street" in a "stony, arid town"), away from the forest. In the forest, the tree would have lived among a "brotherhood with far-lock'd woods" with "kindred" trees and other plants.

Choice A is incorrect because, though monotony is a hallmark of the urban tree's existence, the text does not juxtapose the tree's past and present states (rather, it juxtaposes the urban setting with a natural setting). Choice B is incorrect because, while the text describes the fulfillment associated with nature and contrasts that with the urban setting, it does not describe nature by depicting the activities in a dreary and unappealing town. Choice C is incorrect because, while the text describes the tree's unpleasant situation in a man-made environment, it does not discuss how human activity has changed a natural setting.

Question 7: Choice D
Cross-Text Connections
Difficulty - **Hard** | Topic - **Science**

Choice D is the best answer because Text 2 describes relatively recent research on K28 and KTD1 in yeast as a "scrupulous examination." Text 1 describes research into exactly the topic mentioned in Text 2. Though Text 2 does note that there were sometimes decades separating different investigations of toxins in yeast, this text primarily notes that this research builds towards recent discoveries and does not adopt a negative tone towards the research itself.

Choice A is incorrect because Text 2 approvingly mentions research involving how "yeast counteracts K28 using the KTD1 protein." The author of this text would approve of both the research into K28 and the research into KTD1 as mentioned in Text 1 and would not single out one of these research projects as deficient. Choice B is incorrect because only Text 1 discusses the "widespread" and household use of yeast; Text 2 does not address this issue directly. Choice C is incorrect because Text 2 does not indicate any specific criticisms of research into yeast, even though the time gaps noted in Text 2 may seem unusual. Instead, Text 2 notes "breakthroughs" that were simply spaced somewhat far apart in time.

Question 8: Choice A
Central Ideas and Details
Difficulty - **Hard** | Topic - **Humanities**

Choice A is the best answer because the text contrasts movie now-popular posters that "present overwhelming amounts of information" with "iconic movie posters" in a manner that favors the second type of poster. This analysis in favor of more "minimalistic" posters relies on the poster for Rosemary's Baby as a core example that deviates sharply from the practices of overcrowding cited at the beginning of the text.

Choice B is incorrect because the text does not draw a causal connection between movie poster choices. Instead, the text indicates that minimalistic posters such as the poster for Rosemary's Baby are preferable to crowded posters without indicating that the poster for Rosemary's Baby represents a reaction to other poster types. Choice C is incorrect because it neglects the text's discussion of more appealing "minimalistic" posters and criticizes the overcrowded posters on a faulty basis. These overcrowded posters are unappealing to the writer of the text but do not, on the basis of the evidence, alienate other moviegoers as well. Choice D is incorrect because it does not discuss the crowded posters and features a faulty assumption about Rosemary's Baby. The writer approves of the poster for Rosemary's Baby but does not in fact indicate whether the film itself is a classic.

Question 9: Choice B
Central Ideas and Details
Difficulty - **Hard** | Topic - **Science**

Choice B is the best answer because the passage requires an answer referring to capybaras' natural tendency to enjoy wading in hot springs. Choose B, since it connects this preference to a decision to use capybaras as the subject of a research study on the benefits of hot springs.

Choice A is incorrect because the passage states that capybaras enjoy soaking in hot springs, but does NOT stipulate that they intentionally do so to reap skincare benefits. Choice B is incorrect because the passage implies that the study of capybaras was used to determine if hot springs might aid humans, not that human benefits are already known and understood. Choice D is incorrect because the passage describes capybaras as the choice of research subject because they readily gravitate to hot springs, not because they are larger and slower.

Question 10: Choice B
Quantitative Command of Evidence
Difficulty - **Medium** | Topic - **Social Studies**

Choice B is the best answer because it shows that "the growth mindset students . . . achieved the best results" by the end of the study. Moreover, it concedes that the growth mindset students earned relatively low scores on the second quiz, which aligns with the claim that they were "possibly disoriented by their initial instructions."

Choice A is incorrect because, though it shows that the growth mindset students outperformed the goal mindset students after the second quiz, it does not say that the growth mindset students outperformed the control students too. Choice C is incorrect because, though it says that the growth mindset students improved by more than two points, it does not show that they "achieved the best results." Choice D is incorrect because, though it is about the growth mindset students' improvement, it does not show that the growth mindset students outperformed the other groups.

Question 11: Choice B
Quantitative Command of Evidence
Difficulty - **Hard** | Topic - **Science**

Choice B is the best answer because the text must be completed with an indication that some of the properties cited in the table are not correlated. Hyperion has a density that is lower than that of a moon closer to Saturn and a moon farther from Saturn; logically, there is not a direct correlation (positive or negative trend) between moon density and distance from Saturn.

Choice A is incorrect because the evidence presented simply involves comparisons of the orbital periods of three moons. To prove or disprove a correlation, it would be necessary to compare two different types of evidence (such as density and orbital period) to determine whether these evidence types are correlated. Choice C is incorrect because it presents the statistics for two moons without indicating whether there is a correlation. It is possible that higher density is correlated with a lower orbital period based on this evidence, since a third moon is not mentioned to support or undermine the correlation. Choice D is incorrect because this evidence offers comparisons for a few different properties without clearly indicating whether a correlation is being established. It is possible based on this evidence that greater distance in fact correlates with lower density since a third moon is not mentioned.

Question 12: Choice C
Textual Command of Evidence
Difficulty - **Hard** | Topic - **Social Studies**

Choice C is the best answer because the journalist's claim that "a few luxury car brands" can be connected to the problems with oversized cars would be weakened by information on problematic oversized cars from non-luxury brands. If "More than half" of the problematic oversized vehicles were "marketed for affordability," then cars other than the luxury cars cited by the journalist would be most problematic.

Choice A is incorrect because it introduces a new criterion (oversized by width) that does not clearly relate to luxury and non-luxury cars. It is possible that the luxury cars are still problematic by length even if their widths vary. Choice B is incorrect because it would in fact support the journalist's claim that luxury cars are problematic in terms of parking and management. Choice D is incorrect because it indicates that certain car models were discontinued without clearly indicating whether these models were luxury cars. This choice does not directly indicate which cars, if any, were in fact most problematic.

Question 13: Choice A
Textual Command of Evidence
Difficulty - **Hard** | Topic - **Literature**

Choice A is the best answer because "I have always considered myself cleverer than any of the people surrounding me" supports the claim that the "Underground Man . . . expresses high regard for his own abilities," and the statement that he "never could look people straight in the face" supports the claim that that he "admits that he is incapable of asserting himself."

Choice B is incorrect because, though it paints the Underground Man as passive, it does not suggest that he expresses high regard for his own abilities. Choice C is incorrect because, though it denigrates "direct" people, it does not suggest that the narrator expresses high regard for his own abilities. Choice D is incorrect because, though it refers to respecting oneself, it does not suggest that the narrator expresses high regard for his own abilities or that he has trouble asserting himself.

Question 14: Choice C
Inferences
Difficulty - **Hard** | Topic - **Science**

Choice C is the best answer because the claim that "tinier and tinier Brookesia lizards have been discovered" is supported by the examples of the small Brookesia micra and the smaller Brookesia nana. The logical extension of this would be an

even smaller Brookesia. Moreover, the end of choice C is consistent with the statement that Brookesia are "adept at eluding fieldwork zoologists."

Choice A is incorrect because, while it is about size, growing larger over time would reverse the claim that "tinier and tinier Brookesia lizards have been discovered." Choice B is incorrect because, though the passage mentions Brookesia chameleons and Madagascar's plantlife, the claim is not about plants. Choice D is incorrect because, though the text discusses Brookesia micra and Brookesia nana, nothing in the passage suggests that they are a single species.

Question 15: Choice C
Inferences
Difficulty - **Hard** | Topic - **Science**

Choice C is the best answer because the presumption of dreaming about singing rests on the similarities between the brainwave pattern observed during REM sleep and the brainwave pattern exhibited when singing. Thus, if that brainwave pattern observed during REM sleep also matched that of silent activities, it would not solely be associated with singing.

Choice A is incorrect because, though it is about waking and sleeping brainwave patterns, a correlation between a different pattern of REM sleep brainwaves and those observed during a second signature activity of the zebra finches would strengthen rather than weaken the claim that REM brainwave patterns are associated with specific signature activities. Choice B is incorrect because, though it points out a difference in sleeping versus waking brainwaves, it does not provide a difference in sleeping versus waking brainwaves for singing. Choice D is incorrect because, though it may seem to distance dreaming about singing from actually singing, the biologists' claim does not rest on temporal closeness between dreaming about singing and actually singing.

Question 16: Choice D
Form, Structure, and Sense
Difficulty - **Easy** | Topic - **History**

Choice D is the best answer because the sentence requires the finite verb form "led" to create an independent clause. The verb form should take the subject "needs." The other subject-finite verb pair in the sentence is located in a dependent clause, so it could not be the main subject-verb pair of the sentence.

Choice A is incorrect because the nonfinite verb form "to be leading" is the infinitive form, which does not create an independent clause. Choice B is incorrect because the nonfinite verb form "leading" is the present participle, which leaves the sentence without an independent clause. Choice C is incorrect because the nonfinite verb form "to lead" is the infinitive form, which does not create an independent clause.

Question 17: Choice A
Form, Structure, and Sense
Difficulty - **Hard** | Topic - **History**

Choice A is the best answer because the dependent clause "Arguably . . . otherwise" should describe a "presidency" as noted. The phrasing "Chester A. Arthur's administration" would properly present a "presidency" after the modifier that begins the sentence.

Choice B is incorrect because a single "Act" or a single piece of legislation cannot logically be described as a "presidency." Choice C is incorrect because "the passage" of a single piece of legislation cannot logically be described as a presidency; instead, a presidency might involve a single action of this sort along with other actions Choice D is incorrect because, though Arthur was a president, Arthur himself should not be described as a "presidency" or a group administration. All of these false answers introduce modifier errors.

Question 18: Choice A
Boundaries
Difficulty - **Hard** | Topic - **History**

Choice A is the best answer because a colon can be followed by an independent clause construction that explains content introduced previously. Here, the "historical commonality" mentioned earlier is explained by the independent clause "each state . . . statehood" in a further description of conditions in Vermont and Texas.

Choice B is incorrect because the word "with" creates a dependent clause, yet a colon should normally be followed by an independent clause, an item, or a list of items. Choice C is incorrect because the comma creates a comma splice that wrongly coordinates the independent clauses "these states . . . commonality" and "each state . . . statehood." Choice D is incorrect because it creates a dependent clause that is not grammatically correct in terms of verb form, since "with each state existed" wrongly introduces a finite verb into a prepositional phrase that, at best, should be written as "with each state existing."

Question 19: Choice C
Form, Structure, and Sense
Difficulty - **Hard** | Topic - **Humanities**

Choice C is the best answer because the plural verb "suggest" agrees with the plural subject "art critics." The subject may be hard to locate due to the intervening clause ("who understand . . . 'rivalry'").

Choice A is incorrect because the singular verb "suggests" does not agree with the plural subject. Choice B is incorrect because the singular verb "has suggested" does not agree with the plural subject. Choice D is incorrect because the singular verb "is suggesting" does not agree with the plural subject.

Question 20: Choice C
Form, Structure, and Sense
Difficulty - **Medium** | Topic - **Science**

Choice C is the best answer because the modifier ("with their . . . broad wings") must modify the noun immediately after it. That phrase is describing fruit bats, so "fruit bats" must be the beginning of the correct answer.

Choice A is incorrect because it would make the modifier modify "difference," which is not what has furry faces and broad wings. Choice B is incorrect because it would make the modifier modify "humans," which do not have furry faces and broad wings. Choice D is incorrect because it would make the modifier modify "humans" rather than "fruit bats."

Question 21: Choice D
Boundaries
Difficulty - **Hard** | Topic - **Humanities**

Choice D is the best answer because the content that follows the colon properly uses the independent clause "artists . . . wide" to further explain a situation mentioned earlier, namely the manner in which Rubens planned out and executed "the paintings attributed to him." In the content after the colon, other elements are properly coordinated as dependent clauses ("after . . . composition") or as further independent clauses ("Rubens . . . embellishments") connected to the independent clause "artists . . . wide."

Choice A is incorrect because the absence of punctuation before the word "after" creates a single long and awkward independent clause in the beginning of the sentence. This independent clause is then followed by a comma and a second independent clause, and a comma splice results. Choice B is incorrect because the absence of the word "after" causes "they . . . composition" to function as an independent clause and thus introduces a comma splice. Choice C is incorrect because the comma positions "after . . . composition" as a dependent clause, and a comma splice results when this dependent content is factored out of the sentence.

Question 22: Choice A
Form, Structure, and Sense
Difficulty - **Hard** | Topic - **Social Studies**

Choice A is the best answer because the noun that occurs directly after the dependent clause "Translated . . . energy" should refer to a word or term that could be translated. The term "axé," which the text connects to a lively city and which could logically be translated as "energy" for this reason, appropriately fits the modifying dependent clause.

Choice B is incorrect because the people designated by "they" could not themselves be translated and would instead use a specific term, which other people could translate. Choice C is incorrect because a "culture" could not be "Translated" itself; instead, a single term used by a culture would be translated. Choice D is incorrect because a "cultural fusion" is not a single word that could be translated; instead, cultural fusion is a process that may involve translation as part of a broader scenario. All of these false answers introduce modifier errors.

Question 23: Choice C
Transitions
Difficulty - **Hard** | Topic - **Science**

Choice C is the best answer because "moreover" signals that "seek[ing] out ways to alleviate any harmful effects already incurred" is an additional skill related to "quickly withdraw[ing] from harmful scenarios." This transition properly signals an extension relationship.

Choice A is incorrect because "before then" introduces a reverse chronological relationship, which wrongly indicates that octopuses learned "to seek out ways to alleviate any harmful effects already incurred" before they "learned to quickly withdraw from harmful scenarios." Choice B is incorrect because "regardless" introduces a contrast relationship, which wrongly indicates that octopuses learned "to seek out ways to alleviate any harmful effects already incurred" despite the fact that they "learned to quickly withdraw from harmful scenarios." Choice D is incorrect because "for this reason" introduces a causal relationship, which wrongly indicates that octopuses learned "to seek out ways to alleviate any harmful effects already incurred" because they "learned to quickly withdraw from harmful scenarios."

Question 24: Choice D
Transitions
Difficulty - **Hard** | Topic - **Science**

Choice D is the best answer because "accordingly" signals that "material scientists and engineers are searching for ways to create superconductors that are not so situation specific" because many superconductors "only exhibit their superconducting properties at extremely low temperatures." This transition properly signals a causal relationship.

Choice A is incorrect because "by contrast" introduces an alternative relationship, which wrongly indicates that the search for more situation-flexible superconductors constitutes a parallel comparison with superconducting properties. Choice B is incorrect because "in theory" introduces a contrast relationship, which wrongly indicates that scientists and engineers are theoretically but not actually "searching for ways to create superconductors that are not so situation specific." Choice C is incorrect because "as noted" introduces a reiteration relationship, which wrongly indicates that the search "for ways to create superconductors that are not so situation specific" is a restatement of the fact that superconductors "only exhibit their superconducting properties at extremely low temperatures."

Question 25: Choice C
Transitions
Difficulty - **Hard** | Topic - **Science**

Choice C is the best answer because "at present" signals that "different freshwater dolphin species inhabit rivers in India, Cambodia, and Brazil" in the current moment, whereas "China's Yangtze River Dolphin was declared extinct" in the past. This transition properly signals a temporal relationship.

Choice A is incorrect because "in other words" introduces a reiteration relationship, which wrongly indicates that "different freshwater dolphin species inhabit[ing] rivers in India, Cambodia, and Brazil" is the same thing as "China's Yangtze River Dolphin [being] declared extinct." Choice B is incorrect because "accordingly" introduces a causal relationship, which wrongly indicates that "different freshwater dolphin species inhabit rivers in India, Cambodia, and Brazil" because "China's Yangtze River Dolphin was declared extinct." Choice D is incorrect because "in retrospect" introduces a correction relationship, which wrongly indicates that the notion that "China's Yangtze River Dolphin was declared extinct" should be viewed differently in light of the fact that "different freshwater dolphin species inhabit rivers in India, Cambodia, and Brazil."

Question 26: Choice D
Rhetorical Synthesis
Difficulty - **Hard** | Topic - **Humanities**

Choice D is the best answer because it notes a very general fact about the Underground City by mentioning the "cultural institutions and various businesses" that are present. This choice then effectively supports the general statement with more specific details by noting that "bookstores, restaurants, and arts venues such as the Salle Wilfrid-Pelletier" can be accessed through the Underground City.

Choice A is incorrect because it notes a single specific feature of the Underground City by describing the Salle Wilfrid-Pelletier but does not provide a general statement as required by the student's goal. Choice B is incorrect because it provides two general statements about the Underground City, noting first the range of venues and second the loose organization but not indicating more precise facts or information to support either statement. Choice C is incorrect because it presents specific information about a single venue, the Museum of Contemporary Art, that can be accessed through the Underground City but does not present a general statement about the Underground City itself.

Question 27: Choice B
Rhetorical Synthesis
Difficulty - **Hard** | Topic - **Science**

Choice B is the best answer because it explains that global temperature increases may cause the geographic ranges for some snake species to expand by 2070. This choice is consistent with the student's goal of "explain[ing] why the geographic ranges for some snake species could change by 2070."

Choice A is incorrect because, though it states that the geographic ranges for some snake species might expand by 2070, it does not explain why. Choice C is incorrect because, though it states that the geographic ranges for the European horned viper might expand by 2070, it does not explain why. Choice D is incorrect because, though it gives an explanation for why the geographic ranges for some snake species might contract by 2070, that explanation is not consistent with the student's notes.

No Test Content on This Page

Reading and Writing

27 QUESTIONS

1

Marking the presumed _____ of the Solar System, the Kuiper Belt is a vast expanse of rocky fragments and icy shards. Perhaps, however, the Kuiper Belt does not define the Solar System's outer limits exactly as was once thought: new research from NASA's New Horizons spacecraft hints that the Kuiper Belt is larger than was once assumed—or even that there is a second belt beyond the Kuiper's final reaches.

Which choice completes the text with the most logical and precise word or phrase?

A) potential

B) origin

C) transference

D) boundary

2

Sociologist Basak Kus once faulted one of America's iconic companies, General Electric, for _____ its original focus on industrial manufacturing and expanding into seemingly unrelated business sectors, particularly finance. This was Kus's stance in a 2015 article; arguably, GE has returned to its industrial roots since then.

Which choice completes the text with the most logical and precise word or phrase?

A) diluting

B) redoubling

C) corroborating

D) proclaiming

CONTINUE

3

This text is adapted from Ivan Turgenev's 1859 novel *A House of Gentlefolk*. The character described here, Christopher Theodor Gottlieb Lemm, was born in the east German region of Saxony and eventually relocated to Russia.

[Lemm's] father played the French horn, his mother the harp; he himself was practicing on three different instruments by the time he was five. At eight years old he was left an orphan, and from his tenth year he began to earn his bread by his art. He led a wandering life for many years, and performed everywhere in restaurants, at fairs, at peasants' weddings, and at balls. <u>At last he got into an orchestra and constantly rising in it, he obtained the position of director.</u>

Which choice best describes the function of the underlined sentence in the text as a whole?

A) It communicates the excitement that Lemm feels upon leaving behind his lifestyle as a wandering musician.

B) It raises uncertainties about Lemm's ability to maintain his respected position in the orchestra.

C) It signals Lemm's arrival at a position of authority after pursuing music over a long period of time.

D) It highlights Lemm's awareness of different audiences as central to his success as a musician.

4

Surveying the two major US political parties over a two-year period, the Pew Research Center observed the same likelihood to switch to the opposing party among Democratic and Republican voters. <u>By the metrics of this study, 9% of voters who identified as Democrats in 2018 identified as Republicans in 2020, and 9% of voters who identified as Republicans identified as Democrats by the end of the same period.</u> Moreover, party-switching voters mirrored one another in terms of political involvement. The less engaged a voter was in the preferred 2018 political party, the more likely that voter was to switch party by 2020.

Which choice best describes the purpose of the underlined portion in the text as a whole?

A) It summarizes the methods of researchers who cataloged a surprising difference between Democratic and Republican voting tendencies.

B) It recapitulates findings from a study that indicates a parallel between Democratic and Republican voters.

C) It indicates a discrepancy between Democratic and Republican voters while explaining how one recent initiative reduced this discrepancy.

D) It notes the hypothesis behind a survey of Democratic and Republican voters while cautioning that some survey results remain inconclusive.

5

Text 1
Fluorocarbons represent a health hazard when present in considerable concentrations. Present in aerosol sprays and in the foam used in fire extinguishers, these often-gaseous substances can cause respiratory illness if they are not isolated in airtight metal containers—like those being refined by an international group of researchers. Materials scientists from Cornell University, the Korea Institute of Science and Technology, and Southern Methodist University are creating "metal organic frameworks" that can accommodate multiple fluorocarbons and absorb fluorocarbons before they leak out.

Text 2
The manufacture of versatile plastics and coatings hinges on the use of fluorocarbons, substances that are often associated with aerosols and foams and are often considered health hazards in liquid and gaseous forms. However, fluorocarbons have also been used in the manufacture of plastics that are toxic: the US Environmental Protection Agency notes that cast-off plastic food containers created with fluorocarbon-based chemicals present a growing health and environmental danger.

Which choice best describes how Text 1 and Text 2 relate to each other?

A) Text 1 profiles as a project that would address fluorocarbon-related liabilities, while Text 2 specifies a few of the difficulties that the same project has encountered.

B) Text 1 outlines the problems that accompany gaseous and liquid fluorocarbon substances, while Text 2 explains how fluorocarbons are problematic in another physical form.

C) Text 1 focuses on the industrial uses of fluorocarbons and a few associated dangers, while Text 2 cautions that fluorocarbons are ultimately too dangerous for daily use.

D) Text 1 describes an effort to develop safer containers for fluorocarbon-based products, while Text 2 argues that new materials must be developed before fluorocarbons can be handled safely.

6

This text is adapted from Phoebe Cary's 1902 poem "A Leak in the Dike." Peter, a young boy who lives in the Netherlands, is on his way to visit the old man.

> And now, with his face all glowing,
> And eyes as bright as the day
> With the thoughts of his pleasant errand,
> He trudged along the way;
> And soon his joyous prattle
> Made glad a lonesome place—
> Alas! if only the blind old man
> Could have seen that happy face!
> Yet he somehow caught the brightness
> Which his voice and presence lent;
> And he felt the sunshine come and go
> As Peter came and went.

Which choice best states the main idea of the text?

A) Peter's presence is a source of happiness for the old man.

B) The old man is eager to help Peter.

C) The sunshine makes the old man remember distant events.

D) Peter is too young to understand the old man's sadness.

7

Massive climatic and weather manipulations can be safely and affordably explored by researchers equipped with the right software—researchers like Alan Robock. In a research inquiry that was publicized in 2020, Robock and colleagues examined how geoengineering, or artificially altering temperature and atmospheric conditions, could impact apple yields in Himachal Pradesh, a province in India. Technically, Robock did not need to travel to India to determine that geoengineering could "backfire if it ended suddenly." He relied on software simulations to reach this conclusion.

According to the text, what is true about Robock's approach to geoengineering in Himachal Pradesh?

A) Robock's conclusions have been challenged by researchers who visited the province.

B) Robock developed the simulation software that his research employed.

C) Robock could explore geoengineering without manipulating the province's actual climate.

D) Robock's colleagues developed competing geoengineering simulations.

8

The 1936 photograph *Migrant Mother* would become a symbol of the plight of displaced farm workers during the Great Depression as well as one of photographer Dorothea Lange's best known images. This image places its central subject, Florence Owens Thompson, in extreme close-up. Still, the now-iconic *Migrant Mother* was not the only image of Thompson that Lange captured: among the others are photographs of Thompson and her children (who flank her in the *Migrant Mother* image) taken from farther back to include the group's tent-like shelter and rather barren surroundings.

Which choice best states the main idea of the text?

A) Lange's *Migrant Mother* photograph has risen to iconic status despite doubts about its central subject's identity.

B) Lange took multiple photographs of Thompson, and at least one differs significantly from the close-up *Migrant Mother*.

C) Lange edited out Thompson's surroundings in the well-known *Migrant Mother* photograph.

D) Several Lange photographs depict farm workers such as Thompson.

CONTINUE

9

Among first-person narrators, Christopher Boone, the teenage protagonist of Mark Haddon's *The Curious Incident of the Dog in the Night-Time* (2003), exhibits an unusual trait: he is rigorously truthful. Typically, first-person narrators are designed to engage in some level of deception or exaggeration for the sake of psychological interest. Yet Christopher, claims one scholar, is interesting because he finds even slight exaggerations objectionable and is profoundly upset by the deceptive narratives of Haddon's other characters.

Which finding, if true, would directly support the scholar's characterization of Christopher Boone?

A) Christopher spends part of the novel attempting to solve a mystery and provides evasive answers when other characters ask him about this "detective work."

B) Despite his ability to comprehend advanced mathematical concepts, Christopher often struggles to understand the motives of the adults around him, including his own father and mother.

C) In the novel, Christopher discovers that his father has not been fully truthful about a family conflict, and Christopher's former respect for his father quickly deteriorates.

D) Several chapters of Haddon's novel serve more as commentaries on random topics that interest Christopher than as narrative segments that move the central plot of the novel forward.

10

Eskers, or mineral deposits left behind as glaciers recede, have been found in Iceland and have been studied as part of a joint project from Northern Arizona University and two US government agencies, NASA and the US Geological Survey. For the scientists involved, studying eskers is not simply or even primarily a way of understanding Iceland's terrain. Rather, these specialists claim, Iceland's eskers are comparable to features on Mars and may, through analogy, facilitate a deeper understanding of the natural history of this planet.

Which finding, if true, would best support the claim of the specialists as noted in the text?

A) One of the researchers involved in the project, Lauren Edgar of the US Geological Survey, has previously used comparative studies of Earth-based and Moon-based geology.

B) Edgar has identified a group of "sinuous ridges" on Mars, and comparisons between these ridges and Iceland's eskers might explain how Mars's terrain changed over time.

C) Kristen Bennett of the US Geological Survey, a project researcher, has noticed landforms on Mars that resemble eskers but cautions that the researchers are unsure whether they are "seeing an esker on Mars or an inverted channel,"

D) Explaining the significance of the Iceland-based study, Edgar has noted that humans study "the Moon and other planets in part to better understand our own."

CONTINUE

11

Gases in "Empty Space" Air for Potato Chip Bags

Sample Bag	Percent Nitrogen	Percent Hydrogen	Percent Carbon Dioxide
Brand 1	98	0.8	0.6
Brand 2	98	0.9	0.5
Brand 3	99	0.9	0.1
Brand 4	99	0.8	0.1

Vilified by consumers for presumably taking up bag space that could have accommodated more food, the air in potato chip bags actually serves a valuable purpose. This air, in fact, is not identical to the air we breathe but is composed of purified nitrogen that helps to keep the potato chips fresh; there are inevitably be traces of other gases, which can lead to the potato chips going stale more quickly. Thus, a consumer who is evaluating four different brands (labeled 1 through 4) and wants to purchase the chips that would remain freshest the longest in an unopened bag would be advised to buy _____

Which choice most effectively completes the text with relevant information from the table?

A) brand 1

B) brand 2.

C) either brand 2 or brand 3.

D) either brand 3 or brand 4.

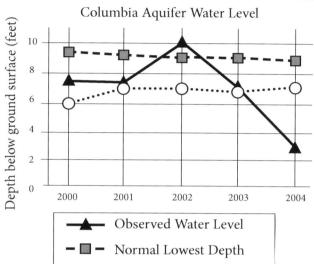

12

Columbia Aquifer Water Level

— ▲ — Observed Water Level

– ■ – Normal Lowest Depth

··· O ··· Normal Highest Depth

Located in southwestern Delaware, the Columbia Aquifer is an underground supply of water housed in semipermeable minerals. The surface level of an aquifer's water supply will fluctuate over time, as water extraction (by households and utilities companies, for instance) lowers the aquifer's water surface level farther below the surface of the ground; conversely, heavy precipitation and other sources of inflow will raise the aquifer's water surface level closer to the surface of the ground. For the Columbia Aquifer, increased water extraction most likely occurred between _____

Which choice most effectively uses data from the graph to support the underlined claim?

A) 2000 and 2001.

B) 2001 and 2002.

C) 2002 and 2003.

D) 2003 and 2004.

13

During his lifetime, Donald Featherstone had 57 plastic flamingos on his lawn. The number was no coincidence: in 1957, Featherstone, a sculptor who made his living as a plastics designer, developed the first-ever lawn flamingo for the Union Products company in Massachusetts. At first, Featherstone had been hesitant about corporate work. Eventually, he went on to enjoy a respected 43 year-long career with Union Products and embraced the pink flamingo as a personal symbol. In this context, Featherstone's own lawn flamingo grouping is best understood as _____

Which choice most logically completes the text?

A) an acknowledgment of Featherstone's origins as a sculptor.

B) a subtle criticism of Featherstone's long-running corporate work.

C) a celebration of the versatility of plastics in art and advertising.

D) a tribute to a significant development in Featherstone's life.

14

Late in December of 1894, the Amateur Golf Association of the United States was founded. This _____ were due, at least in part, to the fact that two different golfing clubs had hosted entirely different "national" championships earlier that year—and avoiding such inconsistencies while promoting a thriving sport would be among the Association's duties.

Which choice completes the text so that it conforms to the conventions of Standard English?

A) organization's beginnings

B) organization's beginning's

C) organizations beginnings

D) organizations beginning's

15

Part art historical reflection, part creative writing platform, the Abang-guard project was _____ former security guards at the Metropolitan Museum of Art. The three co-founders—Maureen Catbagan, Jevijoe Vitung, and Louisa Lam—have reassessed Asian American art from the past 100 years; Lam, a poet, has also recorded readings of her work for the Abang-guard website.

Which choice completes the text so that it conforms to the conventions of Standard English?

A) founded; by

B) founded by—

C) founded, by

D) founded by

16

Completing an unfinished work by a composer of unmatched talents _____ like an impossible task, but computer scientist Ahmed Elgammal and collaborators have used artificial intelligence to shape out the missing portions of Ludwig van Beethoven's Tenth Symphony, which the great 19th century composer completed only in fragments.

Which choice completes the text with the most logical and precise word or phrase?

A) were seeming

B) seem

C) seems

D) have seemed

17

Historians commonly _____ "gunpowder empires"—the Ottoman, the Safavid, and the Mughal—that dominated southern and western Asia for centuries. Regardless of the common category, these world powers did not actually use gunpowder with equal success, and musket-wielding Ottoman soldiers easily defeated Safavid cavalry forces in battle.

Which choice completes the text so that it conforms to the conventions of Standard English?

A) cite: three

B) cite three,

C) cite three

D) cite, three

18

Labeling bagels as vegan (that is, as produced without direct use of any animal-based food products) both helps cafes appeal to vegan customers _____ a reality of classic bagel recipes: most bagels have traditionally been produced without any use of eggs or dairy products.

Which choice completes the text so that it conforms to the conventions of Standard English?

A) and reflects

B) reflects

C) reflecting

D) and reflecting

CONTINUE

19

The first Earth Day, which was first observed in April of 1970, was not the only environmental awareness initiative that represented a defining moment that year. Taking place only months later, in December of 1970, _____ appreciation for the natural world in government policy.

Which choice completes the text so that it conforms to the conventions of Standard English?

A) it was the Environmental Protection Agency that, through its founding, enshrined

B) the Environmental Protection Agency was founded to enshrine

C) the newly-founded Environmental Protection Agency enshrined

D) the founding of the Environmental Protection Agency enshrined

20

Sometimes, slow and steady really does win the race, as participants in motorcycle "slow races" know. Participants in a race of this sort must keep from tipping over—sometimes navigating around a small obstacle, more often simply keeping inside a demarcated lane—while _____ towards a finish line, with the last person to reach the end without tipping declared the winner.

Which choice completes the text so that it conforms to the conventions of Standard English?

A) you maneuver

B) one maneuvers

C) it maneuvers

D) they maneuver

21

Jamaican-Canadian artist Tau Lewis conveys her multifaceted vision through a single _____ salvaged fabric, which Lewis then fashions into works ranging from wall-mounted and mask-like compositions that she calls "soft portraits" to an installation centered on a single gargantuan figure and adorned with hanging strands of cloth.

Which choice completes the text so that it conforms to the conventions of Standard English?

A) medium; of

B) medium:

C) medium: of

D) medium

22

As Turkey's head of state in the aftermath of World War I, Mustafa Kemal Ataturk devoted his energies to a series of reforms that restructured political institutions and religious customs in the mid 1920s. _____ he shifted focus somewhat, devoting his energies to educational projects, including the adoption of a Europeanized alphabet for the Turkish language, in the late 1920s.

Which choice completes the text so that it conforms to the conventions of Standard English?

A) Then,

B) Nonetheless,

C) For instance,

D) Simultaneously,

23

Professor Tim Michaelis of Northern Illinois University specializes in the psychology behind frugality. _____ he has studied whether entrepreneurs who embrace a frugality mindset of extreme resourcefulness are setting their businesses on the path to success or whether, instead, they are becoming overly cautious and focusing on needlessly small details.

Which choice completes the text with the most logical transition?

A) Granted,

B) By contrast,

C) In particular,

D) On the other hand,

24

Providing in-flight food can be at best a burden and at most an obligation for some high-volume airlines. _____ some airlines have treated airline food as a thrilling culinary challenge, one that carries an air of prestige: Singapore Air, for one, recently partnered with acclaimed chef Alfred Portale to customize recipes for high-altitude flights.

Which choice completes the text with the most logical transition?

A) To this end,

B) For example,

C) Likewise,

D) Still,

25

You will find, if you go far back enough in the history of evolution, that some of the very earliest animals resembled sea-bound plants. Nonetheless, the seemingly rudimentary marine animals of 580 million years ago, notes University of Cambridge zoologist Emily Mitchell, "mixed up the water and enabled resources to spread more widely" in prehistoric seas. _____ new species began to develop as new concentrations of resources stimulated evolution.

Which choice completes the text with the most logical transition?

A) In consequence,

B) Conversely,

C) For instance,

D) Paradoxically,

26

While researching a topic, a student has taken the following notes:

- The Platonic Solids are three-dimensional shapes with special properties.

- Each face of a given Platonic Solid takes the shape of a regular polygon.

- One common Platonic Solid is the cube, which has six square faces.

- The Platonic Solid with the fewest faces is the tetrahedron, which has four triangular faces.

- The Platonic Solid with the most faces is the icosahedron, which has twenty triangular faces.

The student wants to call attention to a similarity between the faces of two specific Platonic Solids. Which choice most effectively uses relevant information from the notes to accomplish this goal?

A) The icosahedron is a Platonic Solid with twenty faces, and the tetrahedron is a Platonic Solid with four faces.

B) Platonic Solids, which have faces that take the forms of regular polygons, include the cube, icosahedron, and tetrahedron.

C) The tetrahedron, like the icosahedron, has triangular faces, though these two Platonic Solids have different numbers of faces.

D) Platonic Solids exist in three dimensions but can be classified according to the two-dimensional shapes, such as squares and triangles, that form their faces.

27

While researching a topic, a student has taken the following notes:

- Singer-songwriter Bob Dylan wrote the song "Mr Tambourine Man" in the mid 1960s.

- He performed the song in May of 1964 and recorded the song in June of the same year.

- A version of this song was included in Dylan's 1965 album *Bringing It All Back Home*.

- The folk-rock band The Byrds recorded a version of "Mr Tambourine Man" in 1965.

- This version of the song was included in *Mr Tambourine Man*, the album that The Byrds released in June of 1965.

The student wants to provide a brief history of the two versions of "Mr Tambourine Man" for an audience unfamiliar with The Byrds. Which choice most effectively uses relevant information from the notes to accomplish this goal?

A) Written and first performed by Bob Dylan, "Mr Tambourine Man" was performed in a second version by The Byrds, a folk-rock band whose 1965 album was titled after this song.

B) Bob Dylan, a singer and songwriter, wrote "Mr Tambourine Man" and recorded a version of this song in 1964; one year later, a version of "Mr Tambourine Man" appeared on an album by The Byrds.

C) Bob Dylan wrote "Mr Tambourine Man" in the mid 1960s, and he then performed and recorded the song in 1964, while The Byrds produced a version of "Mr Tambourine Man" in 1965.

D) Roughly one year after Bob Dylan recorded a version of "Mr Tambourine Man," The Byrds produced a version of the song; this second version was released in June of 1965 as part of a larger album.

STOP
**If you finish these exercises, you may check your work on this section only.
Do not turn to any other section in the book.**

No Test Content on This Page

Reading and Writing

27 QUESTIONS

1

Dialogue was regarded by some modernist authors as _____ narration that revealed the inner thoughts of characters, but for Ivy Compton-Burnett, who reversed this premise to treat interior narration as relatively minor in novels like *Parents and Children*, dialogue was primary.

Which choice completes the text with the most logical and precise word or phrase?

A) grounded in

B) crafted from

C) despised by

D) secondary to

2

To meet energy needs without relying on a _____ facility, regions of the United States rely on what Daniel Cohan, a professor of environmental engineering, calls "virtual power plants": networks of interrelated factories, generators, transmission lines, and storage units that can be configured as sweeping yet coherent matrices, with specialists known as "grid managers" overseeing energy supply and demand.

Which choice completes the text with the most logical and precise word or phrase?

A) heterogeneous

B) versatile

C) regulated

D) centralized

CONTINUE

3

This text is adapted from Murasaki Shikibu's circa 1020 CE novel *The Tale of Genji*, translated into English by Arthur Whaley. Genji is the son of a Japanese emperor. In this scene, he is secretly observing the people around him.

It amused [Genji] very much to see people behaving quite <u>naturally</u> together. He had lived in an atmosphere of ceremony and reserve. This peep at everyday life was a most exciting novelty.

As used in the text, what does the word "naturally" most nearly mean?

A) Predictably

B) Spontaneously

C) Uniformly

D) Legitimately

4

NASA's Perseverance Mars Rover does not capture Martian atmosphere samples as part of its primary mission, which instead involves drilling mineral samples from the planet's surface. Yet through an interesting _____ effect of this activity, the Perseverance mission has in fact yielded Martian air samples, since the rock samples often contain small gas pockets.

Which choice completes the text with the most logical and precise word or phrase?

A) collateral

B) submissive

C) cryptic

D) stipulated

5

Viewers who expect complete self-effacement on the part of a documentary director often find themselves disappointed by the films of Werner Herzog, a German documentarian who regularly _____ his chosen subjects—often speaking just off-camera about the philosophical conundrums that the individuals in his films face.

Which choice completes the text with the most logical and precise word or phrase?

A) attenuates

B) opines about

C) digresses from

D) exacerbates

6

Towards the middle of the 19th century, historians interested in vast economic forces began to challenge the _____ of historical models attributing epochal change to the influence of individual "great men." While this latter mode still had important proponents, such as Thomas Carlyle and Ralph Waldo Emerson, so-called "great man" theories never returned to their former dominance.

Which choice completes the text with the most logical and precise word or phrase?

A) jurisdiction

B) congeniality

C) ambiguity

D) hegemony

7

Alessandro Antonietti, a scientist involved in the cognitive study of aging, is convinced that growing older unlocks some forms of creativity. Together with colleagues from the University of Brescia and the Catholic University of the Sacred Heart, Antonietti conducted research that, for him, challenges the concept of an inevitable late-in-life "decrease of intellectual efficiency. This is true only of some aspects of cognitive functioning, but not of creativity and humor." In fact, Antonietti revealed that "divergent thinking"—a process of drawing unconventional connections—flourishes among older people.

Which choice best states the main purpose of the text?

A) To demonstrate how Antonietti's findings overturn assumptions central to an earlier research project

B) To illustrate a correlation between humor and old age by comparing Antonietti's work to similar studies

C) To distinguish between intellectual efficiency and divergent thinking by presenting Antonietti's viewpoint

D) To offer Antonietti's perspective on how aging actually impacts older adults

8

High-resolution telescopes are frequently launched into outer space, <u>mainly because Earth's atmosphere would cloud these telescopes' images of distant stars, galaxies, and nebulae</u>. This approach above-the-atmosphere nonetheless limits how powerful an orbiting telescope can be: a telescope mirror (central to imaging) that is too wide or too heavy cannot be launched from Earth. For NASA engineers who want to create wider telescope mirrors, one promising way around these constraints is to construct a telescope mirror in space using liquefied metal, an approach central to the Fluidic Telescope (FLUTE) endeavor.

Which choice best describes the function of the underlined portion?

A) It emphasizes one of the liabilities of the large orbiting telescopes that have already been launched beyond the atmosphere.

B) It pinpoints a few of the deficiencies in image resolution that the FLUTE project was designed to address.

C) It specifies the reason that telescopes are launched from Earth despite other limitations associated with orbiting telescopes.

D) It underscores the innovative nature of the FLUTE project through contrast with an earlier endeavor.

CONTINUE ➡

9

This text is adapted from Maurice Baring's 1920 poem "Russia." Here, the speaker personifies and directly addresses the nation of Russia itself.

> What can the secret link between us be?
> Why does your song's unresting ebb and flow
> Speak to me in a language that I know?
> Why does the burden of your mystery
> Come like the message of a friend to me?
> Why do I love your vasts of corn or snow,
> The tears and laughter of your sleepless woe,
> The murmur of your brown immensity?

Which choice best states the main idea of the text?

A) The speaker feels an intense connection to Russia while nonetheless interrogating the causes of this bond.

B) The speaker seeks a stronger understanding of life in Russia even though such knowledge is construed as unattainable.

C) The speaker draws upon the history of Russia in order to make careful predictions about the nation's future.

D) The speaker evokes a specific scene from a journey through Russia in hopes of resolving an uncertainty.

10

The sketch comedy show *Saturday Night Live* (*SNL*) has played a complex role in American politics since its late 1970s debut. Very often, *Saturday Night Live* cast members have staged short sketches based on events such as presidential debates, White House press conferences, and campaign rallies, with the various cast members playing exaggerated versions of well-known political figures. However, as one television and media critic has claimed, these representations do not merely reflect political realities: sometimes, the caricatures on *Saturday Night Live* meaningfully have shaped how political figures are perceived.

Which quotation from an article about *Saturday Night Live* best illustrates the critic's claim?

A) "From the beginning, *SNL* balanced topical satire with madcap physical comedy, the latter exemplified by the antics of original cast member John Belushi."

B) "Accuracy on small points was secondary to broader satire for many of *SNL*'s first performers: Dan Aykryod, who depicted President Jimmy Carter, had a mustache, but Jimmy Carter did not."

C) "In his portrayal of President Gerald Ford as bumbling and oblivious, Chevy Chase, one of the very first *SNL* cast members, did more than any political ad to effectively create the image of Ford as a dope and a lightweight."

D) "*SNL* found new life in the 1980s as a cast led by Eddie Murphy returned to the show's roots in topical satire, with Phil Hartman memorably depicting president Ronald Reagan and Murphy himself lampooning the inequalities in American society."

165   CONTINUE

11

Broadcaster Adrian Chiles recalls that some of his presentations were "de-ummed" in the 1990s—that is, that his producers edited Chiles's recordings to remove vocalizations like "um" and "er." Thought to represent hesitation or uncertainty and, thus, to reduce a listener's confidence in an "umming" speaker, the verbal tics like Chiles's may in fact impart various benefits to listeners, including—as researchers associated with the University of Edinburgh have claimed—better retention of specific pieces of information.

Which finding, if true, would best support the University of Edinburgh researchers' claim?

A) In 2023, Chiles published the newspaper article "I thought my umming and erring made for better radio. I was wrong" to clarify that his style of delivery was, to an extent, meant to establish a better connection with his radio audiences.

B) Chiles is a respected broadcast journalist, and the Edinburgh researchers have noted that other halting speakers, such as former US President George W. Bush, might have used vocalizations such as "um" for dramatic effect.

C) In part, the Edinburgh researchers gauged word responses by assessing N400, a measure of cerebral voltage that is most pronounced when a person hears a surprising word; hesitations such as "um" caused N400 to be relatively high for expected words and relatively low for unexpected words.

D) Comparing an "erred" version of a 160-word sentence to a fluently spoken version of the same sentence, the Edinburgh researchers found that experiment participants remembered the final word of the sentence better when this word was preceded by a verbal hesitation.

12

Doctor Faustus is a play written by Christopher Marlowe between 1592 and 1593. In the play, Faustus himself expresses dissatisfaction with some of the studies that he has pursued, as is evident when _____

Which choice best uses a quotation from *Doctor Faustus* to illustrate the claim?

A) he asks whether "to dispute well, [is] logic's chiefest end? / Affords this art no greater miracle?" and resolves to "read no more; thou hast attain'd that end."

B) he speaks aloud his determination to "Be a physician, Faustus; heap up gold, / And be eterniz'd for some wondrous cure."

C) his thoughts turn to the "world of profit and delight, / Of power, of honour, of omnipotence" that "Is promis'd to the studious artizan!"

D) another character advises Faustus to lay a particular "book aside, And gaze not on it," only to have Faustus respond by anticipating a "desperate enterprise" and knowledge of a "strange philosophy."

13

Reaction Times for 5 Students, Visual and
Auditory Stimuli; Experiment Administered in 2024

Experiment Participant	Auditory stimulus (milliseconds)	Visual stimulus (milliseconds)
Student 1, Age 16	220	231
Student 2, Age 18	216	235
Student 3, Age 19	207	195
Student 4, Age 20	231	253
Student 5, Age 20	244	263

In a 2015 study, Aditya Jain, Ramta Bansal, and colleagues assessed how quickly 120 medical students (typically between the ages 18 and 20) responded to auditory and visual stimuli. For this group, there was a weighted difference of roughy 20 milliseconds between auditory and visual stimuli, with a faster response for the auditory stimuli. A college student attempted to reproduce Jain and Bansal's research in 2024, yet experiment results that resembled those of the 2015 experiment participants were achieved by _____

Which choice completes the text with relevant and accurate information from the table?

A) student 2 only.

B) students 2 and 3 only.

C) students 1, 3, and 4 only.

D) students 2, 4, and 5 only.

14

Leadbeater's Possum holds an iconic status in the Australian state of Victoria, serving as Victoria's "faunal emblem" or state mammal. Nonetheless, this small marsupial faces difficult chances of survival in the wild—so difficult, in fact, that Leadbeater's Possum was mistakenly declared extinct early in the 1900s. Subsequent "rediscoveries" of the Possum generally (in 1961) and of presumably extinct lowland variety of the possum (in 1986) took place in the wild; conservationists currently monitor a few dozen Leadbeater's Possums in controlled preserve-like settings, ensuring that _____

Which choice most logically completes the text?

A) the survival of Leadbeater's Possum would be likely even though it has become impossible to return this animal to the wild.

B) any future announcements concerning the Leadbeater Possum's extinction are not based solely on random observations of populations in the wild.

C) conservationists searching for Leadbeater's Possum in the wild no longer confuse the lowland variety with other varieties of this mammal.

D) mistaken "rediscoveries" of Leadbeater's Possum populations cease to hinder conservation efforts.

15

The speed of individual sea turtles does not pose an obstacle to researchers interested in the movements of these creatures on land. Rather, adult sea turtles that crawl on land to lay eggs may do so over a wide expanse of seaside sand, so both the movements of the parent sea turtles and of the newly-hatched sea turtles that crawl towards the sea are widely dispersed. To perform more effective surveys of such turtle populations, R.C. Mickey and Dave Thompson of the United States Geological Survey have relied on a fast-moving, four-wheeled utility task vehicle (UTV), which enables _____

Which choice most logically completes the text?

A) researchers to study the relatively fast movements of turtles that have reached the sea.

B) investigation of sea turtle populations in a manner that does not alert the sea turtles themselves.

C) initiatives to redistribute sea turtles groups to areas that researchers visit more often.

D) research surveying newly-hatched turtles spread along a wide expanse of shoreline.

16

Kazuo Ishiguro's 2021 release *Klara and the Sun* is, like its author's earlier novels *The Remains of the Day* _____ an understated character study of a protagonist devoted to serving others—in this case, Klara herself, an "Artificial Friend" who inhabits a fanciful future society.

Which choice completes the text so that it conforms to the conventions of Standard English?

A) (1989) and *Never Let Me Go* (2005)

B) (1989) and *Never Let Me Go* (2005):

C) (1989), and *Never Let Me Go* (2005),

D) (1989) and *Never Let Me Go* (2005),

17

Bioethics, as a formal field of study, at times defies easy classification within university departments. Already an area that would naturally be of interest to practicing doctors (who would flock to medical schools) and genomicists (who would more likely perform _____ it is also the province of humanist scholars, who trace some tenets of bioethical thought to the Greek philosopher Aristotle.

Which choice completes the text so that it conforms to the conventions of Standard English?

A) research in biology departments)

B) research) in biology departments,

C) research), in biology departments,

D) research in biology departments),

18

Before the advent of some of today's influential large data models, sociologist Catriona Mirrlees-Black performed meticulous surveys of legal and jurisdictional statistics. She and collaborator Sarah Randall _____ some of these studies around 2015, though Catriona Mirrlees-Black was investigating area-by-area Australian legal statistics on her own around 1992.

Which choice completes the text so that it conforms to the conventions of Standard English?

A) has conducted

B) was conducting

C) conducted

D) conducts

19

Remarkable for her longevity, French actress Jeanne Louise Calment (1875-1997) claimed to have met the acclaimed painter Vincent van Gogh early in her lifetime; by Calment's account, he had been a customer at her parents' store. This experience would return in a film project, director Michael Rubbo's *Vincent and* _____ that Calment completed late in her lifetime.

Which choice completes the text so that it conforms to the conventions of Standard English?

A) *Me* (released in 1990);

B) *Me,* (released in 1990)

C) *Me,* (released in 1990),

D) *Me* (released in 1990),

20

New research into the movements of Earth's core posits that the molten matter at Earth's interior is rotating somewhat faster than the rest of the _____ historical data on earthquakes that took place over almost three decades (1967-1995), Xiaodong Song and Paul Richards determined that seismic waves are passing more and more rapidly through Earth's interior—a fact that suggests a relatively fast-moving core.

Which choice completes the text so that it conforms to the conventions of Standard English?

A) planet, by using

B) planet; using

C) planet, using

D) planet by using

21

Rarely seen even now because they dwell underground, _____ partially because caecilians (unlike amphibians such as frogs) have minimal bone structures and partially because the caecilians of earlier epochs lived underground as well.

Which choice completes the text so that it conforms to the conventions of Standard English?

A) amphibians, which include the elongated and legless caecilians, have left few known traces in the fossil record,

B) few known traces of the elongated and legless amphibians known as caecilians are in the fossil record,

C) there are few known fossil record traces of the elongated and legless amphibians known as caecilians,

D) caecilians, which are elongated and legless amphibians, have left few known traces in the fossil record,

22

Large plant-eating dinosaurs generally avoided equatorial regions, gravitating to temperate areas and leaving the tropics to smaller carnivorous _____ Jessica Whiteside, a biochemist, resource dispersion explains this pattern: the scattered shrubs of the prehistoric tropics, which experienced harsh high temperatures, could not support larger herbivores.

Which choice completes the text so that it conforms to the conventions of Standard English?

A) dinosaurs, instead for

B) dinosaurs, instead, for

C) dinosaurs. Instead, for

D) dinosaurs instead. For

23

What's the best way to study jellyfish in Michigan—a state without a seaside? The answer to this question, for researchers at Eastern Michigan University, is twofold: seek out the lesser-known freshwater jellyfish in Michigan's lakes, then investigate these creatures through an intensive lab-based course. _____ notes biology professor Cara Shillington, such work gives students "a better idea of what it means to be a scientist" through local resourcefulness.

Which choice completes the text with the most logical transition?

A) Indeed,

B) Nevertheless,

C) Finally,

D) For example,

24

Historically, some African civilizations such as the Kongo Kingdom (1301-1665) revolved around hereditary heads of state and centralized government. However, sophisticated political structures also developed from less hierarchical approaches. The Igbo clans of West Africa represent one instance of a loose federation; _____ the landlocked villages of the Congo Basin represented a decentralized model very different from the seaside Kongo Kingdom's.

Which choice completes the text with the most logical transition?

A) by contrast,

B) for example,

C) similarly,

D) as a result,

25

Determining the total biomass of a forest is a matter of determining which measurements actually correlate with biomass and which, in contrast, at first seem useful but are actually uninformative. As plant biologists Marie Antoine and Steve Sillett explain, assessing individual trees' near-the-ground diameters to estimate a forest's total biomass is a questionable method; _____ evaluating the heights of individual tall trees provides useful inferences of biomass.

Which choice completes the text with the most logical transition?

A) more broadly,

B) in addition,

C) instead,

D) by this logic,

CONTINUE →

26

While researching a topic, a student has taken the following notes:

- French painter Paul Cézanne influenced representational art in the late 1800s and early 1900s through his experiments with stark color and geometric form.

- He revisited subjects frequently, painting hundreds of versions of a single landscape or a single portrait subject.

- Cézanne's wife, Hortense, was born in 1850 and was a nineteen year-old assistant bookbinder when she met Cézanne.

- Among Cézanne's many images of his wife are four related paintings depicting Madame Cézanne in a red dress.

- Today, these "red dress" paintings are split among museums in four locations: São Paulo, Basel, Chicago, and New York City.

The student wants to indicate a similarity between Cézanne's portraits of his wife and Cézanne's paintings of other subjects. Which choice most effectively uses relevant information from the notes to accomplish this goal?

A) Cézanne's wife Hortense is the subject of four paintings now split among museums in São Paulo, Basel, Chicago, and New York City.

B) In the mid 1800s, Cézanne met his future wife, Hortense; his many images of her would include four paintings of Hortense in a red dress.

C) Often, Cézanne produced multiple images of the same landscape or portrait subject, experimenting with stark color and geometric form.

D) Cézanne frequently created multiple images of portrait subjects, including his wife Hortense, who was depicted in a red dress in four paintings.

27

While researching a topic, a student has taken the following notes:

- Chipmunks are found throughout the US in several states east of the Mississippi River.

- These small burrowing rodents mostly live to the west of the Piedmont in North Carolina.

- The Piedmont is a plateau in the middle of North Carolina.

- Chipmunks were found to the east of the Piedmont in 2024.

- The North Carolina Wildlife Resource Commission asked North Carolina residents to photograph any chipmunks discovered in this expanded range.

The student wants to emphasize how the geographic range of chipmunks has shifted by noting specific regions of North Carolina. Which choice most effectively uses relevant information from the notes to accomplish this goal?

A) Typically found to the west of North Carolina's Piedmont, chipmunks were found to the east of this plateau in 2024.

B) In 2024, chipmunks expanded their range in North Carolina when some of these animals moved from the Piedmont to an area west of this plateau.

C) The North Carolina Wildlife Resource Commission has requested photographic footage of chipmunks, which can be found near North Carolina's Piedmont region.

D) Found east of the Mississippi River, chipmunks can also be found in a few different areas of North Carolina.

STOP
**If you finish these exercises, you may check your work on this section only.
Do not turn to any other section in the book.**

Answer Key

Test 5 Modules
— Pages 150-171 —

Pages 150-160 Module 1: Baseline					
1	D	10	B	19	D
2	A	11	D	20	D
3	C	12	B	21	B
4	B	13	D	22	A
5	B	14	A	23	C
6	A	15	D	24	D
7	C	16	C	25	A
8	B	17	C	26	C
9	C	18	A	27	A

Pages 162-171 Module 2: Hard					
1	D	10	C	19	D
2	D	11	D	20	B
3	B	12	A	21	D
4	A	13	D	22	D
5	B	14	B	23	A
6	D	15	D	24	C
7	D	16	D	25	C
8	C	17	D	26	D
9	A	18	C	27	A

Want to learn more?

Visit prepvantagetutoring.com for Digital SAT updates
and for the research sources for our passages

Module 1: Baseline
— Pages 150-160 —

Question 1: Choice D
Word in Context
Difficulty - **Easy** | Topic - **Science**

Choice D is the best answer because the blank must mean essentially the same thing as "outer limits." "Boundary" means the outer edge of something, so it fits.

Choice A is incorrect because "potential" refers to the ability to do something that has not yet occurred, whereas a future action or process is not mentioned. Choice B is incorrect because, while the origin of the Solar System is of scientific interest, the Kuiper Belt marks the "outer limits," not the beginning, of the Solar System. Choice C is incorrect because the Solar System is not being transferred to anything.

Question 2: Choice A
Word in Context
Difficulty - **Medium** | Topic - **Social Studies**

Choice A is the best answer because General Electric decreased "its original focus on industrial manufacturing [by] expanding into seemingly unrelated business sectors." "Diluting" appropriately conveys that GE focused less on industrial manufacturing by virtue of expanding into other sectors.

Choice B is incorrect because, though it conveys a change in amount, "redoubling" would mean that GE focused more on industrial manufacturing by expanding into other sectors. Choice C is incorrect because, though businesses sometimes have synergistic ventures, "corroborating" would indicate that GE verified its focus on industrial manufacturing by expanding into other sectors. Choice D is incorrect because "proclaiming" would indicate that Kus faulted GE for announcing its focus on industrial manufacturing, whereas there is nothing about an announcement in the passage.

Question 3: Choice C
Text Structure and Purpose
Difficulty - **Medium** | Topic - **Literature**

Choice C is the best answer because the underlined sentence shows a change in Lemm's fortune from wandering musician to successful orchestra director. Moreover, this change occurs after Lemm had been pursuing music for many years.

Choice A is incorrect because, while the underlined sentence shows that Lemm left behind his lifestyle as a wandering musician, it does not show his feelings about it. Choice B is incorrect because, while the underlined sentence mentions Lemm's respected position in the orchestra, it does not raise uncertainties about Lemm's ability to maintain that position. Choice D is incorrect because, while the audiences of wandering musicians are different from those of orchestras, the underlined sentence does not mention audiences or Lemm's awareness of them.

Question 4: Choice B
Text Structure and Purpose
Difficulty - **Medium** | Topic - **Social Studies**

Choice B is the best answer because the first sentence of the passage introduces a research finding: Democratic and Republican voters are equally likely to eventually switch to voting for the opposing party. B reinforces and provides specific data to expand on this finding.

Choice A is incorrect because the sentence does not provide any information about specific methodology, and because it suggests a similarity (NOT a difference) in the behavior of Democratic and Republican voters. Choice C is incorrect because the sentence highlights a similarity, NOT a discrepancy. Choice D is incorrect because it affirms research findings rather than indicating a lack of evidence or conclusion.

Question 5: Choice B
Cross-Text Connections
Difficulty - **Medium** | Topic - **Science**

Choice B is the best answer because Text 1 outlines the dangers of gaseous and liquid fluorocarbons, while Text 2 explains the dangers of fluorocarbons in solid plastics, which constitute "another physical form" when compared to gaseous and liquid fluorocarbon substances.

Choice A is incorrect because, though Text 1 profiles a project that would address fluorocarbon-related liabilities, Text 2 does not discuss that project. Choice C is incorrect because, though the texts focus on the uses and dangers of fluorocarbons, Text 2 does not say that fluorocarbons are too dangerous for daily use. Choice D is incorrect because, though Text 1 describes an effort to develop safer containers for fluorocarbon-based products, Text 2 does not argue for the development of new materials.

Question 6: Choice A
Central Ideas and Details
Difficulty - **Easy** | Topic - **Literature**

Choice A is the best answer because the old man "caught the brightness [that Peter's] voice and presence lent" and "felt the sunshine" caused by Peter's presence. Moreover, Peter "made glad a lonesome place." Thus, Peter's presence is a source of happiness for the old man.

Choice B is incorrect because, though the old man likes Peter, the poem does mention assistance. Choice C is incorrect because, though the poem mentions sunshine, sunshine does not make the old man remember distant events. Choice D is incorrect because, though the text implies that the old man would otherwise be lonely, it does not suggest that Peter is too young to understand the old man's sadness.

Question 7: Choice C
Central Ideas and Details
Difficulty - **Medium** | Topic - **Science**

Choice C is the best answer because the text states that "Robock did not need to travel to India to determine that geoengineering could "backfire if it ended suddenly." He relied on software simulations to reach this conclusion." Thus, he could use computer models rather than manipulating the province's actual climate.

Choice A is incorrect because, though it might seem optimal to visit the province, the text does not mention any researchers who disagree with Robuck. Choice B is incorrect because, though Robock used simulation software, the text does not say that he developed it. Choice D is incorrect because, though Robock's colleagues were involved in his geoengineering simulations, the text does not say that they developed competing simulations.

Question 8: Choice B
Central Ideas and Details
Difficulty - **Medium** | Topic - **Humanities**

Choice B is the best answer because Migrant Mother, which "places . . . Thompson, in extreme close-up, . . . was not the only image of Thompson that Lange captured." Moreover, the other images included "photographs of Thompson and her children . . . taken from farther back to include the group's tent-like shelter and rather barren surroundings." Thus, the content and composition of those photographs differ significantly from those of Migrant Mother.

Choice A is incorrect because, though Lange's Migrant Mother photograph has risen to iconic status, there are no doubts about its central subject's identity. Choice C is incorrect because, though Thompson's surroundings are not seen in the well-known Migrant Mother photograph, they were not edited out but rather were not included in the first place. Choice D is incorrect because, though Lange took several photographs of Thompson, the text does not say that she photographed other farm workers.

Question 9: Choice C
Textual Command of Evidence
Difficulty - **Medium** | Topic - **Humanities**

Choice C is the best answer because Christopher's loss of respect for his father due to his father's dishonesty supports the scholar's claim that Christopher is "meticulously truthful" and "finds even slight exaggerations objectionable."

Choice A is incorrect because, though attempting to solve a mystery is a search for truth, providing evasive answers does not constitute being "meticulously truthful." Choice B is incorrect because, though Christopher is described as being different from other characters, that difference is in honesty, not in understanding motives. Choice D is incorrect because, though it is about Haddon's novel, it is not about Christopher's unique honesty.

Question 10: Choice B
Textual Command of Evidence
Difficulty - **Medium** | Topic - **Science**

Choice B is the best answer because the claim of the specialists requires a valid comparison between geological features on Mars and in Iceland. This choice presents a group of ridges on Mars and indicates that "comparisons between these ridges and Iceland's eskers" could explain the evolution of Mars's terrain; this choice effectively presents an "analogy" that would logically lead to an improved understanding of conditions on Mars.

Choice A is incorrect because it introduces a possible connection between Earth and the Moon, not the required connection between Earth and Mars. Choice C is incorrect because it introduces a connection between Mars and the eskers on Earth but calls the validity of this connection into question; instead, the correct choice should indicate that a comparison would "facilitate a deeper understanding." Choice D is incorrect because it creates a broad comparison that parallels Earth with "the Moon and other planets"; it is not clear that Mars is one of the planets that is being mentioned.

Question 11: Choice D
Quantitative Command of Evidence
Difficulty - **Medium** | Topic - **Science**

Choice D is the best answer because the passage states that "nitrogen . . . helps to keep the potato chips fresh" and that "traces of other gases . . . can lead to the potato chips going stale more quickly than usual." Thus, the consumer should buy a brand with the highest percentage of nitrogen. The table shows that brands 3 and 4 are tied for the highest percentage of nitrogen (99%).

Choice A is incorrect because, though 98% is a high percentage, it is not the highest one in the table. Choice B is incorrect because, though 98% is a high percentage, brands 3 and 4 have an even higher percentage of nitrogen. Choice C is incorrect because, though it includes one brand (brand 3) that is tied for the highest percentage of nitrogen, it also includes a brand (brand 2) that has a lower percentage of nitrogen.

Question 12: Choice B
Quantitative Command of Evidence
Difficulty - **Hard** | Topic - **Science**

Choice B is the best answer because in 2001, the observed water level was quite close to the surface (just above the normal minimum); by 2002, the observed water level had lowered substantially, and slightly exceeded the normal maximum depth below the surface. Since the passage stipulates that water extraction lowers the aquifer's water surface level, it can be inferred that water extraction occurred between 2001 and 2002, contributing to the lowered water level.

Choice A is incorrect because the aquifer water level remained relatively stable between 2000 and 2001. Choice C is incorrect because the water level increased sharply between 2002 and 2003 (evidenced by a decrease in the depth below the surface); water extraction typically leads water levels to decrease, not increase. Choice D is incorrect because between 2003 and 2004, the depth below the surface continued to decline, reflecting rising water levels.

Question 13: Choice D
Inferences
Difficulty - **Hard** | Topic - **History**

Choice D is the best answer because "the number [57] was no coincidence" since it matched the last two digits of the year that "Featherstone . . . developed the first-ever lawn flamingo." Thus, the number 57 is understood as a reference to that development in 1957.

Choice A is incorrect because, while the number 57 is an acknowledgment of an event in Featherstone's life, it is not an acknowledgment of his origins as a sculptor. Choice B is incorrect because, though Featherstone was initially hesitant to engage in corporate work, the number 57 celebrates his corporate work. Choice C is incorrect because, though the number 57 celebrates an event, it does not celebrate the versatility of plastics.

Question 14: Choice A
Form, Structure, and Sense
Difficulty - **Medium** | Topic - **History**

Choice A is the best answer because the singular possessive "organization's" properly indicates that the beginnings are of the Amateur Golf Association. The plural noun "beginnings" is necessary because it is the subject of the verb "were."

Choice B is incorrect because the singular possessive "beginning's" results in a possessive adjective where there should be a noun, thereby leaving "were" without a subject. Choice C is incorrect because the plural noun "organizations" does not match the singular "Amateur Golf Association" and because "organizations" and "beginnings" cannot both be the subject of the verb "were." Choice D is incorrect because the plural noun "organizations" does not match the singular "Amateur Golf Association" and because the singular possessive "beginning's" lacks an object.

Question 15: Choice D
Boundaries
Difficulty - **Easy** | Topic - **Humanities**

Choice D is the best answer because the essential phrase ("founded by") is not set off with, or interrupted by, a punctuation mark. This phrase should be incorporated into the rest of the sentence in this manner, since other options treat an essential phrase as nonessential.

Choice A is incorrect because it treats "by former . . . of Art" as an independent clause. Choice B is incorrect because it separates the founders from "founded by," thereby producing an incomplete clause before the dash. Choice C is incorrect because it treats "by former . . . of Art" as nonessential, thereby producing an incomplete independent clause. All of these false answers result in incomplete independent clauses.

Question 16: Choice C
Form, Structure, and Sense
Difficulty - **Medium** | Topic - **Humanities**

Choice C is the best answer because "completing" is the singular subject of the underlined singular verb "seems."

The subject may be hard to identify due to the intervening prepositional phrase and the fact that the subject is a gerund.

Choice A is incorrect because the plural verb "were seeming" does not agree with the singular subject. Choice B is incorrect because the plural verb "seem" does not agree with the singular subject. Choice D is incorrect because the plural verb "have seemed" does not agree with the singular subject.

Question 17: Choice C
Boundaries
Difficulty - **Easy** | Topic - **History**

Choice C is the best answer because the essential phrase ("cite three") is not set off with, or interrupted by, a punctuation mark. This phrase should be incorporated into the rest of the sentence in this manner, since other options treat an essential phrase as nonessential.

Choice A is incorrect because it treats "Historians commonly cite" as a complete independent clause, which it is not because the verb "cite" requires an object (a colon requires an independent clause before it). Choice B is incorrect because it cuts the phrase "three gunpowder empires" with a comma and because it treats "three" as the complete object of the verb "cite." Choice D is incorrect because it omits the object of the verb "cite" from the independent clause.

Question 18: Choice A
Boundaries
Difficulty - **Medium** | Topic - **Social Studies**

Choice A is the best answer because the sentence requires the finite verb form "reflects" to create a parallel list of verbs with the "both . . . and" construction. The verb form should take the subject "labeling." The underlined verb form must be parallel with "helps" because those two verbs form a list of what labeling bagels as vegan does.

Choice B is incorrect because the finite verb form "reflects" without "and" fuses the two items in the list without a proper boundary. Choice C is incorrect because the nonfinite verb form "reflecting" (a present participle) makes "reflecting a reality of classic bagel recipes" a consequence of helping cafes appeal to vegan customers rather than a separate item in the list. Choice D is incorrect because the nonfinite verb form "and reflecting" is the present participle, so it fails to create a parallel list with "helps."

Question 19: Choice D
Form, Structure, and Sense
Difficulty - **Hard** | Topic - **History**

Choice D is the best answer because the modifier ("taking place . . . of 1970") must modify the noun immediately after it. The founding of the Environmental Protection Agency is what took place in December of 1970, so "the founding of the Environmental Protection Agency" must be the beginning of the correct answer.

Choice A is incorrect because it would make the modifier modify "it," which refers to the Environmental Protection Agency, not its founding. Choice B is incorrect because it would make the modifier modify "Environmental Protection Agency," which is illogical since an agency cannot occur at a specific time. Choice C is incorrect because it would make the modifier modify "Environmental Protection Agency" rather than its founding.

Question 20: Choice D
Form, Structure, and Sense
Difficulty - **Medium** | Topic - **Social Studies**

Choice D is the best answer because "participants" is the plural antecedent of the underlined plural pronoun "they" and the plural subject of the underlined plural verb "maneuver." The subject may be hard to locate due to the interrupter phrase ("in a race . . . while") separating the antecedent from the pronoun and the verb.

Choice A is incorrect because the second-person singular pronoun "you" does not agree with the plural antecedent. Choice B is incorrect because the third-person singular pronoun "one" does not agree with the plural antecedent. Choice C is incorrect because the third-person singular pronoun "it" does not agree with the plural antecedent.

Question 21: Choice B
Boundaries
Difficulty - **Hard** | Topic - **Humanities**

Choice B is the best answer because the colon properly concludes the independent clause "Jamaican-Canadian" and introduces content that explains the "single medium" that Lewis uses. This content is structured as an item, "repurposed fabric," followed by a long dependent clause that explains how the fabric functions in Lewis's art.

Choice A is incorrect because it uses a semicolon to introduce a dependent clause that begins with "of," but semicolons should introduce independent clauses. Choice C is incorrect because it introduces "of" to place two dependent clauses after a colon instead of following the colon with an explanatory independent clause, item, or list of items. Choice D is incorrect because it avoids punctuation to create the improperly fused phrase "single medium repurposed fabric," but the "repurposed fabric" describes the "medium" further and should be set off with punctuation.

Question 22: Choice A
Transitions
Difficulty - **Hard** | Topic - **History**

Choice A is the best answer because "then" signals that Ataturk's educational projects of the late 1920s occurred after his reforms in the mid 1920s. This transition properly signals a temporal relationship.

Choice B is incorrect because "nonetheless" introduces a contrast relationship, which wrongly indicates that Ataturk's educational projects of the late 1920s go against his reforms of the mid 1920s. Choice C is incorrect because "for instance" introduces a support relationship, which wrongly indicates that Ataturk's educational projects of the late 1920s are examples of his reforms in the mid 1920s. Choice D is incorrect because, while "simultaneously" introduces a temporal relationship, it wrongly indicates that Ataturk's educational projects of the late 1920s occurred during his mid 1920s reforms..

Question 23: Choice C
Transitions
Difficulty - **Medium** | Topic - **Social Studies**

Choice C is the best answer because "in particular" signals that studying frugal entrepreneurs is an example of studying frugal people. This transition properly signals a support relationship.

Choice A is incorrect because "granted" introduces a caveat relationship, which wrongly indicates that studying frugal entrepreneurs is an exception to studying frugal people. Choice B is incorrect because "by contrast" introduces an opposing relationship, which wrongly indicates that studying frugal entrepreneurs is different from studying frugal people. Choice D is incorrect because "on the other hand" introduces an opposing relationship, which wrongly indicates that studying frugal entrepreneurs is incongruous with studying frugal people.

Question 24: Choice D
Transitions
Difficulty - **Medium** | Topic - **Social Studies**

Choice D is the best answer because "still" signals that airlines like Singapore Air have made efforts to create prestigious airline food despite the fact that many other airlines view

"providing in-flight food [to] be at best a burden and at most an obligation." This transition properly signals a contrast relationship.

Choice A is incorrect because "to this end" introduces a goal relationship, which wrongly indicates that some airlines have made efforts to create prestigious airline food in order to make other airlines view "providing in-flight food [as] at best a burden and at most an obligation." Choice B is incorrect because "for example" introduces a support relationship, which wrongly indicates that making efforts to create prestigious airline food is an example of viewing "in-flight food [to] be at best a burden and at most an obligation." Choice C is incorrect because "likewise" introduces a similarity relationship, which wrongly indicates that creating prestigious airline food is similar to viewing "in-flight food [as] at best a burden and at most an obligation."

Question 25: Choice A
Transitions
Difficulty - **Medium** | Topic - **Science**

Choice A is the best answer because "in consequence" signals that "new concentrations of resources stimulated evolution" because "marine animals . . . [had] 'mixed up the water and enabled resources to spread more widely' in prehistoric seas." This transition properly signals a causal relationship.

Choice B is incorrect because "conversely" introduces a contrast relationship, which wrongly indicates that "new concentrations of resources stimulat[ing] evolution" is incongruent with "marine animals . . . 'mix[ing] up the water and enabl[ing] resources to spread more widely' in prehistoric seas." Choice C is incorrect because "for instance" introduces a support relationship, which wrongly indicates that "new concentrations of resources stimulat[ing] evolution" is an example of "marine animals . . . 'mix[ing] up the water and enabl[ing] resources to spread more widely' in prehistoric seas." Choice D is incorrect because "paradoxically" introduces a tension relationship, which wrongly indicates that "new concentrations of resources stimulat[ing] evolution" is logically inconsistent with "marine animals . . . 'mix[ing] up the water and enabl[ing] resources to spread more widely' in prehistoric seas."

Question 26: Choice C
Rhetorical Synthesis
Difficulty - **Medium** | Topic - **Science**

Choice C is the best answer because it mentions two different Platonic Solids (the tetrahedron and the icosahedron), and it states a similarity between them (they both have triangular faces). This choice is consistent with the student's goal of "call[ing] attention to a similarity between the faces of two different Platonic Solids."

Choice A is incorrect because, though it mentions two different Platonic Solids, it does not state a similarity between them. Choice B is incorrect because, though it discusses Platonic Solids, it lists three, rather than two, of the solids. Choice D is incorrect because, though it discusses a shared trait among all Platonic Solids, it does not focus on only two of the solids.

Question 27: Choice A
Rhetorical Synthesis
Difficulty - **Hard** | Topic - **Humanities**

Choice A is the best answer because it concisely summarizes virtually all of the information recorded in the passage. It eliminates unnecessary repetition and uses one date (1965) to situate the time range of these events, rather than repeating multiple dates.

Choice B is incorrect because it omits key information about The Byrds, who are mentioned but not in a manner that would introduce their achievements to a reader unfamiliar with The Byrds as a band. Choice C is incorrect because it focuses unnecessarily on Dylan's process of writing and recording the song, rather than providing a more balanced overview of multiple musicians (Dylan and The Byrds) engaging with the same song. Choice D is incorrect because it limits information about Dylan writing and recording the song, placing the focus primarily on The Byrds (but does not mention that the album was titled after the song). This choice also presents The Byrds with minimal context that would be problematic for a reader unfamiliar with The Byrds.

Module 2: Hard
— Pages 162-171 —

Question 1: Choice D
Word in Context
Difficulty - **Easy** | Topic - **Humanities**

Choice D is the best answer because, by treating "interior narration as relatively minor" and "dialogue [as] primary," Compton-Burnett "reversed th[e] premise" of treating "narration that revealed the inner thoughts of characters" as primary. Therefore, the status quo among some modernist authors was to treat interior narration as primary and dialogue as secondary.

Choice A is incorrect because, though grounding dialogue in inner thoughts might make dialogue seem less important than inner thoughts, that would not provide a strong enough foil for treating "interior narration as relatively minor" and "dialogue [as] primary." Choice B is incorrect because, though crafting dialogue from inner thoughts might make inner thoughts seem fundamental, that would not provide a parallel comparison to treating "interior narration as relatively minor" and "dialogue [as] primary." Choice C is incorrect because something can be despised only by a person, not by a thing (narration).

Question 2: Choice D
Word in Context
Difficulty - **Hard** | Topic - **Social Studies**

Choice D is the best answer because the passage describes how some regions of the United States function without a singular and predominant power facility. Choose D to convey the meaning of a system in which multiple functions and services are gathered together in a single, unified location.

Choice A is incorrect because it implies diversity and variety, rather than a site where multiple functions are brought together. Choice B is incorrect because it implies something that can serve multiple purposes and be utilized in different ways. Choice C is incorrect because it implies protocol and oversight.

Question 3: Choice B
Word in Context
Difficulty - **Medium** | Topic - **Literature**

Choice B is the best answer because the underlined word is contrasted with "ceremony and reserve" since "this peep at everyday life was a most exciting novelty." "Spontaneously" appropriately conveys that people are behaving without adherence to preset procedures.

Choice A is incorrect because, though "everyday life" might sound predictable, the narrator is making the point that

Digital SAT Reading and Writing: Test 5

people are not behaving according to ceremony. Choice C is incorrect because, though "everyday life" might sound repetitive, people are acting sincerely rather than letting customs consume their individuality. Choice D is incorrect because, though people are acting sincerely, Genji is not assessing the validity of their actions.

Question 4: Choice A
Word in Context
Difficulty - **Hard** | Topic - **Science**

Choice A is the best answer because, though "captur[ing] Martian atmosphere samples" is not the Perseverance Mars Rover's primary mission, "the Perseverance mission has in fact yielded Martian air samples." Thus, the rover collects Martian atmosphere samples as a side effect of its primary mission. "Collateral" appropriately fits the context of scientific missions.

Choice B is incorrect because, though capturing Martian atmosphere samples is not as important in the rover's mission as "drilling mineral samples from the planet's surface" is, only a living thing can be submissive. Choice C is incorrect because, though Martian samples might seem hard to understand, the fact that the rover collects gaseous samples is not difficult to decipher. Choice D is incorrect because, though the rover is doing what it is designed to do, the secondary effect being discussed is not being demanded or required in an agreement.

Question 5: Choice B
Word in Context
Difficulty - **Hard** | Topic - **Humanities**

Choice B is the best answer because Herzog "speak[s] just off-camera about the philosophical conundrums that the individuals in his films face." Thus, the underlined words must indicate that Herzog talks about his subjects. "Opines about" appropriately fits the context of talking about the inner thoughts of documentary characters.

Choice A is incorrect because, though Herzog's commentary may decrease the focus on the characters' own statements, Herzog does not diminish or weaken his subjects. Choice C is incorrect because, though Herzog might be a distraction for some viewers, he is not veering off-topic. Choice D is incorrect because, though Herzog adds his views of his characters' philosophical conundrums to his films, he does not augment the negative traits of characters.

Question 6: Choice D
Word in Context
Difficulty - **Hard** | Topic - **History**

Choice D is the best answer because the "so-called 'great man' theories" experienced "former dominance." Thus, they were accepted as correct by the majority of historians. "Hegemony" appropriately fits the context of theories and historical models.

Choice A is incorrect because, though epochal change is within the professional jurisdiction of historians, there is nothing to suggest that anyone is challenging whether epochal change is in fact within the purview of historians. Choice B is incorrect because, though the popularity of models is discussed, only people can be congenial. Choice C is incorrect because, though differing historical models are discussed, the historical models described by the underlined word agreed with each other.

Question 7: Choice D
Text Structure and Purpose
Difficulty - **Hard** | Topic - **Social Studies**

Choice D is the best answer because the text describes Antonietti's opinion and findings regarding how aging affects the human brain's capabilities. Specifically, he "is convinced that growing older unlocks some forms of creativity," and his study "revealed that 'divergent thinking' . . . flourishes among older people."

Choice A is incorrect because, though Antonietti's work "challenges the concept of" an old-age decline in intellectual efficiency, that concept was not central to an earlier research project. Choice B is incorrect because, though the text mentions that divergent thinking, which is central to humor, does not decline with age, it does not compare Antonietti's work to similar studies. Choice C is incorrect because, though intellectual efficiency and divergent thinking are not the same thing, the text does not use Antonietti's viewpoint to contrast them.

Question 8: Choice C
Text Structure and Purpose
Difficulty - **Hard** | Topic - **Science**

Choice C is the best answer because the underlined text explains why "high-resolution telescopes are frequently launched into outer space" despite the fact that launching a telescope from Earth "limits how powerful an orbiting telescope can be."

Choice A is incorrect because, though the passage states a limitation of the large orbiting telescopes that have already

Unauthorized copying or reuse of any part of this page is illegal   **179** been launched beyond the atmosphere, the underlined portion is about telescopes orbiting in Earth's atmosphere. Choice B is incorrect because, though the FLUTE project was designed to address limitations on mirror size, which is relevant to imaging, the underlined portion does not pinpoint specific deficiencies in image resolution. Choice D is incorrect because, though the passage shows how the FLUTE project differs from current methods, the underlined portion does not contrast the FLUTE project with an earlier endeavor.

Question 9: Choice A
Central Ideas and Details
Difficulty - **Hard** | Topic - **Literature**

Choice A is the best answer because the speaker expresses both strong connection to Russia (he "love[s] your vasts of corn or snow") but also wonders about the source of this connection: "What can the secret link between us be?" Choose A to reflect that the speaker expresses love for Russia while also wondering about the source of that love.

Choice B is incorrect because the passage focuses on a speaker pondering the source of his strong attachment to Russia, NOT seeking a stronger understanding of life in this country. Choice C is incorrect because the lines in the passage do not describe any information about Russia's history. Choice D is incorrect because the lines in the passage evoke general imagery about Russia ("your vasts of corn or snow") but does NOT evoke a specific scene from a journey through Russia.

Question 10: Choice C
Textual Command of Evidence
Difficulty - **Hard** | Topic - **Humanities**

Choice C is the best answer because it states that Chevy Chase's unflattering portrayal of President Gerald Ford "did more than any political ad to effectively create the image of Ford as a dope and a lightweight." This supports the critic's claim that SNL "representations do not merely reflect political realities: sometimes, the caricatures on Saturday Night Live meaningfully have shaped how political figures are perceived."

Choice A is incorrect because, though it is partly about SNL's topical satire, it does not show how SNL shaped public opinion of political figures. Choice B is incorrect because, though it references an instance of SNL's political satire, it does not show how "the caricatures on Saturday Night Live meaningfully have shaped how political figures are perceived." Choice D is incorrect because, though it references two examples of SNL's political satire, it does not show how that satire shaped public opinion of political figures.

Question 11: Choice D
Textual Command of Evidence
Difficulty - **Hard** | Topic - **Social Studies**

Choice D is the best answer because it notes that verbal hesitations help "experimental participants" to remember information in an exercise involving a 160-word sentence. This information would support the researchers' claim that verbal hesitations lead to "better retention of specific pieces of information."

Choice A is incorrect because it introduces one broadcaster's intentions and a possible benefit of verbal hesitations ("a better connection") that is different from the benefit ("better retention") cited by the Edinburgh researchers. It is possible that the listeners would feel connected to Chiles without remembering specific information with greater clarity. Choice B is incorrect because it associates verbal hesitations with positive effects in terms of reputation and emphasis, not positive effects in terms of memory. Choice C is incorrect because it provides details about the procedures used by the Edinburgh researchers, not a statement of benefits or positive outcomes related to memory.

Question 12: Choice A
Textual Command of Evidence
Difficulty - **Hard** | Topic - **Literature**

Choice A is the best answer because in these lines, Faustus expresses frustration with "logic" (learning and education) and decides to cease reading. Choose A to reflect that these lines provide evidence that Faustus eventually becomes dissatisfied with his studies.

Choice B is incorrect because these lines involve Faustus expressing ambitions, NOT dissatisfaction with studies and learning. Choice C is incorrect because these lines reflect the aspirations that tempted Faustus to pursue studies, NOT his eventual frustration with those studies. Choice D is incorrect because it shows someone else advising Faustus not to pursue study of a certain text, rather than Faustus himself becoming dissatisfied with studying and learning.

Question 13: Choice D
Quantitative Command of Evidence
Difficulty - **Hard** | Topic - **Social Studies**

Choice D is the best answer because results that "resembled those of the 2015 study" would naturally feature the same 18-20 age group and a comparable set of outcomes, namely "a faster response for the auditory stimuli" for each participants. Students 2, 4, and 5 were all in the required age range and achieved auditory responses that were faster than the visual responses by 20 milliseconds; the original 2015 study achieved very similar results, as noted in the text.

Choice A is incorrect because students 4 and 5 achieved results that were in line with the results of the 2015 study; this choice wrongly assumes that student 2 was the only student to do so. Choice B is incorrect because student 3 had a relatively fast response to the visual stimulus and a relatively slow response to the auditory stimulus; the 2015 study yielded the the opposite results. Choice C is incorrect because student 1, at age 16, did not fit the required 18-20 age group for the 2015 study and because, in a departure from the 2015 results, student 3 had a relatively fast response to the visual stimulus and a relatively slow response to the auditory stimulus.

Question 14: Choice B
Inferences
Difficulty - **Hard** | Topic - **Science**

Choice B is the best answer because the Leadbeater's Possum was wrongly declared extinct and was then "rediscovered" based solely on random observations of populations in the wild. Thus, conservationists currently monitor Leadbeater's Possums in controlled settings to get more accurate information about them so as to avoid more incorrect announcements concerning the Leadbeater Possum.

Choice A is incorrect because, though captive possums might be more likely to survive than wild possums, the text does not say that. Choice C is incorrect because, though the text mentions the lowland variety and other varieties of the Leadbeater's Possum, it is not about confusing one for the other. Choice D is incorrect because, though there were mistaken "rediscoveries" of Leadbeater's Possum, the text does not say that those mistaken "rediscoveries" hindered conservation efforts.

Question 15: Choice D
Inferences
Difficulty - **Hard** | Topic - **Science**

Choice D is the best answer because the passage explains that turtles and their hatchlings can be spread out across large expanses of shoreline. A fast-moving vehicle allows researchers to efficiently cover large terrains, and inspect turtles located in dispersed locations.

Choice A is incorrect because the passage describes a land-based vehicle, which cannot enter the ocean and thus would not help researchers attempting to study turtles once they have entered water. Choice B is incorrect because the passage does not mention whether the vehicles are disruptive to the turtles, and focuses instead on how it makes research more efficient for the scientists. Choice C is incorrect because the

passage focuses on research that aims to survey turtles in dispersed locations, NOT relocate them.

Question 16: Choice D
Boundaries
Difficulty - **Hard** | Topic - **Humanities**

Choice D is the best answer because the phrase "like . . . (2005)" should be set off with two commas to form a single dependent clause. When this clause is disregarded, the grammatically correct main independent clause "Kazuo . . . others" results.

Choice A is incorrect because it does not feature the second comma that is necessary to set off the dependent clause. Choice B is incorrect because it introduces a colon that splits parts of the independent clause "Kazuo...others"; the content that remains in front of the colon, "Kazuo . . . is," does not form an independent clause on its own. Choice C is incorrect because it uses a single comma to split two nouns (the names of the novels) that are grammatically connected by "and"; this choice disrupts the construction of a single dependent clause that links two ideas together to name earlier novels.

Question 17: Choice D
Boundaries
Difficulty - **Hard** | Topic - **Social Studies**

Choice D is the best answer because the nonessential phrase ("who would . . . departments") is enclosed by parentheses, and the dependent clause ("Already an . . . departments)") is followed by a comma. The sentence should be punctuated in this manner, since other options treat part of the nonessential phrase as essential or fail to separate the dependent clause from the independent clause ("it is also . . . Aristotle").

Choice A is incorrect because it does not separate the dependent clause from the independent clause. Choice B is incorrect because it excludes "in biology departments" from the parenthetical phrase, thereby stating that bioethics would be of interest to genomicists in biology departments rather than to genomicists. Choice C is incorrect because it treats "in biology departments" as an introductory phrase in the independent clause. All of these false answers result in errors in nonessential phrases.

Question 18: Choice C
Form, Structure, and Sense
Difficulty - **Medium** | Topic - **Social Studies**

Choice C is the best answer because the passage describes an action that began in the past and has now concluded (conducting research in 2015). It therefore requires the verb "to conduct" to be conjugated in the simple past tense.

Choice A is incorrect because it conjugates the auxiliary verb (have) in the singular, whereas two subjects are performing the action. Choice B is incorrect because it utilizes the continuous tense (including a conjugated form of the auxiliary verb to be). Choice D is incorrect because it utilizes the present tense, whereas the sentence requires the past tense to require an action that began and concluded in the past.

Question 19: Choice D
Boundaries
Difficulty - **Hard** | Topic - **History**

Choice D is the best answer because it properly uses two commas to set aside the dependent phase describing the "film project." The content between parentheses is also properly punctuated to function as a description internal to the dependent phrase; "released in 1990" effectively refers to the film Vincent and Me, and the phrase "director Michael Rubbo's Vincent and Me" is properly punctuated as dependent if the content between parentheses is removed.

Choice A is incorrect because it introduces a semicolon to punctuate a single dependent phrase, but semicolons can only coordinate independent clauses or punctuate lists with internally punctuated complex items. Choice B is incorrect because it places the content between parentheses outside the dependent phrase that names the film, but this content should be grouped so that "released in 1990" properly modifies "Michael Rubbo's Vincent and Me." Choice C is incorrect because it places a second comma after the name of the film and would thus result in two consecutive commas without any content if the content in parentheses (which is normally the first dependent content to be factored out of a given sentence construction) is removed.

Question 20: Choice B
Boundaries
Difficulty - **Hard** | Topic - **Science**

Choice B is the best answer because the semicolon properly configures the two independent clauses "New research . . . planet" and "Xiaodong . . . interior." This choice properly places a dependent clause that describes the actions of the researchers after the semicolon, and this placement does not disrupt the structure of the independent clauses.

Choice A is incorrect because it places a long dependent clause that is placed between commas between two independent clauses. This structure creates a comma splice when the dependent clause is disregarded. Choice C is incorrect because it places a long dependent clause between two independent clauses and thus creates a comma splice. Instead, a period or semicolon is needed to configure the independent clauses. Choice D is incorrect because it results in a run-on sentence that fuses an independent and dependent clause; the later

punctuation of a single comma before "Xiaodong Song" results in a comma splice.

Question 21: Choice D
Form, Structure, and Sense
Difficulty - **Hard** | Topic - **Science**

Choice D is the best answer because the modifier ("Rarely seen . . . underground") must modify the noun immediately after it. Caecilians are the animals that are "rarely seen . . . because they dwell underground," so "caecilians" must be the beginning of the correct answer.

Choice A is incorrect because it would make the modifier modify "amphibians" in general rather than only caecilians. That would be incorrect because many amphibians are often seen above ground. Choice B is incorrect because it would make the modifier modify "few known traces," which are not subterranean organisms. Choice C is incorrect because it would make the modifier modify "few known fossil record traces," which are not subterranean organisms.

Question 22: Choice D
Boundaries
Difficulty - **Hard** | Topic - **Science**

Choice D is the best answer because it uses a period to coordinate two independent clauses, "Large . . . regions" and "resource . . . patterns." Dependent clauses occur at the end of the first independent clause and at the beginning of the second, and these clauses are properly punctuated with commas so that they can be factored out to create a construction involving two independent clauses and a single period.

Choice A is incorrect because it creates a comma splice by joining two independent clauses and a few different intervening clauses with commas in the absence of coordinating conjunctions such as "but" or "and." Choice B is incorrect because it creates a comma splice by featuring a comma after "instead" rather than placing a period at this logical break in the sentence construction. Choice C is incorrect because it creates an illogical relationship by grouping "instead" in the second sentence clause. The contrast is presented entirely in the first sentence, which notes groups of larger and smaller dinosaurs with different survival strategies. Placing the "instead" in the second sentence indicates that a new and contrasting explanation is being presented, not that the text is building upon a previous explanation of how two groups of dinosaurs survived.

Question 23: Choice A
Transitions
Difficulty - **Hard** | Topic - **Science**

Choice A is the best answer because "indeed" signals that the fact that students get "a better idea of what it means to be a scientist" is a consequence of the fact that Eastern Michigan University's method is "the best way to study jellyfish in Michigan." This transition properly signals an extension relationship.

Choice B is incorrect because "nevertheless" introduces a contrast relationship, which wrongly indicates that students get "a better idea of what it means to be a scientist" despite the fact that Eastern Michigan University's method is "the best way to study jellyfish in Michigan." Choice C is incorrect because "finally" introduces a temporal relationship, which wrongly indicates that students get "a better idea of what it means to be a scientist" after Eastern Michigan University's method of studying jellyfish is optimal. Choice D is incorrect because "for example" introduces a support relationship, which wrongly indicates that students getting "a better idea of what it means to be a scientist" is an example of Eastern Michigan University's method of studying jellyfish in Michigan.

Question 24: Choice C
Transitions
Difficulty - **Hard** | Topic - **History**

Choice C is the best answer because "similarly" signals that the Congo Basin villages' system of governance differed from that of the Kongo Kingdom, just as the Igbo clans' system of governance differed from that of the Kongo Kingdom. This transition properly signals an alike relationship.

Choice A is incorrect because "by contrast" introduces an opposing relationship, which wrongly indicates that the Congo Basin villages' system of governance did not differ substantially from that of the Kongo Kingdom. Choice B is incorrect because "for example" introduces a support relationship, which wrongly indicates that the Congo Basin villages' system of governance is an example of the Igbo clans' system. Choice D is incorrect because "as a result" introduces a causal relationship, which wrongly indicates that the Congo Basin villages' system of governance is a consequence of the Igbo clans' system.

Question 25: Choice C
Transitions
Difficulty - **Hard** | Topic - **Science**

Choice C is the best answer because "instead" signals that "evaluating the heights of individual tall trees" is a more accurate alternative to "assessing individual trees' near-the-ground diameters to estimate a forest's total biomass." This transition properly signals an opposing relationship.

Choice A is incorrect because "more broadly" introduces a generalization relationship, which wrongly indicates that the usefulness of "evaluating the heights of individual tall trees" is a more generalized version of the lack of usefulness of "assessing individual trees' near-the-ground diameters to estimate a forest's total biomass." Choice B is incorrect because "in addition" introduces an extension relationship, which wrongly indicates that the usefulness of "evaluating the heights of individual tall trees" is an extension of the error inherent in "assessing individual trees' near-the-ground diameters to estimate a forest's total biomass." Choice D is incorrect because "by this logic" introduces a parallel relationship, which wrongly indicates that "evaluating the heights of individual tall trees" should be useful in estimating total biomass because "assessing individual trees' near-the-ground diameters" is not useful for that purpose.

Question 26: Choice D
Rhetorical Synthesis
Difficulty - **Hard** | Topic - **Humanities**

Choice D is the best answer because it notes that Cezanne created "multiple images of individual portrait subjects," in line with the reference to "hundreds of versions" of single subjects in the notes. This broader practice of revisiting subjects was notable for "including [Cezanne's] wife Hortense," so that D properly places the "red dress" portraits in the context of a broader practice.

Choice A is incorrect because it refers to the paintings of Hortense without directly indicating a "similarity" involving these paintings and other works. Choice B is incorrect because it simply addresses Cezanne's many depictions of Hortense without considering "other" painting or portrait subjects. Choice C is incorrect because it addresses Cezanne's broad approach without noting "Cezanne's portraits of his wife" as a more specific group, as required by the student's goal.

Question 27: Choice A
Rhetorical Synthesis
Difficulty - **Hard** | Topic - **Science**

Choice A is the best answer because it indicates a specific set of locations while indicating that chipmunks were found in new areas of North Carolina. At one point found predominantly "to the west of North Carolina's Piedmont," chipmunks also reached locations east of the Piedmont by 2024. This choice both provides relevant details to fit the student's goal and accurately reflects the content of the notes.

Choice B is incorrect because it does not accurately reflect the notes, which state that chipmunks "were found to the east of the Piedmont in 2024," not to the west, as their geographic range shifted. Choice C is incorrect because it notes an area where chipmunks can be found but does not specify a shift or change in a manner that fits the student's goal. Choice D is incorrect because it notes generally that chipmunks can be found in North Carolina but does not specify a shift involving different regions of the state.

No Test Content on This Page

Reading and Writing

27 QUESTIONS

The questions in this section address a number of important reading and writing skills. Each question includes one or more passages, which may include a table or graph. Read each passage and question carefully, and then choose the best answer to the question based on the passage(s).

All questions in this section are multiple-choice with four answer choices. Each question has a single best answer.

1

The works of Irish poet W.B. Yeats (1869-1939) contain several memorable phrases and symbols that later authors have used in book titles. Chinua Achebe's *Things Fall Apart* has a title _____ Yeats's poem "The Second Coming," which is also the source for the title of Joan Didion's *Slouching Towards Bethlehem.*

Which choice completes the text with the most logical and precise word or phrase?

A) taken from

B) irrelevant to

C) rejected by

D) allied with

2

Hoping to enable the safe movements of wildlife, ecologists installed two small wildlife underpasses beneath the highway that runs alongside Canada's Kouchibouguac National Park. These _____ are scaled to allow salamanders, frogs, and other small amphibians to reach new areas without risk.

Which choice completes the text with the most logical and precise word or phrase?

A) monuments

B) intrusions

C) passages

D) barriers

3

Reconciling narrative, movement, and sculptural form, Hellenistic art often depicted individuals with implied backstories and highly physical professions in a state of _____ , as exemplified by the 100 BCE metal figure sculpture Boxer at Rest. Here, a seated prizefighter looks calmly upward as he awaits a new round of competition.

Which choice completes the text with the most logical and precise word or phrase?

A) decline

B) repose

C) haplessness

D) verification

4

The effect of winning the coveted Nobel Prize in Literature, though reliably beneficial, is by no means uniform for the authors who attain this honor. For some, such as American novelist Toni Morrison, winning the Nobel _____ an already legendary reputation. For others, such as German-Romanian author Herta Müller, the Nobel secured a vastly expanded audience.

Which choice completes the text with the most logical and precise word or phrase?

A) bolstered

B) replaced

C) abbreviated

D) specified

5

During the American Civil War, the Confederacy attempted to create an alliance with Britain based on commercial ties, assuming that British imports of cotton, which the Confederacy produced in abundance, would be pivotal. This plan involved _____ : British merchants could also source cotton from Egypt, and the alliance never materialized.

Which choice completes the text with the most logical and precise word or phrase?

A) an epiphany

B) an admission

C) a miscalculation

D) a grievance

CONTINUE

6

Artificial intelligence programs can write recipes, travel itineraries, and entire essays. Can these programs, however, write useful journalism? Writing in the Columbia Journalism Review in 2024, Felix M. Simon posed at least a tentative answer to this question. His article "Artificial Intelligence in the News" argues that digital programs represent a "retooling," not a "fundamental change in the needs and motives of news organizations," a conclusion that Simon qualified by citing the uncertainties introduced by increasingly powerful content-creating algorithms.

Which choice best describes the overall structure of the text?

A) It demonstrates the appeal of artificial intelligence for journalists, asks whether such appeal is justified, and argues that artificial intelligence will ultimately be harmful to journalism.

B) It notes existing uses of artificial intelligence, questions the applicability of artificial intelligence to journalism, and explains how one observer views journalistic trends.

C) It explains why journalists are unwilling to use artificial intelligence, summarizes the opinion of one observer, and illustrates how that observer arrived at a balanced position.

D) It criticizes current uses of artificial intelligence in journalism, proposes a new set of uses, and cites an observer who finds these new uses valid.

7

Intimidating in appearance, the teeth that give saber-toothed tigers their name were in fact fragile—so fragile, in fact, that these teeth might not have been particularly useful in hunting. This possibility has led paleontologist Julie Meachen to a different hypothesis for how saber-toothed tigers hunted. Rather than relying directly on their teeth and jaws, claims Meachen, these prehistoric large cats developed powerful forearms that were instrumental in capturing prey.

What does the text indicate about the large teeth of saber-toothed tigers?

A) The teeth were too fragile to serve any practical use for the tigers.

B) The teeth were not central to the tigers' hunting approach, according to Meachen.

C) Meachen has found few fossilized teeth due to their fragility.

D) Tigers with damaged teeth were often incapable of catching prey.

8

Keisha Oliver works as an artist, a professor, and a historian—with a focus on the art and culture of the Bahamas. This multidisciplinary approach has yielded writings of considerable scope, such Oliver's contributions to the 2019 volume *A–Z Caribbean Art*, along with projects that focus more minutely on underrepresented artists. As a research fellow at the Clark Art Institute, Oliver has dedicated much of her recent attention to formative Bahamian artists from the 1950s; her goal is to bring greater awareness to "marginalized voices within this period of Bahamian visual culture."

According to the text, what is true about Oliver's research fellowship at the Clark Art Institute?

A) Oliver has departed from the multidisciplinary approach of her other projects.

B) Oliver is completing a new installment of *A–Z Caribbean Art*.

C) Oliver's research subjects include artists and historians from the Bahamas.

D) Oliver is working to increase the visibility of 1950s Bahamian artists.

9

Statistics for the Forbidden City

Number of Individual Compounds	90
Total Number of Buildings	980
Area Covered (square meters)	720,000
Maximum width of Moat (meters)	52

The Forbidden City is a separated area of Beijing and served as the seat of power for China's emperors from the early 1400s CE onwards. This massive district is divided into multiple walled compounds. All of the individual buildings in the Forbidden City can be bound within the compounds, and these compounds are organized so that _____

Which choice most logically completes the statement with information from the table?

A) at least one of the compounds is home to multiple buildings.

B) the largest compounds are bordered by the moat of the Forbidden City.

C) each compound building covers roughly 720 square meters.

D) no compound has more than 10 buildings.

CONTINUE ▶

10

"The Three Strangers" is a 1883 short story by Thomas Hardy. In this text, Hardy's narrator evokes the scenery of rural England while also expressing uncertainty about an aspect of the scene that is being described: _____

Which quotation from "The Three Strangers" most effectively illustrates the claim?

A) "Among the few features of agricultural England which retain an appearance but little modified by the lapse of centuries, may be reckoned the high, grassy and furzy downs, coombs, or ewe-leases, as they are indifferently called, that fill a large area of certain counties in the south and south-west."

B) "Fifty years ago such a lonely cottage stood on such a down, and may possibly be standing there now. In spite of its loneliness, however, the spot, by actual measurement, was not more than five miles from a county-town."

C) "Though the wind up here blew unmistakably when it did blow, and the rain hit hard whenever it fell, the various weathers of the winter season were not quite so formidable on the coomb as they were imagined to be by dwellers on low ground."

D) "A glance into the [cottage] at eight o'clock on this eventful evening would have resulted in the opinion that it was as cozy and comfortable a nook as could be wished for in boisterous weather." HARD

To facilitate the detection of endotoxins in drinking water and other liquids, Joanna Aizenberg and Xiaoguang Wang have developed a testing method with several advantages. Their approach, which involves observing the movements of minute water droplets and noting motions indicative of toxic particles, is highly cost-efficient and detects low-concentration toxins, but one molecular chemist claims that this method might be unsuitable for detecting some types of toxic substances.

Which finding, if true, would most effectively support the molecular chemist's claim?

A) Aizenberg and Wang's method has only detected endotoxins classified as amphiphiles, and it remains unclear whether other toxins could be detected by similar means.

B) Before Aizenberg and Wang developed their method, the only means of detecting comparably small concentrations of endotoxins involved significant costs and the use of rare biological substances in the testing process.

C) The endotoxins that Aizenberg and Wang's method targets can be found in varying amounts in drinking water.

D) Aizenberg and Wang find their method beneficial because it allows researchers to easily visualize the presence of a few different types of endotoxins.

At least two different geological shifts created Puerto Rico's Luquillo Mountains. Roughly 37 to 28 million years ago, the movements of Earth's tectonic plates began pushing the underlying volcanic rock of the mountain range upward. Then, roughly 4 million years ago, additional tectonic movements pushed the mountains higher and redistributed their soil layers—the latter transformation giving rise to the mountains' current rainforest ecosystem, according to natural scientists Jane Willenbring and Maria Uriarte. In contrast to today's mountain range, the Luquillo Mountain range of 40 million years ago most likely _____

Which choice most logically completes the text?

A) did not support a rainforest ecosystem as understood by Willenbring and Uriarte but would have been characterized by high temperatures due to ongoing volcanic activity.

B) supported evenly distributed soil layers that, as a result of volcanic and tectonic activity, were mixed in a manner that facilitated the higher temperatures required for a rainforest ecosystem.

C) featured a relatively large number of relatively small mountains that would have resisted soil redistribution, at least in the absence of tectonic activity.

D) consisted of lower mountains and would have supported an ecosystem different from the rainforest ecosystem noted by Willenbring and Uriarte.

13

Shipping massive quantities of goods from seaport to seaport is a traditional method of global commerce; it continues to be a central method nonetheless, as explained by Myrto Kalouptsidi and colleagues. According to a 2023 report by Kalouptsidi, "more than 80% of traded goods (amounting to 11 billion tons and about $20 trillion) are carried by ships," meaning a trade disruption to the entirety of the sea-based shipping network would impact most of the world's commerce. In contrast, a trade disruption isolated to other methods, such as air-based transportation of goods, _____

Which choice most logically completes the text?

A) should affect considerably less than 80% of all traded goods.

B) would cause the global shipping network to expand.

C) is likely to be of no interest to Kalouptsidi.

D) could impact seaport shipping and other traditional methods.

Thailand, over the past 30 years, has adhered to a language learning policy that balances local heritage and globalized communication, according to Thom Huebner of San José State University. While Thailand's students begin learning English as a medium of global dialogue in the first _____ Huebner stresses that Thailand's linguistic diversity—"70 languages representing five distinct language families"—also guides curricula.

Which choice completes the text so that it conforms to the conventions of Standard English?

A) grade though

B) grade, though

C) grade,

D) grade

15

Holding remarkable potential for powering entire settlements on the Moon yet challenging to produce at least for now, _____ and new discoveries could facilitate fission reactions—which involve the splitting of atomic nuclei, thus unlocking enormous reserves of energy—in lightweight, portable generators.

Which choice completes the text so that it conforms to the conventions of Standard English?

A) NASA engineers are currently investigating fission energy,

B) there is a current investigation of fission energy by NASA engineers,

C) fission energy is currently being investigated by NASA engineers,

D) NASA engineers' current investigation is of fission energy,

16

Fashion designer Ashish Gupta gravitates to striking pinks, blues, and greens, crafting pieces that accentuate these tie-die shades with _____ Gupta's attention-grabbing style subtly combines cultural influences that appear rather distant, from opulent shades of India's traditional saris to the pastels favored by British and American teenagers in the 1950s.

Which choice completes the text so that it conforms to the conventions of Standard English?

A) sequins, however;

B) sequins, however

C) sequins. However,

D) sequins, however,

17

Feldspar, a mineral which _____ up 60% of Earth's crust, consists of a crystalline structure of aluminum, silicon, and oxygen atoms; these three elements combine with traces of others (including sodium and potassium) in different feldspar formations.

Which choice completes the text so that it conforms to the conventions of Standard English?

A) make

B) are making

C) makes

D) were making

18

The Indian Pueblo Cultural Center of Albuquerque acknowledges and promotes the fact that the term "Pueblo" encompasses a variety of _____ the Center calls itself a "gateway to the 19 Pueblos of New Mexico" and uses this framework of multiple Pueblo tribes when introducing visitors to the roughly 4500 artifacts in its collection.

Which choice completes the text so that it conforms to the conventions of Standard English?

A) traditions, indeed

B) traditions, indeed,

C) traditions indeed,

D) traditions; indeed,

19

Surreal, dancelike, and built upon poses and postures that alternately convey calculated awkwardness and physical grace, _____ with Jones—heavily costumed, but capable of expressive, acrobatic movement even then—playing otherworldly characters in several of del Toro's fantasy epics.

Which choice completes the text so that it conforms to the conventions of Standard English?

A) actor Doug Jones's performances are central to the films of Mexican director Guillermo del Toro,

B) Mexican director Guillermo del Toro's films feature actor Doug Jones as a central performer,

C) actor Doug Jones is a central performer in the films of Mexican director Guillermo del Toro,

D) the films of Mexican director Guillermo del Toro feature central performances by actor Doug Jones,

20

Deposits of volcanic rock and ash have a unique nomenclature of their own. The entire deposits are themselves known as _____ these deposits are made up of small rocks known as "matrix particles" and larger rocks known as "clasts."

Which choice completes the text so that it conforms to the conventions of Standard English?

A) "lahars"

B) "lahars,"

C) "lahars" and

D) "lahars," and

21

Under the phenomenon of "automation bias," professionals who rely on computerized systems disregard useful intuitions if these insights are not quickly confirmed by computerized programs. _____ as business strategist Bryce Hoffman notes, automation bias leads to an over-trusting approach to artificial intelligence (AI) in high-stakes pursuits such as navigation and finance, even when that same AI delivers faulty information.

Which choice completes the text with the most logical transition?

A) In theory,

B) To that end,

C) Regardless,

D) Moreover,

22

Peat, a spongy topsoil material consisting of decomposed moss and other vegetation, has traditionally been used to start small controlled blazes but is now proving its worth in large-scale energy production. _____ a power plant reliant on dried peat was opened in Rwanda around 2017. Plans for a second, larger plant soon followed.

Which choice completes the text with the most logical transition?

A) In fact,

B) Nevertheless,

C) In retrospect,

D) As noted,

CONTINUE ➤

23

Public speaking was important across ancient cultures. Among the Greeks of Aristotle's time, giving speeches was a civic duty. _____ among the ancient Romans, public speaking was held in high regard: this discipline even became a rigorous realm of study due to the influence of Quintilian, author of the 12-segment treatise *Principles of Oratory*.

Which choice completes the text with the most logical transition?

A) More broadly,

B) Likewise,

C) Nonetheless,

D) In other words,

24

Located in modern-day Iran, the Dezful Bridge was built around 250 CE by the Sassanid Empire, a regional power that, at the time, was in conflict with the Roman Empire. _____ this ancient stonework bridge predates current protocols for the preservation of historic sites, yet the Sassanids and later empires such as the Safavids undertook repairs and kept the bridge intact as the centuries passed.

Which choice completes the text with the most logical transition?

A) Previously,

B) In the end,

C) However,

D) Of course,

25

The trickster gods of ancient African mythologies perform a variety of secondary roles. Anansi, a trickster deity traceable to Ghanaian culture, also functions as a clever and mostly benign storyteller. _____ Ekwensu, a Nigerian trickster god, serves as a god of war and, naturally, is seen as a destructive force.

Which choice completes the text with the most logical transition?

A) By contrast,

B) For instance,

C) Therefore,

D) For this reason,

CONTINUE

26

While researching a topic, a student has taken the following notes:

- The Borobudur Temple compound was built in the 8th and 9th centuries.

- This Buddhist compound is located on Java, one of the largest islands that makes up modern-day Indonesia.

- The compound's structures are laid out in the form of a lotus, one of the sacred plants of Buddhism.

- Several stupas, or domed structures made of stone, can be found throughout the compound.

- Some of the stone carvings on these stupas call to mind lotus leaves.

The student wants to describe the Borobudur compound, with particular attention to multiple uses of the lotus motif. Which choice most effectively uses relevant information from the notes to accomplish this goal?

A) Built after between the 8th and 9th centuries, the Borobudur Temple compound is notable for the stupas, or domed structures, that it features.

B) The Borobudur Temple is located on the Indonesian island of Java and features stone carvings that recall the leaves of the lotus, a sacred plant in Buddhist tradition.

C) Laid out in the shape of a lotus leaf, the Borobudur Temple also features carvings reminiscent of lotus leaves on several of its stone stupas.

D) Carvings that call to mind the lotus leaf can be found in the Borobudur Temple, a Buddhist compound on the island of Java.

27

While researching a topic, a student has taken the following notes:

- The LUCAS machine is a device used by first responders and emergency medical technicians.

- LUCAS stands for Lund University Cardiac Arrest System.

- A LUCAS machine administers chest compressions to revive a patient whose heart has stopped or has begun to beat irregularly.

- The machine administers identical compressions that can create a steady rhythm.

- The machine can also administer compressions in a moving vehicle.

- A human first responder is more likely to administer non-identical compressions and would most likely find the movements of a vehicle disruptive.

The student wants to call attention to a few different benefits of the LUCAS machine. Which choice most effectively uses relevant information from the notes to accomplish this goal?

A) Unlike a human responder, a LUCAS machine administers identical compressions and could effectively do so in a moving vehicle.

B) Although a LUCAS machine does not operate well in a moving vehicle, it can revive a patient whose heart has stopped by administering identical chest compressions.

C) The name of the LUCAS machine involves an abbreviation of Lund University Cardiac Arrest System; this machine is used by first responders.

D) Human first responders administer chest compressions to revive cardiac arrest patients, but these compressions are often non-identical.

STOP
If you finish these exercises, you may check your work on this section only.
Do not turn to any other section in the book.

Reading and Writing

27 QUESTIONS

1

Snow leopards are not themselves migratory animals; rather, their hunting patterns are _____ the movements of migratory herds of goats and sheep, which move through mountain territories that may be split between competing snow leopard adults. Despite this dependence, one adult snow leopard will often be wary of invading another's range to "poach" sheep or goats.

Which choice completes the text with the most logical and precise word or phrase?

A) independent of

B) intrinsic to

C) reliant on

D) merited by

2

For assessing products without unwisely _____ extensive expenditures of time and capital, a judicious company will often develop a prototype known as a minimum viable product (MVP) for trial runs. Testing a MVP or even a series of MVPs, not a nearly-finished product, enables continuous improvement as the final product nears fruition—preventing, moreover, the need for costly and unforeseen corrections to a semi-finished product.

Which choice completes the text with the most logical and precise word or phrase?

A) monetizing

B) committing to

C) nullifying

D) digressing from

CONTINUE ▶

3

Harvard University paleontologist Megan Whitney has followed the evolution of tusks backwards to a single group of prehistoric creatures: the dicynodonts. Common ancestors of today's large-tusked elephants and walruses, these tusked land-dwellers do not, at least _____ , call to mind their descendants; dicynodonts had cartilaginous beaks of a sort exhibited by no mammal species, and their tusks were by no means prominent.

Which choice completes the text with the most logical and precise word or phrase?

A) superficially

B) provocatively

C) arbitrarily

D) strenuously

4

Indoor cat trees—with their multiple levels and scratchable surfaces—provide cats with more than climbing-based exercise. Even an indoor cat needs "vertical space," according to veterinarian Megan Conrad, since vertically-oriented activities such as surveying land and pouncing upon prey are _____ mammals that, like cats, have predatory propensities even when domesticated.

Which choice completes the text with the most logical and precise word or phrase?

A) inherent to

B) peripheral for

C) inchoate for

D) rationalized by

5

Sometimes, Broadway plays that were widely maligned during their initial theatrical runs find a second life as cultural curiosities—their questionable creative choices inspiring ongoing fascination. Among dramas, *Moose Murders* (1983) has risen to this form of _____ , as has *Spiderman: Turn Off the Dark* (2010) among musicals.

Which choice completes the text with the most logical and precise word or phrase?

A) indignation

B) fallaciousness

C) notoriety

D) vehemence

6

Found in European and North American forests, the wolf lichen is threatened across its large geographic range. Fortunately, scientists from the University of Barcelona are arriving at a new understanding of this symbiotic organism's survival mechanisms: a lichen itself is made up of a fungus in interdependence with an algae, and wolf lichens are themselves interdependent on very old trees. As trees die out, explains research author Sergi Munné-Bosch, they provide refuge for wolf lichens, since "the worse off these trees are, the more useful they are" for supporting other organisms.

Which choice best states the main purpose of the text?

A) To investigate the reasons for declines in wolf lichen populations across different ecosystems

B) To demonstrate how wolf lichens exhibit the interdependent relationship which is characteristic of lichens overall

C) To highlight a recently-investigated situation which facilitates the survival of wolf lichens

D) To refute the argument that very old trees do not serve a valuable ecological purpose

CONTINUE

7

This text is adapted from Rebecca Harding Davis's 1861 short story "Life in the Iron Mills."

Can you see how foggy the day is? As I stand here, idly tapping the windowpane, and looking out through the rain at the dirty back-yard and the coalboats below, fragments of an old story float up before me—a story of this house into which I happened to come to-day. You may think it a tiresome story enough, as foggy as the day, sharpened by no sudden flashes of pain or pleasure [that] I know: only the outline of a dull life, that long since, with thousands of dull lives like its own, was vainly lived.

Which choice best states the main purpose of the text?

A) To illustrate how a familiar and unappealing scene evokes a particular narrative in the speaker's mind

B) To demonstrate how a chance encounter led the speaker to reflect more deeply on events from the distant past

C) To suggest that bleak settings are paradoxically capable of inspiring elevated and noble thoughts

D) To establish a parallel between the condition of a single area and the economic problems facing a large group of people

8

Cell biologists speak of a "point of no return" in cell division: a point in the replication process (known as mitosis) after which a cellular split becomes irreversible. The reality may be more complicated, though. At the National Cancer Institute of the National Institutes of Health, researchers have determined that as many as 15% of cells can exit mitosis if mitogens, the signaling proteins that prompt cellular splits, are inhibited early on. This knowledge holds the promise of new therapies that target malignant cancers early in their growth stages or successfully blunt intermediate growth stages.

Which choice best describes the purpose of the underlined portion in the text as a whole?

A) It presents findings that call into question the methods used to determine whether a cell is entering or reversing the process of cell division.

B) It provides evidence that qualifies a seemingly absolute understanding of the "point of no return" in mitosis.

C) It clarifies how mitogens prompt cell division by contrasting how the "point of no return" operates in different groups of cells.

D) It summarizes findings that resulted from an investigation of malignant cancers and that could explain the behavior of other groups of cells.

CONTINUE

9

Text 1

The communal spirit of folk music is evident in the emphasis on music festivals characteristic of the contemporary folk scene: the New York Metropolitan Area alone is home to the Hudson West Folk Festival, the Washington Square Park Folk Festival, and the Brooklyn Folk Festival, to name but a few. Still, the prevalent image of folk music—which some of these festivals embrace in their promotional materials—is of a lone singer or guitarist onstage, not of an aggregate of voices, instruments, and styles.

Text 2

<u>Collaboration has been central to the history of American folk music</u>, even when the folk musician in question is a figure as legendary and, by some interpretations, as solitary as Pete Seeger. Dubbed the "Father of American Folk Music," Seeger was also one member of the influential Almanac Singers, an early 1940s group of over half a dozen members who, as pictured singing along together on the cover of the album *Talking Union* (1941), advertised their music as a synthesis of individual contributions.

Based on the texts, how would the author of Text 1 respond to the underlined claim in Text 2?

A) By faulting the author of Text 2 for highlighting Seeger's contributions to the Almanac Singers while neglecting Singer's individual status

B) By asserting that factors other than collaboration explain why folk music has increased in popularity over the past several decades

C) By calling attention to a recent tendency that appears to be unaligned with the historical trend noted in Text 2

D) By concurring that collaboration guides folk music but noting that current folk audiences mostly avoid communal events

10

Uses of Plant Produce by Farm Size for 2010

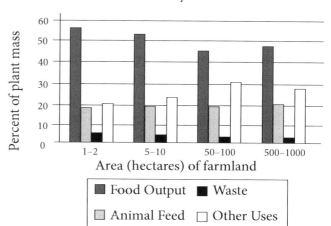

In 2010, researchers gathered international statistics that indicate how, on average, farms of various sizes allocated cropland based on the end usage of the food produced on their land. Larger farms are generally viewed as more efficient than smaller farms. However, farm efficiency is not normally measured by comparing the percent allocation of a farm's land for usable product (food output) to the percent allocation for producing food (the total for animal feed, waste, and other uses), as indicated by the fact that _____

Which choice most effectively completes the statement with information from the graph?

A) both large (50–100 hectares) and very large (500–1000 hectares) farms allocated roughly 30% of their land for "other uses" beyond food output.

B) the smallest farms considered (1–2 hectares) allocated more than 50% of their land for food output and less than 20% of their land for animal feed.

C) farms of 50–100 hectares allocated less than 50% of their land for food output while farms of 5–10 hectares allocated more than 50% of their land for food output.

D) farms of 500–1000 hectares allocated roughly 28% of their land for non-output uses, excluding waste and animal feed.

11

Constituting over 40 percent of the world's mammal species, rodents also impart important ecological benefits to the diverse environments that they inhabit, according to Abbi Gazzard and colleagues. To make their case in a recent article in The Conversation, these environmental and biological scientists cite a 2011 study by Laura Prugh and Justin Brashares, who themselves determined that kangaroo rats act as "ecosystems engineers" in a beneficial manner.

Which finding from Prugh and Brashares's research, if true, would best support Gazzard and colleagues' claim?

A) Prugh, through fieldwork, directly observed that kangaroo rat burrows consist of an "extensive network of tunnels that extend more than three feet underground" and designed the study for manageable monitoring of a few kangaroo rat populations in California grassland.

B) The burrows that kangaroo rats create will sometimes be taken over by kangaroo rat predators such as snakes and small foxes, as Prugh and Brashares noted.

C) Contrary to some of their initial expectations, Prugh and Brashares determined that "plant productivity was markedly higher" and that plant diversity improved in areas where kangaroo rats were actively burrowing.

D) Prugh and Brashares concluded that the effects of kangaroo rats on California grassland ecosystems "often varied annually" and had some connection to factors such as yearly precipitation.

12

Waged between 1652 and 1784, the Anglo-Dutch Wars were four conflicts involving competition for control of international shipping. Ultimately, the Wars resulted in the 18th-century ascendancy of the British and a less powerful role for the Dutch. Evaluating the cumulative effects of the Wars, one historian has claimed that the final outcome, which can be understood as a British victory, should be understood as the product of a few decisive and relatively short stages in the Wars.

Which finding, if true, would provide the most effective support for the historian's claim?

A) At the time of each Anglo-Dutch War, the Dutch followed a system of government best classified as a republic; the British, between the first war and the fourth, mostly followed a model of constitutional monarchy, with a more republican model during the English Civil War (1642-1651).

B) Despite leaving the Dutch navy in a position of commercial dominance, the First Anglo-Dutch War (1652-1654) demonstrated that British ships were more powerful and that the British shipbuilding industry could support a larger navy than Dutch shipbuilding could.

C) The Second Anglo-Dutch War (1665-1667) was the only of the wars in which the Dutch could be considered the victors, though some of the problems faced by the British were linked to internal crises such as the Great Fire of London (1666).

D) The Fourth Anglo-Dutch War (1780-1784) was in part linked to Dutch involvement in the American Revolution but was notable primarily because, unlike previous Anglo-Dutch conflicts, it decisively limited Dutch influence over maritime commerce.

13

Costs and Profits USD per for Three Publishers

Company	Cost per Book		Profit per Book	
	Offset	Print on Demand	Offset	Print on Demand
Publisher 1	7.47	4.79	3.12	4.34
Publisher 2	4.21	4.39	2.33	3.09
Publisher 3	6.12	4.39	7.74	7.01

At present, paperback books can be printed under one of two arrangements: offset printing (in which large numbers of a book are printed in one batch, then stored for eventual sale) and print on demand (in which books are printed one at a time or few at a time for individual customers). Offset printing is sometimes depicted as the method that more effectively lowers costs and increases profits, but the experiences of three publishers challenge this idea, as is evident from statistics for _____

Which choice completes the statement with accurate and relevant information from the table?

A) profitability per book for Publisher 1 and Publisher 3.

B) cost per book and profitability per book for Publisher 1.

C) profitability per book for Publisher 2 and Publisher 3.

D) cost per book and profitability per book for Publisher 3.

14

Nutritional scientists have long questioned the idea that consumption of carbonated water correlates with diminished bone health; some of the data that supports these doubts was gathered in the course of the Framingham Heart Study, a multi-decade assessment of the health of multiple adult patients. Granted, the Framingham statistics suggest that carbonated drinks such as sweetened sodas can adversely affect bone health in men, but effects of this sort most likely have no causal connection to carbonation and are better explained by the other properties of the beverages consumed.

Which finding, if true, would best support the underlined statement?

A) The Framingham study revealed that the effects of drinking carbonated beverages on bone density are also localized to specific bones, with the hip bones of women especially vulnerable.

B) Research from the Harvard Medical School indicates that the phosphates used as flavor enhancers in some sugary carbonated beverages are the ingredients that would prove most detrimental to bone density.

C) Carbonated beverages can be highly acidic, and Claudia Hammond of the British Broadcasting Corporation has reported that some sodas have a powerfully acidic pH of 2.5, compared to water's neutral pH of 7.

D) Studies of the detrimental effects of carbonated beverages often assume prolonged contact between the teeth of an experiment participant and the beverage being consumed, a setup that does not reflect how most people in fact consume carbonated beverages.

CONTINUE ➤

15

Major metropolitan centers such as Tokyo have experienced a boom in small (200 to 300 square-foot) apartments, many custom-designed in new buildings instead of being carved out of large spaces in older structures. The lingering challenge is to sell these spaces by making them seem efficient, not cramped. Green Residential, a property management firm, has put forward a set of design principles—maximized natural lighting, removal of clutter, and an 80-20 rule (a color scheme that is 80 percent neutral colors, 20 percent vivid accents)—to preclude visual overload.

Which choice best describes the overall structure of the text?

A) It describes a trend involving urban living spaces, then explains a few strategies for overcoming a specific challenge associated with that trend.

B) It emphasizes the factors that have led a specific type of living space to become more popular, then examines the likelihood of an imminent decrease in popularity.

C) It highlights the appeal of smaller living spaces, then explains how owners of these spaces can use a few different strategies to make living in these spaces more fulfilling.

D) It investigates a demographic change that has led to a new urban living arrangement, then describes how one company has responded to this change.

16

Insects seldom remain in family units, though there are exceptions such as the earwig, an insect known to build maternal nests and care for its young soon after they hatch. For biologist Barbara Thorne, termites could be an even more intriguing exception. Termites live in multi-generational colonies, observes Thorne, because branching out to found new colonies can pose risks for younger generations of termites and because, as their parents die off, younger termites can assume dominance of an already well-structured colony. These family unit tendencies among termites _____

Which choice most logically completes the text?

A) cause the number of termite colonies in a given area to progressively decrease, leading to the eventual dominance of a few long-established colonies.

B) result in a generational structure that increases conflicts between groups of younger and older insects within individual termite colonies.

C) differ from those of earwigs in that termites often form family units composed almost entirely of mature insects.

D) concern a life stage and set of motives that are very different from those that explain family unit tendencies among earwigs.

CONTINUE

17

Under a planned economy, a hyper-centralized government rather than an aggregate of meaningfully autonomous companies controls economic decisions. Planning of this sort is widely seen as historically disastrous—since the failed Soviet Union, after all, had a planned economy model—but is not the only sort of economic planning that experts have assessed. Daniel Pellathy of the University of Tennessee, for one, conceptualizes "planning" in terms of the supply chains and management software that help individual companies to thrive, and this version of economic planning _____

Which choice most logically completes the text?

A) has proven viable in countries that once followed planned economy models closely resembling that of the Soviet Union.

B) functions in such a manner that companies can operate without necessarily following the orders of a hyper-centralized government.

C) is not seen as historically disastrous despite the fact that only a few of the companies that use this sort of planning ultimately thrive.

D) enables national governments to become more efficient and less centralized as individual companies work more closely together.

18

New research on giant kelp has revealed that this underwater plant can adapt to nutrient shortages. As a team from the University of California, Santa Barbara, discovered through fieldwork and lab trials, kelp thrives on two _____ and treats them as interchangeable: an ammonium shortage, for instance, is not a problem if urea is abundant.

Which choice completes the text so that it conforms to the conventions of Standard English?

A) nutrients, urea and ammonium

B) nutrients, urea, and ammonium,

C) nutrients urea and ammonium

D) nutrients, urea and ammonium,

19

Widely assumed to be indigenous to northern Africa, camels spread across the ancient world, and works of statuary depicting camels in fact _____ tombs of Chinese dignitaries, for instance, were often part of elaborate installations with pathways flanked by sculptures; stone figures of resting camels have been located along these walkways.

Which choice completes the text so that it conforms to the conventions of Standard English?

A) appeared. In China, the

B) appeared in China, the

C) appeared: in China. The

D) appeared in China. The

20

Perhaps the most unusual distinction that Toronto has earned is its status as "The Raccoon Capital of the World." Indeed, the city's raccoons have been widespread recently, with the count estimated at 100,000 in 2017 and then at 200,000 in _____ instead of directly reducing the raccoon count, Toronto now promotes measures—warning visitors against feeding raccoons, for example— to discourage the raccoons from becoming bothersome.

Which choice completes the text so that it conforms to the conventions of Standard English?

A) 2022, now:

B) 2022, now

C) 2022. Now,

D) 2022, now,

CONTINUE

21

Moral ambiguity is central to Shakespearean tragedies, though scholars have cited exceptions. One essay written by Susan Snyder and published by the Folger Shakespeare Library suggests that Macbeth, Shakespeare's famous antihero, should not be seen as _____ the same realm of moral uncertainty as Shakespeare protagonists like Othello and Hamlet: Macbeth, instead, is aware of and unrepentant about his immorality.

Which choice completes the text so that it conforms to the conventions of Standard English?

A) to be inhabiting

B) to inhabit

C) inhabits

D) inhabiting

22

By reassessing evidence from a 1991 archaeological dig in Argentina, researchers Ophélie Lebrasseur and Cinthia Abbona have reclassified the remains of a large foxlike animal and have further determined that this _____ was most likely domesticated by humans 1,500 years ago.

Which choice completes the text so that it conforms to the conventions of Standard English?

A) species now, identified as *Dusicyon avus*,

B) species now identified, as *Dusicyon avus*

C) species, now identified as *Dusicyon avus*

D) species, now identified as *Dusicyon avus*,

23

Relatively few of today's most prevalent cephalopods, other than the spiral-shelled nautilus, have shells. The same, _____ cannot be said of the ancestors of these ocean creatures, which had arrays of soft tentacles that protruded from shells of various shapes. To investigate how these now-extinct cephalopods moved, David Peterman, Kathleen Ritterbush, and colleagues have used 3D-printed physical models of ancient cephalopods, suspending the models in dynamic water tanks.

Which choice completes the text with the most logical transition?

A) previously,

B) however,

C) furthermore,

D) increasingly,

24

In the cinematic technique known as a tracking shot, a single camera follows a character's movements for an extended, uninterrupted period. This is a difficult technique to sustain, in part because a true tracking shot must follow a single unbroken "take" of a scene. _____ one of the few films formatted to seem like a single tracking shot, Alfred Hitchcock's *Rope* (1948), is really ten tracking shots spliced together to create the illusion of continuity.

Which choice completes the text with the most logical transition?

A) Rather,

B) Nonetheless,

C) In fact,

D) To some extent,

25

While researching a topic, a student has taken the following notes:

- Insect biologists Susan Kirmse and Caroline S. Chaboo have investigated biodiversity among beetles in the Amazon rainforest.

- The Amazon forest canopy is an upper layer of vegetation formed by the tops of trees.

- Several of the trees in the canopy either have flowers of their own or act as supports for flowering plants.

- Kirmse and Chaboo have focused on beetles that dwell in flowering trees.

- The researchers note that there are almost 16,000 distinct tree species in the Amazon.

- Their findings indicate that there could be as many as 400,000 beetle species in these trees.

The student wants to introduce Kirmse and Chaboo's findings to an audience unfamiliar with the Amazon forest canopy. Which choice most effectively uses relevant information from the notes to accomplish this goal?

A) Kirmse and Chaboo investigated the trees of the Amazon forest canopy, and several of these trees support various sorts of flowers as well as groups of beetles.

B) According to Kirmse and Chaboo, up to 400,000 beetle species could inhabit the flowering trees of the Amazon rainforest's canopy, an upper layer formed by treetop vegetation.

C) In the Amazon forest canopy, an upper layer of vegetation that consists primarily of treetops, there are almost 16,000 different tree species, some of which are inhabited by beetles.

D) Kirmse and Chaboo, in assessing the biodiversity of the Amazon rainforest, determined that the canopy could be home to 400,000 beetle species.

CONTINUE

26

While researching a topic, a student has taken the following notes:

- Amphibious vehicles can operate both on land and on the water.

- Some amphibious vehicles have car-sized wheels for movement on land and boat-like bodies for movement over water.

- Sherp is a company that produces vehicles with small compartment-like bodies and large tractor-sized wheels.

- Sherp's vehicles have been advertised both as amphibious vehicles and as all-terrain vehicles.

- Many Sherp vehicles can navigate boggy and swampy terrain.

The student wants to explain the physical differences between Sherp's vehicles and other amphibious vehicles. Which choice most effectively uses relevant information from the notes to accomplish this goal?

A) Sherp produces amphibious vehicles with tractor-sized wheels and boat-like bodies, yet other amphibious vehicles have car-sized wheels.

B) Departing from the boat-like bodies and car-sized wheels of amphibious vehicles, Sherp's vehicles have compartment-like bodies and tractor-sized wheels.

C) Like other amphibious vehicles, the vehicles that Sherp produces can operate on land and on water, and Sherp's vehicles can also handle boggy terrain.

D) While vehicles with car-sized wheels and boat-like bodies are classified as amphibious vehicles, Sherp's vehicles have been classified as all-terrain vehicles.

27

While researching a topic, a student has taken the following notes:

- The Universal Declaration of Human Rights provides an overview of the private, political, and civil rights that modern nations should respect.

- It was ratified by the United Nations General Assembly on December 10, 1948.

- Eleanor Roosevelt, a former First Lady of the United States, was one important proponent of the Declaration.

- Roosevelt was a UN delegate and a respected humanitarian figure.

- Other important proponents of the Declaration were Lebanese diplomat Charles Habib Malik and Canadian diplomat Charles Humphrey.

The student wants to make and support a generalization about the ratification of the Universal Declaration of Human Rights. Which choice most effectively uses relevant information from the notes to accomplish this goal?

A) Eleanor Roosevelt, Charles Habib Malik, and Charles Humphrey were some of the proponents of the Universal Declaration of Human Rights.

B) Advocates of the Universal Declaration of Human Rights hailed from different countries: Eleanor Roosevelt was from the US, while Charles Humphrey was from Canada.

C) On December 10, 1948, the United Nations General Assembly ratified the Universal Declaration of Human Rights.

D) The Universal Declaration of Human Rights was promoted by UN delegate Eleanor Roosevelt, who had once held a different position: First Lady of the United States.

STOP
If you finish these exercises, you may check your work on this section only.
Do not turn to any other section in the book.

No Test Content on This Page

Answer Key

Test 6 Modules
— Pages 186-206 —

Pages 186-195 Module 1: Baseline								
1	A	10	B	19	A
2	C	11	A	20	D
3	B	12	D	21	D
4	A	13	A	22	A
5	C	14	C	23	B
6	B	15	C	24	D
7	B	16	C	25	A
8	D	17	C	26	C
9	A	18	D	27	A

Pages 196-206 Module 2: Hard								
1	C	10	C	19	D
2	B	11	C	20	C
3	A	12	D	21	D
4	A	13	B	22	D
5	C	14	B	23	B
6	C	15	A	24	C
7	A	16	D	25	B
8	B	17	B	26	B
9	C	18	D	27	B

Want to learn more?

Visit prepvantagetutoring.com for Digital SAT updates
and for the research sources for our passages

Module 1: Baseline
— Pages 186-195 —

Question 1: Choice A
Word in Context
Difficulty - **Easy** | Topic - **Humanities**

Choice A is the best answer because Yeats's works "contain several memorable phrases and symbols that later authors have used in book titles." Moreover, the passage states that "The Second Coming" was "also the source for the title of Joan Didion's Slouching Towards Bethlehem." Thus, the clause before that must show that "The Second Coming" was the source for a title from Things Fall Apart. "Taken from" appropriately conveys that "Chinua Achebe's Things Fall Apart has a title" that comes from "The Second Coming."

Choice B is incorrect because, though Yeats's work may be irrelevant to certain later texts, the passage states that "The Second Coming" was "also the source for the title of Joan Didion's Slouching Towards Bethlehem," so it must not have been irrelevant to the author mentioned just prior to that. Choice C is incorrect because, though authors can reject the work of earlier authors, the passage states that "The Second Coming" was "also the source for the title of Joan Didion's Slouching Towards Bethlehem," so it must not have been rejected by the author mentioned just prior to that. Choice D is incorrect because, though it is reasonable to infer that Achebe agrees with or likes Yeats's phrasing, the text does not mention Achebe teaming up with Yeats.

Question 2: Choice C
Word in Context
Difficulty - **Easy** | Topic - **Science**

Choice C is the best answer because the underlined word refers to "two small wildlife underpasses beneath the highway." Thus, the underlined word must mean something akin to "tunnels." "Passages" appropriately conveys that the underpasses provide safe pathways for wildlife to cross under the highway.

Choice A is incorrect because, though monuments can be installed, the "two small wildlife underpasses" are pathways, not monuments. Choice B is incorrect because, though the "small wildlife underpasses" were carved into the ground, they are not intruding on anything. Choice D is incorrect because, though scientists sometimes use barriers to alter the routes of wildlife, the "two small wildlife underpasses" are thoroughfares, not blockades.

Question 3: Choice B
Word in Context
Difficulty - **Hard** | Topic - **Humanities**

Choice B is the best answer because the prizefighter is "at rest" and "seated," so he is in an inactive position. "Repose" appropriately conveys that the figures are in relaxed states.

Choice A is incorrect because, though "decline" would provide a contrast with "highly physical professions," the prizefighter "awaits a new round of competition," so he is still active in his boxing career. Choice C is incorrect because, though a boxer might sit out from a competition if the competition is not going well, the prizefighter "awaits a new round of competition," so there is nothing to indicate that the prizefighter is in an unfortunate or unlucky state. Choice D is incorrect because, though an implied backstory might need to be verified, there is nothing in the passage about corroborating or proving any information.

Question 4: Choice A
Word in Context
Difficulty - **Medium** | Topic - **Humanities**

Choice A is the best answer because the passage contrasts the experience of Morrison, who was already famous, with that of Müller, who was not. "Bolstered" correctly indicates that winning the Nobel augmented rather than created Morrison's "legendary reputation."

Choice B is incorrect because, though Morrison's reputation changed as a result of winning the Nobel, "replaced" would incorrectly indicate that winning the Nobel ended her "already legendary reputation." Choice C is incorrect because, though Morrison's reputation was affected by winning the Nobel, "abbreviated" would incorrectly indicate that winning the Nobel cut short Morrison's "already legendary reputation." Choice D is incorrect because, though winning the Nobel is a specific achievement, "specified" would incorrectly indicate that winning the Nobel identified Morrison's "already legendary reputation."

Question 5: Choice C
Word in Context
Difficulty - **Medium** | Topic - **History**

Choice C is the best answer because the "assum[ption] that British imports of cotton" turned out to be incorrect. Thus, the planned alliance based on that assumption "never materialized." "A miscalculation" appropriately conveys that the assumption underlying the plan was wrong.

Choice A is incorrect because, though the Confederacy eventually realized that it had been incorrect in its assumption, the plan did not involve that epiphany. Choice B is incorrect because, though the Confederacy likely admitted that it had been incorrect in its assumption, the plan did not involve that admission. Choice D is incorrect because, though the fact that "British merchants could also source cotton from Egypt" was detrimental to the Confederacy, that was not a matter of unfair treatment.

Question 6: Choice B
Text Structure and Purpose
Difficulty - **Medium** | Topic - **Social Studies**

Choice B is the best answer because the text begins by listing what "artificial intelligence programs can write," then asks whether they can "write useful journalism." After that, it quotes Felix M. Simon's answer to that question.

Choice A is incorrect because, though the text does ask a question about artificial intelligence and journalism, the part of the text that appears before the question is not about journalists. Choice C is incorrect because, though the text presents one observer's opinion, it does not explain why journalists are unwilling to use artificial intelligence. Choice D is incorrect because, though the text discusses a potential new use of artificial intelligence, it is questioning rather than proposing that new use.

Question 7: Choice B
Central Ideas and Details
Difficulty - **Medium** | Topic - **Science**

Choice B is the best answer because saber-toothed tigers "developed powerful forearms that were instrumental in capturing prey" instead of "relying directly on their teeth and jaws." Thus, the teeth were not the tigers' primary way to capture prey.

Choice A is incorrect because, though "these teeth might not have been particularly useful in hunting," the text does not say that they served no practical use. Choice C is incorrect because, though the teeth are fragile, the text does not say that Meachen has found few teeth because of that. Choice D

is incorrect because, though the tigers may have used their teeth to some extent while hunting, the forearms were more important for hunting, so tigers with damaged teeth would still likely be able to catch prey.

Question 8: Choice D
Central Ideas and Details
Difficulty - **Medium** | Topic - **Humanities**

Choice D is the best answer because the passage describes various aspects of Oliver's career, and spotlights the research she is performing as a fellow at the Clark Art Institute. Since the passage stipulates that Oliver's research in this period focused on "formative Bahamian artists from the 1950s," choose D to best align with this content.

Choice A is incorrect because the passage mentions that Oliver has taken a multidisciplinary approach throughout her career, and does not specify that she deviated from this approach during her fellowship. Choice B is incorrect because the passage implies that the A-Z Caribbean Art project was completed prior to Oliver's fellowship. Choice C is incorrect because the passage implies that Oliver herself could be classified as a historian, but NOT that she studies other historians (her research focuses primarily on artists).

Question 9: Choice A
Quantitative Command of Evidence
Difficulty - **Medium** | Topic - **History**

Choice A is the best answer because the table shows that there are more buildings (980) than compounds (90). Thus, it cannot be the case that each compound has only one building.

Choice B is incorrect because, though the table includes compounds and a moat, it says nothing about the largest compounds in particular. Choice C is incorrect because, though the average footprint of a building is roughly 720 square meters, the buildings need not all be the same size. Choice D is incorrect because, if no compound had more than 10 buildings, the maximum number of buildings would be 900, which is less than the actual number of buildings (980). Thus, at least one compound has more than 10 buildings.

Question 10: Choice B
Textual Command of Evidence
Difficulty - **Medium** | Topic - **Literature**

Choice B is the best answer because the claim that the "narrator evokes the scenery of rural England" is supported by "such a lonely cottage stood on such a down" and "the spot, by actual measurement, was not more than five miles from a county-town." Moreover, the claim that the narrator "express[es] some uncertainty about the scene that is being described" is supported by "may possibly be standing there now."

Choice A is incorrect because, though it describes "features of agricultural England," it does not express uncertainty about those features. Choice C is incorrect because, though it describes the weather of rural England, it does not express uncertainty. Choice D is incorrect because, though it describes a hypothetical scene, the fact that the scene is hypothetical does not make the narrator uncertain about it.

Question 11: Choice A
Textual Command of Evidence
Difficulty - **Medium** | Topic - **Science**

Choice A is the best answer because its reference to an exception supports the molecular chemist's claim that the researchers' method "might be unsuitable for detecting some types of toxic substances." If Wang and Aizenberg's method has only detected "endotoxins classified as amphiphiles and might not be useful in detecting other substances, then this method is limited in a manner that fits the claim of the molecular chemist as explained in the passage.

Choice B is incorrect because it explains that Aizenberg and Wang's method represents an improvement upon earlier methods; instead of indicating benefits of the new detection method, the correct choice should call attention to a limitation. Choice C is incorrect because it notes a source of various endotoxins without indicating that Aizenberg and Wang's method might not be helpful in detecting specific endotoxins from this group. Choice D is incorrect because it calls attention to a possible asset of Aizenberg and Wang's method without noting limitations as required by the molecular chemist's claim.

Question 12: Choice D
Inferences
Difficulty - **Hard** | Topic - **Science**

Choice D is the best answer because the first geological shift "began pushing the underlying volcanic rock of the mountain range upward," then the second geological shift "pushed the mountains higher and . . . [gave] rise to the mountains' current rainforest ecosystem." Thus, before those two shifts, the mountains would have been lower and would have had a different ecosystem.

Choice A is incorrect because, though the mountains would not have supported the rainforest ecosystem that exists there now, they would not have had high temperatures and ongoing volcanic activity. Choice B is incorrect because, though the soil layers would have been distributed differently than they are now, the geological shifts that made the mountains hospitable to a rainforest ecosystem had not yet occurred 40

million years ago. Choice C is incorrect because, though the mountains would have been lower, there is nothing to suggest that there were a relatively large number of mountains 40 million years ago.

Question 13: Choice A
Inferences
Difficulty - **Medium** | Topic - **Social Studies**

Choice A is the best answer because "more than 80% of traded goods . . . are carried by ships," so less than 20% of traded goods are carried by other methods. Therefore, a trade disruption isolated to other methods would affect less than 20% of traded goods, which is considerably less than 80%. Moreover, "in contrast" sets up a parallel comparison with the prior sentence, so the correct answer should contrast with "impact[ing] most of the world's commerce."

Choice B is incorrect because, though it is possible for new routes to be added to compensate for the disruption of other routes, the text does not say that. Choice C is incorrect because, though Kalouptsidi discusses goods carried by ships, there is nothing to suggest that Kalouptsidi has no interest in other methods of shipping goods. Choice D is incorrect because, though disruptions in one mode of transport could affect other modes of transport, the text does not say that.

Question 14: Choice C
Boundaries
Difficulty - **Medium** | Topic - **Social Studies**

Choice C is the best answer because the sentence begins with a dependent clause and then features an independent clause beginning with "Huebner stresses." The single comma after the dependent clause should be used to separate this clause from the independent clause.

Choice A is incorrect because it introduces the transition "though" (unnecessary since "While" establishes a contrast) and wrongly fuses an opening dependent clause with an independent clause. Choice B is incorrect because the transition "though" turns the independent clause into a dependent clause; as a result, this choice creates a sentence without an independent clause. Choice D is incorrect because it entirely avoids punctuation in a manner that fuses an opening dependent clause with an independent clause.

Question 15: Choice C
Form, Structure, and Sense
Difficulty - **Hard** | Topic - **Science**

Choice C is the best answer because the modifier ("Holding . . . for now") must modify the noun immediately after it. Fission energy is what holds "remarkable potential" and what is "challenging to produce," so "fission energy" must be the beginning of the correct answer.

Choice A is incorrect because it would make the modifier modify "NASA engineers," which do not hold "remarkable potential for powering entire settlements on the Moon." Choice B is incorrect because it would make the modifier modify "current investigation," which does not hold "remarkable potential for powering entire settlements on the Moon." Choice D is incorrect because it would make the modifier modify "current investigation," which does not hold "remarkable potential for powering entire settlements on the Moon."

Question 16: Choice C
Boundaries
Difficulty - **Medium** | Topic - **Humanities**

Choice C is the best answer because it separates two independent clauses with a period. The first independent clause ("Fashion . . . sequins") and the second independent clause ("However . . . distant") should be separated in this manner, since other options produce comma splices and changes in meaning.

Choice A is incorrect because it includes "however" in the first independent clause, thereby making it a contrasting statement to a missing prior statement rather than to the second independent clause. Choice B is incorrect because it uses a comma to join two independent clauses. Choice D is incorrect because it sets off "however" with commas, thereby treating it as nonessential and fusing the two independent clauses without proper punctuation. All of these false answers result in errors in the coordination of independent clauses.

Question 17: Choice C
Form, Structure, and Sense
Difficulty - **Easy** | Topic - **Science**

Choice C is the best answer because "a mineral" is the singular subject of the underlined singular verb "makes." The subject may be hard to locate due to its location in a nonessential phrase.

Choice A is incorrect because the plural verb "make" does not agree with the singular subject. Choice B is incorrect because the plural verb "are making" does not agree with the singular subject. Choice D is incorrect because the plural verb "were making" does not agree with the singular subject.

Question 18: Choice D
Boundaries
Difficulty - **Medium** | Topic - **Humanities**

Choice D is the best answer because the sentence contains two independent clauses, "The Indian . . . traditions" and "the Center . . . collection." To coordinate two independent clauses, a semicolon is appropriate and the word "indeed" can be set off as dependent content.

Choice A is incorrect because it introduces a comma splice and wrongly attempts to use "indeed" (which functions as dependent content) to connect independent clauses. Choice B is incorrect because it does not feature a transition or punctuation (semicolon, period) that can connect independent clauses, even though "indeed" is set off as dependent. Choice C is incorrect because it introduces a comma splice by only featuring a comma after "indeed," not transitions or punctuation appropriate for connecting independent clauses.

Question 19: Choice A
Form, Structure, and Sense
Difficulty - **Hard** | Topic - **Humanities**

Choice A is the best answer because the modifier that begins the sentence describes something that is "dancelike" and involves movement, particularly movements that indicate "awkwardness" and "grace." The "performances" of a single individual, Doug Jones, would be logically described by the modifier that begins the sentence.

Choice B is incorrect because the modifier must refer to physical movements that are "dancelike," namely Jones's "expressive, acrobatic" performances, instead of to a larger film. The "poses and postures" mentioned in the modifier most logically describes Jones's movements rather than the broader "fantasy epics" that del Toro creates. Choice C is incorrect because the modifier should describe a specific type of performance, not the person giving the performance, as "dancelike." Choice D is incorrect because del Toro's films feature Jones's movements among the films' components. This choice would wrongly indicate that the films, which are larger "fantasy epics," are instead entirely dancelike and built on gestures in the manner of a single actor's performance.

Question 20: Choice D
Boundaries
Difficulty - **Easy** | Topic - **Science**

Choice D is the best answer because it correctly separates the two independent clauses ("The entire . . . 'lahars'" and "these deposits . . . as 'clasts'") with a comma and a coordinating conjunction ("and"). The clauses should be joined in this manner, since other options result in run-on sentences and comma splices.

Choice A is incorrect because it fuses two independent clauses without any punctuation between them. Choice B is incorrect because a comma without a coordinating conjunction cannot join two independent clauses. Choice C is incorrect because it fuses two independent clauses with a coordinating conjunction ("and") but no punctuation. All of these false answers result in errors in the coordination of independent clauses.

Question 21: Choice D
Transitions
Difficulty - **Medium** | Topic - **Social Studies**

Choice D is the best answer because the fact that "automation bias leads to an over-trusting approach to artificial intelligence" is a consequence of automation bias in general. This transition properly signals an extension relationship.

Choice A is incorrect because "in theory" introduces an error relationship, which wrongly indicates that the fact that "automation bias leads to an over-trusting approach to artificial intelligence" is a theoretically true but actually false claim. Choice B is incorrect because "to that end" introduces a goal relationship, which wrongly indicates that "an over-trusting approach to artificial intelligence" is a means of achieving the goal of automation bias. Choice C is incorrect because "regardless" introduces an opposing relationship, which indicates that "an over-trusting approach to artificial intelligence" exists despite automation bias.

Question 22: Choice A
Transitions
Difficulty - **Medium** | Topic - **Science**

Choice A is the best answer because the "power plant reliant on dried peat" is evidence of the usefulness of peat for energy production. This transition properly signals a support relationship.

Choice B is incorrect because "nevertheless" introduces an opposing relationship, which wrongly indicates that the "power plant reliant on dried peat" exists despite the usefulness of peat for energy production. Choice C is incorrect because "in retrospect" introduces an error relationship, which wrongly indicates that the "power plant reliant on dried peat" is a correction of a false idea about the usefulness of peat for energy production. Choice D is incorrect because "as noted" introduces a reiteration relationship, which wrongly indicates that the "power plant reliant on dried peat" has already been mentioned in the paragraph.

Question 23: Choice B
Transitions
Difficulty - **Medium** | Topic - **History**

Choice B is the best answer because "likewise" signals that public speaking was regarded in the same way in Greece and in Rome. The passage begins with the idea that multiple civilizations held public speaking "in high regard" and uses positive statements about public speaking as a "civic duty" in Greece and a "rigorous realm of study" in Rome to support this idea.

Choice A is incorrect because "more broadly" introduces a generalization relationship, which wrongly indicates that public speaking in ancient Rome is a broader version of public speaking in ancient Greece. Choice C is incorrect because "nonetheless" introduces a contrast relationship, which wrongly indicates that the role or reputation of public speaking in ancient Rome was dissimilar to the role or reputation of public speaking in ancient Greece. Instead, both of the civilizations in question valued public speaking. Choice D is incorrect because "in other words" introduces a reiteration relationship, which wrongly indicates that ancient Rome was ancient Greece.

Question 24: Choice D
Transitions
Difficulty - **Hard** | Topic - **History**

Choice D is the best answer because "of course" signals that 250 CE "pre-dates current protocols for the preservation of historic sites." This transition properly signals an inherent relationship.

Choice A is incorrect because "previously" introduces a reverse chronological relationship, which wrongly indicates that the bridge predated current protocols before something else in the passage occurred. Choice B is incorrect because "in the end" introduces a conclusion relationship, which wrongly indicates that the fact that the "ancient stonework bridge pre-dates current protocols for the preservation of historic sites" is the conclusion of the text. Choice C is incorrect because "however" introduces a contrast relationship, which wrongly indicates that the Dezful Bridge "pre-dates current protocols for the preservation of historic sites" despite the fact that it was built around 250 CE.

Question 25: Choice A
Transitions
Difficulty - **Medium** | Topic - **Humanities**

Choice A is the best answer because "by contrast" signals that being "a god of war . . . seen as a destructive force" contrasts with being a "mostly benign storyteller." This transition properly signals an opposing relationship.

Choice B is incorrect because "for instance" introduces a support relationship, which wrongly indicates that being "a god of war . . . seen as a destructive force" is an example of being a "mostly benign storyteller." Choice C is incorrect because "therefore" introduces a causal relationship, which wrongly indicates that Ekwensu's role as "a god of war" is a result of Anansi serving as a "mostly benign storyteller." Choice D is incorrect because "for this reason" introduces a causal relationship, which wrongly indicates that Ekwensu is "a god of war . . . seen as a destructive force" because Anansi is a "mostly benign storyteller."

Question 26: Choice C
Rhetorical Synthesis
Difficulty - **Medium** | Topic - **Humanities**

Choice C is the best answer because it states the overall lotus leaf shape of the Borobudur compound, and it mentions the "carvings reminiscent of lotus leaves." This choice is consistent with the student's goal of "describ[ing] the Borobudur compound, with particular attention to multiple uses of the lotus motif."

Choice A is incorrect because, though it discusses the Borobudur Temple compound, it does not mention the lotus leaf motif. Choice B is incorrect because, though it discusses "carvings that recall the leaves of the lotus," it does not state an additional use of the lotus leaf shape, so it does not describe "multiple uses of the lotus motif." Choice D is incorrect because, though it discusses "carvings that call to mind the lotus leaf," it does not describe "multiple uses of the lotus motif."

Question 27: Choice A
Rhetorical Synthesis
Difficulty - **Medium** | Topic - **Science**

Choice A is the best answer because it states two things (administer identical compressions and administer compressions in a moving vehicle) that a LUCAS machine can do that a human responder cannot do. This choice is consistent with the student's goal of "call[ing] attention to a few different benefits of the LUCAS machine."

Choice B is incorrect because, though it discusses the capabilities of the LUCAS machine, it does not explain that the LUCAS machine can do what human responders cannot do. Choice C is incorrect because, though it discusses the LUCAS machine, it does not state any benefits of the machine. Choice D is incorrect because, though it discusses a deficiency of human responders, it does not say how the LUCAS machine operates better than human responders do.

Module 2: Hard
— Pages 196-206 —

Question 1: Choice C
Word in Context
Difficulty - **Medium** | Topic - **Science**

Choice C is the best answer because the passage explains how snow leopards depend on the movement of prey animals from place to place. C captures the meaning of interdependence and snow leopards needing their prey to move between different locations in a region.

Choice A is incorrect because it implies that there is no connection between the hunting behavior of snow leopards and the movement of the animals they feed on. Choice B is incorrect because it implies that migratory animals are an essential characteristic of snow leopards, rather than a distinct entity existing in a predator-prey relationship. Choice D is incorrect because it implies that snow leopards are deserving of their prey moving between different locations

Question 2: Choice B
Word in Context
Difficulty - **Hard** | Topic - **Social Studies**

Choice B is the best answer because MVPs are meant to help a company to avoid "extensive expenditures of time and capital." "Without unwisely committing to" conveys that the company is not bound to invest "extensive expenditures of time and capital" during product testing.

Choice A is incorrect because, though the text is partly about money, expenditures of capital are already financial, so they cannot be monetized. Choice C is incorrect because, though the company seeks to avoid excessive expenditures, they are not rendering them void. Choice D is incorrect because, though the company seeks to avoid excessive expenditures, they are not deviating from the expenditures but rather are minimizing them.

Question 3: Choice A
Word in Context
Difficulty - **Hard** | Topic - **Science**

Choice A is the best answer because "beaks" and "tusks" are traits of outward appearance. "Superficially" correctly indicates that the "ancestors of today's large-tusked elephants and walruses" do not resemble their descendants in outward appearance.

Choice B is incorrect because, though the traits of animals are of interest to paleontologists, "provocatively" incorrectly indicates that the "ancestors of today's large-tusked elephants and walruses" do not resemble their descendants in a way that arouses interest. Choice C is incorrect because, though the mutations that drive evolution are random, "arbitrarily" incorrectly indicates that the "ancestors of today's large-tusked elephants and walruses" do not resemble their descendants in random ways. Choice D is incorrect because, though paleontology requires hard work, "strenuously" incorrectly indicates that the "ancestors of today's large-tusked elephants and walruses" do not resemble their descendants in laborious ways.

Question 4: Choice A
Word in Context
Difficulty - **Hard** | Topic - **Science**

Choice A is the best answer because the text describes how "predatory propensities" exist in cats "even when domesticated." Thus, they are innate. "Inherent to" appropriately fits the context of innate animal traits.

Choice B is incorrect because, though predation is not as significant for domesticated cats, the text argues that the propensity for "vertically-oriented activities" has not been dulled by domestication. Choice C is incorrect because, though cat trees are far more basic than real trees, there is nothing to suggest that the "predatory propensities" of domestic cats are more basic than those of wild cats. Choice D is incorrect because, though the "predatory propensities" of cats exist for an evolutionary reason, the mammals are not justifying their own behaviors.

Question 5: Choice C
Word in Context
Difficulty - **Hard** | Topic - **Humanities**

Choice C is the best answer because the plays were "maligned," so they acquired bad reputations. Moreover, they became subjects of "ongoing fascination" for negative reasons ("their questionable creative choices"). "Notoriety" appropriately fits the context of negative fame.

Choice A is incorrect because, though the writers of the plays were likely angry about their works receiving negative reviews, a play cannot feel emotions. Choice B is incorrect because, though the plays were fictional, fallaciousness does not cause "fascination." Choice D is incorrect because, though the plays were maligned, only a person can be vehement.

Question 6: Choice C
Text Structure and Purpose
Difficulty - **Hard** | Topic - **Science**

Choice C is the best answer because the passage focuses on how wolf lichens survive in the wild, as elucidated by a study ("scientists from the University of Barcelona are arriving at a new understanding of this symbiotic organism's survival mechanisms"). Moreover, these survival mechanisms center on interdependence.

Choice A is incorrect because, though the text states that "the wolf lichen is threatened," that is not the focus of the text. Rather, the lichen's survival mechanisms are the focus. Choice B is incorrect because, though the text states that all lichens are made of two symbiotic organisms, the text states that "wolf lichens are themselves interdependent on very old trees," not that all lichens depend on very old trees. Choice D is incorrect because, though the text states that very old trees serve a valuable ecological purpose, that statement is not a rebuttal of the opposite view.

Question 7: Choice A
Text Structure and Purpose
Difficulty - **Hard** | Topic - **Literature**

Choice A is the best answer because the speaker keeps referencing unappealing descriptions, such as "foggy," "idly," "dirty," "tiresome," and "dull." Moreover, the speaker is familiar with the surroundings, which make "fragments of an old story" come to mind. Thus, the scene evokes a particular narrative in the speaker's mind.

Choice B is incorrect because, though the "house into which I happened to come to-day" may be a chance encounter, there is nothing to suggest that the speaker has not already reflected deeply on past events. Choice C is incorrect because, while the setting is bleak, the thoughts that it inspires are not elevated or noble. Choice D is incorrect because, though the passage establishes a parallel, that parallel is not between the condition of a single area and the economic problems facing a large group of people but rather between "a dull life" and "thousands of [other] dull lives."

Question 8: Choice B
Text Structure and Purpose
Difficulty - **Hard** | Topic - **Science**

Choice B is the best answer because it gives an example to support the prior sentence ("The reality . . . though"). That sentence qualifies the absolute nature of the "point of no return" in the first sentence.

Choice A is incorrect because, though the underlined text presents findings that call into question a claim, the claim that is being questioned is the absolute nature of the "point of no return," not any scientific methods. Choice C is incorrect because, though the underlined text states that mitogens prompt cell division, it does not contrast how the "point of no return" operates in different groups of cells. Choice D is incorrect because, though the underlined text discusses research that was done at the National Cancer Institute, the text does not say that the cells in that study were cancer cells.

Question 9: Choice C
Cross-Text Connections
Difficulty - **Hard** | Topic - **Humanities**

Choice C is the best answer because, though the author of Text 1 agrees that "collaboration has been central to the history of American folk music," Text 1 points out that "the prevalent image of folk music—which some of these festivals embrace in their promotional materials—is of a lone singer or guitarist onstage." A lone performer seems incongruous with the communal spirit of folk music.

Choice A is incorrect because, though Text 1 is partly about individualism versus collaboration in folk music, the underlined claim in Text 2 is not about Seeger. Choice B is incorrect because, though factors other than collaboration might explain why folk music has increased in popularity over the past several decades, the underlined claim in Text 2 is not about popularity. Choice D is incorrect because, though the author of Text 1 agrees that collaboration guides folk music, the underlined claim in Text 2 is not about current folk audiences.

Question 10: Choice C
Quantitative Command of Evidence
Difficulty - **Hard** | Topic - **Social Studies**

Choice C is the best answer because it provides a comparison of food output allocation between larger farms (50–100 hectares) and smaller farms (5-10 hectares). Moreover, the comparison supports the claim that large farms would not be viewed as more efficient "by comparing the percent allocation of a farm's land for usable product (food output),"

as the larger of the two size categories discussed in Choice C has the lower food output allocation.

Choice A is incorrect because, though it is true that "both large (50–100 hectares) and very large (500–1000 hectares) farms allocated roughly 30% of their land for 'other uses,'" Choice A is only about larger farms (50–100 hectares and 500–1000 hectares), so it fails to provide a comparison between larger farms and smaller farms (1-2 hectares or 5-10 hectares). Choice B is incorrect because, though it is true that "the smallest farms considered (1–2 hectares) allocated more than 50% of their land for food output and less than 20% of their land for animal feed," Choice B fails to provide a comparison between different categories of farms. Choice D is incorrect because, though it is true that "farms of 500–1000 hectares allocated roughly 28% of their land for non-output uses, excluding waste and animal feed," Choice D fails to provide a comparison between farms in different size categories.

Question 11: Choice C
Textual Command of Evidence
Difficulty - **Hard** | Topic - **Science**

Choice C is the best answer because Gazzard and colleagues' claim is that rodents "impart important ecological benefits to the diverse environments that they inhabit." A finding that shows an ecological benefit of kangaroo rats would support this claim. Choice C fulfills this goal by stating that plant productivity and diversity improved in areas where kangaroo rats were actively burrowing.

Choice A is incorrect because, though it is about Prugh and Brashares's study, it does not present an ecological benefit of kangaroo rats. Choice B is incorrect because, though it shows that kangaroo rats benefit their predators, all prey species benefit their predators, so that phenomenon is not unique to rodents. Choice D is incorrect because, though it is about the effects of kangaroo rats on ecosystems, it merely states that those effects varied rather than stating that they were positive.

Question 12: Choice D
Textual Command of Evidence
Difficulty - **Hard** | Topic - **History**

Choice D is the best answer because the historian's claim is that "the final outcome [of a British victory over the Dutch] should be understood as the product of a few decisive and relatively short stages in the Wars." Choice D supports this claim by stating that a very limited time period (1780-1784) was "notable" in that "it decisively limited Dutch influence over maritime commerce."

Choice A is incorrect because, though it is about short time periods during the Anglo-Dutch Wars, it is about systems of governments rather than a British victory over the Dutch. Choice B is incorrect because, though it lists some advantages of the British navy, it primarily states that the Dutch navy was in a position of dominance, which does not support the claim of a British victory. Choice C is incorrect because, though it suggests that the British won three of the four wars, it is also about the problems faced by the British, which does not support the claim of a British victory.

Question 13: Choice B
Quantitative Command of Evidence
Difficulty - **Medium** | Topic - **Social Studies**

Choice B is the best answer because the information must undermine the claim that "offset printing is sometimes depicted as the method that more effectively lowers costs and increases profits." This claim is undermined by the cost per book and profitability per book for Publisher 1, which shows that offset printing has a higher cost per book and a lower profit per book.

Choice A is incorrect because, though Publisher 1 had a higher profit per book for print on demand books, Publisher 3 did not. Choice C is incorrect because, though Publisher 2 had a lower profit for offset books, Publisher 3 did not. Choice D is incorrect because, though Publisher 3's cost per book was higher for offset books, Publisher 3's profit per book was also higher for offset books.

Question 14: Choice B
Textual Command of Evidence
Difficulty - **Hard** | Topic - **Science**

Choice B is the best answer because the notion that phosphates, which are for flavor enhancement rather than carbonation, are the ingredients that are most detrimental to bone density supports the claim that bone problems "have no causal connection to carbonation and are better explained by the other properties of the beverages consumed."

Choice A is incorrect because, though it is about the detrimental effects of carbonated beverages on bone health, it is not about which components of carbonated beverages cause those detrimental effects. Choice C is incorrect because, though it is true that carbonated beverages are acidic, Choice C is not about which components of carbonated beverages affect bone health. Choice D is incorrect because, though it casts doubt on studies about carbonated beverages and bone health, it does not say whether carbonation damages bones.

Question 15: Choice A
Text Structure and Purpose
Difficulty - **Hard** | Topic - **Social Studies**

Choice A is the best answer because the text begins by stating the "boom in small (200 to 300 square-foot) apartments" in large cities. It then states the "challenge is to sell these spaces by making them seem efficient, not cramped," followed by a few ways to achieve that goal.

Choice B is incorrect because, though the text is about a specific type of living space that has become more popular, it does not list the factors that have led to that popularity, nor does it examine the likelihood of an imminent decrease in popularity. Choice C is incorrect because, though the text highlights the growing popularity of smaller living spaces, it explains how sellers, not owners, of these spaces can make these spaces seem more appealing. Choice D is incorrect because, though the passage highlights the growing popularity of a new urban living arrangement, it does not investigate a demographic change.

Question 16: Choice D
Inferences
Difficulty - **Hard** | Topic - **Science**

Choice D is the best answer because "termites could be an even more intriguing exception" to insect family unit tendencies than earwigs are. Thus, termites are different from earwigs insofar as family unit tendencies are concerned.

Choice A is incorrect because, though the passage suggests that the number of termite colonies does not increase, it does not suggest that it decreases. Choice B is incorrect because, though the text mentions groups of younger and older insects within individual termite colonies, it does not mention conflict. Choice C is incorrect because, though the text suggests that the family unit tendencies of termites differ from those of earwigs, it also says that "termites live in multi-generational colonies," which include "younger generations of termites."

Question 17: Choice B
Inferences
Difficulty - **Hard** | Topic - **Social Studies**

Choice B is the best answer because "a hyper-centralized government . . . is not the only sort of economic planning that experts have assessed." Thus, the text suggests that Pellathy's concept of planning is not reliant on a hyper-centralized government.

Choice A is incorrect because, though Pellathy's concept of a planned economy is contrasted with the Soviet Union's version, the text immediately before Pelathy is introduced says that a Soviet-style government "is not the only sort of economic planning that experts have assessed," which suggests only that Pelathy's concept is different from the Soviet version; it does not suggest that certain countries have adopted that structure. Choice C is incorrect because, though the passage discusses failure, it portrays Pellathy's concept of a planned economy in a positive light. Choice D is incorrect because, though Pellathy's concept of a planned economy is contrasted with a hyper-centralized government, it is about "individual companies," not governments.

Question 18: Choice D
Boundaries
Difficulty - **Easy** | Topic - **Science**

Choice D is the best answer because it uses the commas to set off a dependent phrase that properly explains what the "nutrients" are. The main independent clause remains properly constructed if the phrase "urea and ammonium" is omitted.

Choice A is incorrect because it avoids the second comma that would be necessary to set off the dependent phrase "urea and ammonium" before the independent clause continues. Choice B is incorrect because it breaks the connected pairing "urea and ammonium" with a single comma and makes it seem as though the passage is presenting a three-part list, not a two-part further description of the "nutrients." Choice C is incorrect because it avoids any commas and thus runs together the nouns "nutrients" and "urea" as though they are a single term, yet "urea" should further specify one of the "nutrients" in a dependent phrase.

Question 19: Choice D
Boundaries
Difficulty - **Hard** | Topic - **History**

Choice D is the best answer because it properly coordinates multiple independent clauses ("camels . . . world," "works . . . China," and "The tombs . . . sculptures") with periods and with commas combined with coordinating conjunctions. Moreover, this choice avoids splitting logically connected content using unnecessary punctuation; the sentence structure connects the phrase "appeared in China" to meaningfully indicate where the sculptures of camels appeared using a single independent clause.

Choice A is incorrect because it splits the phrase identifying where the sculptures of camels appeared. As a result, the sentence features the incomplete and uninformative independent clause "works of statuary depicting camels in fact appeared. Choice B is incorrect because it uses the comma after "China" to wrongly introduce a comma splice. Choice C is incorrect because it splits the phrase "appeared

in China" with an unnecessary colon and further follows the colon with a prepositional phrase, note a list of discrete items or an independent clause.

Question 20: Choice C
Boundaries
Difficulty - **Hard** | Topic - **Science**

Choice C is the best answer because the period is properly used to coordinate two independent clauses, "the city's . . . recently" and "Toronto's . . . bothersome." In this instance, portions of the text that should be treated as dependent clauses ("with . . . 2022," "Now," "instead . . . count") are properly set off from the independent clauses with commas.

Choice A is incorrect because the word "now" should describe a further situation presented in a new clause construction ("Toronto's . . . bothersome"). Instead, this version illogically groups "now" with earlier content to suggest that 2022, a year that has already passed, is happening "now." Choice B is incorrect because it creates a comma splice by placing a long dependent clause ("now . . . count") between two independent clauses joined with only a comma. Choice D is incorrect because it creates a comma splice by avoiding a period, a semicolon, or a coordinating conjunction; the dependent clauses are properly configured but the independent clauses cannot be joined with only a comma.

Question 21: Choice D
Form, Structure, and Sense
Difficulty - **Hard** | Topic - **Humanities**

Choice D is the best answer because the sentence requires the nonfinite verb form "inhabiting" to create a dependent clause. The verb should be in the gerund form to show that inhabiting the same realm of moral uncertainty as other Shakespeare protagonists is a perception ("seen as inhabiting").

Choice A is incorrect because the verb form "to be inhabiting," while nonfinite, has the infinitive "to be," which is not used in the "seen as -ing" construction. Choice B is incorrect because the verb form "to inhabit," while nonfinite, is the infinitive form, which is not used in the "seen as -ing" construction. Choice C is incorrect because the finite verb form "inhabits" would create an independent clause where an adverbial phrase should be.

Question 22: Choice D
Boundaries
Difficulty - **Hard** | Topic - **Science**

Choice D is the best answer because the dependent clause "now . . . Dusicyon avus" is properly set off from the independent clause "researchers . . . ago" with two commas.

This construction situates the dependent clause as an effective further description of the "species" mentioned earlier.

Choice A is incorrect because it creates an illogical independent clause indicating that a species domesticated "1,500 years ago" was also domesticated "now." The word "now" should be grouped with the word "identified" in the dependent clause to logically indicate that the identification of the animal, not its domestication, was recent. Choice B is incorrect because it introduces a single comma that creates the incomplete independent clause "researchers . . . identified" and sets off content needed for the independent clause (the verb "was") in a faulty dependent clause. Choice C is incorrect because it omits the second comma that is necessary to set off "now . . . Dusicyon avus" as a dependent clause that further describes the "species."

Question 23: Choice B
Transitions
Difficulty - **Hard** | Topic - **Science**

Choice B is the best answer because "however" signals that the fact that the ancestors of modern cephalopods "had arrays of soft tentacles that protruded from shells of various shapes" is true despite the fact that "few of today's most prevalent cephalopods . . . have shells." This transition properly signals a contrast relationship.

Choice A is incorrect because "previously" introduces a reverse chronological relationship, which wrongly indicates that assuming that the ancestors of modern cephalopods resembled their descendants was incorrect before those descendants were known to lack shells. Choice C is incorrect because "furthermore" introduces an extension relationship, which wrongly indicates that the shells of the ancestors of modern cephalopods are consistent with the lack of shells in their descendants. Choice D is incorrect because "increasingly" introduces an augmentation relationship, which wrongly indicates that categorizing the ancestors of modern cephalopods as lacking shells has become a more incorrect statement over time.

Question 24: Choice C
Transitions
Difficulty - **Hard** | Topic - **Humanities**

Choice C is the best answer because "in fact" signals that Alfred Hitchcock's Rope consisting of ten rather than one tracking shot supports the claim that "a tracking shot . . is a difficult technique to sustain" for an entire film. This transition properly signals a support relationship.

Choice A is incorrect because "rather" introduces a contrast relationship, which wrongly indicates that Alfred Hitchcock's Rope consisting of ten rather than one tracking shot is an

alternative to the claim that "a tracking shot . . is a difficult technique to sustain" for an entire film. Choice B is incorrect because "nonetheless" introduces an opposing relationship, which wrongly indicates that Alfred Hitchcock's Rope consists of ten rather than one tracking shot despite the fact that "a tracking shot . . is a difficult technique to sustain" for an entire film. Choice D is incorrect because "to some extent" introduces a moderation relationship, which wrongly indicates that Alfred Hitchcock's Rope consists somewhat of ten rather than one tracking shot.

Question 25: Choice B
Rhetorical Synthesis
Difficulty - **Hard** | Topic - **Science**

Choice B is the best answer because it defines what the Amazon forest canopy is, and it states what Kirmse and Chaboo found regarding beetle species. This choice is consistent with the student's goal of "introduc[ing] Kirmse and Chaboo's findings to an audience unfamiliar with the Amazon forest canopy."

Choice A is incorrect because, though it mentions Kirmse and Chaboo, it does not define what the Amazon forest canopy is for an audience unfamiliar with the Amazon forest canopy. Choice C is incorrect because, though it defines what the Amazon forest canopy is, it does not mention Kirmse and Chaboo. Choice D is incorrect because, though it gives Kirmse and Chaboo's findings, it does not explain what the Amazon forest canopy is.

Question 26: Choice B
Rhetorical Synthesis
Difficulty - **Hard** | Topic - **Social Studies**

Choice B is the best answer because it contrasts the bodies and wheels of Sherp's vehicles with those of other amphibious vehicles. This choice is consistent with the student's goal of "explain[ing] the physical differences between Sherp's vehicles and other amphibious vehicles."

Choice A is incorrect because, though it contrasts the wheels of Sherp's vehicles with those of other amphibious vehicles, it does not complete the comparison of their body styles. Choice C is incorrect because, though it discusses Sherp's vehicles and other amphibious vehicles, it gives a similarity, rather than a difference, between them. Choice D is incorrect because, though it discusses amphibious vehicles and mentions Sherp's vehicles, it does not state any physical differences between Sherp's vehicles and other amphibious vehicles.

Question 27: Choice B
Rhetorical Synthesis
Difficulty - **Hard** | Topic - **History**

Choice B is the best answer because it states a generalization about the multinational nature of the advocacy for the Universal Declaration of Human Rights and then supports that generalization with two examples. This choice is consistent with the student's goal of "mak[ing] and support[ing] a generalization about the ratification of the Universal Declaration of Human Rights."

Choice A is incorrect because, though it lists some proponents of the Universal Declaration of Human Rights, it does not give a generalization. Choice C is incorrect because, though it makes a general statement about the ratification of the Universal Declaration of Human Rights, it does not give any supporting details. Choice D is incorrect because, though it discusses a proponent of the Universal Declaration of Human Rights, it does not state a generalization.

Scan here for online questions!

Want even more practice?

We are partnered with EdisonOS, and some of our questions are published on the EdisonOS digital platform.

- If you'd like to explore more digital tests, please visit the website at the following link: https://www.edisonos.com/sat-practice-tests.

Learn more about our strategies and question research!

Visit the background pages prepvantagetutoring.com/digitalreading and prepvantagetutoring.com/digitalwriting for more information

Made in the USA
Middletown, DE
02 June 2025

76416660R00124